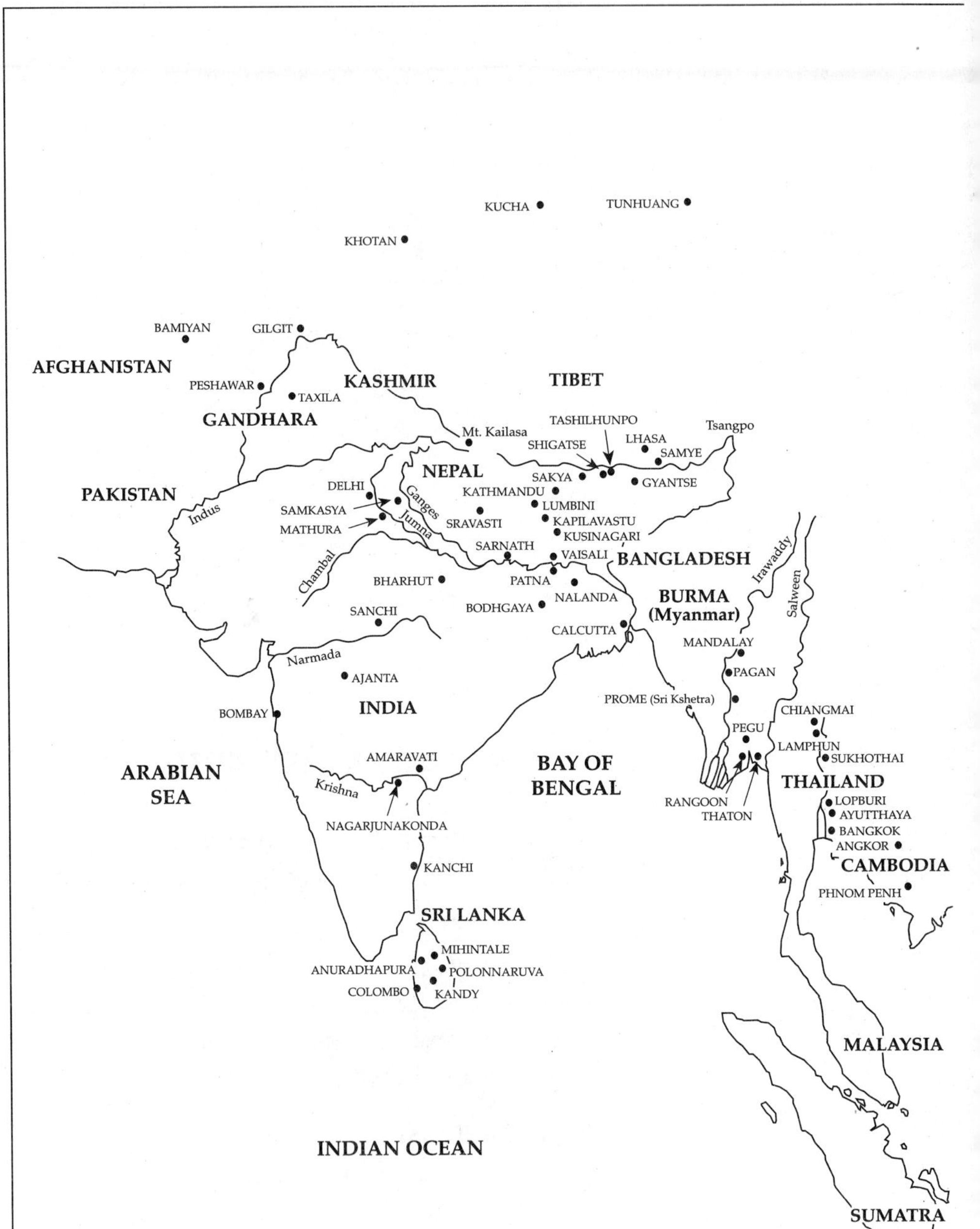
KUCHA
TUNHUANG
KHOTAN
BAMIYAN
GILGIT
AFGHANISTAN
PESHAWAR
TAXILA
KASHMIR
TIBET
GANDHARA
TASHILHUNPO
Tsangpo
Mt. Kailasa
SHIGATSE
LHASA
SAMYE
NEPAL
SAKYA
GYANTSE
PAKISTAN
DELHI
KATHMANDU
LUMBINI
Indus
SAMKASYA
Ganges
SRAVASTI
KAPILAVASTU
MATHURA
Jumna
KUSINAGARI
SARNATH
VAISALI
BANGLADESH
Irawaddy
Chambal
BHARHUT
PATNA
NALANDA
BURMA
(Myanmar)
Salween
BODHGAYA
SANCHI
CALCUTTA
MANDALAY
Narmada
PAGAN
AJANTA
PROME (Sri Kshetra)
INDIA
BOMBAY
CHIANGMAI
PEGU
LAMPHUN
SUKHOTHAI
AMARAVATI
ARABIAN
SEA
BAY OF
BENGAL
THAILAND
Krishna
RANGOON
THATON
LOPBURI
AYUTTHAYA
NAGARJUNAKONDA
BANGKOK
ANGKOR
CAMBODIA
KANCHI
PHNOM PENH
SRI LANKA
MIHINTALE
ANURADHAPURA
POLONNARUVA
COLOMBO
KANDY
MALAYSIA
INDIAN OCEAN
SUMATRA

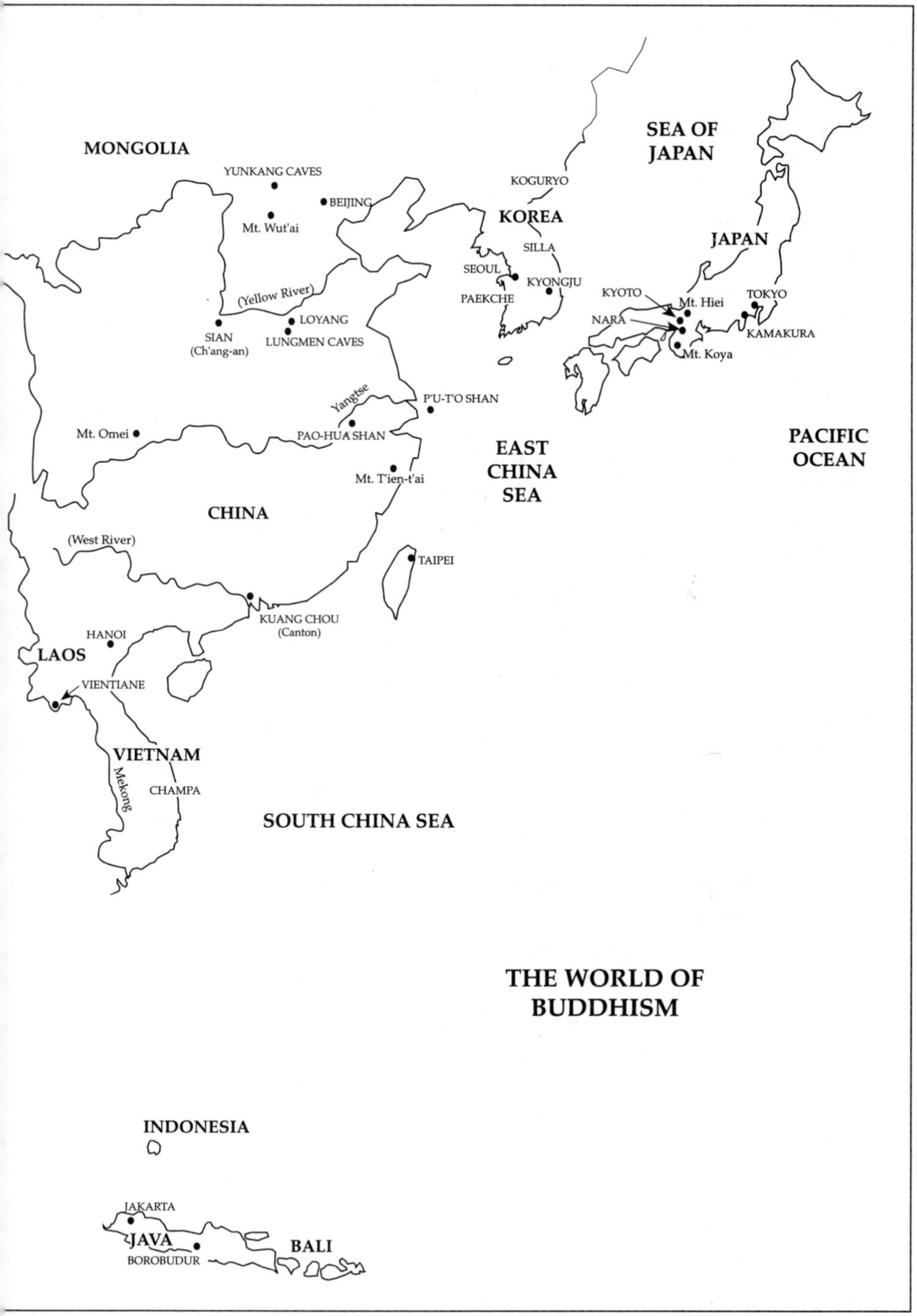
MONGOLIA
YUNKANG CAVES
BEIJING
Mt. Wut'ai
(Yellow River)
SIAN
(Ch'ang-an)
LOYANG
LUNGMEN CAVES
Yangtse
P'U-T'O SHAN
Mt. Omei
PAO-HUA SHAN
Mt. T'ien-t'ai
CHINA
(West River)
TAIPEI
KUANG CHOU
(Canton)
HANOI
LAOS
VIENTIANE
VIETNAM
Mekong
CHAMPA
SOUTH CHINA SEA
KOGURYO
KOREA
SILLA
SEOUL
KYONGJU
PAEKCHE
SEA OF
JAPAN
JAPAN
KYOTO
Mt. Hiei
NARA
Mt. Koya
TOKYO
KAMAKURA
EAST
CHINA
SEA
PACIFIC
OCEAN
THE WORLD OF
BUDDHISM
INDONESIA
JAKARTA
JAVA
BOROBUDUR
BALI

The Religious Life in History Series
CHARLES HALLISEY, *Series Editor*

Understanding Religious Life, Third Edition
Frederick J. Streng

African Cosmos: An Introduction to Religion in Africa
Noel Q. King

The Experience of Buddhism: Sources and Interpretations, Second Edition
John S. Strong

The Buddhist Religion, Fourth Edition
Richard H. Robinson, Willard L. Johnson, and Sandra A. Wawrytko

Chinese Religion: An Introduction, Fifth Edition
Laurence G. Thompson

The Chinese Way in Religion, Second Edition
Jordan Paper and Laurence G. Thompson

The Hindu Religious Tradition
Thomas J. Hopkins

The House of Islam, Third Edition
Kenneth Cragg and R. Marston Speight

Islam from Within: Anthology of a Religion
Kenneth Cragg and R. Marston Speight

Japanese Religion: Unity and Diversity, Third Edition
H. Byron Earhart

Religion in the Japanese Experience: Sources and Interpretations, Second Edition
H. Byron Earhart

The Life of Torah: Readings in the Jewish Religious Experience
Jacob Neusner

The Way of Torah: An Introduction to Judaism, Sixth Edition
Jacob Neusner

Native American Religions: An Introduction
Sam Gill

Native American Traditions: Sources and Interpretations
Sam Gill

The Experience of Buddhism

Sources and Interpretations

SECOND EDITION

John S. Strong
Bates College

WADSWORTH
THOMSON LEARNING

Australia • Canada • Mexico • Singapore • Spain • United Kingdom • United States

WADSWORTH
THOMSON LEARNING™

Publisher: *Eve Howard*
Religion Editor: *Peter Adams*
Assistant Editor: *Kara Kindstrom*
Editorial Assistant: *Chalida Anusasananan*
Marketing Manager: *Dave Garrison*
Marketing Assistant: *Adam Hofmann*
Print/Media Buyer: *Judy Inouye*
Permissions Editor: *Stephanie Keough-Hedges*

Printed in the United States of America
2 3 4 5 6 7 06 05 04 03 02

Library of Congress Cataloging-in-Publication Data

The experience of Buddhism : sources and interpretations / John S. Strong.
p. cm. — (Religious life in history series)
Includes index.
ISBN 0-534-54175-5 (alk. paper)
1. Buddhism. I. Strong, John, [date]– II. Series.

BQ122 .E97 2001
294.3—dc21

2001026898

Production Service: *Scratchgravel Publishing Services*
Copy Editor: *Victoria Nelson*
Cover Designer: *Margarite Reynolds*
Cover Image: *Corbis*
Cover Printer: *Phoenix*
Compositor: *Scratchgravel Publishing Services*
Printer: *Maple-Vail*

Wadsworth/Thomson Learning
10 Davis Drive
Belmont, CA 94002-3098
USA

For more information about our products, contact us:
Thomson Learning Academic Resource Center
1-800-423-0563
http://www.wadsworth.com

International Headquarters
Thomson Learning
International Division
290 Harbor Drive, 2nd Floor
Stamford, CT 06902-7477
USA

UK/Europe/Middle East/South Africa
Thomson Learning
Berkshire House
168-173 High Holborn
London WC1V 7AA
United Kingdom

Asia
Thomson Learning
60 Albert Street, #15-01
Albert Complex
Singapore 189969

Canada
Nelson Thomson Learning
1120 Birchmount Road
Toronto, Ontario M1K 5G4
Canada

This book is printed on acid-free recycled paper.

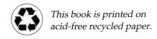

Contents

Preface to the Second Edition

Buddhism has over twenty-five hundred years of history and has taken root, in one form or another and at one time or another, in virtually every country in Asia. In more recent times, it has found a niche in Western nations as well. To present the entirety of the Buddhist experience in a single volume of texts and readings is not possible. Inevitably, an anthology involves selections: topics to be covered, texts to be chosen, passages to be emphasized, balances to be achieved. The choices are virtually endless, and the materials discarded far more numerous than those retained.

In making selections, I have striven for a balance of both "classically important texts" and "previously neglected materials." The former (debunkers of "canons" notwithstanding) are things with which all students of Buddhism should be acquainted; the latter (upholders of "canons" aside) are things that should make us think afresh about the Buddhist tradition. At the same time, I have sought to include materials illustrating many dimensions of the Buddhist religion. I have tried to cover not only history and doctrine but also ritual, myth, community, experience, practice, and daily life. Hence this volume comprises not only translations of Buddhist canonical texts but also noncanonical materials (of various genres, written at various times, in various languages), as well as descriptions of Buddhist rituals and practices by anthropologists, historians of religions, and travelers.

In organizing and introducing this material, I have sought to make it possible to use this anthology in at least two ways: either independently, in its own right, as an introductory survey or sourcebook on Buddhism or as a companion volume to Richard Robinson and Willard Johnson's *The Buddhist Religion: A Historical Introduction.*[1]

To that end, its basic structure follows that of the Robinson and Johnson textbook: Part One is devoted to Buddhism as it primarily developed in South Asia and is roughly organized around the topics of the "Three Jewels," or "refuges," of Buddhism: the Buddha (Chapter 1), the Sangha, or Buddhist community (Chapter 2), and

[1] To that extent, this volume is a replacement for Stephan Beyer's anthology, *The Buddhist Experience* (1974), which is now out of print. It is not, however, either a revision or a new edition of Beyer's work, even though I have used some of his translations and been inspired by his example.

the Dharma, or Buddhist Doctrine (Chapters 3, 4, and 5). (For reasons of expediency, I have here inverted the traditional order of the second and third refuges.)

Part Two is then given over to a consideration of the development of Buddhism outside of India, with separate treatments of Sri Lanka and Southeast Asia (Chapter 6), the Tibetan Cultural Area (Chapter 7), China (Chapter 8), Japan (Chapter 9), and the West (Chapter 10). Readers familiar with the first edition of this work will note here the division of the old chapter on East Asia into two chapters on China and Japan and the addition of a full new chapter on Buddhism in the West. The basic organization of Chapters 6–10 seeks to do justice to Buddhism both in its pan-Asian and its culturally specific aspects. Hence (as is readily apparent from a glance at the Contents) the subsections in these chapters all deal with the same set of eight topics: mythic histories, interactions and syncretism, divisional issues, regulation and reform, rituals and festivals, meditational endeavors, women and the sangha, and sangha and society. Doubtless, many other subjects could have been chosen, but what this parallelism means is that these chapters can be read in two ways: either "vertically," one chapter at a time, in order to get a cultural-historical perspective, or "horizontally," skipping through the chapters one set of subsections at a time, in order to get a pan-Buddhist comparative perspective on these various topics.

In choosing the materials to illustrate these topics, I have followed what might be called a "situational" approach and have tended to give preference to selections that embody Buddhist beliefs and practices in "concrete" examples, such as legends, anecdotes, life stories, sermons, and travelers' accounts, rather than in the more "abstract" presentations of codes, principles, or doctrines. Hence, little systematic attention is paid to the development of Buddhist thought outside of India, though the doctrinal background for its evolution there has been set in the chapters of Part One. The topic "sacred biography," used in the first edition, has been dropped, although some of the old readings under that topic have been retained and incorporated in new ways in the other sections.

With some exceptions (especially in the case of Tibetan materials), selections from Buddhist texts were freshly translated, even when other English translations were available. In some instances, the existing translations were less than accurate, in others, they were dated and couched in archaic language, and in still others there were difficulties in obtaining reprint permissions. Nonetheless, references to other translations are found in the notes, so that readers can look them up if they wish to get a "second opinion" on the meaning of a passage or to place it in its overall textual setting. Likewise, if an alternative translation exists only in French or German, a reference is given to it.

Unless otherwise noted, all translations from Sanskrit and Pali texts are my own, as are the translations from the French in sections 6.5.2 and 7.8.1. In the case of Chinese and Japanese materials, I have either used the translations of other scholars or depended on the help of friends and colleagues in Japan and in the United States, chief among them, Sarah M. Strong. In making translations, I have sought for a balance of accuracy and readability, though sometimes I have sacrificed literalness for the sake of ready comprehension. At times, I have felt it necessary to add significant explanatory material, indicated by square brackets, or to eliminate redundancies or skip passages altogether, indicated by ellipses. Ellipses in square brackets denote the omission of a sizable portion of text.

No work such as this one would be possible without the help and encouragement of numerous individuals. In addition to the many persons who originally helped with the first edition, I would like to thank the following colleagues and friends for their advice and input in preparing this second edition: Roger Corless, Cynthia Ann Humes, Steven Kemper, Jacob Kinnard, Harry Krebs, Todd Lewis, Jan Nattier, Trian Nguyen, Jacqueline Stone, Sarah Strong, and Thanissaro Bhikkhu. I implemented some of their suggestions and not others, but all were helpful. The shortcomings that remain are mine alone.

John S. Strong

The Experience of Buddhism

PART ONE

The Experience of Buddhism in South Asia

CHAPTER 1

The Life Story of the Buddha and Its Ramifications

Though few would doubt the historical existence of the north Indian religious teacher who came to be known as the Buddha (the Awakened One), what we know about his life is legend. Scholars are still debating such fundamental points as the dates of his birth and death, some contending that his life should be placed in the sixth and fifth centuries B.C.E., others inclined to situate it as much as one to two hundred years later (440–360 B.C.E.). As for the historicity of many of the stories told about him, there is widespread disagreement. Did the Buddha's mother really die seven days after his birth? Did he really have no knowledge of sickness, old age, and death until his late twenties, when he went for a drive in his chariot? Did he really attain enlightenment in one night at Bodhgaya? The questions about the Buddha are as numerous as the recorded events of his life, but in answering them we are better off thinking of his biography not as "his history" but as "his story."

This does not mean that all Buddhists were in agreement as to what that story was. Eventually, as we shall see below in the selections dealing with the teachings of the Mahāyāna school (Great Vehicle), some Buddhists came to view the whole of the Buddha's life in a radically different context. But more immediately, different groups of Buddhists retold his story in different ways, emphasizing various events or episodes so as to make it into their story. For example, in recounting the start of the Buddha's religious quest, his Great Departure from home, monks might portray it in such a way as to make it resemble their own ordination rituals, whereby they themselves left home to begin a monastic life. Alternatively, laypersons might choose to emphasize stories of the Buddha's previous lives (jātakas), when he accomplished great deeds of merit as a prince or lay householder. Or the people in a particular community might wish to enhance the prestige of their hometown by "recalling" the time when the Buddha himself visited them, thus eventually fabricating stories of his visits to places far from his homeland (for example, Kashmir, Afghanistan, Sri Lanka, Southeast Asia).

This does not mean that these various stories about the Buddha's life were deliberately made up by people plotting to fulfill their own purposes. That is not the way legends are born. As Clifford Geertz has pointed out, myths or legends are as much "models for" reality as they are "models of" it.[1] In other words, the Buddha's life story was both a blueprint for and a reflection of the lives of Buddhists.

Written or oral texts, however, were not the only ways in which the Buddha's story was told. Early on, art and architecture also became important mediums in which the whole of his life or episodes from it were recalled. Narrative bas-reliefs allowed devotees to retrace visually, and in their own religious emotions, the whole of the Buddha's career from his past lives to his birth, his Great Departure and Enlightenment, his first sermon, and his death and cremation. On a grander scale, stūpas (originally monuments built over the relics of the Buddha), or caityas (commemorative monuments), were built at actual sites associated with events in the Buddha's life story. Thus Buddhist pilgrims, by going on a "grand tour" to visit and venerate these monuments, could themselves relive the life of the deceased Master. In this way pilgrimage, and the devotionalism that went with it, became important factors in the ongoing development of the Buddha's biography.

1.1 THE EIGHT COMMEMORATIVE SHRINES

At first, in the development of Buddhist pilgrimage, particular attention was paid to four major sites, each marking a key event in the story of the Buddha:

1. Lumbinī, just over the north Indian border in what is now Nepal, where the Buddha's mother, Queen Māyā, gave birth to him while holding on to the branch of a tree
2. Bodhgaya, in what is now Bihar, in north India, where the Buddha attained enlightenment, sitting under the Bodhi Tree (Tree of Enlightenment)
3. the Deer Park at Sarnath, near the city of Vārāṇasī (Benares) on the Ganges, where the Buddha preached his first sermon, an event that is called Setting in Motion the Wheel of the Dharma (Doctrine)
4. Kusinārā, or Kuśinagarī, the present town of Kasia, where the Buddha, lying between two sal trees, passed away, no longer to be reborn in this or any other world, an event that is known as his parinirvāṇa (complete extinction)

As time went on, four "secondary" sites of pilgrimage were added to these four major sites to form a group of eight. The identification of the Buddha-stories that took place at these four secondary sites varies somewhat from

[1]Clifford Geertz, "Religion as a Cultural System," in *Reader in Comparative Religion,* 4th ed., ed. William A. Lessa and Evon Z. Vogt (New York: Harper and Row, 1979), p. 81.

one textual or iconographic tradition to another, but for the most part they are said to commemorate seemingly supernatural events, thus emphasizing the Buddha's miraculous powers. It is interesting to note, at the same time, that although the four "major" Buddhist sites listed above were all located in groves of trees in rather out-of-the way places, the four "secondary" ones were situated in what were, at the time, major towns and cities:

1. Śrāvastī, the capital of the kingdom of Kosala, where the Buddha is said to have performed a great display of magical powers
2. Sāṃkāśya, or, less commonly, Kānyakubja, a major center upstream on the Ganges, where the Buddha is said to have come down from heaven after preaching the Dharma to the gods of Indra's (the king of the gods) heaven
3. Rājagṛha, the capital of the kingdom of Magadha, where the Buddha is variously thought to have tamed a maddened elephant or put an end to an incipient schism in the community
4. Vaiśālī, the capital of the Licchavi republic, where the Buddha is variously thought to have been given an offering of honey by a monkey or to have announced his decision not to remain in this world

The following text, extant in both Chinese and Tibetan, lists the eight sites in their "chronological" order in his life and advocates devotion to them.

These are the Eight Great Stūpas:

In King Śuddhodana's capital, Kapilavastu, Lumbinī Garden is where the Buddha was born.

In Magadha, by the Nairañjanā River, under the Bodhi Tree, he attained enlightenment.

In the kingdom of Kāśī, in the city of Benares, he set in motion the Wheel of the Great Dharma in twelve ways.

In the great city of Śrāvastī, in the Jetavana monastery, he put on a display of miracles, throughout the Triple World.

In the country of Sāṃkāśya, in the city of Kānyakubja, he came down from the palace of the Thirty-three gods.

In the great city of Rājagṛha, where there was a schism in the community, the Tathāgata [the Buddha] changed the ways of the heretics and practiced compassion.

In the great city of Vaiśālī, a stūpa marks the spot where the Tathāgata reflected upon the duration of his life.

In the city of Kuśinagarī, the place of the very powerful Malla tribe, between the two sal trees, he entered nirvāṇa.

These are the Eight Great Stūpas. . . . Devout laymen and laywomen . . . who build stūpas and caityas . . . will attain great benefit, win meritorious rewards, and be honored. . . . If they worship these Eight Great Stūpas sincerely in this life, they will be reborn, as soon as they die, in one of the heavens.

Source: Translated from *Aṣṭamahāsthānacaityastotra* (Taishō shinshū daizōkyō, ed. J. Takakusu and K. Watanabe [Tokyo, 1924–29], no. 1685, 32:773a).[2]

1.2 A ROYAL PILGRIM RETRACES THE LIFE OF THE BUDDHA

According to Buddhist legend, one of the greatest builders and worshippers of stūpas and caityas was King Aśoka, who ruled as emperor of all of India in the third century B.C.E. and was one of the most important monarchs in the history of Buddhism. Historically speaking, we know from an inscription on a pillar that still stands at the site (see 2.6.3) that Aśoka himself personally visited Lumbinī, the place of the Buddha's birth. But according to a Sanskrit legend, Aśoka is said to have built no fewer than eighty-four thousand stūpas all over India to enshrine the bodily relics of the Buddha, which he collected and had redistributed throughout his kingdom. For centuries, many pilgrimage sites in India and beyond were thought to be centered on the monuments that Aśoka had built. In the following legend, Aśoka is portrayed as accompanying the Buddhist elder Upagupta, who acts as his guide on a tour not only to Lumbinī but to over thirty sites associated with events in the life of the Buddha. It is a good example of the further elaboration of the legend of the Buddha, especially the early events of his childhood and youth, and of the intimate relationship of that story to the practice of pilgrimage.

King Aśoka then prostrated himself in front of the elder Upagupta and said: "Elder, it is my desire to venerate the places where the Blessed Buddha lived, and to mark them with signs as a favor for people in the future."

Upagupta replied, "Very good, Your Majesty, your intention is a fine one. I will, even today, be your guide." . . . And he took him first of all to the Lumbinī Wood, and stretching out his right hand he said, "In this place, Your Majesty, the Blessed One was born. . . .

"This is the first of the caityas
of the Buddha whose vision is unsurpassed.
Here, as soon as he was born,

[2]Alternative English translations, P. C. Bagchi, "The Eight Great Caityas and Their Cult," *Indian Historical Quarterly* 17 (1941): 241; Hajime Nakamura, "The Aṣṭamahāsthānacaityastotra and the Chinese and Tibetan Versions of a Text Similar to It," in *Indianisme et bouddhisme: mélanges offerts à Mgr. Etienne Lamotte* (Louvain: Université Catholique de Louvain, 1980), p. 261; Susan L. Huntington and John C. Huntington, *Leaves from the Bodhi Tree* (Dayton: Dayton Art Institute, 1990), pp. 531–32.

he took seven steps, and
looked down upon the earth in the four directions,
and uttered these words:
'This is my last birth,
my last sojourn in a womb.' " [. . .]

And King Aśoka gave one hundred thousand pieces of gold to the birthplace of the Buddha, built a caitya there, and went on.

The elder Upagupta then led him to Kapilavastu, and stretching out his right hand, he declared: "Your Majesty, in this place, the bodhisattva was brought to his father, King Śuddhodana, and when he saw that his son's handsome body was adorned with the thirty-two marks of the Great Man, the king prostrated himself fully at his feet.

"And this, Your Majesty, is the ancestral temple of the Śākya tribe. Soon after he was born, the bodhisattva was brought here so that he could venerate the clan deities, but, instead, all the statues of the deities fell at the bodhisattva's feet, and King Śuddhodana declared that his son was a god even for the deities, and so gave him the name 'Devātideva' [God beyond gods].

"In this place, Your Majesty, the bodhisattva was shown to the Brahmins who were learned readers of bodily signs; and over here, the sage Asita predicted that he would become a Buddha in this world.

"In this place, Your Majesty, he was brought up by his aunt Mahāprajāpatī; here he was taught how to write; and here, in the bodhisattva's gymnasium, he trained in the arts appropriate to his lineage: riding an elephant and a horse, driving a chariot, handling a bow, grasping a javelin, using an elephant goad. And in this place, Your Majesty, surrounded by a hundred thousand deities, the bodhisattva pursued pleasure with his sixty thousand wives.

"In this place, distressed by the sight of an old man, a sick man and a corpse, the bodhisattva went out to the woods; and over here, sitting down in the shade of a jambu tree, he rid himself of evil and demeritorious inclinations, and attained the first level of trance, . . . and when it was afternoon and the mealtime was past, the lengthening shadows of the trees slanted toward the east, except for the shadow of the jambu tree, which did not leave the body of the bodhisattva. And witnessing this, King Śuddhodana once again prostrated himself fully in front of his son.

"Through this gate over here, surrounded by a hundred thousand gods, the bodhisattva left Kapilavastu at midnight and here he gave his horse and his ornaments to his groom Chandaka, and sent them back to the city . . . while he went on and entered the forest of asceticism.

"In this place, the bodhisattva met the hunter; he gave him his clothes of Benares silk in exchange for a yellow robe, and wandered forth as a recluse. And here, the potter invited the bodhisattva to his hermitage; here King Bimbisāra offered him half of his kingdom; and here he . . . studied . . . under the sages Udraka and Ārāḍa.

"In this place, the bodhisattva practiced extreme asceticism for six years . . . and then gave it up, realizing this was not the path to highest knowledge.

"In this place, Nandā and Nandabalā, the daughters of a village headman, came to the bodhisattva and gave him sweetened milk-rice . . . and after partaking of it he set out for the seat of enlightenment. And over here, on his way to the Bodhi Tree, the bodhisattva was praised by the nāga king, Kālika." [. . .]

Then the elder Upagupta led King Aśoka to the foot of the Bodhi Tree, stretched out his right hand and said: "In this place, Your Majesty, the bodhisattva used his loving kindness to defeat the forces of Māra, and then realized complete unsurpassed enlightenment [anuttara samyak saṃbodhi]. . . ."

And King Aśoka gave one hundred thousand pieces of gold to the Bodhi Tree, built a caitya there, and went on.

Then the elder Upagupta said to Aśoka: "In this place, the Blessed One received from the divine guardians of the four quarters four stone begging bowls which he joined into a single bowl. And over here, he received an offering of alms food from the merchants Trapuṣa and Bhallika. And here, on his way to Benares, the Blessed One was praised by the Ājīvika Upaga."

Then Upagupta led Aśoka to Ṛṣipatana in Sarnath near Benares, and stretching out his right hand he declared: "In this place, Your Majesty, the Blessed One set in motion . . . the magnificent Wheel of Dharma, in order to bring saṃsāra to a standstill.

"In this place, he converted a thousand long-haired ascetics. And over here, he taught the Dharma to King Bimbisāra, and the king, along with eighty-four thousand deities and several thousand Magadhan Brahmin householders, realized the Four Noble Truths. In this place, he taught the Dharma to Indra, the king of the gods, and Indra, together with eighty-four thousand other deities, realized the Truths. In this place, Śrāvāstī, the Blessed One performed a great miracle. Over here in Sāṃkāśya, surrounded by a host of gods, he came down from the Trāyastriṃśa heaven after spending a rainy season retreat there teaching the Dharma to his mother."

Finally, the elder took King Aśoka to Kuśinagarī, and stretching out . . . his right hand, he said: "In this place, Your Majesty, the Blessed One finished doing the work of a Buddha, and attained the state of complete nirvāṇa without remainder." And he added:

> The great, wise, most compassionate Sage
> converted everyone he was to convert—
> gods, men, asuras, yakṣas, and nāgas.
> Then he went to rest, his mind at ease,
> because there was no one left for him to convert.

Hearing this, Aśoka fainted. His attendants splashed some water on his face, and, as soon as he had regained consciousness, he gave a hundred thousand pieces of gold to the site of the Buddha's parinirvāṇa and built a caitya there.

Source: Translated from *The Divyāvadāna*, ed. P. L. Vaidya, Buddhist Sanskrit Texts, no. 20 (Darbhanga: Mithila Institute, 1959), pp. 248–52.

1.3 THE GREAT DEPARTURE AND ENLIGHTENMENT

Two key events in the legend of the Buddha are his decision to leave his family and home to set out on a religious quest—an event known as his Great Departure—and his attainment, six years later, of bodhi (enlightenment)—an event that transforms him from being a bodhisattva (a being headed for enlightenment) into being a Buddha (an Enlightened or Awakened One).

The story of the Buddha's Great Departure was clearly informed by, and a model for, the ordination ritual of Buddhist monks. One of the first things that the Buddha does after leaving home is to cut his hair, to give up his princely clothes in exchange for the rough garb of an ascetic, and to embark, bowl in hand, on the rounds of a mendicant. The same events are ritually reenacted to this day by Buddhist monks, whose initial ordination ceremony, called their wandering forth (pravrajyā), is marked by the shaving of their head, the exchange of their lay clothes for the robes of a monk, and the acquisition of their begging bowl.

The practice of abandoning one's home to adopt a life of religious mendicancy was, however, already widespread in the Buddha's time. It was, in fact, an age that saw all sorts of youthful questers (śramaṇas), not just Buddhists, seeking out teachers and striving for religious satisfaction in one way or another. It was an age of ferment, in which it was thought that enlightenment, salvation, and escape from the prison of repeated rebirths could come only by "dropping out," by quitting the householder's life with its pleasures and obligations. The Buddha's family—the Śākya tribe—being of royal blood, was clearly opposed to the Buddha's Great Departure.

According to Buddhist legend, at the time of the Buddha's birth, some soothsayers had predicted that if he remained at home and inherited his father's throne, he would become a great cakravartin king, or "world-ruling" monarch. The Buddha's father, Śuddhodana, concerned for the future of his family line, understandably preferred his son's becoming a cakravartin king to his becoming a wandering quester. In the hopes of preventing his son's departure, he therefore made the Buddha a virtual prisoner in the palace, surrounding him with bevies of beautiful women and encouraging his attachment to his principal wife, Yaśodharā, and to his newborn son. But all of this was in vain. The Buddha, on a drive in his chariot through the royal park, came across an old person, a sick person, and a corpse and became deeply distressed by the phenomena of old age, sickness, and death. When, on his next outing, he met a wandering śramaṇa who seemed to be at peace with the world, he was inspired to leave home and become a quester himself. Soon thereafter, according to what is perhaps the best-known version of the story, he was filled with disgust by the sight of the sleeping women of his harem, drooling, dissheveled, and snoring, and turning away from his wife and his child, whom he now called Rāhula (a fetter), he left home.

But Buddhist attitudes towards the family and home were more complex and varied than this account, informed by the misogamist attitudes of male monastics, would seem to indicate. The selection that follows, taken from a Sanskrit text, presents a noted variant to the story given above. Here the Buddha's father still tries to keep him at home, and the Buddha's repulsion at the sight of the harem women is still expressed, but his relationship to his wife and child is radically different. Rāhula is not born on the eve of the Great Departure but only engendered then, when the future Buddha makes love to his wife to prove his manhood and to fulfill his duties to his family. To judge from her dreams, Yaśodharā is clearly aware, at least subconsciously, that her husband is about to leave her, but there ensues an interesting parallelism between his career as a quester and her own pregnancy, which develops at home. When he undertakes asceticism, she does likewise; when he fasts, she fasts; when he gets thin, she does, and the growth of the fetus within her is retarded; when he takes food again, she does so as well, and the growth of Rāhula within her resumes; finally, when he attains enlightenment at Bodhgaya, she gives birth at home, having, according to this legend, borne her son in her womb for six years! Here her son's name, Rāhula, is not associated with the word for fetter but with the divinity Rāhu, who eclipses the moon at the moment of his birth, just as his father, upon attaining enlightenment, is thought to outshine the sun.

The Night of the Great Departure

Then King Śuddhodana met with his brothers, Droṇodana, Śuklodana, and Amṛtodana, and said to them: "The brahmin soothsayers and fortunetellers have predicted that my son . . . will become a cakravartin king if he does not leave home to become a wandering ascetic. Therefore we should watch the bodhisattva carefully . . . and keep the city well guarded."

So they encircled the city of Kapilavastu with seven walls and seven moats, and iron doors were put in each city gate. Very loud bells were attached to the doors, so that whenever the doors were opened, they could be heard up to a distance of a league around. They saw to it that the bodhisattva, in his palace, was constantly attended to by entrancingly beautiful women who danced, sang, and played instruments. Royal ministers, commanding armed men and riders, were posted outside on the walls, and they patrolled everywhere, keeping watch all around. Five hundred men were likewise stationed at the door to the bodhisattva's harem and ordered to sound the alarm in King Śuddhodana's quarters were that door to be opened. [. . .]

Now when the bodhisattva was in his harem, in the absence of other men, the women sought to amuse, delight, and seduce him by playing instruments. And it occurred to him: "Lest others say that the Prince Śākyamuni was not a man, and that he wandered forth without 'paying attention' to Yaśodharā, Gopikā, Mṛgajā, and his other sixty thousand wives, let me now make love to Yaśodharā." He did so, and Yaśodharā became pregnant.

That night, in her sleep, Yaśodharā had eight dreams: she saw her own maternal line cut off, her marvelous couch broken, her bracelets broken, her teeth falling out, the braid of her hair undone, happiness departed from her house, the moon eclipsed by Rāhu, and the sun rising in the east and then setting there again.

And the bodhisattva, going to sleep, had five dreams: he saw himself lying on the great earth, with Mount Meru, the king of mountains, as his pillow, his left arm resting in the great Eastern Ocean, his right arm in the great Western Ocean, and his feet in the great Southern Ocean. He saw an upright grass reed grow out of his navel and reach up as far as the sky. He saw large śakunaka birds, all white with black heads, standing at his feet and up as far as his knees. He saw other birds of various colors (varṇa) coming from the four directions and then becoming one color in front of him. He saw himself walking back and forth over a mountain of feces.

Seeing all this, he was pleased and thought: "From what I have seen in my dreams, it will not be long now before I attain highest knowledge."

Then Yaśodharā told the bodhisattva about her eight dreams, . . . and the bodhisattva reflected: "The dreams Yaśodharā has seen are surely related to her worries about my going away today; thus I will speak so as to make light of them." And in order to explain them away, he interpreted them as follows: "You say your maternal line was cut off, but is it not established? You say your couch was broken, but it is not broken; it is right here. You say your bracelets were broken, but see for yourself, they are not. You say your teeth fell out, but you yourself know they have not. You say the braid of your hair was undone, but it is itself; look, it is not undone. You say that 'happiness has left my house,' but for a woman, a husband is happiness, and I am right here. You say the moon was eclipsed by Rāhu, but is that not the moon over there? You say the sun rose in the east and then set there again, but it is now midnight and the sun has not yet risen, so how can it have set?"

At this explanation, Yaśodharā remained quiet. But then she said: "Lord, wherever you go, take me there with you." And the bodhisattva, thinking he was going to nirvāṇa [and would show her the way there], said, "So be it; where I am going, I will take you."

Now Indra, Brahmā, and the other gods, knowing the thoughts of the bodhisattva, approached him and said: . . . "Get up, get up, well-minded one! Leave this place and set out into the world! Upon reaching omniscience, you will save all beings."

The bodhisattva replied: "Do you not see, Indra? I am trapped in a net like the king of beasts. The city of Kapila is completely surrounded by a great many troops, with lots of horses, elephants, chariots, and very capable men bearing bows, swords, and scimitars . . ."

Indra said: "Good sir, recall your former vow, and the past Buddha Dīpaṃkara's prediction [see 1.4.1], that having abandoned this world that is afflicted by suffering, you would wander forth from your home. We gods will arrange it so that you will be able to dwell in the forest this very day, free from all hindrances."

Hearing this, the bodhisattva was very pleased. Then Indra, Lord of the gods and causer of sleepiness, gave orders to Pāñcika, the great yakṣa general: "My friend, bring on sleep, and the bodhisattva will come down from his palace!" So he brought on sleep, and the bodhisattva came out.

Then, as had been prearranged by Indra, the bodhisattva came across his attendant Chandaka, and saw that Chandaka had succumbed to a deep sleep. With some effort, he managed to rouse him and spoke to him this verse:

"Ho! Chanda! Get up, and from the stable,
quickly fetch me Kanthaka,
that jewel of a horse;
I am determined to set out for the forest of asceticism
which previous Buddhas enjoyed
and which brings satisfaction to sages. . . ."

Then the bodhisattva, seeing that the king of horses, Kanthaka, stood ready, . . . mounted him, and with Chandaka holding on behind, he flew up into the air. This was out of the bodhisattva's bodhisattva-power, as well as out of the divine power of the gods.

And because of the departure of the bodhisattva, the divinities who inhabited the harem of the palace began to cry, and the tears of those crying divinities began to fall onto the earth. And Chandaka said: "Prince, drops of water are falling. Why is the god making it rain?" The bodhisattva replied: "The god is not raining, but, because of my departure, the deities who dwell in the harem of the palace are crying; their tears are falling down everywhere." And Chandaka, his own eyes filled with tears, heaved a long emotional sigh, and remained silent.

Then the bodhisattva, turning his whole body around to the right like an elephant, considered the following matter: "This for me is the last night on which I will have lain with a woman." And he further reflected: "I will depart through the eastern gate; were I to go out through another gate, my father, the king, would be upset that I, as prince, did not come to see him and take my leave at this final moment." Therefore he went and gazed upon King Śuddhodana, who was sleeping soundly. He circumambulated him and said: "Father, I am leaving not out of lack of respect, not out of lack of reverence, but for no other reason than that I wish to liberate the world, which is afflicted by old age and death, from the fear of the suffering that comes with old age and death. . . ."

Then, surrounded by several hundreds of thousands of deities headed by Indra and Brahmā, the bodhisattva crossed over to the other side. . . . And, unsheathing his sword, which was like a blue lotus, he cut off his hairknot and threw it very high into the air. It was taken by Indra, king of the gods, and received with great honor by the deities in his heaven, who instituted a Festival of the Hairknot. Also, the faithful brahmin householders in that place established a caitya called the Keśagrahaṇa [Receiving of the Hair] Shrine, which the monks still venerate today. . . .

Receipt of the Robes

[After he had sent Chandaka back to Kapilavastu, together with the horse Kanthaka], there arose the matter of obtaining the bodhisattva's robes. Long ago, in that peerless city, there lived a certain householder who was rich, the possessor of great fortune and felicity, the owner of vast estates, as wealthy and well endowed as the god Vaiśravaṇa. He had married a woman from a family of equal status. They dallied, embraced, and made love, and a son was born. Similarly, in time, ten sons were born, and all of them, wandering forth from the householder's life, became enlightened on their own as pratyekabuddhas. Their mother was then old; she offered to them some robes of hemp, but they said: "Mother, we are going to attain parinirvāṇa. We have no use for these, but King Śuddhodana will have a son named Śākyamuni who will attain unsurpassed complete enlightenment. You should pass these robes on to him. In that way, you will obtain great meritorious rewards."

After saying this, they performed the miracle of simultaneously glittering with both fire and rain showers, and passed away into complete final nirvāṇa. The old woman, at the time of her death, gave the robes to her daughter, telling her everything that had happened. In time, that daughter too became sick, and she, about to succumb to death, placed the robes on a tree, requesting the deity who dwelt in that tree to give them to the son of King Śuddhodana.

Now Indra, king of the gods, sees everything that happens down below. Thus, he went down and took the robes, and then, taking on the form of a hunter ravaged by old age, he dressed himself in those robes and went and stood on the bodhisattva's path, holding a bow and some arrows. And in due time, the bodhisattva came along that path and saw the hunter dressed in the monastic robe, . . . and he said to the man: "Ho! fellow! Those hempen clothes are fit for one who has wandered forth. Take these garments of Benares silk, and give me those in exchange."

The hunter replied: "Prince, I cannot give you these robes, because if I do, there may be others who will say that I deprived a royal prince of his life in order to steal his garments of Benares silk."

The bodhisattva said: "Ho, fellow! The whole world knows me and the kind of power that I have. Who is able to deprive me of life? Who would believe that you could kill me? Give without fear."

Thereupon, Indra fell at the feet of the bodhisattva and presented to him the hempen robes, and he received the bodhisattva's silken robes in exchange, . . . and taking them, he established among the gods in his heaven the Festival of the Benares Silk Robes. And the faithful brahmin householders in that place built a caitya called the Reception of the Monastic Robes Shrine, and the monks still venerate it to this day. . . .

Now the robes of hemp did not fit the bodhisattva's body, so he said: "Oh! May my hempen robes fit my body!" And just as soon as he had uttered those words, the hempen robes became the right size. This also was due to the bodhisattva's bodhisattva-power and to the divine power of the deities. . . .

Meeting with King Bimbisāra

Then the bodhisattva reflected: "The city of Kapilavastu is still near. It would be best not to stay here; the Śākya men could cause a commotion. Therefore, let me cross the Ganges."

So he crossed the Ganges and, walking along, reached the city of Rājagṛha. Being skilled in all the arts and crafts, the bodhisattva then made a begging bowl of oleander leaves and . . . entered Rājagṛha to go questing for alms. At that time, King Bimbisāra was walking on the terrace of his palace. He saw the bodhisattva and, impressed by his demeanor, had his bowl filled with food. . . . [He then later went to visit him on nearby Mount Pāṇḍava.]

"I want to give you, for your enjoyment," he declared, "a bevy of women, unsurpassed riches. . . ."

"O, King," replied the bodhisattva, "I am a kṣatriya, a Śākya, I belong to the solar clan, descendant of Ikṣvāku. I come from Kosala, a kingdom near the Himālayas. It is filled with riches and grain; I do not long for sensual pleasures."

"Sir," Bimbisāra then asked him, "for what purpose did you wander forth?"

The bodhisattva answered: "For unsurpassed complete enlightenment."

The king said: "Sir, when you attain unsurpassed complete enlightenment, then please turn your thoughts to me."

"I will do so," the bodhisattva replied, and he departed from Rājagṛha.

Study with Various Teachers

Not far from there, near Vulture's Peak, there was a hermitage of ascetics, and that is where the bodhisattva now went. He stayed there and meditated, engaging in those ascetics' practices. If they stood on one foot for a portion of the day, the bodhisattva did so for two portions. If they engaged in the painful practice of sitting between four fires with the sun shining overhead for one portion of the day, the bodhisattva did so for two. In this way they were amazed, and began to call him the great quester. . . .

The bodhisattva asked them: "Sirs, what is the purpose of your practice?"

And some said, "We want to gain the status of the god Indra"; and others said, "We want to gain the status of Brahmā"; and still others said, "We want to gain the status of Māra."

And the bodhisattva thought, "Indeed, these ascetics are caught in a whirlpool, practicing a wrong path."

So, finding that path inadequate, he went to the hermitage of Ārāḍa Kālāma. . . . He asked Ārāḍa what sorts of dharmas he had realized.

"O, Gautama," answered Ārāḍa, "everything up to the stage of nothingness."

The bodhisattva then declared: "The faith of Ārāḍa Kālāma is also my faith. The determination, the mindfulness, the concentration, the wisdom of Ārāḍa Kālāma are also my determination, mindfulness, concentration, and wisdom. The dharmas that Ārāḍa Kālāma has realized, up to the stage of nothingness, I will realize." . . .

[The bodhisattva then followed and completed all of Ārāḍa's practices, but he was not fulfilled by them.] "This path," he declared, "is not adequate for knowledge, not adequate for seeing, not adequate for unsurpassed total enlightenment."

And having thus determined Ārāḍa's path to be insufficient, the bodhisattva went to Udraka Rāmaputra. . . . He asked Udraka what sorts of dharmas he had realized.

"O, Gautama," Udraka replied, "everything up to the stage of neither perception nor nonperception."

The bodhisattva then declared: "The faith of Udraka Rāmaputra is also my faith. The determination, mindfulness, concentration, and wisdom of Udraka Rāmaputra are also my determination, mindfulness, concentration and wisdom. The dharmas that Udraka Rāmaputra has realized, up to the stage of neither perception nor non-perception, I will realize." . . .

[The bodhisattva then followed and completed all of Udraka's practices, but he was not fulfilled by them either.] "This path too," he declared, "is not adequate for knowledge, not adequate for seeing, not adequate for unsurpassed total enlightenment."

And having thus determined that path to be insufficient, the bodhisattva went on.

The Practice of Austerities

Now King Śuddhodana, overcome by sorrow for his son, constantly sent out messengers to search for the bodhisattva. In this way, he learned that the bodhisattva had left Udraka Rāmaputra, departed Rājagṛha, and was wandering around without any attendants. Having heard that, he sent three hundred servants to attend to him. And in the same royal city, the Śākya Suprabuddha, Queen Māyā's father, heard the same news, and he sent two hundred servants. So the bodhisattva, surrounded by five hundred attendants, wandered in the forest of asceticism.

Soon, he reflected: "Dwelling in crowds is no good for discipline in ascetic practices and is antithetical to the search for the deathless state. Therefore I will retain five servants only and send the others away." So he kept two from the maternal side and three from the paternal side, and they attended to his needs.

Now, with his entourage of five attendants, he went on a journey to the south of Gayā, to Urubilvā, the village of Senāpati. There he found a lovely spot, a grove of trees near the Nairañjanā River. . . . And he sat himself firmly down at the base of a tree, clenched his teeth, placed the tip of his tongue on his palate, and grabbed, gathered, and pressed hard his thoughts with his mind. . . . [And he began to fast.] As he gradually took smaller and smaller amounts of food, his backbone became like a string of beads, and his buttocks became like the foot of a camel. Taking hold of his body from the front, he found he held it at the back. Taking hold of it from the back, he found he held it in front. He rubbed and stroked his body with his hands, and where he did so his hairs readily fell off. [. . .]

In the meantime, King Śuddhodana heard that the bodhisattva was practicing austerities, and he sent 250 spies to report on his activities. And Suprabuddha as well sent 250 spies. And they, every day, sent various reports back to Kapilavastu: "The bodhisattva is carrying out such and such an austerity." "He is eating a meal of one sesame seed, one grain of rice, one jujube, one pulse pod, one bean . . ." "He is sleeping on darbha grass."

Learning all this, King Śuddhodana became very worried about his son, and, his eyes clouded with tears, his heart and mind in torment, he suffered himself and began to make his own bed on darbha grass.

And the bodhisattva's wife, Princess Yaśodharā, . . . learning the news about her husband, was overcome with sorrow for him, and, her face wet with tears, her ornaments and garlands cast aside, despondent, she too undertook austerities. She too began to eat meals of one sesame seed, one grain of rice, one jujube, one pulse pod, one bean, and she slept on a bed of straw. As a result, the child in her womb wasted away.

King Śuddhodana heard of her condition and reflected: "If Yaśodharā continues every day to receive news of the bodhisattva, and thereby to be stricken with sorrow for her husband, and to persist miserably in her asceticism, she will not be able to bear this fetus, and it will perish."

Therefore he undertook measures to ensure that no more news of the bodhisattva be told to Yaśodharā. . . . The spies were instructed to communicate any information about the bodhisattva only to Śuddhodana. And keeping what he heard secret, and hiding his own distress from Yaśodharā, he deceived the whole harem, and Yaśodharā regained her health. . . .

Meanwhile, the bodhisattva, who was practicing bodily austerities, thought: "No one engaged in the discipline of great ascetic striving has ever transcended suffering; therefore this path as well is not adequate for knowledge, not adequate for seeing, not adequate for unsurpassed total enlightenment." And he began to relax his strenuousness; and his body, which had been suppressed, became calm, . . . and his mind, which had been repressed, became one-pointed.

And he reflected: "What is the way that is adequate for knowledge, for seeing, for unsurpassed total enlightenment?" Then it occurred to him: "I remember when, as a boy, I sat down in the shade of the jambu tree while attending a festival at the place of my father Śuddhodana; at that time, I attained a trance state that was free from sensual desires, free from sinful and demeritorious things, thoughtful, reflective, arising from discrimination, and blissful. That must be the way, that must be the path that is adequate for knowledge, for seeing, for unsurpassed total enlightenment. . . ."

So the bodhisattva began to take substantial food, porridge and gruel, and he rubbed his limbs with ghee and oil, and he took a warm bath. . . . And gradually he regained his bodily strength, his vigor and energy, and, in time, he went to the village of Senāyani. There, lived a villager named Sena. He had two daughters, Nandā and Nandabalā. They had heard that the bodhisattva was the prince of the Śākyas, who had been born in the foothills of the Himālayas on the banks of the Bhāgīratha River, not far from the hermitage of the sage Kapila, and that brahmin soothsayers had predicted he would become a cakravartin king. . . . So they prepared for him, in a crystal bowl, some sweetened milk-rice condensed sixteen times. . . .

Then the bodhisattva consumed the milk-rice, and, after washing the bowl, he threw it into the Nairañjanā River. There the nāgas took hold of it. But the gods are aware of what happens down below, and Indra, king of the gods, took on the form of a garuḍa bird, stirred up the waters of the Nairañjanā, terrified the nāgas, took away the bowl, and instituted a Festival of the Bowl among the gods in his heaven.

Then the bodhisattva asked Nandā and Nandabalā: "What did you seek by virtue of your gift?"

They replied: "Blessed One, as a result of the merit of our gift and of our resolution, we would like to have you, the Prince of the Śākyas, as our husband, . . . you who, the soothsayers predicted, would become a cakravartin king."

The bodhisattva replied: "This is not possible; I am one who has wandered forth and have no desire for sensual pleasures."

They said: "Blessed One, if that is the case, let the meritorious fruit of this act of giving be your highest enlightenment." [. . .]

Enlightenment Obtained

Then, having received some grass from the grass-cutter Svastika, the bodhisattva approached the foot of the Bodhi Tree, by the road pointed out to him by the gods. Getting there, he prepared a broad, nicely arranged, firmly established seat of grass. . . . And mounting this adamantine throne, he sat down with his legs crossed like a sleeping snake-king's coils. Holding his body upright and fixing his mind in front of him, he resolved: "I will not uncross my legs until the destruction of defilements has been attained." [. . .]

And in the first watch of the night, he inclined his mind toward achieving firsthand knowledge of the field of supernatural powers, . . . and he set himself to the task of remembering, in a firsthand way, his former births. . . . He recalled his many various previous existences: one birth, two, three, four, . . . ten, twenty, thirty, forty, fifty, a thousand, . . . many thousands, . . . many hundreds of thousands. . . .

And in the second watch of the night, he inclined his mind to achieving firsthand knowledge of the transmigration of beings from one existence to another. With his pure divine eye transcending human sight, he saw beings dying and being reborn, of good caste and bad, low and high, in good rebirths, in unfortunate ones. . . . They were wandering in saṃsāra according to the evil inclinations of their sensual desires, birth, and ignorance. . . .

Then in the third watch of the night, he declared his intention to achieve direct perception of the destruction of evil inclinations, and disciplining himself and persevering, he meditated on the dharmas that are conducive to enlightenment. . . . And he truly realized: "This is the Noble Truth of Suffering; this is the Origination of Suffering; this is the Cessation of Suffering; this is the Noble Truth of the Way leading to the Cessation of Suffering." Knowing that and seeing that, he was then released from thoughts inclined to sensual desire, he was released from thoughts inclined to rebirth, he was released from thoughts inclined to ignorance. And released, he had a realization of his liberation: "Destroyed is my birth; consumed is my striving; done is what had to be done; I will not be born into another existence!" Thus the Blessed One attained to the highest enlightenment. . . .

Birth of Rāhula

When the Buddha attained highest enlightenment, Māra, . . . the evil-minded One, was angry. Making himself invisible, he spitefully had his godlings announce to the city of Kapilavastu: "The bodhisattva

Śākyamuni, after practicing austerities and mounting the adamantine throne, has died on his seat of grass."

Hearing this, King Śuddhodana, together with his harem, the princes, and his ministers, was stricken with great sorrow, as was the whole population of Kapilavastu. And . . . Yaśodharā, remembering the qualities of her husband, fainted and fell on the ground. Recovering her senses when some water was sprinkled on her face, she lamented incessantly, her face ever filled with tears, her words choked with sobs, the women of the harem trying to console her.

Soon, however, seeing that her behavior was in response to a deception, some divinities who had faith in the Buddha declared, "The bodhisattva is not dead, but he has attained highest knowledge."

Hearing this, King Śuddhodana, together with his entourage and the population of Kapilavastu, was transported with great joy.

Now when the Blessed One attained highest knowledge, Yaśodharā gave birth to a son. . . . And King Śuddhodana, seeing this good fortune, was pleased, happy, delighted, filled with highest joy. He arranged for a great celebration in the city of Kapilavastu. . . . And because, at the time of the boy's birth, Rāhu had caused an eclipse of the moon, the bodhisattva's son was given the name Rāhula.

Source: Translated from *The Gilgit Manuscript of the Saṃghabhedavastu, Being the 17th and Last Section of the Vinaya of the Mūlasarvāstivādin,* ed. Raniero Gnoli (Rome: Istituto Italiano per il Medio ed Estremo Oriente, 1977), 1:78–119.

1.4 REMEMBERING PAST LIVES

According to tradition, as we have just seen, during the three watches of the night of his enlightenment under the Bodhi Tree, the Buddha had a number of distinct experiences. In the first watch, he is said to have remembered systematically all of his previous lives, thereby not only showing his mastery over time but also reviewing the course of his karmic history. For it rapidly became clear, in the Buddhist tradition, that an achievement such as Buddhahood was not the result of the quest of a single lifetime, lasting only a few years, but the end product of a long series of previous lives devoted to the accumulation of merit and the practices of perfection necessary for the making of a Buddha. The story of the Buddha, therefore, was quickly extended to include hundreds of tales of his previous lives (jātakas), in which he is generally portrayed as the hero.

1.4.1 Planting the Seeds of Buddhahood

The number of one's previous lives is theoretically infinite, for the course of rebirth is beginningless. The process of becoming a Buddha, however, is not. It starts, as in the following jātaka story of Sumati (who in other versions of this tale is known as Megha or Sumedha), with a simple devotional gesture, such as the offering of some flowers, and with the making of a firm resolution, or vow, to attain Buddhahood at some time in the future. These relatively simple religious acts are seen as tremendously effective because they are directed toward and confirmed by a previous fully enlightened Buddha, in this case the past Buddha Dīpaṃkara.

And here we come to another dimension of the developing tradition: early on, perhaps from the very start of Buddhism, it was thought that "our" Buddha, Siddhārtha Gautama, the sage of the Śākyas (Śākyamuni), was but one of a whole series of Buddhas who had succeeded one another over the aeons. Various lists of these previous Buddhas, sometimes specified as six or twenty-four but theoretically infinite in number, were established, as were lists of future Buddhas, also variously numbered but focusing on the next Buddha, Maitreya, presently awaiting his "turn" in residence in one of the Buddhist heavens.

In this vast scenario, however, one important rule seems to have been invariable: to become a Buddha, one first has to meet a Buddha and be inspired or awakened by him to begin the long process of the bodhisattva path, which may last hundreds of lifetimes but which will eventually lead to Buddhahood. The story of Sumati, then, is the legend of the bodhisattva Śākyamuni's "first" jātaka, the tale of his initial awakening, when he met the past Buddha Dīpaṃkara, long ago.

[Then the Buddha, recalling his former life, said to the monks: At that time,] there appeared in the world a Blessed Buddha named Dīpaṃkara, completely enlightened as to knowledge and conduct, a Perfected One, knowing the world, the unsurpassed guide of those who are to be converted, a teacher of gods and humans.

Wandering here and there in the land, the Buddha Dīpaṃkara came to the royal capital of Dīpāvatī. There, ruled a king named Dīpa, who spread prosperity, abundance, peace, and plenty among the people. And King Dīpa invited the Buddha Dīpaṃkara to enter the city with a resolute mind.

Now in a neighboring kingdom there was another king, named Vāsava. He proclaimed a twelve-year sacrifice, at the end of which he put on display five great presents: a golden water jar with a handle, a golden food bowl, a couch made of four kinds of gems, five hundred pieces of gold, and a maiden adorned with all her jewelry. These, he declared, would be given to whatever brahmin was most accomplished in knowledge of the Vedas.

Not too far away, dwelt two youths who had studied the Veda. Knowing that it was the custom to give their preceptor a preceptor's fee and their teacher a teacher's fee, they were wondering how they would do this when they heard what King Vāsava had proclaimed. "Those presents are as good as ours," they thought, "for who is there more learned and knowledgeable than us?" With this in mind, they set out for the great city of King Vāsava.

In the meantime, the king had a vision of a divinity, who said to him: "Your Majesty, of the two youths who are coming, Sumati and Mati, give the offerings to Sumati. You have carried out a sacrifice for twelve years;

from the meritorious fruit of that act, you can now make a great offering to the youth Sumati, who is of the highest rank. . . ."

When the king saw the two youths approaching, filled with grace and charm, . . . he thought he should do what was recommended by the gods, so he went up to the first youth and asked, "Sir, are you Sumati?"

Sumati replied, "I am."

Then King Vāsava seated young Sumati on the highest seat, regaled him with food, and presented him with the five presents. The young Sumati accepted the first four of them, but he did not accept the gift of the maiden. "I am celibate," he explained.

The girl, seeing how gracious and charming young Sumati was, was filled with desire and love and pleaded with him, saying, "Brahmin, take me."

But he replied, "I cannot take you."

Now since King Vāsava had given away that girl as a present, he could not take her back again, . . . so she went away to Dīpāvatī, the city of King Dīpa. Upon arrival there, she removed all of her jewelry and gave it to a garland maker, asking him, in return, to provide her every day with blue lotuses so that she could worship the gods.

In the meantime, Sumati took the four presents he had accepted and went and gave them to his teacher. His teacher agreed to accept three of them, but he gave the five hundred gold pieces back to Sumati. That very night, Sumati had ten dreams: he dreamed that he drank the great ocean; that he flew through the air; that he touched and clasped with his hand both the sun and the moon; that he harnessed the chariot of the king; and that he saw ascetics, white elephants, geese, lions, a great rock, and mountains. He then woke up and thought, "Who can clarify for me the meaning of these dreams?"

Not far from there lived an ascetic endowed with five supernatural powers. Accordingly, the young Sumati went to him . . . and asked him to interpret his dreams.

The ascetic said: "I cannot clarify the meaning of these dreams for you, but go to the royal city of Dīpāvatī. King Dīpa has invited the Buddha Dīpaṃkara there, . . . [and] he will be able to interpret your dreams. . . ."

Now, in the royal city of Dīpāvatī, King Dīpa had requisitioned all the flowers from all the flower merchants in the land, thinking that in seven days, he would welcome the Buddha Dīpaṃkara into the city. . . . And when all the flowers had been gathered by the king, the girl, who was now a devout worshipper of the gods, went to her garland maker and said, "Give me some blue lotuses; I wish to carry out the service of the gods."

But the garland maker replied, "Today, the king has taken all of the blossoms for Dīpaṃkara's entrance into the city."

She said, "Go back again to the lotus pool and see if, through my merit, you cannot find some blue lotus flowers that have not been taken away."

The garland maker went there and saw that, through the power of her merit, seven blue lotuses had appeared in the pool.

"Please pluck them," she asked.

The garland maker replied: "I cannot pick them; I will be blamed by the king's men. . . ."

But she insisted: "Pluck these blossoms and give them to me; they have appeared on account of my merits."

"How will you get them into the city without the knowledge of the king's men?"

"Pluck them, sir, and I will enter the city with them hidden in a water pot."

Thus reassured, the garland maker plucked the blossoms and gave them to her. She took them, hid them in a jar, filled the jar with water, and set out for the city.

Now, just at that time, young Sumati arrived in that place, and he reflected: "I should pay homage to the Blessed Buddha when I see him, but with what?" So he went from one garland maker's house to another, inquiring everywhere after flowers, but he did not find a single blossom. . . .

Then, in his search, he came to that garden and met the girl just as she was leaving. Out of the power of her merit, the blue lotuses suddenly emerged from her water pot.

Seeing them, Sumati said to her, "Give me five of those lotuses, and in exchange I will give you five hundred pieces of gold."

The girl said to Sumati: "Formerly you wanted to have nothing to do with me; now, you ask me for my lotuses. I will not give them to you!" But then she went on: "What will you do with them?"

Sumati replied, "I wish to honor the Blessed Buddha."

Thereupon, the girl said: "I too wish to give flowers to the Buddha. So what am I to do with these gold pieces? But I will give you these lotuses on one condition: if you, at the time of your offering them to the Buddha, make a formal, earnest wish to have me as your wife in life after life, saying, 'May she become my spouse in repeated existences.' "

To this Sumati agreed, . . . and the girl gave him five lotuses and retained two for herself. . . .

Then, starting at the city gate, King Dīpa had the road cleared of all stones, gravel, and potsherds. He had flags, banners, and archways put up, bands of cloth fastened, and perfumed water and sandalwood powder sprinkled about. . . . And taking a hundred-ribbed umbrella, the king set out to meet the Buddha Dīpaṃkara. And so did King Vāsava [who had come to the city] and all of their ministers. And King Dīpa fell at the feet of the Blessed Buddha and declared: "Blessed One, take possession of this place."

Then the Blessed One, at the head of the community of monks, proceeded to enter into the city with proper mental preparation. And King Dīpa held a hundred-spoked umbrella for the altogether enlightened Dīpaṃkara, and so did his ministers, and so did King Vāsava and his ministers, but through his supernatural power, the Blessed One made it so that each and every one of them felt "I am holding the umbrella over the Blessed One!" . . .

Then the Blessed One, with proper mental preparation, set his foot down on the threshold stone of the city gate, . . . and immediately the earth shook in six ways. It shivered, shook, quaked, trembled, grumbled, and rumbled. It is the norm, whenever Blessed Buddhas set their foot down on the threshold stone of the city gate with proper mental preparation, that various extraordinary marvels occur. The insane recover their minds, the blind can see again, the deaf become able to hear, the mute become able to speak, the lame become able to walk; women's difficult pregnancies become regular; those who are bound by fetters find their bonds have loosened; those who have been attached to enmity in birth after birth suddenly become full of love; calves break their tethers and are united with their mothers; elephants trumpet, horses neigh, bulls bellow, and parrots, myna birds, cuckoos, and pheasants warble delightfully; musical instruments, without being struck, make a sweet sound; ornaments put in boxes tinkle pleasantly; the places on earth that are high are made low, and the places that are low are lifted up; stones, gravel, and potsherds disappear; from midair, deities throw down divine blossoms, lotuses, lilies, aloe powder, sandalwood powder, tagara powder, tamāla leaves, and divine māndāra flowers. . . .

And there in the royal city of Dīpāvatī, hundreds of thousands of living beings paid homage to the Buddha Dīpaṃkara with flowers and incense and perfumes. Sumati and the girl also followed the Blessed One, holding their lotuses, but they were not able to get near him, surrounded as he was by the great crowd of people intending to worship him.

But the Blessed One then reflected: "This young Sumati is to become a great source of merit to this large crowd of people." So he magically fashioned a tumultuous rainstorm. In that way, the crowd dispersed, and, now that there was more room, Sumati was able to see the entrancing sight of the Blessed One, and great faith was engendered in him. Filled with faith, he tossed his five lotuses toward the Buddha Dīpaṃkara; just as they fell, the Blessed One magically fashioned them into a canopy of flowers the size of a wagon wheel, which, suspended in the air, followed him when he moved and remained stationary when he stopped.

When the girl saw this, faith was engendered in her also, and she tossed her two lotuses to the Blessed One. And again, just as they fell, they were magically fashioned into canopies the size of wagon wheels and took up their position on either side of the Buddha's head.

Now, in that place, a lot of mud had been created by the heavy downpour. So the young Sumati went up to the Blessed Buddha, and on the muddy ground in front of him, he spread out his long hair and spoke this verse:

"If I am to become a Buddha, awakened to enlightenment, may you tread with your feet on my hair—on my birth, old age, and death."

And the Buddha Dīpaṃkara trod upon the young Sumati's locks . . . and he made a prediction about him: "Freed from human existence, you will become an effective Teacher, for the sake of the world. Born among the Śākyas, as the epitome of the Triple World, the Lamp of all Beings, you will be known as Śākyamuni."

When young Sumati had received this prediction from the Buddha Dīpaṃkara, he, at that very moment, rose up into the air to the height of seven palm trees. And his hair fell out, and other even better hair appeared in its place. And a great many people, seeing him aloft in midair, made this firm resolve: "When this one attains to the highest knowledge, may we become his disciples."

And the girl too made a vow: "When you fulfill your resolve to become a Buddha, a guide, then I would be your wife, your constant companion in the Dharma. When you become completely enlightened, a most excellent trainer of the world, then I would, at that time, become your disciple. . . ."

And King Vāsava taking the hair that had fallen from Sumati's head, counted eighty thousand strands of it. His ministers then said to him: "Lord, give each of us one of these hairs, and we will enshrine them in caityas."

So the king gave his ministers one hair each, and they, each going to their own districts, set up a caitya. . . .

[What do you think monks? asked the Buddha.] He who was in that time King Vāsava, he is now King Bimbisāra; and those who were his eighty thousand ministers are now eighty thousand deities; . . . and she who was the girl, is now Yaśodharā; and he who was Sumati—that was myself, practicing the bodhisattva path.

Source: Translated from *The Divyāvadāna*, ed. E. B. Cowell and R. A. Neil (Cambridge: Cambridge University Press, 1886), pp. 246–53.[3]

1.4.2 The Last Past Life: The Story of Vessantara

Of the hundreds of tales that were and still are told by Buddhists about the exploits of the Buddha in his previous lives, the one that stands out as being the most popular is the Vessantara jātaka. There are many versions of this tale, which in South and Southeast Asia is as well known as the biography of the Buddha Gautama himself.

It recounts the penultimate life of the Buddha as Prince Vessantara, during which he perfected the practice of giving (dāna) and exhibited the sort of utter generosity that is born from compassion for others and from the realization of the truths of selflessness and impermanence. There is nothing that Vessantara will not give if it is asked of him. He gives away the white elephant of state to a neighboring kingdom, something that gets him in trouble with his own people. They chase him and his family away, but still he gives: his possessions, and then the chariot he is riding in. Together with his wife and children he proceeds on foot, and he seemingly reaps the rewards of his virtue, for the gods, and nature itself, end up providing him with food and a place to live. But then there are further tests: a wandering brahmin comes and asks for his children; another comes and requests his wife. Vessantara gives them all away, glad to be of service.

The Vessantara story is truly a poignant one, but its appeal is many faceted. Vessantara is an impressive example of someone who has taken one of the most commonly advocated lay practices of Buddhism—giving—to its furthest

---

[3]Alternative German translation, Heinrich Zimmer, *Karman: ein buddhistischer Legendenkranz* (Munich: Verlag F. Bruckmann, 1925), pp. 42–60.

limits. Buddhists were not blind to some of the ethical difficulties involved in this practice. In a semicanonical text, *The Questions of King Milinda*, Milinda points out that Vessantara's generosity, though perhaps worthy of admiration, brought grief and suffering to his children and his wife. The monk Nāgasena, whom he is questioning, admits as much but then suggests that the end justifies the means; Vessantara's actions are comparable to rushing a sick person to a doctor by bullock cart, even though it inflicts pain on the bullocks. In the tale itself, the Buddha, remembering his own previous life, appears to say something similar: "It is not that he disliked his children but that he loved omniscience more." By perfecting practices such as dāna, he could become a Buddha, and by becoming a Buddha, he could help everyone.

In some versions of the story, after Vessantara proves his generosity, everything is restored to him. Like Job in the Bible, he was only being tested by the gods. In the following Pali verse rendition of the tale, presented as being recounted by the Buddha himself in the first person, this does not happen, and Vessantara ends up possessionless, wifeless, without children, and alone in a hermitage. Interestingly, it might be noted that this is much the same situation as that of a Buddhist monk, which Vessantara has here achieved though still a layperson.

My mother, Phusatī, had borne me for nine months when, while circumambulating the city, she gave birth to me in the Street of the Merchants.

My name came neither from the maternal nor the paternal side of my family; because I was born there, in the Street of the Merchants, I was called Vessantara [Among the Merchants].

When I was eight years old, a mere boy, seated in the palace, I thought of making offerings.

I would give my heart, my eyes, and my flesh—even my blood! I announced I would give my body, if anyone were to ask me for it!

The sincerity of my thoughts was so unshakable and steadfast that Earth trembled, even up to the pleasure gardens of the gods on Mount Meru.

Every fortnight, on the uposatha days of the full and the new moon, I mounted the elephant Paccaya and went out to make offerings.

One day, brahmins from the kingdom of Kalinga approached me and asked me for my elephant, who was considered to be auspicious and brought good fortune to the state.

"Our country," they declared, "is suffering from drought, scarcity of food, a great famine; give us your excellent all-white elephant, the acme of its kind."

I did not hesitate. I gave what the brahmins asked me for. I did not keep back anything, I rejoiced at my gift.

It was not in my nature to turn down any request that came my way. I would not break my resolve. . . .

Taking the elephant by the trunk, I sprinkled water from a jeweled vase in my hand, and by this gesture gave the elephant to the brahmins.

As I was doing this, once again, Earth trembled, even up to the pleasure gardens of the gods on Mount Meru.

Because I gave away the state elephant, the people of my country, Sivi, were angry. They assembled and voted to send me away from my own kingdom, saying, "Let him go to Mount Vaṅka."

Unshakable and steadfast, I asked those who were throwing me out to grant me one wish: to be able to bestow another gift.

Thus asked, the people of Sivi accorded me my one wish, and I, beating a ceremonial drum, gave the great gift.

Then there was a great clamor, a frightful tumult; because of a gift, they had driven me out, but now I was giving gifts again!

I gave away elephants, horses, chariots, male and female slaves, cattle, money! I made the great gift! And then I left the city.

And when I was leaving the city, I turned to look at it one last time, and then too Earth trembled, even up to the pleasure gardens of the gods on Mount Meru.

At a great crossroads, I gave away my four-horsed chariot, and standing there by myself, without an attendant, I said to my wife, Maddī:

"You carry Kaṇhā; she is light and younger. I will take Jāli, her brother, who is heavier."

Maddī took up Kaṇhājinā, who was like a white lotus flower, and I took up the young noble Jāli, who was like the golden disk of the sun.

We four persons, well-born, refined, nobles, trod along that road, rough and smooth, heading for Mount Vaṅka.

We asked whomever we met, going or coming along the road, "What is the way to Mount Vaṅka?"

And they, seeing us, uttered words of pity and expressed their sorrow: "Mount Vaṅka is far away."

When the children saw on a hillside trees laden with fruit, they whined on account of those fruits.

And seeing the children crying, those great tall trees, quite on their own, bent down and extended their branches to them.

Seeing this miraculous, marvelous, astonishing thing, Maddī, lovely in every limb, sang out in praise:

"A miracle! Marvelous, astonishing in this world! Because of Vessantara's glory, the trees have bent down of their own accord."

And out of compassion for the children, the spirits shortened the road, . . . and departing from there, we arrived at Mount Vaṅka.

The king of the gods then spoke to the deity Vissakamma, who was endowed with great supernatural powers: "Build for them a hermitage, a pleasant well-made hut out of leaves."

Hearing Indra's command, Vissakamma did as he was told. And entering the quiet and peaceful grove, we four dwelt there on the mountain.

I and Queen Maddī, and both Jāli and Kaṇhājinā, dwelt there in the hermitage, comforting one another.

I was not useless: I watched over the children in the hermitage. And Maddī gathered fruit; she provided for three people besides herself.

While I was dwelling in the grove, a wanderer came to me and asked me to give him the children, both Jāli and Kaṇhājinā.

Seeing the supplicant there, I was filled with joy. And taking hold of both children, I gave them to the brahmin, Jūjaka.

While I was giving up my own children, again Earth trembled, even up to the pleasure gardens of the gods on Mount Meru.

Then, once more, Indra descended, and, taking on the form of a brahmin, he asked me to give him my virtuous, devoted wife, Maddī.

Taking Maddī by the hand, I gave her to him, filling his hands with water. I was gladdened by my resolve.

When Maddī was being given away, the deities in the sky rejoiced. And then too Earth trembled, even up to the pleasure gardens of the gods on Mount Meru.

I did not think twice about abandoning Jāli, my daughter, Kaṇhājinā, and my devoted wife, Maddī; it was all done for enlightenment.

It is not that I hated the children nor that I disliked Maddī, but that I loved omniscience. That is why I gave away those who were dear to me. . . .

Source: Translated from *Cariyāpiṭaka*, ed. Richard Morris (London: Pali Text Society, 1882), pp. 7–10.[4]

1.5 VIEWING THE COSMOS

In the second watch of the night of his enlightenment, as we have seen, the Buddha is said to have used the supernatural power of his divine eye to survey the entire world and all the beings in it, as they were dying out of and being reborn into the various realms of rebirth. One of the epithets of the Buddha is that he "knows the world." He can directly perceive the situation of all beings everywhere—not just humans but also animals, ghosts, denizens of hell, gods—and he is aware of their suffering. Such an experience is significant for a number of reasons. First of all, it demonstrates the Buddha's mastery over the element of space; second, it reflects his compassion for the beings of the universe; finally, as a total survey of the universe and all modes of rebirth in it, it confirms the fact that there is, in the whole of saṃsāra, no place of refuge, no escape from suffering.

1.5.1 The Hierarchy of Beings

A number of these themes are reiterated in the following passage, repeated verbatim in many Buddhist Sanskrit legends, where the vision of the cosmos, and the compassion that goes with it, are associated with the Buddha's smile, a cosmic smile that illuminates the entire universe and alleviates the pain of beings in it.

---

[4]Alternative English translation, I. B. Horner, *Minor Anthologies of the Pali Canon, Part 3* (London: Pali Text Society, 1975), pp. 10–14.

Now it is the norm that whenever Blessed Buddhas manifest their smile, blue, yellow, red, and dazzlingly white rays issue forth from their mouth, and some go down and some go up. Those that go down enter the Sañjīva, Kālasūtra, Raurava, Mahāraurava, Tapana, Pratāpana, Avīci, Arbuda, Nirarbuda, Aṭaṭa, Hahava, Huhuva, Utpala, Padma, and Mahāpadma hells. And in the hells that are hot, they become cold; and in the hells that are cold, they become hot. In this manner, the various sufferings of the hell-beings are allayed, and they ask themselves: "What is happening to us? Have we ended our stay here? Have we been reborn elsewhere?"

But then, in order to engender their faith, the Blessed One creates a magical image of himself, and seeing this image, they realize: "We have not left this place, nor have we been reborn elsewhere, but this being was not to be seen before; it must be by his power that our various sufferings have been alleviated." Their minds fill with faith at the sight of the magical image of the Buddha, they cast off the karma they have yet to suffer in the hells, and they take birth among gods or humans, where they become vessels of the Truth.

Those rays that go upward, enter the abodes of the various gods: the Cāturmahārājika, Trayastriṃśat, Yāma, Tuṣita, Nirmāṇarati, Paranirmitavaśavartin, Brahmakāyika, Brahmapurohita, Mahābrahma, Parīttābha, Apramāṇābha, Ābhāsvara, Parīttaśubha, Apramāṇaśubha, Śubhakṛtsna, Anabhraka, Puṇyaprasava, Bṛhatphala, Abṛha, Atapa, Sudṛśa, Sudarśana, and Akaniṣṭha heavens. In those heavens, they proclaim the facts of impermanence, suffering, emptiness, and nonself. . . .

After thus coursing through the great trichiliocosm, all of the rays then return to the Buddha's body. And if the Buddha wants to reveal a past action, they disappear into him from the back; but if he wants to reveal a future action, they disappear into him from the front. If he wants to reveal a rebirth in hell, they vanish into the sole of his foot; if he wants to reveal a rebirth as an animal, they vanish into his heel; if he wants to reveal a rebirth as a hungry ghost, they vanish into his toes; if he wants to reveal a rebirth as a human being, they vanish into his knees; if he wants to reveal the kingship of a balacakravartin [a world ruler who conquers by the force of arms], they vanish into his left hand; if he wants to reveal the kingship of a cakravartin [a world ruler who conquers by virtue of his righteousness], they vanish into his right hand; if he wants to reveal the enlightenment of a disciple, they vanish into his mouth; if he wants to reveal the enlightenment of a pratyekabuddha, they vanish into his ūrṇā [the growth of hair in the middle of the Buddha's forehead]; if he wants to predict the unsurpassed total enlightenment of a Buddha, they vanish into his uṣṇīṣa [the protuberance on the top of his head].

Source: Translated from *Avadānaśataka*, ed. P. L. Vaidya, Buddhist Sanskrit Texts, no. 19 (Darbhanga: Mithila Institute, 1959), p. 297.[5]

[5]Alternative French translation, Léon Feer, *Avadāna-çataka: cent légendes bouddhiques* (Paris: E. Leroux, 1891), pp. 10–11.

1.5.2 Karma and the Six Realms of Rebirth

Another aspect of the Buddha's second watch vision of the beings in the cosmos is, of course, his understanding of their karma, of the deeds they did to merit rebirth into or out of the various realms of the universe. The law of karma is a doctrine that Buddhism inherited from its greater Indian religious context. Simply put, it states that any moral act, good or bad, will bring about a correspondingly positive or negative result, either in this or in a future lifetime.

Buddhist tales of karma, just like the fire-and-brimstone sermons of Christian preachers describing hell, often have an admonitory purpose: to encourage good deeds and the avoidance of bad ones. What fascinated Buddhists, however, were the specifics of retribution, the particular acts committed and the particular sufferings or rewards that resulted from them.

A system of five (later, six) realms or "courses" (gatis) of rebirth came to be standard: the realms of humans, gods, animals, hell-beings, hungry ghosts, and (later) "titans" (asuras, or demonic antiheroes). The first two of these realms were deemed fortunate and the rest unfortunate, "fortune" and "misfortune" being measured not only by the amount of suffering involved in the realms but also by the access they afforded to the teachings of the Buddha.

Within these realms, however, all sorts of subdivisions came to be specified. This was, in part, a response to a need to elaborate on the workings of karma: Was it better to be reborn as a jackal or as a pig? Was it better to be a hungry stray dog or an intestinal parasite in the stomach of a rich person's well-fed dog? And what karmic deeds might result in any of these situations?

At the same time, just as there were obviously different species of animals and different castes and socioeconomic situations of humans, so too there were elaborated different "species" of hell-beings, of hungry ghosts, and of gods. Thus, whole texts were devoted to elaborating upon the categories of rebirth. The following work, attributed to the Buddhist poet Dhārmika Subhūti, is a relatively late example of the genre, though it has its roots in the Buddhist Canon itself.

"Beings reap the fruit of actions—good or bad—which they themselves have done (there is no other doer) with their body, speech, and mind."

Thus thinking, the compassionate Teacher, master of the Triple World, proclaimed, for the sake of all beings, which acts had which fruits.

That is what I will speak of today, in brief, having heard what was said by the Buddha: the good deeds and the bad, to be done or shunned.

Hell Realm

People who slay living beings, out of greed, delusion, fear, or anger or who rear them in order to harm them are surely going to the Sañjīva hell.

It is called "Sañjīva" because beings there, during many thousands of years, are killed only to be revived (saṃjīvanti) and killed again and again.

People who have angered their mother or father or relations or friends, who slander and lie, are destined for the Kālasūtra hell.

It is known as "Kālasūtra" because beings there are cut up with burning hot saws, the way lumber is cut, along lines made with a black chalkline (kālasūtra).

People who have killed goats, sheep, jackals, hare, rats, deer, boar, and other living creatures are going to the Saṃghāta hell.

This hell is commonly given the name "Saṃghāta" because the beings there are all piled in a heap (saṃghāta), and, in that state, slaughtered together.

People who have made creatures suffer bodily and mental anguish and who are cheats and deceivers are going to the Raurava hell.

It is known as "Raurava" because beings there, continuously burned by an intense fire, let out a dreadful cry (ghoraṃ ravaṃ).

People who have taken the wealth of kings, brahmins, or teachers and caused them suffering and those who take back what they have given are going to the Great Raurava hell.

It is called "Great Raurava" because of the great dreadfulness of the cries there and of the greatness of the heat of its fire. These are greater than those of the Raurava hell.

The person who causes creatures to be burned in a forest fire or any other fire will burn in the Tāpana hell, wailing in the midst of a great conflagration.

In this world it is given the name "Tāpana" because beings there suffer continuously from the intense burning torment (tāpana).

The person who is a nihilist, who declares the interchangeability of Dharma and non-Dharma, or who leads beings into misdirected ascetic practices will burn in the Pratāpana hell.

It is said to be "Pratāpana" because the intense fire there makes beings suffer an even greater torment (pratāpana) than they do in the Tāpana hell.

People who have angered beings of great virtue or who have killed a disciple of the Buddha or their mother or father or teacher will be reborn in the Avīci hell.

It is called "Avīci" because beings there are burned by such a horrible fire that even their bones are melted, and because, in the midst of their suffering, there is no interval (na vīci) allowing them any respite. . . .

Animal Realm

By passionate attachment to sensual pleasures, people are reborn as geese, pigeons, donkeys, and other passionate animals; those who have erred through stupidity are reborn as worms.

Anger and malice cause rebirth as snakes; the prideful become lions; haughtiness causes rebirth as an ass or a dog.

As a result of jealousy, envy, aversion, and so on, beings become monkeys after death; those who are scurrilous, impudent, or of wanton nature will become crows.

As a result of killing, tying up, and whipping cattle and horses, beings are reborn as noxious spiders and scorpions.

People who are hostile and selfish become, after death, tigers, cats, jackals, bears, vultures, wolves, or other meat eaters.

People who are generous benefactors, yet get angry and are cruel, become nāgas with great wealth; those who liberally give up their possessions, yet who get angry and are arrogant, become lordly garuḍas.

Evil deeds of body, speech, and mind result in rebirth as an animal. Therefore, refrain from doing even the slightest such action.

Hungry Ghost (Preta) Realm

People who steal food become kaṭapūtana pretas, who are deprived of energy and who feed on corpses.

Those who harm children and out of desire lead them astray are reborn as kaṭapūtanas, feeding on fetal matter.

People who are vile and utterly wretched, selfish and ever-lusting, are reborn after death as pretas with goiters.

The person who hinders the practice of dāna and who gives nothing himself will become an emaciated preta with a big belly and a mouth the size of a needle.

The person who hoards his wealth for the sake of his family, without enjoying it or giving it away, is reborn as a preta who receives only what is given as funeral offerings made to the dead.

The person who wishes to deprive others of their wealth and who gives only to regret it immediately becomes a preta consuming excrement, phlegm, and vomit.

The person who, out of anger, speaks unkind words that cut to the quick will, as a result of that act, be for a long time a preta with a flaming mouth.

And the person who causes strife, who has a fierce disposition and no pity, will become a preta agitated by fear, feeding on worms and various kinds of insects. . . .

Human Realm

Among gods, asuras, and humans, nonviolence leads to a long life; violence gives rise to a short life. Thus, one should abstain from violence.

Leprosy, consumption, fever, madness, and other human diseases are due to killing, tying up, and whipping creatures.

People who steal others' property and give out nothing whatsoever will never themselves become wealthy, strive as they may.

One who takes goods that were not given but who also gives gifts will, after death, first become wealthy but then exceedingly poor.

One who neither steals nor gives nor is excessively niggardly will, with great effort, obtain a lasting fortune in the next life.

People who do not steal others' property, who are generous and free from greed, obtain what they wish: great wealth that cannot be taken away.

One who, in this world, makes donations of alms food will be reborn ever-happy: endowed with long life, good complexion, strength, good fortune, and good health.

One who makes offerings of clothes will become modest, good looking, and well dressed, enjoying life and cutting a handsome figure.

People who happily, without regret, make a donation of a dwelling, will, in a future life, be endowed with palaces and everything they want.

By virtue of a gift of a lamp, a person will come to have good eyes; by the gift of a musical instrument, a good voice; by the gift of beds and seats, ease and comfort. [. . .]

He who abstains from the wives of others will obtain the wives he desires; and he who stays away from his own wives, when the place and time are not right, will again be reborn as a man.

The man who does not restrain his thoughts and unites with the wives of others, or who finds delight in illicit parts of the body, will be reborn as a woman.

But the woman who is of good morals and little passion, who abhors her femaleness and constantly aspires to masculinity, will be reborn as a man. [. . .]

All karmic rewards resemble the acts of which they are the natural outcome: suffering from sin, happiness from good deeds, and a mixture of the two from a mixed deed.

Asura Realm

One who is always practicing guile and deception but who does no injury, who is quarrelsome but generous, will become an asura-lord.

Deity Realm

Those who do not long for pleasure for themselves and who do not rejoice in possessions become one of the four great divine kings, foremost of the planetary deities.

People who revere their mother, father, and family elders, who are generous, patient, and do not delight in strife, will be reborn among the gods of the Trayastriṃśat heaven.

Those who are not fond of quarreling, whose minds do not delight in strife, who undertake only what is good, will go to the Suyāma heaven.

People of great learning, who are wise upholders of the Dharma, who desire liberation, go to the Tuṣita heaven.

People who themselves are inclined toward morality, giving, and discipline and who make strenuous efforts are certainly on their way to the Nirmāṇarati heaven.

Superior people possessing goodness, surpassing others in the virtues because of their giving, discipline, and self-control, will certainly become gods in the Parinirmitavaśavartin heaven.

By moral conduct one reaches heaven; even more so by meditation. From seeing all things as they are, one comes to the ultimate end of saṃsāra.

Source: Translated from Dhārmika Subhūti, *Ṣaḍgatikārikā*, ed. Paul Mus, in Paul Mus, *La lumière sur les six voies* (Paris: Institut d'Ethnologie, 1939), pp. 217–89.[6]

[6]Alternative French translation, by Mus, *La lumière*, pp. 216–88.

1.6 REALIZING THE FOUR NOBLE TRUTHS

In the third watch of the night of his enlightenment, the Buddha is said to have realized, among other things, the Four Noble Truths. If the experience of the first watch of the night can be termed "karmalogical" (having to do with the karmic deeds of the Buddha in his past life) and the second watch experience is thought of as "cosmological" (having to do with the various realms of rebirth in the cosmos), this third watch can be labeled "dharmalogical" (having to do with the realization of the Buddha's Dharma, or "Doctrine").

In any case, the Four Noble Truths, which do form a sort of doctrinal core of Buddhism, are said to have been the subject of the Buddha's first sermon, at the Deer Park in Sarnath near Benares, an event known as the Setting in Motion of the Wheel of the Dharma. This sermon was delivered to the five men, Ājñāta Kauṇḍinya and his companions, who were to become the Buddha's first monastic disciples. The sermon, therefore, marks not only the first preaching of the Dharma but also the establishment of the monastic community.

The Four Noble Truths can be stated as follows:

1. that life in all the realms of rebirth is, by definition, ultimately unsatisfactory, suffering (duḥkha)
2. that there is a reason for this suffering, an origination (samudaya) of it, which is connected to our ongoing desire, a thirst that we cannot assuage, a clinging to possessions, to persons, to life itself
3. that there is, however, such a thing as freedom from or the cessation (nirodha) of this unsatisfactory state, this suffering, which will come with the rooting out (rather than the mere assuagement) of that ongoing thirst
4. that the way to do this is to practice the so-called Noble Eightfold Path

This Path (mārga) is the same as the realization of the Middle Way, between the extremes of indulgence and asceticism, and it is for this reason that the Buddha (as in the selection below) often preached the Middle Way along with the Four Noble Truths.

Finally, it should be pointed out that the Buddha is said to have realized each of the Four Noble Truths in three ways: first, he came to "see" them; second, he engaged in "developing" them through practice; and third, he fully realized them in such a way that he had "nothing more to learn" about them. In this way, the Wheel of the Dharma was "thrice-turned," and the Four Noble Truths together have twelve aspects. The *Dharmacakrapravartana sūtra* (*Sūtra on Setting in Motion the Wheel of the Dharma*) was incorporated into many Buddhist texts, both Pali and Sanskrit. The following is from a Sanskrit work said to be the Vinaya of the Mahāsāṃghika-Lokottaravādin school.

Thus have I heard: Once, when the Blessed One was dwelling in Benares, at the Deer Park in Ṛṣivadana, he spoke to the "Fortunate Five," the group of elders who were his first disciples.

"Monks," he said, "for one who has wandered forth, there are two extremes. What two? On the one hand, there is attachment to sensual pleasures; this is vulgar, common, ignoble, purposeless, not conducive to a chaste and studious life, to disgust with the world, to aversion from passion, to cessation, monkhood, enlightenment, or nirvāṇa. On the other hand, there is addiction to exhausting the self through asceticism; this is suffering, ignoble, and purposeless. Monks, for one who has wandered forth, these are the two extremes. Staying with the Tathāgata's Noble Doctrine and Disciple, away from both of these extremes, is the middle course, fully realized [by the Buddha], bringing about insight, and conducive to tranquillity, disgust with the world, aversion from passion, cessation, monkhood, enlightenment, and nirvāṇa. . . .

"Furthermore, monks, there are Four Noble Truths. What four? The Noble Truth of suffering, the Noble Truth of the origination of suffering, the Noble Truth of the cessation of suffering, and the Noble Truth of the way leading to the cessation of suffering.

"Now, monks, what is the Noble Truth of suffering? Just this: Birth is suffering, old age is suffering, sickness is suffering, death is suffering. Involvement with what is unpleasant is suffering. Separation from what is pleasant is suffering. Also, not getting what one wants and strives for is suffering. And form (rūpa) is suffering, feeling (vedanā) is suffering, perception (saṃjñā) is suffering, karmic constituents (saṃskāras) are suffering, consciousness (vijñāna) is suffering; in sum, these five agglomerations (skandhas), which are the basis of clinging to existence, are suffering. This, monks, is the Noble Truth of suffering.

"And what is the [second] Noble Truth of the origination of suffering? It is the thirst for further existence, which comes along with pleasure and passion and brings passing enjoyment here and there. This, monks, is the Noble Truth of the origination of suffering.

"And what is the [third] Noble Truth of the cessation of suffering? It is this: the destruction without remainder of this very thirst for further existence, which comes along with pleasure and passion, bringing passing enjoyment here and there. It is without passion. It is cessation, forsaking, abandoning, renunciation. This, monks, is the Noble Truth of the cessation of suffering.

"And what is the Noble Truth of the way leading to the cessation of suffering? Just this: the Eightfold Noble Path, consisting of right views, right intention, right effort, right action, right livelihood, right speech, right mindfulness, right meditation. This, monks, is the Noble Truth of the way leading to the cessation of suffering.

" 'This is suffering. . . . This is the origination of suffering. . . . This is the cessation of suffering. . . . This is the way that leads to the cessation of suffering': monks, from these basic mental realizations, according to doctrines that were not handed down from previous teachers, there were produced in me knowledge, insight, understanding, enlightenment, intelligence, and wisdom; illumination became manifest.

" 'This Noble Truth of suffering is to be thoroughly known. . . . This origination of suffering is to be given up. . . . This Noble Truth of the cessation of suffering is to be realized. . . . This Noble Truth of the way leading to the cessation of suffering is to be cultivated': monks, from this basic mental realization, according to doctrines that were not handed down from previous teachers, there were produced in me knowledge, insight, understanding, enlightenment, intelligence, and wisdom; illumination became manifest.

" 'This Noble Truth of suffering has come to be known thoroughly. . . . This origination of suffering has been given up. . . . This Noble Truth of the cessation of suffering has been realized. . . . This Noble Truth of the way leading to the cessation of suffering has been actualized': monks, from this basic mental realization, according to doctrines that were not handed down from previous teachers, there were produced in me knowledge, insight, understanding, enlightenment, intelligence, and wisdom; illumination became manifest.

"And monks, as long as I did not perceive, with right wisdom, these Four Noble Truths as they are, thrice-turned and in their twelve aspects, I could not claim to have fully attained unsurpassed complete enlightenment, nor would there be produced knowledge in me, nor would I have realized certain emancipation of the mind. But since, monks, I did perceive, with right wisdom, these Four Noble Truths as they are, thrice-turned and in their twelve aspects, I know I have fully attained unsurpassed complete enlightenment. Knowledge was produced in me, and I did realize certain emancipation of the mind, liberation through wisdom."

Thus the Buddha spoke while he was residing in Benares, at the Deer Park in Ṛṣivadana. And hearing this explanation, the Venerable Ājñāta Kauṇḍinya's understanding was awakened, and he attained the perfectly pure, pristine, unstained Dharma-eye into the nature of things. . . .

Source: Translated from *Mahāvastu*, ed. Emile Sénart (Paris: Imprimerie Nationale, 1897), 3:330–34.[7]

1.7 THE "DEATH" AND PARINIRVĀṆA OF THE BUDDHA

Ājñāta Kauṇḍinya and his companions, as we have seen, became the first Buddhist monks and formed the initial core of what was to become the Buddhist monastic community. Soon, however, other disciples were attracted to the Buddha and his Teaching, and the new religion grew steadily (see 2.1).

The Buddha is said to have spent forty-five years wandering through northern India, preaching his Dharma, making converts, and firmly establishing his community. But like all compounded things, he too was subject to impermanence, and according to the legend, at age eighty, his "final extinction" (parinirvāṇa) took place in the small town of Kuśinagarī, between two śala trees. To this day, all over the world, this event marks the beginning (year 0) of the Buddhist calendar.

---

[7]Alternative English translation, J. J. Jones, *The Mahāvastu* (London: Luzac, 1956), 3:322–27.

The parinirvāṇa can also be called the "death" of the Buddha, with the understanding that, by it, the Buddha is thought to have put an end to the process of death and rebirth, the cycle of suffering. So, although the Buddha is no longer "alive" after his parinirvāṇa, neither is he "dead" in the usual sense of the term, because he is not subsequently "reborn" anywhere, in any realm. The question of where the Buddha exists, or whether he exists at all, "in" or "after" his parinirvāṇa, is one of those inquiries that the Buddha himself, during his lifetime, is said to have labeled as "not conducive to edification," so I shall not even address it here.

It is more interesting, perhaps, to look at the stories of the various events leading up to and immediately following the Buddha's parinirvāṇa. Quite early on, legends arose, such as the following Sanskrit *Sūtra of the Great Extinction,* recounting not only the Buddha's final words of advice to his followers but also the preparation of his body for cremation and the disposal of his relics thereafter.

Arrival at Kuśinagarī

Then the Blessed One, traveling through the land of the Mallas, went to Kuśinagarī, where he dwelt in the grove of the twin śala trees, in the territory of the Mallas. There, the time of his parinirvāṇa being near, he said to the Venerable Ānanda: "Ānanda, set the Tathāgata's couch out between the two śala trees, with its head pointing north; for today, in the middle watch of the night, the Tathāgata will attain parinirvāṇa, the element of complete extinction."

The Venerable Ānanda did so; then, standing to one side, he announced: "Lord, the Tathāgata's couch has been set out in between the two śala trees, with its head pointing north." And the Blessed One approached the couch and lay down on his right side, one foot on top of the other, . . . attentive, aware, his mind bent on the thought of nirvāṇa.

Then Ānanda, standing in back of the Blessed One, leaned against the couch, and wept. "Too soon," he exclaimed, "too soon the Blessed One, the Well-Gone-One, will attain parinirvāṇa! Too soon the Eye of the World will be put out! In the past, monks from various regions used to come from all over to see and to venerate the Blessed One, and the Blessed One would preach the Dharma to them. . . . But from now on, those who used to come to listen to the Buddha will have heard that he has attained parinirvāṇa, and they will no longer make the journey. Thus the great rejoicing in the Dharma will cease. . . ."

But the Blessed One said to the Venerable Ānanda: "Do not grieve, Ānanda, do not be depressed! You have served me well, with body, speech, and mind, in ways that were loving, unparalleled, immeasurable, helpful, and pleasing. All the completely enlightened Buddhas of the past also had attendants who served them, just as you have served me. So do not grieve, Ānanda, do not be depressed! For how could it be that something born, living, fashioned, karmically constituted, . . . dependently arisen, should not be subject to decay, to change, decline, destruction, . . . and dissolution?" [. . .]

Paying Homage to the Buddha's Body

Now at that time, the Venerable Upamāna was standing in front of the Blessed One, fanning him. And the Blessed One said to him: "Monk! Don't stand in front of me!"

And the Venerable Ānanda said: "I have served the Blessed One for over twenty years, but I have never heard him use such harsh language as he just did with the Venerable Upamāna. What is the reason for this?"

And the Blessed One explained: "Right now, myriads of deities are looking down from the sky and, upset, they are grumbling: 'The appearance of fully enlightened Buddhas in the world is as rare an event as the blossoming of the udumbara tree, and today this Buddha is going to enter parinirvāṇa in the middle watch of the night, but this prominent monk is standing in front of him, so that we have to try to look around him. Because of him, we are unable to see the Blessed One, or to approach and pay homage to him.' That is why I asked the Venerable Upamāna to move. . . ."

Then the Venerable Ānanda said to the Blessed One: "Lord, how should we pay homage to the Blessed One's body after his parinirvāṇa?"

"Ānanda, do not worry yourself about the homage to the body of the Buddha; the faithful Brahmanical householders will take care of that."

"But how, Lord, are they to take care of it?"

"Ānanda, they should do what they they would do for the funeral of a cakravartin king."

"And how, Lord, is it with cakravartin kings?"

"The body of a cakravartin king is wrapped in new cotton cloth and cotton wool, five hundred layers of each, and once so wrapped, it is placed in an iron coffin filled with oil, which is then covered with another iron coffin. A funeral pyre of fragrant wood is piled up, set afire, and later extinguished with cow's milk. Then the bones are placed in a golden urn, which is carried on a golden palanquin to a great crossroads, where a stūpa is built, on which umbrellas, flags, and banners are set up, . . . and to which homage and worship are paid with offerings of perfumes, garlands, flowers, incense, and music." [. . .]

Last Words of the Buddha

Then the Blessed One said: "It may be that after I am gone some of you monks will think: 'Our Master has attained parinirvāṇa; we are now without a teacher, without hope of salvation!' You should not see things in that way. The prātimokṣa list of precepts [see 2.3.1] to be recited every fortnight, which I taught you, will henceforth be your Master and your salvation. The sangha may, in due time, abolish certain minor and secondary rules of conduct if it so wishes, . . . for that will lead to your dwelling in harmony.

"And, monks, henceforth, a more recently ordained monk should not address a senior monk by calling him by his personal name or his clan name, but he should call him 'Reverend Sir' or 'Venerable One.' And a senior monk should be kind to a junior monk and help him pay attention to his bowl, his robe, the carrying sling for his bowl, his drinking vessel, his belt, his subject of study, his topic of inquiry, his explanations, and his practice of yoga. . . .

"Furthermore, monks, there are four places on earth that laymen and laywomen endowed with faith should recall all their lives. Which four? The places where, [as pilgrims], they will say: 'Here the Blessed One was born; here, he attained unsurpassed complete enlightenment; here he set in motion, three times and in twelve ways, the Wheel of the Dharma; and here he attained the state of complete nirvāṇa.' Going to these places, after my death, they should circumambulate the shrines there and pay homage to them. . . . All those who do so, with minds filled with faith for me, will, at the time of their death, be reborn in heaven. . . ."

Then the Blessed One said to the monks: "Monks, do not hesitate to ask me, if you have any doubts or uncertainties about the Buddha, the Dharma, and the Sangha or about suffering—its origination, its cessation, or the path to its cessation—and I will elucidate these points for you. It may be that you are feeling: 'Why should we trouble the Master with our questions now?' Do not think that, but make your doubts known, as one monk to another, one friend to another, and I will clarify them."

And [when no monks had any questions], the Venerable Ānanda said . . . : "Not a single monk in this assembly has any doubt, any uncertainty as to the points raised earlier! This has been done by the Tathāgata for the sake of those people who will follow hereafter."

Then the Blessed One took off his outer robe and said: "Monks, gaze now upon the body of the Tathāgata! Examine the body of the Tathāgata! For the sight of a completely enlightened Buddha is as rare an event as the blossoming of the udumbara tree. And, monks, do not break into lamentations after I am gone, for all karmically constituted things are subject to passing away." Those were the last words of the Buddha. [. . .]

The Distribution of the Relics

[There follows an account of the preparation of the body of the Buddha in the manner described above and of its cremation, an event that is delayed by seven days until the arrival of the Buddha's disciple Mahākāśyapa. After the cremation fire is extinguished, the Mallas of Kuśinagarī then gather up the remains of the Buddha's body (bones and ashes) with the intention of building a stūpa over them. But shortly thereafter, representatives of seven other cities and kingdoms (Pāpā, Calakalpā, Viṣṇudvīpa, Rāmagrāma, Vaiśālī, Kapilavastu, and Magadha) arrive and lay claim to the Buddha's remains as well. But the Mallas are not willing to give up their claim to the relics, and soon matters come to a head: armed parties gather, ready to fight in what the tradition came to know as the "war over the relics." At the last moment, however, bloodshed is avoided by the intervention of the brahmin Droṇa, known in this version of the story as the brahmin Dhūmrasagotra]:

Now the brahmin Dhūmrasagotra knew that the various parties arranged in battle formation would quickly come to kill one another, so . . . he approached the Mallas of Kuśinagarī and said: "May the honorable Mallas of Kuśinagarī here assembled listen to me! For many years, the

Blessed One, peaceful and not given to passion, celebrated tolerance and preached forbearance. Now, departing from his peacefulness, from his passionlessness, from his advocacy of patience, you are ready to kill one another on account of his bodily relics! I propose to divide right away the relics of the Blessed Gautama into eight shares, [so that each of the contending parties may get a portion]. . . . To this the Mallas of Kuśinagarī agreed.

Then the brahmin Dhūmrasagotra went and [similarly announced his intention to the seven other parties involved. And when they too had all agreed to his plan], he divided the relics of the Blessed One into eight shares.

He gave the first share to the Mallas of Kuśinagarī, who erected a stūpa in Kuśinagarī, surmounted it with umbrellas, flags, and banners, instituted a festival in its honor, and paid homage to it, worshipping and venerating it with perfumes, garlands, flowers, incense, and music.

The second share he gave to the Mallas of Pāpā, and they likewise erected a stūpa for the bodily relics of the Blessed One, in Pāpā, and similarly paid homage to it.

The third share he gave to the Bulakas of Calakalpā, who likewise erected a stūpa, and similarly paid homage.

The fourth share he gave to the Krauḍyas of Rāmagrāma. . . .

The fifth share he gave to the brahmins of Viṣṇudvīpa. . . .

The sixth share he gave to the Licchavis of Vaiśālī. . . .

The seventh share he gave to the Śākyas of Kapilavastu. . . .

And the eighth share he gave to Varṣākāra, the prime minister of Magadha, whose king, Ajātaśatru, son of Vaidehi, erected a stūpa for the bodily relics of the Blessed One, surmounted it with umbrellas, flags, and banners, instituted a festival in its honor, and paid homage to it, worshipping and venerating it with perfumes, garlands, flowers, incense, and music.

And the urn in which the bones of the Buddha had first been placed was given to the brahmin Dhūmrasagotra, and he built a stūpa over the urn in his hometown of Droṇagrāma and paid homage to it in the same manner.

Then, a young man named Pippalāyana, who was sitting in the assembly, said to the Mallas of Kuśinagarī: "May the honorable Mallas of Kuśinagarī here assembled listen to me! For many years, the Blessed One was dear to my people. Now he has attained parinirvāṇa in your village. We deserve a share of his bodily relics, but since those relics have been divided, give us the ashes of his cremation fire, and we will erect a stūpa over them in Pippalavatī, and pay homage to it. The Mallas of Kuśinagarī then gave the youth Pippalāyana the ash-relics. . . .

Thus, at that time, there were eight stūpas for the bodily relics of the Blessed One, one for the urn, and one for the ashes of his cremation fire.

Source: Translated from *Das Mahāparinirvāṇasūtra*, ed. Ernst Waldschmidt, Abhandlungen der deutschen Akademie der Wissenschaften zu Berlin, Philologish-historische Klasse, 1949–50 (Berlin: Akademie Verlag, 1950–51), pp. 292–300, 356–60, 386–94, 442–50.

1.8 A STORY OF A BUDDHA IMAGE

The legend of the Buddha does not end with his death. As we have just seen, relics and the stūpas enshrining them were a means of remembering the Buddha after his parinirvāṇa, but they were not the only ones. As centers of Buddhist pilgrimage developed and Buddhist devotional art flourished, devotees found additional ways of recalling the presence of the Blessed One. At first, in art, he and the places where he had been were represented by symbols such as footsteps, thrones, trees, wheels of the Dharma, and the like, but eventually, after a number of centuries, anthropomorphic images and statues of him came to the fore.

Scholars have much debated the issue of when (probably around the first century C.E.), where (probably in northwestern India), and by whom the first images of the Buddha were made, but Buddhist legends did not hesitate to assert that depictions of him had already been fashioned during his lifetime. Thus the famous sandalwood image of King Udrāyaṇa is said to have been carved by artists so that people could venerate it while the Buddha himself was absent in one of the heavens, preaching the Dharma to his mother and the assembled deities. Such an image was clearly seen as a substitute for the Buddha in his absence and was itself thought to be "alive" in a variety of ways. Stories are told of its standing up, preaching the Dharma, making converts, and so on.

In the following tale, the image featured is also a sandalwood image, but one made by King Pasenadi of Kosala so that the inhabitants of Śrāvastī will have something to worship when the Buddha is out of town. As the story makes clear, however, the image is destined to become something more than that once the Buddha becomes permanently "absent" in parinirvāṇa.

One day, the Blessed One, seeing some persons in this world who were ready for conversion, left the great Jetavana monastery and went to their country in order to preach to them. Just then, however, King Pasenadi of Kosala decided to visit the Buddha. Together with his men, he took some perfumes, garlands, and other things needed for worship, left the city and, in the midst of a large entourage, went to the Jetavana. Not finding the Buddha in residence there, he became perturbed and said: "Sirs, without the Buddha, the Jetavana is empty!" And the king's men and the people likewise, failing to find the Buddha in his residence, became perturbed, and said to one another: "Friends, without the Buddha, this world is indeed empty, without protection or refuge!" Given this, they venerated the dwelling place of the Blessed One with their various perfumes, flowers, etc., and then left. And all of them, starting with the king, were upset and filled with sorrow as they went home.

Later, after teaching the Dharma to potential converts in different countries and awakening them to the fruit of the path, the Buddha returned to the great monastery in the Jetavana. Hearing that he was back, King Pasenadi of Kosala rejoiced greatly, and taking once more the various things needed for worship, he left the city and went to the Jetavana.

Approaching the Blessed One, he saluted him respectfully, sat down to one side, and said: "Yesterday, sir, a large group of citizens of Śrāvastī came here to the Jetavana to worship the Awakened One. Not finding the Buddha in, they were filled with sorrow and went home disappointed. Sir, even though you are still alive, when you go to another place, the people, unable to behold your body, become miserable, feeling that they are without a protector. This makes them wonder how they will ever find refuge and be happy, once you pass into final nirvāṇa and are no more. Therefore, sir, these many people would like to have an image of the Blessed One, in this world, that they can venerate. Please allow me to have a statue made of you that can be honored and worshiped by men and gods."

Hearing these words of Pasenadi, and considering the wellbeing of the whole world, the Master, in order to make his religion last, then allowed the king to have an image of himself made. [. . .] Pasenadi was filled with happiness; he worshiped the Blessed One with perfumes, flowers, etc., and returned home, intending to make a Buddha-statue that would benefit the whole world. He had the most excellent sandalwood tree brought from the sandalwood forest, had it finely carved and made into a very pleasing statue of the Buddha. He had it repeatedly rubbed with oil, covered with a pair of the best monastic robes the color of red lacquer, and set on a high seat spread with fine cloth. When the king saw the Buddha statue sitting there, glowing as though it were alive, he said repeatedly "now I have completed this Buddha statue," and his mind was permeated with delight in the Buddha.

Then he had a great pavilion built and had it adorned with the seven kinds of gems and various sorts of ornaments, and suffused with perfumes. In that pavilion, he spread a very worthy seat and set the Buddha statue there. He worshipped that image intently, and then went to see the Buddha at the Jetavana. After saluting him, he sat down to one side and said: "Sir, I have completed the image that you allowed; it glows with light as though it were alive. I would like you to come tomorrow to see your own form; that would please me greatly."

The Master accepted the king's invitation by remaining silent. Understanding that his silence meant consent, the king rose, venerated the Blessed One, and went back to the city. The next day, the Master, surrounded by his disciples, went to the king's palace, and approached the great pavilion in order to see the statue in his own likeness. At that moment, however, the Buddha statue made from the most excellent sandalwood, seeing the Buddha arriving, . . . acquired as it were a devout mind and a living body, and thought: "Now that the most excellent living Buddha is coming here, it is improper for me to be seated on the highest seat. I must show respect for him." As though thinking thus, the statue, so as to honor the Buddha, put one foot down from its seat, thereby showing signs of getting up to go meet the Blessed One. Seeing the Buddha statue doing this, the Master raised his right hand . . . , and, restraining the image, said this verse:

"Friend, stay there. Soon, O statue, I will be entering parinirvāṇa; therefore, you should remain behind so that my religion will last into the future for five thousand years. . . .

"Today, I commit my Order to you; for the sake of the wellbeing of the whole world, stay with my religion."

Source: Translated from *Paññāsa-jātaka or Zimme Paṇṇāsa,* ed. Padmanabh S. Jaini (London: Pali Text Society, 1983), 2:414, 424–35.[8]

1.9 THE FUTURE BUDDHA MAITREYA

The memory and presence of the Buddha were kept alive in relics and images as well as in his Teaching long after his passing away, and they continue to be so today. But as we have seen, the Buddha known as Gautama Śākyamuni was not the only Buddha. He was but the most recent of a long line of Buddhas who had succeeded one another over the aeons, a line that, moreover, was not destined to end with him. For just as Buddhist legends tell of Buddhas of the past, so too they tell of Buddhas of the future, enlightened masters who are yet to come and who will continue the cycle.

By far the most famous of these future Buddhas is Maitreya (Pali: Metteyya), whose cult has been very widespread. Indeed, Buddhists today can perhaps best be thought of as living devotionally in between two Buddhas, trying to recollect, on the one hand, the glories of Śākyamuni, and looking forward, on the other hand, to the coming of Maitreya.

Maitreya is presently thought to be residing in the Tuṣita heaven, in his penultimate life, awaiting the time for his rebirth in this world. Generally speaking, however, his advent is seen as being still some way off, for a number of developments are supposed to precede it. It has been a common belief in Buddhism that after the Buddha Śākyamuni's parinirvāṇa, his teaching would go into decline. Indeed, according to one tradition, the Buddha's Dharma will, over a period of five thousand years, be successively affected by five "disappearances." First, the ability to attain nirvāṇa will be lost; then the practice of the path and the maintenance of the precepts will disappear; then the knowledge of the scriptures will die out as, one by one, the texts of the Canon are forgotten; then the very symbols of the religion, such as Buddha images or the wearing of yellow robes by monks, will be lost; and finally, the relics of the Buddha, no longer honored, will vanish.

But then, materially at least, things will gradually get better and better until eventually there will come a great, glorious king, named Śaṅkha, who will rule over a golden age of wonder and plenty. And it is his rule that will mark the advent of Maitreya, who like Śākyamuni before him will become a Buddha and restore the Dharma in all its purity, making it once again comparatively easy to attain enlightenment. Consequently, as the following passages from a Sanskrit text entitled *The Prediction about Maitreya* make clear, it is very important to practice meritorious deeds so as to be reborn at the time and in the place of Maitreya and not to "miss" his coming by doing things that will result in rebirth in some hell or hungry-ghost realm (or in some foreign country), where one will not be able to benefit from his preaching.

[8]Alternative English translation, Padmanabh S. Jaini, *Apocryphal Birth-Stories* (London: Pali Text Society, 1986), 2:103–04, 114–16.

The very wise Śāriputra, mighty general of the Dharma, questioned the Master out of compassion for the world: "Once, in the midst of a discourse, you mentioned the Order of the future Buddha, a leader of the world named Maitreya. Please explain further to me about his power and also his supernatural endowments. I would like to hear about them, O Best of Men."

The Blessed One replied: "Listen, and I will explain to you the might of this Buddha Maitreya, most excellent personage.

"At that time, for many leagues around, the oceans will dry up; the roads will become easily passable for cakravartin kings, and Jambudvīpa [India] will be flat like a field extending in every direction for ten thousand leagues, a dwelling place for all creatures. And the human beings in those various regions will do good deeds, they will be nonviolent, nonvengeful, very prosperous, and happy. And the surface of the ground will be even, free from thorns and covered with green grass that yields gently when one jumps onto it and is soft like cotton. It will be sweet-smelling, and a delicious rice will grow there without any labor. And the trees will have garments of different colors hanging from them. . . .

"And the beings there will have good skin and large bodies and be very strong; and they will be intelligent, free from defilements, without fault, and long-lived. They will suffer only from three troubles: desires, old age, and indigestion. Women will get married only when they are five hundred years old.

"And at that time there will be a city called Ketumatī. It will be the residence of beings who work for the welfare of all creatures, and will be twelve leagues in length and seven leagues wide, a delightful, meritorious, pure city. . . . It will have a resplendent king named Śaṅkha, a powerful cakravartin ruler over four continents, endowed with the seven jewels of kingship and having a four-fold army. This lord of the earth will engender a thousand sons and extend his protection throughout the world as far as the ocean, which he will rule according to Dharma. . . . And this king will have a brahmin priest named Subrāhman. This teacher will be very learned, knowing the four Vedas. . . . And he will have a wife named Brahmāvatī, who will be beautiful, graceful, gloriously attractive.

"Then Maitreya, foremost of humans, will descend from Tuṣita heaven and take his final birth in her womb. She will bear him for ten lunar months; then she, the virtuous mother of Maitreya, will go to a flowering park, and, neither sitting nor lying but standing, holding on to the branch of a tree, she will give birth to Maitreya. He, the best of men, will come out of her right side and shine like the sun that has emerged from the clouds, as unsullied by the impurities of the womb as a lotus is by water. And he will fill the whole Triple World with his splendor.

"Then Indra, the thousand-eyed king of the gods, . . . will pick up the just-born child, the Best of Men, the wonderful Maitreya, resplendent, endowed with the thirty-two signs of the Great Man. But he, hardly born, will say: "Let me go, let me go, thousand-eyed one," and, hardly born, he will walk seven steps, and at each step there will grow a lotus or a jewel. And he will gaze in the four directions and declare these words: "This is my last birth; there will be no more rebirth for me; I shall not return again, but, free from defilement, will attain nirvāṇa."

[There follows an account of Maitreya's growing up, leaving home and attaining enlightenment, and preaching the Dharma that, with some exceptions, parallels the life story of Śākyamuni. Then, having gathered hundreds of thousands of disciples around him, Maitreya declares]: "All of you were seen by the Buddha Śākyamuni, the best of sages, the savior, the lord of the world, the embodiment of the true Dharma. He set you on the road to liberation, directed toward my Teaching. Because of the devotional offerings you made to Śākyamuni, such as parasols, flags, banners, incense, flowers, and unguents, you have come to my Teaching. Because of your offerings to the stūpas of Śākyamuni, of saffron water and sandalwood unguents, you have come to my Teaching. Because you always took refuge in the Buddha, Dharma, and Sangha, and did meritorious deeds, you have come to my Teaching. Because you received the moral precepts that were taught by Śākyamuni and kept them meticulously, you have come to my Teaching. Because you made donations to the Sangha of food, drink, robes, and various kinds of medicines, you have come to my Teaching. . . .

Source: Translated from *Āryamaitreya vyākaraṇa,* ed. Nalinaksha Dutt, *Gilgit Manuscripts* (Calcutta, 1959), 4:187–207.[9]

---

[9]Alternative French translation, Sylvain Lévi, "Maitreya le consolateur," *Etudes d'orientalisme publiées par le Musée Guimet à la mémoire de Raymonde Linossier* (Paris: E. Leroux, 1932), pp. 390–95. Partial English translation, Edward Conze, *Buddhist Scriptures* (Harmondsworth: Penguin Books, 1959), pp. 238–41.

CHAPTER 2

The Experience of the Sangha

Part of the Buddha's greatness lay in the fact that he did not just preach a doctrine to those who would listen to him; he also organized his followers into a community, the Buddhist sangha. At the time of the Buddha and subsequently, one could be affiliated with the Buddhist religion in a number of ways. Indeed, Buddhist texts commonly speak of the sangha as being a "fourfold" community, as consisting of monks, nuns, laymen, and laywomen. The relationships among these groups and their respective relationships to the Buddha and enlightenment were topics of concern almost from the start. Nevertheless, the people in these groups shared a common experience—conversion to the Buddha's way—giving them a common affiliation and identity that distinguished them from their non-Buddhist neighbors.

2.1 TALES OF CONVERSION

Buddhist literature is full of stories of conversion. Some are psychologically poignant, telling of people who turn to the Blessed One when they are truly at loose ends. Others are incredibly elaborate, tracing the roots of a person's movement of faith back through numerous previous lives. Still others are relatively straightforward and simple. We shall start with some stories about laypersons before moving on to recount tales of monks and nuns.

2.1.1 The First Disciples of the Buddha

In selection 1.6, we saw that, as a result of the Buddha's first sermon, Kauṇḍinya and his companions became the first monastic members of the Buddhist community. They, however, were not the Buddha's first disciples. Even before his first sermon the Buddha had converted two merchants, who, according to legend, did not become ordained but remained laymen. Shortly after his enlightenment, before going to the Deer Park at Sarnath, the Buddha is said to have met and preached the Dharma to two men, who, in the Pali tradition, are called Tapassu and Bhallika. They responded by taking "double refuge" in him and his teaching (there being as yet no formal sangha that they could join).

It is noteworthy that this movement of faith on their part is not portrayed as accidental. Not only are they goaded into it by a divinity who was their mother in a previous existence, but also, according to the selection below, it is something that, unbeknownst to them, they themselves willed eons ago at the time of the previous Buddha Padumuttara.

Significantly also, Tapassu and Bhallika are portrayed as doing some of the things that, in this tradition, characterize the lives of laypersons: they make offerings of material goods (food) to monks (in this case, the Buddha himself), and they interest themselves in the veneration of relics (in this case, some hairs from the Buddha's head).

Long ago, at the time of the past Buddha Padumuttara, two brothers were reborn in a good family in Haṃsavatī. One day, after listening to the Master preach the Dharma and witnessing his establishment of two lay disciples as "foremost of those taking refuge," those two brothers made a formal resolution, aspiring to attain that same status for themselves in the future.

For one hundred thousand aeons, they were reborn repeatedly in saṃsāra, in the realms of gods and humans, until, just prior to our own Buddha [Gotama]'s attainment of omniscience, they were reborn in a propertied family, in the city of Asitañjana. The elder was called Tapassu and the younger Bhallika. They lived as householders, and in time they owned five hundred oxen and went about doing the business of merchants.

When our bodhisattva obtained omniscience, he remained near the seat of enlightenment in Bodhgaya for seven weeks, contemplating his achievement. Then, in the eighth week, he sat at the foot of the tree Rājāyatana. Soon, those merchants came to that place, together with their five hundred oxen.

Now their mother in a previous life had been reborn in that place as a divinity. She reflected: "Buddhas ought to be given food. Indeed, this one should not go much farther without any. My two sons, who are now here in this place, should be caused to make food offerings to the Buddha." Thus she caused the five hundred yoked oxen to stop in their tracks.

"Now, what's this?" reflected the brothers as they contemplated the omen. . . .

The divinity then took on the form of a man and said to them: "Do not be afraid! I am not different from you; I am not a demon, or a ghoul, or a nāga. Indeed, in a past life, I was your mother, and I have now become the local deity of this place. The Buddha sits at the foot of the Rājāyatana tree; you should offer most excellent alms to him."

When they heard this, the brothers rejoiced, and approached the Master, bearing alms of rice cakes and sweets on a gold platter. "Good sir," they declared, "take this food."

The Master considered what had been done by previous Buddhas [and resolved to accept their offering. But he realized he had no bowl.] So, the four great divine kings came and offered him bowls made of stone. The Master, saying, "May the merit of their deed be great," declared that the four bowls should become one, and that is what happened. Then the merchants placed the rice cakes and sweets into the bowl of the Tathāgata and offered him water when he was finished. And at the conclusion of his meal, they saluted the Master and sat down to one side.

Then the Master preached the Dharma to them, and at the conclusion of the sermon they took double refuge in the Buddha and the Dharma. Then they saluted the Master and, wishing to return to their own city, said: "Good sir, give us a memento of yourself that we can worship."

The Master then rubbed his head with his right hand and gave the two men eight handfuls of hair relics. The two men made golden boxes for the relics, and, taking them to their own city, Asitañjana, they erected a shrine for the living hair relics, there at the city gate. On each festival day, a blue ray of light still issues forth from the shrine.

Source: Translated from *Manorathapūraṇī: Buddhaghosa's Commentary on the Anguttara Nikāya,* ed. M. Walleser and H. Kopf (London: Pali Text Society, 1924), 1:382–84.

2.1.2 The Laywoman Sujātā

Tapassu and Bhallika were the first male lay disciples of the Buddha. The first female lay disciple was Sujātā. Laywomen have always played an important role in the Buddhist community, but the story of Sujātā is noteworthy for a number of reasons. She was not only the Buddha's first female disciple of any kind (it took a while before the Buddha was willing to ordain women as nuns, see 2.1.4), but she was, in a sense, a devotee of the Buddha even before his Buddhahood and even before she knew who he was. In the Pali tradition,[1] it is she who gives the Buddha the offering of milk-rice that marks the end of his practice of extreme asceticism and that sustains him throughout the attainment of his enlightenment and for seven weeks thereafter until, in fact, the food offering made by Tapassu and Bhallika. Her devotional offering as first laywoman, then, and theirs as first laymen serve to frame the story of the Buddha's enlightenment, to mark by ritual food offerings the beginning and the end of the enlightenment narrative.

Sujātā, however, has no idea that she is making an offering to the bodhisattva (at that point he is not yet the Buddha). Instead, she thinks that she is seeing a tree spirit to whom she once prayed for help in getting a son and who has now graciously manifested himself in person to accept her promised gift of thanks. Nevertheless, her offering has important karmic repercussions. Her son, Yasa, eventually becomes an important early disciple of

[1]In the Sanskrit tradition, as we saw in 1.3, this role was taken on by the sisters Nandā and Nandabalā.

the Buddha, and she herself, at that time, is converted to the Dharma and takes refuge in the Three Jewels. Thus, despite her early encounter with the Buddha under the tree, it is only through her family—through its male members—that she eventually comes to the sangha.

Long ago, at the time of the past Buddha Padumuttara, a woman was born into a good family in Haṃsavatī. One day, after listening to the Master preach the Dharma and witnessing his establishment of a laywoman as "foremost of those taking refuge," she made a formal resolution, aspiring to attain that same status herself.

For one hundred thousand aeons, she was repeatedly reborn in saṃsāra, in the realms of gods and humans, until just before our own Master Gotama's birth, she was reborn in the house of the landlord Senāni in the village of Senāni in Uruvelā. Once she had come of age, she made this promise to the god of a banyan tree: "If, once I am married to someone of the same caste, my first child is a son, I will, every year, make a food offering to you."

Her wish was successful and a son, Yasa, was born to her. Then, on the full moon day of the month of Visākha, when coincidentally the six years of the bodhisatta's practice of extreme asceticism were just about over [see 1.3], she got up early in the morning and milked her cow before dawn, thinking, "Today, I will make that food offering!" The cow's calves had not yet suckled, but as soon as a new pot was put under the udder, the milk flowed out of its own accord. Marveling at this, Sujātā took the milk in her own hand and directed it into the new pot, and she herself put it on the fire to cook. And when that milk-rice started to boil, great bubbles appeared, and auspiciously turned to the right. So that in bursting they would not splash over the sides, the god Brahmā held an umbrella [as a lid over the pot], . . . while Indra regulated the fire, and the gods of the four directions added a divine nutritive essence to the milk-rice.

Beholding all these marvels, Sujātā said to her servant Puṇṇā: "It has been a long time since I have seen so many good omens; go quickly and prepare the place of the god!"

"Yes, mistress," she answered, and as told, she hurried to the foot of the banyan tree.

Now the bodhisatta had gotten up early, and waiting for the time of the begging round, he was sitting under that tree. And Puṇṇā, arriving at that pure place, mistook him for the tree god. She went back to Sujātā and said: "The divinity himself is seated at the foot of the tree!"

Sujātā replied, "Ah! If what you say is true, then it was he who gave me my son!" And putting on all of her ornaments, she piled the milk-rice on a golden plate worth a hundred thousand pieces of gold, enclosed it in another golden bowl, wrapped it in a white cloth, added wreaths of sweet-smelling garlands, picked it up, and set forth. When she saw the Great Man, there arose in her an overpowering gladness, and she bowed down very low in front of him, touching her head to the ground. Uncovering the dish of milk-rice, she offered it to the Blessed One with her own hand, saying, "Just as my wish has been fulfilled, so may yours be accomplished." Then she went away.

The bodhisatta went to the bank of the Nerañjanā River and put the golden dish down there on the shore; he bathed, got out, fashioned the milk-rice into four balls, and ate it. He then washed the dish in the river, and in due course he went to the seat of enlightenment, attained omniscience, spent seven times seven days contemplating his enlightenment, and set in motion the excellent wheel of the Dharma at the Deer Park of Isipatana.

In the meantime, Sujātā's son, Yasa, had grown, and the Buddha, realizing that he had within him the conditions necessary for enlightenment, went and sat down under another tree planning to encounter him. Young Yasa, finding the door to his harem open at midnight, was suddenly full of restlessness. Muttering: "How depressing! How distressing [is this life of sensual pleasure]!" he left his house, went out of the city, happened across the Blessed One, heard from him the teaching of the Dharma, and attained the first three fruits of the path.

Then his father, searching for him, followed his tracks until he too came to the Blessed One. He asked what had happened to his son. The Master, however, concealed young Yasa by making him invisible and preached the Dharma to his father. At the end of the sermon, Yasa's father attained the fruit of entering the stream, and Yasa [who, though invisible, had been listening], became an arhat. The Blessed One then ordained Yasa simply by saying, "Come, monk," and as soon as he heard those words, the characteristics of a layman in him disappeared and he became like a great elder, bearing a begging bowl and all the requisites of a monk, which had been magically created.

Yasa's father invited the Buddha to their home. The Blessed One, taking young Yasa as his novice disciple, went to their house, ate a meal, and preached the Dharma. At the end of the sermon, Yasa's mother, Sujātā, . . . also attained the fruit of entering the stream, . . . and at the same time uttered the formula of the threefold refuge. Subsequently, when the Master was assigning statuses to the laywomen, he established her as the foremost laywoman among those taking refuge.

Source: Translated from *Manorathapūraṇī: Buddhaghosa's Commentary on the Anguttara Nikāya,* ed. M. Walleser and H. Kopf (London: Pali Text Society, 1924), 1:402–04.

2.1.3 The Conversion of Śāriputra and Maudgalyāyana

Sujātā, Tapassu, and Bhallika all chose to affiliate themselves with the Buddhist community as laypersons. But the sangha, of course, also comprised monks and nuns, that is, people who had chosen to renounce the householder's life and become monastic followers of the Buddha. The first such disciples were, as we have seen, the "Fortunate Five" monks to whom the Buddha first preached at Sarnath [see 1.6]. But two other monks were eventually to play more significant roles in the sangha and were, in fact, to become the two chief disciples of the Blessed One: the friends Śāriputra and Maudgalyāyana.

A number of early biographies of the Buddha end not with his death but with the story of the conversion of Śāriputra and Maudgalyāyana, as though, with their ordination as monks, the sangha was in good hands and established on a firm foundation. It is appropriate therefore to recount the tale of their conversion as a prime example of the foundation of the male monastic branch of the fourfold community. It is noteworthy, however, that they were not actually converted by the Buddha. In fact, Śāriputra, when he was still called by his given name of Upatiṣya, was converted by the monk Aśvajit, one of the Fortunate Five at Sarnath. And Maudgalyāyana, known then as Kolita, was converted by Śāriputra. It is only then that the two friends went together to find the Buddha and to seek ordination.

At least two things should be noted about their conversion. One of these is simply the power of the Dharma, the Buddha's doctrine. Both Śāriputra and Maudgalyāyana (who, it should be pointed out, have already been wandering ascetics on a quest of their own for some time), are inspired by a single saying of the Buddha: his declaration that he knows the cause of all things in this world and that he knows also their cessation (that is, that he has discovered the second and third Noble Truths). This is enough to bring about their conversion. The second thing that should be noticed is the physical effect of knowledge of the Truth, that is, of salvation. Śāriputra is first attracted to Aśvajit because of the latter's serene disposition, of the way he walks and moves about. And Maudgalyāyana notes the same thing later in his friend Śāriputra. Their story is found in many sources; the following selection is from a Sanskrit sūtra.

At that time, for some reason or another, the wandering ascetic Upatiṣya [later, Śāriputra] had gone to Rājagṛha on an errand. He happened to notice from a distance the Venerable Aśvajit, whose way of moving and looking about, of wearing his robes and holding his bowl, was strikingly serene. He thought: "There are many accomplished renunciants dwelling in Rājagṛha, but I have never seen anyone whose deportment is like this one's. I should ask him who his teacher is and whose Dharma he professes."

Intending to do so, he followed him and then went and stood in a narrow street where the Venerable Aśvajit was about to pass. When the Venerable Aśvajit came close to him, the wandering ascetic Upatiṣya said to him: "Who, monk, is your teacher, and into whose order did you wander forth? Whose Dharma do you profess?"

"Venerable One," Aśvajit replied, "the wanderer Gautama of the Śākya clan is my teacher. He left his family, shaved his hair and beard, and put on yellow robes. With great faith, he wandered forth into the homeless life. He attained unsurpassed complete enlightenment. This Blessed One is my teacher. Into his order I wandered forth. I profess his Dharma."

"Then, Venerable One, teach me that Dharma."

"I am, Venerable One, but a novice, newly ordained. I cannot expound at great length upon all aspects of the teaching of the Blessed One, but I can teach you the gist of it."

"Monk, all I need is the gist. What is the need for many elaborations? Tell me the gist."

The Venerable Aśvajit then recited this verse:

"The Tathāgata has explained the cause of those elements of reality that arise from a cause, and he, the Subdued One, has also spoken of their cessation."

And as soon as the doctrine had been explained to him in this way, the wandering ascetic Upatiṣya's pure, spotless Dharma-eye was opened into the nature of things.

Then, having seen the Dharma, having obtained the Dharma, having understood and penetrated the Dharma intellectually, beyond doubt, beyond uncertainty, the wandering ascetic Upatiṣya . . . got up from his seat, put his upper robe over one shoulder, and, with folded hands, he solemnly declared: "This doctrine of the Holy Ones is immortal, infallible, without sorrow; it has not been seen or heard of before for many myriads of millions of aeons. Where does the Blessed One reside?"

"He is now right here in Rājagṛha, in the Veṇuvana monastery. . . ."

The wandering ascetic Upatiṣya then went to his friend, the wandering ascetic Kolita [later, Maudgalyāyana].

Kolita, seeing Upatiṣya from a distance, said: "Venerable One, your senses are serene, your face is at peace, and the complexion of your skin utterly pure. Did you reach the deathless state?"

"I reached it, Venerable One," Upatiṣya replied.

"Then teach me the Dharma."

And the wandering ascetic Upatiṣya then recited this verse:

"The Tathāgata has explained the cause of those elements of reality that arise from a cause, and he, the Subdued One, has also spoken of their cessation."

"Say it again, Venerable One, say it again."

"The Tathāgata has explained the cause of those elements of reality that arise from a cause, and he, the Subdued One, has also spoken of their cessation."

And as soon as the doctrine had been explained to him in this way, the wandering ascetic Kolita's pure, spotless Dharma-eye was opened into the nature of things.

Then, having seen the Dharma, having obtained the Dharma, having understood and penetrated the Dharma intellectually, beyond doubt, beyond uncertainty, the wandering ascetic Kolita . . . got up from his seat, put his upper robe over one shoulder, and, with folded hands, he solemnly declared: "This doctrine of the Holy Ones is immortal, infallible, without sorrow; it has not been seen or heard of before for many myriads of millions of aeons. Where does the Blessed One reside?"

"He is now right here in Rājagṛha, in the Venuvana monastery. . . ."

"Come, Venerable One, we shall practice the religious life under the Blessed One."

Source: Translated from *Das Catuṣpariṣatsūtra, eine kanonische Lehrschrift über die Begründung der buddhistischen Gemeinde,* ed. Ernst Waldschmidt, Abhandlungen der deutschen Akademie der Wissenschaften zu Berlin, 1960 (Berlin: Akademie Verlag, 1962), 3:374–86.[2]

2.1.4 The Acceptance of Women into the Order

One more branch of the early sangha that was established by the Buddha needs to be considered here: the community of nuns. Though commonly listed second in the usual enumeration of the divisions of the fourfold sangha, the community of nuns was, in fact, the last to be established by the Buddha and, according to legend, was done so with great reluctance.

It is possible to argue that the sexist views found in many Buddhist texts were not so much those of the Buddha himself as those of the gynophobic male monastics who wrote and edited them. It is also possible to argue that, compared with the misogynist views of some of his non-Buddhist peers, the Buddha's attitude toward women was relatively liberal, that he at least admitted their capacity for leading a monastic life and for attaining enlightenment. The following selection, however, suggests that he did so only grudgingly. As it makes clear, it was only after repeated prodding by his own aunt and foster mother, Mahāprajāpatī Gautamī, and by his disciple Ānanda that the Buddha reluctantly agreed to allow for the ordination of women, suggesting, in the same breath, that his action would cut in half the life span of his teaching.

Moreover, the passage goes on to spell out eight special rules for nuns, which had the effect of definitely making them subordinate to and dependent on the community of monks. In fact, these eight rules were only the beginning: throughout the centuries, women being ordained into the sangha found themselves facing a far greater number of rules and regulations than their male counterparts, and partly because of these additional regulations, the lineage and order of nuns eventually died out in many countries. There are concerted efforts today to restore it.

Then Mahāprajāpatī Gautamī, together with her four companions and five hundred other Śākyan women, approached the Blessed One and, after paying obeisance to him, sat down to one side. And Mahāprajāpatī Gautamī said this to the Buddha:

"Blessed One, the appearance of Buddhas in the world is rare; instruction in the True Dharma is difficult to obtain. But now the Blessed One . . . has appeared, and the Dharma whose preaching is conducive to tranquillity and parinirvāṇa is being expounded by him and is causing the

[2]Alternative English translation, Ria Kloppenborg, *The Sūtra on the Foundation of the Buddhist Order* (Leiden: E. J. Brill, 1973), pp. 92–95.

realization of ambrosial nirvāṇa. It would be good if the Blessed One were to allow women to be initiated into his order and ordained as nuns."

The Blessed One said: "Gautamī, do not long for the initiation of women into the order, or for their ordination as nuns."

Now Mahāprajāpatī Gautamī, thinking that the Buddha would not give women a chance to become initiated and ordained, paid obeisance to the Blessed One and took her leave. Then, together with her companions she approached the Śākyan women and said: "The Blessed One will not allow honorable women to be initiated and ordained as nuns. However, let us honorable women cut our own hair, acquire our own monastic robes, and attach ourselves to the Blessed One's party and follow after him, . . . wandering where he wanders throughout the land of Kośala. And if the Blessed One allows it, we will be initiated, and if he does not allow it, we will lead a chaste life in the presence of the Holy Buddha. . . . "

Now the Blessed One, after dwelling as long as he wished in the city of Kapilavastu, set forth to travel through the land of Kośala. And Mahāprajāpatī Gautamī, together with her companions, cut their own hair, acquired their own robes, attached themselves to the Blessed One's party, and followed after him. . . . Wandering through Kośala in the company of a large group of monks, the Blessed One arrived at the city of Śrāvastī. There he dwelt in the Jetavana, Anāthapiṇḍada's park.

Then Mahāprajāpatī Gautamī approached the Blessed One, paid obeisance to him, and sat down to one side. And she said: "Blessed One, the appearance of Buddhas in the world is rare, instruction in the True Dharma is difficult to obtain, but now the Blessed One . . . has appeared, and the Dharma whose preaching is conducive to tranquillity and parinirvāṇa is being expounded by him and causing the realization of ambrosial nirvāṇa. It would be good if the Blessed One were to allow women to be initiated into his order and ordained as nuns."

The Blessed One said: "Gautamī, do not long for the initiation of women into the order or for their ordination as nuns."

And again, Mahāprajāpatī Gautamī, thinking that the Buddha would not give women a chance to become initiated and ordained, paid obeisance to the Blessed One and withdrew to the gateway of the Jetavana. There, she stood crying and scuffing her toes on the ground.

Now a certain monk, seeing her there, went to the Venerable Ānanda, and said: "Venerable Ānanda, Mahāprajāpatī Gautamī is standing crying in the gateway of the Jetavana, scuffing the dirt with her toes. You should go, Ānanda, and find out why she is crying."

Ānanda therefore approached Mahāprajāpatī Gautamī and said to her: "Why are you crying, Gautamī?"

"Indeed, I am crying, Noble Ānanda, because truly the appearance of Buddhas in the world is rare, instruction in the True Dharma is difficult to obtain, and now the Blessed One . . . has appeared, and the Dharma whose preaching is conducive to tranquillity and parinirvāṇa is being expounded by him and causing the realization of ambrosial nirvāṇa, but the Blessed One will not give women a chance to be initiated and ordained into his order and to become nuns. It would be good, Ānanda, if you were to go to the Blessed One so as to obtain permission for women to be initiated and ordained."

"That would be good, Gautamī," agreed the Venerable Ānanda. So, approaching the Buddha, he paid obeisance to him and sat down to one side. Sitting there, he said: "The appearance of Buddhas in the world is rare, instruction in the True Dharma is difficult to obtain, and now the Blessed One . . . has appeared, and the Dharma . . . is being expounded by him and causing the realization of ambrosial nirvāṇa. It would be good if the Blessed One were to allow women to be initiated into his order and ordained as nuns."

Thus addressed, the Blessed One replied to the Venerable Ānanda: "Mother Gautamī should not long for the initiation of women into the order or for their ordination."

Then the Venerable Ānanda . . . after taking leave of the Buddha, went to Mahāprajāpatī Gautamī and told her what had happened.

Upon hearing this, Mahāprajāpatī Gautamī replied: "It would be good, Ānanda, if you were to go to the Blessed One and ask him a second time. . . . "

[So Ānanda went and repeated his request a second time, and] the Blessed One again replied: "Mother Gautamī should not long for the initiation of women into the order or for their ordination as nuns. Such a thing, Ānanda, would be just as though the disease known as kāraṇḍava were to fall upon a ripe field of grain and make it turn to chaff. Just as that would be a great defilement to the field of grain, so it would be a great defilement to the teaching of the Buddha were Mother Gautamī allowed to be initiated into his order and become a nun. Indeed, Ānanda, it would be just as though the disease known as 'red rust' were to fall on a ripe field of sugar cane. Just as that would be a great defilement to the field of sugar cane, so it would be a great defilement to the teaching of the Buddha were Mother Gautamī allowed to be initiated into his order and become a nun. Indeed, Ānanda, it would be just as though a great storm were to fall on a ripe field of rice in such a way as to bring about the destruction and utter ruin beyond hope of recovery of the rice crop. Just as that would be a great defilement to the field of rice, so it would be a great defilement to the teaching of the Buddha, were Mother Gautamī allowed to be initiated into his order and become a nun."

Then the Venerable Ānanda . . . returned to Mahāprajāpatī Gautamī and said to her: "Gautamī, the Blessed One will not give women a chance to be initiated and ordained into his order and to become nuns."

Upon hearing this, Mahāprajāpatī Gautamī replied: "It would be good, Ānanda, if you were to go to the Blessed One and ask him a third time. . . . "

"That would be good, Gautamī," agreed the Venerable Ānanda, and, he went a third time, and paid obeisance to the Buddha and sat down to one side. Sitting there, he said: "Blessed One, how many assemblies of disciples did enlightened Buddhas of the past have?"

The Blessed One replied: "Previous Buddhas, Ānanda, had four assemblies of disciples, to wit, monks, nuns, laymen, and laywomen."

Then the Venerable Ānanda said to the Blessed One: "Blessed One, the four fruits of monastic life—namely, the fruit of a stream-winner, the fruit of a once-returner, the fruit of a nonreturner, and the highest fruit of arhatship—can a woman who is earnest and zealous and who dwells in seclusion realize any of these?"

The Buddha replied: "Yes, Ānanda, a woman who is earnest and zealous and who dwells in seclusion can realize any of these four fruits of the monastic life."

"Well, then," the Venerable Ānanda said to the Blessed One, "since, Blessed One, enlightened Buddhas of the past had four assemblies—namely, monks, nuns, laymen, and laywomen—and since women who are earnest and zealous, and who dwell in seclusion are able to realize the four fruits of the monastic life—namely, the fruit of stream-winnner up to the highest fruit of arhatship—it would be good if the Blessed One were to allow women to be initiated into his order and to be ordained as nuns. Moreover, Mahāprajāpatī Gautamī performed some difficult tasks for the Blessed One; she nourished, fed, and suckled him after his mother had passed away. And for this the Blessed One is grateful and recognizant."

Hearing this, the Blessed One said to Ānanda: "This is true, Ānanda, Mahāprajāpatī Gautamī did perform difficult tasks for the Tathāgata; and she did nourish, feed, and suckle him after his mother passed away. And for this the Tathāgata is grateful and recognizant. But, Ānanda, the Tathāgata, too, performed some difficult tasks for Mahāprajāpatī. Thanks to him, she took refuge in the Buddha, she took refuge in the Dharma, and she took refuge in the Sangha. . . . "

Then the Blessed One reflected: "If I oppose the request of Ānanda a third time, this will cause him mental distress, and the teachings which I have revealed and entrusted to him would become utterly confused in his mind. I would like my true Dharma to last a thousand years, but it is preferable that Ānanda not become mentally distressed and that the revealed teachings not become utterly confused, even though, this way, my true Dharma will abide but five hundred years."

So the Blessed One proclaimed to the Venerable Ānanda: "Ānanda, [I am willing to allow Mahāprajāpatī Gautamī to be initiated and ordained, but first] I wish to make known the eight cardinal rules for nuns, which they should respect, esteem, honor, and venerate for as long as they live. They are like the steadfast banks of the great ocean, like a firm dike that people might build and that floodwaters cannot overflow. What are these eight rules?

1. "Ānanda, a nun, even one who has been ordained for a hundred years, must respectfully salute a monk, even one who has been ordained but a day. This, Ānanda, is the first cardinal rule for nuns, which they should respect, esteem, honor, and venerate as long as they live and steadfastly maintain as though it were the shore of the great ocean.
2. "Starting at age 18, a girl . . . can request full ordination but she must first complete a two-year preliminary course of training in the precepts. Moreover, her full ordination must be obtained from

the communities of both monks and nuns. This, Ānanda, is the second cardinal rule for nuns which they should respect . . . as long as they live and steadfastly maintain as though it were the shore of the great ocean.

3. "It is forbidden for nuns to criticize monks for real or nonexistent offenses; it is not forbidden for monks to criticize nuns for real offenses [though it is for nonexistent ones]. This, Ānanda, is the third cardinal rule for nuns. . . .
4. "Nuns should not receive food, beds, seats, or lodging ahead of monks. This, Ānanda, is the fourth cardinal rule for nuns. . . .
5. "A nun, Ānanda, who violates a cardinal rule of conduct must undergo disciplinary penance for a fortnight in the community of nuns and must seek restitution in front of the communities of both nuns and monks. This, Ānanda, is the fifth cardinal rule for nuns. . . .
6. "Every fortnight on festival days, the nuns should approach the community of monks and ask them for instruction. This Ānanda, is the sixth cardinal rule for nuns. . . .
7. "It is not proper for nuns to enter upon a rains retreat in a residence where there are no monks. This, Ānanda, is the seventh cardinal rule for nuns. . . .
8. "Ānanda, nuns who have finished their rains retreat should request the pravāraṇā ceremony from both communities. This, Ānanda, is the eighth cardinal rule for nuns, which they should respect, esteem, honor, and venerate for as long as they live. These rules are like the steadfast banks of the great ocean. [. . .]

"If, Ānanda, Mahāprajāpatī Gautamī accepts these eight cardinal rules, does not engage in any of the deeds that may occasion expulsion from the community, and observes the precepts, she can, from now on, be a nun, initiated and ordained."

Source: Translated from *Bhikṣuṇī Vinaya [of the Mahāsanghikas]: Manual of Discipline for Buddhist Nuns,* ed. Gustav Roth (Patna: K. P. Jayaswal Research Institute, 1970), pp. 4–18.[3]

2.1.5 The Conversion of Paṭācārā

Despite the extra rules imposed on them, numerous women in ancient India chose to become members of the sangha. Their interest in the Buddha's teachings and their desire to join his community were as varied as those of men but often revolved around reactions to their traditional roles as daughters, wives,

---

[3]With Sanskrit variants in C. M. Ridding and Louis de la Vallée Poussin, "A Fragment of the Sanskrit Vinaya, Bhikṣunikarmavacana," *Bulletin of the School of Oriental Studies* 1 (1920): 124–27. Alternative French translation, Edith Nolot, *Règles de discipline des nonnes bouddhistes,* Publications de l'Institut de Civilisation Indienne, no. 60 (Paris: E. de Boccard, 1991), pp. 2–10.

mothers, or widows. The following example recalls the traumatic life of the nun Paṭācārā, who, having been dealt repeated blows by fate, is close to going permanently insane when she happens across the Buddha preaching a sermon. As in the case of Śāriputra and Maudgalyāyana (see 2.1.3), one verse of the Dharma is enough to change her life.

At the time of the birth of the Buddha, a certain girl was born in Śrāvastī in the household of a guild master. When she had come of age, she secretly became sexually intimate with a workman in her household. In due time, however, her parents decided that she was to marry into a family of the same caste as her own. In desperation, she said to her lover: "Starting tomorrow, a hundred guards will prevent you from seeing me; if you are up to the task, take me away with you right now!"

"All right," he replied, and taking a certain amount of movable wealth, he went with her three or four leagues from the city, where they took up residence in a village. In time, she became pregnant, and when she was about to give birth, she said: "Husband, we are without resources in this place, let us go back and have this child in my family's home."

But he only said: "Shall we go today? Shall we go tomorrow?" Unable to decide, he let time pass.

Seeing him procrastinate in this way, she thought, "This fool will never take me." So, when he was out of the house, she set off on her own, thinking, "I will return home by myself!"

When her husband got back to the house, he did not find her anywhere. He asked the neighbors where she was, and they told him she had gone home. "Because of me, this daughter of a good family has become destitute," he thought, and he set out after her and caught up with her.

There on the road, she went into labor and gave birth. Thus, the very purpose for which they had set out had become accomplished in mid-journey. And thinking, "Why do we now need to go on?" they returned to the village.

Once again, she became pregnant, and everything repeated itself just as it had happened before. This time, however, when she went into labor and gave birth in the middle of the road, great clouds arose in all four directions. She said to her husband: "Husband, unseasonably, storm clouds have arisen all around; try to make me a shelter from the rain."

"I will do so," he replied, and built a hut out of sticks. Then, thinking he would get some grass for the roof, he went off to cut some at the foot of an anthill. But a black snake who lived in the anthill bit him on the foot, and he fell to the ground in that very place.

She spent the whole night, thinking: "He will come back now! He will come back now!" Then she thought: "Surely, he thinks I am a destitute woman, so he has abandoned me on the road and gone away." But when it became light the next day, she followed his tracks and saw him fallen, dead, at the foot of the anthill.

"My man has perished because of me!" she lamented, and taking her younger child on her hip and holding the elder by the hand, she went along the road until she came to a river flowing across her path.

"Now I cannot carry both children across at once," she reflected. "I will leave the elder on this bank, carry the younger one across to the other bank, put him down on a piece of cloth, come back again to get this one, and go on." So she entered the river and carried the baby across. But when, on her way back, she reached the middle of the stream, a hawk, thinking, "Here is a piece of meat," arrived to peck at the infant left on the bank. She waved her hand in order to scare the bird away. Seeing her gesture, the elder boy thought, "She is calling me" and went down into the river. He fell into the stream and was carried away by it. The hawk then carried off the infant, just before she could reach it. Overwhelmed by great sorrow, she went down the middle of the road, wailing this song of lament:

Both my sons are gone
and my husband is dead upon the road!

Thus lamenting, she arrived in Śrāvastī and went to the well-to-do neighborhood where she had lived, but . . . she was not able to find her own home.

"In this place, there is a family of such and such a name," she said. "Which one is their house?"

"Why do you ask about that family? The house where they dwelt was blown down by a great gust of wind, and all of them lost their lives. They are now, young and old, being burned right there, on a single funeral pyre. Look, you can still see the smoke."

Hearing this, she cried: "What are you saying?" And unable to bear even the clothes her body was dressed in, she stripped them off and, crying with outstretched arms the way she had at birth, she went to her family's funeral pyre and gave voice to this lament of total grief:

Both my sons are gone
and my husband is dead upon the road!
And my mother and father and brother
burn on a single pyre!

Again and again she tore off the garments that people gave her and threw them away. . . .

One day, when the Buddha was preaching the Dharma to a great crowd of people, she entered the monastery and stood at the edge of the assembly. The Master, spreading out his pervasive loving-kindness, said to her: "Sister, regain awareness, acquire mindfulness."

As soon as she heard the words of the Master, she became profoundly ashamed and fearful, and she sat down right there on the ground. A man standing nearby threw her his outer garment. She put it on and listened to the Dharma. With reference to her conduct, the Master then recited this verse from the *Dhammapada*:

Neither sons, nor parents, nor kinfolk are a refuge.
Relatives offer no shelter for one seized by Death.
Knowing this situation, the wise, exercising moral restraint,
can quickly clear the way that leads to nirvāṇa.

At the end of the verse, even as she stood there, she became a stream-winner. She approached the Master, venerated him, and asked to be ordained. He agreed to her ordination, telling her to go to the home of the nuns and wander forth there. She was ordained, and it was not long before she obtained arhatship, and grasping the word of the Buddha, she became a master of the book of the discipline (Vinaya). Subsequently, when the Master was seated at the Jetavana and assigning statuses to each of the nuns, he established Paṭācārā as the foremost of those knowing the Vinaya.

Source: Translated from *Manorathapūraṇī: Buddhaghosa's Commentary on the Anguttara Nikāya,* ed. M. Walleser and H. Kopf (London: Pali Text Society, 1924), 1:356–60.[4]

2.1.6 The Conversion of a Lynch Mob

Finally, one more conversion story needs to be related here. In the religiously pluralistic context of ancient India, it is important to remember that the Buddha and his disciples were not always welcome. In some places, in fact, people feared and resented Buddhists as a threat. Some Indian parents, not unlike their modern American counterparts who criticize "cults" and "sects," were worried about these yellow-robed Buddhists, who sought to persuade their children to take up a new faith, shave their heads, "drop out," and become wandering beggars or live together in a commune.

These fears were genuine, and Buddhist legends such as the following one occasionally reflect them. Characteristically, such legends do not have much good to say about the detractors of Buddhism, whom they label "heretics" and whom they generally mock as ineffective in their efforts to stop the True Doctrine and put a halt to the spread of the community.

At that time, the Blessed One was traveling in the country of Kosala and was headed for a brahmin village. The non-Buddhist heretical masters there, learning of the coming of the wanderer Gautama, hastened to visit the families of the brahmin householders.

"May your happiness increase!" they declared to them. "We are leaving!"

"Reverend sirs," the householders responded, "why are you going?"

The heretics replied: "Having seen you rich, we hate to see you ruined. That is why we are leaving!"

"What do you mean, reverend sirs?" the others asked. "Why do you say we shall be ruined?"

"You should know that the wanderer Gautama is coming, at the head of twelve hundred disciples. His band is like a hailstorm that decimates

---

[4]Alternative English translation, Mabel Bode, "Women Leaders of the Buddhist Reformation," *Journal of the Royal Asiatic Society,* 1893, pp. 556–60.

the crops. Countless parents among you will doubtless be deprived of your sons."

The householders said: "But, reverend sirs, if that is the case, we must remain united and support each other. . . . "

The heretics said: "Let us make an agreement, then. We promise to stay here, but you must go and ill-treat the wanderer Gautama."

"We will rough him up!" the brahmin householders declared, and taking swords, sticks, bows, and arrows . . . they headed down the road.

Now, there was in that town an old man who was inclined toward Buddhism. He saw those men and asked them, "Where are you going?"

"We're going to get someone!" they replied.

"Whom are you mad at?" the old man asked.

"The wanderer Gautama!" they answered.

"Go home," the old man told them. "The Blessed One is a great teacher; if you are angry with him, whom would you consider to be a friend?"

But they refused to go back.

The old man then reflected: "People of this sort—it is not possible to convert them by preaching the Dharma. They can only be tamed by the performance of some kind of magical display."

So he went back to the village and set fire to it. The fire rose up on every side, and those who had stayed in the village started screaming. Those who wanted to assault the Buddha heard their cries and were afraid.

"The wanderer Gautama is still far from here," they said to one another, "and already a horrible thing has happened: the village is on fire! We must go back and put out the blaze." They tried to do so, but found they could not.

Soon, however, the Blessed One arrived. "Why are you afraid?" he asked.

The villagers replied: "Our houses are being consumed by the flames, and we can't do anything about it!"

The Buddha then said to them: "I will put the fire out for you. . . . "

And then, just as soon as the Tathāgata had finished speaking, the fire was extinguished by his supernatural powers, and faith was engendered in the hearts of all those brahmin householders.

"Blessed One," they said to the Buddha, "what did we do to merit your coming?"

"It is for your sake that I have come," the Blessed One said to them. And understanding their character and knowing their roots of merit, he preached the Dharma to them, and instructed them in the Four Noble Truths. . . .

Source: Translated from *Mūlasarvāstivāda Vinaya* (Taishō shinshū daizōkyō, ed. J. Takakusu and K. Watanabe [Tokyo, 1924–29], no. 1448, 24:38c).[5]

---

[5]Alternative French translation, Jean Przyluski, "Le Nord-ouest de l'Inde dans le Vinaya des Mūla-Sarvāstivādin et les textes apparentés," *Journal asiatique* 4 (1914): 500–502.

2.2 RITES OF PASSAGE

The word *sangha*, as we have seen, means, in its broadest sense, a community that includes monks, nuns, laymen, and laywomen. The word is most commonly used, however, to refer simply to the monastic community, especially the community of monks. At first, becoming a monk in India seems to have been a relatively simple affair; monks were "chosen" by the Buddha, who simply said to them, "Come, monk," in somewhat the same way, perhaps, that Jesus "made" his disciples by saying, "Follow me." In time, however, ordination rituals became more complex; the distinctions between monks and laypersons hardened, rules and regulations and rituals were worked out, and within the sangha itself hierarchical distinctions developed.

2.2.1 Passage Denied: The Nāga Who Tried to Become a Monk

As the tradition evolved, a number of prerequisites for ordination were established. Buddhists seeking to enter the sangha needed to be of a certain age; to have the permission of their parents; to be free from certain diseases and physical deficiencies; not to be debtors, runaway slaves, or army deserters; and not to have committed certain heinous crimes. They also needed to have sponsors within the monastic community who would agree to act as their preceptor (upādhyāya) and teacher (ācārya). All of these criteria are readily understandable as measures meant to ensure the good reputation of the community. According to the Vinaya, however, there was one other, perhaps more perplexing, criterion: candidates for ordination had to be humans.

In ancient India, where belief in the ability of deities, dead spirits, and supernatural beings of various sorts to take on human form was widespread, this rule made good sense, and to this day, in South and Southeast Asia, candidates are routinely asked, as part of the ritual preliminaries for higher ordination, the intriguing question "Are you a human being?"

In the following story, the legendary reason for that question is set out: it is the tale of a nāga (snake divinity) who managed to join the monastic order and live as a monk until it was discovered that he was not a human being. He was then expelled from the community. Ironically and interestingly, in commemoration of this snake's intense desire to become a monk, and perhaps also to symbolize their liminal status, candidates for ordination are still today referred to as nāgas.

At that time, there was a nāga who was distressed that he had been born as a nāga; he was ashamed of his state and loathed it. He reflected, "How can I quickly free myself from being a nāga and regain human status?" And it occurred to him: "Truly these renunciants, these followers of the Buddha, practitioners of the Dharma, lead peaceful, chaste lives. They speak the truth and practice morality and virtue. If I were to be initiated into their community, surely I would quickly free myself from being a nāga and regain human status."

Then that nāga, taking on the form of a young brahmin, went to the monks and requested initiation. The monks initiated him and granted him full ordination, and he came to live together with another monk in a cell at the edge of the monastery.

Then one day, that other monk got up at night, toward dawn, and stepped outside to practice walking meditation. The nāga, feeling certain that his cellmate had gone off, fell asleep, and in his sleep he took on his natural form. His snake's body filled the whole room, and his coils came out through the windows. Then, his roommate, thinking he would go back inside the cell, opened the door and saw the whole room filled with snake. . . . Terrified at the sight, he screamed.

The other monks came running and said: "Brother, why did you cry out?"

"This whole room is filled with a snake whose coils are coming out the windows!"

Then, because of the noise, the nāga woke up, resumed his human form, and sat down on his own seat.

The monks said to him: "Brother, who are you?"

"Reverend sirs, I am a nāga."

"But why, brother, have you acted in this manner?"

Then the nāga related the whole matter to the monks, and the monks told it to the Buddha. The Buddha, with reference to this case, convened the community of monks and said this to the nāga: "You nāgas cannot advance in the practice of the Dharma and the Vinaya; but go and observe the uposatha twice each fortnight, and in this way you will quickly be freed from being a nāga and will regain human status."

Then the nāga thought, "Apparently I cannot advance in the practice of the Dharma and the discipline." Saddened, anguished, and sobbing, he cried out and went away.

The Blessed One spoke to the monks: "Monks, there are two conditions in which the true nature of a nāga becomes manifest: when he indulges in sexual intercourse with a female of his kind and when he falls asleep feeling certain he is safe. . . . Monks, an animal who is not ordained should not be ordained, and one who is ordained by mistake should be expelled from the community."

Source: Translated from *The Vinaya piṭakaṃ,* ed. Hermann Oldenberg (London: Williams and Norgate, 1879), 1:86–87.[6]

2.2.2 Passage Achieved: Joining the Order

Assuming that one is not a nāga and that one has met the other criteria for wandering forth, there are several ritual stages in the process of becoming a fully ordained monk. First, of course, one has to be a Buddhist layperson

---

[6]Alternative English translation, I. B. Horner, *The Book of the Discipline* (London: Pali Text Society, 1951), 4:110–11.

(upāsaka). This can be accomplished by the simple rite of pronouncing the threefold refuge formula and vowing to uphold the five precepts (see 3.5.1). A more decisive step is the initiation rite called wandering forth (pravrajyā), by which one is accepted into the order as a novice (śrāmaṇera). This rite involves acquiring the robes and bowl of a monk and taking upon oneself five additional precepts, for a total of ten (see 3.5.1). The next step, for which one has to be at least twenty years old, involves higher ordination (upasampadā). By this ritual one becomes a full mendicant (bhikṣu), and one commits oneself to observing over two hundred precepts, which are codified in a listing called the Prātimokṣa. The date of one's ordination thereafter determines one's seniority within the sangha, but here again there are distinct stages. The most noteworthy of these, occurring ten years after one's ordination, is when one becomes an elder (sthavira), a status that allows one, in turn, to become a preceptor to younger monks.

The rules and ritual formulas for all of these stages are set forth in the Buddhist disciplinary code (Vinaya) and in various ordination manuals that are commonly used to this day. A more concise account, however, can be found in the following description of Indian ordination practices by the Chinese monk I-ching, who spent twenty-four years traveling and living in India and Southeast Asia in the seventh century C.E.

In India, the rules concerning the wandering forth of monks into the homeless life are spelled out in detail. I shall only briefly point out some of them here. All those whose faith has been awakened and who wish to be initiated into the Buddhist order approach a preceptor of their own choosing and tell him of their intention. The preceptor, by use of good means, finds out whether they have any impediment that would disqualify them from the monkhood, such as a record of patricide, matricide, or the like. If he discovers no such disqualification, he agrees to their request and accepts them. After accepting a candidate, the preceptor tells him to wait until ten days or a month have passed and then confers on him the five precepts.

The candidate is now called an upāsaka. . . . This marks his entry into the basic teaching of the Buddha. Then the preceptor prepares for the candidate a set of robes, a begging bowl, and a cloth for filtering water, and communicates to the community of monks the candidate's desire to wander forth. With the sangha's consent, he then requests the candidate's teacher (ācārya) to conduct the ceremony.

The candidate is taken to a place apart, where his hair and beard are shaved off by a barber and where he is instructed to take a cold or a warm bath, depending on the season. His preceptor then dresses him in his underrobe and, by the use of good means, verifies whether he is a eunuch or has some other physical disqualification. He is then given his upper garment, which he accepts, touching it reverently with his head. Once he is dressed in his monastic robes, he is presented with his bowl and is now called "one who has wandered forth." Then, in the presence of his preceptor, the ācārya confers on him the ten precepts, either by reciting or by reading them. After he has been instructed in the precepts, he is called a novice (śramaṇera). [. . .]

Once a novice wishing to receive full ordination has become familiar with the religious rituals and has reached the requisite age of twenty, his preceptor, having seen his intention and resolve, prepares for him the six requisites of a monk [three robes, a bowl, a mat, and a water strainer] and asks at least nine other monks to take part in the ceremony. The ordination may be held on a small platform, in a larger demarcated area, or within a naturally bounded area. In the ritual area, the mats belonging to the community may be used, or people may bring their own seats. No cost is spared in preparing incense and flowers. Then the novice is instructed to pay respect three times to each of the monks present. . . .

The preceptor hands him his bowl, and he takes it and shows it to all the assembled monks. If it is a suitable bowl, they give it their approval. . . . Thereupon, the candidate is to accept his bowl according to the Dharma. Then the ācārya who is conducting the ceremony reads or recites . . . the precepts of the Prātimokṣa. When the candidate has received these, he is called "one who is ordained." . . . As soon as the ritual is finished, a measure should quickly be taken of the shadow of the sun [in order to determine the exact time of ordination], and it should be written down. . . .

Source: Translated from I-ching, *Nan hai chi kuei nei fa chuan* (Taishō shinshū daizōkyō, ed. J. Takakusu and K. Watanabe [Tokyo, 1924–29], no. 2125, 54:219a–c).[7]

2.3 THE REGULATION OF THE SANGHA

From the time of its first establishment by the Buddha, the community of monks and nuns in India was ordered by rules and regulations. These are said to have grown in number over the years, as the Buddha himself promulgated new rules for dealing with various situations as the need arose. Eventually, these rules came to be recorded in the Vinaya and codified in the list known as the Prātimokṣa. In the Theravāda tradition (the number of rules varies from one Buddhist sect to another), this list comprises 227 rules for fully ordained monks and 311 rules for fully ordained nuns.

The Prātimokṣa rules are supposed to govern monastic life. They prescribe not only general principles of ethical conduct but also specific modes of behavior with regard to dress, eating, sleeping, cleanliness, and so on. Thus, alongside rules against murder and other felonious crimes, we find regulations governing what kind of robes, bowls, seats, beds, and lodgings are acceptable; restrictions on dealing with members of the opposite sex or with the laity; and injunctions against bad table manners, bad bathroom behavior, and bad study habits.

---

[7]Alternative English translation, Junjiro Takakusu, *A Record of the Buddhist Religion as Practiced in India and the Malay Archipelago, by I-Tsing* (1896, reprint ed., Delhi: Munshiram Manoharlal, 1966), pp. 95–96, 99–100.

2.3.1 Recitation of the Rules

The rules of the Prātimokṣa (or Pāṭimokkha, as in the Pali text below) are arranged in different categories, according to the type of punishment that their violation entails. At the top of the list are those offenses that may result in expulsion from the community. These are followed by violations requiring judgment by a formal meeting of the sangha, which can then decide to put the guilty party on probation or suspend some of their privileges. Next are offenses concerning disallowed possessions, which may require forfeiture of the article in question; offenses requiring confession only; and finally, minor offenses deemed to be simply breaches of polite, proper behavior.

The entirety of the Prātimokṣa, category by category, was intended to be recited twice a month at ceremonies that fully ordained members of the sangha were required to attend and where they were expected to confess any infractions. It is not possible to give all of the rules here, so the following selection will limit itself to the ritual prelude to the recitation of the list and to the rules figuring in the first of the categories mentioned above, those involving expulsion. For monks there were four of these, for nuns, eight. (These eight should not to be confused with the eight cardinal rules imposed on nuns [see 2.1.4].)

[A.] Honorable sirs, may the sangha listen to me. Today is an Uposatha day, falling on the fifteenth day of the fortnight. If it suits the sangha, let the Uposatha ceremony be carried out and the Pāṭimokkha recited. Before we begin, let the Venerable Ones communicate the declarations of purity [made by any sick monks who are absent].

I will now recite the Pāṭimokkha. Everyone should listen to it and pay close attention. Anyone who has committed an infraction of the rules should disclose it. Those who are without infractions should remain silent. I will recognize your purity, Venerable Ones, by your silence. When the question is put to the assembly three times, you should divulge any infraction as though you were being interrogated personally. A monk who remembers an infraction but does not disclose it, after the question has been put three times, is guilty of a deliberate lie. And, Venerable Ones, deliberate lying has been declared by the Blessed One to be an impediment to progress on the path. Therefore, a monk who remembers an infraction and is desirous of purification should disclose it. Disclosing it will be beneficial to him.

These are the four cases involving expulsion:

1. A monk who has undertaken to live his life according to the moral precepts of monks and who has not renounced those moral precepts, or formally announced his inability to follow them, if he indulges in sexual intercourse with another human being, or with an animal, he is expelled and no longer allowed to be a part of the community.
2. A monk who stealthily takes something that was not given to him, in a village or in the forest—if his theft was such that it would

merit his being arrested by the king as a thief and executed, jailed, or exiled, and his being told, "You are a thief, a fool, an aberrant, a sneak!"—he is expelled and no longer allowed to be a part of the community.

3. A monk who intentionally takes the life of another human being, who finds a weapon for someone else and extols the beauty of death, or who incites them to kill themselves by planting thoughts in their minds with words such as these: "Ho, friend, of what use to you is this life of suffering and sin? You would be better off dead!"—such a monk is expelled and no longer allowed to be a part of the community.

4. A monk who lets it be known that he has superhuman attainments, though he has none, or that he has knowledge and insight like those of enlightened persons and who says, "I know this, I see that,"—unless he was mistakenly overestimating his achievements—such a monk is expelled and no longer allowed to be a part of the community, even if later on, . . . wishing to purify himself, he should admit that he was lying, engaging in vain and idle talk, claiming to know when he did not know, claiming to see when he did not see.

Venerable Ones, the four cases involving expulsion have been recited. Any monk who admits to any one of these can no longer reside with the monks. . . .

Venerable Ones, I ask you: "Are you completely pure on these points?"

A second time, I ask you: "Are you completely pure on these points?"

A third time, I ask you: "Are you completely pure on these points?"

The Venerable Ones are completely pure on these points, and therefore they are silent. Of this, I am taking note.

[B.] [When the Pāṭimokkha is recited in the community of nuns, the following extra cases liable to punishment by expulsion are added to the four that apply to monks. These are part of the numerous additional rules imposed on nuns]:

5. A nun who, moved by desire, touches, strokes, takes hold of, or presses up against a man, . . . anywhere between his neck and his knees,— she is expelled and no longer allowed to be a part of the community.

6. A nun who knows that another nun is guilty of an infraction meriting expulsion but who does not reprimand her personally or communicate that fact to others, or does so only after the nun in question has died or been ejected or left— . . . she is expelled and no longer allowed to be a part of the community.

7. A nun who continues to be a follower of a monk who has had some of his privileges suspended by the community, who does not regret his infractions, and who is disrespectful and unfriendly towards the Master's teaching, . . . she should be told by the other nuns, "Sister,

this monk has had some of his privileges suspended by the sangha, . . . do not follow him." And if after being so warned, she continues to be associated with that monk, the other nuns should further urge her, up to three times, to renounce her ways. If she relents by the third reprimand, that is fine, but if she does not relent, she is expelled and no longer allowed to be a part of the community.

8. A nun who, moved by desire, agrees to take the hand of a man, who is similarly so moved or who agrees to hold the corner of his robe, to stand together with him, to converse with him, to go to meet him at an appointed place, to have him come to her, to wait for him in a secluded spot, or to dispose her body for the purpose of indulging in non-Dharmic behavior—she is expelled and no longer allowed to be a part of the community.

Sources: [A.] Translated from *The Pāṭimokkha—227 Fundamental Rules of Bhikkhus,* ed. Ñāṇamoli Thera (Bangkok: Social Science Association Press of Thailand, 1966), pp. 19, 21. [B.] Translated from *The Vinaya piṭakaṃ,* ed. Hermann Oldenberg (London: Williams and Norgate, 1879), 4:213–21.[8]

2.3.2 The Ongoing Interpretation of the Rules

In the Prātimokṣa, we can find certain specifications of some of the particular circumstances in which the monastic rules are to be applied. As time went on, however, new situations arose requiring new refinements of the rules and new applications of them. For example, as various forms of currency developed, questions arose about the rule forbidding the acceptance of "gold and silver"—something requiring confession and forfeiture. Should it be applied to copper coins? to paper money? to checks? to credit cards? Alternatively, should the rule (requiring confession) against the consumption of alcohol or fermented liquor be extended to addictive substances such coffee, tea, or tobacco? to mind-altering substances such as marijuana, cocaine, LSD? to painkillers such as morphine? Some of the principles governing such cases are contained already in the *Book of the Discipline,* but in time Vinaya experts were to develop commentaries and subcommentaries trying to make things as clear as possible. This, in fact, is a process that still goes on today as new questions arise. An example of a recent attempt to spell out the applications of the Theravāda rules for monks on the basis of the texts and commentaries is a work by Thanissaro Bhikkhu, from which the following discussion of the rule against killing animals is taken.

[Rule:] *Should any bhikkhu knowingly deprive an animal of life, it is to be confessed.*

---

[8] [A.] Alternative English translation, Ñāṇamoli Thera, *The Pāṭimokkha,* pp. 18, 20; [B.] alternative English translation, I. B. Horner, *The Book of the Discipline* (London: Pali Text Society, 1951), 3:160–74.

There are five factors for the full offense here.

1. *Object*: a living animal.
2. *Perception:* One perceives it to be a living animal.
3. *Intention:* One knowingly, consciously, deliberately, and purposefully wants to cause its death.
4. *Effort:* whatever one does with the purpose of causing it to die.
5. *Result:* It dies as a result of one's action.

Object. *Animal* here covers all common animals. As the Commentary notes, whether the animal is large or small makes no difference in terms of the penalty, although the size of the animal is one of the factors determining the moral gravity of the act.

Apparently, this factor does not include beings too small to be seen with the naked eye, inasmuch as the classes of medicine allowed in Mahavagga VI include a number of anti-bacterial and anti-viral substances—some mineral salts and the decoctions made from the leaves of some trees, for example, can be antibiotic. The Commentary's example of the smallest extreme to which this rule extends is a bed bug egg. The four "Things Not to Be Done," taught to every bhikkhu immediately after his ordination (Mahavagga I.78.4), say that one should not deprive an animal of life, "even if it is only an ant."

On the other end of the spectrum, there is a parajika [offense entailing expulsion] for deliberately killing a human being, and a thullaccaya [grave offense] for deliberately killing a peta [hungry ghost], yakkha [demon], or nāga.

Perception. If this factor is not fulfilled, there is no offense. For example, if one steps on bed bug eggs, thinking them to be spots of dirt, there is no penalty.

Intention, in the Vibhanga, is described as "having made the decision knowingly, consciously, and purposefully." According to the Commentary, "having made the decision" refers to the moment when one "crushes" one's indecisiveness by taking an act. *Knowingly* means that one knows that "This is a living being." *Consciously* means that one is aware that one's action is depriving the animal of life. *Purposefully* means that one's purpose in acting is to kill the animal.

All of this indicates that this factor is fulfilled only when one acts on a clear and consciously made decision to deprive the animal of life. Thus, for example, if one is sweeping a walk, trying carefully not to kill any insects, and yet some ants happen to die, one does not commit an offense even if one knew that there was the possibility that some might die, since one's purpose in acting was not to cause their death.

Effort. The act of taking life may take the form of any of the six types of action listed under Parajika 3:

using one's own person (e.g., hitting with the hand, kicking, using a knife or a club);

throwing (hurling a stone, shooting an arrow or a gun);

using a stationary device (setting a trap, placing poison in food);

using magical formulae;

using psychic powers;

commanding.

A passage in the Mahavagga (V.10.10) deals with a case of this last instance, in which a depraved bhikkhu tells a layman that he has use for a certain calf's hide, and the layman kills the calf for him. Since the bhikkhu did not give a specific command that the calf be killed, and yet the Buddha said that this action did come under this rule, this shows that there is no room for *kappiyavohara* [allowable practice] in this context. Whatever one says in hopes of inciting someone else to kill an animal would fulfill this factor.

Result. Only if the animal dies does one incur the pacittiya [offense to be confessed] here. The Commentary to Pacittiya 74 imposes a dukkata [offense] on the simple act of striking an animal.

Non-offenses. There is no offense in killing an animal

unintentionally—e.g., accidentally dropping a load that crushes a cat to death;

unthinkingly—e.g., absent-mindedly rubbing one's arm while it is being bitten by mosquitoes;

unknowingly—e.g., walking into a dark room and, without realizing it, stepping on an insect; or

when one's action is motivated by a purpose other than that of causing death—e.g., giving medicine to a sick dog whose system, it turns out, cannot withstand the dosage.

Still, the Commentary states that if one notices even bed bug eggs while cleaning a bed, one should be careful not to damage them. Thus, "out of compassion, one's duties are to be done carefully." Or, in the words of the Subcommentary: "One's duties in looking after one's dwelling are to be done with mindfulness well-established so that such creatures do not die."

Source: Reprinted by permission of the author from Thanissaro Bhikkhu [Geoffrey DeGraff], *The Buddhist Monastic Code* (Valley Center, CA: Metta Forest Monastery, 1994), pp. 420–22.

2.3.3 Rules and Right Attitudes

The recitation of the Prātimokṣa was primarily aimed at ensuring the purity and unity of a local community, that is, of all monks or nuns living within the bounds of a particular monastery. But it could also cause a considerable amount of soul searching on the part of an individual. Failure to confess an infraction was itself a punishable violation of the rules that could, moreover, be denounced by others. And resentment at being denounced by others only compounded the transgression.

The rules thus were not the only thing that governed monastic life; attitude was equally important. Members of the community were expected to have an attitude of humility, of acceptance of their position in the hierarchy of the sangha and in the day-to-day order of things. Jealousy of others and attempts at self-aggrandizement were seen as "blemishes" on one's behavior and detrimental not only to community life but also to spiritual progress. The following text, taken not from the Vinaya but from a sermon attributed to one of the Buddha's disciples, warns monks against slippage into vain hopes and false expectations, an all-too-human pattern of petty egocentricities.

Honorable sirs, when a monk commits an infraction of the rules, it may well happen that he should have the following wish: "May the other monks not find out about it!" But then they do find out about it, and when they do, that monk gets irritated and is distressed, and that irritation and distress are themselves both blemishes.

Then, honorable sirs, when a monk commits an infraction, it may well happen that he should have the following wish: "May the other monks reprimand me in private and not in the midst of the sangha." But then they reprimand him in the midst of the sangha and not in private, and when that happens, he gets irritated and is distressed, and that irritation and distress are themselves both blemishes.

Then, honorable sirs, when a monk commits an infraction, it may well happen that he should have the following wish: "May I be reprimanded by one of my companions and not by someone else." But then he is reprimanded by someone who is not one of his companions, and when that happens, he gets irritated and is distressed, and that irritation and distress are themselves both blemishes.

Then, honorable sirs, when the Master is teaching the Dharma to the monks, it may well happen that a monk should have the following wish: "Oh, may he put his questions to me only and not to some other monk!" But then he does not put his questions to him at all but to someone else, and when that happens, he gets irritated and is distressed, and that irritation and distress are themselves both blemishes.

Then, honorable sirs, when the monks go out on their begging rounds, it may well happen that a monk should have the following wish: "Oh, may I, and not some other monk, be at the head of the line!" But then it so happens that he is not at the head of the line, and when that occurs, he gets irritated and is distressed, and that irritation and distress are themselves both blemishes.

Then, honorable sirs, when the monks are being served a meal . . . , it may well happen that a monk should have the following wish: "Oh, may I, and not some other monk, be given the best seat, the best food and the best drink!" But then he is not given the best seat or the best food and drink, and when that happens, he gets irritated and is distressed, and that irritation and distress are themselves both blemishes.

Then, honorable sirs, when the meal to the monks has been served, it may well happen that a monk should have the following wish: "Oh, may

I, and not some other monk, be asked to say the word of thanks. But then he is not asked to say the word of thanks, and when that happens, he gets irritated and is distressed, and that irritation and distress are themselves both blemishes. . . .

Then, honorable sirs, when the monks have gone into the monastery, it may well happen that a monk should have the following wish: "Oh, may I, and not some other monk, be the one to preach the Dharma!" But then it so happens that he is not the one to preach the Dharma, and when that occurs, he gets irritated and is distressed, and that irritation and distress are themselves both blemishes.

Then, honorable sirs, when the nuns have come to the monastery, it may well happen that a monk should have the following wish: "Oh, may I, and not some other monk, be the one to preach to the nuns!" But then it so happens that he is not the one to preach to the nuns, and when that occurs, he gets irritated and is distressed, and that irritation and distress are themselves both blemishes.

Then, honorable sirs, when the laity have come to the monastery, it may well happen that a monk should have the following wish: "Oh, may I, and not some other monk, be the one to preach to the laity!" But then it so happens that he is not the one to preach to the laity, and when that occurs, he gets irritated and is distressed, and that irritation and distress are themselves both blemishes. . . .

Source: Translated from *Majjhima Nikāya,* ed. V. Trenckner (London: Pali Text Society, 1888), 1:27–30.[9]

2.4 SANGHA SITUATIONS

Rules, as the very existence of the Vinaya implies, were not always followed by Buddhist monastics. Indeed, Buddhist literature is filled with stories of monks and nuns who, in one way or another, violated the rules of the monastic discipline and were reprimanded or punished for it. These stories are interesting not only for what they tell us about the ongoing process of elaboration of the rules of the sangha but also for the real-life situations that they reveal to us. Not all Vinaya violators were depraved, immoral fiends. Many, in fact, were simply following the dictates of their own inclinations in the face of moral dilemmas, or in circumstances in which they, willy-nilly, found themselves.

2.4.1 Nāgasena Disobeys His Master and Preaches to a Layman

The following story features the monk Nāgasena, famous as the interlocutor of King Milinda, whom we shall encounter in Chapter 3. It highlights a dilemma faced by Nāgasena when he was still a young monk: His master asks him to go

---

[9]Alternative English translation, I. B. Horner, *The Collection of Middle Length Sayings* (London: Pali Text Society, 1954), 1:34–38.

on a begging round for him, but to ensure that he does not engage in frivolous conversation with lay donors (or perhaps to make sure that he does not eat any of the food ahead of time!), he orders the young monk to take some water in his mouth and not to swallow it until he gets back. When, however, a layman invites Nāgasena in to preach to him, he finds himself caught betwixt and between the strict demands of his rather rigid teacher, who is concerned with monastic discipline, and his own desire to share the Dharma with others.

Then Nāgasena got a new teacher, who was over eighty years old and was named Kavigupta. In that region there was a lay devotee who was very wise and virtuous and who every day gave food to Kavigupta and his disciples. When it was Nāgasena's turn to go to get food from this layman, Kavigupta told him to fill his mouth with water and keep it there for the duration of his quest for alms at the layman's house.

The lay devotee saw that Nāgasena was young, superior in appearance and demeanor, of great intelligence, and capable of expounding the doctrine of the sūtras. When Nāgasena entered his house, the lay devotee greeted him respectfully and, with folded hands, said: "On many occasions I have given food to the monks, but no one has ever explained the sūtras to me." And he asked Nāgasena to explain a sūtra to him so that his mind would be freed.

Nāgasena then reflected: "My teacher gave me an order to keep this water in my mouth and not to speak. If, now, I spit out the water, I would be disobeying my teacher. What should I do?"

Then he thought: "This lay devotee is intelligent and has lofty aspirations. If I expound a sūtra to him he may well attain the path."

So Nāgasena spat out the water, sat down, and . . . said: "A person should dispense gifts, make merit, and observe the moral precepts set forth in the Buddha's teachings. After death, such a person will be reborn in this world and obtain wealth and nobility. A person who does not violate the precepts will not be reborn in the hells, among hungry ghosts, or among animals. Such a person will be reborn in heaven."

The lay devotee, hearing this explanation, was pleased in his mind. Knowing him to be so [and realizing that he was ready for more profound teachings], Nāgasena went on to expound to him a deeper sūtra: "All things in this world are subject to cessation, impermanent . . . and subject to suffering. And all beings lack independent existence. Those who have reached the path to nirvāṇa do not suffer from birth, old age, sickness, death, worry, or torment. . . . "

When Nāgasena finished expounding this sūtra, the lay devotee attained the fruit of the first path, that of stream-winner, and Nāgasena himself also attained it. The lay devotee was very happy. He prepared for Nāgasena some good food. Nāgasena told the lay devotee first to put the food in his teacher's bowl. . . . He then took it and returned to the monastery.

There, his teacher, Kavigupta, saw him and said: "Today, you have brought back marvelous food. This means you [must have said something to that layman; thus you violated my order, and so] have acted against the sangha. You should accordingly be expelled from the community."

The teacher then told the community of monks to assemble; it did so and sat down. The teacher said: "Nāgasena has violated the laws of our community; we must agree to expel him. . . . "

But then another meditation master, the Venerable Aśvagupta, . . . said: "Do not expel him! Nāgasena is just like a man who, with a single arrow, has hit two targets: He himself has attained the path, and the lay devotee has attained the path."

But the Venerable Kavigupta said: "Even if with one arrow he had hit one hundred targets, he still violated the rules of the community and cannot be allowed to stay in the midst of the order! Others, who follow the rules, will equate violation of the rules with Nāgasena's attainment. . . . "

The community kept silent. And so Nāgasena was expelled by the teacher Kavigupta. Nāgasena prostrated himself in front of his teacher, circumambulated the community of monks, and left the monastery.

He went far into the mountains, sat under a tree, and night and day, without ceasing, he exerted himself, meditating on the Path, until he attained the path of arhatship. He could then fly, he had the divine eye and divine ear, he could read the minds of others, and he knew previous births.

Having attained arhatship, Nāgasena then returned to the monastery, prostrated himself in front of the community of monks, confessed his offense, and asked for reinstatement. The sangha accepted his request.

Source: Translated from *Nāgasenabhikṣu sūtra* (Taishō shinshū daizōkyō, ed. J. Takakusu and K. Watanabe [Tokyo, 1924–29], no. 1670a, 32:694c–695a].[10]

2.4.2 Walls Make Good Neighbors

Monastic life in ancient India tended to have its routines, but it was never entirely free from quirky incidents that lent it variety. At such times, routines broke down and personalities came to the fore. The Buddhist Vinaya methodically tried to cover all sorts of contingencies, to set up rules for all situations that might arise in interactions between members of the monastic community (monks and monks, nuns and nuns, nuns and monks) or between members of the monastic community and the laity. There were always unusual situations, however, especially when there were dealings with non-Buddhists who, as in the following selection, might be near neighbors.

The Blessed One was dwelling in Śrāvastī. At that time, the residence of the Buddhist nuns was separated from the sleeping quarters of some Jain heretics by a wall. One day, the wall fell down. The nun in charge of

---

[10]Alternative English translation, Thich Minh Chau, *Milindapañha and Nāgasenabhikshusūtra (A Comparative Study)* (Calcutta: Firma K. L. Mukhopadhyay, 1964), pp. 39–40. Alternative French translation, Paul Demiéville, "Les versions chinoises du Milindapañha," *Bulletin de l'Ecole Française d'Extrême-Orient* 24 (1924): 85–89.

the residence in that nunnery was named Sthūlanandā. [Upon seeing the naked Jain monks], she declared: "You heretics should rebuild the wall! You are immodest, indecent, devoid of any shame. We honorable women, who are endowed with modesty, see you going in and out at all times, [with what should be hidden visible], and this brings about mental impurity."

But they replied: "It is now the rainy season; when the rains stop, we will build it."

"Do it now!" she retorted.

But they did not.

Getting angry, Sthūlanandā then heaped abuse on them: "May your life spans be cut off, ended! your hopes broken! Drunkards! Asses! You will not do it? Why not? You naked ones are indecent, immodest, lacking in any sense of shame, holders of false views, fallen into ruin! Fix that wall!"

But they answered back: "You witch's whelp! Big fat pumpkin-nun! You'll die before we rebuild that wall!"

Now Sthūlanandā went to the court and reported all this to the authorities. And after recounting everything, she said: "Your honors, act in such a way that the wall be rebuilt."

Now the court officials believed in Buddhism. They said: "Summon those promiscuous Jains!" They were summoned. The court officials said to them: "You sons of witches, naked heretics, drunkards, asses, holders of false views, fallen into ruin! Go and build that wall!" . . . Thus ordered by the court, those unwilling reprobates began to build up the wall, but every day, during the night, the rain caused it to collapse. In this way they went on working for the three months of the monsoon. Then they said: "We have been doing hard work in the mud because of this witch's whelp, this big fat pumpkin-nun!"

And they complained to the families of the lay supporters: "Look, householders, is it right that because of the suit of your venerable nun . . . we have been forced to work for three months?"

The lay householders made these thoughts known to nuns who were associated with their families. Those nuns communicated this to Mahāprajāpatī Gautamī, and Mahāprajāpatī Gautamī told the Buddha. And the Blessed One said: "Summon Sthūlanandā." She was summoned. "Is this true, Nandā?" he asked. [And finding out that it was, he set forth the following rule]:

"If a nun should use quarrelsome language with householders or non-Buddhist wandering mendicants, for a day or so much as a moment, or with novices and workers in the monastery, that is an infraction of the Vinaya."

Source: Translated from *Bhikṣuṇī Vinaya [of the Mahāsanghikas]: Manual of Discipline for Buddhist Nuns,* ed. Gustav Roth (Patna: K. P. Jayaswal Research Institute, 1970), pp. 106–07.[11]

---

[11]Alternative French translation, Edith Nolot, *Règles de discipline des nonnes bouddhistes,* Publications de l'Institut de Civilisation Indienne, no. 60 (Paris: E. de Boccard, 1991), pp. 88–91.

2.4.3 The Community at Kiṭāgiri

In establishing its disciplinary rules, the sangha was often conscious of its own public image, sensitive to the opinions and reactions of the laity. The Vinaya often portrays the laity as wanting their monks and nuns to be reserved and disciplined, "holy" and rather puritanical in their behavior. This was not always necessarily the case, however. In the following story we read of some monks whose relaxed, sociable, fun-loving lifestyle made them popular in the town of Kiṭāgiri in which they resided. Their actions caused a crisis in the larger sangha, however, which was not about to allow such behavior to persist. In the end, the Buddha sent his two chief disciples, Śāriputra (Sāriputta in the Pali text below) and Maudgalyāyana (Moggallāna), to banish the monks in question, not from the sangha itself (their actions did not warrant expulsion or even suspension from monkhood) but from further residence in Kiṭāgiri so that they could not continue to be a bad influence on the laity. This was not necessarily an easy task, because it was not at all clear that the overall sangha, or even the Buddha himself, had any institutionalized authority to tell monks where they could or could not reside. In the long run, Śāriputra and Maudgalyāyana were successful in their efforts at banishment, though, as the end of the present selection hints, such missions were not always easy.

At that time some bad monks, immodest disciples of Assaji and Punabbasu, were living in Kiṭāgiri. There, they engaged in a number of wrong practices: they planted flowering bushes, watered them, plucked the blossoms, and strung them into single-stalked, double-stalked and branching wreaths, flowery headbands, garlands for the hair, and corsages. And they had others do these things, too. Then they took these various garlands and ornaments and sent them to the wives, daughters, girls, daughters-in-law, and female slaves of respectable families. And together with these women, they would then eat from the same dish, drink from the same pitcher, sit on the same seat, and share the same couch, the same mat, the same blanket, and the same sheet. And they would take their meals when they were not supposed to, drink intoxicants, wear garlands, and in various ways dance and sing and play musical instruments and make merry as the women did likewise.

And they played checkers on boards of eight and ten rows, and mentally "in the sky" with no boards at all; they played hopscotch, pick-up-sticks, craps, tipcat, sticks-in-the-hand, and dice; they played at blowing horns made of leaves, . . . at tumbling, at guessing letters traced on one another's backs, at guessing thoughts, and at impersonating others; and they practiced controlling elephants, riding horses, driving chariots, archery, and swordsmanship; they ran back and forth in front of the elephants, horses, and chariots, yelling and clapping their hands; they wrestled and boxed; and, spreading out their robes as though to make a stage, they applauded dancing girls, saying, "Dance here, sister!" . . .

At that time a certain monk, who had just spent the rains retreat near Benares and was on his way to Sāvatthi to see the Buddha, arrived in

Kiṭāgiri. Getting dressed early in the morning, he took his bowl, put on his outer robe, and went into town to beg for food. He was an inspiration to behold; going and coming, whichever way he faced, holding out his bowl and retracting it, he kept his eyes downcast and was perfect in his deportment.

Seeing him, the people of Kiṭāgiri said: "Who is this fellow acting like an idiot, an utter fool, totally stuck-up? Who would ever give him alms? Our masters, the followers of Assaji and Punabbasu, are cordial, congenial, good to talk to, always smiling, and courteous. They aren't stuck-up, but they speak plainly and initiate conversations. It is better to give alms to them!"

One layman, however, seeing that monk wandering for alms in Kiṭāgiri, approached him and said: "Sir, have you managed to get any alms?"

"No, friend, I have not."

"Then come, sir, let us go to my house."

Then that layman took the monk to his house, gave him something to eat, and said:

"Sir, where are you going?"

"I am going to Sāvatthi to see the Buddha."

"Then, sir, in my name, please venerate the Blessed One and tell him that the monastery at Kiṭāgiri has gone bad, that the followers of Assaji and Punabbasu who dwell there are corrupt, immodest monks who engage in all sorts of wrong practices, that those people who formerly had faith and were pious no longer have faith nor are pious, and that those who were formerly fonts of generosity to the sangha have cut off their support. The good monks have left; the bad ones remain. It would be good, sir, if the Buddha could send some monks to Kiṭāgiri so as to reestablish the monastic life there."

"So be it, my friend," answered the monk, and going to Sāvatthi, . . . [he informed the Buddha of everything he had seen and heard at Kiṭāgiri].

The Buddha spoke to his two chief disciples: "Sāriputta and Moggallāna, go to Kiṭāgiri, and there formally banish from Kiṭāgiri those monks who are followers of Assaji and Punabbasu. . . . "

"Lord, how are we to do that to the followers of Assaji and Punabbasu? Those monks are fierce and rough!"

"Well then, take a lot of monks with you!"

"So be it, Lord," Sāriputta and Moggallāna replied. . . .

[There follows a rather elaborate description of the proper format for the act of banishment, which Sāriputta and Moggallāna are then successful in carrying out.]

Source: Translated from *The Vinaya piṭakaṃ,* ed. Hermann Oldenberg (London: Williams and Norgate, 1879), 2:9–13.[12]

---

[12]Alternative English translation, I. B. Horner, *The Book of the Discipline* (London: Pali Text Society, 1951), 5:14–19.

2.5 THE LAITY AND THE SANGHA: COMMONALITIES AND DIFFERENCES

The question of the relationship of laypersons to monastics is a complex one. On the one hand, the monastic sangha itself, in ancient India as well as in modern South and Southeast Asia, comprised both town-dwelling monks, who were primarily preoccupied with meritorious activities such as preserving the Buddha's teachings and imparting them to laypersons, and forest-dwelling monks, whose chief concern was with the practice of meditation and whose inclination was often toward more ascetic practices (see 6.3.1 [B]). Similarly, within the laity, it might be possible to distinguish between ordinary lay householders, who were involved in meritorious activities, and dedicated lay devotees, who were likewise committed to good deeds but whose relationship to the sangha was somewhat more intense, as reflected in their taking upon themselves additional precepts.

The complex relationships of all these groups, however, often boil down to a specific issue: what makes members of the monastic community "special"? In the selections that follow we shall address this issue by focusing on three particular questions: What spiritual or soteriological advantages are to be gained by joining the sangha? In what ways is the practice of meditation open to laypersons? And how do the laity and the monastic sangha relate in the making and sharing of merit?

2.5.1 Why Not Remain a Layperson?

As Buddhism developed in India, Buddhists appear to have joined the order for a wide variety of reasons. Some saw life in the sangha as the only alternative for a situation in lay life that had become intolerable to them. Others apparently decided to become monks because they viewed it as a chance to get a steady supply of good food in return for little physical labor. Some, usually younger sons, entered the sangha when their parents "gave" them to a monastery as novices, to make merit, or to have one fewer mouth to feed. Others saw it as a chance to get an education, to better themselves through enhanced status, or to be companions to a brother, a cousin, or an uncle who had already joined the order. Finally, of course, the motivation of a spiritual quest—a desire for enlightenment—never disappeared.

With regard to the last case, however, an important further question was perhaps inevitable: was it necessary to become a monk in order to attain enlightenment, or could that goal be accomplished as a layperson?

As with many important issues in Buddhism, different Buddhists had different answers. Some schools of thought had it that only fully ordained monks and nuns could attain arhatship. Others, more liberal, were willing to recognize the potential of laypersons. The following selection, featuring once again the elder Nāgasena and his interlocutor King Milinda, taken from a collection of Buddhist tales preserved in Chinese, gives a middle-of-the-road answer: it *is* possible for laypersons to attain enlightenment, but the path there is much easier and quicker for monastics.

Long ago, there was a king named Milinda. He was very intelligent and learned, and there was no subject in which he was not well versed.

He thought that no one could surpass him in knowledge, and so he asked his ministers: "Is there anyone intelligent enough and clever enough in debate to answer any question that I might ask him?"

Now, one of Milinda's ministers used to invite to his home an old monk whose conduct was very pure but who was not very learned. He came to discuss things with the king.

The king asked him: "Those who attain to the path, do they do so while living at home as laypersons, or do they do so by wandering forth as monks?"

The old monk answered: "Both can attain the same path."

The king retorted: "If both can attain it, then why bother wandering forth?"

The old monk was silent, for he did not know what to answer, and King Milinda became more arrogant than ever.

Then, the ministers said to Milinda, "There is another monk, named Nāgasena, who is unusually intelligent and wise and who is now living in the mountains." [. . .]

[The king invited Nāgasena to the capital, and, when the two of them met], the king asked: "Is it by living at home as a layman or by wandering forth as a monk that one can attain the path?"

Nāgasena answered: "Both can attain the same path."

The king replied: "If both can attain the path, then why wander forth?"

Nāgasena said: "Here is a simile: If you send on a journey to a place that is three thousand leagues away a young and strong man on horseback and provide him with all the necessary supplies, equipment, and weapons, will he be able to get there?"

The king replied: "Yes, he will."

Nāgasena went on: "Now, what if you were to send an old man there, riding a decrepit horse, without any provisions, would he get there?"

The king replied: "He could, but even if he had provisions, he might not be able to reach his goal, and it would be even harder for him without provisions."

Nāgasena then said: "To reach the Path by leaving one's home—that is like the journey of the young, strong man; to reach the Path by remaining a householder, that is like the old man's journey."

Source: Translated from *Tsa pao tsang ching* (Taishō shinshū daizōkyō, ed. J. Takakusu and K. Watanabe [Tokyo, 1924–29], no. 203, 4:492c–493b].[13]

2.5.2 Meditation in the Midst of Daily Life

It is sometimes claimed that one of the other things that differentiates laypersons from members of the monastic community is that the former engage in merit-making practices in order to improve their karma and achieve a better

---

[13]Alternative English translations, Junjiro Takakusu, "Chinese Translations of the Milindapañha," *Journal of the Royal Asiatic Society,* 1896, pp. 17–20, and Charles Willemen, *The Storehouse of Sundry Valuables* (Berkeley: Numata Center for Buddhist Translation and Research, 1994), pp. 224–26.

rebirth, whereas the latter meditate in order to transcend the whole karmic process of death and rebirth. Such generalizations, however, can be grossly misleading. For one thing, meditation itself is a merit-making activity, and making merit can be viewed as a form of meditation. For another, it is by no means true that all monks meditate.

It could be argued that certain forms of meditation demand the time, isolation, and freedom from worldly concerns that can come only with a monastic life. But the meditation tradition was supple and varied in its approaches. In the following very short anecdote, we have an example of a meditation technique that was eminently suited to lay life, a practical means of paying attention to one's thoughts. The method was said to have been taught by the elder Śāṇakavāsin to his disciple, the young Upagupta, whom we already met at a later stage in his career in selection 1.2. At this point, Upagupta is still a layman working in his father's perfume shop in the bazaar in Mathurā, in northern India.

The Venerable Śāṇakavāsin went to find Upagupta, who was selling perfumes in the marketplace. Upon seeing him, he said: "My son, as you conduct your business, are your thoughts pure or impure?"

Upagupta replied: "I do not know. What are 'pure thoughts' and what are 'impure thoughts'?"

The Venerable Śāṇakavāsin said: "When people feel desire, passion, and anger toward one another, that is what is called an impure mental state. When their interactions are free from these things, that is a pure mental state. In this way, my son, you can know the origin of your thoughts: when an impure mental state arises, put aside, on your left, a black stone. When a pure mental state arises, put aside, on your right, a white stone. . . . "

On the first day, there were twice as many black stones as white ones. On the second day, there were as many black stones as white ones. And gradually this went on until there were only white stones left and no black ones, only good thoughts left and no bad ones, only decisions according to the Dharma left and none contrary to it.

Source: Translated from *Aśokarājāvadāna* (Taishō shinshū daizōkyō, ed. J. Takakusu and K. Watanabe [Tokyo, 1924–29], no. 2042, 50:117c–118a).[14]

2.5.3 Making and Sharing Merit

It is commonly claimed that the sangha and the laity enjoy a reciprocal or symbiotic relationship in South Asia: laypersons support monks with material donations and thereby receive, in return, not only the Dharma (in the form of teachings) but also merit, which will enable them to attain a better situation

[14]Alternative French translation, Jean Przyluski, *La légende de l'empereur Açoka,* (Paris: Paul Geuthner, 1923), p. 348.

either in this or a future lifetime (see 1.5.2). Making merit, in fact, lies at the basis of much of lay life, even though, of course, laypersons are not the only ones who make merit; monastics are equally interested in it.

The most effective form of making merit is giving (dāna). For the laity, this generally means the giving of food and other supplies to members of the sangha. For the sangha, it may mean the giving of Dharma to the laity, in the form of sermons, sūtra recitations, or spiritual advice. But there are other forms of making merit as well. A common though noncanonical listing sets out ten meritorious types of action, including deeds that can be done by either monks or laypersons: giving, observing moral precepts, meditating, showing respect to one's superiors, attending to their needs, transferring merit to others, rejoicing at the merit of others, listening to the Dharma, preaching the Dharma, and having right beliefs.

One of these meritorious actions, the transfer of one's merit to others, is the subject of the following selection. It is common, on ritual merit-making occasions in South and Southeast Asia today, to see laypersons solemnly pouring water from one vessel into another, or onto the ground, while reciting certain verses. They are thereby signaling their intention to share the merit they have made (by virtue of their donation to the monks or attendance at the ceremony) to other beings, usually their deceased parents or other members of their family. This transference of merit, being an act of generosity and compassion, is itself an act of merit; hence it does not mean a depletion of one's own merit supply but rather an increase of it. (Similarly, one can "cash in" on the merit of others simply by rejoicing at their merit making, for such rejoicing is seen as a meritorious deed in its own right.)

A crucial factor in the efficacity of all this is the monastic community. It is not possible to make offerings directly to one's dead relatives. Rather, it is by making gifts to the monks that one can assure oneself of helping others, for the sangha acts as a sort of merit transfer station (especially between the living and the dead), whereby the goods that are offered in this world can be translated so as to benefit beings elsewhere. The following story concerning an offering made by King Bimbisāra, a contemporary lay supporter of the Buddha, is often cited today as one of the paradigmatic illustrations of the point.

One day, when the Tathāgata was alive, King Bimbisāra made offerings of alms to him; but that night in his palace, some hungry ghosts made a horrible noise and showed themselves. The following day, the king went to the Veṇuvana monastery and told the Tathāgata what had happened.

The Master said: "Great king, ninety-two aeons ago, at the time of the past Buddha Phussa, these ghosts were relatives of yours. They did a misdeed then by eating the gifts of alms that had been offered to the community of monks; as a result, they were reborn in the world of hungry ghosts. Wandering through saṃsāra aeon after aeon, they constantly sought, unsuccessfully, to receive alms from you. Yesterday, you failed to transfer to them the merit of the gift you made, so again they got nothing. That is why they acted as they did."

Bimbisāra then asked: "Venerable sir, what if I were to make an offering now, is it still possible for them to receive its transfer?"

"Yes, it is, great king."

So the next day, King Bimbisāra invited the Buddha, along with the community of monks, to his palace, made a great offering to them, and said, "Venerable sir, may these offerings become divine food and drink for these hungry ghosts." In this way, he successfully effectuated the transfer of his merit.

The following day, however, the hungry ghosts showed themselves again; this time, they were naked. The king went and reported this matter to the Buddha.

The Buddha said: "Great king, you did not make any offering of clothes to them."

So once again, Bimbisāra invited the Buddha, along with the community of monks. He made a great offering of robes to them, and said: "May these robes become divine garments for these hungry ghosts." In this way, he successfully effectuated the transfer of his merit, and, instantaneously, those ghosts who had been relatives of his were clothed in divine raiments; they left behind their hungry-ghost state and acquired divinity.

Source: Translated from *The Commentary on the Dhammapada,* ed. Helmer Smith (London: Pali Text Society, 1925), 1:86–87.[15]

2.5.4 Maudgalyāyana Brings about the Conversion of His Mother

In the last section, the emphasis was on a layman (the king) who alleviated the physical suffering of his dead ancestors by transferring merit to them. A greater responsibility sometimes fell on monks, who, if their parents were not Buddhists, felt the filial duty of converting them. Despite the ritual severing of ties between monks and their families that took place at ordination, there is considerable evidence that individual monks continued to care for the spiritual and, in some cases, material needs of those relatives, especially their parents when they became elderly and had no one else to look out for them. This filial responsibility was sometimes felt even after the parents were deceased, as the following story of the Buddha's disciple, Mahāmaudgalyāyana, makes clear. This tale, in which Mahāmaudgalyāyana convinces the Buddha to preach to his mother, who has been reborn in another world, is taken from a Sanskrit text, but it may lie at the root of a whole epic saga, much developed in East Asia, in which Mahāmaudgalyāyana (known in Chinese as Mulien) searches for his mother and becomes a paradigm of filial piety (see 8.2 and 9.5).

---

[15]Alternative English translation, E. W. Burlingame, *Buddhist Legends* (Cambridge: Harvard University Press, 1921), 1:209–10.

The Blessed One once said: "Monks, truly a mother and a father do what is difficult for their son; they give him milk and show him the many things of this world; they feed, nourish and rear him. If a man were to carry his mother on one shoulder and his father on the other for a full hundred years, or if he were to establish them in supremacy and lordship over this great earth, and give them various riches, such as jewels, pearls, cat's eye, gold, silver, emeralds, . . . [etc.], he would not thereby be doing as much for them as the son who introduces, instructs, establishes and confirms his doubting parents in the fullness of faith, his sinning parents in the fullness of morality, his greedy parents in the fullness of renunciation, or his weak-minded parents in the fullness of wisdom."

Reflecting on this, the Venerable Mahāmaudgalyāyana thought: "I have failed to attend to my mother; I must consider where she has been reborn."

Fixing his attention, he saw that she had been reborn in the Marīcika World System. He then pondered the matter of who it was who was going to convert her and he saw that it was to be the Blessed One. Then he thought: "We here are a long ways from there; I should communicate my purpose to the Buddha. So he said to the Blessed One: "Venerable Sir, the Blessed One once said, 'Truly, a mother and a father do what is difficult for their son. . . .' Now my mother has been reborn in the Marīcika World System and is to be converted by the Blessed One. May the Blessed One have compassion on her and do so."

Then the Buddha said: "Maudgalyāyana, by whose magical power shall we go there?"

"By mine, Blessed One."

So the Buddha and the Venerable Mahāmaudgalyāyana placed their feet on the summit of Mount Meru and set forth, and, in seven days, they reached the Marīcika World System.

From afar, [Maudgalyāyana's mother] Bhadrakanyā saw her son, and, as soon as she saw him, she rushed up to him exclaiming, "Ah! At long last, I see my little boy!"

At that, the crowd of people who had assembled said: "He is an aged wandering monk, and she is a young girl—how can she be his mother?"

But the Venerable Mahāmaudgalyāyana replied, "Sirs, these aggregates [skandhas] of mine were fostered by her; therefore, she is my mother."

Then the Buddha, knowing the disposition, propensity, nature and circumstances of Bhadrakanyā, preached to her a sermon fully penetrating the meaning of the Four Noble Truths. And when Bhadrakanyā had heard it, she . . . was brought to the realization of the fruit of the stream-winner.

Source: Translated from *The Divyāvadāna*, ed. P. L. Vaidya, Buddhist Sanskrit Texts, no. 20 (Darbhanga: Mithila Institute, 1959), pp. 31–32.[16]

[16]Alternative English translation, Joel Tatelman, *The Glorious Deeds of Pūrna* (Richmond: Curzon Press, 2000), pp. 77–79.

2.6 BUDDHISM AND THE STATE: THE KING AND THE COMMUNITY

As the story of King Bimbisāra demonstrates, ordinary people were not the only laypersons with whom the Buddhist monastic community in India came in contact. Virtually from the start, the sangha was also concerned about its relationship to one particular layperson, the king, and he, in turn, was quite naturally interested in the activities of this organized religious community within his domain.

We have seen that according to legend, the Buddha himself was from a royal family and that he gave up a career as a great universal monarch, a cakravartin king, in order to leave home and become a Buddha. The Buddha's great departure and religious quest, however, did not mean that he departed radically from the symbols of kingship. Rather, in Buddhist texts, the two careers—of the Buddha and the cakravartin—tended to be viewed as parallel and complementary. The Buddha undertook to teach the Dharma (the doctrine) to his disciples within his own community. The ideal king undertook to maintain the Dharma (in the broader sense of cosmic order and righteous rule) within the kingdom as a whole. This parallelism led to what has been called the doctrine of the two spheres, or wheels, of Dharma—the Buddhist version, perhaps, of Church and State relationships.

2.6.1 The Two Wheels of Dharma: A Parable

What was the relationship between these two wheels of Dharma? As with all such questions, the answer depended to some extent on who was giving it. Buddhist kings, though leading sponsors and devotees of the sangha, sometimes sought to control it, to "purify" it of "heterodox" elements, sometimes on their own initiative and sometimes at the prompting of a particular group of monks. The sangha, on the other hand, despite its maintenance of the parallelisms between the two wheels of Dharma, tended to see kings as dependent on its moral authority. The following story, incorporated into the Pali canon immediately following a sūtra comparing the Buddha and the cakravartin king, expresses this latter monastic view. Here it is clear that the first wheel, the wheel of kingship, because it lacks perfection, cannot stand alone but depends on being attached to the other wheel, the wheel of the Buddha (whom the story goes on to identify with the chariot maker).

Once, the Blessed One was dwelling in Benares, in the Deer Park at Isipatana.

"Monks," he said, . . . "in former times there was a king named Pacetana, who said to his chariot maker: 'My good chariot maker, six months from now there will be a battle; can you make a new pair of chariot wheels for me by then?'

" 'I can, your majesty,' the chariot maker answered. . . .

"Now, monks, after six months minus six days, . . . King Pacetana said: 'My good chariot maker, six days from now there will be a battle; have you finished the new pair of chariot wheels?'

" 'Your majesty, . . . in these six months minus six days, I have finished one wheel.'

" 'But will you be able, my good chariot maker, in the six days that are left, to finish the second wheel?'

" 'I will, your majesty.' That, monks, is what the chariot maker replied to King Pacetana.

"Now, monks, six days later, the chariot maker had finished the second wheel, and he took the two wheels and went to see King Pacetana. And he said this to him: 'Your majesty, here is the new pair of chariot wheels which I made for you.'

" 'Good chariot maker, what is the difference between the two wheels —the one that you took six months minus six days to make and the other that you finished in six days? I can see no difference between them!'

" 'There is a difference, your majesty. Please observe.'

"Thereupon, monks, the chariot maker set in motion the wheel that he had completed in six days; rolling, it went as far as its momentum carried it, and then, twirling around and around, it settled on the ground. Then, he set in motion the wheel that he had taken six months minus six days to finish; rolling, it went as far as its momentum carried it, and, when it came to a stop, it stayed upright on its rim as surely as though it were attached to an axle."

Source: Translated from *The Anguttara Nikāya,* ed. R. Morris and E. Hardy (London: Pali Text Society, 1885), 1:110–13.[17]

2.6.2 King Udena and the Elder Piṇḍola

Despite such views, the sangha was not so naive as to think that kings always looked to them for support. Numerous Buddhist tales reflect a somewhat different attitude. Caught up in worldly pursuits, kings were viewed with suspicion as fickle and potentially dangerous. They were also seen, however, as objects of ridicule and derision. The following semihumorous story of the encounter between Udena, King of Kosambī, and the elder Piṇḍola manages to combine all of these points.

When the Blessed One was dwelling in Sāvatthi, the Venerable Piṇḍola Bhāradvāja, wishing to spend his siesta in a cool spot, went to Udakavana, King Udena's park on the banks of the Ganges near Kosambī. . . . There, he went into a trance at the foot of a tree near the river to pass the heat of the day.

Now on that day, King Udena had also gone to amuse himself in the park. And for a great part of the day he sported about in the garden and was diverted by songs and dances, until, quite intoxicated, he lay down and went to sleep with his head in the lap of one of his harem girls.

[17]Alternative English translation, F. L. Woodward, *The Book of Gradual Sayings* (London: Pali Text Society, 1932), 1:95–97.

The rest of the women, realizing that the king was asleep, got up and wandered off, gathering flowers and fruits in the garden. [In time, they happened across the elder Piṇḍola and], seeing him, . . . they restrained one another, saying, "Do not make any noise," and quietly approached him, bowed down before him, and sat down around him. The elder then emerged from his trance and began to teach them the Dharma. They listened approvingly, and were pleased.

Now the girl who was sitting with the head of the king in her lap thought, "The others have left me and are having a good time." She became envious of them, so she moved her thigh thus waking the king.

The king, not seeing his harem around him, said: "Where are those wretched women?"

She replied: "Instead of paying attention to you, they went off saying, 'Let's have a good time with a wandering ascetic!'"

The king became enraged and went quickly to the place where the elder was sitting. Some of the women, seeing him coming, said: "Your majesty, we were just listening to the Dharma being taught by this one who has wandered forth." Others did not say anything.

But the king became even more furious and, not bothering to salute the elder, said, "Why did you come here?"

"For seclusion, your majesty," answered Piṇḍola.

"For seclusion!" shouted the king. "You came here for seclusion, and you sit surrounded by my seraglio? Tell me about your seclusion!"

The elder, self-possessed, said nothing, thinking quietly to himself: "This person asks without wishing to understand."

The king then said: "If you do not speak, I will have you eaten by red ants!" And, going himself to a nearby tree, he grabbed a red ants' nest. It broke, and red ants were scattered all over him, biting him painfully. Madder than ever, the king wiped his body clean and, taking another red ants' nest, approached the elder.

Piṇḍola, seeing Udena, thought that if he allowed the king to sin against him in this way, the king would be reborn in an unfortunate realm. So, making use of his supernatural powers, he rose up into the air, and flew away.

Then the women said to King Udena: "Your majesty, when other kings see someone like this who has wandered forth, they make devotional offerings of flowers and perfumes. But you undertook to lay on him a nest of red ants. Indeed, are you trying to destroy your family's lineage?"

At that, King Udena realized his fault, and became silent. Then he asked the park keeper: "Has that elder come here on other days as well?"

"Yes indeed, your majesty."

"Then," said the king, "let me know the next time he comes."

Some days later, the park keeper announced that the elder had come. It is said that the king then went up to him, politely saluted him, apologized, asked questions about the Dharma, and took refuge.

Source: Translated from *Sutta-Nipāta Commentary Being Paramatthajotikā II,* ed. Helmer Smith (London: Pali Text Society, 1917), 2:514–15.

2.6.3 Some Edicts of Aśoka

One of the most famous kings in the history of India was Aśoka, whom Buddhist legend portrays as a great devotee and supporter of the sangha. As we have seen in the account of his pilgrimage with the elder Upagupta in selection 1.2, he became renowned, among other things, as a builder of stūpas.

But Aśoka is also known to us as a historical figure from the edicts and rock inscriptions he had engraved all over his empire, which, when he ruled in the third century B.C.E., extended throughout most of the Indian subcontinent. In these edicts, Aśoka (who calls himself King Devanampriya Priyadarśi, "Beloved of the Gods, Whose View Is Dear") talks a lot about "Dharma" as his policy for rule, something that maintains order without depending on war and oppression and encourages proper moral behavior among citizens.

Scholars have much debated the issue of whether or not Aśoka was referring to Buddhism in his use of the term *Dharma.* His "conversion" experience following his war against the Kingdom of Kalinga makes no mention of the Buddha, and it is likely he had something broader in mind by "Dharma" than just the notion of the Buddhist doctrine. We shall see, however, that a number of his inscriptions refer specifically to his dealings with the Buddhist sangha. In these, he seems to have a double attitude of respect toward and willingness to control the Buddhist community.

Rock Edict XIII

Eight years after his coronation, King Devanampriya Priyadarśi conquered Kalinga. One hundred and fifty thousand persons were deported, one hundred thousand were killed, and many times that number perished. Now that the Kalingans have been taken, Devanampriya is zealous in his study of Dharma, his love of Dharma, and his teaching of Dharma. Devanampriya feels sorrow at having conquered the Kalingans. Indeed, the conquest of a previously unconquered country, which involves killing, dying, and deportation, still impresses itself upon Devanampriya and weighs heavily on his mind.

But this depresses him even more: Living in Kalinga, there were brahmins and recluses, adherents of other sects, and householders who practiced obedience to elders and to their parents and teachers, who behaved courteously toward friends, acquaintances, companions, relatives, slaves, and servants, and who were very devout. They all were injured or killed or separated from those who were dear to them. Even those who themselves were lucky enough to escape harm were affected by the afflictions of their friends, acquaintances, companions, and relatives.

And this weighs heavily on the mind of Devanampriya: all people share in this suffering. For there is no country, other than among the Greeks, where there are no brahmins and recluses, and there is no country where there are people who do not feel some sort of faith. Even if the number of people who were killed in Kalinga, who died, or were deported had been a hundred or a thousand times less, this would still weigh heavily on the mind of Devanampriya.

Devanampriya thinks he should be as patient as he is able to be with those who have wronged him. Even the indigenous tribes whom he has conquered, he now leads to discipline and self-control. From a position of power, he says to them that they too should feel remorse and should not kill.

Indeed, Devanampriya wishes all beings to be safe, restrained, and even-keeled in the face of violence. For Devanampriya considers the foremost form of conquest to be Dharma-conquest. This he has again and again achieved here and in all the borderlands as far as six hundred leagues away, where the Greek king named Antiochos II of Syria reigns, and beyond Antiochos's kingdom in the lands of the four kings, Ptolemy II of Egypt, Antigonos of Macedonia, Magas of Cyrene, and Alexander of Epirus; and, to the south, among the Coḷas and the Pāṇḍyas, as far as Sri Lanka. Everywhere . . . people follow Devanampriya's teaching of Dharma. Even where the envoys of Devanampriya do not go, people have heard of his Dharma, and they conform and will continue to conform to the duties and ordinances promulgated by it. . . .

Pillar Edict VII

King Devanampriya Priyadarśi says: I have had banyan trees planted along the roads in order to provide shade for beasts and people, and I have had mango groves planted. And, I have had wells dug and rest areas built every mile, and here and there I have had watering holes made for the enjoyment of beasts and humans. . . . Of course, previous kings as well have sought to please the people with such facilities, but I am doing this so that people may follow the path of Dharma.

Edicts Specific to Buddhism

[At Maskī]: King Devanampriya Aśoka says: "For more than two years, I have been a layman; one year ago, I approached the sangha, and, since that time, I have been zealous. . . . "

[At Nigalisagar]: Fourteen years after his coronation, King Devanampriya Priyadarśi doubled the size of the stūpa of the [past] Buddha Kanakamuni . . . and came in person to venerate it. . . .

[At Lumbinī]: Twenty years after his coronation, King Devanampriya Priyadarśi came in person to venerate this place, for it is here that the Buddha Śākyamuni was born. . . . Because the Blessed One was born here, the village of Lumbinī is exempt from paying tribute and has its land revenue tax rate fixed at one-eighth.

[At Sāñchī]: . . . Any monk or nun who causes a schism in the sangha will have to wear the white robes of a layperson and will no longer be able to dwell in monastic residence. This order should be made known to both the community of monks and the community of nuns . . . and a copy of this edict should be given to the laity. . . .

[At Bhabra]: To the sangha from Priyadarśi, King of Magadha: "Greetings! May you be free from troubles, and dwell content. You know, Venerable Sirs, the extent of my respect for and faith in the Buddha, Dharma, and Sangha. Venerable Sirs, everything the Buddha said was well said. Nevertheless, please allow me to say something in order to ensure that the True Dharma lasts a long time. Venerable Sirs, these are texts on the Dharma: *The Exaltation of the Vinaya, The Noble Lineage, Dangers of the Future, The Sage's Verses, The Discourse on Saintliness, The Questions of Upatissa,* and *The Sermon to Rāhula,* which the Blessed Buddha gave on the topic of lying. Venerable Sirs, I want many monks and many nuns, as well as laymen and laywomen, to listen often to these texts on the Dharma, and to reflect upon them. . . . "

Source: Translated from *Les inscriptions d'Asoka,* ed. Jules Bloch (Paris: Société Les Belles Lettres, 1950), pp. 125–32, 170, 145–46, 158, 157, 152–53, 154–55.[18]

[18]Alternative English translation, N. A. Nikam and Richard McKeon, *The Edicts of Asoka* (Chicago: University of Chicago Press, 1959), pp. 27–30, 64, 66, 69, 67–68, 66–67.

CHAPTER 3

The Dharma: Some Perspectives of Mainstream Buddhism

As we have just seen, King Aśoka in the third century B.C.E. threatened in one of his edicts to expel from the order any monks or nuns causing a schism in the community, adding that he hoped that the sangha would "remain united a long time." That, of course, was wishful thinking. For several centuries after the Buddha's parinirvāṇa, his teachings were preserved orally, and despite occasional councils that, according to legend, tried to codify his doctrine, some Buddhists "remembered" certain things over others (for example, see 3.6.1). In fact, even before Aśoka's time, the nascent splits in the Buddhist community had become fully apparent divisions, and neither Aśoka nor anyone else was able to put an end to them.

There were many reasons for sectarianism within the sangha. Some splits were due simply to differences in monastic practices that were accentuated by the geographical spread of the religion and the growth of regionalism. Others were related to different attitudes toward the laity. Still others, however, were rooted in philosophical differences, in divergent views about what it was that the Buddha had taught.

It is customary in speaking of the development of the Dharma to oppose the views of the Lesser Vehicle (Hīnayāna) to those of the Greater Vehicle (Mahāyāna). However, since the term *Hīnayāna* was not used by Hīnayānists but was a denigrative designation invented by Mahāyānists for pejorative purposes, it sometimes happens that the word *Theravāda* (the Tradition of the Elders) is used instead. But Theravāda and Hīnayāna do not designate the same thing. The Theravāda was, in fact, but one of many Hīnayāna schools (the traditional number was eighteen) which had varying views on a variety of issues. They also held many doctrines in common. To retain this sense of breadth and commonality, as well as to avoid the pejorative overtones implicit in the notion of a Lesser Vehicle, I will use here the expression *Mainstream Buddhism* instead of Hīnayāna (and instead of Nikāya Buddhism, or Buddhism of the Schools, which has sometimes been suggested as an alternate solution to this problem of nomenclature, as in the first edition of this anthology). *Mainstream Buddhism* is not without its own set of problems, but these are probably fewer than those posed by *Nikāya Buddhism* and certainly fewer than those for Hīnayāna or Theravāda, and it is increasingly being adopted by scholars.[1]

Among the schools of Mainstream Buddhism, the Theravāda is important because it is the only one to have survived as an institution and it now preponderates in Sri Lanka and Southeast Asia. It also managed to have kept intact its canon of scriptures (written in the Pali language), unlike the other Mainstream Buddhist schools, whose canons (written in Sanskrit) have been only partially preserved. But the fuller preservation and readier accessibility of Theravāda texts and traditions should not erase from our minds the historical importance of the other schools, for example, the Sarvāstivādins, the Mahāsāṃghikas, and the Pudgalavādins, which had a tremendous influence on the development and direction of Buddhist doctrine.

For all their differences, however, the Mainstream Buddhist schools also held a large number of views in common. Thus, although we shall pay some attention to divergent opinions at the end of this chapter, we shall focus first on the basic doctrines that held Mainstream Buddhism together. Second, as we shall see, many of these same basic Mainstream Buddhist doctrines were not abandoned by the Mahāyāna. To be sure, Mahāyānists extended them, added to them, reinterpreted them, and critiqued them, but for the most part they did not fundamentally reject them. Many of the doctrines that follow, therefore, can be considered to be basic to the whole of Buddhism.

3.1 PRELIMINARIES: THE LOSS AND PRESERVATION OF THE DHARMA

No Buddhist text of any school was written down until centuries after the lifetime of the Buddha. Therefore, the sources we shall be dealing with, both Pali and Sanskrit, represent not so much "what the Buddha taught" as what certain persons within the community thought the Buddha had taught. Indeed, according to Buddhists themselves, the Buddha's "True Dharma" was subject to the same laws of impermanence and change as anything else. Thus "what the Buddha taught" was bound to be lost, forgotten, transformed, or reinterpreted. The following selection, taken from a Sanskrit Mainstream Buddhist text preserved in Chinese, well illustrates the problem and the process. It tells a story about the Buddha's disciple Ānanda and what can happen to the Dharma in its oral transmission over time. It is all the more poignant when one remembers that Ānanda is the disciple whom tradition credits with having listened to all of the Buddha's sermons, with having remembered everything that he heard, and with having then recited all that he remembered at the First Council held immediately after the Buddha's parinirvāṇa.

[1]On the use of this term, *Mainstream Buddhism,* which was popularized by Paul Harrison, see Paul Williams, *Buddhist Thought* (London: Routledge, 2000), p. 256n.

Once, when the Venerable Ānanda was staying in the Veṇuvana, he overheard a monk reciting a verse from the *Dharmapada:* "It would be better for a man to live a single day and see a marsh fowl than for him to live a hundred years and not see a marsh fowl."

The Venerable Ānanda went up to him and said: "My son, the Buddha did not say that! This is what he said: 'It would be better for a man to live a single day and see the harsh, foul nature of saṃsāra than for him to live a hundred years and not see the harsh, foul nature of saṃsāra.'" . . .

The monk then went to his preceptor and said: "The Venerable Ānanda tells me that the Buddha did not speak this verse."

The monk's preceptor replied: "The Venerable Ānanda is a mistaken, senile old man who can no longer remember the Dharma. Keep on reciting the way you were taught."

Later, Ānanda came by and heard the verse being recited just as before, without change. He said: "My son, did I not tell you the Buddha did not say that?"

The monk replied: "Yes, but my preceptor said, 'Ānanda is getting on in years and cannot remember so well; go on reciting as before.'"

Ānanda reflected: "I myself told him the correct verse, but he did not accept it." Ānanda then contemplated the question of whether anyone would be able to convince this monk to correct his recitation, and he realized: "There is no one who can get him to change. The Buddha's disciples Śāriputra, Maudgalyāyana, and Mahākāśyapa have all entered nirvāṇa; to whom could I now turn as an authority? I shall also enter nirvāṇa."

Source: Translated from *Aśokarājāvadāna* (Taishō shinshū daizōkyō, ed. J. Takakusu and K. Watanabe [Tokyo, 1924–29], no. 2042, 50:115b–c).[2]

3.2 SUFFERING, IMPERMANENCE, AND NO-SELF

We have already seen (in 1.6) that suffering, or unsatisfactoriness (duḥkha, Pali: dukkha) was propounded as the first of the Four Noble Truths. Suffering figures also as the first of the three "marks," or "characteristics," of existence along with impermanence (anitya, Pali: anicca), and no-Self, or the absence of a Self (anātman, Pali: anattā). These three doctrines, of course, are closely interdependent. Things are "suffering," that is, not finally satisfying, because they are impermanent: they do not last forever, or even for a moment, but are in a constant process of change; and partly because of this, there can be no Self, that is, no "abiding ego," no "unchanging me," and consequently no "mine."

[2]Alternative French translation, Jean Przyluski, *La légende de l'empereur Açoka dans les textes indiens et chinois* (Paris: Paul Geuthner, 1923), pp. 335–36.

3.2.1 Impermanence

Many Buddhist texts touch on the theme of impermanence or on the momentariness of the elements of existence, the "dharmas" that in Mainstream Buddhism are the basic constituents of reality. The full implications of the Buddhist doctrine of impermanence, as we shall see, were not without their philosophical convolutions, and these were tackled differently by different schools and worked out even more fully in the Mahāyāna. At a basic level, however, impermanence always meant simply that all beings, all things, having arisen, pass away: they die. The following selection from a Sanskrit text makes the point well.

Thus have I heard: Once the Blessed One was dwelling in Śrāvastī at the Jetavana monastery together with a great company of monks. And he said: "O monks, all karmically constituted things are impermanent; they are not fixed, not comforting, and are characterized by constant change. . . . For all beings, all creatures, all living things, life is limited by death; for them there is no termination of death and rebirth.

"And, monks, those who are householders from prominent families, brahmins, nobles, rich people . . . —their lives too are limited by death; for them there is no termination of death and rebirth.

"And, monks, nobles who have been annointed king, who have attained power and sovereignty over the people, and who have conquered the whole earth—their lives too are limited by death; for them there is no termination of death and rebirth.

"And, monks, brahmanical ascetics who dwell in the forest, who grasp for the fruit of liberation, who enjoy the fruit of liberation, who live by the fruit of liberation—their lives too are limited by death; for them there is no termination of death and rebirth.

"And, monks, those gods of the realm of desire, the four great guardian kings, the gods of the Trāyastriṃśa, Yama, Tuṣita, and other heavens—their lives too are limited by death; for them there is no termination of death and rebirth.

"And, monks, those gods of the realm of form—those who have attained the first, the second, the third, or the fourth trance levels—their lives too are limited by death; for them there is no termination of death and rebirth.

"And, monks, those gods of the formless realm, those who dwell in the contemplation of endless space, those who dwell in the contemplation of endless consciousness, those who dwell in the contemplation of nothingness, and those who dwell in the contemplation of neither perception nor nonperception—their lives too are limited by death; for them there is no termination of death and rebirth. Thus it is for the Triple World.

"And, monks, those arhats who have destroyed all the defilements, who have done what needed to be done, . . . who have attained perfect, utter mastery over their minds—their bodies too are subject to being discarded.

"And, monks, those pratyekabuddhas who, all alone like the horn of a rhinoceros, still their selves and by themselves attain parinirvāṇa—their bodies too are subject to being discarded.

"And, monks, those Tathāgatas, completely enlightened Buddhas, endowed with the ten powers, . . . possessors of the fourfold confidence, namely, the confidence of being able to get over all obstructive dharmas, the confidence of being able to teach all doctrines, the confidence of having discovered the path to nirvāṇa, the confidence of knowing they are rid of all defilements—their bodies too are subject to being discarded.

Source: Translated from *Anityatāsūtra,* ed. Isshi Yamada, in *Indogaku bukkyōgaku kenkyū / Journal of Indian and Buddhist Studies* 20 (1972): 1001–996.

3.2.2 Milinda and the Chariot

The view of impermanence, of course, meant not simply the eventual passing away of all beings; more immediately it affirmed the actual passing away (and arising), from moment to moment, of things, of "dharmas" (the basic constituent elements of reality). This led in Mainstream Buddhism to various scholastic attempts to define a "moment," to answer the question "Just how long do dharmas last?" Some maintained that dharmas existed only in the present, arising and passing away in an instant, in a fraction of the time it takes to blink one's eyes. Others, as we shall see (in 3.6.2), contended that dharmas existed somehow in all three times, past, present, and future. In any case, the impermanence of life was closely related to the doctrine of no-Self, which became one of the hallmarks of Buddhist doctrine.

The notion that there is no abiding entity that can be called the Self (ātman) is not an easy one for Westerners to accept, but it caused difficulties for Buddhists as well. Indeed, it was not long before there was at least one Mainstream Buddhist sect, the so-called Personalists (Pudglavādins), who held that even though there was no Self, there was something called a Person (pudgala, Pali: puggala), which was ineffable, neither the same as nor different from the agglomerations of elements (skandhas) that make up human beings and all of reality.

A great amount of scholastic energy was spent by Buddhists of other schools attempting to refute the Personalist doctrines. In these debates, much of the argument revolved around what was meant by the term *pudgala* as well as by its connotations. But it is important to realize that the Personalists were also concerned with spiritual issues; they worried that if there were not something like a pudgala, one would not be able to explain such things as moral responsibility or karmic continuity from one life to the next. One would not be able to say that a particular individual had made merit or attained enlightenment.

Some of these same concerns are raised in the following Pali text, in which the discussion of no-Self is carried out in a less scholastic context between the monk Nāgasena and King Milinda.

Then King Milinda said this to the Venerable Nāgasena: "By what name, Reverend Sir, are you known?"

"Your majesty, I am known as Nāgasena, and my co-practitioners address me as such. But, your majesty, . . . there is no Person (puggala) to be found here."

Then King Milinda declared: "Listen to me, you five hundred . . . lords and you eighty thousand monks! This Nāgasena says, 'There is no Person to be found here!' Is it possible to agree to that?"

And addressing the Venerable Nāgasena, he said: "If, Venerable Nāgasena, no Person is to be found, who then is it who gives you robes, food, lodgings, medicine—all the requisites for a mendicant? Who is it who enjoys the use of these things? Who keeps the precepts? Who practices meditation? Who experiences the path, the fruits, nirvāṇa? Who kills living beings? Who takes what is not given? Who engages in sinful pleasures? Who tells lies? Who drinks intoxicants? Who commits the five evil deeds that have karmic effects in this lifetime?

"From what you say it follows that there is no such thing as merit or demerit; there is neither doer nor causer of meritorious or demeritorious actions; there is no reward or punishment for good or evil deeds. If, Nāgasena, a man were to kill you, there would be no murder in that! Moreover, Nāgasena, you monks would have neither teacher nor preceptor: you are not even ordained! You say, 'Your majesty, my co-practitioners call me Nāgasena'; well, what is this 'Nāgasena'? Tell me, is the hair of the head 'Nāgasena'?"

"No, it is not, your majesty."

"Is the hair of the body 'Nāgasena'?"

"No, your majesty."

"What about nails, teeth, skin, flesh, sinews, bones, marrow, kidneys, heart, liver, pleura, spleen, lungs, colon, intestines, stomach, feces, bile, phlegm, pus, blood, sweat, fat, tears, lymph, saliva, snot, synovia, urine, brain—are any of these 'Nāgasena'?"

"No, your majesty."

"Well, then, sir, is your physical form (rūpa) 'Nāgasena'?"

"No, your majesty."

"Are feelings (vedanā) 'Nāgasena'?"

"No, your majesty."

"Are perceptions (saññā) 'Nāgasena'?"

"No, your majesty."

"Are karmic constituents (sankhārā) 'Nāgasena'?"

"No, your majesty."

"Is consciousness (viññāṇa) 'Nāgasena'?"

"No, your majesty."

"Perhaps the five skandhas all together—form, feelings, perceptions, karmic constituents, and consciousness—are they 'Nāgasena'?"

"No, your majesty."

"Then is it something other than physical form, feelings, perceptions, karmic constituents, and consciousness that is 'Nāgasena'?"

"No, your majesty."

"Well, my friend, though I question you repeatedly, I do not find any 'Nāgasena.' 'Nāgasena' is but a sound! Who is this 'Nāgasena?' You are lying, my friend, you are telling falsehoods. There is no Nāgasena!"

Then the Venerable Nāgasena said to King Milinda: "Your majesty, you are a delicate, refined nobleman. If, in the middle of the day, you were to walk on the hot, burning, sandy ground and tread on rough, gritty, pebbly sand, your feet would hurt, your body would get tired, your mind would be distressed, and there would arise in you a consciousness of bodily suffering. Tell me, did you come on foot, or did you ride?"

"I did not come on foot, sir, I rode in a chariot."

"If that is the case, your majesty, tell me what is the chariot. Is the pole the chariot?"

"No, it is not, sir."

"Is the axle the chariot?"

"No, sir."

"Are the wheels the chariot?"

"No, sir."

"Is the frame the chariot?"

"No, sir."

"Is the banner staff the chariot?"

"No, sir."

"Is the yoke the chariot?"

"No, sir."

"Are the reins the chariot?"

"No, sir."

"Is the goad the chariot?"

"No, sir."

"Perhaps, your majesty, the pole, the axle, the wheels, the frame, the banner staff, the yoke, the reins, and the goad all together—are they the chariot?"

"No, sir, they are not."

"Then, your majesty, is it something other than the pole, the axle, the wheels, the frame, the banner staff, the yoke, the reins, and the goad that is the chariot?"

"No, sir, it is not."

"Well, your majesty, though I question you repeatedly, I do not find any chariot. 'Chariot' is but a sound! What is this chariot? You are lying, your majesty, you are telling falsehoods. There is no chariot! Your majesty, you are the supreme ruler over the whole of India, who are you afraid of that you should tell a lie? Listen to me, you five hundred . . . lords and you eighty thousand monks! This King Milinda says, 'I came in a chariot!' But when I ask him to tell me what the chariot is, he cannot produce a chariot. Is it possible to agree to such a thing?"

When he had thus spoken, the five hundred . . . lords applauded the Venerable Nāgasena, and said to King Milinda: "Now, your majesty, answer that if you can!"

And King Milinda said to the Venerable Nāgasena: "Good Nāgasena, I did not lie. The word *chariot* comes into existence, dependent on the pole, dependent on the axle, the wheels, the frame, the banner staff, the yoke, the reins, the goad; it is a designation, a description, an appellation, a name."

"Well said, your majesty! You truly understand the chariot! In the same way, your majesty, in my case, the word *Nāgasena* comes into existence, dependent on the hair of the head, dependent on the hair of the body, . . . dependent on the brain, dependent on physical form, on feelings, on perceptions, on karmic constituents, on consciousness. It is a designation, a description, an appellation, nothing but a name. But in the final analysis, the ultimate sense, there is no Person to be found herein. . . . "

Source: Translated from *The Milindapañho,* ed. V. Trenckner, reprint edition with the *Milinda-ṭīkā* (London: Pali Text Society, 1986), pp. 25–28.[3]

3.2.3 Vajirā's Reply to Māra

Nāgasena's use of a chariot as a simile for the Self (or rather for explaining no-Self) was effective in the case of King Milinda, but the image was not original with him. The chariot metaphor is also found in the Pali canon itself, in a dialogue between the nun Vajirā and the Evil One of Buddhism, the divinity Māra. Their discussion is interesting, for it reflects the fact that some Buddhists, at least, saw wrong belief in Self, Person, or some sort of integral "being" as a temptation, held out by Māra himself, into which one might easily slip.

One morning, the nun Vajirā got dressed in her robes, and, taking her bowl, she entered the city of Sāvatthi for alms and went about the town on her begging round. On her way back, after her noonday meal, she entered into the Andhavana woods and seated herself at the foot of a tree to take her midday rest.

Then Māra, the Evil One, wishing to engender fear, shock, and dread in the nun Vajirā and hoping to disturb her meditation, approached her and spoke these verses:

Vajirā, who created this Being?
Where is Being's maker?
Where did Being come from?
Where will it disappear to?

But the nun Vajirā replied:

[3]Alternative English translation, T. W. Rhys Davids, *The Questions of King Milinda* (Oxford: Clarendon Press, 1890), 1:40–45.

Māra, why do you keep coming back to Being?
You are resorting to false views.
There is no Being to be found here—
only a heap of karmic constituents.
Just as the word *chariot* is used,
when we come across a combination of parts,
so we speak conventionally of a Being
when the five skandhas are present.
But, truly, it is only suffering that arises,
suffering that persists and passes away,
nothing other than suffering that arises,
nothing else than suffering that ceases to be.

Source: Translated from *The Samyutta-Nikāya,* ed. Léon Feer (London: Pali Text Society, 1884), 1:134–35.[4]

3.2.4 The Buddha's Silence

Vajirā is able to answer Māra in part because of her realization that it is useless to get involved in discussing the kinds of questions he is asking when the very premise on which they are based is false. In a dialogue preserved in a Chinese text,[5] Nāgasena acts in a similar fashion. When asked by Milinda whether the Self is permanent or impermanent, Nāgasena counters by asking the king whether the fruit of the mango tree in his garden is sweet or sour. Milinda replies that he does not have a mango tree in his garden, so how can he possibly answer the question. "Exactly," retorts Nāgasena.

In the following selection, the Buddha, too, refuses to address the question of Self, but he takes the dialectic one step further: he also refuses to assert that there is no Self, because, even though "no-Self" accords with his doctrine, to make that assertion would call forth in the mind of his ignorant interlocutor a notion of a Self that is being denied, and how can one deny something that has never existed? It is like denying that one has stopped beating one's mother. The Buddha, therefore, prefers silence. In this, he seems to be including the Self in the category of "questions not explicated" (avyākṛta), which comprised such things as whether the universe is finite or infinite and whether the Buddha exists after death or not. At the same time, this move may contain a response to the Personalists, who felt that the Theravādins, with their notion of anātman, sometimes ran the risk of falling into the extreme of annihilationism.

Then Vacchagotta, the wandering ascetic, approached the Blessed One, greeted him courteously, sat down to one side, and said: "Well, now, good Gotama, is there a Self?"

[4]Alternative English translation, C. A. F. Rhys Davids, *The Book of the Kindred Sayings* (London: Pali Text Society, 1917), 1:169–70.

[5]See Edouard Chavannes, *Cinq cents contes et apologues extraits du Tripiṭaka chinois* (Paris: Imprimerie Nationale, 1934), 3:123–24.

The Blessed One remained silent.

"Well, then, good Gotama, is there not a Self?"

Once again, the Blessed One remained silent, and the wandering ascetic Vacchagotta got up and went away.

Soon thereafter, the Venerable Ānanda said to the Blessed One: "Master, why did you not respond to the wandering ascetic Vacchagotta's question?"

"Ānanda, if in response to Vacchagotta's first question I asserted that there is a Self, that would be associating myself with the renouncers and brahmins who are eternalists. But, Ānanda, if in response to his second question I asserted that there is no Self, that would be associating myself with the renouncers and brahmins who are annihilationists.

"Or again, Ānanda, if in response to the wandering ascetic Vacchagotta's first question I asserted that there is a Self, would that be in accord with the knowledge that all elements of reality are without Self?"

"No, it would not, Master."

"But, Ānanda, if in response to Vacchagotta's second question I asserted that there is no Self, the confused Vacchagotta would have been even more confused, saying, 'Formerly, I had a Self, but now it does not exist.'"

Source: Translated from *The Samyutta-Nikāya,* ed. Léon Feer (London: Pali Text Society, 1894), 4:400–401.[6]

3.2.5 Channa Is Taught the Middle Way

It is clear from the Buddha's response (or nonresponse) to Vacchagotta that one of the things he is concerned about is avoiding the extremes of eternalism or annihilationism in which a yes or a no answer would involve him. We have here another expression, in doctrinal terms, of Buddhism as a Middle Way between the extremes of world affirmation (indulgence) and world denial (extreme asceticism), a doctrine that, as we shall see, was much developed in the Mahāyāna. The same point is made, however, in the Theravāda story of the monk Channa, which, moreover, reflects the real struggle Buddhists underwent to grapple with this question of anātman, not just as an intellectual issue but also existentially as a matter of actual realization.

Once several elders were staying in Benares at Isipatana in the Deer Park. One evening, the Venerable Channa came out of his meditational retreat, took his door key, and going from one lodging to the next, he said this to the elders: "Please, venerable sirs, exhort me, teach me, preach to me, so that I may come to see the Dharma!"

[6]Alternative English translation, F. L. Woodward, *The Book of the Kindred Sayings* (London: Pali Text Society, 1927), 4:281–82.

Thus addressed, the elders said this to the Venerable Channa: "Brother Channa, physical form is impermanent, feelings are impermanent, perceptions are impermanent, karmic constituents are impermanent, consciousness is impermanent. Physical form is not the Self, feelings are not the Self, perceptions are not the Self, karmic constituents are not the Self, consciousness is not the Self. . . . "

"I know all of that! . . . " exclaimed the Venerable Channa, "but my mind fails to experience the calming of all conditioned states, the complete rejection of the bases of rebirth, the destruction of craving, the achievement of passionlessness, cessation, nirvāṇa! Agitated, I find no satisfaction, no stability, no release! Attachment arises, and I keep coming back to the thought 'Well, then, what *is* the Self?' I just cannot understand the Dharma in this way. Isn't there anyone who can teach it to me in such a way that I will see it?"

Then it occurred to Channa that the Venerable Ānanda was staying in Kosambī in the Ghosita Park and that the Master had praised and honored him as foremost among his learned co-practitioners. "The Venerable Ānanda," he reflected, "will be able to teach me the Dharma, in such a way that I will come to see it." . . .

So Channa left his lodging, took his robe and bowl, and went to Ghosita Park in Kosambī, where the Venerable Ānanda was staying. There, [after telling him all about his quest and his inability to experience the Truth of the Buddha's teachings, he explained his motivation in coming], saying: "Please, Venerable Ānanda, exhort me, teach me, preach to me, so that I may come to see the Dharma."

"All this is pleasing to me, Channa," Ānanda replied. "You have indeed made things clear. You are like a field ready for planting. Listen to me, for you are capable of truly knowing the Dharma!"

And at these words—that he would really be able to know the Dharma—there arose in the Venerable Channa an exhilarating joy and gladness.

Then the Venerable Ānanda said: "With my own lips, Channa, I will impart to you what I heard from the very lips of the Blessed One, as he was instructing the monk Kaccānagotta. 'Kaccāna,' he said, 'the world, as a rule, depends on dualism: things are said to exist or not to exist. But, Kaccāna, one who sees the arising of the world as it truly happens, with right wisdom, cannot maintain the nonexistence of the world; and one who sees the cessation of the world as it truly happens, with right wisdom, cannot maintain the existence of the world. Kaccāna, for the most part, people in this world seek support in schemes and are tied to tendencies. But those who do not resort to or depend on schemes or mental obstinacies, tendencies and biases, do not decide, "This is my Self."

" 'What arises is suffering; what ceases is suffering—one who knows this has no doubts, is not distracted, has knowledge that does not depend on others. This, Kaccāna, is the extent of right view.

" 'Everything exists—that, Kaccāna, is one extreme. Everything does not exist—that is the other extreme. The Tathāgata, Kaccāna, teaches a doctrine that goes down the middle, avoiding both extremes. Dependent on ignorance are karmic constituents; dependent on karmic constituents is consciousness, and so forth. In this way, this whole mass of suffering arises. But with the doing away of passion and the complete cessation of ignorance comes the cessation of karmic constituents, and so forth. In this way, this whole mass of suffering ceases.' "

"Venerable Ānanda," Channa responded, "this is what we brethren get who have co-practitioners such as you, who are compassionate, who long for our welfare, who are exhorters, teachers. Indeed, by hearing you preach the doctrine, Venerable Ānanda, I have come to realize the Dharma."

Source: Translated from *The Samyutta-Nikāya,* ed. Léon Feer (London: Pali Text Society, 1890), 3:132–35.[7]

3.2.6 The Man Who Lost His Body

Finally, lest it be thought that the realization of anātman was solely a matter of the intellectual or meditational pursuits of monks, it is useful to recall the following story of a layman who willy-nilly comes to a very existential realization of no-Self. This parable, taken from a collection of Buddhist tales preserved in Chinese, is somewhat gruesome but perhaps not utterly fanciful in this day of organ transplants.

Once, a man who had been sent on a long journey found that he had to spend the night alone in a deserted house. In the middle of the night, a demon came in carrying a corpse on his shoulders, which he set down on the floor. Later on, another demon came in and began to berate him angrily: "That dead man belongs to me. How did it come to be in here?"

To this the first demon answered: "He is mine! I got him, and I brought him here myself!"

But the second demon retorted, "I am the one who brought him in." And in this way the two demons fought over the corpse, each one grabbing and pulling it.

Then the first demon [noticing our traveler who was witnessing all this] said: "There is a man here whom we can ask." So the second demon began to question him: "Who brought this dead body in here?"

The traveler reflected: "These two demons are very strong; whether I tell the truth or whether I lie, I am sure to be killed by one or the other of them. So why not tell the truth?" And he declared that it was the first demon who had brought in the corpse.

At that, the second demon got very angry, and grabbing the traveler's hand, he ripped off his arm, and threw it on the ground. But the second demon took an arm from the corpse and attached it to the traveler's body. In the same manner the traveler's other arm, legs, head, and torso were

[7]Alternative English translation, F. L. Woodward, *The Book of the Kindred Sayings* (London: Pali Text Society, 1925), 3:111–14.

ripped off by the first demon, but replaced by the second demon with corresponding parts taken from the corpse. Then the two demons together devoured the [now dismembered, original] body of the traveler, and wiping their mouths, they went away.

The traveler then reflected: "I have just seen these two demons entirely devour the body that my mother and father gave birth to. Now my present body is entirely constituted by the flesh of another. Do I or do I no longer actually have a body? If I say I do, it is someone else's body; if I say I don't, there is nonetheless a body here that looks very real." And so reflecting, he became very troubled and was like one who had lost his mind.

The next day, he set off on the road again and arrived in the kingdom to which he had been heading. There, near a Buddhist stūpa, he saw a group of monks. All that he could say to them was to ask them whether his body existed.

The monks inquired: "Who are you?"

He answered: "I don't even know if I am or am not," and he told them at length all that had happened to him.

The monks said: "This man has learned on his own the nonexistence of the Self; he will easily attain salvation." And turning to him they said: "Not just now, but from its beginning up until the present, your body has all along been devoid of a Self. It was only because of the coming together of the four basic elements that you thought, 'This is my body.' But there is no difference between your former body and that which you have today." In this way, the monks converted the traveler to the Buddhist Path; he cut off all defilements and attained arhatship.

Source: Translated from *Chung ching hsüan tsa p'i yü ching* (Taishō shinshū daizōkyō, ed. J. Takakusu and K. Watanabe [Tokyo, 1924–29], no. 208, 4:531c–532a).[8]

3.3 THE ARISING OF SUFFERING

The realization of anātman puts an end to selfish desires, to the clinging and thirst and ignorance that, according to the second Noble Truth, are responsible for the origination of suffering. But how do desires themselves and this falsely based clinging that keeps one attached to this world originate?

3.3.1 Interdependent Origination

That question is usually answered by the doctrine of interdependent origination (pratītyasamutpāda). This particularly Buddhist theory of causation posits

[8]Alternative French translation, Edouard Chavannes, *Cinq cents contes et apologues extraits du Tripiṭaka chinois* (Paris: Imprimerie Nationale, 1934), 2:72–74. Some details supplied from the *Mahāprajñāpāramitā śāstra* (Taishō shinshū daizōkyō, ed. J. Takakusu and K. Watanabe [Tokyo, 1924–29], no. 1509, 25:148c); French translation, Etienne Lamotte, *Le traité de la grande vertu de sagesse* (Louvain: Institut Orientaliste, 1949–80), pp. 738–40.

not a first cause in time but the two-way dependence of a series of causal links that tie together not only suffering, desire, and ignorance but also the very world as we know it, with its physical forms (including our bodies); our sense perceptions, feelings, and consciousnesses; and the processes of rebirth itself. The basic causal principle at work here is stated as follows: "When this is, that comes to be; from the arising of this, that arises. When this is not, that does not come to be; from the nonarising of this, that does not arise." Another way of putting it is to say that everything is both conditioned and conditioning. What this amounts to is a rejection of the two extremes of absolute determinism (e.g., everything is determined by one's past actions or, alternatively, by an all-powerful deity), and absolute nondeterminism, in which nothing is thought to have a cause. Both views were held by contemporaries of the Buddha.

The doctrine of pratītyasamutpāda has long occupied a central place in Buddhist thought. Indeed, as one text was to put it: "One who sees pratītyasamutpāda sees the Dharma, and one who sees the Dharma sees the Buddha."[9] In a number of traditions, the Buddha is said to have worked the doctrine out fully, along with the Four Noble Truths, during the night of his enlightenment. And later on, key Mahāyāna thinkers such as Nāgārjuna (see 4.3.1) were to give it equal prominence while extending its implications. In the following selection, from the Pali canon, the Buddha's presentation of the doctrine is prefaced by a discussion with a naked ascetic named Kassapa who asks a number of questions about the causes of suffering.

Thus have I heard. Once, when the Blessed One was dwelling in Rājagaha, . . . he got dressed early in the morning, took his bowl and his robe, and went into town for alms. Kassapa, the naked ascetic, saw his coming from a distance. He approached him, they exchanged greetings, and Kassapa, standing to one side, said: "If it is all right, good Gotama, I would like to ask you to explain something."

"Kassapa," the Buddha replied, "this is not a good time for questions; I am visiting houses. . . . "

But Kassapa repeated his request, and added: "I do not have many things to ask, good Gotama."

"Then go ahead and ask if you wish to, Kassapa."

"Good Gotama," Kassapa began, "is the suffering that one suffers caused by oneself?"

"No, it is not, Kassapa," replied the Blessed One.

"Then is the suffering that one suffers caused by someone else?"

"No, it is not, Kassapa."

"Well, then, is it caused both by oneself and by someone else?"

"No, it is not, Kassapa."

"Well, then, . . . does it arise spontaneously?"

"No, it does not."

"Then suffering is nonexistent, good Gotama."

[9] *Śālistambasūtra,* ed. Louis de La Vallée Poussin in *Bouddhisme, études et matériaux: Théorie des douze causes* (Gand: Librairie Scientifique E. Van Goethem, 1914–19), p. 70.

"No, Kassapa, it is not nonexistent; there *is* suffering."

"But you do not know it, nor do you see it?"

"Not so, Kassapa, I both know it and see it."

"Good Gotama, to all these questions that I have asked you . . . you have answered no. So please tell me, please teach me about suffering."

"Kassapa, if you say, 'The same individual who does a deed experiences its results'—what you called 'suffering caused by oneself'—then you fall into the view of eternalism. But if you say, 'One individual does a deed and another experiences its results'—what a sufferer would call 'suffering caused by another'—then you fall into the view of annihilationism. Kassapa, avoiding these two extremes, the Tathāgata teaches the Dharma in the manner of a Middle Way:

"Conditioned by ignorance are karmic constituents; conditioned by karmic constituents is consciousness; conditioned by consciousness is individuality (name and form); conditioned by individuality are the six senses; conditioned by the six senses is contact; conditioned by contact is feeling; conditioned by feeling is desire; conditioned by desire is clinging; conditioned by clinging is becoming; conditioned by becoming is rebirth; conditioned by rebirth are old age, death, sorrow, lamentation, suffering, depression, and dismay. In this way, this whole great heap of suffering originates.

"But from the complete cessation and dissipation of ignorance comes the cessation of karmic constituents; and from the complete cessation and dissipation of karmic constituents comes the cessation of consciousness; and from the complete cessation and dissipation of consciousness comes the cessation of individuality; and from the complete cessation of individuality . . . [and so forth until]: from the complete cessation and dissipation of rebirth comes the cessation of old age, death, sorrow, lamentation, suffering, depression, and dismay. In this way, this whole great heap of suffering ceases."

Source: Translated from *The Samyutta-Nikāya,* ed. Léon Feer (London: Pali Text Society, 1888), 2:18–21.[10]

3.3.2 The Evolution of the World

The doctrine of pratītyasamutpāda was not the only way in which Buddhists addressed the issue of the origination of suffering. The following selection takes a more mythological tack. It tells of an earlier time, before the world as we know it existed, before beings had bodies and knew suffering, and describes how they lost that world and evolved into their present states. It is the closest thing in Buddhism to a creation myth or to a story of the Fall, but, of course, it is neither. For as the text itself makes clear, this is not a tale of "*the* Beginning" of the world but only of the start of a new cycle of cosmic history, of the reevolution of the world, and the beings that populate this world are not utterly new and pure, for they have karma left over from previous lives in

---

[10]Alternative English translation, F. L. Woodward, *The Book of the Kindred Sayings* (London: Pali Text Society, 1922), 2:14–16.

previous worlds and that is what impels them in the process of reevolution. Still, the text is sometimes called the *Sūtra on Knowing the Beginning* (*Aggañña sutta*). It is found in several versions in both Pali and Sanskrit works. The following is taken from a text said to be part of the Vinaya of the Mahāsāṃghika sect, whose view of the Buddha we shall encounter again in selection 3.6.3.

O monks, eventually there comes a time when, after a long period, this world starts to wind down. And as the world is winding down, beings for the most part are reborn out of it, in the Realm of the Radiant Gods. Eventually, after another long period, it happens that this world that has ended begins to reevolve. And as it is reevolving, settling, and becoming established, certain beings, in order to work out their karma, fall from the Realm of the Radiant Gods and come to be once again in this world. These beings by nature are self-luminescent and move through the air. They are made of mind, feed on joy, dwell in bliss, and go where they will.

When at first they reappear, there is no knowledge in the world of the sun and the moon. And likewise there is no knowledge of the forms of the stars, of the paths of the constellations, of night and day, month and fortnight, seasons and years. . . .

Eventually, this Great Earth appears; it is like a pool of water. It is pretty and savory and tastes just like pure sweet honey, and in physical appearance it is like the scum on milk or ghee.

Now, monks, it happens that a certain being, fickle and greedy by nature, tastes some of this earth-essence with his finger. He enjoys its color, its smell, and its savor. Then other beings, seeing what he has done, imitate him. They also taste some of the earth-essence with their fingers, and they too take pleasure in its color, its smell, its savor.

Then, on another occasion, that being takes a morsel of earth-essence and eats it, and the other beings too, seeing what he has done, imitate him. . . . And because they take morsels of earth-essence and eat them, in due course their bodies become heavy, solid, and hard, and their former qualities—of being self-luminescent, of moving through the air, being made of mind, feeding on joy, dwelling in bliss, and going where they will—disappear. And when this happens, the sun and the moon and likewise the forms of the stars, the paths of the constellations, night and day, month and fortnight, seasons and years come to be known in the world.

Now, monks, for a very long time these beings continue to consume this earth-essence. It is their food, what they eat, and it shapes them. Those who eat a lot of it take on an ugly appearance, whereas those who consume only a little of it become good looking. And the ones who are good looking become contemptuous of those who are ugly. "We are handsome," they declare, "and you look bad." While they go on in this way, convinced of their own superior beauty, proud and arrogant, the earth-essence disappears. And there appear instead "earth-puffs," which are like mushrooms. They are pretty and sweet smelling and taste just like pure honey. . . .

For a very long time, these beings continue to consume these earth-puffs. . . . And those who eat a lot of them take on an ugly appearance, whereas those who consume only a little become good looking. And the ones who are good looking become contemptuous of those who are ugly. "We are handsome," they declare, "and you look bad." While they go on in this way, convinced of their own superior beauty, proud and arrogant, the earth-puffs disappear. And there appears instead a creeper that is like bindweed. It is pretty and sweet smelling and savory, and it tastes just like pure honey. [. . .]

Now, monks, for a very long time, these beings continue to consume this creeper. . . . And those who eat a lot of it take on an ugly appearance, whereas those who consume only a little of it become good looking. And the ones who are good looking become contemptuous of those who are ugly. "We are handsome," they declare, "and you look bad." While they go on in this way, convinced of their own superior beauty, proud and arrogant, the creeper disappears. And there appears instead a rice that is huskless, polished, and sweet smelling. If it is reaped in the evening, by daybreak it has grown back, sprouted, and ripened, as though it had never been cut. If it is reaped in the morning, by evening it has grown back, sprouted, and ripened, as though it had never been cut. [. . .]

Now monks, when those beings eat the rice that is huskless, polished, and sweet smelling, bodily features of femininity appear in those who are women, and bodily features of masculinity appear in those who are men. Then, overflowing thoughts of passion for each other arise in their minds; they are pleased with each other, consumed by passion for each other, and have illicit sex together.

Then, other beings see them having illicit sex together and throw sticks and clods of dirt and dust at them. . . . Nowadays, when a girl is carried off to be married, people throw sticks and clods of dirt. In this way, they repeat an ancient primeval custom without realizing the meaning of it. In former times, it was thought to be immoral, profane, and undisciplined, but nowadays it is deemed moral, sacred, and disciplined. . . .

Then, it occurs to a certain being who has gone out to gather rice that he is needlessly wearying himself. "Why," he reflects, "should I go on tiring myself by getting rice for supper in the evening and rice for breakfast in the morning, when I could be gathering it for both evening and morning meals just once a day?" And that is what he begins to do.

Then, one evening, some other being says to him: "Come, my friend, let's go get some rice."

But the first being replies: "You go, friend. I already brought back rice for both evening and morning meals."

Then it occurs to that second being: "This is a wonderful way of doing things! Why, I could be gathering rice all at once for two or three days!" And that is what he begins to do.

Then, monks, it happens that a third being says to him: "Come, my friend, let's go get some rice."

And he replies: "You go, my friend. I already brought back rice for two or three days."

Then it occurs to that third being: "Now this is a wonderful way of doing things! Why, I could be gathering rice all at once for four or five days!" And that is what he begins to do.

But because these beings are now hoarding and consuming that rice that is huskless, polished, and sweet smelling, husks and reddish coatings begin to appear on it. And if it is reaped in the evening, by daybreak it has not sprouted, ripened, or grown back, and it is clear that it has been cut.

Then, those beings quickly assemble together and take counsel with one another: . . . "Now what if we were to divide the rice fields and draw boundaries between them?"

And that, monks, is what those beings do, declaring, "This field is yours, and this field is mine."

Then it occurs to one of those beings who has gone to gather rice: "How will I get my livelihood if my allotment of rice is destroyed? Why don't I now go and steal someone else's rice?"

And so that being, while guarding his own share of rice, goes and steals somebody else's portion. But another being happens to see him stealing that other person's portion, and he goes up to him and says, "Ho, my friend, you have taken someone else's rice!"

To which he replies: "Yes, my friend, but it will not happen again."

Nonetheless, it occurs a second time . . . and a third time. He goes and steals somebody else's portion, and another being sees him. But this time, that other being goes up to him and beats him with a stick, and says: "This is the third time, friend, that you have taken someone else's rice!"

Then that being holds up his arms, wails, and cries out: "Friends, immorality has appeared in the world! Irreligion has appeared in the world, for the taking up of sticks is now known!" But, the first being throws his stick on the ground, holds up his arms, wails, and cries out: "Friends, immorality and irreligion have appeared in the world, because stealing and lying are now known!"

In this way, monks, these three evil and demeritorious things first come to be known in the world: theft, lying, and violence. . . .

[The myth then goes on to recount the origins of kingship and the taxation system. The beings get together and decide they need to elect someone to maintain order in their world and mete out punishment where punishment is due. That person becomes the first "king," known as the Great Elected One (Mahāsammata), and is compensated for his role by being assigned a share of the crops of each of the beings in the world.]

Source: Translated from *Mahāvastu avadāna,* ed. S. Bagchi, Buddhist Sanskrit Texts, no. 14 (Darbhanga: Mithila Institute, 1970), 1:280–89.[11]

---

[11]Alternative English translation, J. J. Jones, *The Mahāvastu* (London: Pali Text Society, 1949), 1:285–93.

3.4 THE CESSATION OF SUFFERING

The third Noble Truth, the cessation (nirodha) of suffering, comes with the realization of nirvāṇa. The problem of nirvāṇa, like the problem of anātman, is one of the classic questions of Buddhism and is much debated by Buddhists and non-Buddhists alike. Buddhist texts commonly distinguish between two forms of nirvāṇa: the "nirvāṇa with a remaining substratum of existence" and the "nirvāṇa without a remaining substratum of existence." The first of these can be equated with enlightenment (bodhi). It means that the person attaining nirvāṇa, though freed from desire and the accumulation of new karma and though destined not to be reborn again, nonetheless still remains present in the world and lives out his or her life span within it. The second form can be equated with parinirvāṇa and means that the one attaining nirvāṇa is no longer present, physically or in any other way, in the world.

The word *nirvāṇa* itself means "extinction" or "going out," as when a lamp goes out for want of fuel. It is thus often described in negative terms as the cessation of desire, of ignorance, of suffering, of the endless round of death and rebirth and redeath. But because all these things that "cease" are, in fact, themselves valued negatively, nirvāṇa is naturally viewed as a goal to be sought and so is also sometimes described positively as peace, happiness, or bliss, as something that brings hope, that assures us, as one reputedly early text puts it, that "escape is possible from the born, the become, the made, the conditioned."[12]

The story is sometimes told of two great Buddhist scholars who were having an argument about the nature of nirvāṇa. The one maintained that it was absolutely negative, that it meant annihilation, a complete and total end to being and becoming—that is, nihilism. The other argued that it was transcendentally positive, an ineffably wonderful, desired state, indescribable bliss. Each wrote many books and articles expounding his views and critiquing the other's position. In the end, each succeeded in convincing the other: the nihilist came to see the positive side of nirvāṇa, and the advocate of transcendent bliss came to see the negative side. And having switched their positions, they went on arguing for the rest of their careers! It is perhaps wise to recall, therefore, that according to at least one text in the Pali canon, the Buddha, as with Vacchagotta's question about the Self, refused to address the question of the nature of nirvāṇa. The question itself, he contended, simply misses the mark. What is important is putting an end to suffering, not speculating on what the absence of suffering is or is not like.

3.4.1 Nirvāṇa, Nirvāṇa

Be that as it may, many texts in the Pali canon deal with the question of nirvāṇa. Perhaps one of the most straightforward is the following, which, interestingly in view of the Buddha's silence, is put in the mouth of one of his disciples, Sāriputta. It describes nirvāṇa simply as the destruction of desire (rāga), hatred (dosa), and delusion (moha). These three causes of suffering, sometimes symbolized in Buddhist iconography as a rooster, a snake, and a

[12] *Udāna,* ed. Paul Steinthal (London: Pali Text Society, 1885), p. 81.

pig constantly chasing one another, are seen as the "three poisons" that keep the wheel of saṃsāra turning; nirvāṇa puts a stop to them.

Once, the Venerable Sāriputta was staying at Nālaka Village in Magadha. One day, the wandering ascetic Jambukhādaka approached him, greeted him courteously, sat down to one side, and said: "People are always saying 'nirvāṇa, nirvāṇa,' but tell me, Sāriputta, what is nirvāṇa?"

"The destruction of desire, the destruction of hatred, and the destruction of delusion—that, my friend, is what is called nirvāṇa."

"But is there a path, is there a way to the realization of this nirvāṇa?"

"There is, my friend."

"And what is it, sir?"

"It is the Eightfold Path of the Noble Ones, namely: right views, right intention, right speech, right action, right livelihood, right effort, right mindfulness, and right concentration. This is the Path, this is the way to the realization of this nirvāṇa."

Source: Translated from *The Samyutta-Nikāya,* ed. Léon Feer (London: Pali Text Society, 1894), 4:251–52.[13]

3.4.2 Milinda Asks about Nirvāṇa

We have already had occasion to witness the argumentative style of King Milinda and to see how the elder Nāgasena deals with his questions. Milinda is not loath to ask even the most elementary things about nirvāṇa, and Nāgasena is never reluctant to respond. Sometimes their logic is a bit weak and their argumentation a bit devious, but the questions are nonetheless genuine and the answers remain interesting.

"Tell me, Nāgasena, is nirvāṇa pure bliss, or does it involve suffering?"

"It is pure bliss, your majesty, and devoid of any suffering."

"We find it hard to believe, Nāgasena, that nirvāṇa is pure bliss, and we conclude that it must be involved with suffering. Why? Because, Nāgasena, we see that those who seek nirvāṇa torment and afflict their bodies and minds. They observe restraints in standing, walking, sitting, lying, and eating, keep themselves from sleeping, repress their senses, and renounce wealth, property, relatives, and friends. But those who are blissful, who are happy in this world, enjoy and cultivate the delights of the senses. With their eyes, they enjoy and cultivate all sorts of charming, beautiful forms; with their ears, they enjoy and cultivate all sorts of charming, beautiful sounds—songs and music; with their noses, they

[13]Alternative English translation, F. L. Woodward, *The Book of the Kindred Sayings* (London: Pali Text Society, 1927), 4:170–71.

enjoy and cultivate all sorts of charming, beautiful scents—flowers, fruits, leaves, bark, roots, and resin; with their tongues, they enjoy and cultivate all sorts of charming, beautiful tastes—solid and soft foods that are chewed, licked, drunk, or tasted; with their sense of touch, they enjoy and cultivate all sorts of charming, beautiful tactile sensations—smooth and subtle, soft and tender; and with their minds, they enjoy and cultivate all sorts of charming, beautiful thoughts and ideas—meritorious and demeritorious, pure and impure.

"You, however, stop and destroy, break and cut off, hinder and restrain the cultivation of your visual, aural, olfactory, gustatory, tactile, and mental senses. Thus, you afflict your body and afflict your mind, and with your afflicted body you feel bodily suffering, and with your afflicted mind you feel mental suffering. No wonder the wandering ascetic Māgandiya reproached the Blessed One, saying that he was a repressionist! This is why I say that nirvāṇa is involved with suffering."

"No, your majesty, nirvāṇa has nothing to do with suffering. You say that it does, but what you call "suffering" is not "nirvāṇa"; it is preliminary to the realization of nirvāṇa, it is the quest for nirvāṇa. Nirvāṇa itself is pure bliss and not mixed with suffering at all. Let me give you an example. Do kings, your majesty, know such a thing as the 'bliss of kingship'?"

"Indeed, they do."

"Now, your majesty, is this bliss of kingship involved with suffering?"

"No, it is not."

"But, your majesty, what about when kings have to put down a disturbance in a border region and subdue the inhabitants of the area? Surrounded by their ministers and troops, they must set out, and tormented by gadflies and mosquitoes, wind and heat, running over even and uneven ground, engaging in great battles, they come to fear for their lives. . . . "

"But, Nāgasena, that is not what is called the 'bliss of kingship'; that is preliminary to it, part of the quest for it. Through suffering, the king seeks sovereignty, and then he enjoys the bliss of kingship. Thus, Nāgasena, the bliss of kingship is itself devoid of suffering. It is one thing, and suffering is another."

"Just so, your majesty, nirvāṇa, too, is pure bliss and is not involved with suffering." [. . .]

"Venerable Nāgasena, you keep referring to nirvāṇa; can you enlighten me as to the form, makeup, age, or size of this nirvāṇa by means of some simile, explanation, reason, or inference?"

"Your majesty, nirvāṇa cannot be compared to anything. It is not possible to elucidate its form, makeup, age, or size by means of any simile, explanation, reason, or inference."

"But, Nāgasena, nirvāṇa is something real; I find it hard to accept that it should be impossible, by any means whatsoever, to make me understand its form, makeup, age, or size. You can explain it to me."

"All right, your majesty, I will explain it. Is there, your majesty, such a thing as the ocean?"

"Indeed, there is."

"Well, then, suppose someone were to put to you the following questions: 'Your majesty, how much water is in the ocean? How many creatures live in it?' How would you answer such questions?"

"If I were asked that, Nāgasena, I would reply: 'You idiot, you are asking me the unaskable. No one should ask those questions; they are irrelevant. Topographers have not examined the ocean; it is not possible to measure the amount of water in it or to count the number of creatures who live there.' That, Nāgasena, is the reply I would give."

"But, your majesty, the ocean is something real; why would you give such a reply? You ought to count and show that there is *X* amount of water in the ocean, and that *N* number of creatures live there."

"That is not possible, Nāgasena. The question is beyond my scope."

"Just so, your majesty. Just as you cannot measure the water or count the creatures in the ocean, even though it is something real, so you cannot give an idea of the form, makeup, age, or size of nirvāṇa, even though it is something real. . . . Your majesty, even if someone who had mastered magical powers were able to count the waters and the creatures in the ocean, that same person would not be able to explain by any means the form, makeup, age, or size of nirvāṇa." [. . .]

"Venerable Nāgasena, you say that nirvāṇa is not past, not future, not present, not produced, not unproduced, not producible. In that case, Nāgasena, does the person who realizes nirvāṇa through right practice realize something that was already produced, or does he first produce it and then realize it?"

"Neither one, your majesty. The person who realizes nirvāṇa through right practice neither realizes something that was already produced nor first produces something and then realizes it. Even so, the element of nirvāṇa, which is realized through right practice, exists."

"Nāgasena, do not clarify this question by obscuring it! Please explain it plainly and clearly. . . . "

"All right, your majesty. There is this thing called nirvāṇa, which is peaceful, blissful, and exalted, and that is what a person realizes through right practice, by means of understanding karmic constituents according to the teachings of the Buddha, and wisdom. Just as a student may realize knowledge according to the instruction of his teacher, just so, your majesty, one may realize nirvāṇa through right practice, according to the instruction of the Buddha. And how is nirvāṇa to be recognized? It can be recognized through its safety, its freedom from mishap and danger, its tranquillity, its peacefulness, its blissfulness, its pleasantness, its excellence, its purity, its coolness. Your majesty, it is like a man who is being burned by a fire, a great pile of flaming sticks of wood; when by means of a great effort he escapes from there, out into the open where there is no fire, he realizes utter bliss. Similarly, your majesty, through right practice and proper concentration one can realize the utter bliss of nirvāṇa, in which the torment of the threefold fire of desire, hatred, and delusion has gone out." [. . .]

"Venerable Nāgasena, things in this world come about due to karma, causes, and climatic changes. Tell me, is there anything not due to any of these reasons?"

"There are two such things in this world, your majesty: space and nirvāṇa. Neither of them is due to karma, causes, or climatic changes."

"Venerable Nāgasena, do not sully the word of the Buddha! Do not expound on a question while lacking knowledge! . . . Nāgasena, what you say about space is correct: it is due neither to karma, nor causes, nor climatic changes. But, Nāgasena, in hundreds of ways the Blessed One explained to his disciples the path to the realization of nirvāṇa, but now you say nirvāṇa is not due to any cause!"

"It is true, your majesty, that the Blessed One explained to his disciples the path to the realization of nirvāṇa in hundreds of ways, but he never explained the cause of the appearance of nirvāṇa."

"Venerable Nāgasena! Here we are going from darkness into greater darkness, from the woods deeper into the woods, from a thicket to a denser thicket. What you are saying is that there is a cause for the realization of nirvāṇa but no cause for the thing itself. But if, Nāgasena, there is a cause for the realization of nirvāṇa, it itself must have a cause one can look for. Nāgasena, a son has a father; therefore, one expects that father to have a father. A student has a teacher; therefore, one expects that teacher to have a teacher. A shoot has a seed; therefore, one expects that seed to have a seed. Just so, Nāgasena, if the realization of nirvāṇa has a cause, one expects its appearance to have a cause. . . . "

"Your majesty, nirvāṇa cannot be made to arise, and no cause for its appearance has been proclaimed. . . .

Source: Translated from *The Milindapañho,* ed. V. Trenckner, reprint edition with the *Milinda-ṭīkā* (London: Pali Text Society, 1986), pp. 313–17, 323–24, 268–69.[14]

3.4.3 The Attainment of Two Arhats

Discourses about nirvāṇa are an important source of information on Buddhist views on the subject, but they are not the only one. A number of texts also provide us with what amounts to personal testimonials of monks and nuns attaining nirvāṇa. Such experiences are sometimes portrayed as sudden breakthroughs to understanding, dramatic awakenings to reality-as-it-is, and the verbal expressions of such enlightenment experiences are called "lion's roars." In other cases, however, the attainment of nirvāṇa is associated with much quieter experiences, like snow slipping off a leaf or, as in the second example below, like rain falling on the roof.

The *Verses of the Elders* and the *Verses of the Eldresses* (*Theragāthā* and *Therīgāthā*) are Pali canonical texts that contain several hundred "songs of enlightenment" uttered by monks and nuns upon their attainment of nirvāṇa, their becoming arhats. Arhats, as we have seen, attain enlightenment through their own efforts, by following the teaching of a Buddha. In this they differ

[14]Alternative English translation, T. W. Rhys Davids, *The Questions of King Milinda* (Oxford: Clarendon Press, 1894), 2:181–87, 195–97, 103–4.

from Buddhas, who find their own path to enlightenment and then preach that path to others, and pratyekabuddhas, who find their own path but then keep it to themselves. Though the two selections that follow are illustrative of the arhat ideal that preponderated in the Theravāda tradition, it should not be forgotten that Mainstream Buddhism kept open the possibility of all three of the above attainments. Indeed, schools like the Sarvāstivādins compiled whole anthologies of stories (for example, the *Avadānaśataka*) recounting the various paths and attainments of Buddhas, pratyekabuddhas, and arhats (both male and female).

[A.] [As we saw in 2.1.5, the nun Paṭācāra joined the sangha after suffering the loss of her entire family and almost going insane. As a nun, she then went on to attain nirvāṇa, something that occurred to her after taking a bath and getting ready for bed, just as she was putting out the lamp in her cell (nirvāṇa literally means "extinction"). She later recounted the experience as follows]:

> Ploughing their fields, sowing seeds in the earth, men look after their wives and children, and prosper.
> Why can't I, who keep the precepts and follow the teachings of the Master, attain nirvāṇa? I am neither lazy nor conceited!
> After washing my feet, I note the water, and watch it going down the drain; that makes me collect and control my mind as though it were a noble thoroughbred horse.
> Then taking a lamp, I enter my cell; thinking of going to sleep, I sit down on my bed;
> With a pin, I pull out the wick. The lamp goes out: nirvāṇa. My mind is freed.

[B.] [The monk Girimānanda was invited by King Bimbisāra to dwell on the grounds of his palace, but then the king neglected to give him a place to live. As a result the monk stayed out in the open, and in compassion for him the gods stopped the rains from coming, thus causing a drought. The king worried about the drought, discovered what he had done, and sought to rectify the situation by building a proper hermitage hut for Girimānanda. Once it was built, the rains began to fall, and the elder, sheltered and dry, at peace and able to meditate, attained nirvāṇa. He expressed his enlightenment with the following verses]:

> The gods have sent the rain; it is like a sweet song. In my thatched hut, comfortable, out of the wind, I dwell appeased. So, rain, gods, if you wish.
> The gods have sent the rain; it is like a sweet song. In my thatched hut, comfortable, out of the wind, I dwell, my mind at ease. So rain, gods, if you wish.
> The gods have sent the rain; it is like a sweet song. In my thatched hut, comfortable, out of the wind, I dwell, free from desire. So rain, gods, if you wish.
> The gods have sent the rain; it is like a sweet song. In my thatched hut, comfortable, out of the wind, I dwell, free from hatred. So rain, gods, if you wish.

The gods have sent the rain; it is like a sweet song. In my thatched hut, comfortable, out of the wind, I dwell, free from delusion. So rain, gods, if you wish.

Source: Translated from *Thera- and Therī-gāthā,* ed. Hermann Oldenberg and Richard Pischel (London: Pali Text Society, 1883), pp. 134–35, 38.[15]

3.5 THE PATH

Buddhists, of course, did not simply affirm the possibility of the attainment of nirvāṇa, described in the verses just cited as the absence of desire, hatred, and delusion. They also outlined a path for the elimination of desire, hatred, and delusion. The Noble Eightfold Path, as we saw in 1.6, set forth a method for attaining enlightenment that consisted of right views, right intention, right speech, right action, right livelihood, right effort, right mindfulness, and right concentration. Another way of describing it was to divide it into three basic components: moral practice (or lifestyle), wisdom (or intellectual insight), and meditation (or contemplative technique). These three components are like the legs of a tripod: they depend on one another and reinforce one another to the extent that you cannot have one without the others.

3.5.1 The Refuges and the Precepts

The very first step in embarking on the path, whether as a layperson or as a monk or nun, is to take refuge in the Three Jewels (the Buddha, the Dharma, and the Sangha). In Theravāda countries today, the refuge formula is commonly recited in Pali by monastics and laity alike on virtually every Buddhist occasion, and some repeat it every day as part of their own personal religious routine. It represents, therefore, not only a commitment but also a recommitment to the Buddhist way. It is usually followed by a (re)commitment to upholding the five precepts, another mark of one's embarcation on the path. These five precepts are to abstain from killing, stealing, unchastity, lying, and drinking intoxicants. (For the third precept, laypersons commit themselves not to complete chastity but to avoiding sexual misconduct.) In addition, on special occasions, as a sort of further embarcation on the path, laypersons may take on three more precepts, usually for a limited period of time: not to eat after noon, to abstain from going to public entertainments and from adorning their persons in any way, and not to use high or broad beds (that is, to sit on mats on the floor). Buddhist novices, when they become novices, commit themselves permanently to these same precepts, plus an additional one: abstaining from the personal use of money. (This is thought to make a total of ten precepts, because in this listing the "seventh" precept, to abstain from public entertainments and personal adornment, is divided into two.)

[15]Alternative English translation, K. R. Norman, *The Elders' Verses* (London: Pali Text Society, 1969–71), 2:14–15, 1:36–37. For the first selection, see also Susan Murcott, *The First Buddhist Women* (Berkeley: Parallax Press, 1991), pp. 33–34.

The following selection, from a Buddhist catechism included in the Pali canon, gives the threefold refuge formula and the ten precepts. Because these formulas are so frequently on the lips of Buddhists in South and Southeast Asia, I have provided the Pali text, along with a translation.

Namo tassa Bhagavato arahato sammā sambuddhassa. "Praise to the Blessed One, the arhat, the completely enlightened One."

Buddhaṃ saraṇaṃ gacchāmi: "I take refuge in the Buddha."

Dhammaṃ saraṇaṃ gacchāmi: "I take refuge in the Dharma."

Saṅghaṃ saraṇaṃ gacchāmi: "I take refuge in the Sangha."

Dutiyaṃ pi Buddhaṃ saraṇaṃ gacchāmi: "A second time, I take refuge in the Buddha."

Dutiyaṃ pi Dhammaṃ saraṇaṃ gacchāmi: "A second time, I take refuge in the Dharma."

Dutiyaṃ pi Saṅghaṃ saraṇaṃ gacchāmi: "A second time, I take refuge in the Sangha."

Tatiyaṃ pi Buddhaṃ saraṇaṃ gacchāmi: "A third time, I take refuge in the Buddha."

Tatiyaṃ pi Dhammaṃ saraṇaṃ gacchāmi: "A third time, I take refuge in the Dharma."

Tatiyaṃ pi Saṅghaṃ saraṇaṃ gacchāmi: "A third time, I take refuge in the Sangha."

1. *Pāṇātipātā veramaṇī sikkhāpadaṃ samādiyāmi:* "I take up the precept to refrain from taking life."
2. *Adinnādānā veramaṇī sikkhāpadaṃ samādiyāmi:* "I take up the precept to refrain from taking what is not given."
3. *Abrahmacariyā* [or *Kamesumicchācārā*] *veramaṇī sikkhāpadaṃ samādiyāmi:* "I take up the precept to refrain from unchastity [or illicit sexual relations]."
4. *Musāvādā veramaṇī sikkhāpadaṃ samādiyāmi:* "I take up the precept to refrain from speaking falsely."
5. *Surāmeraya-majjapamādaṭṭhāna veramaṇī sikkhāpadaṃ samādiyāmi:* "I take up the precept to refrain from intoxicating drinks, which result in heedlessness."
6. *Vikālabhojanā veramaṇī sikkhāpadaṃ samādiyāmi:* "I take up the precept to refrain from eating at the wrong time."
7. *Naccagītavāditavisūkadassanā veramaṇī sikkhāpadaṃ samādiyāmi:* "I take up the precept to refrain from attending events where there are dancing, singing, music, or acrobatic exhibitions."
8. *Mālāgandhavilepanadhāraṇa-maṇḍanavibhūsanaṭṭhānā veramaṇī sikkhāpadaṃ samādiyāmi:* "I take up the precept to refrain from wearing garlands, perfumes, unguents, ornaments, or cosmetics."

9. *Uccāsayanamahāsayanā veramaṇī sikkhāpadaṃ samādiyāmi:* "I take up the precept to refrain from using high or broad beds."
10. *Jātarūparajatapaṭiggahaṇā veramaṇī sikkhāpadaṃ samādiyāmi:* "I take up the precept to refrain from accepting gold or silver."

Source: Translated from *The Khuddaka-pāṭha,* ed. Helmer Smith (London: Pali Text Society, 1915), pp. 1–2.[16]

3.5.2 Moral Conduct of Monks

Separated from their contexts, the ten precepts may seem to be purely proscriptive in nature, essentially a list of "Thou shalt nots." The practice of the precepts, however, as well as of the Buddhist Path in general, also involved positive moral actions. In the following selection, some of these are spelled out. Although this passage, too, ends up with a list of proscriptions, it starts off by showing what the rules of restraint might mean to a newly ordained monk as a positive paradigm for life.

"Life in a household is confining and polluting; the monastic life is like open air. Living in a home, it is not easy to lead an utterly fulfilling, pure, chaste, and studious life, polished like mother of pearl. Why don't I, therefore, cut off my hair and beard, put on a yellow robe, leave home, and adopt the homeless life?"

Thus thinking, a householder or his son . . . abandons his accumulated wealth, whether great or small, and leaves behind the circle of his relations, whether many or few. And once he has wandered forth, he lives . . . endowed with good conduct, careful of the slightest transgressions, undertaking to observe the precepts, doing meritorious deeds of body, speech, and mind and leading a pure life, perfect in morality. . . .

In what ways . . . is a monk perfect in morality? Forsaking the taking of life, he abstains from killing. Having laid down his stick and his sword, he lives in modesty, showing kindness, compassion, and concern for the welfare of all living beings. Such is his moral conduct.

Forsaking the taking of what is not given, he abstains from theft. He lives, openly accepting and expecting gifts, keeping himself pure. Such is his moral conduct.

Forsaking unchastity, he leads a chaste life, aloof, abstaining from the vulgar practice of sex. Such is his moral conduct.

Forsaking uttering falsehoods, he abstains from lying. He . . . speaks the truth and is reliable, open, and trustworthy, not deceiving the world. Such is his moral conduct.

Forsaking malicious speech, he abstains from slander. What he hears here he does not repeat there so as to create factions; and what he hears

---

[16]Alternative English translation, Bhikkhu Ñāṇamoli, *The Minor Readings* (London: Pali Text Society, 1960), pp. 1–2.

there he does not repeat here for the same reason. In this way, he reconciles those who are at odds, he encourages those who are united, and he rejoices, delights, and takes pleasure in concord and promotes it when he speaks. Such is his moral conduct.

Forsaking harsh speech, he abstains from rudeness. Instead, he speaks words that are blameless, pleasing to the ear, kind, heart-warming, polite, delightful, and charming to many people. Such is his moral conduct.

Forsaking frivolous talk, he abstains from trivial conversations. His speech is timely, factual, and to the point, dealing with Dharma and the Vinaya. At the right time, he speaks words that are worth treasuring, that are reasonable, well defined, and purposeful. Such is his moral conduct.

He refrains from harvesting seeds or plants. He takes one meal a day and refrains from eating after noon or at night. He avoids watching shows that involve dancing, singing, and music. He abstains from bodily ornaments or jewelry and from wearing garlands, perfumes, or cosmetics. He does not use high or large beds. He refuses to accept gold or silver. . . .

Source: Translated from "Sāmaññaphala sutta" in *Dīgha Nikāya,* ed. T. W. Rhys Davids and J. Estlin Carpenter (London: Pali Text Society, 1890), 1:63–64.[17]

3.5.3 Sayings on the Path

The interdependent relationship of the three components of the Path—moral practice, wisdom, and meditation—was worked out systematically in the Theravāda tradition in such works as the *Visuddhimagga* (*The Path of Purity*) of the great fifth-century scholar Buddhaghosa. But it is found also in some of the earliest canonical texts. The following selections are from the *Udānavarga*, the Sanskrit counterpart to the better known Pali text, the *Dhammapada.* Both works are collections of aphorisms rather loosely organized topically into different chapters. Some of these chapters focus on doctrinal concepts (such as karmic constituents), others on moral concerns (such as desires), and still others on meditational techniques (such as mindfulness). There are thirty-three such topics in the *Udānavarga.* In the translation that follows, I have selected at least one verse from each chapter.

1.1 Don't be sluggish! Don't be drowsy! But take delight in your minds! Listen and I will proclaim what was uttered by the Buddha.

1.3 Alas, all karmically constituted things are impermanent; their nature is to rise and fall. Coming into being, they cease to be; happiness comes in, bringing them to rest.

2.1 Desire, I know your origin! You are due to mistaken perceptions. But I will not mistake you, so for me you will not exist!

[17]Alternative English translation, Maurice Walshe, *Thus Have I Heard: The Long Discourses of the Buddha* (London: Wisdom Books, 1987), pp. 99–100.

3.16 A weed that has been cut down will grow back again if its roots are not hacked away. So too latent craving, if not rooted out, will result in suffering again and again.

4.27 A monk who delights in vigilance and looks fearfully upon heedlessness can extricate himself from evil states like an elephant in a pool of mud.

5.5 Never associate with things that are dear to you or things that you dislike. Not seeing what is dear and seeing what is disliked: both entail suffering.

6.1 A wise man keeps the moral precepts, eager for three happinesses: approbation, wealth, and, after death, the joy of heaven.

7.5 Use your body to make merit, and use your speech as well. Make merit with your mind, and attain limitless freedom from attachments.

8.1 One who speaks lies goes to hell. So does one who claims his own deed was done by another. Both are said to be the same; after death they will become low-born humans in another place.

9.19 Rust eats away the very metal it grows on. Just so, the very deeds of those whose conduct is not tranquil will lead them to unfortunate rebirths.

10.10 One who desires the presence of the Noble Ones and who delights in hearing the True Dharma and who wipes away the stain of selfishness is said to be a person of faith.

11.13 A shaved head does not make a man a monk, for he may lack restraint and speak untruths. How can one still touched by longing and greed be called a recluse?

12.5 All karmically constituted things are impermanent. When, with wisdom, one can see this, one turns away from suffering. This is the path to purity.

12.6 All karmically constituted things are suffering. When, with wisdom, one can see this, one turns away from suffering. This is the path to purity.

12.7 All karmically constituted things are empty. When, with wisdom, one can see this, one turns away from suffering. This is the path to purity.

12.8 *All things* are without a Self. When, with wisdom, one can see this, one turns away from suffering. This is the path to purity.

13.10 If one wishes to live happily, attentive to the aims of renunciation, one should delight in whatever happens and cherish the one Dharma.

13.11 If one wishes to live happily, attentive to the aims of renunciation, one should not despise the robes, food, or drink of the sangha.

14.9 "He yelled at me! He spoke to me! He bested me! He conquered me!" Those who dwell upon such things will never bring a rest to animosity.

15.2 With body and mind both alert, a monk should always be mindful, whether standing or sitting or lying down. With his mind thus established, he will attain distinction in a later life; having then attained distinction, he will no longer be subject to death.

16.15 For the pure, it is always a holy night. For the pure, every day is a "sabbath." For the pure with acts unsullied, it is always time for religious practice.

16.16 Weeds are the bane of fields, and desire is the bane of beings. Thus a gift to those who are free from desire bears great fruit.

17.5 Do not treat a misdeed lightly, thinking, "It will not come back to me." Drops of water, dripping slowly, can fill even a large pot; so, too, misdeeds will fill up fools, bit by little bit.

17.6 Do not treat a good deed lightly, thinking, "It will not come back to me." Drops of water, dripping slowly, can fill even a large pot; so, too, good deeds will fill the wise, bit by little bit.

17.10 Washermen wash with water, fletchers straighten arrowshafts, carpenters master wood, and the wise tame their selves.

18.3 Cut down the forest, not the tree; it is the forest that causes fear! But monks who uproot the forest will be in nirvāṇa, forest-free.

19.8 This cart does not go to that place, but one who is subdued, through discipline and self-control, can get there on his own.

20.1 One should abandon anger, jettison arrogance, and overcome all fetters. Desires do not befall the one who has nothing and is not attached to mind and body.

21.9 The glorious Buddhas who are intent on meditation and who delight in the tranquillity of renunciation: the gods themselves ever long for them.

22.17 One's ears hear a lot, one's eyes see a lot; the wise person ought not to believe everything seen or heard.

23.2 Sitting alone, sleeping alone, walking alone: alert, one should delight in being by oneself, dwelling alone in the forest.

24.6 It is better to live a single day and see the arising and passing away of things than to live a hundred years and never realize it.

25.23 A fool may sing praises, and a wise man, blame, but it is better to be blamed by the wise man than praised by the fool.

26.7 Hunger is the greatest of diseases, but karmic constituents are truly suffering. Knowing this to be the way things are, one reaches the supreme nirvāṇa.

27.37 There is said to be a difference between having insight and having views; like day and night they are not known to overlap.

28.1 To refrain from all misdeeds, to attain merit, to purify one's thoughts completely: this is the teaching of the Buddha.

29.38 In the air one leaves no footprints; outside the order there is no recluse. Fools delight in idle fancies; Tathāgatas are free of them.

30.14 Happy are those whose minds delight in Dharma, who without clinging have reached nirvāṇa and find joy in the application of mindfulness to the seven factors of enlightenment—

30.15 Happy are those whose minds delight in Dharma, who without clinging have reached nirvāṇa and find joy in the establishment of supernatural powers, and delight in the Eightfold Path—

30.16 Happily they eat begged food, and happily they wear their robes. Pleasant are their cloisters, in the mountains or in the caves.

31.23 "Things" follow after Thought, are junior to Thought, are whisked into being by Thought; speak or act with a Mind that is irritated, and suffering will ensue, just as the cart wheel follows in the ox's track.

31.24 "Things" follow after Thought, are junior to Thought, are whisked into being by Thought; speak or act with a Mind that is tranquil, and happiness will ensue, just as one is trailed by one's shadow.

32.81 Monks keep the precepts, meditators deal with emptiness, yogins are involved with perseverance; happiness comes with nirvāṇa.

33.76 When the elements of reality appear to the zealous one in meditation, when he understands suffering and its cause, then all his doubts disappear.

Source: Translated from *Udānavarga,* ed. Franz Bernhard (Göttingen: Vandenhoeck & Ruprecht, 1965), vol. 1, passim.

3.5.4 Mindfulness

As the notion of the Path developed, Buddhism came to recognize two major forms of meditation: tranquilization of the mind (śamatha), which is a form of meditative absorption involving trances, and insight meditation (vipāśyana), whereby the meditator gains direct understanding of the nature of things. Both forms, however, demand that the meditator develop mindfulness (smṛti, Pali: sati), and have the powers of concentration necessary to "apply the mind" to particular topics of meditation. The Theravāda tradition developed a list of no fewer than forty subjects of meditation, suitable for different personality types and including things such as simple physical devices (for example, a flat disk of clay) intended to develop one's powers of concentration, immaterial ethical attitudes (such as loving kindness for all beings), hard-to-grasp states of mind (such as "neither perception nor nonperception"), and graphic reminders of impermanence and no-Self (such as corpses in various states of decomposition). Which meditation topic one used depended on one's character and on the recommendation of one's meditation master, but most people started off by focusing their attention on their breathing. That is, at any rate, what is described first in the following selection.

Monks, there is one road, one path for beings to purify themselves, to transcend sorrow and grief, to overcome suffering and melancholy, to attain the right way, to realize nirvāṇa: that is the fourfold establishment of mindfulness. What are the four mindfulnesses? They are . . . the mindful contemplation of the body, . . . the mindful contemplation of the feelings, . . . the mindful contemplation of thoughts, . . . and the mindful contemplation of the elements of reality. . . .

1. How does a monk practice the mindful contemplation of the body? In this way: He goes to the forest, or to the foot of a tree, or to an empty room, and he sits down, cross-legged, keeps his back straight, and directs his mindfulness in front of him. Mindfully, he breathes in, mindfully, he

breathes out; breathing in a long breath, he knows "I am breathing in a long breath"; breathing out a long breath, he knows "I am breathing out a long breath"; breathing in a short breath, he knows "I am breathing in a short breath"; breathing out a short breath, he knows "I am breathing out a short breath." . . . He should be like a lathe operator who knows that "I am making a long turn" when he is making a long turn and that "I am making a short turn" when he is making a short turn. . . . Thus, O monks, a monk practices mindfully contemplating the body per se [in three ways]: first, he stays focused on his own body, or on the body of another, or on both his own body and the body of another; second, with regard to the body, he stays focused on the phenomena of origination, or passing away, or both origination and passing away; third, he sustains the awareness "this is the body" in so far as wisdom and recollection allow, and he remains detached, not clinging to anything in the world. . . .

Furthermore, when a monk is walking, he knows "I am walking," and when he is standing, knows "I am standing," and when he is sitting, knows "I am sitting," and when he is lying down, knows "I am lying down." Whatever posture his body may take, he knows that he is taking it. . . . Thus, O monks, a monk practices mindfully contemplating the body per se [in three ways]: first, he stays focused on his own body . . . [as above].

And also, a monk is fully mindful of what he is doing, both going and coming, looking straight ahead and looking away, holding out his bowl or retracting it, putting on his robes, carrying his bowl, eating, drinking, chewing, tasting, defecating, urinating, moving, standing, sitting, sleeping, waking, talking, being quiet. . . . Thus, O monks, a monk practices mindfully contemplating the body per se [in three ways]: first, he stays focused on his own body . . . [as above].

And also, a monk considers his body per se, from the soles of his feet upward and from the top of his head downward, wrapped as it is in skin and filled with all sorts of impurities. He reflects, "In this body, there is hair, body-hair, nails, teeth, skin, flesh, sinews, bones, marrow, kidneys, heart, liver, pleura, spleen, lungs, colon, intestines, stomach, feces, bile, phlegm, pus, blood, sweat, fat, tears, lymph, saliva, snot, synovia, and urine." . . . Thus, O monks, a monk practices mindfully contemplating the body per se [in three ways]: first, he stays focused on his own body . . . [as above].

And also, a monk considers his body . . . with regard to the elements that compose it. He reflects, "In this body, there is earth, water, fire, and air. . . . " He should think of these elements that make up the body as though they were pieces of the carcass of a cow that a butcher had slaughtered and displayed in a market. . . . Thus, O monks, a monk practices mindfully contemplating the body per se [in three ways]: first, he stays focused on his own body . . . [as above].

And also, if a monk should see a corpse abandoned in a cemetery, dead one day or two or three, swollen, turning blue, and beginning to fester, he should concentrate on his own body and think, "This body of mine is just like that one; it has the same nature, and it will not escape this fate." . . . And should he see a corpse abandoned in a cemetery, being eaten by crows, hawks, vultures, dogs, jackals, or various kinds of vermin, he should concentrate on his own body and think, "This body of mine is just like that one; it has the same nature, and it will not escape this fate." . . . And should he see a corpse abandoned in a cemetery, a skeleton still covered with some flesh and blood and held together by tendons, or without flesh but smeared with blood and still held together, or without flesh or blood but still held together, or just bones no longer held together but scattered in different directions—here the bones of a hand, there the bones of a foot, here a tibia, there a femur, here a hipbone, there a backbone, over there a skull—he should concentrate on his own body and think, "This body of mine is just like that; it has the same nature, and it will not escape this fate." . . . And should he see a corpse abandoned in a cemetery, bones bleached white as shells, old bones in a heap, bones that have completely decayed and become dust—he should concentrate on his own body and think, "This body of mine is just like that; it has the same nature, and it will not escape this fate." . . . Thus, O monks, a monk practices mindfully contemplating the body per se [in three ways]: first, he stays focused on his own body . . . [as above].

2. And how, monks, does a monk practice the mindful contemplation of feelings? In this way: Experiencing a pleasant feeling, he knows "I am experiencing a pleasant feeling"; experiencing an unpleasant feeling, he knows "I am experiencing an unpleasant feeling." Experiencing a feeling that is neither pleasant nor unpleasant, he knows "I am experiencing a feeling that is neither pleasant nor unpleasant." Experiencing a pleasant physical feeling, he knows "I am experiencing a pleasant physical feeling"; experiencing a pleasant spiritual feeling, he knows "I am experiencing a pleasant spiritual feeling"; experiencing an unpleasant physical feeling, . . . an unpleasant spiritual feeling, . . . a physical feeling that is neither pleasant nor unpleasant, . . . a spiritual feeling that is neither pleasant nor unpleasant, he knows he is experiencing those feelings. . . . Thus, O monks, a monk practices mindfully contemplating feelings per se [in three ways]: first, he stays focused on his own feelings, or on the feelings of another, or on both his own feelings and the feelings of another; second, with regard to feelings, he stays focused on the phenomena of origination, or passing away, or both origination and passing away; third, he sustains the awareness "this is a feeling" in so far as wisdom and recollection allow, and remains detached, not clinging to anything in the world. . . .

3. And how, O monks, does a monk practice the mindful contemplation of thoughts? In this way: He knows a passionate thought to be a passionate thought; he knows a passionless thought to be a passionless thought; he knows a hate-filled thought to be a hate-filled thought; he knows a hate-free thought to be a hate-free thought; he knows a deluded thought to be a deluded thought; he knows an undeluded thought to be an undeluded thought; he knows an attentive thought to be an attentive thought; he knows a distracted thought to be a distracted thought; he knows a lofty thought, . . . a lowly thought, . . . a mediocre thought, . . . a supreme thought, . . . a concentrated thought, . . . a diffused thought, . . . a thought that is free, . . . a thought that is still bound, . . . to be such

thoughts as they are. . . . Thus, O monks, a monk practices mindfully contemplating thoughts per se [in three ways]: first, he stays focused on his own thoughts, or on the thoughts of another, or or on both his own thoughts and the thoughts of another; second, with regard to thoughts, he stays focused on the phenomena of origination, or passing away, or both origination and passing away; third, he sustains the awareness "this is a thought" in so far as wisdom and recollection allow, and remains detached, not clinging to anything in the world. . . .

4. And how, monks, does a monk practice the mindful contemplation of the elements of reality? In this way: He practices the mindful contemplation of the elements of reality with regard to the five hindrances. And how does he do that? In this way: When there is within him sensual excitement, he knows that "sensual excitement is occurring within me"; when there is within him no sensual excitement, he knows that "sensual excitement is not occurring within me." . . . When there is within him some ill will, he knows that "ill will is occurring within me"; when there is within him no ill will, he knows "ill will is not occuring within me." . . . And similarly he knows the presence and the absence within himself of laziness and lethargy, agitation and worry, and doubt. . . . Thus, O monks, a monk practices mindfully contemplating elements of reality per se [in three ways]: first, he stays focused on elements of reality within himself, or on elements of reality outside of himself, or on elements of reality both inside and outside of himself; second, with regard to elements of reality, he stays focused on the phenomena of origination, or passing away, or both origination and passing away; third, he sustains the awareness "this is an element of reality" in so far as wisdom and recollection allow, and remains detached, not clinging to anything in the world.

A monk also practices the mindful contemplation of the elements of reality with regard to the five aggregates of attachment. And how does he do that? In this way: He reflects "Such is physical form, such is the origin of physical form, such is the passing away of physical form." "Such is feeling, such is the origin of feeling, such is the passing away of feeling." "Such is perception, such is the origin of perception, such is the passing away of perception." "Such are karmic constituents, such is the origin of karmic constituents, such is the passing away of karmic constituents." "Such is consciousness, such is the origin of consciousness, such is the passing away of consciousness. . . . "

A monk also practices the mindful contemplation of the elements of reality with regard to the six senses and sense-objects. How does he do this? In this way: He knows his eyes, he knows visible forms, and he knows the attachments that develop in connection with the two of them. . . . And similarly he knows his ears, and he knows sounds. . . . He knows his nose and he knows smells. . . . He knows his tongue and he knows tastes. . . . He knows his body and he knows tactile things. . . . He knows his mind and he knows thoughts. And he knows the attachments that develop in connection with any of them. . . .

A monk also practices the mindful contemplation of the elements of reality with regard to the seven factors of enlightenment. How does he do that? In this way: When the first factor of enlightenment, which is mindfulness, is within him, he knows it to be present; when it is not within him, he knows it to be absent. . . . And similarly, he knows the presence and absence within himself of the other factors of enlightenment: the investigation of Dharma, . . . energetic effort, . . . enthusiasm, . . . serenity, . . . meditative concentration, . . . and equanimity. . . .

A monk also practices the mindful contemplation of the elements of reality with regard to the Four Noble Truths. How does he do that? In this way: He knows "suffering" the way it really is, and he knows "the origination of suffering" the way it really is, and he knows "the cessation of suffering" the way it really is, and he knows "the way leading to the cessation of suffering" the way it really is. . . .

Source: Translated from "Satipaṭṭhānasutta" in *The Majjhima-Nikāya,* ed. V. Trenckner (London: Pali Text Society, 1888), 1:55–63.[18]

3.5.5 The Practice of Meditation

In addition to outlining the techniques and subjects of meditation, Buddhist texts may contain practical advice of a more down-to-earth type, in order to help meditators, especially beginners, deal with some of the hindrances that may interfere with their practice. The following selection, from a work by the second century C.E. Buddhist poet Aśvaghoṣa, contains his rendition of the advice that the Buddha reputedly gave to his handsome half-brother, Nanda. Nanda had been very much attached to his beautiful wife and had been living in marital bliss when the Buddha, hoping to lead him to a different form of bliss, more or less shanghaied him into joining the sangha. The following passages are from a later episode, when the Buddha takes it upon himself to exhort young Nanda in his practice of meditation and instructs him in some of the practicalities of doing so.

Now after closing the windows of the senses with the shutters of mindfulness, you should know the proper measure of food that is conducive to meditation and good health. For too much food obstructs the flow of one's breathing, leads to lethargy and sleep, and saps one's strength. And just as too much food produces purposelessness, the consumption of too little food is debilitating. For excessive fasting takes away from the body its substance, its glow, its vitality, its ability to act, and its strength. Just as too heavy a weight will cause scales to go down, too light a weight will make them go up, and the correct weight will keep them even, so too it is with food and the body. . . . Thus, as a practitioner of meditation you should feed your body not out of desire for food or love of it but solely for the purpose of subduing hunger.

After spending the day in mental concentration, self-controlled, you should shake off sleepiness and throughout the night as well submit

[18]Alternative English translation, I. B. Horner, *The Middle Length Sayings* (London: Pali Text Society, 1954), 1:70–82.

yourself to the discipline of yoga. Do not think that your awareness is endowed with the qualities of awareness when, in the midst of it, drowsiness manifests itself in your heart. When sleepiness threatens, you should resolve upon exertion and steadfastness, strength and courage. You should recite clearly those texts that have been taught to you, and you should teach them to others and think about them yourself. To stay awake constantly, splash water on your face, look around in all directions, and look at the stars. . . . Fear, joy, and grief can win out over sleepiness; therefore, at the onset of sleepiness you should foster these three. You should bring on fear by thinking of the coming of death, joy by remembering you have embraced the Dharma, and sorrow by musing upon the boundless sufferings that come with rebirth. By this and other means, my friend, you should seek to stay awake. For what wise person would wish to spend his life unproductively in bed? . . . The first of the three watches of the night, you should spend in practice, but then you should resort to lying down, for the sake of resting your body. You should lie on your right side, staying awake in your heart, your mind tranquil, fixed on the thought of light. In the third watch, get up and, either walking or sitting, continue your practice of yoga, your mind pure, your senses under control. . . .

Furthermore, my friend, you should choose a place to practice that is isolated, quiet, and conducive to yoga; keeping the body in solitude makes for a mind that is aloof. But if your mind is not at peace, if you are passionate and do not opt for a solitary lifestyle, you will get hurt; it is like someone who has missed the path and is walking on the ground full of thorns. One who delights in being alone, eats anywhere, wears anything, and resides by himself is known as one who accomplishes his purpose. For he has tasted tranquillity, his mind is made up, and he avoids the company of others as though it were a thorn.

Sit down cross-legged in some solitary place, hold your back straight, and direct your mindfulness in front of you, to the tip of your nose, your forehead, or the space between your eyebrows. Make your wandering mind focus entirely on one thing. Now if that mental affliction—a lustful imagination—should rear its head, do not abide it but brush it off as though it were dust on your clothes. For even if you have consciously rid yourself of desires, . . . there remains an innate proclivity toward them, like a fire hidden in the ashes. This, my friend, must be extinguished by meditation, like a fire put out by water. Otherwise, from that innate proclivity, desires will grow back again, as plants do from a seed. Only by its destruction will they cease to be, as plants whose roots are destroyed. . . .

Now if malice or thoughts of violence should unsettle your mind, you should use their antidotes to make it calm, the way a jewel settles muddied water. Know that their antidotes are love and compassion, for the opposition between them is eternal, like that between light and darkness. Those who have controlled wickedness but still harbor malicious thoughts throw dirt onto themselves, the way an elephant does after a bath. What noble, compassionate person could wish to impose further suffering on mortals who are already afflicted by sickness, death, old age, and so forth? . . . Therefore, abandon what is demeritorious, and meditate on what is meritorious, for that will cause you to attain your goals in this world, as well as the ultimate goal. . . .

Now if your thoughts should turn to the prosperity or lack thereof of your own family members, you should examine the inherent nature of the world of living beings in order to suppress them. Among beings who are being dragged along through saṃsāra by the force of karma, who is a stranger, who is a relative? It is due to delusion that one person seems attached to another. Your relative in a past life has become a stranger, and in a future life a stranger may become a relative. Just as birds assemble here and there in the evening to roost, so it is with the closeness of relatives and strangers from one birth to the next. . . . He who was your beloved relative in another existence—what is he to you now, or you to him? Therefore, you should not let your mind dwell on thoughts of your family; in saṃsāra there is no steady distinction between relatives and nonrelatives. . . .

Now if thoughts should arise in your mind that this country or that country is peaceful or fortunate or that alms are easy to get there, discard them, my friend, and do not dwell on them in any way whatsoever. For you know that the whole world everywhere is plagued by one problem or another. . . . Whether by cold, heat, disease, or danger, people are always being oppressed; nowhere in this world is there a refuge. There is no country where fear does not exist, where the people are not in terror of old age, sickness, and death. . . .

Now if you should have any thoughts that assume that there is no death, make efforts to ward them off, as though they were an illness you had come down with. Not even for a moment should you trust in the continuity of life. Like a tiger lying in wait, death can strike down the unsuspecting at any time. Do not think "I am strong, I am young." Death does not consider age but kills in all circumstances. Realizing the world to be insubstantial and ephemeral like a bubble, what sane person could ever fail to take death into consideration?

In summation then, my friend, in order to avoid having all of these thoughts, you should become a master of mindfulness. . . . In order to obtain gold, one must wash away the dirt—first the big clods and then, to cleanse it further, the smaller ones, until finally one retains pure particles of gold. Just so, in order to obtain liberation, one must discipline the mind and wash away from it first the big clods of one's faults and then, to purify it further, the smaller ones until finally one retains pure particles of Dharma.

Source: Translated from *The Saundarananda of Aśvaghoṣa,* ed. E. H. Johnston (reprint edition, Delhi: Motilal Banarsidass, 1975), pp. 96–111.[19]

3.5.6 How to Walk on Water and Fly through the Air

Meditators who are very advanced in the practice of concentration and adept at entering the various trances that come with tranquillity (śamatha) meditation are said to have developed such control over their minds that they can

---

[19]Alternative English translation, Johnston, *The Saundarananda,* part 2, pp. 77–87.

visualize at will any object of meditation, even if it is not physically in front of them. Thus, for example, if they have been concentrating on a clay disk, the so-called "earth-device," they no longer need to look at it but can visually call it to mind anywhere, with their eyes open or closed. With further efforts, by means of "sustained resolve," such visualizations can be made to last even beyond the period of actual concentration (as though, perhaps, we could control and regulate the visual after-images that sometimes flash in our minds after we look hard at something for a long time). Finally, with still further practice, such visualizations can be extended to the other senses as well, so that meditators have the power not only to "see" things in their "mind's eye" but also to hear, smell, taste, and touch them. They can, in other words, mentally "create" a completely convincing reality.

At this point, which is thought to come in the fourth trance level of śamatha meditation, adepts are ready to develop so-called supernatural, or "magical," powers such as walking through walls, diving into the earth, walking on water, or flying through the air. In his *Visuddhimagga,* Buddhaghosa is quite straightforward about how this is done: It starts simply by concentratedly developing the image and after-image of the earth-device and then imposing it upon one's perception of water or thin air. Once this has been done, it is simply a matter of hopping on. Unfortunately, Buddhaghosa is less clear about how the meditator makes others perceive this meditationally created reality.

Walking on water and flying through the air were generally seen as attractive by-products of advanced stages of meditation but not as aims in themselves. In fact, Buddhist texts are careful to warn against infatuation with such supernatural powers. The Vinaya has a rule against the demonstration of them in public, and they are roundly seen as potentially dangerous byways that can lead a meditator to stray from the road to complete enlightenment, the road that ends with arhatship or Buddhahood.

If you want to walk on water without breaking its surface, you should enter a trance focused on the earth-device and, coming out of it, mentally mark out an area, thinking, "May the water in this place become earth." Then you should do the meditation . . . and make a firm resolution. And with the sustaining of that resolution, the area of water that had been marked off becomes earth, and you walk on that. . . . Not only can you walk on it, you can adopt any posture you wish such as sitting, standing, lying. . . . The water becomes earth for oneself only; for everyone else it remains water, and fish, turtles, and birds swim about there as they like. However, if you want to make it become earth for others as well, you can do so. When the time set for it to remain so comes to an end, it becomes water again. . . .

If you who want to fly through the air like a bird, you should enter a trance focused on the earth-device, and come out of it. If you want to fly cross-legged, you should mentally mark off an area the size of a seat to sit down crosslegged on. . . . If you want to fly lying down, you should mark off an area the size of a bed. If you want to stroll through the air, you should mark off an area the size of a path. Then you should do the meditation . . . and make a firm resolution: "May the air in such and such a space become earth," and, with that resolve, it becomes earth. . . .

But if you fly through the air, you should also have obtained the divine eye. Why? So as to be able to see mountains, trees, and other obstacles you might meet on the way. . . . What should you do when you see them? You should go into the fourth trance, come out of it, do the necessary meditation, and firmly resolve: "May these mountains, trees, and other obstacles become space. . . . " What is more, you should have the divine eye so as to be able to come down in an isolated spot. Otherwise, you might land in a public place, in a bathing place, or at a city gate and so be visible to many people.

Source: Translated from *Visuddhimagga,* ed. Henry Clarke Warren and D. D. Kosambi (Cambridge, MA: Harvard University Press, 1950), pp. 333–34.[20]

3.5.7 The Trance of Cessation

Extraordinary powers such as flying through the air are said to be achievable by a meditator in the fourth trance, the highest level of the realm of form. But śamatha meditation does not stop there. Indeed, the meditator is encouraged to proceed beyond the realm of form to the trances of the formless realm, in which concentration moves from its focus on material objects to successive one-pointed contemplations of the spheres of infinite space, infinite consciousness, nothingness, and then neither perception nor nonperception. All of this can culminate in what is known as the trance of cessation (nirodha), a state in which all mental and most bodily functions are suspended. The meditator in such a state does not have thoughts, feelings, or sensory awareness of either the outside or the inside world. Indeed, it is said that meditators, before entering cessation, must set a time limit for their trance or predetermine circumstances that would occasion their emergence from it, lest they not be able to get out of it. For, because they are immune to all sensory stimuli, no amount of shouting or shaking would serve to awaken them. Typically, the time limit set for the trance of cessation seems to be no more than seven days, although Buddhist legends do recount the cases of monks who, rather than dying, enter into cessation with the intention of emerging from it only at the time of the future Buddha Maitreya.

The relationship of the trance of nirodha to nirvāṇa is not easily explained. Sometimes the two terms are very nearly equated; in both states, the normal processes of karmic continuity are interrupted. Alternatively, the trance of cessation, because it is not permanent, is seen as a meditative foretaste of nirvāṇa in this life, something that inspires one to go on. On the other hand, it should be noted that the Buddha did not attain nirvāṇa or pass into parinirvāṇa from the trance of cessation, but only after redescending to the level of the fourth trance, still in the realm of form and consciousness. This too may be another expression of the Buddhist notion of the Middle Path.

[20]Alternative English translation, Bhikkhu Ñyāṇamoli, *The Path of Purification* (reprint edition, Berkeley: Shambhala Publications, 1976), 1:433–35.

What then is the trance of cessation? It is the shutting down, by means of progressive cessation, of the mind and all mental factors. . . .

Why do people enter the trance? They become tired of the arising and falling of karmic constituents and enter the trance thinking, "May we dwell in bliss by becoming without thought, and here and now experience the cessation that is nirvāṇa."

How does entrance into the trance occur? . . . A monk who wishes to enter the trance of cessation finishes his meal, cleans his hands and feet, and sits down on a specially prepared seat in a secluded place. He crosses his legs, sits up straight, and establishes mindfulness in front of him. He then enters the first level of trance and, emerging from it, has insight into the fact that it is constituted by elements that are impermanent, suffering, and devoid of any Self. . . . Then he enters the second trance level and, emerging from it, has insight into the fact that it is similarly so constituted. And so it is with the third trance level, the fourth trance level, the trance of the sphere of infinite space, and the trance of the sphere of infinite consciousness. He has insight into the fact that all of them are constituted by elements that are impermanent, suffering, and devoid of any Self.

Then he enters the trance of the sphere of nothingness and, emerging from it, carries out the fourfold preparation:

(1) He resolves that no damage will come to the property of others, . . . that such things as his robe and bowl, the seat he is on, and the room he is in will not be damaged or destroyed by fire, flood, wind, thieves, rats, and the like while he is in a trance. . . .

(2) He resolves that he will emerge from his trance should his services be required by the sangha . . . for the carrying out of any formal sangha business. . . .

(3) He resolves that he will emerge from his trance should he be called by the teacher . . . for the imparting of the Dharma. . . .

(4) He determines how long his remaining life span is, so that his trance will not be cut off by death. . . .

Now when, after emerging from the trance of the sphere of nothingness, he has carried out this fourfold preparation, he enters the trance of neither perception nor nonperception. Then, after one or two moments of thought have passed, he achieves mindlessness, he reaches the trance of cessation. Why do his thoughts not continue after one or two moments? Because he is applying himself to cessation. This monk, who has yoked together both tranquillity and insight and has mounted through the eight trances, is practicing progressive cessation; he is not striving for the trance of the sphere of neither perception nor nonperception.

If a monk enters the trance of the sphere of neither perception nor nonperception without carrying out the fourfold preparation upon emerging from the trance of the sphere of nothingness, he will not be able to achieve mindlessness and will have to return to the sphere of nothingness. . . .

What is the duration of the trance? It lasts for the length of time the monk has set for it, unless it is interrupted by death, by duty to the sangha, or by a call from the teacher.

How does one emerge from it? Emergence from the trance of cessation is of two types: for a nonreturner, by the attaining of the fruit of non-returning; for an arhat, by attaining the fruit of arhatship.

Toward what is the mind of one who emerges from the trance inclined? It is inclined toward nirvāṇa. . . .

What is the difference between one who is dead and one who is in the trance of cessation? . . . When a monk is dead, when he has passed away, all the elements that constitute his body, speech, and mind cease and are still; his life is ended, his bodily warmth subsides, and he is cut off from the sphere of the senses. When a monk enters the trance of cessation, . . . all the elements that constitute his body, speech, and mind cease and are still, but his life is not ended, his bodily warmth does not subside, and he is not cut off from the sphere of the senses.

Is the trance of cessation karmically constituted or not? It should not be thought of as karmically constituted or not karmically constituted, as worldly or supramundane. Why? Because it does not have independent self-existence. But since one who attains it comes to attain it, it *can* be thought of as being produced, not unproduced.

Source: Translated from *Visuddhimagga of Buddhaghosācariya,* ed. Henry Clarke Warren and D. D. Kosambi (Cambridge, MA: Harvard University Press, 1950), pp. 604, 607–11.[21]

3.6 DOCTRINAL ISSUES

The Mainstream Buddhist schools as a group were basically in agreement about the nature and thrust of the Four Noble Truths. That, at any rate, was the opinion of Vasumitra, a scholar of the fourth century C.E., who wrote a treatise on the origins of Buddhist sectarianism. But there were, of course, issues that separated the schools from one another and doctrinal stances for which particular sects were known. We have already had occasion to encounter the Personalist view (in 3.2.2). In the following selections, we shall first review the history of Buddhist schisms from a Theravādin perspective and then look at selected views of two other schools: the notion of the existence of all dharmas in all three times adopted by the Sarvāstivādins, and the view of the Buddha maintained by the Mahāsāṃghikas.

3.6.1 A Theravādin Claim to Orthodoxy

The history of Mainstream Buddhist schools is closely bound up to traditions concerning the Buddhist councils. According to these accounts, most of which are of questionable historicity, some elders gathered immediately after the

---

[21]Alternative English translation, Bhikkhu Ñāṇamoli, *The Path of Purification* (Colombo: R. Semage, 1956), pp. 824, 828–33.

parinirvāṇa of the Buddha in order to compile and preserve his teachings. This was the First Council, held at Rājagṛha. One hundred years later, a Second Council was supposedly held at Vaiśālī, at which the expulsion of certain "heretics" was confirmed. In the selection that follows, these "heretics" are accused of various wrong *practices* (not beliefs); in time, however, some *doctrinal* issues were read back into this situation. It is claimed by some that the end result of this council was a split between the school of the elders and the school of the Mahāsāṃghikas (see 3.6.3), although whether the latter had anything to do with the heretical practices of the monks at Vaiśālī is unlikely. A century or so later, at the time of King Aśoka (see 2.6.3), a Third Council was held that resulted, among other things, in the splitting off of the school of the Sarvāstivādins (see 3.6.2). By this time, however, a number of other sects had emerged. In fact, traditionally, it is said that there developed eighteen different Mainstream Buddhist schools. Some of these coexisted side by side in India for many centuries. Obviously, the question of who split off from whom and who represents the "true" or "original" community of the Buddha depends a lot on the sectarian group to which one happens to belong. The following account of all this is written from the perspective of the Theravādin sect, the only one of the Mainstream Buddhist schools that has survived institutionally up to the present.

At the time of the Buddha's parinirvāṇa in Kusināra, . . . seven hundred thousand disciples of the Buddha assembled. The elder Kassapa was the leader of this assembly . . . and he chose five hundred of the most prominent arhats to hold a Dharma Council. . . . At this council there were many monks, the original depositories of the Teaching, who had all attained perfection . . . : Kassapa, the foremost of those advocating ascetic practices; Ānanda, the foremost of those widely learned in the sūtras; Upāli, the foremost of those in matters of the Vinaya, . . . and many others.

These five hundred elders recited together the Dharma and the Vinaya. Because theirs was a compilation made by a council of elders, it is called the Theravāda (the Tradition of the Elders). They compiled the Dharma and the Vinaya by asking Upāli about the Vinaya and the wise Ānanda about the Dharma. These two elders were perfect in their knowledge of the true Dharma, which they had obtained from the Buddha himself. . . . Because these elders who held the First Council were the original depositories of the Teaching, the Theravāda is also called the "original tradition."

When 100 years had passed and a second century was begun, a great schism occurred in the Theravāda. In Vaiśālī, twelve thousand Vajjiputtas assembled and upheld ten points as being part of the doctrine of the Buddha. They claimed that it was permissible (1) to store salt in a horn, (2) to eat when the sun's shadow was two fingers' breadth past noon; (3) to go to town to beg again after having eaten in the monastery; (4) to hold assemblies separately from other monks dwelling in the same residence; (5) to approve an act of the sangha when the whole sangha was not present; (6) to justify one's actions as being in accord with another's example; (7) to drink buttermilk; (9) to drink toddy; and (10) to use mats without fringes. All these were contrary to the Dharma, contrary to the Vinaya, and divergent from the teaching of the Master. . . .

In order to suppress these teachings, many disciples of the Buddha . . . assembled. Among them were eight great monks, . . . and they refuted the doctrine of the ten points and expelled those evil heretics. They then chose seven hundred monks from among the most prominent arhats and held a Dharma Council at Vaiśālī. It lasted eight months and is known as the Second Council.

The wrongdoers, the Vajjiputtaka monks who had been expelled by the elders, then formed a separate faction, and a great number of them—ten thousand in all—assembled and held a council of their own. This council was called the Great Council. These Great Council monks [Mahāsaṃgītikas] maintained perverse doctrines. They broke up the original compilation of the teachings and made another one. They took sūtras that were collected in one place and put them together elsewhere. They disrupted the standard organization of the Dharma into five parts. Understanding neither what was explained nor what was left unexplained, neither what was explicit nor what was inferred, these monks put some sayings of the Buddha together with others where they did not belong. Blinded by literal meanings, they destroyed the intent of the teachings. They rejected parts of the profound Dharma and Vinaya and created instead counterfeit sūtras and a false Vinaya.

These Mahāsaṃgītikas were the first schismatics, but their example was followed by many others. Thus, a split soon occurred within their own community between the Gokulikas and the Ekabyohāras. Then the Gokulikas split into two . . . and there was yet another subsect . . . forming altogether five traditions that stemmed from the Mahāsaṃgītikas.

In the pure tradition of the elders, other schisms occurred: the Mahiṃsāsakas and the Vajjiputtakās formed two factions. From the Vajjiputtakas, four sects arose. . . . And later, from the Vajjiputtakas, two sects emerged, the Sabbatthivādas [Sarvāstivādins] and the Dhammaguttas [Dharmaguptas]. From the Sabbatthivādas [one, two, and eventually three more sects split off in turn].

Altogether there were eighteen sects: seventeen schismatic traditions and one orthodoxy. The most excellent Theravāda is like a great banyan tree: it represents the complete teaching of the Buddha with nothing added to it and nothing taken away. The other sects grew from it like thorns on a tree.

Source: Translated from *Dīpavaṃsa,* ed. Hermann Oldenberg (reprint edition, New Delhi: Asian Educational Services, 1982), pp. 34–37.[22]

3.6.2 The Sarvāstivādins on Time

The Sarvāstivādins, mentioned in the listing above, emerged as a sect around the time of King Aśoka. By then, the doctrine of impermanence, which viewed

---

[22]Alternative English translation, Oldenberg, *Dīpavaṃsa,* pp. 138–42.

the elements of existence (dharmas) as momentary phenomena, arising and passing away in a single present instant, was causing many thinkers to reflect on the problem of how to account for the apparent continuity of things, for the relationship of such distinct, momentary dharmas to one another. The Sarvāstivādins, in particular, were concerned about this issue (among others). If only the present exists, they worried, what happens to the doctrine of karma, which wants to claim the efficacity and reality of past causes and future fruits? This, at first, seems a somewhat bizarre concern, until it is remembered that Buddhists generally accepted the view that the perceptibility of something implies its existence, for only existing things (dharmas) can actually be perceived. Thus, the fact of perception requires at least the reality of both the perceiving subject and the perceived object. Given this assumption, the question was asked how one could claim that the Buddha (for example) could *perceive* an event of a person's past life if that past event did not in some sense exist? Similarly, if a future thing (for example, the karmic effect of one's present deed) did not in some sense exist, how could it be accurately foretold? And if past karmic causes or future karmic effects did not exist, that is, were not perceptible, what did that do to the reality of the doctrine of karma?

The Sarvāstivādins sought their own solution to these questions in the simple affirmation that past and future dharmas, as well as present ones, do "exist" and also are cognizable. This was not to argue that past and future dharmas are in all respects like present ones. Various Sarvāstivādin scholars, in fact, sought to distinguish them in a variety of ways. One solution was to claim that although past and future dharmas can be said to exist, they differ from present ones in that they lack "activity," or "function" (kāritra).

Such a "solution," of course, was not without its own obscurities and philosophical difficulties, and it implied a particular understanding of what was meant by "existence." Indeed, the Sarvāstivādin theory as a whole was hotly disputed by other Mainstream Buddhist schools (for example, the Theravādins), and later attacked by Mahāyānists as well. But the Sarvāstivādin tradition was as important for the problems it addressed as for the solutions it propounded. It insisted on a metaphysic that would allow for both the assertion of impermanence and for the maintenance of a sense of continuity from one time frame to the next. The context of controversy with the Theravādins is reflected in the following selection, from the fourth book of the Sarvāstivādin *Abhidharma*, which reads like the transcript of a possible debate.

The Theravādin monk Maudgalyāyana said, "The past and the future do not exist; only the present and dharmas that are not karmically constituted [such as nirvāṇa] exist."

In this regard, one should ask, "Did the Buddha not state, and state well, in a sūtra, that there are three roots of demerit: greed, hatred, and delusion?"

He must answer, "That is so."

Then one should ask, "In regard to greed, which is a root of demerit, are there not some who have perceived it in the past, who perceive it now, and who will perceive it in the future as being demeritorious?"

He will answer, "That is so."

Then one should ask, "Then what is this thing that is perceived—is it past, present, or future?"

If he says that what is perceived is past, respond that the past exists. Because it can be perceived, one cannot claim that the past does not exist; to do so is not in accord with logic.

If he says that what is perceived is future, respond that the future exists. Because it can be perceived, one cannot claim that the future does not exist; to do so is not in accord with logic.

If he says that what is perceived is present, respond that it follows that one person is holding two thoughts at the same time—the thought of the object perceived and the thought of the subject perceiving. That is not in accord with logic.

If he does not admit that one person is holding two thoughts at the same time, . . . he should not respond that what one perceives is present. To do so is not in accord with logic.

If he says that one does not perceive the past, present, or future, then there is no one who has perceived in the past, who is perceiving now, or who will perceive in the future a root of demerit as being demeritorious.

If there is no one who has seen this, who sees it now, or who will see it, there is no one who has been disgusted, who is disgusted, or who will be disgusted with greed (which is a root of demerit). If that is so, there is no one who has become detached, who is becoming detached, or who will become detached from greed. If that is so, there is no one who has been, who is, or who will be liberated from greed. And if that is so, there is no one who has attained, who is attaining, or who will attain nirvāṇa.

Source: Translated from Devaśarman, *Vijñānakāya* (Taishō shinshū daizōkyō, ed. J. Takakusu and K. Watanabe [Tokyo, 1924–29], no. 1539, 26:531a–b).[23]

3.6.3 The Mahāsāṃghikas on the Buddha

Another point of dispute among the Mainstream Buddhist schools was the nature of the Buddha. Some, as we have seen, maintained that the Buddha was essentially a historical figure who, though endowed with great powers and wisdom, was not fundamentally to be distinguished from the rest of humanity. Others, however, tended to magnify and exalt the Buddha, asserting that his real nature was eternal and fundamentally different from that of the world. The Mahāsāṃghikas were of the latter opinion. For them, the Buddha was essentially transcendent, though he conformed to the ways of the world. Thus, he seemed to exert himself but felt no fatigue, he washed regularly though no dirt ever adhered to his body, he sat in the shade but the sun did not oppress him, he took medicine though he was never really sick. According to

[23] Alternative French translation, Louis de La Vallée Poussin, "La controverse du temps et du pudgala dans le Vijñānakāya," *Etudes asiatiques* (Paris, 1925), 1:346–47. Much the same issue is argued out, but from the Theravādin perspective, in the fifth book of the Pali Abhidhamma; see S. Z. Aung and C. A. F. Rhys Davids, *Points of Controversy* (London: Pali Text Society, 1915), pp. 84ff.

tradition, the Mahāsāṃghikas were one of the earliest sects to form, arising about one hundred years after the parinirvāṇa of the Buddha and foreshadowing in their doctrines many of the later views of the Mahāyāna. The following selection lists succinctly the doctrines they maintained about the Buddha.

Together, the Mahāsāṃghikas and its three related subsects maintained that:

All Blessed Buddhas are supramundane; all Tathāgatas are without defilement; all Tathāgatas, whenever they speak, preach the Dharma; the Buddha can speak the whole Dharma in a single sound; nothing the Buddha says is without meaning; the Tathāgata's physical body is boundless; the Tathāgata's power is boundless; the length of the Buddha's life is boundless; the Buddha never ceases to convert beings by planting the seed of faith in their hearts; the Buddha never sleeps or dreams; the Tathāgata answers questions instantly without having to think of the answer; . . . in a single thought, instantaneously, the Buddha understands all dharmas; in a single thought linked to wisdom, instantaneously, the Buddha knows all dharmas; Blessed Buddhas retain constant knowledge of the destruction of past karma and knowledge of the nonproduction of future karma up until their parinirvāṇa.

Source: Translated from Vasumitra, *Samayabhedoparacanacakra* (Taishō shinshū daizōkyō, ed. J. Takakusu and K. Watanabe [Tokyo, 1924–29], no. 2031, 49:15b–c).[24]

[24]Alternative French translation, André Bareau, "Trois traités sur les sectes bouddhiques," *Journal asiatique* 242 (1954): 238–40.

CHAPTER 4

The Dharma: Some Mahāyāna Perspectives

The Mahāyāna, or "Great Vehicle," is the type of Buddhism that predominates today in China, Korea, Japan, Vietnam, and Tibet, but historically it has been influential throughout the whole of the Buddhist world. It is generally thought to have started in India around the first century B.C.E., but how and why it originated are a matter of great dispute. Some scholars contend that it began as a lay movement, a breakaway reaction against the ever-growing elitism of conservative monks and against monastic monopolies on enlightenment and the definition of doctrine, not to mention on the increasing wealth of the sangha. Others add that these new groups of laypersons were centered on the cult of stūpas, with all the devotionalism that implied. This view, however, has been countered by those who maintain that the laity had little to do with the new movement. Instead, they see the origins of the Mahāyāna in groups of monks who found their identity and meaning in certain new scriptures and who were part of a cult not of stūpas but of books.[1]

It is probably wrong to think of the Mahāyāna as having resulted from some sort of schism, if by schism we mean some sort of divergence in practice and belief such that one group is unable or unwilling to live in community with another. One scholar, in fact, prefers to talk of the Mahāyāna not as a sect or school but as a vision or motivation.[2] In any case, whatever their view of its origins, scholars are, for the most part, inclined to talk of "emergences" and "evolutions" of the Mahāyāna rather than of radical departures. Clearly, it is possible to point to many Mahāyānist elements within early Buddhism and within Mainstream Buddhist schools (for example, the Mahāsāṃghikas); at the same time, it is indisputable that it took centuries for some of the Mahāyāna's fundamental doctrines to emerge fully.

[1]On the origins of the Mahāyāna and the various views of Etienne Lamotte, Akira Hirasawa, and Gregory Schopen, see Paul Williams, *Mahāyāna Buddhism: The Doctrinal Foundations* (London: Routledge, 1989), ch. 1.

[2]Paul Williams, *Buddhist Thought* (London: Routledge, 2000), p. 99.

It may be better, therefore, to think of the Mahāyāna as a movement that had a tendency to take certain elements of early Buddhism and extend them to the limits of their logic, expanding, embellishing, and sometimes questioning them in the process. For example, to the anātman doctrine, which asserted that people have no selves but can be analyzed as consisting of an ever-changing combination of certain fundamental elements of reality (dharmas), Mahāyānists asked: "Is it wise to stop our analysis at those elements of reality? Should we not go one step further and assert not only the 'no-Self of persons' but also the 'no-Self of dharmas'?" Or to the claim that compassion for others was a good thing, Mahāyānists posed the question "Then would it not be even better to have a *great* compassion for *all* living beings, everywhere, at all times?" And to the thought that enlightened beings motivated by compassion (such as Buddhas) are supposed to guide others to enlightenment and have the power to prolong their lives here on earth in order to do so, they said: "Then shouldn't they prolong their lives indefinitely so as to help all living beings, everywhere, attain enlightenment and escape from saṃsāra? And if all beings are ultimately destined for enlightenment, does that not imply that all beings have within themselves the potential for enlightenment, the guarantee of enlightenment, for all intents and purposes, the actuality of enlightenment? And if the Buddha was a great man, who had great compassion and who knew how to employ his magical powers as skillful means for converting others, perhaps his whole life was but one great manifestation of his magical powers. Perhaps the events of the historical Gautama's life—his birth, enlightenment, first sermon, and parinirvāṇa—were but a clever display of magical powers. Maybe the 'real' Buddha was not the historical Buddha but a transcendent, eternal figure. And if this real Buddha could use his magical powers to project other Buddhas, was there one Buddha, or many Buddhas, or no Buddha?"

It is unlikely, of course, that any of these lines of thought was pursued in so simplistic a manner, but these questions do point to what has been called the "speculatively ambitious" nature of Mahāyāna thought.[3] In the selections that follow, we will be able to view some of the results of that speculation.

4.1 PRELIMINARY: THE PARABLE OF THE BURNING HOUSE

In the year 654 C.E., some time after he had returned to China from the sixteen years he had spent traveling and studying in India, the great Chinese Mahāyāna Buddhist scholar and pilgrim Hsüan-tsang wrote a letter to a monk he had met at Bodhgaya, the Venerable Prajñādeva. After thanking him for some gifts of cloth he had received, Hsüan-tsang recalls the time the two of them had participated in a debate in India, in front of the king at Kanyākubja. "It was unavoidable," he declares, "that there had been bitter arguments" as

[3]The term is from Hajime Nakamura, "Buddhism, Schools of: Mahāyāna Buddhism," *Encyclopedia of Religion,* ed. Mircea Eliade (New York: Macmillan, 1987), 2:457.

one party had upheld the views of the Mahāyāna and the other the teachings of the Hīnayāna. "Thus," he apologizes, "I probably offended you during the debate, but as soon as the meeting was over, all resentment cleared immediately." And he goes on to praise Prajñādeva as "a good scholar of great eloquence and noble character" and wishes him the best in spreading the true Dharma.

Then, however, Hsüan-tsang's tone appears to change. Declaring that there is no doctrine as perfect as the Mahāyāna, he regrets that his friend does not have faith in it, telling him he is like someone opting for a goat or deer cart instead of an ox cart, and he openly berates him: "Learned scholar that you are, why are you so persistent in your biased views? It befits you to embrace the right views of Mahāyāna teachings at an early date, so that you will not repent at the moment of death."[4]

Hsüan-tsang's mixture of compassion and contempt is not atypical of the Mahāyānists' assessment of themselves, as a school, *vis-à-vis* what they pejoratively called the Hīnayāna, or "Lesser Vehicle." It is important, however, to note that in these discussions Mahāyānists do not speak only in terms of an opposition between the greater and the lesser vehicles. More commonly, a threefold distinction (already found in certain Mainstream Buddhist texts) is drawn between the bodhisattva-yāna (the vehicle of the bodhisattva, sometimes also called the Buddha-yāna), the pratyekabuddha-yāna (the vehicle of solitary Buddhas—those who attain enlightenment on their own, without the immediate help of a teacher, but who do not then go on to share their enlightenment with others by preaching), and the śrāvaka-yāna (the vehicle of disciples, or of "hearers"—those who attain enlightenment as the result of being taught the Dharma by others, usually the Buddha).

The bodhisattva vehicle corresponds, of course, to the Mahāyāna, while the other two belong to the Hīnāyana. The three are sometimes compared to three animals crossing a river: an elephant (the bodhisattva), who has no trouble whatsoever; a horse (the pratyekabuddha), who if the current is strong, may not be able to cross in a straight line; and a rabbit (the śrāvaka), who *can* make it across but who has no idea of how deep the water is because he never touches the bottom.[5]

Another simile, referred to by Hsüan-tsang, is that between an ox-drawn carriage (the bodhisattva-yāna), and a goat cart and a deer cart (the pratyekabuddha-yāna and the śrāvaka-yāna). The *Lotus Sūtra*'s "Parable of the Burning House," in which this analogy is classically set forth, does not, however, stop at drawing distinctions between these three yānas. Instead, it goes one step further to maintain that ultimately there are not three separate vehicles but only one great one (the Mahāyāna), which is the best vehicle, the one true vehicle. The others were held out only as a skillful means in communicating his teaching and attracting followers. The Buddha spoke of them in order to entice "his children" (all sentient beings) out of the "burn-

[4] *The Life of Hsuan-Tsang Compiled by Monk Hui-li,* trans. Li Yung-hsi (Peking: Chinese Buddhist Association, 1959), pp. 239–40.

[5] This metaphor is found in a Central Asian Buddhist text, *The Book of Zambasta: A Khotanese Poem on Buddhism,* ed. and trans. R. E. Emmerick (London: Oxford University Press, 1968), pp. 188–89.

ing house" (a symbol for saṃsāra). Does this mean that there is no Lesser Vehicle or that the Hīnayāna and the Mahāyāna are really the same? And does the end of liberation from saṃsāra justify the Buddha's misleading preaching of Nikāya Buddhism? These and other dilemmas are all raised in the following selection, which remains one of the best known pieces of Mahāyāna literature.

Śāriputra, let us suppose that somewhere, in a village, a town, a city, a country, a region, a kingdom, or a capital, there was a householder who was . . . wealthy and enjoying life. Suppose that he had a great mansion, lofty, vast, built long ago, housing several hundred people. And suppose that this mansion had a single door, that it was covered with thatch, that its terraces were collapsing, that the bases of its pillars were rotting away, and that its walls, partitions, and plaster were falling to pieces. And suppose that all of a sudden the whole mansion burst forth into flames, that the householder managed himself to get out, but that he had several little boys who were still inside.

Now, Śāriputra, let us suppose the following: when this man saw his house ablaze everywhere, engulfed in flames, he was thoroughly frightened and alarmed, and he thought: "Fortunately, I was quickly able to get out of this burning house through the door, without getting burned by those flames, but my sons, my little boys, are still inside, playing with their playthings, enjoying and amusing themselves. They do not know, do not realize, do not understand that the house is on fire, and are not upset. Even caught in that inferno, being burned by those flames, in fact, suffering a great deal, they are oblivious to their suffering, and the thought of getting out does not occur to them."

Now, Śāriputra, this man was strong and had powerful arms, so at first he thought, "I am strong-armed and powerful; what if I were to gather all these little boys together in a bunch and carry them all out of the house?"

But then it occurred to him: "This house has a single entrance, and its door is shut. Those little boys are thoughtless and panicky and of an age when they are apt to be foolish. What if they start running about when I call them to me? They will experience misfortune and come to disaster in the flames. Therefore I should first try to warn them of the danger."

So he called out to the little boys: "Come, my children, get out! The house is ablaze with a mass of flames! Do not stay there, or you will all be burned in the conflagration and come to misfortune and disaster!"

But the little boys did not pay any attention to the words of the man, though he desired only their well-being. They were not perturbed, not afraid, not frightened. They did not reflect, did not dash out of the house, did not understand, did not comprehend even the meaning of the word "conflagration." Instead, they ran around playing here and there, occasionally gazing out at their father. Why? Simply because of their being foolish children.

So then, Śāriputra, the man thought: "The house is burning, ablaze, a mass of flames. I do not wish for my little boys to come to misfortune and disaster in this inferno. Therefore, I should by some skillful means cause these children to come out of the house." Now the man knew the mental dispositions of his children and understood their interests, and he knew that there were many kinds of toys that pleased them, that they wanted and desired and that were dear and captivating to them but that were hard to obtain. . . . So he said to them: "Children, all of those toys that are pleasing to you, that are marvelous and wonderful, that you ardently long to possess, of various colors and many kinds—for instance, little ox carts, goat carts, and deer carts—so dear and captivating; well, I have put all of them outside the gate of the house so that you can play with them. Come on! Run out of the house! I will give each of you whatever you need and want. Come quickly! Come out for the sake of these playthings!"

Then the little boys, hearing the names of the toys that were pleasing to them, that they so wished for, so imagined having, and so longed for, . . . quickly dashed out of the burning house at great speed, not waiting for one another and calling out: "Who will be first? Who will be foremost?" . . .

Then the man, seeing his children out of the house safe and sound and knowing them to be out of danger, sat down in the open village square, conscious of his joy and delight, free from sorrow, his troubles gone, without worry. But his children went up to him and said: "Daddy, give us now those various pleasing toys—the little ox carts, and the goat carts, and the deer carts."

However, Śāriputra, that man then gave his children . . . ox carts only. They were made of seven precious materials, equipped with railings, hung with strings of bells, high and lofty, adorned with marvelous and wonderful jewels, brightened by garlands of gems, decorated with wreaths of flowers. . . . And, Śāriputra, that man reflected: "I am very wealthy and have many treasures and storehouses; I could give other vehicles to these my children, but why should I? All of these children are my children, and all of them are dear and delightful to me. I should think of all of my children as being equal and the same [and should give all of them the best vehicle]." . . .

Now what do you think, Śāriputra, did that man tell a lie to his children by first promising them three vehicles and then later giving them only great vehicles, the best vehicles?

Śāriputra said: "No indeed, Blessed One! No indeed! There is no reason to think that in this case that man was a liar, because he was using skillful means in order to get his children to come out of the burning house, and that gave them the gift of life. Moreover, Blessed One, in addition to getting back their very lives, they also received all those toys. But, Blessed One, even if that man had not given them a single cart, he would still not have been a liar. How so? Because, Blessed One, that man first reflected: 'By the use of skillful means, I will liberate these children from a great heap of suffering. . . .'"

Well said, Śāriputra, well said! You have spoken well. In just this way, the Tathāgata too . . . is father of the world; he has attained the highest perfection of the knowledge of great skillful means, he is greatly compassionate, his mind is unwearied, and his concern is for the well-being of others. He appears in this threefold universe, which is like a burning house being consumed by a mass of suffering and sadness—a shelter with an old roof—in order to liberate from desire, hatred, and delusion those beings who remain ensnared in a veil of darkness—the obscuring blindness of ignorance, of birth, old age, sickness, death, sorrow, grief, suffering, sadness, and irritation—and in order to stimulate them toward unsurpassed, complete enlightenment. . . . And he sees that even as they are buffeted by this mass of suffering, they play, enjoy and amuse themselves, without being perturbed or afraid or frightened, without knowing or realizing or being upset or trying to escape. Even there, in that threefold universe that is like a burning house, they enjoy themselves and run about. For though they are being afflicted by a great deal of suffering, the thought that they are suffering does not occur to them.

So, Śāriputra, the Tathāgata realizes: "I am indeed the father of these beings. I must liberate them from such a great mass of suffering and give the immeasurable, inconceivable bliss of Buddhahood, for them to enjoy. . . ." But, Śāriputra, if I should declare to these beings the strength and knowledge and self-confidence of the Tathāgata by saying to them: "I have the power of knowledge; I have supernatural faculties," without employing skillful means, they would not thereby escape. Why? Because they covet the objects of the five senses, they are not free from the desires of this Triple World. . . .

Therefore, Śāriputra, the Tathāgata must be just like that strong-armed man who refrained from using the strength of his arms, and, employing skillful means, enticed his children out of the burning house . . . by speaking of three vehicles, that is to say, the disciples' vehicle, the pratyekabuddhas' vehicle, and the bodhisattvas' vehicle.

By referring to these three vehicles, he attracts the beings and says to them: "Do not, in this Triple World that is like a burning house, take pleasure in lowly forms, sounds, odors, tastes, and touches. . . . Flee from this Triple World! The three vehicles are yours: the disciples' vehicle, the pratyekabuddhas' vehicle, and the bodhisattvas' vehicle. In this, let me assure you that I will give you the three vehicles; apply yourselves to escaping from the Triple World!" [. . .]

But then, Śāriputra, just as that man who saw his children out of the house, safe and sound, free from danger, . . . gave them only one highest great vehicle, so too, Śāriputra, the completely enlightened arhat, the Tathāgata, when he sees many millions of beings liberated from the Triple World, freed from suffering, fear, terror, and calamity, escaped by the door of the Buddha's teaching . . . and having realized nirvāṇa, . . . brings about the parinirvāṇa of all beings by means of the Buddha-vehicle, knowing them to be his children. He does not teach an individual, personal parinirvāṇa for each of these beings; rather, he causes all those beings to attain parinirvāṇa by means of the great parinirvāṇa, the Tathāgata-parinirvāṇa. And furthermore, Śāriputra, the Tathāgata gives to those beings who have been liberated from the Triple World enjoyable "playthings"—the noble and transcendentally blissful practices of the same type: meditation, liberation, concentration, and trance. And, Śāriputra, just as that man was not a liar when he held out to his children the prospect of three vehicles but then gave them a single great vehicle, . . . so too, Śāriputra, the completely enlightened arhat, the Tathāgata, is not a liar when, using skillful means, he first holds out the prospect of three vehicles and then leads beings to parinirvāṇa by means of a single great vehicle.

Source: Translated from *Saddharmapuṇḍarīka-sūtra,* ed. U. Wogihara and C. Tsuchida (Tokyo: Seigo Kenkyūkai, 1934–35), pp. 70–76.[6]

4.2 BASIC PERSPECTIVES: THE PERFECTION OF WISDOM

Chronological discussions of Mahāyāna doctrine usually start with references to the *Perfection of Wisdom* (*Prajñāpāramitā*) sūtras. This voluminous literature began appearing around the beginning of the Common Era and continued to be produced, expanded, and distilled for the next thousand years in India. The longest *Perfection of Wisdom* sūtra, in 100,000 verses, is truly a magnum opus; the shortest, in one letter ("A"), you have just read. The fact that in this school of thought the meaning of these two texts can be said to be the same should alert us that we are entering a world where language can operate in strange ways. It can be both a trap and a liberation. Prajñāpāramitā literally means the "wisdom gone beyond," and engaging in this literature is somewhat like playing a game of transcendental leapfrog in which the hurdles come in binary pairs. As soon as one jump is made beyond, say, the assertion of something, it is time to make the next jump, beyond its negation. This is a campaign against stumbling at the barriers of thoughts, things, words.

4.2.1 Rāhulabhadra's Verses in Praise of Perfect Wisdom

It is important to remember, however, that all this text is within a particular ideological context. The following verses are found as a preface to a number of different *Perfection of Wisdom* sūtras, including what was most likely the oldest such text, the *Perfection of Wisdom in Eight Thousand Lines* (*Aṣṭasāhasrikā prajñāpāramitā sūtra*). The verses are attributed to Rāhulabhadra, who, according to Tibetan tradition, was one of the eighty-four "accomplished ones" (siddhas) of Indian Buddhism and, reputedly, a teacher of the great philosopher Nāgārjuna (see 4.3.1). His verses are important, for they reflect not only the budding philosophy of transcendent wisdom that goes beyond binary opposites but also the devotional aspect of the school, the fact that here Prajñāpāramitā is treated both as a concept (or nonconcept) and as a goddess, in fact, the Mother of the Buddhas, for it is from her that enlightenment comes.

---

1. Praise to you, Prajñāpāramitā,
   unmeasured, beyond imagining!
   You whose body is irreproachable
   are viewed by those beyond reproach.

[6]Alternative English translation, Hendrik Kern, *Saddharma-puṇḍarīka or The Lotus of the True Law* (Oxford: Clarendon Press, 1884), pp. 72–82.

2. You are untainted like empty space,
beyond discourse, beyond words,
The one who truly sees you
sees the Tathāgata.
3. The wise can discern no difference
between you, rich in noble qualities,
and the Buddha, guru of the world:
it is like moon and moonlight.
4. O fond recipient of devotion,
forebear of the Buddha-Dharma,
compassionate souls who come to you
easily achieve magnanimity beyond compare.
5. You, whose mental disposition is pure,
whose sight is liberating,
success surely awaits anyone
who duly looks upon you, even but once.
6. You are the affectionate mother,
the begetter and nourisher,
of all those heroes who achieved
self-discipline for the sake of others.
7. Good Lady, since the compassionate Buddhas,
gurus of the world, are your sons,
you are thus the grandmother
of all beings.
8. O Irreproachable One, you appear
when all the untainted perfections appear,
just as the stars come out
with the crescent moon.
9. Reaching out to potential converts,
the Tathāgatas praise you everywhere
as having many forms and diverse names,
though you be One.
10. Just as dewdrops evaporate
when touched by the rays of the sun,
so do the faults and theories of professors
dissolve in your presence.
11. In your fierce manifestation,
you engender fear in fools;
in your benign manifestation,
you enable the wise to breathe easily.
12. O Mother, how can anyone who embraces you,
without asserting ownership,
feel desire or hatred
for anything else?
13. You do not come from anywhere,
you are not going anywhere;
there is no place at all
where the wise can apprehend you.
14. Thus those who do not see you
are the ones who reach you,
and reaching you they become free from suffering.
How utterly wonderful this is!

15. Seeing you, one is bound to suffering,
not seeing you, one is also bound.
Seeing you, one is freed from suffering,
not seeing you, one is also freed.
16. You are amazing! You are profound!
You are illustrious! You are not easily known.
Like a magic show,
you are both seen and not seen.
17. Buddhas, pratyekabuddhas, and
disciples have honored you.
You are the one path to liberation;
there is no other—that is certain.
18. Out of compassion for bodily beings, and following
common usage so that they can understand,
Lords of the World [Buddhas] speak of you,
and speak not.
19. Who here is able to praise you,
you who are featureless and without makeup?
Not attached to anything whatever,
you have transcended the whole realm of speech.
20. Nevertheless, since there is a conventional language,
we employ its words to praise you,
though you are beyond praise.
Being satisfied with this, we attain repose.
21. May the praise that I have piled up
by my eulogy of Prajñāpāramitā
quickly make the whole world
intent upon wisdom without peer.

Source: Translated from *Prajñāpāramitāstotra,* ed. Etienne Lamotte, in *Le traité de la grande vertu de sagesse* (Louvain: Institut Orientaliste, 1949–80), pp. 1061–65n. The five verses not edited there are taken from Rajendralal Mitra, *The Sanskrit Buddhist Literature of Nepal* (Calcutta: Asiatic Society of Bengal, 1882), pp. 190–92.[7]

4.2.2 The Heart Sūtra

Rāhulabhadra's verses already introduce us to a number of paradoxes, but they are not that difficult to sort out. Buddhas both *speak* of the Perfection of Wisdom and yet do not "speak" of it. If one merely "sees" the Truth (and one becomes attached to thinking one has found it), one is still bound to suffering; but if one truly *sees* it, one is freed from suffering. Consequently, if one does not truly *see* it, one cannot be liberated and so remains bound, whereas if one manages to resist the temptation to merely "see" it, one is freed.

Such paradoxes are taken even further in the *Heart Sūtra,* which is perhaps the best known *Perfection of Wisdom* text and which to this day is commonly

---

[7]Alternative English translation, Edward Conze, *Buddhist Texts through the Ages* (New York: Harper and Row, 1954), pp. 147–49.

recited, by monks and laity alike, throughout the whole of East Asia and Tibet. Suffice it to point out here a number of its features.

First, in the framework of the text the attempt of the Mahāyāna to distinguish itself from what it called the Hīnayāna is not completely absent. The sūtra is put in the mouth of Avalokiteśvara, one of the most famous bodhisattvas of the Mahāyāna tradition (see 5.2.1), and it is addressed to Śāriputra, a disciple of the Buddha and consequently a representative of Mainstream Buddhism. Moreover, the topics addressed are, for the most part, familiar to us from early Buddhism: the five aggregates (skandhas), the various sense organs, and consciousness—all the categories of the Abhidharma schools of analysis.

Second, all of these elements are here declared to be "empty" (śūnya). The notion of emptiness (śūnyatā) is of central importance to Mahāyāna thought, and we shall encounter it again in the texts that follow. As the *Heart Sūtra* makes clear, empty means "empty of any inherent self-existence" (svabhāva). Svabhāva was a category that was much affirmed by the Mainstream Buddhist Abhidharma schools. It implies that all elements of reality have something like an essential self-identity, an essence of their own that is permanent, inalienable, and intrinsic. That view is here denied. All things are said to be empty of such a nature. That does not signify, however, that emptiness therefore means that these things do not exist; it simply means that they do not exist in the way the Abhidharmists thought they existed. (And to the extent that we tend to think, more or less, like Abhidharmists, this means that they do not exist in the way we think they exist.)

Finally, attention should be called here to the mantra inserted at the end of this sūtra. Here is a formula that not only sums up the whole of the sūtra but also is supposed to be potently effective in saving beings from suffering, regardless of understanding.

Oṃ! Praise to the Blessed Noble Prajñāpāramitā!

The bodhisattva, Noble Avalokiteśvara, while carrying out his practice in profound transcendent wisdom, contemplated the five aggregates, and he saw that they were empty of inherent self-existence.

Here, O Śāriputra, form is emptiness, and emptiness is form. Form is not other than emptiness, and emptiness not other than form; whatever is form, that is emptiness, and whatever is emptiness, that is form. So it is also for [the four other aggregates]: feelings, perceptions, karmic constituents, and consciousness.

Here, O Śāriputra, all elements of reality are empty, without characteristic; they do not come into being, they do not cease; they are not defiled, not undefiled; not defective, not perfect.

Therefore, O Śāriputra, in emptiness, there are [none of the five aggregates]: no form, no feelings, no perceptions, no karmic constituents, no consciousness; there are [none of the six psychophysical sense organs]: no eye, ear, nose, tongue, body, or mind; there are [none of the six psychophysical sense objects]: no forms, sounds, odors, tastes, touchable, or thinkable things; there are [none of the eighteen psychophysical elements that correspond to the sense organs, the sense objects, and the six consciousnesses that connect them]: no eye-element, and so forth up to no mental consciousness element; there are [none of the links of interdependent origination]: no ignorance or elimination of ignorance, and so forth up to no old age and death or elimination of old age and death; there are [none of the Four Noble Truths]: no suffering, origination of suffering, cessation of suffering, or path to the cessation of suffering; there is no knowledge, no attainment, no nonattainment.

Therefore, O Śāriputra, because of his nonattainment, a bodhisattva relies on the perfection of wisdom and stays free from mental hindrances. And because of this freedom from mental hindrances, he is unafraid, he moves beyond error, and is assured of attaining nirvāṇa. All the various Buddhas of the past, present, and future have attained unsurpassed, complete enlightenment, after relying on the perfection of wisdom.

Therefore, one should know the great mantra of Prajñāpāramitā, the mantra of the great spell, the unsurpassed mantra, the peerless mantra, the mantra that soothes all suffering. Because it is not false, it is true. The mantra of Prajñāpāramitā is spoken as follows: gate, gate, paragate, parasaṃgate, bodhi svāhā (gone, gone, gone beyond, utterly gone beyond: enlightenment!).

Source: Translated from "The Prajñāpāramitā-hṛdaya-sūtra," ed. Edward Conze, in *Thirty Years of Buddhist Studies* (London: Bruno Cassirer, 1967), pp. 148–67.[8]

4.2.3 The Perfection of Wisdom as the Middle Way

Another important theme of the *Perfection of Wisdom* literature, as indeed of the whole of the Mahāyāna, is that of the Middle Way, which avoids the two extremes. In the Buddha's biography, of course, these two extremes are defined as the life of the palace—self-indulgence and full affirmation of the things of this world—and the life of extreme asceticism—self-mortification and utter denial of the things of this world. We have already seen how, even in the Pali canon (see 3.2.5), this Middle Way was interpreted more philosophically as the path between the extremes of eternalism and nihilism, of existence and nonexistence. In the following selection, taken from the Chinese translation of a commentary (wrongly attributed to Nāgārjuna) on the *Great Perfection of Wisdom Sūtra,* we find a whole series of other extremes proposed. The Perfection of Wisdom always shuns them both, even when the Middle Way itself becomes a new extreme!

Everlasting—that is one extreme; passing away—that is another extreme; give up these two extremes to go on the Middle Way—that is the Perfection of Wisdom. Permanence is one extreme, impermanence is an-

---

[8]Alternative English translation, Edward Conze, *Buddhist Wisdom Books* (London: George Allen and Unwin, 1958), pp. 77–107.

other; give up these two extremes to go on the Middle Way—that is the Perfection of Wisdom. . . . Form is one extreme, formlessness is another; the visible is one extreme, the invisible is another; aversion is one extreme, nonaversion is another; . . . depravity is one extreme, purity is another; this world is one extreme, the supramundane is another; . . . ignorance is one extreme, the extinction of ignorance is another; old age and death are one extreme, the cessation of old age and death is another; the existence of all dharmas is one extreme, the nonexistence of all dharmas is another; give up these two extremes to go on the Middle Way—that is the Perfection of Wisdom.

Bodhisattva is one extreme, the six perfections are another; Buddha is one extreme, bodhi is another; give up these two extremes to go on the Middle Way—that is the Perfection of Wisdom. The six internal sense organs are one extreme, the six external sense objects are another; give up these two extremes to go on the Middle Way—that is the Perfection of Wisdom. "This is the Perfection of Wisdom"—that is one extreme, "this is not the Perfection of Wisdom"—that is another; give up these two extremes to go on the Middle Way—that is the Perfection of Wisdom.

Source: Translated from *Mahāprajñāpāramitāśāstra* (Taishō shinshū daizōkyō, ed. J. Takakusu and K. Watanabe [Tokyo, 1924–29], no. 1509, 25:370a–b].[9]

4.3 PHILOSOPHICAL FORMULATIONS

The *Perfection of Wisdom* literature set many of the doctrinal themes of the Mahāyāna, but these were further developed and elaborated by various schools of thought. In India, it is possible to distinguish two principal schools of Mahāyāna philosophy: the Mādhyamika school, founded by Nāgārjuna (first to second century C.E.?) and Āryadeva (about 170–270 C.E.), and continued by such thinkers as Buddhapālita (about 470–540), Bhāvaviveka (about 490–570), Candrakīrti (600–650), and Śāntideva (about 650–750); and the Vijñānavāda, or Yogacāra, school, which is associated with such figures as Maitreyanātha (about 270–350) (who is sometimes identified with the bodhisattva Maitreya), the brothers Asanga (about 310–390) and Vasubandhu (about 320–400), Dignāga (480–540), Sthiramati (510–570), Dharmapāla (530–561), Śāntirakṣita (about ?–788), and Kamalaśīla (about 740–795), the latter two also being involved in a philosophical rapprochement with the Mādhyamikas.

Mahāyāna philosophy, however, was not limited to these two major philosophical schools. In addition, there arose less organized currents of thought, such as the Tathāgatagarbha doctrine and the Avataṃsaka doctrine of interpenetration and totality, which were developed in certain sūtras that were highly influential. In what follows, we shall sample all of these by means of some classic representative texts.

---

[9]Alternative English translation, K. Venkata Ramanan, *Nāgārjuna's Philosophy as Presented in the Mahā-Prajñāpāramitā-śāstra* (Tokyo: Tuttle, 1966), pp. 108–9.

4.3.1 Nāgārjuna: Verses on the Noble Truths and on Nirvāṇa

Nāgārjuna, the founder of the Mādhyamika school and one of the great philosophers of world history, can be viewed, first, as a systematizer of Perfection of Wisdom doctrines. He too is preoccupied with the doctrine of emptiness, but his genius was in spelling out its implications for the rest of Buddhist thought.

Nāgārjuna's works are subtle and profound, and for the most part they are rather densely packed into concise verses. It may be helpful, therefore, to make a few preliminary points to be kept in mind in reading the following selections, taken from the 24th and 25th chapters of one of his most important works, his *Mūlamadhyamakakārikaḥ* (*Stanzas on the Middle Way*).

First, it should be noted that Nāgārjuna here presents his arguments as responses to objections raised by philosophical opponents. Indeed, his method is said to have been merely to show that the philosophical assertions of others were ultimately untenable, and not to establish a philosophical position of his own. According to him, any assertion of a "Truth" can ultimately be dismantled, can be reduced to absurdity and shown to be inconsistent, because it necessarily freezes the reality it is supposed to express. Nāgārjuna realizes that were his views to be hypostatized in any way, they too would be untenable. Hence, he is wary of falling into the trap he springs on his opponents. He claims to set up no tenets of his own, only to demolish the tenets of others.

Because of this, some have asserted that Nāgārjuna is only a nay-sayer, a nihilist, denying all realities. To conclude this, however, would be a dangerous misunderstanding. For one thing, Nāgārjuna is such a thoroughgoing "nay-sayer" that he says no even to nihilism. For another, there is a distinct difference between denying reality and denying descriptions of reality. Nāgārjuna was acutely aware of the hypostatic powers of language, and for him, to "assert" that reality did not exist would be just as absurd as "asserting" that it did.

In this regard, mention should be made of the doctrine of the two truths: ultimate truth (paramarthasatya), sometimes called the "highest object truth," and conventional truth (saṃvṛtisatya), sometimes called "relative truth." Nāgārjuna mentions this theory of two truths only in passing in the passage below, but it is basic to his whole enterprise and to the Buddhist attempt at enlightening beings: conventional truths, expressed in conventional language, are needed in order to teach about the ultimate, about emptiness. Otherwise, no approach, no progress is possible for unenlightened beings caught in saṃsāra.

It is important to realize that Nāgārjuna had a keen appreciation of the dynamics of reality. He, in fact, equates emptiness (śūnyatā) with interdependent origination (pratītyasamutpāda), thus causing some scholars to translate "śūnyatā" not as "emptiness" but as "relativity." Because "things" (dharmas) are empty of any inherent, separate, unchangeable, permanent, essential self-existence (svabhāva), it is possible for relativity, for interdependence, to occur. It is possible for things to interact, to come into contact with one another, to change, to come into existence, to pass away. If "things" were *not* empty, that is, if they *did* have svabhāva, it would be impossible for them—for their "essence"—to change, interact, or grow, because their "essence," their "inherent nature," what makes them "them," is by definition unchangeable, separate, and permanent. For Nāgārjuna, the world of svabhāva is a frozen landscape in which there can be no movement, no change, no interaction, no relativity. And to those who would object and say, "But the world is not like that!" Nāgārjuna would reply: "Precisely! That is why the world is emptiness."

In the first of the two passages below, from chapter 24 of his *Stanzas on the Middle Way*, Nāgārjuna, using the logic just described, reacts to an opponent who seems to think that emptiness means that the Four Noble Truths, and consequently the whole of Buddhism, are devoid of reality. Not so, Nāgārjuna retorts, it is only without emptiness, that is, with svabhāva, that that would be the case. In the second passage (chapter 25), the argument turns to nirvāṇa. Here another dimension of Nāgārjuna's thought emerges: On the one hand, because of the special nature of nirvāṇa, Nāgārjuna has to push his "nay-saying" further and ends with the famous tetralemma, the fourfold negation of the Buddha in nirvāṇa as neither existing, nor nonexisting, nor both existing and nonexisting, nor neither existing nor nonexisting. On the other hand, because much the same language could be applied to saṃsāra, Nāgārjuna is led to conclude that nirvāṇa and saṃsāra are not distinct, not separable. At this point, the dialectic has come full circle.

Chapter 24: On the Four Noble Truths

[An opponent argues:]

1. If everything is empty, there can be no arising or passing away, and it follows that the Four Noble Truths [which involve the arising and passing away of suffering] do not exist.
2. And because the Four Noble Truths do not exist, there can be no understanding [of the truth of suffering], no abandonment [of the cause of suffering], no practice [of the Path], no realization [of nirvāṇa].
3. Nor, without these, can there be any knowledge of the four fruits [of the Path: stream-winner, once-returner, nonreturner, and arhatship]; and without these, there can be no individuals who are established in the four fruits, and none who are on the four paths toward them.
4. And if these eight kinds of individuals do not exist, there can be no sangha. And since the Four Noble Truths do not exist either, no true Dharma can be found.
5. And if neither the sangha nor the Dharma exists, how can there be a Buddha? Thus, in speaking of emptiness, you contradict the Three Jewels [Buddha, Dharma, and Sangha].
6. And you deny the reality of the fruits, of good and bad, and of all worldly conventions.

[Nāgārjuna replies:]

7. To this we say that you do not know what emptiness is all about. You are therefore distressed by emptiness and [what you wrongly see as the] implications of emptiness.

8. In teaching the Dharma, Buddhas resort to two truths: worldly conventional truth and ultimate truth.
9. Those who do not know the distinction between these two truths do not understand the deep reality in the Buddha's Teaching.
10. The ultimate cannot be taught without resorting to conventions; and without recourse to the ultimate, one cannot reach nirvāṇa.
11. Emptiness, poorly perceived, destroys those of slight intelligence, like a snake badly grasped or magical knowledge misapplied.
12. That is why the Buddha was at first averse to teaching the Dharma; he thought that it would be difficult for those of slight intelligence to fathom it.
13. You have repeatedly objected to emptiness, but your faulty condemnation has nothing to do with our views, and does not apply to what is empty.
14. What is linked to emptiness is linked to everything; what is not linked to emptiness is linked to nothing.
15. You, putting off onto us your own deficiencies, are like someone who mounts a horse and then forgets he is on it.
16. If you view the true existence of existing things from [the perspective of each thing having] its own inherent self-existence [svabhāva], you will necessarily see those existing things as having neither cause nor condition, [as being totally unconnected to anything].
17. And you will deny cause and effect as well as [the possibility of there being] a doer, a deed, a doing, an origin, a cessation, or a fruit [of the Path].
18. Interdependent origination—that is what we call emptiness. That is a conventional designation. It is also the Middle Way.
19. There can be found no element of reality [dharma] that is not interdependently originated; therefore, there can be found no element of reality whatsoever that is *not* empty.
20. If everything were *not* empty, there could be no arising or passing away, and it would follow that the Four Noble Truths [which involve the arising and passing away of suffering] did not exist.
21. How could suffering *not* be interdependently originated? Indeed, suffering is said to be impermanent; thus it cannot be found to exist if it has its own [permanent] inherent self-existence.
22. And furthermore, how could there be an arising of suffering having its own inherent self-existence? Because for one who denies emptiness, there is no arising.
23. Nor could a cessation of suffering having its own inherent self-existence be found to exist; by insisting on the notion of inherent self-existence, you deny cessation.
24. Finally, if there is such a thing as inherent self-existence, there can be no practice of the Path. But that Path is cultivated, so it cannot be found to have its own inherent self-existence. [. . .]

31. According to your view, it follows that the Enlightened One is independent of his enlightenment, and enlightenment is independent of the Enlightened One!
32. According to your view, people who, by virtue of their own inherent self-existence, are [defined as being] unenlightened, will never attain enlightenment, even by means of the practices of a bodhisattva.
33. And no good or bad will be done by anyone, for what can be done by what is not-empty? That which has its own inherent self-existence does not act.
34. Indeed, acccording to your view, a fruit would be found to exist without [reference to having been brought about by] a good or bad deed, because for you a fruit is not found to be fashioned by good or bad deeds.
35. But if according to your view, a fruit *is* fashioned by good or bad deeds, how can that fruit that has *originated* from a good or bad deed not be empty?
36. When you deny emptiness, which is interdependent origination, you deny all worldly transactions.
37. For one who denies emptiness, there would be nothing at all to be done, doing would never get started, and a doer would not be doing.
38. According to the theory of inherent self-existence, the world should be [unchanging]: neither coming into being nor ceasing, utterly uniform and devoid of varying situations.
39. In the absence of emptiness, there could not be found to exist either the attainment of what has not yet been attained, or the bringing to an end of suffering, or the abandonment of all defilements.
40. One who perceives interdependent origination also perceives this: suffering, the origination of suffering, the cessation of suffering, as well as the path to the cessation of suffering.

Chapter 25: On Nirvāṇa

[An opponent argues:]

1. If everything is empty, there can be no arising or passing away; therefore, by what abandonment, by what cessation can nirvāṇa be expected?

[Nāgārjuna replies:]

2. [It is only] if everything is *not* empty that there can be no arising or passing away [and that one can ask]: by what abandonment, by what cessation can nirvāṇa be expected?
3. This is said about nirvāṇa: no abandonment, no attainment, no annihilation, no eternality, no cessation, no arising.

4. Nirvāṇa is not a thing, for then it would follow that it would be characterized by old age and death, for no thing is free from old age and death.
5. And if nirvāṇa were a thing, it would be karmically constituted, for no thing anywhere has ever been found not to be karmically constituted.
6. And if nirvāṇa were a thing, how could it not be dependent on other things, for no independent thing has ever been found.
7. If nirvāṇa is not a thing, can it be that it is a "nonthing"? [No, because] wherever there is no thing, neither can there be a nonthing.
8. And if nirvāṇa were a nonthing, how could it not be dependent on other things, for no independent nonthing has ever been found.
9. The state of moving restlessly to and fro [in saṃsāra] is dependent and conditioned; independent and unconditioned, it is said to be nirvāṇa.
10. The Buddha said that both existence and freedom from existence are abandoned. Therefore it is fitting to say that nirvāṇa is not a thing and not a nonthing.
11. If nirvāṇa were *both* a thing and a nonthing, liberation would also be *both* a thing and a nonthing, but that does not make sense.
12. If nirvāṇa were *both* a thing and a nonthing, it would not be independent [of other things], for both [things and nonthings] are dependent.
13. And how could nirvāṇa be both a thing and a nonthing? Nirvāṇa is not karmically constituted, but things and nonthings are.
14. [And anyhow,] how could nirvāṇa be both a thing and a nonthing? Like light and darkness, these two are opposites and cannot both exist at the same place.
15. Only if things and nonthings are established can the proposition "Nirvāṇa is *neither* a thing nor a nonthing" be established.
16. But how could it be asserted that nirvāṇa was found to be "neither a thing nor a nonthing?"
17. It is not asserted that the Blessed One exists after his passing away; nor is it asserted that he does not exist, that he both exists and does not exist, or that he neither exists nor does not exist.
18. Even while he is living, it is not asserted that the Blessed One exists; nor is it asserted that he does not exist, both exists and does not exist, or neither exists nor does not exist.
19. There is no distinction whatsoever between saṃsāra and nirvāṇa; and there is no distinction whatsoever between nirvāṇa and saṃsāra.
20. The limit of nirvāṇa and the limit of saṃsāra: one cannot find even the slightest difference between them.

21. Views about such things as the finitude or infinitude of the state coming after death, are related to the issue of nirvāṇa having beginning and ending limits.
22. Given that all elements of reality are empty, what is infinite? What is finite? What is both finite and infinite? What is neither finite nor infinite?
23. What is just this? What is that other? What is eternal? What is noneternal? What is both eternal and noneternal? What is neither eternal nor noneternal?
24. Ceasing to fancy everything and falsely to imagine it as real is good; nowhere did the Buddha ever teach any such element of reality.

Source: Translated from Nāgārjuna, *Mūlamadhyamakakārikaḥ,* ed. J. W. de Jong (Adyar: Adyar Library and Research Centre, 1977), pp. 34–40.[10]

4.3.2 The Ongoing Dialectic

Despite Nāgārjuna's advocacy of the Middle Way, and his precautions against nihilistic interpretations, the doctrine of emptiness presented in the *Perfection of Wisdom* literature was seen by some as being too negativistic or, perhaps more accurately, as being in need of interpretation so that it would not be viewed negativistically. The *Saṃdhinirmocana sūtra* (*The Unraveling of Hidden Intentions,* or *Explanation of Mysteries*), a text of the early third century C.E., reflects this view in its account of the "Three Turnings of the Wheel of the Dharma." According to this, the Buddha, when he preached his first sermon in the Deer Park near Benares, denied the existence of the Ātman but affirmed the reality of dharmas. This was the doctrine of Mainstream Buddhism. Later, in the so-called second turning of the Wheel of the Dharma, the Buddha proclaimed the emptiness of those dharmas and posited the Absolute in negative terms. This was the doctrine of the *Perfection of Wisdom* literature. According to the *Saṃdhinirmocana sūtra,* both of these views are true but conventional, in need of interpretation in order to be understood properly. The third turning of the Wheel of the Dharma, with which the *Saṃdhinirmocana sūtra* wishes to identify itself, claims to represent the Buddha's views of the Absolute explicitly, directly, without hidden meaning. Doctrinally, the *Saṃdhinirmocana sūtra* marks the transition between the *Perfection of Wisdom* texts and the full development of the Vijñānavāda school. Its later chapters, in fact, contain a presentation of many basic Mind-Only Vijñānavāda views.

[10]Alternative English translations, Frederick Streng, *Emptiness: A Study in Religious Meaning* (Nashville: Abingdon Press, 1967), pp. 212–17; David Kalupahana, *Nāgārjuna: The Philosophy of the Middle Way* (Albany: State University of New York Press, 1986), pp. 326–69; Kenneth Inada, *Nāgārjuna: A Translation of His Mūlamadhyamakakārikā with an Introductory Essay* (Tokyo, 1970), pp. 143–59; and Jay L. Garfield, *The Fundamental Wisdom of the Middle Way* (New York: Oxford University Press, 1995), pp. 293–334.

One of these is the subject of the following selection: the view of the threefold absence of inherent self-existence (niḥsvabhāvatā). To this threefold denial of inherent self-existence corresponds the assertion of the three aspects, or natures (trisvabhāva), of reality, a sort of Vijñānavādin counterpart to the Mādhyamika notion of the two truths. Elements of reality (dharmas) can be thought of as having a falsely constructed, or imaginary, nature (parikalpita svabhāva). This is involved in attributing to them inherent self-existence, which they do not have. This is also the world of subject-object dualism in which we, ignorantly, live our lives. But dharmas are also said to have a "dependent nature" (paratantra svabhāva); here the separation and false conception of objects disappears and we see only their underlying interconnections, their dependently originated nature. Finally, there is what is called the "perfected nature" (parinişpanna svabhāva), which amounts to permanently seeing reality in its suchness (tathatā), as it truly is, as one does in meditation.

Sometimes, the three natures are distinguished by the simile of a mirage. When we see a mirage and think what we see is water—that is the falsely constructed nature. When we see a mirage and realize that what we are seeing is not water but a phenomenon caused by other things (heat waves, glare)—that is the interdependent nature. When we see a mirage, know that both the notions of water and of mirage are ultimately false, and see what is actually there, realizing that it is inherently neither water nor mirage—that is the perfected nature.

Then the bodhisattva Paramārthasamudgata said this to the Blessed One: "Blessed One, once, when I found myself alone, I had this reflection: 'On several occasions, the Blessed One has spoken of the inherent characteristics of the five skandhas, . . . of the Four Noble Truths, . . . of the eighteen dhātus, . . . of the four applications of mindfulness, . . . of the Noble Eightfold Path. . . . However, on another occasion, the Blessed One stated that all dharmas are *without* inherent self-existence, are not originated, not destroyed, originally peaceful, of the nature of nirvāṇa.' I would like to ask: What was the hidden intention of the Blessed One in describing things in this way?"

The Blessed One replied: "Your thought is good and legitimate. . . . Listen and I will tell you the hidden intention with which I teach that all dharmas are without inherent self-existence, not originated, not destroyed, originally peaceful, of the nature of nirvāṇa.

"When I teach that, I do so with reference to the threefold lack of inherent self-existence of all dharmas, to wit: the lack of inherent self-existence with regard to character, the lack of inherent self-existence with regard to origination, and the ultimate lack of inherent self-existence.

"What, then, Paramārthasamudgata, is the lack of inherent self-existence of dharmas with regard to their character? It is the falsely constructed [parikalpita] character. How so? Because its character is established by names and conventions and is not inherently established, it is called the lack of inherent self-existence with regard to character.

"And what, Paramārthasamudgata, is the lack of inherent self-existence of dharmas with regard to their origination? It is the dependent [paratantra] character of dharmas. How so? Because its character originates not by itself but through the power of causation by something other than itself, it is called the lack of inherent self-existence with regard to origination.

"And what, Paramārthasamudgata, is the ultimate lack of inherent self-existence of dharmas? Those dharmas that are interdependently originated, and so have no inherent self-existence due to their origination, also have an ultimate lack of inherent self-existence. How so? Paramārthasamudgata, that which, in dharmas, is the object of purification, that is what I call the Ultimate. This object of purification does not have the character of dependence. That is why it is said to have an ultimate lack of inherent self-existence. Moreover, Paramārthasamudgata, the perfected (parinispanna) character of dharmas is also said to be the ultimate lack of inherent self-existence. How so? Paramārthasamudgata, the non-self of dharmas is called their lack of inherent self-existence. That is the Ultimate. Since the Ultimate is made manifest by the lack of inherent self-existence of all dharmas, it is said to be the ultimate lack of inherent self-existence."

Source: Translated from Etienne Lamotte, *Saṃdhinirmocana sūtra: L'explication des mystères* (Louvain: Université de Louvain, 1935), pp. 65–69.[11]

4.3.3 Vasubandhu: Types of Consciousness

Approximately two hundred years after Nāgārjuna was establishing the Mādhyamika and one hundred years after the *Saṃdhinirmocana sūtra* was being compiled, the monk Vasubandhu converted to the Mahāyāna and helped further establish the Vijñānavāda school, also known as the Yogacāra, or the Cittamātra, school. In English, it is often referred to as the Mind-Only, or the Consciousness-Only, school.

One of the preoccupations of this school was the analysis of consciousness. For the Vijñānavādins, that was equivalent to an analysis of reality-as-we-know-it, because like all Buddhists they believed that we know reality only through the consciousnesses that come with our senses and our minds.

Vijñānavāda is sometimes called a philosophically "idealist" school, implying that it does not believe in the reality of the external world, that it sees the world and everything as being somehow "unreal"—nothing but a projection of our consciousness. Vasubandhu would probably have found such a statement bizarre and still based on a mistaken subject-object dualism. He is not trying to show the *unreality* of the world but rather to analyze its *reality.* That reality is characterized by the absence of subject-object dualism.

In a sense, subject-object dualism is the "villain" for Vasubandhu the way inherent self-existence was the "villain" for Nāgārjuna. And just as the

[11]Alternative French translation, Lamotte, *Saṃdhinirmocana sūtra,* pp. 192–94.

Mādhyamikas called on emptiness to deal with their problem, the Vijñānavādins call on consciousness-only to handle theirs. At times this consciousness-only ultimately seems to resemble emptiness, but at others it seems that some real assertions about it are possible.

In unpacking their notion of reality, the Vijñānavādins were very good at distinguishing between types of consciousness and eventually developed a system of eight consciousnesses. The first six of these they shared with the Mainstream Buddhist schools: the five consciousnesses associated with the five physical senses (that is, the consciousnesses involved in seeing, hearing, smelling, tasting, and touching) and the mental consciousness associated with the brain seen as one of the sense organs (that is, the consciousness involved in thinking). To these were added a seventh consciousness called the mind (manas), which is chiefly involved in our giving to ourselves (and to objects) a false sense of individuality, and an eighth consciousness called the storehouse consciousness (ālaya-vijñāna), or the "granary consciousness," which is said to contain all the "seeds" for what become "consciousness-moments" or "consciousness-events" (what we usually called reality). Ultimately, then, reality might be envisioned as but a series of seeds (bījā) in the granary consciousness that sprout, germinate, are harvested, and are once again stored, all in the granary consciousness. Sometimes, in this connection, the notion of vāsanā (the residual impressions, traces, or impregnations of mental, verbal, and physical events) is used instead of, or in addition to, the notion of seeds.

In the following selection from his quite condensed work, the *Treatise on Consciousness-Only in Thirty Stanzas,* Vasubandhu begins with the granary consciousness. He then moves on to manas and the other six senses, and sees fit to list all of the mental states or factors that can accompany those consciousnesses. In sum, then, in this part of his work he gives us an Abhidharmic list of elements of reality (dharmas), all of which are seen as part of, or associated with, consciousness. He then turns to assert that all of this elaboration amounts to making ultimately false discriminations (vikalpa); it is therefore "merely perception" (vijñaptimātra). And he further warns against reifying the notion "all this is merely perception" and setting it up as though it itself were some sort of external object of perception.

The original text is in verse, but as sentences often overlap from one stanza to another, it has here been translated as prose.

. . . The transformation of consciousness is of three kinds: coming to fruition, intellectualizing, and perceiving sense-objects.

The consciousness that is called "coming to fruition" is the granary consciousness (ālaya-vijñāna); it comprises all of the seeds (bīja). Its substratum, its disposition, its perceptions cannot be discerned, but it is always accompanied by the following factors: linkage to sense objects, attention, feeling, conceptualization, and volition. Its feelings are [neither pleasant nor unpleasant but] neutral, and it is undefiled and karmically indeterminate. . . . Its behavior is like the current of a stream. At arhatship, there occurs in it a fundamental revolution.

The intellectualizing consciousness is called "the mind" [manas]. As it develops, it is dependent on the granary consciousness and takes it as its object. It is karmically indeterminate but obstructed by four defilements to which it is always connected. These are called false view of the Self, delusion about the Self, pride of the Self, and love of the Self. Whenever the mind comes into being, it is accompanied by linkage to sense objects and by the other mental factors: attention, feeling, conceptualization, and volition. It ceases to exist at arhatship, or in the trance of cessation, or on the supramundane path. That is the second transformation of consciousness.

The third transformation concerns the consciousnesses dependent on the six senses: [the visual, auditory, olfactory, gustatory, tactile, and mental consciousnesses]. They are meritorious and/or demeritorious. They are accompanied by the three kinds of feeling [that is, pleasant, unpleasant, and neutral sensations], and they are connected to the following mental factors: the five mental factors that accompany them everywhere; the five special [mental factors which are not always present]; the meritorious mental states; the defilements, which are demeritorious; and the secondary defilements, which are also demeritorious.

First, the five mental factors that accompany the sense consciousnesses everywhere are: linkage to sense objects, attention, feeling, conceptualization, and volition.

The special mental factors are: zeal, resolve, mindfulness, concentration, and wisdom.

The meritorious mental states are: faith, modesty, fear of blame, lack of desire, lack of hatred, lack of delusion, striving, serenity, carefulness, and noninjury.

The defilements are: greed, hatred, confusion, pride, false views, and doubt.

The secondary defilements are: anger, enmity, disparaging others, irritation, envy, selfishness, deception, guile, assault, immodesty, nonfear of blame, sluggishness, excitability, lack of faith, sloth, carelessness, loss of mindfulness, distraction, and nondiscernment; there are also remorse and sleepiness, reflection and investigation, two pairs which are double factors [that can be either defiled or undefiled].

The first five sense consciousnesses [that is, the visual, auditory, olfactory, gustatory, and tactile consciousnesses] arise in the granary consciousness, either together or not, depending on conditions. They are like waves on the water. The sixth sense consciousness, the mental consciousness, always arises with them except in a situation where there is no recognition; in the two trance states where there is no mental consciousness; in dreamless sleep; in fainting; or in unconsciousness.

The whole transformation of consciousness is itself ultimately a false discrimination, and because it is a false discrimination, it does not exist. Therefore, all this is merely perception.

The granary consciousness contains all the seeds; its transformation takes place according to a process of give and take between it and the false discriminations to which it gives rise [and which in turn affect it. This process leaves in the granary consciousness] residual impressions [vāsanā] of actions, which along with the residual impressions of dualistic grasping give rise to a new "coming to fruition" when the former "fruition" has died out. [. . .]

As long as consciousness is not content with being perception only, there will continue to be a tendency toward dualistic grasping. This is so even with the thought "All this is perception only." If you come to apprehend this and set it up in front of you, you are not being content with "this only." But when consciousness truly no longer apprehends any object of consciousness, it abides as consciousness only; for when what it grasps does not exist, there is no grasping. It is then free of thought, nondependent, transcendent knowledge. This is the fundamental revolution of all consciousness, the destruction of the double depravity. This element is also free from evil attachments, unimaginable, meritorious, constant, blissful. It is the liberation body, which is called the Dharma body of the Buddha.

Source: Translated from Vasubandhu, *Triṃśikāvijñaptikārikā,* ed. Stefan Anacker, *Seven Works of Vasubandhu* (Delhi: Motilal Banarsidass, 1984), pp. 422–23.[12]

4.3.4 In Praise of the Bodies of the Buddha

In the final line of his *Thirty Stanzas,* Vasubandhu makes reference to various notions of the body of the Buddha. In fact, another doctrine that is associated with the Vijñānavādin school but that was broadly influential in the whole of Mahāyāna Buddhism was the doctrine of the three bodies (trikāya) of the Buddha. Some attempt was made to associate this doctrine with the three natures doctrine (see 4.3.2), but more simply this was a scheme that distinguished the dharma body (dharmakāya) of the Buddha, sometimes also called his essential body, or self-existent body (svabhāvikakāya); the body of shared enjoyment (saṃbhogakāya), sometimes also called the body of bliss; and the magically fashioned body, or transformation body (nirmāṇakāya). The dharmakāya was thought to be transcendent and ineffable, the saṃbhogakāya to be a sort of glorified body in which the Buddha preached to assemblies of bodhisattvas, and the nirmāṇakāya to be an expression of the Buddha's skillful means, a projection in this world for the sake of preaching to human beings. In the Mahāyāna, the body that the Buddha had when he lived in this world as Gautama was such a nirmāṇakāya.

Several texts on the bodies of the Buddha could be quoted here. One of the most straightforward, however, is the following short piece, which is actually a hymn in praise of the bodies of the Buddha. By the end of the fourth century it had already attained a certain popularity among Mahāyānists. A transcription of the Sanskrit original was preserved in both the Chinese and Tibetan canons.

---

[12]Alternative English translation, Anacker, *Seven Works,* pp. 186–89.

I venerate the incomparable Dharma body of the Buddhas, to be realized by oneself, which is neither one nor many, the basis for the great accomplishment of one's own purpose and that of others, neither being nor nonbeing, like empty space, of a single taste, whose inherent nature is hard to comprehend; which is unstained, unchanging, benign, peerless, all-pervading, free from discursive thought.

I venerate the enjoyment body, which is supramundane, inconceivable, the fruit of hundreds of good deeds, powerful, which spreads great brilliance in the midst of the assembly to the delight of the wise, which uninterruptedly proclaims the lofty sound of the good Dharma throughout the Buddha worlds, which is established in the great kingship of the Dharma.

I venerate the magically fashioned body of the Buddhas, which can shine forth anywhere like a fire, in order to "cook" beings to perfection; which, tranquil, repeatedly reveals in different places the Wheel of the Dharma leading to complete enlightenment; which employs many forms and takes away the terror of the three realms of existence by the skillful means of taking on various bodies; which, with great purpose, seeks out beings in the ten directions.

With devotion I pay homage to the three bodies of the Buddhas, who have as their one concern the good of all beings, who bring the immeasurable merits of the Mahāyāna, who eliminate the wrong paths of mind and speech. May the merit that I have accumulated, seed of enlightenment, procure for me the three bodies; may I enjoin the whole world to follow the path to enlightenment.

Source: Translated from *Trikāyastava,* ed. Sylvain Lévi, in Edouard Chavannes, "Les inscriptions chinoises de Bodh-gaya," *Revue de l'histoire des religions* 34 (1896): 19–20.[13]

4.3.5 Queen Śrīmālā Explains the Womb of the Tathāgata

In addition to the various theories of the bodies of the Buddha, there occurred another development in Mahāyāna buddhology: the evolution of the theory of a "Buddha within." This came to center on the notion of the Tathāgatagarbha, that is, the womb or embryo of the Tathāgata, a doctrine that was of central importance in several major Mahāyāna sūtras and was very influential in a number of ways in later Mahāyāna thought.

The basic concept behind the Tathāgatagarbha theory is that living beings all have within them the potentiality for enlightenment, that all of us are potential Buddhas. The Tathāgatagarbha is thus the presence of Buddhahood within us, even as we are unenlightened, living in saṃsāra. Freed from the defilements of saṃsāra, the Tathāgatagarbha is none other than the Dharma body of the Buddha.

---

[13]Alternative English translation (of the first three stanzas), George N. Roerich, *The Blue Annals* (Calcutta: Asiatic Society of Bengal, 1949), p. 2.

The word *garbha* means womb, or matrix, but it can also mean embryo, or seed. Hence, as the doctrine evolved, different traditions took it in different directions. On the one hand, it came to be seen as a seed, as the germ for eventual enlightenment, and as such it was associated with such things as bodhicitta, the "mind of enlightenment" (see selection 4.4.2). On the other hand, it also came to be seen as a matrix, an environment in which enlightenment could develop, and as such it was associated with such things as the granary consciousness (ālayavijñāna). In fact, in certain later texts (for example, the *Lankāvatāra sūtra*), the Tathāgatagarbha is explicitly identified with the ālayavijñāna.

The notion of the Tathāgatagarbha was to find important resonances in later Mahāyāna thought outside of India. In East Asia, for example, it can be associated with the Zen notion of the Buddha-mind, or Buddha-nature, to be found within us through the process of meditation; in Tibet, it helps us understand notions such as the "self-existent intrinsic awareness" (rang-byung rig-pa) featured in certain schools of thought, such as Dzog-chen.

The following presentation of the Tathāgatagarbha doctrine is taken from a sermon that Queen Śrīmālā, a laywoman and the daughter of King Prasenajit of Kośala, is reputed to have preached to the Buddha himself.

Blessed One, of the Four Noble Truths, three are impermanent and one is permanent. Why is that? Because three of the truths [suffering, its origination, and the path to its cessation] refer to things that are karmically constituted; and what is karmically constituted is impermanent; and things that are impermanent are false and deluding, untrue, impermanent, and unreliable. Therefore, the three truths mentioned above are ultimately untrue, impermanent, and unreliable.

The truth of the cessation of suffering, however, is apart from that which is karmically constituted; and anything apart from what is karmically constituted is permanent; and things that are permanent are not false and deluding, but they are true, permanent, and reliable. Therefore the truth of the cessation of suffering is the ultimate one. . . .

But, Blessed One, what is called the cessation of suffering does not mean the destruction of dharmas, because the cessation of suffering has no beginning, was not created, does not arise, and does not become exhausted; distinct from what is exhaustible, it is permanent, unchangeable, inherently pure, and apart from the storehouse of the defilements. Blessed One, . . . when it is not apart from the storehouse of defilements, this Dharma body of the Tathāgata is called the Tathāgatagarbha. . . .

Blessed One, if there were no such thing as the Tathāgatagarbha, there would be no turning away from suffering and no longing for nirvāṇa. Why is that? Because the six sense-based consciousnesses [the eye, ear, nose, taste, tongue, and mind consciousnesses], and their accompanying mental faculty (the manas)—these seven—are momentary and discontinuous and cannot retain the impression of suffering. Thus they cannot bring about revulsion from suffering or longing for nirvāṇa.

But, Blessed One, the Tathāgatagarbha is without beginning, it does not arise or cease, and it can retain the impression of suffering; so it can bring about revulsion from suffering and longing for nirvāṇa.

Blessed One, the Tathāgatagarbha is not a Self, nor a living being, nor a soul, nor a person. The Tathāgatagarbha is not for those who believe in a real person, who have heterodox views, or who are confused by emptiness. Blessed One, the Tathāgatagarbha is the womb of the Dharma realm, the womb of the Dharma body, the womb of the supramundane, the womb of intrinsic purity.

Source: Translated from *Śrīmālādevī siṃhanāda sūtra* (Taishō shinshū daizōkyō, ed. J. Takakusu and K. Watanabe [Tokyo, 1924–29], no. 353, 12:221c–222a, 221c, and 222b).[14]

4.3.6 Sudhana's Vision of the Cosmos

Finally, one more aspect of Mahāyāna thought needs to be considered here. If the Tathāgatagarbha theory develops the notion of the potentiality of Buddhahood within saṃsāra, the Avataṃsaka doctrine tells of the total interpenetration of Buddhahood and saṃsāra. One of the earliest expressions of Avataṃsaka thought can be found in the *Gaṇḍavyūha sūtra* (second century C.E.?), which might be described as an epic adventure with philosophical, cosmological, and soteriological implications. It tells the story of Sudhana, who in his quest for enlightenment visits over fifty teachers, each of whom instructs him and sends him on his way to yet another master. His pilgrimage culminates in visits to Maitreya (the future Buddha), and to the bodhisattva Samantabhadra, in whose body he perceives the totality of the cosmos.

This vision is reflective of Avataṃsaka doctrine (and the *Gaṇḍavyūha sūtra* itself was, in fact, later incorporated into the massive *Buddha-Avataṃsaka sūtra*). The Avataṃsaka view of the world could simplistically be described as the flip side of the Mādhyamika. Rather than destroying the notion of svabhāva (inherent self-existence) by proclaiming the *emptiness* of all elements of reality (dharmas), the Avataṃsaka destroys the same notion by proclaiming the utter "fullness" of all dharmas. Each and every element of reality contains and is itself contained in each and every other element of reality in the entire infinite cosmos. All the Buddhas of all the universes can be found in a single speck of dust—in all specks of dust—in all the universes. Sometimes, in order to explain this view, the simile of a hall of mirrors is used: a person sitting in the middle of a polyhedral chamber, the walls, floor, and ceiling of which are entirely mirrored, would be reflected in all those mirrors, and

[14] Alternative English translation, Diana Mary Paul, *The Buddhist Feminine Ideal* (Missoula: Scholars Press, 1980), pp. 203–7, 192, 215; see also Garma C. C. Chang, *A Treasury of Mahāyāna Sūtras* (University Park: Pennsylvania State University Press, 1983), pp. 378–81 (which translates Taishō shinshū daizōkyō, no. 310, 11:677a–c); and Alex Wayman and Hideko Wayman, *The Lion's Roar of Queen Śrīmālā* (New York: Columbia University Press, 1974), pp. 100, 98–99, and 104–6.

the reflections in all those mirrors, in turn, reflected in all those mirrors, and so on ad infinitum. Another analogy might be the case of a perfectly floodlit stadium, so that the shadows cast in one direction by the players on the field are canceled out by the lights that are coming in the other direction. Then, in this shadowless world, imagine that the players (dharmas) themselves are not solid, shadow-casting bodies but lights . . .

Such a world view commonly calls to mind words such as totality, interpenetration, luminosity, infinity. It portrays reality not as we commonly see it in our ignorance but as it truly is. It is a view of the dharmadhātu, the Dharma realm, as perceived by a completely enlightened being. The following final vision of Sudhana tries to describe it.

Then Sudhana, the son of the guild-master, reflecting upon the body of the bodhisattva Samantabhadra, saw in every single pore of that body untold quadrillions of Buddha fields being entirely filled up with Buddhas. And in every single one of those quadrillions of Buddha fields he saw Tathāgatas surrounded by countless assemblies of bodhisattvas. And he saw that all those quadrillions of fields had various bases, various forms, various arrangements, various surrounding mountains, various clouds covering the sky, various Buddhas arising, various proclamations of the Dharma. And just as he saw all this in every single pore, so too he saw it in all the pores without exception, in all the major and minor physical marks, in all the major and minor limbs of Samantabhadra's body. In every single one he saw quadrillions of fields, from which issued clouds of fashioned Buddha bodies, equal to the number of atoms in all Buddha fields, pervading all of the world systems in the ten directions, bringing beings to the maturity of unsurpassed complete enlightenment.

Then Sudhana, the son of the guild-master, guided by the words and instructions of the bodhisattva Samantabhadra, entered into all the world systems within the body of Samantabhadra and brought beings there to maturity. Moreover, the meritorious roots and knowledge accumulated by Sudhana, the son of the guild-master, during his meetings, audiences, and service to spiritual friends as numerous as the atoms of a Buddha field, did not amount to even a hundredth, a thousandth, a hundred thousandth, a billionth, of the meritorious roots he accumulated by virtue of his audience with Samantabhadra. In one moment of thought, he entered more Buddha fields, . . . in a single pore of the body of Samantabhadra than the whole series of fields he had entered from the time of his arousing the thought of enlightenment to the time of his audience with Samantabhadra. And as it was for one pore, so it was for all pores. Proceeding, in each moment of thought, through world systems as numerous as the atoms in countless Buddha fields, he still did not arrive at the end. . . .

He explored one Buddha field for an aeon. He explored another for as many aeons as there are atoms in countless Buddha fields, without ever leaving that field. In each and every moment of thought, he entered quadrillions of Buddha fields and brought beings there to the maturity that is unsurpassed complete enlightenment.

And gradually he came to equal the bodhisattva Samantabhadra in his quadrillions of vows and practices; he came to equal all the Tathāgatas; he came to equal them in the pervasion of all fields; he came to equal them in the fulfillment of practices; . . . he came to equal them in turning the Wheel of the Dharma; he came to equal them in the purity of knowledge; he came to equal them in voice and speaking; he came to equal them in great love, in great compassion, and in the inconceivable liberation of bodhisattvas.

Source: Translated from *Gaṇḍavyūhasūtra,* ed. P. L. Vaidya, Buddhist Sanskrit Texts, No. 5 (Darbhanga: Mithila Institute, 1960), pp. 427–28.

4.4 THE BODHISATTVA PATH

As we have seen, one of the hallmarks of Mahāyāna Buddhism is its emphasis on and elaboration of the doctrine of the bodhisattva. Most simply, the word *bodhisattva* can be defined as meaning "a being headed for Buddhahood," that is, a being in whom the aspiration for complete enlightenment has been roused. In Mainstream Buddhism, the word refers primarily to the Buddha Gautama prior to his enlightenment (in all of his past lives as a bodhisattva), and to the future Buddha Maitreya, who is presently a bodhisattva, awaiting his turn for Buddhahood. In the Mahāyāna, however, every sentient being can be seen as ultimately "headed for Buddhahood" and so is potentially or actually on the bodhisattva path.

4.4.1 The Necessity of Compassion

The motivating force behind the actual practice of the bodhisattva path is the element of compassion, the desire to help alleviate the sufferings of others, either by guiding them to enlightenment or by assisting in more material ways. This factor, it is sometimes claimed, is one of the things that differentiated the bodhisattva from the arhat, and in some contexts, as we shall see, it led to the notion of bodhisattvas who reject the option of arhatship in order to continue to work in saṃsāra for the welfare of all sentient beings. More immediately, as the following selection by Kamalaśīla (eighth century) makes clear, the development of compassion for others can be seen as a crucial first step on the bodhisattva path.

One who wishes to gain omniscience swiftly must strive in three things: in compassion, in the thought of enlightenment, and in meditation. And one should practice compassion from the very outset, for we know that compassion alone is the first cause of all the qualities of Buddhahood. As we read in scripture:

> Blessed One, a bodhisattva should not practice too many things at once: for if a bodhisattva can master and truly understand just one thing, then

> he will hold all the qualities of Buddhahood in the palm of his hand. And what is this one thing? It is great compassion: Blessed One, it is through compassion that a bodhisattva holds all the qualities of Buddhahood in the palm of his hand. . . .

And again we read:

> The great compassion of a bodhisattva does not perish. And why is that? Because it precedes all else. Just as a man's breath precedes his ability to live, the great compassion of a bodhisattva precedes his endowment with all the merit and knowledge of the Great Vehicle.

And again we read:

> What is the beginning of a bodhisattva's practice, and what is its abode? Great compassion is the beginning of a bodhisattva's practice, and it abides among living beings.

Thus a bodhisattva is impelled only by the desire to help others, with no regard for himself; and he sets out upon a long and arduous path, ever exerting himself to acquire merit and knowledge. As we read in scripture: "When his compassion aims to bring all beings to maturity, there is no happiness at all which he will not renounce. . . ."

Now this compassion grows through an increasing concern for beings who suffer; and thus he should meditate upon these beings, that throughout the Triple World they are ever tormented with the three-fold suffering of their condition.

Thus the Blessed One has shown us that those in hell are sunk in unremitting and burning pain; he has shown us, too, that the hungry ghosts feel pain both sharp and keen, their bodies withered with the ache of unbearable hunger and thirst, who cannot find in a hundred years even a wretched piece of filth to eat. And we ourselves can see how animals suffer many pains, maiming and slaughtering each other in mutual rage; how some are bound and beaten, their noses split for rings, their bodies castrated, tormented on all sides; how they weary, their reluctant bodies exhausted in bearing their hard and heavy loads. . . .

And we can see, too, how humans can suffer the pains of hell, for thieves have their limbs cut off, are impaled and hanged, and endure the sufferings of hell; the poor and powerless suffer the hunger and thirst of hungry ghosts; slaves suffer the bondage and beatings of animals, owned by the strong, belonging to others, tormented. For humans endure immeasurable pain: they seek each other out to torture and betray; they are separated from their loved ones and forced to serve those that they despise.

Even those called rich and happy will meet with death: sunk in the abyss of their evil ways, they gather the sinful deeds which will be for them their pain in hell; they stand above a dizzy precipice; and they truly suffer, who stand in the cause of suffering.

Even the gods themselves in the realm of desire have minds which blaze with the fires of sharp lust, darkened and distracted: they find not a moment for peace or calm. . . .

And thus one understands that the entire world is licked by the blazing flames of suffering; and one meditates upon compassion for all beings, for one knows that they abhor their pain as one does one's own.

One meditates first, then, upon those whom one loves; one sees how they must bear the many sufferings we have described; they are all the same as oneself, and one sees no difference among them.

Then one meditates upon those to whom one is neutral: one considers that in the beginningless world there is no being who has not been one's kinsman a hundred times, and one awakens compassion for them as for those one loves.

Then one meditates upon one's enemies also, and one realizes that they are all the same as oneself is, and one awakens compassion for one's enemies even as for those one loves.

And thus gradually one meditates upon all beings in the ten directions: one awakens one's compassion for all beings equally, that they are as dear as one's own suffering children, that they are one's own family, and one wishes to lead them out of pain. Then is one's compassion made perfect, and it is called great compassion.

Source: From Stephan Beyer, *The Buddhist Experience* (Encino, CA: Dickenson, 1974), pp. 99–101 (slightly altered). Reprinted by permission of Wadsworth, Inc.[15]

4.4.2 Developing the Thought of Enlightenment

The bodhisattva path, in the Mahāyāna tradition, has been elaborately described in a number of ways. Reference is usually made to the practice of the six (or ten) perfections (pāramitā) (see 4.4.3). Sometimes these are correlated to the schema of progression through ten bodhisattva stages (bhūmi) whereby one moves from the first, the "Joyous Stage," through to the last, the stage of Buddhahood known as the "Cloud of Dharma Stage."[16] Before embarking on either of these courses, however, a bodhisattva must first develop the thought of enlightenment (bodhicitta) or, more precisely, the "mind fixed on enlightenment by means of a vow" (bodhipraṇidhicitta). This event marks the start of one's aspiration to Buddhahood, and it can be understood as the initial experience of embarking on the path, akin to the step taken by the Buddha Gautama, in his previous life long ago, under the past Buddha Dīpaṃkara (see 1.4.1). What was legendary and biographical in the case of Gautama, however, became ritual and meditational in the Mahāyāna and extended to everyone. This is significant, for though the arousing of bodhicitta was theoretically something to be done once at the start of the bodhisattva path, in fact, ritually, it became something to be repeated often, the repetition serving to renew one's dedication.

---

[15]Original text of *Bhāvanākrama* by Kamalaśila in Giuseppe Tucci, *Minor Buddhist Texts* (Rome: Istituto Italiano per il Medio ed Estremo Oriente, 1958), 2:187ff.

[16]On the ten bodhisattva stages, see Edward Conze, *The Large Sutra on Perfect Wisdom* (Berkeley: University of California Press, 1975), pp. 163-78.

There are several preliminary phases to the act of arousing the mind set on enlightenment. The following selection from the *Bodhicaryāvatāra* [*Entering the Path of Enlightenment*], by the eighth-century poet Śāntideva, describes them well. The ritual begins with praise and worship of the Buddhas (magnified by the visualization of tremendous offerings), followed by a number of steps: reaffirming refuge, confessing one's faults and sins, expressing thanks for the merits of others, supplicating the Buddhas for help, and making a declaration of altruism leading up to a more formal bodhisattva vow.

Worship and Devotion

So as to obtain this gem of the mind set on enlightenment, I make devotional offerings to the Tathāgatas, to the immaculate jewel of the good Dharma, and to the Sangha, consisting of the sons of the Buddha, who are oceans of virtue.

However many flowers and fruits, medicinal plants, and precious gems there are in the world, as well as clear delightful waters;

and mountains made of jewels, and forest retreats where solitude is pleasant, where the creepers are resplendent with blossoms and the trees laden with fruit;

and sweet-smelling incenses from, among other places, the worlds of the gods; and wish-granting trees, and trees made of gems, and ponds bedecked with lotuses, made enchanting by the loud cries of wild geese;

and cultivated and uncultivated crops, and other things to honor those deserving devotional offerings; everything stretching as far as the limits of space, even those things that cannot be grasped—

All this I mentally give to the most eminent sages and their sons. . . .

Refuge and Confession

And I sing the praises of these oceans of virtue, with verses, with a flood of utterances. May the clouds of my hymns reach them without fail.

I go to the Buddha for refuge, taking enlightenment as my highest aim; and I go to the Dharma for refuge, as well as to the troop of bodhisattvas.

With folded hands, I make this confession to the Buddhas, spread out in all directions, as well as to the greatly compassionate bodhisattvas:

"Consumed by remorse, I hereby confess the evil deeds that I, no better than a beast, have committed or caused others to commit, either here in this life or throughout beginningless saṃsāra; and I confess the things that I deludedly took pleasure in and that led to self-destruction.

"And I confess all the wrongs that I have done with my body, speech, and mind, lacking respect for the Three Jewels, my parents, my teachers, and others; and the cruel evil deeds that I, guilty of many faults, have committed.

"Lords, how can I be rid of this burden? Help me quickly, lest death arrive soon while my pile of evil is still undiminished. . . .

"Lords, accept the sins I have committed. What was not good, I will not do again. . . ."

Rejoicing at the Merit of Others and Supplicating the Buddhas

And I joyously applaud the good done by all beings that results in the cessation of the suffering of rebirth in the lower realms. May all those who suffer be happy!

And I applaud the liberation of embodied beings from the sufferings of saṃsāra, and I applaud the bodhisattvahood and Buddhahood of those so liberated.

And I applaud the Teachers, who are oceans of resolution, who bring happiness and welfare to all beings.

And with folded hands, I request the Buddhas in all directions to be a lamp of Dharma for those who have fallen into suffering because of their delusion.

With folded hands, I ask the Victorious Ones, who desire cessation, to stay in this world for endless aeons lest it remain blind.

Altruistic Intent

May I too, through whatever good I have accomplished by doing all this, become one who works for the complete alleviation of the sufferings of all beings.

May I be medicine for the sick; may I also be their physician and attend to them until their disease no longer recurs.

With showers of food and water, may I eliminate the pain of hunger and thirst, and during the intermediate periods of great famine between aeons, may I *be* food and drink.

And may I be an inexhaustible storehouse for the poor, and may I always be first in being ready to serve them in various ways.

So that all beings may achieve their aims, may I sacrifice, without regret, the bodies, as well as the pleasures that I have had, and the merit of all the good that I have accomplished and will accomplish in the past, present, and future.

Nirvāṇa means to renounce everything. My mind is set on nirvāṇa, so because I am to renounce everything, it is best for me to give it to others.

I therefore dedicate this self of mine to the happiness of all beings. Let them smite me, constantly mock me, or throw dirt at me.

Let them make sport with my body, laugh, and make fun of me! I have given my body away to them: what could its misfortune mean to me?

Let them do to me whatever pleases them, but let no one suffer any mishap on my account.

Whether they direct toward me thoughts that are angry or kindly, may those very thoughts be a constant cause for their achieving all their aims.

Those who accuse me falsely, others who do me wrong, and still others who deride me—may they attain enlightenment!

May I be a protector of the unprotected, a guide for travelers on the way, a boat, a bridge, a means of crossing for those who seek the other shore.

For all creatures, may I be a light for those who need a light, a bed for those who need a bed, and a slave for those who need a slave.

For all creatures, may I be a wish-fulfilling gem, a vase of fortune, a spell that works, a true panacea, a wish-granting tree, a cow of plenty. . . .

Just as the Buddhas of the past grasped the mind set on enlightenment and went on to follow the bodhisattva-training,

so too will I give rise to the mind set on enlightenment for the well-being of the world, and so will I train in the stages of the bodhisattva discipline.

Source: Translated from *Bodhicaryāvatāra of Śāntideva,* ed. P. L. Vaidya, Buddhist Sanskrit Texts, no. 12 (Darbhanga: Mithila Institute, 1960), pp. 1–43.[17]

4.4.3 The Practice of the Perfections

The act of arousing the mind set on enlightenment was formalized and fixed by the making of a vow (praṇidhāna). Equivalents of this vow can already be found in Mainstream Buddhist texts. In its simplest form, the vow is a solemn commitment by the bodhisattva to use his or her own life and enlightenment not for the sake of a personal achievement or bliss but to assist others who are still on the path toward enlightenment. As one early formulaic declaration has it: "After crossing over the stream of saṃsāra, may I help others across; being freed, may I free others; being comforted, may I comfort others; gone to nirvāṇa, may I lead others there."[18] As time went on, however, such vows

---

[17]Alternative English translation, Marion Matics, *Entering the Path of Enlightenment* (New York: Macmillan, 1970), pp. 143–55.

[18]See Har Dayal, *The Bodhisattva Doctrine in Buddhist Sanskrit Literature* (reprint ed., Delhi: Motilal Banarsidass, 1970), p. 65.

became more elaborate and detailed. Whole lists of promises (see 5.4.1 and 5.4.2) were developed, and the bodhisattva's Buddhahood was made contingent upon their fulfillment.

Be this as it may, once a bodhisattva had made his or her vow and embarked on the bodhisattva path, there followed the phase that Śāntideva calls the actual "progression toward enlightenment" (bodhiprasthāna). One way in which this is described is in terms of the practice of the six perfections (pāramitās): giving (dāna), morality (śīlā), forbearance (kṣānti, sometimes translated as "patience" or "stamina"), striving (vīrya, sometimes translated as "heroism" or "energy"), meditation (dhyāna), and wisdom (prajñā). To this list are sometimes added four more perfections to make a total of ten: skillful means (upāya), firm resolution or vow (praṇidhāna), strength or power (bala), and knowledge (jñāna).

The perfections, of course, are not unique to the Mahāyāna. Many of the same qualities are said, in Mainstream Buddhist texts, to have been pursued and fulfilled by the bodhisattva Gautama in his previous lives and are illustrated by jātaka tales of his self-sacrifice, utter dedication, and so on (see, for example, 1.4.2). The following verses have been chosen from various chapters of a Mahāyānist text, the *Compendium on the Perfections,* by the poet Āryaśūra. Each chapter of the text is supposed to illustrate one of the perfections. I have selected a few verses from each.

The Perfection of Giving (Dāna)

After respectfully taking refuge in the Three Jewels and firmly setting their mind on enlightenment by means of a vow, bodhisattvas who wish to advance to the level of the Tathāgatas should first practice exchanging their own situation for that of others.

Then they should discipline themselves in the way of giving, so focused on the welfare of the world that should anyone ask them for their own body, they would give it without shrinking in any way from their resolve. . . .

Thinking, "For the sake of the world, I will achieve various Buddha qualities such as long life, effectiveness as a preacher, and power, and I will offer material objects to beings in order to gather them to me and make them into ready recipients of the good Dharma," wise bodhisattvas make gifts of food and of drink, not in order to attain prosperity or heaven in another life but for the benefit of the world and so as to allay humankind's thirst for impurities.

The Perfection of Morality (Śīlā)

In a nutshell, this is what is called morality: control of body, speech, and mind. Those who are fully disciplined in this regard will effortlessly achieve purity in these three things.

Bodhisattvas who wish to establish in morality all beings in the boundless world systems, should attend to morality for the well-being of the world. That is what the wise call "the perfection of morality."

The Perfection of Forbearance (Kṣānti)

How can the eye get angry? It is nothing but an eye. And the ear or any of the other sense organs—how can they get angry? But a tolerance that regards the senses in such a way is not forbearance in the ultimate sense.

Likewise, a speaker and speech are impermanent; so too are my hearing and my thinking. But a tolerance that is based on making such distinctions between impermanent realities—that is not called the highest forbearance.

There is no doer of wrongful deeds, nor anyone to whom wrongful deeds are done. But a tolerance that is merely successful because it is based on perceiving the nonself of persons is not forbearance that is intent upon transcendence.

The doctrines of impermanence, suffering, impurity, and absence of separate self-identity seem good to me, and their opposites do not. But such a tolerance, which is based on the elimination of contraries, evolves out of a dualist view and is not forbearance in the ultimate sense.

However, when the process of falsely discriminating things as being the same, better, or worse ceases completely, that is what those who walk the path of nondualism call the unsurpassed forbearance whose range is inconceivable.

The Perfection of Striving (Vīrya)

When the all-prevailing power of forbearance has grown, bodhisattvas heroically begin all sorts of amazing feats, employing the great power of their striving, by which they surpass even the deities.

Without striving it is hard for bodhisattvas to finish worldly acts, even when their completion is easily envisioned. But nothing whatsoever can be accomplished except by marching forward, without thinking of getting tired.

The lesser person is unable even to get started. The middling person sets off but gets discouraged. But those bodhisattvas of the Greater Vehicle, who march forward without slowing down, set nirvāṇa aside for the sake of others and undertake their task.

The Perfection of Meditation (Dhyāna)

Thinking, "This is the time for me to cultivate wisdom but not to enter the nirvāṇa [of arhats], for I am unable to attain my own nirvāṇa without quenching the suffering of others," bodhisattvas consider the well-being of the world, and, impatiently eager to become Buddhas, they undertake the practice of meditation with constant diligence.

The Perfection of Wisdom (Prajñā)

These meritorious practices, starting with giving, are even more resplendent when they are ruled by wisdom, just as ornaments made of gold shine brighter when they are set with a jewel.

For in these practices that can proceed independently in developing their own aims, there is a commonality of purpose that wisdom instills throughout all of them and that is like the continuity the mind gives to the senses.

Just as a bodily frame, which is unsuited for activities and devoid of vitality, has no luster, so do these accomplishments lack luster when they are rendered dumb by being disconnected to wisdom.

Source: Translated from Āryaśūra, *Pāramitāsamāsa,* ed. Carol Meadows, in *Ārya-Śūra's Compendium of the Perfections* (Bonn: Indica et Tibetica Verlag, 1986), pp. 156, 160, 176, 190, 200, 202, 206, 220, 238, 240.[19]

4.4.4 The Skillful Means of Vimalakīrti

Finally, one more aspect of the bodhisattva path needs to be emphasized here: the bodhisattvas' use of skillful means (upāya) in expressing their compassion for others. We have already seen an example of the Buddha's use of upāya in the parable of the burning house (see 4.1). Like the Buddha, bodhisattvas did not always act in predictable or straitlaced fashion in creatively teaching others the path. Indeed, when the bodhisattva's upāya is coupled with the freedom that comes from their liberating vision of the Perfection of Wisdom, the result could sometimes be rather eccentric behavior, prototypical, perhaps, of Zen masters or Tibetan gurus.

One bodhisattva who was famous in this regard was Vimalakīrti, whose story is told in a sūtra bearing his name. In a series of encounters, Vimalakīrti, with his Perfection of Wisdom perspective, manages to unsettle various disciples of the Buddha (śrāvakas), as well as a number of his fellow bodhisattvas, while leading them along the path to true enlightenment. In addition, Vimalakīrti is not even a monk but a householder, a layperson, something that added to his popularity in certain Chinese Buddhist circles, where this sūtra became famous.

The Skillful Means of Vimalakīrti

And in the city there lived an elder named Vimalakīrti, who dwelt there as a skillful means for the salvation of human beings. For he used his measureless wealth to convert the poor, and his own pure virtue to convert those who broke the precepts; he controlled himself with patience to convert the scornful, and strove with diligence to convert the lazy; he used his calm meditation to convert the confused, and his firm wisdom to convert the ignorant.

He wore the white robes of a layman but observed the pure conduct of a recluse; he lived the household life but was not attached to the world. He had a wife and children but ever practiced the religious life: he kept a household but ever delighted in solitude.

[19] Alternative English translation, Meadows, *Ārya-Śūra's Compendium,* pp. 157, 161, 177, 191, 201, 203, 207, 221, 239, 241.

He wore jewels and ornaments but adorned his body with the signs of greatness; he ate and drank but delighted in the taste of meditation. He went to the gambling hall but worked for the salvation of men; he took on the ways of the heretics but never strayed from the true faith; he knew all the worldly texts but ever delighted in the teachings of the Buddha.

And truly he was honored by all as the best among the worthy, for he upheld justice; he converted the old and the young.

He knew all businesses, but he took no pleasure in the worldly profits he gained. Rather he went out upon the streets to benefit all living creatures: he entered the courts to defend the oppressed; he attended the debates to lead the people to righteousness; he went to the schools to educate the untaught; he entered the brothels to show the follies of lust; he went to the wine houses to make firm the wills of men.

When he was with the elders, he was the most honored among them and taught them the highest teachings; when he was with the householders, he was the most honored among them and taught them to cast aside attachment; when he was with the warriors, he was the most honored among them and taught them forbearance.

When he was with the priests, he was the most honored among them and taught them humility; when he was with the judges, he was the most honored among them and taught them justice; when he was with the princes, he was the most honored among them and taught them loyalty.

When he was in the inner palace, he was the most honored person there, and he converted all the harem girls to virtue; when he was with the common people, he was the most honored among them and taught them the power of merit. . . .

The Illness of Vimalakīrti

And thus with innumerable skillful means, the elder Vimalakīrti brought benefit to living creatures, and using his skillful means he made his body appear to be sick.

And the kings and ministers, the elders and householders, the priests and princes heard of his illness, and thousands upon thousands of people came to inquire after his health. And Vimalakīrti made use of his illness to receive them and to preach to them the Law.

True Meditation

And the elder Vimalakīrti thought to himself: "Here I am sick and upon my bed, yet the Blessed One has no compassion upon me, nor does he think of me."

But the Blessed One knew his thoughts.

So the Buddha said to Śāriputra: "Go and call on Vimalakīrti, and inquire about his illness."

And Śāriputra said to the Buddha: "Blessed One, I am not worthy to call on him and inquire about his illness. For I remember that once I was sitting quietly in meditation at the foot of a tree, and Vimalakīrti came up to me and said:

'Śāriputra, to sit quietly is not necessarily to sit in meditation. But rather to sit in meditation is to let neither your body nor your mind appear in the universe; it is to let all your activities appear without arising from your trance of cessation.

'To sit in meditation is to act like everyone else while casting aside no quality of enlightenment; it is to let your mind neither abide within or wander without.

'To sit in meditation is to be unmoved by error while you practice all that conduces to enlightenment; it is to enter nirvāṇa without cutting off the passions of the world.

'It is when you can sit like this that you win the seal of the Buddhas.'

"And when I heard this, Blessed One, I remained silent and could make no reply. That is why I am not worthy to call on him and inquire about his illness. . . ."

True Nirvāṇa

Then the Buddha said to the great Kātyāyana: "Go and call on Vimalakīrti and inquire about his illness."

And the great Kātyāyana said to the Buddha: "Blessed One, I am not worthy to call on him and inquire about his illness. For I remember that once the Buddha had preached an outline of the Law to a group of monks, and I was expanding upon it, teaching them the meaning of impermanence, and suffering, and emptiness, and not-Self, and nirvāṇa; and Vimalakīrti came up to me and said:

'Kātyāyana, do not use arising and ceasing thoughts to teach about reality. For all events ultimately neither arise nor cease: that is the meaning of impermanence. And the five aggregates are empty and occur nowhere: that is the meaning of suffering.

'No event ever really happens: that is the meaning of emptiness. Self and not-Self are the same: that is the meaning of not-Self. And events have never been as they are, and so will never cease: that is the meaning of nirvāṇa.'

"And when he taught this teaching, the minds of all the monks gained freedom. That is why I am not worthy to call on him and inquire about his illness."

True Purity

Then the Buddha said to Upāli: "Go and call on Vimalakīrti, and inquire about his illness."

And Upāli said to the Buddha: "Blessed One, I am not worthy to call on him and inquire about his illness. For I remember that once two monks had committed an offense, and they were so ashamed that they dared not tell the Buddha.

"And they confessed to me, and said: 'Resolve our doubt and our remorse, that we may cleanse our guilt.' So I was teaching them in accordance with the Law and Vimalakīrti came up to me and said:

'Upāli, do not aggravate the sin of these two monks, but rather wipe it out at once, without tormenting their minds. For the true nature of their sin abides neither within nor without, nor does it abide in between.

'The Buddha has said that living creatures are impure when their minds are impure, and pure when their minds are pure. And the mind abides neither within nor without, nor does it abide in between: as their minds are, so are their sins. Every event is the same, and does not depart from reality. Upāli, tell me, is your mind impure when it gains its freedom?'

"I said that it was not.

'And even so the minds of all living creatures are without impurity. Misconceptions are impurity: purity is to be without misconceptions. Error is impurity: purity is to be without error. Clinging to a self is impurity: purity is to be without clinging.

'All events arise and cease, and do not abide: like an illusion, like lightning, events do not wait for each other, and do not stay for an instant. All events are false vision: like a dream, like fire, like the moon in water, like an image in a mirror, they are born of false vision.

'He who knows this is said to be a keeper of the rule; he who knows this is said to be truly free.'

"And the two monks said: 'This is the highest wisdom, and it is beyond the ability of Upāli: he is the highest in keeping the rule, yet he cannot explain it. . . . '

"And the two monks had their doubt and remorse resolved, and awakened the thought of supreme and perfect enlightenment. That is why I am not worthy to call on him and inquire about his illness. . . ."

True Enlightenment

Then the Buddha said to the bodhisattva Maitreya: "Go and call on Vimalakīrti, and inquire about his illness."

And Maitreya said to the Buddha: "Blessed One, I am not worthy to call on him and inquire about his illness. For I remember that once I was preaching to the King of the Gods and his retinue, explaining the conduct of one who can no longer be turned back from enlightenment, and Vimalakīrti came up to me and said:

'Maitreya, the Blessed One has prophesied that in one more life you will attain to supreme and perfect enlightenment. Tell me, for which life did you receive this prophecy? Is it the past, or the future, or the present?

'For if it is the past, then your past life is already finished; if it is the future, then your future life has not yet come; if it is the present, then your present life does not abide. For the Buddha has said that at this very moment you are born, and are decaying and passing away.

'And if you received the prophecy for no lifetime at all, then no lifetime at all is the fixed abode of nirvāṇa; and in nirvāṇa there is no receiving of prophecy, and no attaining to supreme and perfect enlightenment.

'Maitreya, tell me, how did you receive the prophecy that in one more life you would attain to enlightenment? Did you receive the prophecy from the birth of reality? Did you receive the prophecy from the cessation of reality?

'If you received the prophecy from the birth of reality, then reality has no birth; if you received the prophecy from the cessation of reality, then reality has no cessation.

'All living creatures are reality; all events are reality; all the saints and sages are reality; even Maitreya is reality.

'If Maitreya receives a prophecy, then all living creatures should receive a prophecy, for reality is always the same and never different.

'If Maitreya attains to supreme and perfect enlightenment, then all living creatures should attain to it, for all living creatures are the manifestation of enlightenment.

'If Maitreya gains nirvāṇa, then all living creatures should gain nirvāṇa; for the Buddhas know that all living creatures are already calm and ceased, and this is nirvāṇa; and they shall not cease hereafter.

'Therefore do not mislead these sons of heaven with your teachings; for there is no such thing as awakening the thought of enlightenment, and there is no such thing as turning back from it.

'But rather you should urge these sons of heaven to give up thinking that enlightenment is something real, or something different; for enlightenment cannot be attained by the body, and it cannot be attained by the mind.

'Enlightenment is calm cessation, for there all manifestations cease. Enlightenment is nonseeing, for it is beyond all connection. Enlightenment is nonaction, for it is without thought. Enlightenment is cutting off, for it sees nothing as real. Enlightenment is separation, for it imposes nothing upon reality. . . . '

"Blessed One, when Vimalakīrti taught this teaching, two hundred sons of heaven realized that no event in this world is truly real. That is why I am not worthy to call on him and inquire about his illness. . . ."

The Visit of Mañjuśrī

Then the Buddha said to the bodhisattva Mañjuśrī: "Go and call on Vimalakīrti, and inquire about his illness."

And Mañjuśrī said to the Buddha: "Blessed One, this excellent man is hard to answer. Deeply he has reached reality; skillfully he teaches the essentials of the Law. His eloquence is unhindered and his insight boundless: he knows all that a bodhisattva must do, and has penetrated into all the secret treasures of the Buddha. He has overcome the Evil One, and exercises magic powers: he has gained both wisdom and skillful means. But I will accept the command of the Buddha, and go and inquire about his illness."

And all the bodhisattvas who were present—the great disciples and the kings of the four heavens—all thought to themselves: "Now these two great men shall meet together; surely they will discuss the wonderful Law."

So eight thousand bodhisattvas, and five hundred disciples, and hundreds of thousands of men and gods followed after Mañjuśrī to the house of Vimalakīrti. . . .

The Buddha Way

And Mañjuśrī asked Vimalakīrti: "How does a bodhisattva set forth on the Way of the Buddha?"

And Vimalakīrti replied: "If a bodhisattva treads what is not the Way, then he has set forth on the Way of the Buddha."

And Mañjuśrī asked: "How does a bodhisattva tread what is not the Way?"

And Vimalakīrti replied: "A bodhisattva walks among those who have committed the most grievous sins, yet feels no anger; he goes to the deepest hell, yet has neither sin nor stain. . . .

"He may seem to be aged and sick, but he has cut off all disease, and has no fear of death; he may seem to be born with property, but he ever looks upon impermanence, and desires nothing. He may seem to have wives and concubines, but he is far from the swamp of desire; he may seem to be dull and stammering, but he is perfect in eloquence and unfailing in memory; he may seem to have entered the wrong crossing, but he saves all living creatures. He may seem to be in the world, but he has cut off the causes of becoming; and he may seem to be in nirvāṇa, but he has not cut off arising and ceasing.

"And if a bodhisattva thus can tread what is not the Way, then he has set forth on the Way of the Buddha."

And then Vimalakīrti asked Mañjuśrī: "What is the seed of Buddhahood?"

And Mañjuśrī replied: "The body is the seed of Buddhahood; ignorance and craving are the seeds of Buddhahood; lust and hatred and delusion are the seeds of Buddhahood. . . . The senses are the seeds of Buddhahood; evil and passion are the seeds of Buddhahood. . . . Whoever sees the unconditioned, and enters into the fixed abode of nirvāṇa, cannot awaken the thought of supreme and perfect enlightenment. For the lotus flower does not grow on the high dry plain, but in the muddy swamp; and only in the swamp of passion are there living creatures to produce the qualities of Buddhahood. . . ."

Entering the Gate of Oneness

And Vimalakīrti said to all the bodhisattvas: "Gentlemen, tell me, how does a bodhisattva enter the gate of oneness? Each of you tell me in your own way."

So the bodhisattva Dharmavikurvaṇa said: "Gentlemen, arising and ceasing are two. But events have never arisen, so now they do not cease. To realize that no event in this world is truly real is to enter the gate of oneness. . . ."

The bodhisattva Candrottara said: "Darkness and light are two. If there is neither darkness nor light, then they are two no longer. For when you enter the trance of cessation there is neither darkness nor light; and so it is with all events. To enter into this state of peace is to enter the gate of oneness. . . ."

The bodhisattva Ratnamudrāhasta said: "To delight in nirvāṇa and despise the world are two. If you neither delight in nirvāṇa nor loathe the world, then they are two no longer. For if there were bondage there could be freedom; but if there has never been bondage, then who would seek for freedom? If there is neither bondage nor freedom, then there is neither delight nor loathing. This is to enter the gate of oneness."

The bodhisattva Maṇikūṭarāja said: "The right and the wrong are two. If you abide in the right, then you do not discriminate between the right and the wrong. To be free of these two is to enter the gate of oneness."

The bodhisattva Satyarata said: "Reality and unreality are two. But he who truly sees does not see reality; so how could he see unreality? For it is not what the eye can see; only the eye of wisdom can see it; and the eye of wisdom neither sees nor does not see. This is to enter the gate of oneness."

And thus each of the bodhisattvas spoke in turn; and they asked Mañjuśrī what it was to enter the gate of oneness.

Mañjuśrī said: "I think that when you can neither speak nor talk of any event, when you neither indicate nor know any thing, when you pass beyond both questions and answers, this is to enter the gate of oneness."

And then Mañjuśrī said to Vimalakīrti: "Sir, each of us has spoken. Tell us how a bodhisattva enters the gate of oneness."

And Vimalakīrti kept silent, and did not say a word. . . .

Source: Reprinted by permission of Wadsworth, Inc. from Stephan Beyer, *The Buddhist Experience* (Encino, CA: Dickenson, 1974), pp. 219–25 (slightly altered).[20]

---

[20]Original text, *Vimalakīrtinirdeśa sūtra* (Taishō shinshū daizōkyō, ed. J. Takakusu and K. Watanabe [Tokyo, 1924–29], no. 475, 14:539a–551c).

CHAPTER 5

Saviors and Siddhas: The Mahāyāna Pantheon and Tantric Buddhism

The history of Mahāyāna thought is in part the history of great sūtras, in part the history of great philosophical thinkers who were influential in developing doctrine, and in part the elaboration of the bodhisattva path. But it is also the history of an exuberance of mythological thinking, which sought to illustrate the practice of that path with the paradigms of great bodhisattvas and Buddhas, and it is the history of the development of alternative means to enlightenment. In the sections that follow, we shall look at some of these further evolutions in Mahāyāna thought by focusing first on the development of the Buddhism of devotion, which centered on certain savior figures of the growing Mahāyāna pantheon. We shall then examine some of the principles and practices of Tantric Buddhism, concentrating in particular on the visionary tradition of meditation.

5.1 THE LIFE SPAN OF THE TATHĀGATA

One important area where Mahāyānists departed from earlier Mainstream Buddhist views lay in their understanding of the person of the Buddha Śākyamuni. Though still recognized as the "founder" of the tradition, Śākyamuni was, in the Mahāyāna, magnified and apotheosized in such a way that he was no longer thought of as a strictly historical figure (albeit an exceptional one). In particular, the view developed that his time as the Buddha was not limited to a mere eighty years on earth. Rather, as a transcendent Savior whose life is immeasurable, he was thought to exist eternally. The *locus classicus* for this new Mahāyāna vision of Śākyamuni was the *Lotus Sūtra*. The selection that follows, however, is taken from a later text, the *Sūtra of Golden Light*, which expresses the doctrine in a somewhat more straightforward manner in its account of the bodhisattva Ruciraketu's doubts about the life span of Śākyamuni.

Śākyamuni, however, was not the only Buddha in the Mahāyāna pantheon. With the unlimited extension of his life span, what had once been (in Mainstream Buddhism) a plurality of short-lived Buddhas existing in time and succeeding one another over the aeons, now became a multiplicity of infinitely long-lived Buddhas existing in space and spread out in world systems in the various cardinal directions. The cult of these so-called celestial Buddhas, savior figures such as Amitābha, Akṣobhya, and Bhaiṣajyaguru quickly became an important feature of the Mahāyāna, and it will be dealt with below in section 5.4. Some of these figures already appear in the selection that follows, however, as witnesses to Śākyamuni's glory.

At that time, in the great city of Rājagṛha, there dwelt a bodhisattva named Ruciraketu. He had served a past Buddha, under whom he had planted roots of merit, and then he honored many hundreds of thousands of millions of billions of Buddhas.

One day, this thought occurred to him: "What is the cause, what is the underlying reason that the Blessed Śākyamuni Buddha had a life span that was limited to just eighty years? Indeed, did the Blessed One not declare that there are two causes, two reasons, for long life—abstaining from taking life and making offerings of food? Now the Blessed Śākyamuni abstained from taking life for incalculable hundreds of thousands of millions of billions of aeons! And as he gave his possessions, so too he gave himself as food to beings, satiating those who were hungry with the flesh, blood, bones, and marrow of his own body!"

Now, while Ruciraketu was thus recollecting the qualities of the Buddha his house suddenly became vast and spread out. Transformed by the Tathāgata, it became made of cat's eye, studded with many divine gems, suffused with more-than-heavenly perfumes. And in that house, in the four directions, there appeared four seats made of divine gems; and on those seats, divine cushions, covered with bejeweled cotton cloth; and on those cushions, divine lotuses . . . also studded with gems. And on those lotuses, there appeared, seated on lion thrones, four Blessed Buddhas: in the East, the Tathāgata Akṣobhya; in the South, the Tathāgata Ratnaketu; in the West, the Tathāgata Amitāyus; and in the North, the Tathāgata Dundubhisvara.

Then, just as the great city of Rājagṛha was suffused with a great shining light, the trichiliomegachiliocosm and world systems in all ten directions as numerous as the sands of the Ganges also became suffused with light. Divine blossoms came down in showers, and divine musical instruments were heard; and all the beings in the trichiliomegachiliocosm became endowed with divine bliss, through the power of the Buddhas. Those who were born blind were able to see, the deaf could hear, those who were mad regained their senses, those who were distracted became attentive, the naked were clothed, the hungry ate their fill, the thirsty had their thirsts quenched, the diseased were cured of their illness, and the handicapped recovered full use of their limbs. In general, many marvelous things happened in the world.

Then the bodhisattva Ruciraketu, seeing those Blessed Buddhas, was astonished: "How can this be?" he wondered. And, pleased, glad, elated, delighted, giving rise to joy and happiness, he saluted those Buddhas with folded hands. But while recollecting those Blessed Buddhas, and then recollecting the qualities of the Buddha Śākyamuni, he considered again the life span of the latter and remained puzzled: "How can this be? Why is it that the Blessed Śākyamuni had a life span that was limited to just eighty years?"

Then, those Blessed Buddhas, mindful and conscious of what the bodhisattva Ruciraketu was thinking, said to him: "O son of a good family, do not think that the life span of the Blessed Śākyamuni was limited in this way. Apart from fully enlightened Buddhas, we do not perceive anyone—in the world of gods, Māras, and Brahmās or among śramaṇas, brahmins, divinities, humans, or asuras—who is capable of understanding from one end to the other the life span of the Blessed Tathāgata Śākyamuni."

As soon as those Blessed Buddhas had uttered this explanation of the life span of the Tathāgata, by the power of the Buddha, the gods dwelling in the realms of desire and of form, such as nāgas, yakṣas, gandharvas, asuras, garuḍas, kiṃnaras, and mahoragas, as well as many hundreds of thousands of millions of billions of bodhisattvas, all assembled in that house of the bodhisattva Ruciraketu. And then those Tathāgatas delighted that whole congregation with these verses explaining the life span of the Blessed Śākyamuni:

> "It is possible to count the drops of water in all the seas, but no one can measure the life of Śākyamuni.
> "It is possible to number the atoms of Mount Meru, but no one can measure the life of Śākyamuni.
> "As many atoms as there are on earth, it is possible to count them all, but not to figure the life of the Buddha.
> "Someone may wish somehow to measure space, but no one can measure the life of Śākyamuni.
> "Talk of aeons and millions of aeons will come to a standstill; the Buddha cannot be arrived at by counting. . . .
> "Therefore, do not be confused; do not have a single doubt: no full measure of the life span of the Buddha can be obtained."

Source: Translated from *Suvarṇaprabhāsa sūtra*, ed. S. Bagchi, Buddhist Sanskrit Texts, no. 8 (Darbhanga: Mithila Institute, 1967), pp. 4–6.[1]

5.2 SAVIOR BODHISATTVAS

The bodhisattva path described in 4.4 was not just a set of ideals and practices, it was also a catalyst for the development of legends about great bodhisattvas and about even greater Buddhas, who had fulfilled all their bodhisattva vows. Here we enter the realm of mythology—of the Mahāyāna pantheon peopled by "savior bodhisattvas" (also called "celestial bodhisattvas") and "savior," or "celestial," Buddhas and of the wonderful Buddha fields, or Pure Lands, that developed around them. Here we also enter the

---

[1]Alternative English translation, R. E. Emmerick, *The Sūtra of Golden Light* (London: Luzac, 1970), pp. 3–5.

realm of the devotional cult of individual Buddhas and bodhisattvas, the "Buddhism of Faith," which grew not only in India but also took root throughout the Mahāyāna world in China, Japan, and Tibet. As this cult developed, Avalokiteśvara, Mañjuśrī, Kṣitigarbha, Tārā, and other bodhisattvas who were thought to be far advanced on the path all became renowned as figures who were dedicated to saving all sentient beings as part of their bodhisattva practice.

5.2.1 The Compassion of Avalokiteśvara

In the story of Vimalakīrti (see 4.4.4), we have already had an example of a bodhisattva's use of skillful means to fulfill the role of teacher. But being "saved" did not just mean being guided or goaded into a better understanding of the perfection of wisdom; it also meant being rescued from specific situations of suffering—from monsters, murderers, shipwrecks, and the like. The bodhisattvas' compassionate role, therefore, quickly expanded, so that in addition to being perceived as guides on the path to enlightenment, they were seen as figures who could be relied upon for help in more down-to-earth difficulties. They became savior bodhisattvas in the fullest sense of the term.

Early on, Avalokiteśvara, the embodiment of compassion, became famous as this kind of savior bodhisattva. Always available to succor and help out suffering sentient beings, he was renowned for his ability to take on a multiplicity of forms in doing so. In China and Japan, in fact, Avalokiteśvara permanently became known in female form as the so-called Goddess of Mercy, Kuan-yin (Japanese: Kannon).

One of the most famous texts on the compassion of Avalokiteśvara/Kuan-yin is the chapter devoted to him/her in the *Lotus Sūtra*, translated in the selection that follows. In this text, in order to call on Avalokiteśvara's aid one has to "recollect him," to remember him with mindfulness (anusmṛti). In time, however, it was also possible to do this with the aid of Avalokiteśvara's own mantra, the famous "OṂ MAṆI PADME HŪṂ," much used in Tibet, where Avalokiteśvara became a guardian deity of the country as a whole.

. . . Listen to the course of conduct of Avalokiteśvara. Listen and I will explain how, for unimaginable hundreds of aeons, he purified himself by reaffirming his vows in the presence of thousands of millions of Buddhas.

The systematic visual and auditory recollection of the bodhisattva Avalokiteśvara will, without fail, result in this world in the elimination of all the sufferings and sorrows of living beings.

If an evil-minded fiend, intent on killing you, throws you in a pit of coals, recall Avalokiteśvara, and the fire will be extinguished as though it were sprayed with water.

If someone throws you into the depths of the ocean, the abode of nāgas, monsters, and demonic beings, recall Avalokiteśvara, the king of the waters, and you will never drown.

If an evil-minded fiend, intent on killing you, tosses you off the top of Mount Meru, recall Avalokiteśvara, and you will be upheld in midair like the sun.

If someone, intent on killing you, hurls down upon your head rocky missiles the size of mountains as hard as diamonds, recall Avalokiteśvara, and not a hair on your body will be hurt.

If hosts of enemies surround you, swords in hand and intending to do you harm, recall Avalokiteśvara, and right away their hearts will be filled with friendliness.

If you are led to the execution ground and given over to the executioners, recall Avalokiteśvara, and their swords will fall into pieces.

If you are bound in stocks made of wood or with iron shackles, recall Avalokiteśvara, and your bonds will immediately be broken.

Powerful spells, magical formulas, herbal concoctions, and ghosts and goblins can all destroy the body, recall Avalokiteśvara, and they will go back whence they came.

If you are surrounded by yakṣas, nāgas, asuras, ghosts and ghouls who sap your strength, recall Avalokiteśvara, and not a hair on your body will be hurt.

If you are surrounded by ferocious beasts and wild animals, fearsome with their sharp teeth and claws, recall Avalokiteśvara, and they will immediately go off in all directions.

If you are surrounded by malicious and terrible cobras, spitting venom at your eyes as though their heads were emitting fiery rays, recall Avalokiteśvara, and immediately they will lose their poison.

If a heavy downpour falls from thunderclouds emitting bolts of lightning, recall Avalokiteśvara, and the storm will instantaneously be calmed.

Seeing beings oppressed by hundreds of sorrows and afflicted by many sufferings, he looks down upon the world, including the gods, and protects it. . . .

Recall, recall, and do not doubt that pure being, Avalokiteśvara! In the face of death, misfortune, and calamity, he is a protector, a refuge, a recourse.

He, Avalokiteśvara, has perfected all qualities, and he looks upon all beings with pity and loving kindness. Virtuous—a great ocean of virtue—he is worthy of praise.

He has compassion for the world and will one day in the future become a Buddha. I bow down before him, Avalokiteśvara, who puts an end to all suffering, fear, and sorrow.

Source: Translated from *Saddharmapuṇḍarīka-sūtra*, ed. U. Wogihara and C. Tsuchida (Tokyo: Seigo Kenkyūkai, 1934–35), pp. 366–72.[2]

5.2.2 The Multiple Forms of Tārā

Another favorite savior bodhisattva in both Indian and Tibetan Buddhism was the "goddess" Tārā, who is sometimes paired with Avalokiteśvara. Tārā, like Avalokiteśvara, could take on a variety of forms. She could be benign and comforting and was tireless in the assistance she provided to the oppressed

---

[2] Alternative English translation, Hendrik Kern, *Saddharma-puṇḍarīka or The Lotus of the True Law* (Oxford: Clarendon Press, 1884), pp. 413–17.

and downtrodden; but she could also be ferocious, specializing not only in saving sentient beings from their enemies but also in fiercely destroying those enemies. She too had a short mantra (OṂ TĀRE TUTTĀRE TURE SVĀHĀ) by which she could be invoked. The following selection is from a Sanskrit work in praise of Tārā, attributed to Sarvajñanamitra, an Indian monk of the late seventh or early eighth century.

Oṃ! Praise to the Blessed Noble Tārā! [. . .]

Your compassion truly extends equally to all beings on the pathways of rebirth; therefore, I am surely among those whom it embraces.

Your unequaled capacity to save beings shines like the sun on the dark passions, the impurities of the whole world; and I too suffer and am tormented! Oh! The impure misdeeds that I have committed!

Woe! Woe! Ill-fated am I! I am blind, even in the light of the sun! I am thirsty even on the banks of a refreshing icy mountain stream! I am poor even with access to abundant jewels in the mines of the Isle of Gems! Being without refuge, I make you my protector, Blessed Lady, you who are the support of the whole world.

Even a mother gets tired of a baby who constantly cries for milk. Even a father gets angry at a son who daily asks for things he does not have. But you, like a great wish-granting tree, fulfill the desires of this Triple World. You never fail to grant the requests of all those who reverence you. [. . .]

When those who are injured—whose limbs are being fed on by vermin that have attached themselves to their oozing open wounds, smelling of flesh, flowing with blood, suppurating with stinking pus, filled with impurities due to their past evil deeds—devote themselves . . . to service at your feet, their physical bodies become beautiful like gold, and their eyes like lotuses.

Those in whose ear the gurus have not repeated the sacred texts (as though they were putting alms in a bowl) and those who, lacking a wealth of knowledge, become mute in the fellowship of the learned—they will become the Lord of Speech as a result of devotion to you. . . .

Those whose loins are covered with rags that are torn and dark with dirt from lying on the ground; who pick lice and seek food from others in a broken pot—they will gain universal sovereignty over the earth by propitiating you. . . .

Those who are tired of seeking ways in which to make a living by bartering, by carrying out a trade, or by being employed in the service of others and who fail to get money even though they have amassed merit in previous lives—by turning to you who surpass the gods, Mother of the destitute, they . . . will obtain a treasure of gold spewed forth from the earth. [. . .]

Some see you in your fierce form, striking out with bright weapons uplifted and swinging, breaking and pervading the sky, your arms entwined with bracelets that are hooded serpents. Taking on this frightful aspect, you scare enemies away, your laughter causes great tumult, like the rolling and striking of a great drum. . . .

But for others, in each of your hairs is visible the expanse of heaven and earth wherein dwell in bliss the gods Brahmā, Indra, and Rudra as well as humans, maruts, siddhas, gandharvas, and nāgas. And all directions are pervaded by hundreds of Buddhas without end, which you have magically fashioned. Worthy of worship by the Triple World, in your own being, you contain all creatures. . . .

Some see you red like the sun whose rays are redder than red lacquer or vermillion. Others see you blue like dust made of the pulverized fragments of a magnificent precious sapphire. And some see you white, more dazzling than the churned ocean of milk and brighter than gold. Your form, like a crystal, takes on various aspects, changing according to the different things that are placed near it.

Source: Translated from *Āryatārāsragdharāstotra,* ed. Godefroy de Blonay, *Matériaux pour servir à l'étude de la déesse buddhique Tārā* (Paris: Emile Bouillon, 1895), pp. 34–39.[3]

5.2.3 Samantabhadra and the Reciters of the *Lotus Sūtra*

The bodhisattva Samantabhadra was relatively late in gaining popularity in India, but he achieved some importance in East Asia, where he is known as P'u-hsien (Chinese) or Fugen (Japanese) and is famed in his own right as well as for the great white elephant on which he is said to ride. He is often paired with Mañjuśrī, the prime bodhisattva of wisdom. In the *Lotus Sūtra,* however, from which the following selection is taken, he is given a specialized role as the protector of all those who preserve the sūtra by reciting it.

Then the great bodhisattva Samantabhadra . . . went to Vulture's Peak and approached the Blessed One. He saluted him by prostrating himself at his feet, then circumambulated him seven times and said: "Blessed One, I have come here from the Buddha field of the Blessed Tathāgata Ratnatejobhyudgata, since I have heard that in this world system the Blessed Tathāgata Śākyamuni is preaching a discourse on the Dharma, the *Lotus of the Wonderful Law,* and I wish to hear it. . . .

[Then, having heard the sūtra expounded], the great bodhisattva Samantabhadra said: "Blessed One, in later times, in a later period, . . . I will protect all those monks who recite this Dharma discourse. I will ensure their well-being, preserve them from persecution, protect them from malignant poisons, so that no one looking for a way to oppress them will be able to get at them: neither Māra, nor his sons, nor his daughters, nor others of his followers and neither gods, nor demons, nor hungry ghosts, nor ghouls, nor evil spirits, nor spectres.

"Blessed One, I will always constantly guarantee the protection of one who recites this Dharma. And when a Dharma-reciter who applies himself to this sūtra mounts the walkway to practice walking meditation, I

---

[3]Alternative French translation, in de Blonay, *Matériaux,* pp. 41–47.

will mount my six-tusked white elephant and, surrounded by a host of bodhisattvas, go to his hut and safeguard his recitation of the Dharma.

"And when that Dharma-reciter, applying himself to this sūtra, forgets so much as a word or a syllable of the text, I will mount my six-tusked white elephant, appear to him in person, and repeat the whole Dharma discourse for him. And seeing my actual self and hearing from me the whole Dharma discourse, without lacunae, he will become happy, delighted, exultant, . . . and he will make heroic efforts in his recitation and, upon seeing me, will immediately acquire samādhi and be endowed with various spells to ensure his protection."

Source: Translated from *Saddharmapuṇḍarīka-sūtra,* ed. U. Wogihara and C. Tsuchida (Tokyo: Seigo Kenkyūkai, 1934–35), pp. 384–86.[4]

5.3 SAVIOR TEXTS

Samantabhadra's function in the *Lotus Sūtra*—to protect those who rehearse and venerate the sūtra itself—reflects the growing magical, salvific function of Buddhist scriptures. Indeed, in the Mahāyāna the personae of bodhisattvas were not the only agents of salvation; the very texts in which they figured, because they contained and conveyed the Dharma, came to be seen as having the power both to enlighten and to protect beings who turned to them. And the intervention of a Samantabhadra figure to ensure protection was by no means always needed: the text itself came to be seen as quite capable of doing so on its own. Just as the power of bodhisattvas could be called upon by the recitation of their particular mantras, the power of texts could likewise be captured by the recitation or copying of a portion of the text, a chapter, a verse, or even just the title.

This gave rise, in the Mahāyāna, to the phenomenon of self-laudatory texts, sūtras that devote a few lines or a chapter to the praise of their own preservation, recitation, and power. Indeed, in other portions of the *Lotus Sūtra,* we can read how those who commit to memory or copy out but a portion of it will be guaranteed immense soteriological benefits. In time, whole Buddhist sects came to be focused on the salvific power of such texts, the prime example, perhaps, being the Japanese Nichiren sect, where the primacy of the *Lotus Sūtra* is much emphasized and the mantra in praise of its title (Namu Myōhō renge kyō—"Praise to the *Lotus Sūtra* of the Wonderful Dharma") is much chanted (see 9.7).

In time, also, some sūtras appeared that were almost entirely self-laudatory in nature, as the following selection testifies. Here the emphasis is not so much on the recitation of the text as on its writing, its copying—something that was seen as a powerful, protective act of praise and merit. The following example comes from a relatively obscure text, the *Aparimitāyuh Sūtra* (*Discourse on Unbounded Life*).

[4]Alternative English translation, Hendrik Kern, *Saddharma-puṇḍarīka or The Lotus of the True Law* (Oxford: Clarendon Press, 1884), pp. 431–34.

Oṃ! Praise to the Blessed One, the king of immeasurable life, . . . the arhat, the completely enlightened Buddha.

Whoever copies or sponsors the copying of this *Aparimitāyuḥ sūtra* will never be reborn in the hells, nor among animals, nor in the world of Yama, nor in any of the places of inopportune rebirth; and wherever they are reborn, they will, in each birth, be able to remember their previous lives. . . .

Whoever copies or sponsors the copying of this *Aparimitāyuḥ sūtra* will thereby have caused to be written the 84,000 sections of the Dharma. . . .

Whoever copies or sponsors the copying of this *Aparimitāyuḥ sūtra* will thereby have built and established 84,000 stūpas. . . .

Whoever copies or sponsors the copying of this *Aparimitāyuḥ sūtra* will never unwittingly commit any of the five deeds that result in immediate retribution in hell. [. . .]

Whoever copies or sponsors the copying of this *Aparimitāyuḥ sūtra* will be followed everywhere by the four celestial guardian kings, who will ensure his or her protection. . . .

Whoever copies or sponsors the copying of this *Aparimitāyuḥ sūtra* will be reborn in the Sukhāvatī world system, Buddha field of the Tathāgata Amitābha. . . .

Whoever copies or sponsors the copying of this *Aparimitāyuḥ sūtra* will never be reborn as a woman. . . .

Whoever, for the sake of teaching this *Aparimitāyuḥ sūtra*, would give so much as a penny, it would be as though he or she had given a gift by filling up the trichiliomegachiliocosm with the seven precious gems.

Indeed, if one were to venerate, with offerings of the seven precious gems, all the Tathāgatas of the past, . . . it would still be possible to measure the merit thereby accumulated, but it is not possible to measure the amount of merit that comes from this *Aparimitāyuḥ sūtra*.

Source: Translated from *Aparimitāyuḥ sūtra*, Sanskrit text ed. A. K. Rudolf Hoernle, *Manuscript Remains of Buddhist Literature found in Eastern Turkestan* (Oxford: Clarendon Press, 1916), pp. 309ff.

5.4 CELESTIAL BUDDHAS AND PURE LANDS

Savior texts such as the *Aparimitāyuḥ sūtra* and bodhisattvas such as Tārā and Avalokiteśvara were effective in dealing with the problems of this world, but they were not, of course, the only figures in the Mahāyāna pantheon. An equally important role must be assigned to those bodhisattvas who, by fulfilling their vows, had become celestial, or savior, Buddhas such as Amitābha, Akṣobhya, Ratnasambhava, and Bhaiṣajyaguru.

It is sometimes asked how these Buddhas differ from the savior bodhisattvas who are often closely associated with them. Are they simply "more advanced" beings on the same path, or are they radically different in nature? The question is not easy to answer, and it is rendered more complex by the twin assertions that Buddhahood is one of the things that bodhisattvas will not attain without assisting other sentient beings to final enlightenment, and that Buddhas, being totally transcendent, are not supposed to be able to intercede personally in everyday worldly affairs. The problem can be elucidated, however, by a consideration of two features of the careers of these celestial Buddhas: first, their vows and second, their Pure Lands.

The mythology of the celestial Buddhas likes to feature the vows that they made long ago when they were still bodhisattvas. Typically, these often-elaborate vows are set in conditional terms, expressing a desire on the part of the bodhisattva *not* to become a Buddha *unless* such and such items specified in the vow have been fulfilled. For example, in one Pure Land text, Dharmākara (the bodhisattva who eventually becomes the Buddha Amitābha) makes a series of vows (see below) and then reflects: "Having made these world-surpassing vows, I am certain to attain the unsurpassable Way. But, I pledge that, if my vows are not fulfilled, I will not realize perfect awakening. If I do not become a generous donor for endless cosmic ages, rescuing everywhere the destitute and the suffering, I pledge I will not realize perfect awakening."[5] Such statements, however, are presented as having been made long ago. In the meantime, the bodhisattva making them (in this case, Dharmākara) *has* gone on to become a "full" Buddha (in this case, Amitābha). What this amounts to, then, is the ultimate guarantee of the genuineness of his vows, for, in a certain sense, they have already been fulfilled.

Obviously, one of the things to which this mythology opened the door was a mushrooming among devotees of the sentiment of faith, of reliance on the vows or former vows of Buddhas for one's own attainment of enlightenment and one's own benefit in this world.

Buddhas, however, are sometimes portrayed as not being supposed to intervene directly in the affairs of human beings. Unlike bodhisattvas, who might be said to be "in this world though not of it," celestial Buddhas are "neither of it nor in it." Instead, they reside in transcendent, utterly wonderful "other worlds"—not ordinary heavens but Pure Lands—where they wait to welcome devotees. As a consequence, their compassion tends to be more centripetal than that of the great bodhisattvas. Rather than going out to help sentient beings, they attract them to themselves.

5.4.1 Amitābha and His Pure Land

One of the best known of the celestial Buddhas is the Tathāgata Amitābha, who dwells in the Western Pure Land of Sukhāvatī (the Land of Bliss). In the *Larger Sukhāvatī vyūha sūtra,* the forty-eight (or forty-six; the number varies) vows he made long ago as the bodhisattva Dharmākara are listed. These conditional vows lie at the basis of what was eventually to become, in the Pure Land tradition of China and Japan, a very sophisticated theology of salvation by means of faith in the grace of this Buddha, but for the most part they describe characteristics of Amitābha's future Pure Land, Sukhāvatī.

[5]Luis O. Gómez, *The Land of Bliss: The Paradise of the Buddha of Measureless Light* (Honolulu: University of Hawai'i Press, 1996), p. 172. Original text: *Larger Sukhāvatī vyūha sūtra* (Taishō shinshū daizōkyō, ed. J. Takakusu and K. Watanabe [Tokyo, 1924–29], no. 360, 12:269b).

Amitābha's vows are too numerous to spell out fully here, but a summary can be given.[6] Dharmākara first promises that his Pure Land will have certain characteristics: it will be a place where there will be no unfortunate realms of rebirth (vow 1) and no danger of falling into any of them (vow 2); where all beings will have golden skin (vow 3) and there will be no difference between gods and humans (vow 4); where all beings will be endowed with magical powers (vow 5), such as the ability to remember former births (vow 6), the divine eye (vow 7), the divine ear (vow 8), and mind-reading powers (vow 9); where there will be no notion of personal possessions (vow 10); and where there will be no beings who are not fixed in the truth (vow 11). Dharmākara further promises not to attain Buddhahood if anyone should be able to count his disciples (vow 12); if the light of his body is measurable (vow 13), or if the life span of beings in his Pure Land (vow 14) or his own life span (vow 15) are measurable; or even if the word *demeritorious* is known there (vow 16); or if all Buddhas everywhere do not praise his name (vow 17).

There then follows, in Chinese versions of the text, Dharmākara's famous Eighteenth Vow, which is not fully stated in the Sanskrit text but which became of key importance in the Chinese and Japanese Pure Land tradition. In it, Dharmākara guarantees entry into his Pure Land to anyone who repeats his name as many as ten times and thinks on him with faith. Indeed, to this day, millions of Buddhists in East Asia seek to make good on this vow by sincerely chanting "Praise to the Buddha Amitābha" (Japanese: Namu Amida Butsu), desiring rebirth in his Pure Land.

Dharmākara then goes on to promise to appear to people at the moment of their death (another important feature of East Asian Pure Land mythology) and, in another vow not found in the Sanskrit text, to make sure that all beings in his Pure Land are endowed with the thirty-two marks of a Great Man. The next several vows (nos. 20–32 in the Sanskrit text) all promise beings in his Pure Land ease of access to various sorts of things: opportunities to worship, the wherewithal to do so, and abilities to fathom doctrine, to know things. Moreover, beings there will be freed from rebirth (vow 33), freed from being women (vow 34), clothed in new monastic robes (vow 36), and free from pain (vow 37); the jewel-trees there will produce magnificent ornaments (vow 38); Buddhas and bodhisattvas everywhere will praise Amitābha's name (vows 35 and 39); and beings in his Pure Land will easily attain knowledge, powers, and various meditative trances (vows 40–46).

These vows give us some idea of what Amitābha's Sukhāvatī is like, but the Pure Land texts do not rest at that. They go on to describe its features in detail, features that make it much resemble a paradise. The following passage is from the Sanskrit text of the "Smaller Description of the Land of Bliss."

Then the Blessed One spoke to the Venerable Śāriputra: "Śāriputra, over a hundred thousand billion Buddha fields to the west of here, there is a Buddha field called the world of Sukhāvatī. And there dwells a

[6] For the full text, see "Sukhāvatīvyūhaḥ [vistaramātṛkā]," in *Mahāyāna-sūtra-saṃgraha,* ed. P. L. Vaidya, Buddhist Sanskrit Texts, no. 17 (Darbhanga: Mithila Institute, 1961), pp. 225–30; English translation, F. Max Muller, in *Buddhist Mahāyāna Texts,* ed. E. B. Cowell (Oxford: Clarendon Press, 1894), part 2, pp. 12–22.

Tathāgata, an altogether enlightened Buddha named Amitāyus [Amitābha]. . . . Now what do you think, Śāriputra, why do they call that world the land of bliss? Because, Śāriputra, in that world, Sukhāvatī, beings do not experience suffering [duḥkha], neither with their body nor with their mind, and the things causing happiness are innumerable. . . .

"Śāriputra, Sukhāvatī is adorned and enclosed by seven railings, seven rows of palm trees and strings of bells. And it is beautiful and embellished with four kinds of precious materials: gold, silver, lapis lazuli, and crystal. . . . And, Śāriputra, there are lotus pools there made of seven precious materials: gold, silver, lapis lazuli, crystal, red pearls, diamonds, and coral. They are filled with water endowed with eight good qualities . . . and they are strewn with sand of gold. And going down into those lotus pools, from all four sides, are four flights of steps, beautiful, and embellished with four precious materials, . . . and all around the lotus pools jewel-trees are growing, beautiful, and embellished with seven precious materials. . . . And in those lotus pools, lotuses are growing: various kinds of blue ones, and various kinds of yellow ones, and various kinds of red ones, and various kinds of white ones, beautiful, beautifully colored, beautifully resplendent, beautiful to look at, and as big around as the wheel of a cart. . . .

"Furthermore, Śāriputra, in that Buddha field, divine musical instruments are always playing, and the earth is pleasant and golden colored. And in that Buddha field, three times each night and three times each day, showers of blossoms fall, divine mandārava blossoms. And the beings there, during the time it takes to eat one morning meal, can pay homage to a hundred thousand billion Buddhas, by going to other universes. And after showering each Tathāgata with a hundred thousand billion flowers, they return to their own world in time for a nap. . . .

"Furthermore, Śāriputra, in that Buddha field, there are geese, snipe, and peacocks. Three times each night and three times each day, they come and sing together, each uttering its own cries. . . . And when the people there hear that sound, they become mindful of the Buddha, mindful of the Dharma, and mindful of the Sangha. Now, Śāriputra, [because of these birds] are you thinking that there are beings who have been reborn in that Buddha land as animals? That is not the way you should see it. Why? Because, in that Buddha field, Śāriputra, no one is born as a hell being, an animal, or a hungry ghost in the dominion of Yama the god of the dead. These birds were magically fashioned by the Tathāgata Amitāyus, and their cries are the sound of the Dharma. With such marvelous Buddha-field qualities, Śāriputra, is that Buddha field Sukhāvatī arrayed."

Source: Translated from "Sukhāvatīvyūhaḥ [saṃkṣiptamātṛkā]," in *Mahāyāna-sūtra-saṃgraha*, ed. P. L. Vaidya, Buddhist Sanskrit Texts, no. 17 (Darbhanga: Mithila Institute, 1961), pp. 254–55.[7]

---

[7]Alternative English translation, Luis O. Gómez, *The Land of Bliss: The Paradise of the Buddha of Measureless Light* (Honolulu: University of Hawai'i Press, 1996), pp. 16–18.

5.4.2 The Twelve Vows of Bhaiṣajyaguru

Sukhāvatī, the Land of Bliss in the west, was, of course, not the only Pure Land, and the Tathāgata Amitābha not the only celestial Buddha to become the object of a cult. The so-called Buddha of Medicine, or Healing Buddha, Bhaiṣajyaguru, also attained a tremendous popularity in East Asia. His cult has its origins in India, however, where he especially appealed to people who found themselves plagued by sickness or all sorts of other sufferings. In the following Sanskrit text, the Buddha Śākyamuni tells the bodhisattva Mañjuśrī about Bhaiṣajyaguru's vows.

The Buddha then said: "Listen, Mañjuśrī, and pay careful attention to what I say."

"I shall," said the ever-youthful Mañjuśrī, and he gave ear to the Blessed One.

"East of here, Mañjuśrī, beyond Buddha fields as numerous as the sands of ten Ganges rivers, there is a world called Vaidūryanirbhāsa. There dwells a fully enlightened Tathāgata named Bhaiṣajyaguru Vaidūryaprabha (Lord of Medicine Resplendent as Lapis Lazuli). He is perfect in wisdom and good conduct, accomplished and knowing the world, an unsurpassed guide of those who are to be trained, a teacher of gods and humans, a Blessed Buddha. Now, Mañjuśrī, that Blessed Tathāgata Bhaiṣajyaguru Vaidūryaprabha, long ago, carrying out the practices of a bodhisattva, made these twelve great vows:

1. " 'When I, in the future, am awakened to unsurpassed complete enlightenment, then may innumerable, inconceivable, unmeasurable world systems be lit up, warmed and illuminated by the brilliant glow of my body. And may the bodies of all beings become endowed, as mine is, with the thirty-two marks and the eighty minor signs of the Great Man.
2. " 'When I, in the future, have attained enlightenment, may my body be absolutely pure, inside and out, like a priceless jewel of lapis lazuli; because my body is large, may it be endowed with a most excellent brilliance and radiance, may its rays surpass those of the sun and the moon and give light everywhere, so that beings born in that world system, even those who are out in the dark, gloomy night, can see to go their various ways and do good deeds.
3. " 'When I have attained enlightenment, may I, through my inconceivable wisdom and the use of my unmeasurable skillful means, be a supporter of beings, providing for their protection, food, and enjoyment; and may those who are in some way deformed no longer be so.
4. " 'When I have attained enlightenment, may those beings who are following a heretical path, or the disciples' path, the pratyeka-

buddhas' path join the Mahāyāna, the path to unsurpassed enlightenment.

5. " 'When I have attained enlightenment, may beings in my order lead chaste and studious lives, and may they be perfect and well-restrained in their observance of the precepts; and if any of them happen to be deficient in morality, may they not be reborn in a lower state of rebirth, after hearing my name.
6. " 'When I have attained enlightenment, may beings who are physically disabled; whose senses are impaired; who have bad skin color; who are deaf and mute, lame, humpbacked, albino, maimed, blind, or mad; and whose bodies are otherwise defective have their senses restored and their limbs made wholesome, after hearing my name.
7. " 'When I have attained enlightenment, may those beings who are afflicted by various diseases, without shelter or refuge, without the aid of medicine, helpless, poor, and suffering, be cured of all their illnesses, should my name fall upon their ears; may they be free from sickness and grief right up until enlightenment.
8. " 'When I have attained enlightenment, any woman who is afflicted by the hundreds of various disadvantages of womanhood and who wishes to be liberated from being reborn as a loathsome female should bear my name in mind, and she will no longer be reborn in the female state, right up until enlightenment.
9. " 'When I have attained enlightenment, all those beings who have been caught by Māra's noose, who are closely tied to various wrong views—may I free them from all of Māra's heretical entrapments, instill in them correct views, and consequently show them the way of the bodhisattva.
10. " 'When I have attained enlightenment, may those beings who are smitten by fear of the king, imprisoned in shackles, condemned to die, plagued by many hallucinations, dishonored, and afflicted by sufferings of body, speech, and mind be liberated from all fears and oppression by the meritorious power of the hearing of my name.
11. " 'When I have attained enlightenment, those beings who are suffering the pangs of hunger or who, in their search for food and drink, were caused unwillingly to commit evil deeds—if they bear my name in their minds, I will satiate their bodies with foods that look, smell, and taste good.
12. " 'When I have attained enlightenment, any beings who have no clothes, who are poor, who are plagued by cold and heat and mosquito bites and suffering day and night—if they bear my name in their minds, I will clothe them in wonderful garments, dyed various colors; and I will bring them pleasures in various ways, by means of jewels, ornaments, perfumes, garlands, unguents, and the sounds of song and musical instruments; in these ways I will fulfill all the wishes of all beings.'

"These, Mañjuśrī, are the twelve vows that were made long ago by the Blessed Bhaiṣajyaguru Vaidūryaprabha, Tathāgata, arhat, completely enlightened one, as he was carrying out the practices of a bodhisattva."

Source: Translated from *Bhaiṣajyaguruvaidūryaprabharāja sūtra,* ed. Nalinaksha Dutt, *Gilgit Manuscripts* (Srinagar: Government Research Department, 1939), 1:2–7.

5.4.3 How to Be Reborn in Akṣobhya's Land

The importance of faith and invocation as means of being reborn in the Pure Land was much emphasized by the Amidist schools that developed in China and Japan. But this should not obscure the fact that in other texts, other ways—more complementary than contradictory—of getting to the Pure Land were advocated. One of these is the practice of visualization, a meditative technique that we have already encountered, which takes as its object of concentration, of "construction," the characteristics of the Pure Land and of the body of the Buddha. In the *Amitāyur-dhyāna sūtra,*[8] for example, one starts by contemplating the setting sun (appropriately in the West) and proceeds to visualize various features of the Pure Land of Sukhāvatī—the water, the land, the jewel-trees—before moving on to the lotus throne of the Buddha and finally the Body of Amitābha itself. If all this is too difficult and complicated, an alternative is then proposed: simply to repeat the name of the Buddha, "Namu Amida Butsu."

In addition to visualization, however, some texts stressed the importance of moral discipline and lifestyle. The following verses suggest that access to the Buddha Akṣobhya's Pure Land was to be had by observing the precepts and doing good, meritorious deeds. The importance of Akṣobhya's cult should not be overlooked. In some ways, his Pure Land of Abhirati, located in the East, was but a counterpart to Amitābha's Pure Land of Sukhāvatī in the West, but in other ways it differed significantly from it. Of special note was the fact that women could be reborn as women in Abhirati and could even give birth there, without labor pains. This was not the case in the Pure Lands of Amitābha and Bhaiṣajyaguru, where women, in gaining rebirth, became men. Moreover, it is evident in the Abhirati texts that the earliest notions of a Pure Land were ones that featured it not as a concession to the rank and file but as something that individual Buddhists should establish for themselves just as Akṣobhya did.[9] In this way, one might not only aspire to "be born in Akṣobhya's Land" but to "give birth to a land like Akṣobhya's" by virtue of one's actions and merit. The following passage is from the *Mahāparinirvāṇa sūtra,* a Mahāyāna text that is not primarily concerned with Akṣobhya but that pauses long enough to do justice to his cult.

[8] English translation, Junjiro Takakusu, "Meditation on Buddha Amitāyus," in *Buddhist Mahāyāna Texts,* ed. E. B. Cowell (Oxford: Clarendon Press, 1894), part 2, pp. 161–201.

[9] See Jan Nattier, "The Realm of Akṣobhya: A Missing Piece in the History of Pure Land Buddhism," *Journal of the International Association of Buddhist Studies* 23 (2000): 71–102.

Do no injury to living beings,
Hold firmly to all the rules of restraint,
Accept the Buddha's exquisite teaching,
And you will be born in Akṣobhya's Land.

Do not steal other people's property,
Always be kind and generous to all,
Everywhere build habitations for monks,
And you will be born in Akṣobhya's Land.

Do not ravish others' wives and daughters,
Do not take your own wife at the wrong time,
Have your bed in keeping with the precepts,
And you will be born in Akṣobhya's Land.

Keep watch on your mouth and avoid false speech
Either for your own sake or for others,
In search of advantage or out of fear,
And you will be born in Akṣobhya's Land.

Do not slander any good acquaintance,
Keep far away from evil company,
Let your mouth always speak agreeably,
And you will be born in Akṣobhya's Land.

Be the same as all the bodhisattvas,
Always free from evil utterances,
So that men will gladly hear what you say,
And you will be born in Akṣobhya's Land.

Even when you are playing and laughing
Do not utter inappropriate words,
Be careful always to speak timely words,
And you will be born in Akṣobhya's Land.

Seeing others receive gain and service,
Let your thoughts be always those of gladness,
Never let knots of jealousy be tied,
And you will be born in Akṣobhya's Land.

Cause no affliction to living beings,
Let your thoughts always be those of kindness,
Do not employ evil expedients,
And you will be born in Akṣobhya's Land.

Perverted views say there is no giving
To one's parents, no past and no future.
If you do not entertain such notions,
Then you will be born in Akṣobhya's Land.

Dig good wells beside roads in the desert,
Plant and cultivate orchards of fruit trees,
Always give nourishment to mendicants,
And you will be born in Akṣobhya's Land.

If to the Buddha, Doctrine and Order
You offer one incense lamp in worship
Or even present a single flower,
Then you will be born in Akṣobhya's Land.

If either because of apprehension
Or for the sake of profit or merit
You write out one stanza of this scripture,
Then you will be born in Akṣobhya's Land.

If, for the hope of profit and fortune
In the course of one day you are able
To read and recite this scriptural text,
Then you will be born in Akṣobhya's Land.

If, for the sake of supreme enlightenment
Throughout a whole day and throughout one night
You adhere to the eight rules of fasting,
Then you will be born in Akṣobhya's Land.

If you do not reside in the same place
As those who violate the chief precepts
And scold slanderers of the expanded texts,
Then you will be born in Akṣobhya's Land.

If you can give charity to the sick,
Even if it is just a piece of fruit
And giving them a pleasant, cheering glance,
Then you will be born in Akṣobhya's Land.

If you do not steal the Order's offerings
But guard the property of the Buddha
And paint and sweep Buddha and Order's sites,
Then you will be born in Akṣobhya's Land.

If you make images and Buddha-shrines,
Even if they are only a thumb's size,
And if you always take delight in them,
Then you will be born in Akṣobhya's Land.

If for the sake of this scriptural text
Your own body, your wealth and your treasures
You give to the preacher of the Doctrine,
Then you will be born in Akṣobhya's Land.

If you are able to listen, write down,
Receive, and remember and read and recite
All the Buddha's reservoir of secrets,
Then you will be born in Akṣobhya's Land.

Source: Reprinted by permission of the publisher from Richard Robinson, *Chinese Buddhist Verse* (London: John Murray, 1954), pp. 61–63.[10]

---

[10]Original text: *Mahāpariṇirvāṇa sūtra* (Taishō shinshū daizōkyō, ed. J. Takakusu and K. Watanabe [Tokyo, 1924–29], no. 375, 12:734a–b).

5.5 TANTRIC BUDDHISM, OR THE VAJRAYĀNA

Tantric Buddhism is based on the Tantras, a category of texts commonly distinguished from the sūtras. The first appearance of the Tantras is very difficult to date (fourth century C.E.?), and the area of their origin within India is still much disputed. Tantric Buddhism is sometimes considered as a final outgrowth of the Mahāyāna, but it is sufficiently distinct as a movement that it is perhaps best to consider it as a "vehicle" in itself. As such it is often called the Vajrayāna (Diamond, Thunderbolt, or Adamantine Vehicle) or the Mantrayāna (Mantra Vehicle).

The complexities of Tantric Buddhism cannot be gone into here, but a number of its features need to be highlighted. First, taking seriously the Mādhyamika doctrine of the inseparability of nirvāṇa and saṃsāra, the Tantras asserted that enlightenment could be attained by means of the things of this world itself, by means of one's own body, one's own speech, one's own mind. To make the point even more graphically (and to reassert, perhaps, through iconoclastic and eccentric language and behavior the freedom from convention that comes with liberation), some Tantrics sought out the equation with nirvāṇa by involvement in some of the most impure forms of saṃsāra—meat eating, wine drinking, sex.

More generally, the Vajrayāna sought to enable one to become identified, in one's own body, speech, and mind, with the enlightened Buddha. This process of identification could be accomplished in this lifetime (the Vajrayāna was commonly seen as a shortcut to enlightenment) by means of certain rituals and visualizations. Calling upon all the powers of concentration that had long been utilized in Buddhist yogic techniques, assuming the constructs of the Mind to be as real as the Vijñānavādins asserted them to be, and basing themselves on the full potential of emptiness, Tantric meditators developed visualization practices whereby they could envision an enlightened Buddha (or several Buddhas) and themselves as merging.

Such visualizations made much use of the creative and transformative power of letters and words, either chanted as mantras or visualized as seed syllables, of different colors, and of their different relations to the Buddhas. They also used mudrās, symbolic hand gestures adopted by both the meditator and the visualized figures of the Buddhas and bodhisattvas, as well as maṇḍalas, structured arenas, sacred worlds in themselves, in which one could symbolically arrange or find arranged many visualized figures of Buddhas and bodhisattvas. It is clear in all of this that ritual and iconography play important roles in Tantric Buddhism.

At the same time, in the Tantras the theme of the creative union of polar opposites came to the fore. Buddhism had always sought a Middle Way between the extremes of world denial and world affirmation. One way of doing this was to seek to combine, to merge perfectly, inclinations in the two directions. Thus a bodhisattva should have both wisdom (prajñā) and skillful means (upāya) and should be involved in both emptiness (śūnyatā) and compassion (karuṇā). In Tantric Buddhism, the symbols for expressing such polarities and their union mushroomed: sun and moon, vowels and consonants, right and left. But one of the most prevalent images that developed was that of female and male, the union of which effected the union of wisdom and means, of the understanding of emptiness and compassionate involvement with the forms of this world.

5.5.1 Tantra against a Mādhyamika Background

In early Buddhist literature, a saying is sometimes quoted to the effect that people who trip and fall on the ground must get up again by supporting themselves on the very ground that made them stumble. In the following selection, from a text that is attributed to a monk called Āryadeva II (in order to distinguish him from Nāgārjuna's disciple, Āryadeva I), this principle is extended to the whole of life in this world and reinterpreted in the context of the Mādhyamika notion of the nonduality of nirvāṇa and saṃsāra.

Those who do not see things as they are think in terms of saṃsāra and nirvāṇa. Those who see things as they are think of neither saṃsāra nor nirvāṇa.

For false discrimination is the "great grabber" that causes one to sink in the ocean of saṃsāra. Free from false discrimination, great beings are released from the bonds of becoming.

Unenlightened people are afflicted by the poison that is the poison of doubt. Having uprooted it completely, one who is compassionate should continue practicing.

Just as pure crystal takes on the colors of other objects, so too the jewel of the mind is colored by its false imaginings.

By nature, the jewel of the mind is free from the colorations of false imaginings; it is originally pure, unproduced, without inherent self-existence, immaculate.

Therefore, because of this fundamental purity of the mind, one should strive to do everything that fools condemn, by means of union with one's own tutelary deity. . . .

One who has aroused the thought of enlightenment and set his mind on Buddhahood should not try to deny or get out of the world.

One who, in contemplating the world, does not see it as originally pure, unproduced, without inherent self-existence, and immaculate is not a Buddha and is not liberated.

What should we do? Where can we obtain the various powers of becoming? Someone who is overcome by poison can become poison-free by the use of some more poison [as an antidote].

Similarly, water in the ear can be washed out by water, and a thorn removed by a thorn. In this way, the wise can get rid of passion by means of passion itself.

Just as a washerman gets the dirt out of clothes by means of dirt, so too the wise resort to vices to get rid of vices.

Source: Translated from *Cittaviśuddhiprakaraṇa of Āryadeva,* ed. Prabhubhai B. Patel (Shantiniketan: Visvabharati, 1949), pp. 2–3.[11]

---

[11] Alternative English translation of some of these verses, David Snellgrove, in Edward Conze, *Buddhist Texts through the Ages* (New York: Harper and Row, 1954), p. 221.

5.5.2 The Perfection of Nonduality

Some of the implications of this lack of distinction between saṃsāra and nirvāṇa are borne out in the practices or visualization-meditations (sādhanas) of Tantric adepts. We shall start with a relatively short text written in the ninth century C.E. by a yogin named Lakṣminkarādevī. She was the sister of King Indrabhūti and achieved fame as one of the eighty-four siddhas (perfected ones) of the Indo-Tibetan Vajrayāna. In her work she sets forth a method of unconventional ritual-meditational acts designed to help one break through this world of conventional reality, this world of attachment to "things," to "ideas," and to the "dos and don'ts" that go with them. Indeed, in a world that is marked by emptiness, in which saṃsāra and nirvāṇa are indistinguishable, nothing (or everything) is sacred, and Lakṣminkarādevī, like later Zen masters, can even advocate murdering the Buddha. At the same time, it must be realized that Lakṣminkarādevī is also using here the conventions of what was called "twilight language," in which certain terms likely to shock not only mean what they say but also stand as symbols for a whole set of other connotations. Thus, for example, when she speaks of "feces, urine, and semen," she is also calling to mind delusion, hatred, and desire; the Buddhas Vairocana, Akṣobhya, and Amitābha; and body, speech, and mind (bodhicitta).

Oṃ. Homage to Vajrasattva [Diamond Being]!

I bow my head before Vajrasattva, resplendent by nature, omniscient, originator of the Triple World, deliverer of desired fruit! I will speak briefly about the supreme sādhana of Vajrasattva. . . .

Even in a hundred billion aeons, one who does not have true yoga will fail to succeed through the practice of restraints, vows, fasting, uttering mantras, or meditating.

The mantrayānist should always practice true meditation by making devotional offerings of such things as feces, urine, and semen as well as snot.

The yogin should always make devotional offerings, employing wisdom and skillful means, to his mother and sister, as well as his daughter and niece.

The yogin should always make devotional offerings, by means of meditation on knowledge and Vajra, to any woman who is missing a limb, who is vile, an artisan, an outcaste.

These are the seed syllable mantras of the Truth: OṂ AḤ HŪṂ.

Those terrifying deeds that bind living beings are the very ones that will liberate them from their bonds of becoming when accompanied by skillful means.

Every day, the yogin should carry out the sacraments that originated in the five divine families of the Tathāgatas, and make devotional offerings of flesh mixed with seminal "milk" produced on various occasions.

Having aspired to complete enlightenment, the mantrayānist should contemplate the ocean of knowledge with a smile on his face and his eyes wide open.

Everything that abides in the Triple World, whether it be stationary or moving, should be seen, by means of true yoga, as having Vajra.

Those who follow other traditions or who are marked by being of mixed caste should not be despised; they too are transformations of Vajrasattva.

Treating all beings equally—they have all come into existence without a Self—the mantrayānist should always meditate upon his body, which is pure by nature.

The Lord delights in receiving offerings made with skillful means such as perfumes, garlands, cloth, incense, and such things as song, music, and dance.

The yogin should not undertake painful practices, such as fasting, bathing, purification; also he should quit his village responsibilities.

He should not venerate gods who are made of wood, stone, or clay but should always make devotional offerings to his own body, by inward concentration.

He should make devotional offerings to the Vajra-bearer with feces and urine mixed with honey together with the flesh of the five [animals: cow, dog, horse, elephant, and human].

By means of true meditation, he should make devotional offerings to the deity dwelling in the body, with the self-born flowers of women together with seminal "milk" produced on various occasions.

He should seize the property of others; he should have intercourse with their wives. He should tell lies; and he should kill all the Buddhas.

He should not build caityas or other monuments made of stone or clay. He should take no delight in books. He should not make maṇḍalas, even in his dreams, neither in body, speech, or mind.

The knower of mantras should not be disgusted by anything at all, for Vajrasattva himself is physically present, abiding in all things. And the mantrayānist should pay no attention to the differences between such things as where one can go and where one cannot go, what one can eat and what one cannot eat, what one can drink and what one cannot drink.

For the sake of his accomplishment, the knower of the secret truth should eat the creatures produced from the body of all beings and those excreted by Vairocana.

A woman sprung from any caste should not disgust him; indeed she is Blessed Wisdom incarnate in a conventional form.

You need pay no attention to lunar dates, constellations, or fasts. One who is endowed with the knowledge of nonduality will accomplish Buddhahood.

What is the use of so much talk? The knower of the Truth, by means of true yoga, will see everything that there is to perceive. . . .

Source: Translated from *Advayasiddhi*, ed. Malati J. Shendge (Baroda: Oriental Institute, 1964), pp. 15–23.[12]

5.5.3 Worship in a Tantric Context

In Tantric Buddhism, visualization was ritual and ritual was visualization, and both, when properly done, were magical, meaningful, dynamic processes that

[12] Alternative English translation, Shendge, *Advayasiddhi*, pp. 24–30.

were soteriologically effective. But visualizations and the mantras and symbolic gestures that accompany them also became important features of ritual worship, of routine practices such as going for refuge, confessing one's faults, making meritorious offerings to one's teacher or to the Buddha, and so forth. Often such visualizations were preliminary practices incorporated into meditative sādhanas aimed at realizing identification with a divinity, but they could also be, as in the following selection from a manual for Buddhist laypersons, ways of practicing one's daily devotions, ways that had the advantage of being able to be done anywhere and of greatly enhancing, at least mentally, the magnificence of one's worship (and the magnitude of one's offerings).

When the third watch of the night has passed, you should get out of bed, cup your hands in devotion, bow your head down to the ground, and say:

"OṂ! I worship the feet of all the Tathāgatas through union with their body, speech, and mind.

"OṂ! I present myself for service in the worship of all the Tathāgatas, by pervading the whole realm of reality with the Vajra of my body, speech, and mind. O, you who are the Vajra Being [Vajrasattva] of all the Tathāgatas, give me a firm basis!

"OṂ! I present myself for initiation into the worship of all the Tathāgatas. O, you who are the Vajra Jewel [Vajraratna] of all the Tathāgatas, initiate me!

"OṂ! I present myself for the duty of the worship of all the Tathāgatas. O, you who are the Vajra Duty [Vajradharma] of all the Tathāgatas, set me in motion!

"OṂ! I present myself for the effectuation of the worship of all the Tathāgatas. O, you who are the Vajra Action [Vajrakarma] of all the Tathāgatas, have me carry it out!

"And I engender the Vajra Mind of the knowledge of all things by giving rise to the thought that is equal to the Vajra Knowledge of all Tathāgatas, in order to attain a realization of the true essence of reality equal to my roots of merit."

Such is the ritual to be done . . . .

Then, after kneeling and touching your head to the ground, you should brush your teeth. . . . And over the water held in your hand [for rinsing the mouth] you should recite: "OṂ! You whose elements are pure, cleanse me of all sins, take away all my misconceptions, HŪṂ!"

Then you should wash your face with water over which you have chanted seven times: "OṂ! Lotus, Lotus. . . . You who are lovely, Lotus of my eyes, HŪṂ! HŪṂ! HŪṂ!" In this way, you will become well liked by all human beings and will suffer from no disease of the eyes.

Then, in your meditation chamber on a comfortable seat, you should contemplate the divinity of your choice, and if you tire of meditation, you should recite mantras. . . .

When the sun has risen, you should immediately offer water that has been purified to Jambhala [the Lord of the Waters]. . . . Then you should do the following ritual visualization: In front of you a red syllable YAṂ appears; it becomes an eight-petaled lotus; on top of it there appears a white syllable A; it becomes the disk of the moon; the whole becomes pale red: wisdom and means together. And on top of that, a yellow JAṂ appears [which is Jambhala himself]. He is in samādhi, in union with his consort Vasudhārā. On his head is the golden Buddha Ratnasambhava. He is bedecked with all his ornaments, his stomach protrudes, he is small in stature, and he is wearing a garland of blue lotuses.

Then, on your right hand, you should visualize the syllables OṂ on your wrist, HŪṂ in the middle of your hand, BLŪṂ at the tips of your fingers, and SAḤ at the base of your fingers. And you should recite the following mantra over your hand: "OṂ! To the Lord of Waters, SVĀHĀ!" And with your cupped hand, drink the five nectars of immortality (or, alternatively, perfumed water) saying: "OṂ HŪṂ BLŪṂ SAḤ."

Then you should offer 108 handfuls of water to Jambhala, for as the Blessed One has said, "One who, with a firm mind and fervent faith, makes such an offering will soon become like Jambhala."

Then, in a pure place, offer 108 handfuls of water to the hungry ghosts while reciting this mantra: "OṂ! This water is for all hungry ghosts. SVĀHĀ!"

Next, without delay, you should make a clay caitya. . . . The ritual is as follows: "OṂ! Praise to the Blessed One, . . . the completely enlightened Tathāgata arhat! OṂ! O subtle, unequaled, quiet, subdued, unreachable, independent, glorious nirvāṇa. . . . SVĀHĀ!"

After reciting this over a lump of clay or sand twenty-one times, you should fashion it into a caitya, saying, "As many as there are atoms in this lump of clay may there be that number of billions of caityas made!" And then set the caitya up with the stanza: "The Tathāgata has explained the cause of those elements of reality that arise from a cause, as well as their cessation. Of this, the great monk has spoken."

Then you should make an offering of flowers to the caitya, reciting the following mantra: "OṂ! Flowers, flowers, great flowers, good flowers, arisen from flowers, source of flowers, moving beyond flowers, covered with flowers, SVĀHĀ!" And for each of the flowers that you offer, it is as though you were giving a billion flowers.

Then you should pay homage to the caitya, saying: "OṂ! Praise to the Blessed One, . . . the completely enlightened Tathāgata arhat! OṂ! Jewels, jewels, great jewels, jewel-victory, SVĀHĀ!" And for each time you venerate the caitya, it is as though you were venerating it a billion times.

Then comes the ritual smiting [or consecration of the image]:

With the mantra "OṂ! Mother Earth, SVĀHĀ!" you should take up the clay. With "OṂ! To the Vajra-born, SVĀHĀ!" shape it into an image. With "OṂ! Clean and pure, SVĀHĀ!" coat it with oil. With "OṂ! Womb of the Vajra-realm, SVĀHĀ!" complete the image. With "OṂ! Womb of the Dharma-realm, SVĀHĀ!" complete the mudrās. With "OṂ! Vajra hammer, smash, HŪṂ! PHAṬ! SVĀHĀ!" smash [the demons]! With "OṂ! Pleasure of the Dharma, SVĀHĀ!" call out [the Buddha in the image]. With "OṂ! Well-established Vajra, SVĀHĀ!" establish its basis [in the image]. With "OṂ! Womb of the Dharma-realm blazing with the splendor of the jewels of all the Tathāgatas, SVĀHĀ!" fix it there. With "OṂ! Pure essence womb of the Dharma-realm, come, be off, SVĀHĀ!" you should dismiss it. And with

"OṂ! Womb of the realm of space, SVĀHĀ!" you should ask for forgiveness for any ritual errors committed. Then, place what is now an object of worship in a pure place. . . .

In worshiping the Buddha, you should first symbolically bathe the image by stroking it with a peacock feather and reciting the bath mantra. . . . Then make these offerings:

> OṂ! ĀḤ! Vajra goods! HŪṂ! SVĀHĀ!
> OṂ! ĀḤ! Vajra garments! HŪṂ! SVĀHĀ!
> OṂ! ĀḤ! Vajra flowers! HŪṂ! SVĀHĀ!
> OṂ! ĀḤ! Vajra incense! HŪṂ! SVĀHĀ!
> OṂ! ĀḤ! Vajra lights! HŪṂ! SVĀHĀ!
> OṂ! ĀḤ! Vajra food! HŪṂ! SVĀHĀ!

Source: Translated from *Ādikarmapradīpa,* ed. Louis de La Vallée Poussin, *Bouddhisme, études et matériaux* (London: Luzac, 1898), pp. 190–93.[13]

5.5.4 The Meditator Becomes the God

Visualizations, of course, were not restricted to use in devotional worship. They were also put to work in Tantric meditations (sādhanas) which had as their aim a double identification: that of the meditator with the Buddha/divinity being visualized and that of the Buddha/divinity with the visualizing meditator. These two realizations, of course, occurred together, but they might be thought of as reflecting the complementary processes of the Tantric path: the quest for wisdom and the expression of compassion.

In the following sādhana, described by the sixteenth century Tibetan monk Pema Karpo, there are several processes of identification with the divinity, and overall the meditation is a visionary endeavor that is fast paced, is constantly changing, and mixes down-to-earth images with syllables, sounds, abstract doctrines, body parts, colors, Buddhas, bodhisattvas, divinities, and so forth. Important in all of this are not only verbal elements and mental elements of the meditation but also the whole physiology of the meditator with its bodily channels and yogic cakras. Truly, this sādhana involves the coordination of body, speech, and mind.

It is often hard to follow in this visualized world what is inside and what is outside, what is the meditator and what is the tutelary deity (the meditator's yidam—here Cakrasamvara, who emanates and is emanated from all the letters of the alphabet), and what is the Buddha (here in one of his "fierce" forms as Heruka). Indeed, unifications of all these figures in the "father-mother" (Tibetan: yab-yum) sexual mode and interpenetrations and identifications are part of the whole purpose of the visualization. But not forever: as in all such meditations, there is, in the end, a systematic dissolution of all the visions. Emptiness is what has made the whole process possible, and to emptiness the process returns; and the meditator comes back to the world, but not unchanged.

---

[13]Alternative English translation, Stephan Beyer, *The Buddhist Experience* (Encino, CA: Dickenson, 1974), pp. 57–59.

We shall start our selection toward the end of the sādhana, at the point where the meditator, having already gone through several transformations, identifies himself with the deity in his fierce manifestation, then visualizes himself united in yab-yum embrace with his consort, and then further generates the maṇḍala of the deity within his heart.

And my body is colored white; I have four heads and twelve arms; my right foot is stretched out, trampling upon the breast of the red Lady Night-of-Time; and my left foot is slightly bent, trampling upon the forehead of the blue Creator-of-Terror. My head in front is white, my head on the left is green, my head in the rear is red, and my head on the right is yellow, and each of my faces has three eyes.

I have matted and piled hair, marked with a jewel, a crossed vajra, and a crescent moon; on each of my heads is a diadem of five dried human skulls; and I have made a necklace of fifty dripping human heads. I am adorned with the six signs of ferocity: wheel and earrings and necklace and bracelets and girdle and ashes of the dead. . . .

And upon my lap is the Mother; her body is colored red; she has one head and two hands; and her face has three eyes.

Her left hand holds a skull-bowl filled with entrails, and with this arm she embraces the Father; her right hand holds a vajra aloft to the sky, with a terrifying gesture; on her head is a diadem of five dried human skulls, and she has made a necklace of fifty human skulls; her hair hangs free, and she is adorned with the five signs of ferocity.

And the calves of her legs embrace the thighs of the Blessed One, and we both stand in the midst of the blazing fire of knowledge.

On a moon at the tops of the heads of both Father and Mother is OṂ; on a sun at our necks is ĀḤ; on a sun at our hearts is HŪṂ. And SVĀ is at the break of our waists; ĀḤ is on our sexual organs; and HĀ is between our thighs.

In the secret place of the Father appears the syllable HŪṂ which transforms into a white vajra; on its tip appears the syllable BAṂ, which transforms into a red gem; and the hole is blocked by a yellow PHAṬ.

In the Mother's place of space appears the syllable ĀḤ, which transforms into a red lotus; in its center appears the syllable OṂ, which transforms into its white anthers; and the hole is blocked by a yellow PHAṬ.

And the Father and Mother enter into union, and the vajra is within the lotus; and by the sound of the bliss thereof, and by the light which radiates forth from our hearts, we invite all those whose accomplishment of deity is innate, and all those whom we have cleansed and transformed into the maṇḍala of the Blessed Cakrasamvara.

And they all enter into union in the sky before me: they melt into Great Bliss and enter through my mouth; they descend my central channel; they pass through my vajra, and fall and mix into the lotus of the Mother. . . .

In my heart is an eight-petaled lotus and in its center stands the god himself, the same as I am, but only four fingers tall; on the four petals in the four directions are the four goddesses of the central lotus, and in the intermediate directions are the four offerings. And in the twenty-four places of my body, as I touch each place with the ring finger of my left hand, there appear the twenty-four syllables PUṂ JĀṂ OṂ AṂ GOṂ RAṂ DEṂ MĀ KAṂ OṂ TRIṂ KOṂ KĀṂ LAṂ KĀṂ HIṂ PREṂ GREṂ SAUṂ SUṂ NAṂ SIṂ MAṂ KUṂ!

And these syllables melt into light and become the twenty-four great places of pilgrimage in the world: the fields and solitary places, the assembly places and cemeteries. And in this divine pavilion of radiance within my body there appear all the deities of my maṇḍala; and each place of pilgrimage is a stage on the path to enlightenment, and all the gods and goddesses therein are the qualities which lead to enlightenment. . . .

And the eight Ladies who guard the gates of the maṇḍala stand at the portals of my mouth and nose and penis and anus and left ear and eyes and right ear.

And my body has become the world, and my whole body is filled with the maṇḍala.

And I grasp the ego of the unchanging body and speech and mind of all Those Who Have Come: OṂ ĀḤ HŪṂ! I am the very self whose essence is the diamond of the body and speech and mind of all the gods and goddesses! OṂ! All events are diamond pure, diamond pure am I! [. . .]

And the deity himself is upon a lotus in my heart, and in his heart is a moon, and upon the moon in his heart is the syllable HŪṂ.

And the dot of the HŪṂ is the essence of the five Buddhas, and its light is like a rainbow halo; and in the midst thereof I clearly see the whole maṇḍala and its retinue.

And every time my breath goes out, the divine hosts of the Blessed Cakrasamvara radiate forth on the tips of beams of light, to purify the world of inanimate objects into a divine palace, and the beings of the world of animate objects into a divine maṇḍala like themselves. And then my breath gathers them all back into me; and this happens over and over again as I breathe.

Then the syllable HŪṂ appears where the secret places of the Father and Mother join together; and then it appears on the tip of my penis, within the vagina of the Mother; and thereby my mind and my breath are firmly fixed within my central channel; and this alone is the very highest of recitations of the mantra.

Then the mantra issues forth with light from the HŪṂ in my heart; it descends the diamond path; it passes through the central channel; it circles through my vajra into the lotus of the goddess and upward from mouth to mouth.

And this is the forward recitation of the mantra; if the direction is reversed, upward through the diamond path and into the mouth of the goddess, this is the fierce recitation; and I practice each of these in turn.

And I recite the mantras in a whisper. . . .

The final emptiness. The vowels and consonants issue forth from my right nostril, with five-colored beams of light; and on the tips of these beams of light there radiate forth the deities of the maṇḍala; they purify the entire Triple World and render it into the essence of their divine body and speech and mind.

And the whole world is made equal to these gods and goddesses, whose deity is forever innate; and the world is gathered back into me with the vowels and consonants; they enter through my left nostril and reach the level of my navel.

And the vowels and consonants transform into a moon of red and white radiance: the gods and goddesses transform into a white and red syllable HŪṂ.

And the syllable HŪṂ transforms into a two-armed Blessed One, Father and Mother, doing the sport of lust; and by the sound of their inner experience of spontaneous joy, the whole maṇḍala is aroused and satiated with Great Bliss.

And the cemeteries are gathered into the gates; and the gates into the central lotus, and the lotus into me, the Lord at the center of the maṇḍala: and I am gathered into the Father and Mother at my navel.

And the Father and Mother melt into light and transform once more into the moon and its syllable HŪṂ.

And the moon dissolves into the HŪṂ, and the U-vowel into the HA, and the HA into the head-stroke, and the head-stroke into the crescent, and the crescent into the dot; and the dot dissolves into Pure Sound.

And my mind is bound to the Pure Sound, and as it grows fainter and fainter I enter into the inconceivability which imposes no constructs upon reality.

The return to the world. And then there arises the Pure Sound, and from that there arises the syllable HŪṂ, and from the syllable HŪṂ the maṇḍala instantaneously appears again: and I am the god himself in the world.

Source: Reprinted by permission of Wadsworth, Inc. from Stephan Beyer, *The Buddhist Experience* (Encino, CA: Dickenson, 1974), pp. 146–53.[14]

5.5.5 Offering the World-Maṇḍala to One's Guru

Within the Tantric Buddhist system of training, one's guru (teacher) occupies a position of prime importance. In some ways, because gurus are present in this world and active as compassionate guides, their disciples are to think of them as prior even to the Buddha or, as in the following text, as embodiments of the Buddha, the Dharma, and the Sangha combined. Indeed, in Tibet, the guru is often added as a "fourth refuge" to the traditional formula of taking refuge in the Triple Gem.

There are many ritual expressions of devotion to one's guru. One of these is the offering of a maṇḍala. The word *maṇḍala* literally means "circle." In

---

[14]Original text: Pad-ma dkar-po, *Snyan-rgyud yi-bzhin nor-bu'i bskyed-pa'i rim-pa rgyas-pa 'dod-pa'i re-skong zhes bya-ba* [The Process of Generation of the Wishing Gem of the Ear-Whispered Teachings] (Dalhousie: Phun-tshogs chos-'khor gling, n.d.), folios 1–19.

Vajrayāna Buddhism it generally refers to a directionally organized diagram of divinities (usually Buddhas and bodhisattvas) that is at once a representation macrocosmically of the whole of reality and microcosmically of the mystical physiology of the meditator. In the present instance, however, *maṇḍala* refers to a representation of the world—the Buddhist cosmos consisting of Mount Meru surrounded by the four continents, in the midst of the great ocean, encircled by the cosmic fence. Monastics and laypersons who carry out this ritual offering today often make use of small world-maṇḍala "kits," a flat metal pan complete with encircling rings, on which they can symbolically construct the cosmos by heaping up small piles of grain to represent each of its continents and other features, all the while chanting mantras and visualizing the "real" things. In this way they can make a total offering of the entire cosmos to their guru or to any other object of devotion, who may well also be visualized.

You should make a maṇḍala offering to your guru. Why? Because it is said, "The guru is like all the Buddhas," and also, "The guru should be seen as the Buddha, Dharma, and Sangha." [. . .]

This is the ritual: Saying, "OṂ! ĀḤ! HŪṂ!" you assure the protection of the place and of yourself. Saying, "OṂ! HRĪṂ! SVĀHĀ!" you establish your seat. Saying, "OṂ! ĀḤ! Vajra-ground, HŪṂ!" you take possession of the ground.

Reciting "OṂ! Vajrasattva, throw out all obstructions! HŪṂ! PHAṬ!" you take cow dung and purify the place and prepare the surface of the maṇḍala-disk. With "OṂ! ĀḤ! Vajra-fence, HŪṂ!" you [encircle the world with a fence and] establish its basis.

Then you should take some flowers, over which you have recited a mantra, and saying, "OṂ! Best of Vajra-gurus, accept my worship and my offering, HŪṂ!" you should offer them in the middle [of the prepared surface]. Then you should wash your hands.

Then, in the middle of the surface, place and visualize the establishment of a four-sided Mount Meru, with eight summits, its east side made of silver, its south side made of lapis lazuli, its west side made of crystal, and its north side made of gold. And in the middle, on top of a lion's throne made of gems, in the center of an eight-petaled lotus, you should see your glorious guru, bedecked with various ornaments. . . .

Then, on the four sides of Mount Meru, you should distinguish the four cosmic continents: Pūrvavideha in the East, in the shape of a half-moon and white; Jambudvīpa in the South, triangular and golden; Aparagodānīya in the West, round and red; and Uttarakuru in the North, square and blue. And you should visualize each and every one of these continents as filled with rubies, sapphires, lapis lazuli, emeralds, diamonds, pearls, and coral.

Then you should take the flowers previously given and offer them again in the center of the maṇḍala, saying, "OṂ! HŪṂ! Praise to the guru in the center!" And offer them above the maṇḍala, saying, "OṂ! Praise to the Vajra-guru!"

Then you should honor the four continents in the four directions:

"OṂ! YAṂ! Praise to Pūrvavideha!
"OṂ! RAṂ! Praise to Jambudvīpa!
"OṂ! LAṂ! Praise to Aparagodānīya!
"OṂ! VAṂ! Praise to Uttarakuru!"

Then you should honor the subcontinents, visualizing them in the intermediate directions:

"OṂ! YĀ! Praise to Dehavideha!
"OṂ! RĀ! Praise to Ambara!
"OṂ! LĀ! Praise to Kurukaurava!
"OṂ! VĀ! Praise to Śākhā Uttarmañjarya!"

And you should honor the [first four regalia-treasures of a great cakravartin king,] visualizing them on the four continents surrounding Mount Meru:

"OṂ! YA! Praise to the Elephant-treasure!
"OṂ! RA! Praise to the Adviser-treasure!
"OṂ! LA! Praise to the Horse-treasure!
"OṂ! VA! Praise to the Woman-treasure!"

And you should honor the [four other regalia-treasures of a great cakravartin king,] visualizing them on the subcontinents in the intermediate directions:

"OṂ! YĀḤ! Praise to the Sword-treasure!
"OṂ! RĀḤ! Praise to the Gem-treasure!
"OṂ! LĀḤ! Praise to the Wheel-treasure!
"OṂ! VĀḤ! Praise to the Great Wealth-treasure!"

And you should offer flowers, in front of and behind Mount Meru, visualizing them as the sun and the moon and saying:

"OṂ! ĀḤ! Praise to the Moon!
"OṂ! ĀḤ! Praise to the Sun!"

And as you recite all these mantras, all of these things come into being of their own accord, and you should offer them to your guru. Taking flowers between your outstretched hands, you should visualize everything as filled with precious gems, and say:

"Praise to you, Praise to you,
Praise to you, Praise, Praise!
With devotion, I praise you,
my guru and my master, be gracious to me!"

Source: Translated from "Ādikarmapradīpa," in Louis de La Vallée Poussin, *Bouddhisme, études et matériaux* (London: Luzac, 1898), pp. 194–97.[15]

---

[15]Alternative English translation, Stephan Beyer, *The Buddhist Experience* (Encino, CA: Dickenson, 1974), pp. 60–61.

5.5.6 Songs of a Mad Saint

For all of its emphasis on realization through transformation of the self and the world and its graphic visualizations, Tantric Buddhism did not escape the processes of systematization and institutionalization. Indeed, in time, the Vajrayāna came to be an academic discipline, part of the curriculum of the monastic universities, and initiations into sādhanas came to be seen as transitional points in one's monastic career. This, however, was not universally the case, for alongside the ranks of monastic Tantrics there were also iconoclasts, homeless wanderers, who expressed in their antinomian behavior the visionary trips of the sādhanas.

Sometimes, these wanderers are said to form what is called the Sahajiyā movement, a variety of Tantra that differed from the mainstream less in its doctrines than in its lifestyle. The Sahajiyā "saints" were long-haired eccentrics who sought not only to be free from rules and restrictions but also to challenge and ridicule them. Wandering about, often with their sexual companions, openly engaging in drunken and licentious behavior, sometimes quite insane, they spoke of Wisdom as a great Whore and sought to shock both the monastic and the social establishments. Some of these "saints" composed songs about their experiences, spontaneous poems that were written in vernacular dialects and were filled with references to their practices, both physical and meditational. The following example is taken from the songs of Kāṇha, who lived in Bengal in the ninth century C.E.

The path is blocked by vowels and consonants.
Kāṇha is disconsolate when he sees it.
Kāṇha, where will you go to make your abode?
You are indifferent to all the objects of your mind.
There are three, there are three, but the three are separate:
Kāṇha says: it is existence separates them.
Whatever comes goes away:
Kāṇha is disconsolate at all this coming and going.
Hey, Kāṇha! The palace of the Conquerors is found nearby.
Kāṇha says: I don't understand this.

He tramples the solid posts of reality.
He tears off the bonds which encompass him.
Kāṇha frolics, rutting with wine.
He enters the lotus lake of the spontaneous and finds peace.
The more the elephant lusts for his mate
The more he drips the musk of Suchness.
All the creatures of the six destinies are pure in essence:
Neither being nor nonbeing has a hairtip of impurity.
The ten precious strengths radiate in the ten directions.
Tame the elephant of ignorance with nondefilement.

His staff holds firm the power of his channels,
His drum unstruck gives forth warlike sounds:
Kāṇha, the skullbearer, the yogin, has set out to practice:
He wanders alone in the city of his body.

The vowels and consonants are made his anklets,
The sun and moon are made his earrings.
He smears himself with the ashes of lust, hatred, and delusion,
He takes supreme freedom to be his string of pearls.
He has slain his mother-in-law and sisters-in-law within the house,
He has slain his mother: Kāṇha has become a skullbearer.

Hey, Whore, your hut is outside the city.
You stroke the brahman boys and go away.
Hey, Whore, I shall join together with you,
I, the shameless Kāṇha, the naked yogin, the skullbearer.
The lotus is one, its petals sixty-four:
I climb upon it and dance with the Whore.
Hey, Whore, honestly I ask you:
In whose boat do you come and go?
The Whore sells string as well as wicker baskets.
For your sake I have given up dancing.
You are a Whore, I a skullbearer.
For your sake I have put on a garland of bones.

I play chess on the board of compassion:
Instructed by my true guru, I capture the chessmen of existence.
Two are removed. Ha! I checkmate the king.
The Conqueror's palace is near, Kāṇha,
In the direction of the castle.
First I take up the pawns and slay them.
I take up the rook and crush the five men.
The bishop sends the king to nirvāṇa.
I keep them from moving, I capture the chessmen of existence.
Kāṇha says: I offer a good stake.
I count out sixty-four squares and take them.

Eight maidens form my boat of the three refuges.
My body is compassion, emptiness my mistress.
I have crossed the sea of existence like an illusion, a dream.
I feel the flow of waves in the middle.
I make the five [Tathāgatas] my oars:
Row your body, Kāṇha, that net of illusion.
Smell, touch, taste: whatever they may be
They are like a waking dream.
My mind is the helmsman in the boat of emptiness:
Kāṇha has gone to live with Bliss.

Easily I ply the triple world.
I sleep in the play of Bliss.
Hey, Whore! How is your flirting?
The patricians are outside, the skullbearers within.
Hey, Whore! You have spoiled everything.
For no reason you have spoiled the moon.
Some people say you are ugly,
But wise men cling to your neck.
Kāṇha sings of his low-caste lover:
There is no better whore than you.

Existence and nirvāṇa are the two drums,
Mind and breath are the two cymbals:
The bass drum resounds *jaa jaa* "Victory victory"
As Kāṇha goes off to marry the Whore.
The whore is married, birth is eaten up,
The dowry is the highest Law.
Day and night pass in lovemaking.
The night is brightened with my Lady's flame.
The yogin who is devoted to the Whore
Does not leave her for a moment: he is drunk with the spontaneous.

The mind is a tree, the five senses its branches,
Desires its many leaves and fruits.
Cut it down with the axe of the true guru's word.
Kāṇha says: the tree will not appear again.
The tree grows with the water of good and evil.
The wise man cuts it down at the command of his guru.
Whoever doesn't know the secret of cutting it down—
The fool slips and falls, and experiences it as existence.
The tree is emptiness, the axe is the sky:
Cut down the tree! Leave neither root nor branch.

He strikes at existence with the arm of emptiness.
He steals the stores of delusion and eats them.
He is asleep.
He does not know the difference between himself and others.
The naked Kāṇha sleeps in the spontaneous.
Neither aware nor feeling, he has gone full asleep.
And dreams in Bliss that he sets all beings free.
In a dream I saw the empty world
Spinning about, neither coming nor going.
I shall make the great yogin my friend:
The scholars don't see things my way.

The objects of the mind are rubbish.
Texts and traditions are piles of bricks.
Tell me how you can speak of the spontaneous
Where body, speech, and mind do not enter.
The guru teaches his disciple in vain.
How can he speak of what is beyond the path of speech?
The more he says, the more he is an old humbug.
The guru is dumb, and the disciple is deaf.
Kāṇha says: what is the jewel of the Conqueror like?
It is like the dumb enlightening the deaf.

The mind spontaneously is full of emptiness.
Do not grieve when you lose your body.
Tell me how Kāṇha doesn't exist any more:
Every day he spreads through the triple world, and measures it.
The fool is sad when he sees the seen destroyed.
Does a breaking wave dry up the ocean?
The fool does not see how the world is:
He does not see the butter in the milk.

Nothing comes or goes in reality.
That's the reality that Kāṇha plays in.

Source: Reprinted by permission of Wadsworth, Inc. from Stephan Beyer, *The Buddhist Experience* (Encino, CA: Dickenson, 1974), pp. 258–61.[16]

5.5.7 The Story of the Yoginī Maṇibhadrā

Kāṇha and the Sahajiyā saints notwithstanding, the lifestyle of Tantric adepts was not all freedom and flaunting of convention. The union of wisdom and means in this very body, speech, and mind could, in fact, take on many different expressions.

In the following story of Maṇibhadrā, one of the the eighty-four siddhas of the Indo-Tibetan tradition, we have an example of a person who appears, at least for a time, to harmonize her practice and realization with the routines of her daily life.

In the town of Agarce there lived a wealthy householder, who had a thirteen year old daughter. She was betrothed to a man of her own caste, and as was the custom the young woman lived in her parents' house until she was old enough to be her husband's wife. During this period the Guru Kukkuripa came to her house begging food.

"What a fine handsome man you are!" the girl told him. "Why do you wear patched robes and beg your food when you could take a wife and live comfortably?"

"I am terrified of the wheel of rebirth, and I am trying to find the great joy of liberation from it," Kukkuripa told her. "If I do not take this opportunity, in my next life I may not be so lucky. This human birth is really a precious chance, and if I break my vows of chastity by taking a wife, all my hopes and aspirations will be shattered and I'll be afflicted with many kinds of grief. When I realized that, I gave up the pursuit of women."

The girl was impressed by Kukkuripa and trusted him. After she had offered him good food, she said, "Please show me the way to liberation."

"I live in the cremation ground," Kukkuripa replied. "If you so desire, come to me there."

Preoccupied with the significance of the Guru's words, Maṇibhadrā, for that was her name, neglected her work for the rest of the day, and then at nightfall she went to the cremation ground. Kukkuripa recognized her spiritual maturity and gave her the Saṃvara initiation and empowerment together with instruction in the union of creative and fulfillment meditation. Thereafter she remained in solitude for seven days, establishing herself in the practice of her sādhana. But when she returned

[16]Original text: *Hājār Bacharer Purāna Bāṅgālā Bauddha Gān O Dohā* [*Buddhist Songs in Old Bengali*], ed. Haraprasad Sastri (Calcutta: Bangiya Sahitya Parisat, 1916), with the emendations of Tarapada Mukherji, *The Old Bengali Language and Text* (Calcutta: University of Calcutta, 1963).

home her parents beat her and reviled her. Maṇibhadrā defended herself, "There is no one in the universe who has not been either father or mother to me," she said. "Besides, a pure blood line and a good family upbringing do not free a girl from the grip of saṃsāra. So relying upon a Guru, I have decided to practice a sādhana that can bring me liberation. I have already begun."

Her words mollified her parents, who could find nothing to answer her with, and putting all thought of her housework out of her mind, Maṇibhadrā began to practice her sādhana one-pointedly. After a year, when her betrothed came to take her to his own house, she accompanied him without demur. In her new home she performed everything that was expected of her cheerfully and uncomplainingly, always speaking modestly and sweetly, thus controlling both her body and speech. In good time, she gave birth to a son and a daughter and brought them up in an exemplary manner.

Twelve years had passed since she met her Guru and formed her aspiration, then one morning as she returned from the stream with a pitcher full of water, she tripped over a root and fell down, breaking her pot. In the afternoon, after she had been missed from the house, her husband came looking for her and found her gazing fixedly at the broken pitcher. When he asked her what was the matter, she continued to stare, evidently not having heard him. All her family and neighbors came to try to distract her, but she remained silent and unmoving until nightfall, and then she expressed her realization in these words:

Sentient beings from beginningless time
Break their vessels, their lives ended,
But why do they return home?
Today I have broken my vessel
But abandoning my saṃsāra home
I go on to pure pleasure.
The Guru is truly wonderful!
If you desire happiness, rely on him.

So saying, Maṇibhadrā floated into the sky and taught the people of Agarce for twenty-one days. Thereafter she attained the Ḍākinī's Paradise.

Source: Reprinted by permission of the publisher from Keith Dowman, *Masters of Mahāmudrā: Songs and Histories of the Eighty-Four Buddhist Siddhas* (Albany: State University of New York Press, 1985), pp. 313–15.

PART TWO

The Development of Buddhism outside India

CHAPTER 6

Buddhists and the Practice of Buddhism: Sri Lanka and Southeast Asia

It is one of the ironies of the history of Buddhism that as an institution it was not destined to thrive forever in the land of its birth. Indeed, except for pockets here and there in outlying regions, Buddhism died out in India even as it was blossoming and sending forth new shoots in places as far away as Japan. Today, most Buddhists in India are either Tibetan refugees or recent Indian converts to the religion, the majority of them being members of the untouchable *mahār* caste, who were led en masse to Buddhism by their charismatic leader, B. R. Ambedkar, in the 1950s.

There were many reasons for the gradual demise of Buddhism in India, including Muslim invasions, the physical destruction of monasteries, syncretism with various forms of Hinduism, and internal decay. Whatever the cause, by the time the Tibetan pilgrim Dharmasvāmin visited northern India in 1234–36 C.E., he found Bodhgaya, Nalanda, and other sacred sites to be semideserted and largely devastated. Monastic libraries had been destroyed. The temple at Bodhgaya, always the heart of the Buddhist sacred world, had been walled shut, and a substitute statue of the Buddha had been placed in it. Moreover, images of Śiva had been drawn on the plastered-over gates, hoping to deter non-Buddhist looters, while the four monks who lived there in hiding were constantly fearful of marauding troops.[1]

Long before that, however, Buddhism had already spread throughout the whole of South and Southeast Asia. The Buddhism that exists in Sri Lanka, Myanmar (formerly Burma), Thailand, Laos, and Cambodia today calls itself Theravāda. This does not mean that it should be equated with the Buddhism that was taught by the Buddha. Nor does it mean that other religions, especially indigenous forms of spirit worship, and other non-Theravāda forms of Buddhism (Mainstream, Mahāyāna, and Tantric traditions) have not existed in these lands, where they have influenced Therāvada "orthodoxy" in a variety of ways. Nor does it mean that the Buddhism that is practiced in Thailand, for example, is identical to that practiced in Myanmar or in Sri Lanka or

[1]See George Roerich, *Biography of Dharmasvāmin* (Patna: K. P. Jayaswal Research Institute, 1959), p. 64.

in other Theravāda countries. Though commonalities certainly do exist, the history and cultures of these nations are naturally different and have variously affected the "Theravāda" tradition in them. In what follows, by looking at selections grouped under eight topics, we can only begin to give a feel for some of the richness and variety of the practice of Buddhism in these regions.

6.1 MYTHIC HISTORIES

6.1.1 The Buddha's Visit to Sri Lanka and the Conversion of King Tissa

In one of his rock edicts (see 2.6.3), King Aśoka speaks of sending out Dharma-messengers to all sorts of outlying regions, to the hellenized kingdoms in the northwest but also as far south as the island of Sri Lanka. Similarly, Theravāda accounts recall the story of the elder Moggaliputta Tissa, who sent out missionaries immediately following the Third Buddhist Council, which is said to have been held under Aśoka's auspices. Elders were dispatched to convert various lands in the Indian peninsula, as well as to Sri Lanka and Southeast Asia, two mission fields that were to become the special homelands of the Theravāda. According to the fifth-century chronicle of Sri Lankan Buddhism, the *Mahāvaṃsa*, the missionary monk who was sent to Sri Lanka was none other than King Aśoka's son, Mahinda, who was also an enlightened Buddhist monk. In those days, the king of Sri Lanka was named Devānaṃpiya Tissa, and it is upon him that Mahinda focused his efforts, for conversion of the king meant conversion of the island.

It should be said, however, that Mahinda's way had been well paved, because, according to Sri Lankan myth, over two hundred years before the elder's arrival, the Buddha himself had three times visited the island, chasing away all the demons from its territory and declaring that it would become a homeland for his Dharma. The overall story of the conversion of Sri Lanka to Buddhism is thus a mythic history of many layers. The following selection recounts only the tale of the Buddha's first visit to the island and the story of Mahinda's encounter with King Tissa.

In the ninth month after his enlightenment, at the full moon of December, the Conqueror [the Buddha] came to Sri Lanka in order to purify it. For the Buddha knew that Sri Lanka was a place where his religion would shine forth but that the demons on the island, which was full of demons, would first have to be driven off.

The Buddha also knew that in the middle of Sri Lanka, by the side of a river, there was a delightful place . . . called Mahānāga, which was a meeting ground for demons. And he knew that a great gathering of all the demons on the island was to take place there.

Arriving at that great assembly of demons, the Buddha hovered in midair above their heads, at the site of [what is today] the Mahiyangaṇa stūpa, and he greatly upset them by causing a fearful storm of rain, wind, and darkness. Badly frightened, the demons pleaded with the fearless Conqueror, and he, bestower of fearlessness, said to them: "Demons, I will free you from your fear and suffering, but you must first all give me a place here where I can sit down."

The demons said to the Buddha: "Sir, we will give you the whole island, but please relieve us of our fear."

Accordingly, the Buddha made the storm stop and brought an end to their fear, to the cold and the dark. He then put a skin rug down on the piece of ground they had given him. Sitting there, he magically stretched that skin out and caused a ring of fire to burn all around its perimeter. Oppressed by the heat, the demons stayed beyond the circumference of the ever increasing circle of fire. Then the Buddha caused the island of Giridīpa to come near, and when the demons had all taken refuge on that island, he set it back where it had been. Then he shrank his skin rug back down to size, the gods assembled, and he preached the Dharma to them. . . .

[There follows an account of two more visits of the Buddha to Sri Lanka, these too being preparations for the arrival of Aśoka's son, Mahinda, and for his conversion of the humans of the island, headed by their king, Tissa.]

King Tissa, the beloved of the gods, arranged water festivities for the townspeople and himself set out to enjoy the pleasures of the hunt. With a company of forty thousand men, he went quickly, on foot, to Mount Missaka. The local divinity of that mountain wished to have him meet Mahinda and the other elders, so he took on the form of a large deer browsing in the bush. Seeing it, the king thought: "It is not sporting to shoot an animal unawares," so he twanged his bowstring, and the deer ran off up the mountain. The king ran after it, but in running, the deer led him to the elders, and as soon as the lord of men came to see the elder Mahinda, the deer itself disappeared.

The elder Mahinda reflected: "The king will become very frightened if he sees many men," so, [using his magical powers, he made all of his fellow elders invisible and] appeared to the king all alone. Even so, the king was still somewhat afraid, so the elder said: "Come, O Tissa." But at the sound of his name, "Tissa," the king reflected: "[This person knows my name.] He must be a demon!"

But the elder, reading the king's mind, reassured him: "Your majesty, we are monks, disciples of the King of Dharma. Out of compassion for you, we have come here from India."

Upon hearing this, the king was no longer afraid. Remembering the letter that his friend, [Aśoka, the emperor of India, had sent to him, informing him about Buddhism,] he thought, "So these are monks," and putting down his bow and arrow, he approached the elder, exchanged greetings with him, and sat down nearby. Then his men came up and stood around him.

Then the great elder Mahinda caused the other elders who had come with him to become visible once again.

Seeing them, the king asked: "When did they get here?"

"They came with me," replied the elder.

"Are there more monks like them in India?" the king inquired.

Mahinda replied: "India is ablaze with yellow robes, and many of the Buddha's disciples there are arhats who have mastered the threefold learning, are endowed with magical powers, are able to read the minds of others, and have the divine ear."

The king then asked: "How did you come here?"

"We came neither by land, nor by sea," Mahinda replied, so the king knew they had come through the air.

Then, in order to test [the king's ability to understand the Dharma], the elder, endowed with great wisdom, gently asked him a question . . . : "What is the name of this tree, your majesty?"

"This tree is called a mango."

"Is there any mango besides this one?"

"There are many mango trees."

"And besides those other mangoes and this mango, are there any trees?"

"Sir, there are many such trees, but they are not mango trees."

"And besides those other mangoes and those trees which are not mangoes, are there any trees?"

"Sir, there is *this* mango tree."

"You are a wise man, your majesty. Tell me, are there many people who are related to you?"

"Yes, sir, many people."

"And are there some who are not related to you, your majesty?"

"Even more than those who are my relatives."

"And besides those relatives and those who are not related to you, is there anyone else?"

"There is *me,* sir."

"Well done, your majesty, you are a wise man."

And having ascertained that he was a wise person, the elder Mahinda preached to King Tissa a sūtra, and as soon as he had finished the sermon, the king took the three refuges, along with his forty thousand men.

Source: Translated from *The Mahāvaṃsa,* ed. Wilhelm Geiger (London: Pali Text Society, 1908), pp. 4–5, 103–5.[2]

6.1.2 The Relic at Haripuñjaya

Apocryphal stories telling of the Buddha's mythical visits to faraway places were intended not only to recount the conversion of various countries but also to give sacred pedigrees to specific holy sites. Thus, the story of the Buddha and the demons recounted above has importance for the whole of Sri Lanka, but it is also intimately associated with the important Sri Lankan pilgrimage site of Mahiyaṅgaṇa; and the tale of Mahinda and Tissa at Mount Missaka is important to Mihintale, near the ancient Sri Lankan capital of Anurādhapura.

---

[2]Alternative English translation, Wilhelm Geiger, *The Mahāvaṃsa or the Great Chronicle of Ceylon* (orig. pub., 1912; reprint ed., Colombo: Government Publications Bureau, 1960), pp. 3–5, 91–93.

Similar legends can be found throughout Southeast Asia, for according to local traditions the Buddha is said to have visited holy sites not only in Sri Lanka but also in Thailand, Myanmar, and Laos. Some of these accounts feature the discovery of a relic of the Buddha at a particular spot. Often such relics are said to have been left there by the Buddha himself, or to have been enshrined there by King Aśoka and then forgotten. In any case, their rediscovery serves to consecrate the site and is often connected to the establishment of a kingdom and the founding of a city, as in the following story featuring the finding of a relic in an unlikely place—a latrine—at what was to become the great royal temple of Haripuñjaya in the city of Lamphun in northern Thailand.

One day, when King Ādicca had gone to the royal privy, some crow droppings fell on his head. "What the . . . ?" said the king looking up . . . and again the crow released some droppings, this time into his mouth, and then it flew away. The king, upset, ordered his men to hunt down the crow. Obeying his command, they searched and captured the bird and brought it to him. The king, in his anger, wanted to kill the crow and asked his ministers: "Doesn't this crow deserve to die?" His ministers, however, replied: "Lord, do not have it killed; rather consult the astrologers." When questioned by the king, the astrologers said: "Your Majesty, [this means] blessings will be yours."

The king therefore had the crow kept in a cage, and, that night, he had a dream. In his dream, a divinity came and said to him: "Your Majesty, if you want to understand the whole of this matter, put a seven-day-old baby in with the crow and have it brought it up in its presence." The king did so and, after seven years, the child, brought up in the presence of the crow, had learned both crow-speech and human-speech. Then the child's mother presented her son to the king, and the king asked him to explain the crow's actions. The boy spoke with the crow, and the latter said: "Son, my ancestor, the white king of the crows, is very old; he told me that this was a place where a relic of the Buddha had been deposited and ordered me to guard it. He now lives in the Himalayas; if the king wants to know more about this matter, I can ask him to come." The boy related all this to the king; the latter promptly had the old crow-king summoned . . . and he arrived in Haripuñjaya seven days later. King Ādicca then gave the crow-king a perch in the palace courtyard, fed him some crow-food, and asked the boy who knew crow-speech to question him. And this is what the crow-king said: "Once, when our Buddha [Śākyamuni] was alive, he was dwelling in Benares. Early one morning, he took his robes and bowl and . . . flying through the air, he came down [near here], in a forest-village where he then went on his almsround. The people dwelling in that village were moved by the sight of the Buddha and gave him some food. The Blessed One preached the Dharma to them, established them in the three refuges and five precepts, and departing through the air from that place, he landed here. Placing his bowl on this flat rock, he ate his meal. After he had finished eating, he made this prediction: "In the future, after the parinirvāṇa of the Tathāgata, there will be a great city in this place.

There a king named Ādicca will rule, and during his reign, a relic of the Tathāgata will be enshrined here."

The boy communicated everything the crow had said to the king, and the latter, very pleased at learning this, had the royal privy taken away, had the site leveled, had it perfumed with incense and made into a pure place. He then had the drum of proclamation beaten throughout the city, and after bathing, he put on his royal ornaments, gathered the many things needed for worship, and went to the place. Asking the communities of monks dwelling in the whole city to pay homage to that place, venerating it himself with cupped hands, he invoked the relic in this way:

> After piling up merit for many aeons,
> and suffering much for the sake of the world
> and striving for a very long time,
> Śākyamuni attained complete buddhahood.
>
> Having done this, may the Blessed One who is compassionate
> release us all from suffering.
> May he show us an astonishing miracle
> so as to cut off the doubts of the whole world.
>
> And [so that we may know] whether all that was said by the crow-king
> about what was said by the Buddha
> is so or not so,
> may he display a wonder before our very eyes.

As he was making this invocation, the golden reliquary that had been made formerly by the Dharma-king Aśoka rose up to a height of three cubits, by the power of the deities, and stayed there, emitting rays of six colors. Seeing this miracle of the relic, the king and all those who dwelled in the city were struck with amazement; overjoyed, uttering cries of "Sādhu!" they honored and praised it with many lights, incense, perfumes, garlands, and ornaments.

Then King Ādicca wished to have the reliquary moved elsewhere . . . but it immediately sank back into the earth and disappeared. Again, the king honored and praised the relic and invoked it. And when he had done so in various multiple ways, once again it emerged, in its reliquary, rose up to a height of three cubits and stayed there, emitting rays of six colors. Then the king placed the reliquary that had been made by King Aśoka inside a casket that was adorned with many jewels, and putting it right there on top of the rock, he built over it a palace-like stūpa, twelve cubits high, with four pillars and four doors. This was 1,383 years after King Aśoka distributed the relics throughout the whole of Jambudvīpa, in the sixteenth year of King Ādicca's coronation, that the great relic of Haripuñjaya was made manifest.

Source: Translated from *Jinakālamālīpakaraṇam*, ed. A. P. Buddhadatta (London: Luzac & Co., 1962), pp. 78–80.[3]

---

[3]Alternative English translation, N. A. Jayawickrama, *The Sheaf of Garlands of the Epochs of the Conqueror* (London: Pali Text Society, 1968), pp. 106–109.

6.2 INTERACTIONS AND SYNCRETISM: BUDDHISM AND THE WORSHIP OF THE PHĪ AT A FESTIVAL IN LAOS

Wherever Theravāda Buddhism has become the dominant religious ideology, it has also tended to coexist with beliefs in indigenous spirits and deities. In part this is due to the Theravāda understanding of the Buddha himself: he is a "converter," he is a "refuge," but he is not an active "protector." Though devotees may well turn to him in their soteriological concerns, he has basically transcended this world and does not interfere directly in the mundane concerns of people. Thus, in Sri Lanka and Southeast Asia, the Buddha occupies a position at the top or, perhaps better, "above the top" of a large pantheon of spirits who are concerned with mundane affairs. This pantheon is not always well organized, but it includes regional and local divinities, guardians of towns and villages, spirits of the dead, and demonic and autochtonous forces concerned with illness, fertility, protection, success, failure, and the like.

The relationship of the worship of these spirits (called *nat* in Myanmar, and *phī* in Thailand and Laos) and the practice of Buddhism has long retained the interest of scholars. Although the situation can be quite complex, Buddhists in these countries do not generally see any contradiction between their veneration of the Buddha and their veneration of these deities. And though rituals toward them may vary (for example, certain indigenous spirits may be offered animal sacrifices or whiskey, while the Buddha and the more buddhaized spirits will receive only cooked food and flowers), often, in festivals, there is a mixture of elements that may baffle Westerners brought up in more exclusively monotheistic traditions.

The following description of the Rocket Festival (Bun Bangfai), a Buddhist/spirit cult celebration that is widely held throughout Laos and northern Thailand, illustrates some of the syncretic mix involved. Generally, the festival can be seen as a fertility cult that also honors the spirit of a particular village (phībān). At the same time, the celebration is the occasion for competition (in the form of the launching of bamboo rockets) between different villages in a given area. But since these rockets are generally made by Buddhist monks and since the villages owe their identity to a large extent to their association with a particular monastery-temple (wat), this competition has Buddhist ramifications as well. The situation is described and analyzed in the following article by the French anthropologist, Georges Condominas.

The Phī and Buddhism

Theravāda Buddhism is the official religion of Laos, of its neighbors to the south and west (Burma, Cambodia, and Thailand), and of Sri Lanka. In all these countries a cult of the "spirits" (*phī* in Lao) remains strong, having mingled so profoundly with Buddhism that the religion as actually practiced by the people represents a syncretism of the two. However, in all these countries Buddhism is predominant in the ideology and is the religion professed. [. . .]

The term phī encompasses a number of diverse notions such as "soul of the dead," "malevolent spirit," "guardian spirit," "nature deity," and the like. In fact, the majority of the Lao devote considerable attention and effort to the phī, whether asking them for favors or simply for their protection, escaping their pranks, or repairing the damage and curing the ills they have caused. In general, the phī do not require any substantial public ritual structures comparable to the Buddhist monastery. [. . .]

This essay focuses on the cult of protective spirits at the village level—that is, on the phībān. . . . The sanctuary of the village's guardian spirit is the *hō phībān*. The hō is generally built in the forest and hence stands apart from the village complex, which is dominated by the spacious buildings of the Buddhist wat [the monastery-temple]. . . . One might take the hō as one of the two sacred nodes unifying the village, the other being the wat. In terms of its unifying function the hō phībān might be viewed as something of an animist equivalent of the wat. However, the hō phībān by no means echoes the wat's outward appearance. It usually consists of a simple hut on stilts of wood and bamboo, approximately two to two and a half meters in height and one or two meters in width, depending on whether the hō is single or double. The buildings of the wat, on the other hand, are centrally located, more substantial, and constructed of more permanent materials. . . . The different locations of the wat and the hō are understandable. The wat represents the Buddhist principles which govern men directly, whereas the hō phībān represents the land on which the village is established and from which the villagers obtain their food and principal resources. . . .

The master of the cult of the village's guardian spirit is designated the *chaocham phībān*. One might think that, because of his responsibilities to the village guardian spirit, the chaocham might sometimes set himself up as a rival to the head of the village wat. This does not occur, however, for actually the chaocham is usually a good Buddhist who would never believe that the rites he performs in honor of the village spirits run counter to his worship of the Buddha. In fact, before the chaocham goes to the hō phībān to honor the spirit, he goes first to give alms to the monks. [. . .]

Feeding the Spirit of the Village and the Rocket Festival

The chaocham's role as a mediator working on behalf of the entire village collectively is most strongly emphasized in the ceremony of Līang Phībān ("feeding the spirit of the village"). All villagers participate in this ceremony, which is performed twice yearly, in the first and the sixth lunar months. . . .

In [some] villages, the Līang Phībān ceremony and the Rocket Festival (Bun Bangfai) are merged. In this case the village is open to outsiders; gunpowder is sent to surrounding villages so that the villagers may make fireworks, which they bring to the host village to be entered in a contest. Neighboring villages which have not received any powder may send only monks and, of course, spectators.

What does the Rocket Festival represent? For one thing, along with Bun Phavet it is the equivalent of our fairs, bringing together large numbers of people. Bun Phavet is a Buddhist ceremony consisting in the ritual reading of the story of Prince Vessantara, the penultimate incarnation of the Buddha [see 1.4.2]. Though the Buddhist associations of the Rocket

Festival are less clear, it is still regarded by most Lao villagers as a Buddhist ceremony. They suppose that it commemorates the Visākhabūjā, the triple anniversary of the Buddha's birth, enlightenment, and death. However, some Lao see in this ritual "the survival of ancient pagan customs. . . . Occurring at the beginning of the rainy season, Bun Bangfai is nothing other than an invocation to Phanhā Thāen (God of Heaven) to ensure the fecundity of the paddy fields and the abundance of the harvests." [. . .]

The villages and other participating groups are given about ten days in which to make their rockets. They must prepare charcoal, construct the body of the rocket, find an appropriate "tail" (a good stick of bamboo, ten meters or so in length, and preferably from a single shoot), squeeze the explosive into the body of the rocket, assemble the parts, decorate the rocket with bands of brightly colored paper, and so on. Interestingly, monks are usually the best rocket makers in a village, and they are invariably the inhabitants with the greatest amount of time to devote to such tasks. Oddly enough, in making the rocket to represent their wat, the monks play their most important role in the Rocket Festival.

The festival lasts two days, though most of the activity takes place during the two afternoons. The general outline is as follows: Late in the morning of the first day, bands of costumed youths and a few older men circulate in the village singing off-color songs, stopping to give special renditions to anyone who offers them drinks. Their disguises are imaginative and depend entirely on each man's fancy, though as invariably happens at carnivals several men disguise themselves as women. (No women actually take part in these goings-on.) One member of such a band always brandishes an object to remind everyone, even if unconsciously, that the Rocket Festival is a fertility rite. This object, a wooden phallus painted red and about half a meter long, is usually displayed intermittently to the crowd in a very realistic manner. . . .

Early in the afternoon (or somewhat later if there is a Buddhist ceremony such as an ordination on the first day of the Rocket Festival) the chaocham goes to the spirit's sanctuary. He is accompanied by a procession of villagers, who are also joined by the band of youthful revelers. At the sanctuary the chaocham makes an offering to the phībān, accompanied by a prayer. The village's rockets are also presented to the phībān, their "heads" placed on the platform of the sanctuary. . . . The tumult which follows the chaocham's prayer is sometimes preceded by the lighting of miniature fireworks and firing a gun into the air. . . .

Leaving the sanctuary of the village spirit, the procession moves toward the wat. The rockets previously presented to the village spirit are then placed on a platform which stands in the court of the pagoda and on which the rockets from other villages have already been arranged. Before the arrival of the procession the nāngthīam [female mediums] have already begun to dance before the rockets. They are elaborately costumed in turban, scarf, belt, and tunic of silk. They dance individually or together in front of the rockets displayed in their bamboo mounts. . . . The principal musical accompaniment is provided by a drum suspended from the shoulder and struck by both hands. A pair of little cymbals and one or more khāen [panpipes] often complete the ensemble. Nowadays this highly rhythmic music is often drowned out by a blaring loudspeaker, powered by a generator, which has been rented for the occasion by some pious soul. While they dance, the mediums swig alcohol from bottles which faithful clients offer them. The dance grows steadily wilder, stopping only as the nāngthīam are possessed by their respective spirits (phī). . . . At the end of the afternoon a procession takes place [three times] around the *sālā* (convocation hall) of the monastery. One of the nāngthīam armed with a pair of sabers dances at its head. She is followed by the orchestra, the chaocham, and the other mediums, also dancing. Some of the men carry the mount on which the rockets have been placed, and if the invited villages have also made mounts to transport their rockets, the parade is quite spectacular. . . .

The second day's festivities consist principally of the lighting of the rockets. Early in the afternoon, after the monks and laity have eaten, the rockets are brought noisily to the "launching ground" at the edge of the village's largest tract of rice fields. A little cluster of trees serves as the launching ramp, with two or three large sticks of bamboo tied together by lateral rungs attached almost vertically to the trees. The rockets are lit one at a time. Their takeoff is watched closely by the crowd and provokes either the wild enthusiasm of its makers and of those who have placed bets on it if it performs properly, or the equally noisy sarcasm of the crowd if it falls in a cloud of smoke a few meters from the launching ramp. The rocket that travels farthest wins a prize of two or three hundred kip, which is set out in a small moneybox at the wat. [. . .]

Travelers and anthropologists have often noted how well Theravāda Buddhism has adjusted to the belief in phī and its associated cult—not only in Laos but in all the countries where this great religion holds sway. More often than not, the role of the phī cult has been considered secondary and even negligible—a collection of peasant superstitions surviving surreptitiously in the shadow of the Buddhist great tradition. However, in contemporary rural Lao society the cult of the phī is restricted to no such minor role. It is on a par with Buddhism, with which it forms an integrated whole.

We have seen that the altar of the village spirit, the hō phībān, constitutes one of the two religious poles of the village community, the other being the Buddhist monastery, the wat. How is it that most authors have minimized the role of the spirit cult? For one thing, these observers were themselves followers of a major religious tradition and, in general, had little interest outside such great traditions and the evolved metaphysical systems associated with them. They regarded other manifestations of religion as so many curious and disparate superstitions. And, it is true, appearances offer some support to their preconceptions. Everyone identifies himself [or herself] as a Buddhist, and the only religious monument, an outstanding one at that in terms of its size and the quality of its materials, is the wat, which clearly dominates the village community. The hō phībān, by contrast, is merely a little hut, hidden in the brush far from the other buildings of the village.

The wat serves many of the functions necessary to community life: primarily temple and monastery, to be sure, it is also town hall, ceremonial center, school, warehouse, and inn. The hō phībān is a place of worship and nothing else. The Buddhist ceremonies associated with the wat open the village to its neighbors who are invited to attend, while the Līang Phībān ritual closes it to outsiders (except when the ritual is accompanied by a Rocket Festival, which is characterized today as Buddhist). Differences between these two institutions express distinctive functions. The wat, an expression of the adopted great tradition, answers the needs of the people as members of a spiritual community, and it is the place of assembly for the group as a social and political entity. The jurisdiction of the hō phībān, on the other hand, is not the community as a social entity but rather the natural ecological system that nurtures its members, above all the land which provides food, shelter, and clothing. The phībān belongs to the world of nature, and it is there that it takes refuge.

Source: Reprinted by permission of the publisher from Georges Condominas, "Phībān Cults in Rural Laos," *Change and Persistence in Thai Society,* ed. G. William Skinner and A. Thomas Kirsch (Ithaca: Cornell University Press, 1975), pp. 252, 254, 257–58, 262–63, 264–69, 271–73 (slightly altered).

6.3 DIVISIONAL ISSUES

Once a religion becomes established in a country, it does not usually take long for disagreements to arise among its followers over what aspects of the faith should be emphasized. We have already seen that in India the Buddhist sangha was affected by sectarianism within a few generations of the death of its founder. Much the same was true in Sri Lanka and Southeast Asia. Indeed, the chronicles of ancient Sri Lanka testify repeatedly to the varying fortunes and interrelationships of at least three major sectarian groups on the island, centered on the Mahāvihāra, Abhayagiri, and Jetavana monasteries. Scholars have much debated the views and doctrinal alignment of these three factions. Like political parties, they changed their stances over the years, depending on whether they were "in power," that is, on whether or not they had the favor of the king, for support of the king was often more of a bone of contention than doctrinal disagreements. Generally speaking, however, the Abhayagiri seems to have been more liberally receptive to changes in Buddhist doctrine (Mahāyāna, Tantra, and so on) coming from India, whereas the Mahāvihāra presented its own history as a more or less constant struggle against three things it tended to lump together: fragmentation of the sangha, laxity in discipline, and the corrupting influences of South Indian imports. The Mahāvihāra itself was not without its own evolution, however, and not without its own influence on other lands: eventually its views spread to Myanmar and Southeast Asia, where in some ways they can be said still to represent the dominant Theravāda "orthodoxy."

6.3.1 Practice versus Study

This kind of sectarianism, however, was not the only divisive force in South and Southeast Asia. Another important division that had its roots in India and is found in all Theravāda countries was that between monks who sought to emphasize practice (the maintenance of the precepts and the practice of meditation) and those who sought to emphasize learning (the study and preservation of the Buddhist scriptures). Alternatively, these two groups are sometimes identified as ascetics and Dharma-reciters, or as forest-dwelling monks and town- or village-dwelling monks, or as followers of the vocation of meditation and followers of the vocation of books. However this polarity is characterized, it represents not so much a sectarian division as a distinction of alternative lifestyles, based on differing notions of whether the main thrust of Buddhist practice should be the preservation of the teachings or the pursuit of perfection.

In the selections that follow, the perspectives of both these views are represented. The first text, excerpted from a Pali "exhortation" preserved in Thailand, somewhat sardonically defines the vocation of scholarly learning as nothing but the rote memorization of texts and recounts the advocacy by the Buddha's disciple Mahākassapa of the practice of meditation, which is also associated with a number of optional ascetic practices. The second selection then spells out more precisely what these thirteen ascetic practices are. These are praised here, but in other texts they are associated with the views of the Buddha's cousin and archrival, Devadatta. Finally, the third selection, from one of Buddhaghosa's commentaries, recalls a crisis that is supposed to have occurred in Sri Lanka in the first century B.C.E, when a famine threatened the continued oral preservation of the Buddhist tradition. As a result of this, we are told (in the *Mahāvaṃsa*), a decision was made to set the Buddha's teachings down in writing, and primary emphasis was put on learning, on the maintenance of the textual tradition. It is perhaps not surprising that Buddhaghosa, a prominent and established scholar himself, should have supported this view.

[A.] Then the elder Kassapa asked the Blessed One: "Reverend sir, what are the vocations [open for monks]?"

"There are two: the vocation of books and the vocation of meditation."

"What is the vocation of books?"

"Kassapa, in the vocation of books, a monk memorizes one section of the canon, two sections of the canon, or all the texts of the entire canon. But in the vocation of meditation, a monk cultivates insight into the perishable nature of existence until he reaches arhatship."

"Reverend sir, I wandered forth and became a monk when I was already old; I cannot follow the vocation of books, so I will follow the vocation of meditation."

Then, speaking of the vocation of meditation, the Blessed One said: "That is good, Kassapa, the Buddhas praised the thirteen ascetic practices. . . . "

[B.] What are the dhutānga? There are thirteen practices: two practices with regard to robes, namely, wearing rubbish-heap robes and owning only three robes; five practices with regard to alms, namely, begging for food, systematic begging, eating in one sitting, eating a measured amount, and not eating after time; five practices with regard to beds and seats, namely, staying in an undisturbed place, staying under a tree, staying in an exposed place, staying in a graveyard, and staying wherever one happens to be; and there is also one practice with regard to energetic rigor, namely, constantly sitting and never lying down. . . .

1. What is meant by accepting rubbish-heap robes? The refusal of robes offered by householders.
2. What is meant by accepting three robes? The refusal of additional robes.
3. What is meant by begging for one's food? The refusal of invitations to eat at laypersons' houses.
4. What is meant by systematic begging? The refusal to skip houses on one's begging round [and only go to those places where one knows one will receive food].
5. What is meant by eating at one sitting? Not sitting down to eat some more after one has finished.
6. What is meant by eating a measured amount? Giving up the desire to indulge oneself.
7. What is meant by not eating after time? Giving up the expectation to eat again after the meal is over.
8. What is meant by staying in an undisturbed place? The refusal to dwell in a village.
9. What is meant by staying under a tree? The refusal to dwell in a building.
10. What is meant by staying in an exposed place? The refusal of a sheltered place.
11. What is meant by staying in a graveyard? The refusal of a better place.
12. What is meant by staying wherever one happens to be? The giving up of the desire for a pleasant place.
13. What is meant by always sitting and never lying down? The refusal to lie down to sleep.

[C.] If learning disappears, practice disappears, and if learning stays, practice stays. Once, on this island [of Sri Lanka], Indra, the king of gods, fashioned a great raft and announced to the monks: "There will soon occur a frightful calamity; the rains will not come on time, and lacking the basic provisions needed for monastic life, monks will not be able to maintain the learning. So, reverend sirs, embark upon this great raft, and go overseas; in this way you will manage to preserve your lives. . . ."

However, when they reached the other shore of the ocean, some sixty monks got together and decided that they really ought not to go on, but should stay on the island in order to preserve the Tripiṭaka. So they returned to Sri Lanka and went to the region of Dakkhiṇamalaya, where they survived on tubers and roots and leaves. Working as a group, they sat down and repeated the teachings, and working individually, they . . . rested, each in his own place, and thought about the teaching. In this way, for twelve years, they fully rehearsed the Tripiṭaka, along with the commentaries.

When the frightful famine had passed, the seven hundred monks who had gone on, and who had in their own places recited the Tripiṭaka and the commentaries without losing a single syllable or a single letter, came back to Sri Lanka and went to the Maṇḍalārāma Monastery in the land of Kallagāma.

Hearing of the arrival of these elders, the sixty monks who had stayed behind on the island went to see them, and, together, they went over the Tripiṭaka, and saw that not one syllable or letter was different.

Then a question arose: "What is the basis of the Buddhist order, learning or practice?"

The ascetic elders said, "Practice is the basis."

The Dharma-reciter elders said, "Learning is the basis. . . ."

[In order to support their view, the ascetic elders] quoted a sūtra wherein the Buddha told the monk Subhadda: "If, Subhadda, the monks continue in right conduct, the world will not be empty of arhats, for the teaching of the Master . . . has its root in practice, has practice as its essence, and stands supported by practice."

Hearing this, the Dharma-reciters quoted a sūtra too: " . . . When the sūtras are preserved, practice is preserved; if learning stays, the tranquillity of yoga will not fly away."

In the face of this sūtra, the ascetic elders were quieted, and the words of the Dharma-reciters won the day. . . . Thus, truly, even if a hundred or a thousand monks were found to undertake the practice of meditation, without learning there would be no realization of the Noble Path.

Sources: A. Translated from *Paṃsukūlānisaṃsaṃ,* ed. Ginette Martini, *Bulletin de l'Ecole Française d'Extrême-orient* 60 (1973): 68.[4] B. Translated from *Vimuttimagga* (Taishō shinshū daizōkyō, ed. J. Takakusu and K. Watanabe [Tokyo, 1924–29], no. 1648, 32:404b–c).[5] C. *Manorathapūraṇī: Buddhaghosa's Commentary on the Anguttara Nikāya,* ed. M. Walleser and H. Kopf (London: Pali Text Society, 1924), 1:91–93.

6.3.2 The Great Robes Controversy

The divergence between practice and study would appear to reflect a significant difference in orientation on the basic nature of the Buddhist enterprise. Other times the divisive issues were seemingly less fundamental, although they may have been felt just as intensely. The selection that follows, for example, features a controversy that wracked the Burmese Sangha throughout most of the eighteenth century. This was the dispute between the "pārupana" monks, who practiced covering both shoulders with their robes when they went out on their begging rounds, and the "ekaṃsika" monks, who maintained that the proper mode of dress while outside the monastery was to put the robe over one shoulder and to leave the other bare. This controversy cut

---

[4]Alternative French translation, Martini, *Paṃsukūlānisaṃsaṃ,* p. 72.

[5]Alternative English translation, N. R. M. Ehara, Soma Thera, and Kheminda Thera, *The Path of Freedom* (Colombo: M. D. Gunasena, 1961), pp. 27–28.

across other divisions such as that between forest-monks and town-monks, meditators and scholars. Nor was it limited to Myanmar; even today, in Sri Lanka, monks who belong to one of the sects (the Siyam Nikāya) still bare one shoulder when out of the monastery, in contradistinction to the members of the other two sects, who cover theirs.

It is hard to comprehend fully the intensity this issue took on, and scholars are still debating some of its ramifications. Part of the problem was the interference of various Burmese kings, who, under the influence of different monastic advisors, tended to favor one party or the other and to make decrees that all monks in their kingdom should dress in a particular way. When one king, however, in a spirit of conciliation, proposed allowing monks to do whatever they wished to on this matter, he was not listened to; clearly, there were some in the sangha who were not willing to compromise on this issue regardless of royal involvement. Underlying this stringency, perhaps, was a more fundamental disagreement between monks who felt they should follow texts, the "Word of the Buddha," and those who felt they should follow the tradition of their lineage. Thus the two-shoulderites tended to support their position on the grounds of a Vinaya passage that said they should "go out covered," while the one-shoulderites claimed they were merely observing the practice that their teachers, and their teachers' teachers, had passed on to them. Both sides, however, were willing to use the debate tactics of the other, the two-shoulderites claiming their ultimate teacher was the Buddha himself and the one-shoulderites invoking (or perhaps forging) an obscure subcommentary that, they claimed, gave their position scriptural authority. In the end, the two-shoulderites won out, after a series of debates in which their opponents were deemed unable to substantiate their position. At least, that is the claim of the following account, clearly written by a two-shoulderite, which features the "heroic" resistance of a monk named Munindaghosa who continued to cover both shoulders at a time when the king favored his opponents, the one-shoulderites.

Now the king asked his ministers: "In my kingdom, do all the monks follow the opinion of my teacher [and bare one shoulder on their begging rounds] or do they not?

The ministers replied: "Your majesty, in the village of Nīpa, in Kukhana township, there lives an elder named Munindaghosa. He instructs his own followers to cover [both shoulders] and has attracted much attention."

The king said: "Summon him, and have the great elders gather in the Assembly Hall and admonish this elder who does not know the true nature of the Vinaya. Let them teach him proper behavior."

The ministers did so; the great elders gathered in the Assembly Hall, summoned Munindaghosa, and admonished him. One of those great elders, who had regard for the words of the king and of the head of the sangha (but *not* for the words of the Blessed Buddha), said this to the elder Munindaghosa: "Brother, all of the monks in Myanmar follow the order of the king and of the head of the sangha, and have now become 'one-shoulderites.' You alone, together with your followers, persist in observing the practice of covering [both shoulders]. Why are you so stubborn and haughty and why don't you give up this wrong practice?"

The Elder Munindhaghosa looked that elder straight in the eye and replied: "I previously heard that you were modest, friendly, and wishing to follow the discipline, but a man such as that would not say such things; this is not right! If you think me of little merit, shameful, and pathetic, and want to insult me, don't do it in front of my teacher, knowing that I am his disciple. . . ."

At that the elder asked him: "Who is your teacher?"

Bowing before the image of the Buddha in the Assembly Hall, Munindaghosa replied: "This is my teacher." He stood up in the midst of the assembly of monks, and then squatting down, he put his hands together in devotion, and declared: "Venerable Sirs, I will give up even my life, but until the end of my days, I will not abandon the rule of the Blessed One who is foremost in the world."

The king, hearing this, reflected that this stubborn and haughty man should not be allowed to dwell in his kingdom but should be sent into exile, and he ordered him banished to a foreign land. Accordingly, the king's men set out with him to that foreign kingdom, but when they reached a region called Mahanga, the headman of Mahanga gave them a bribe and said: "Good sirs, this is a border region of Myanmar [and is far away enough]; you can leave [the elder] right here and go back home."

The king's men accepted the bribe and, leaving him there, returned to the capital. And the elder stayed there [within the borders of Myanmar] instructing monks and novices who came from all four quarters in the practice of covering [both shoulders] just as it is taught in the scriptures. . . .

Eventually, the king came to hear of this, and said: "Now this elder is living in the outskirts of my kingdom, doing something not wanted and forbidden by us. Summon him!"

The king's messengers went there and summoned him. And the elder Munindaghosa reflected: "The king surely now wants to kill me," so he abandoned the precepts, put on the clothes of a layman and went with them. When they reached the city, they took him before the king.

The king said: "I have heard that you, as a monk, persist in attracting more followers, but why have you now become a layperson?"

"Your majesty," answered Munindaghosa, "if you summoned me, wishing to kill me, so be it; but were you to kill me when I had not given up the precepts [and was still a monk] that would be a very bad deed for you. I thought your karma would be less grave if I first returned to lay life. Now if you wish to kill me, you may do so."

The king, however, merely put him in prison, and went off to make war in the kingdom of Siam. And on his way back from doing that, he died. . . .

Source: Translated from *Sāsanavaṃsa*, ed. Mabel Bode (Oxford: Pali Text Society, 1897), pp. 125–27.[6]

---

[6]Alternative English translation, Bimala Churn Law, *The History of Buddha's Religion* (orig. pub., 1952; reprint ed., Delhi: Sri Satguru Publications, 1986), pp. 129–31.

6.4 REGULATION AND REFORM: THE EFFORTS OF KING PARĀKRAMABĀHU

As the previous selection makes clear, the king played a crucial role in regulating or "purifying" the sangha, though how that role was viewed depended, of course, on one's perspective; a king who sought to "reform" (that is, to purge) the sangha could be seen as a purifier and unifier in the eyes of those whom he supported but as a promoter of schism in the eyes of those whom he purged.

From the perspective of Theravāda orthodoxy, one Sri Lankan king who was viewed as a great and successful reformer was Parākramabāhu I. His rule from 1153 to 1186 C.E. was one of the high points of a newly centralized Sri Lankan kingdom with its capital at Polonnaruva. Fortunately, one of Parākramabāhul's rock inscriptions, still extant at Gal Vihāra in Polonnaruva, gives us a glimpse not only of his attempt at reform but also of Buddhist community life in twelfth-century Sri Lanka. Here we are introduced to a world in which monks are encouraged to practice *both* of the traditional monastic "vocations," meditation and study (see 6.3.1). Here also we get a peek at the ongoing relationship of monks and the families they left when they entered the monkhood: they are not allowed to talk to their mothers and sisters in private, but they can go begging for food and medicine to help support them should they become destitute.

Four hundred fifty-three years after the parinirvāṇa of the Buddha, there reigned the great King Vaṭṭagāmaṇi Abhaya. For 1,254 years after his rule, the Order was divided into sects and fell into decay. Then came the great king of kings, Śrī Saṃghabodhi Parākramabāhu. A descendant of the first king Mahāsammata [see 3.3.2], sprung from the Solar race, . . . he was anointed Lord over the whole of Laṅka. While he was pursuing the powers and pleasures of kingship, he became aware of certain persons within the Order who, poisoned by their misbehavior rooted in ignorance and faulty understanding, were headed toward lower realms of rebirth. Repeatedly witnessing such a stain on the utterly pure Buddhist Order, he reflected: "If a great ruler such as I were to do nothing, the Buddhist Order would be lost, and many beings would go to the lower realms of rebirth. The Buddhist Order should last five thousand years; I must attend to it." And having aroused in his heart both wisdom and compassion, he thought; "To whom can I turn to help purify the Teaching . . . so that it will last five thousand years?"

Then he saw that the community of forest monks residing at Mount Udumbara, headed by the great elder Mahākāśyapa, was adorned by gems of the highest quality, that is, the moral virtues they had amassed, cherished, preserved, and amplified by bringing together various good qualities. . . .

And he remembered that long ago, the great king Dharma-Aśoka had turned to the great elder Moggaliputta Tissa, of whom the Buddha himself had spoken in his day, in order to suppress the sinful monks who had gone astray, to purify the Order, and to hold the Third Council for the recitation of the Dharma. So too, King Pārakramabāhu turned to the Mount Udumbara monks to expel several hundred sinful monks and to unite the three sects into one sect, a unification that was not achieved by former kings. . . .

Then, so that the unification of the sangha which he had achieved at great effort, should endure unbroken for five thousand years, and so that members of the community should be endowed with the virtue of having few desires and be diligent in the pursuit of the two vocations of books and meditation, he requested those monks to help protect the Order by giving sermons and instructions. . . . And, headed by the great elder Mahākāśyapa, the community of elders, . . . taking into account the Dharma and the Vinaya, . . . proclaimed the following agreed-upon observances:

" . . . Senior elders should allow no negligence on the part of the disciples and pupils in their charge . . . but should urge them in the vocation of books. . . .

"Those disciples and pupils who are not able to follow fully the vocation of books should at least memorize the *Mūlasikkhā,* and the *Pātimokkha* rules concerned with training, and to recite the [Sinhalese commentary on them]. . . . When they are through memorizing as much as they are able, they should be urged in the vocation of meditation and told a subject of contemplation. . . .

"No monk or novice shall be allowed to go into the town at a forbidden time [sundown to sunrise], except to go begging for food to support their destitute parents, a widowed sister, or a fellow-practitioner, to go to beg for medicine for parents, sisters, or co-practitioners; or to go to recite protective texts (paritta) in a particular place. . . .

"All members of the community—elders, novices, and ordinary monks—should go to bed at midnight . . . in order to rest their bodies. They should get up at dawn and spend some time in the practice of walking meditation. They should practice reciting a text that they know. They should then put on the yellow robe; . . . brush their teeth; attend to the duties . . . with regard to the stūpas, the Bodhi tree, the courtyard, their preceptors, the elders, the sick, and their monastic cells; and then go to the refectory to eat their morning meal and attend to the duties of the refectory. Then, except for those monks who have pressing responsibilities, . . . they should pass their time in the practice of meditation. Also, after the midday meal, they should spend their time in pursuit of the vocations of books and meditation. . . .

"Monks should never speak inappropriate words, either in anger or in jest. They should never converse in private with a member of the opposite sex, even if it be their mother, or with a young boy, even if it be their younger brother. . . .

"If it starts raining while monks are going someplace, they should keep on walking at their natural pace, until they reach some shelter where they will not get wet, unless they are carrying some articles belonging to elder monks that are likely to get damaged by the rain. . . .

"They should not talk while in the midst of worshipping the stūpas or the Bodhi tree, while making offerings of incense or flowers, when brushing their teeth, or when putting their begging bowl in its sling. They should not discuss matters pertaining to the requisites of a monk with laypersons in town. . . .

"A junior monk should practice reciting texts without disturbing those who are meditating. . . . New monks who are being ordained as novices should be examined before their ordination as novices, before their full ordination, before they are taken on as disciples, because each and every son of a good family who is initiated into the community and then ordained is important in the maintenance of the whole Buddhist order."

Source: Translated from "Rock Inscription of Parakkama-Bāhu I," *Epigraphia Zeylanica,* ed. Don Martino DeZilva Wickremasinghe (Colombo: Archaeological Survey of Ceylon, 1912–27), 2:268–72.[7]

6.5 RITUALS AND FESTIVALS

The lives of Buddhists in South and Southeast Asia, both laypersons and monastics, are punctuated by life-cycle rites that mark their passage from one status or situation to another as well as by calendrical celebrations in which the community as a whole, or special groups within it, gather for festivities and for the making of merit. We shall start with an example of a rite of passage from Thailand.

6.5.1 The Death and Funeral of a Northern Thai Saint

Throughout the Buddhist world, death is one of the most important rites of passage at which Buddhist monks officiate. This is especially true when the dying person is himself a famous Buddhist monk. In Thailand, in particular, the funerals of renowned and revered elders can often be very great affairs. Khrūbā Sīwichai (1878–1939) was a famous monk from northern Thailand who owed his "sainthood" to several factors. On one hand, he led a strict, ascetic life; on the other, he was also involved in the world and was renowned for his abilities to inspire communities to undertake great construction projects, building or repairing important religious monuments and assuring easier access to them. Finally, he was also a champion of northern Thai culture and religious tradition, defending it against encroachment from central Thailand, where the forces of the Siamese court were moving to reduce the autonomy of the provinces. The following selection recounts his death and funeral.

In 1935, after having made his peace with the Siamese authorities and having completed his latest undertaking, a road up to the shrine of a Buddha relic on Dōi Suthep, the mountain that rises above Chiang Mai, Khrūbā Sīwichai is said to have begun to age visibly although only 56

[7]Alternative English translation, Nandasena Ratnapala, *The Katikāvatas* (Munich: Münchener Studien zum Sprachwissenschaft, 1971), pp. 127–35.

years old. He returned to his home monastery in Bān Pāng where he sought to rest. However, he was soon persuaded to undertake the leadership of yet another major construction job, in this case a bridge across the Ping River. . . . But his health was not sufficient to the task, and sensing that he was soon going to die he asked his followers to take him back to Bān Pāng. . . .

On 25 July 1938, his condition became much worse and he thought he would not last much longer. . . . He called his followers together and gave them what he thought would be his last words. . . . In fact, he was to live for another seven months. . . .

By February 10 [1939] he was in great pain, being unable to turn over in bed. He asked his disciples to take him outside to lie down to make it easier for the faithful to visit him. He said he would die in a few days. . . .

On February 19 . . . he grew feverish and at 10 P.M. he called his disciples together and spoke to them for the last time: "All beloved disciples, within an hour I shall certainly leave you. I know the time has come. Don't despair. Although my life is coming to an end, I beg you once again to resolve one and all to see to satisfactory completion all those things that have not yet been finished; don't forget them after I have ceased to live. You must take a bottle of honey and pour it in my mouth to prevent decomposition of the corpse because we know well that you all will keep our corpse for a long time. . . ."

[His biographer goes on to say] that at midnight the cocks began to crow—something that is not usual at that hour—that the moon disappeared, and that it became dark. People were startled by the caws of birds. Khrūbā Sīwichai's breath became quieter and quieter and at 12:30 on 20 February 1939, he became still. . . .

After his death, honey was poured into Khrūbā Sīwichai's mouth as he had requested. Even this minimal treatment of the body appeared to be sufficient to prevent [it] from decaying. . . . The corpse was kept at Wat Bān Pāng for three years, where followers from all over northern Thailand came to pay their respects.

Although people from Chiang Mai wished to arrange last rites for Khrūbā Sīwichai in their city, this honor fell to the people of Lamphūn. In 1941, the corpse was brought in procession to Wat Cāmthewī in Lamphūn, a temple with which he had long been associated. The final cremation was not, however, to take place for another five years. Both biographers are silent about why there was such a delay, but it seems likely that World War II was a major factor. . . .

The cremation, held in March 1946, was a grand affair indeed, lasting for fifteen days. A magnificent pyre, planned by the chief monk of the province and designed by a professional architect, was erected at the wat. People from all over the North, including many tribal people who had become his followers during his lifetime, gave of their money and labor for the occasion. . . . A leading sangha official arrived from Bangkok, thus signifying the national sangha's recognition of Khrūbā Sīwichai as a leading monk of the north.

On the day of the cremation, although there had been no sign of rain, it suddenly clouded over and began to sprinkle. People called this a miracle.

Further evidence that Khrūbā Sīwichai had been a particularly holy person . . . was found in the fact that when the coffin was opened to prepare the body for cremation, the corpse was found not to have decayed.

When the cremation was over, a large contingent of policemen had to be posted around the cremation site to prevent the faithful from taking away all the remains. The next day, when the remains were to be collected, the governor of Lamphūn feared that there would be more trouble, so he called in the army from Chiang Mai. A conclave of officials were called together to decide how to make a just division of the relics. His disciples determined to divide the relics into four parts [for enshrinement in four different monasteries in northern Thailand]. . . .

Reliquary shrines were not the only monuments constructed to the memory of Khrūbā Sīwichai. As is the tradition in connection with famous monks, medallions bearing his likeness [to be used as amulets] were struck shortly after his death, and they have continued to be produced to the present day. A number of images of Khrūbā Sīwichai have also been cast, the most famous being one at the foot of Dōi Suthep and another at the reliquary shrine on top of Dōi Suthep. These images have been practically covered by gold leaf affixed by pilgrims who come to the mountain.

Source: Reprinted by permission of the author and publisher from Charles F. Keyes, "Death of Two Buddhist Saints in Thailand," *Journal of the American Academy of Religion, Thematic Studies* 48 (1981): 160–63.

6.5.2 A Festival of Relics in Phnom Penh

As the previous passage makes clear, the search for and veneration of Khrūbā Sīwichai's relics were an important feature of his funeral and its aftermath. Other ritual celebrations take as their focus the relics of the Buddha. Sometimes these are regular calendrical rituals, such as the festival of the Buddha's tooth relic, known as the Esala Perahera, which is held annually in Kandy, Sri Lanka, or the festival of the Buddha's fingerbone relic, which took place every thirty years in medieval China. There were also, however, unique occasions in honor of the "visit" or "tour" of relics not ordinarily seen. Often these celebrations were sponsored by the king or the governing powers, who could thereby show their support for Buddhism. This pattern has continued in modern times. In the 1950s and 1960s (and again in the 1990s), the government of the People's Republic of China, seeking to enhance its relations with South Asian countries, arranged for the Buddha's tooth relic enshrined in Beijing to be taken on tours of Sri Lanka and Myanmar. Even before that, in the early 1950s, the British had, with great fanfare, returned to India the relics of the Buddha's chief disciples, Śāriputra and Mahāmaudgalyāyana, which Alexander Cunningham had uncovered at Sanchi in 1851 and spirited away to the Victoria and Albert Museum in London. Soon thereafter, the Indian government, through the Maha Bodhi Society, sent these same relics on a tour of Sri Lanka. The French colonial government then sponsored their visit, along with a Buddha relic, to Cambodia, where they were received with great ceremony by King Norodom Sihanouk. The atmosphere of that occasion in Phnom Penh in October 1952 has been colorfully and somewhat verbosely evoked by Jean Barthes in the selection that follows.

Virtually the whole of Cambodia, over 500,000 villagers and peasants, have left their towns and land to come to the capital, Phnom Penh, on the occasion of the arrival of the Relics of the Buddha and of those of his two great disciples, Sāriputra and Maudgalyāyana. . . . For a general leave has been given, allowing everyone to accomplish the holy pilgrimage. . . . The great mass of people from the provinces head for the airfield on foot, and are soon met by thousands of vehicles of all types, driven with terrifying fearlessness by people from the city, who are forced to unload their thick sheaths of humanity, still three or four kilometers from their destination. Twice, the sheer numbers of people prevent the passage of the official welcoming delegation, which is also headed for the airfield; the swells of humanity are such that they seem to push along by fits and starts the automobiles of the King [Norodom Sihanouk] and of the High Representatives of France. In this way, it is at an unusually slow pace that the cortège arrives, behind schedule but still in time, at the Phnom Penh airport. . . .

At last, the plane—a special plane from Calcutta—lands on the runway. The king is in his courtly robes covered with gold brocade and red *sampot,* the ritual color for Sunday. Accompanied by his uncle, Prince Monireth, in a white uniform, he approaches the aircraft and they receive the two solid gold reliquaries together with their precious contents. The two reliquaries have the form of dome-shaped Indian stūpas. The larger one, in which there is a minuscule bone of the Buddha, is topped by a small conical spire, its base resting on a stand, the summit ending with a small gold bell suspended from a polyhedral diamond of exceptional size. . . . The second reliquary, containing small bones of the two great disciples of the Sage of Sages, was only a third as high as the first. . . .

Beneath royal umbrellas, the two august bearers of these very venerable Relics, flanked by the princes of the Cambodian Church, the highest religious and civil dignitaries of the kingdom, and Bakous (Brahmanical priests) from the court carrying a ceremonial conch, deposit their precious burden on a stand, placed at the entrance to a hangar bedecked with palm branches and multicolored flags. Seated monks in yellow robes, and officials in ceremonial dress, fill the hall where the praises of the Perfected One soon sound forth.

With the devotions ended, the two reliquaries are then placed, with the same degree of pomp, on an altar underneath a canopy whose roof and columns are smothered with flowers, and the whole is then set on a specially designed vehicle, caparisoned on all four sides with large white pieces of cloth cut across by lines of green flowered garlands. . . .

The procession then starts out in the direction of Phnom Penh, fed, along the route of its slow progress, by the immense crowds that had failed to get to the airfield. On either side of the ten kilometers of the road that links the two endpoints of this sacred way, a dense hedge of Buddhist monks, backed up by ranks of laypeople, stand, flowers and incense sticks in hand, awaiting the chance to salute the three Holy Relics.

Downtown it is just as crowded, for no one would have wanted to miss this imposing procession. Here a Khmer orchestra plays its most melodious compositions; there, an improvised altar on a lovely new cloth has been placed right on the sidewalk, and in the midst of a riot of flowers, swirls of smoke from packs of joss sticks rise up to crown an image of the Buddha. Elsewhere, a temporary stand, covered by sumptuous colored Cambodian cloth, holds Buddhist flags, which Khmer children will wave when the pious procession passes. Even the American Protestant pastor is there in front of the headquarters of the Evangelical Mission, distributing edifying pamphlets of . . . Christian propaganda!

We have now arrived at the Silver Pagoda, where Prince Suramarith, the king's father, and an ecclesiastical dignitary place the reliquaries inside the temple itself. At 9:00 P.M., the king is welcomed by the highest authorities of the kingdom and by all the delegates invited to the ceremony for the solemn reception. The president of the Maha Bodhi Society of Calcutta gives a speech, the king, after saying a few words in reply, withdraws, but not without having been able to contemplate and honor the uncovered Relics presented to him by the Indian delegation after opening for him the two reliquaries.

That night most of the Cambodian dwellings in the capital remained illuminated. The same was true on the following nights up until the 11th of October, the last day of the festivities. Every house flew the Buddhist flag, most often flanked by French and Cambodian flags, and, depending on the identity of its inhabitants, the Chinese flag or some other emblem reflecting the nationality of the household. . . .

The next day, starting at 8:00 A.M., a huge procession formed at the Silver Pagoda in order to parade the Relics around the city. Four lictors, with golden helmets and crimson tunics, went first; next came the marching band of the Guards and a Cambodian orchestra, followed by two rows of Khmer officers-in-training. Then came the automobile bearing the relics, not being driven but being pulled by men dressed all in red. Then the parade of decorated floats, sponsored by various Buddhist Societies or other related groups, and, behind each one of these, the important delegates from each of these groups: Hindus from India who see in the Buddha an avatar of Vishnu; Malay Muslims, whose presence might surprise a European unused to so much mutual tolerance; they even brought along an orchestra dominated by an accordion player playing a Western dance tune. . . . On a float representing a stūpa, some Vietnamese Theravādin bhikkhus stand with the abbot of their monastery; further along, Mahāyānist monks of the same nationality mix with Chinese monks. Caodaism is also worthily represented: a truck made to look like a large rock, marked with the Eye of the Ineffable. The whole scene is completed by a statue of the Buddha in meditation, while young Vietnamese Caodaist girls sing hymns as they wave little flags the color of their sect. . . . The Khmers, men or women, prefer to assemble in the monasteries visited by the procession, if they do not decide more simply to throng its route. . . . Each evening, this same crowd will push through the doors of the royal monastery to attend the display of the relics in their opened reliquaries. The vendors of flowers and incense sticks occupy the courtyards of Wat Preah-Keo—the Cambodian name for "Silver Pagoda"—an expression which designates but does not translate it. Bouquets and packets of joss sticks are available to suit every budget, and who is not able to spend one piaster? For no one would dare enter empty-handed! Once in the courtyard, there is a rush towards the gratings that surround the temple. Inside, the monks on duty move back and forth slowly, one holds the relic of the Buddha enshrined in its monstrance, another those of the two disciples of the Perfected One. The lids of the reliquaries have been taken off ahead of time, and, uncovered, but under a little crystal ampulla, each person can see the precious remains of the Ones whom he or she loves. . . . Homage payed, the visitor then places his flowers, candles, or joss sticks in a great piece of cloth carried by two employees following behind the monks. . . . [Nearby], there is a chest intended to receive the further offerings of the faithful. It is replaced by another as soon as it is full. Among the devotees, many women, more respectful of their tradition than educated in its doctrines, strip themselves of their gold ornaments: necklaces, bracelets, earrrings, etc., all are offered to the Buddha so as to acquire merit. . . .

Source: Translated from Jean Barthes, "Les reliques sacrées à Phnom-Penh," *France-Asie* 8, no. 78 (1952): 951–56.

6.5.3 Magical Rites: The Chanting of Pirit

Another important dimension of Buddhist ritual is what one scholar has called its apotropaic aspect[8]—its "magical" use to ensure protection against a host of actual or potential threats such as accidents, sickness, drought, flood, danger, and violence. In Theravāda countries there are many ways, both Buddhist and non-Buddhist, for dealing with such problems, but a common method is the chanting of Pali texts known as paritta (Sinhalese: pirit), literally meaning "protection." Pirit texts are for the most part sūtras, or portions of sūtras, extracted from the Pali canon. Typically, monks will be asked to chant them in a ceremony that is intended to evoke the power of the Buddha, the Dharma, and the Sangha and to communicate that power to all those present by means of a cotton thread and sanctified water. This magical rite may perhaps best be understood as preventative exorcism. The chanting of the Buddha's Dharma by his Sangha, because it evokes so much good, is thought to be inimical to the forces of evil and keep them at bay, erecting a sort of magical barrier against them. At the same time, of course, the chanting of the Dharma makes merit, which is expected to have beneficial karmic effects.

There is a common belief that most of the afflictions that men suffer from are due to the malice of demons or evil spirits and there are a number of ceremonies by which it is supposed that their anger can be ap-

[8]See Melford E. Spiro, *Buddhism and Society* (Berkeley: University of California Press, 1982), ch. 6.

peased. But the only ceremony that is professed to have the sanction of the Buddha is the pirit ceremony. It is therefore one of the . . . ceremonials of great significance in the domestic and social life of the Sinhalese people. No household or social function, no religious festival or ceremony is complete without the chanting of pirit. . . .

The essence of the ceremony consists in chanting certain selected sacred texts by Buddhist monks holding in their hands a long thread called the pirit nūla, which is twisted round the neck of a new clay pot filled with water—the pūrṇa kumbha—while the other end of the thread is held by the assembled who squat on the floor. When the chanting is concluded, the thread sanctified by the chanting is broken into pieces and tied round the wrist and neck of those assembled and at the same time the sanctified water is sprinkled on all. In short it is a service of blessing.

A gāthā [verse] that is well known and often repeated, commending the chanting of pirit, speaks of the healing powers of the parittas and the rich blessings they bring:

> To ward off all calamities, to bring to fulfilment all rich blessings, for the destruction of all suffering, for the destruction of all fear, and for the destruction of all disease and sickness, recite ye the parittas.

There is a well-known story which is often recalled when pirit ceremonies are held: . . . There were two brahmins who became ascetics and practiced austerities for [a long time]. One of them returned to the world and having procured cattle and money, married and had a son who was named Dīghāyu [Long Life]. One day when the other ascetic came to the city, his friend and companion, now a householder, visited him with his wife and child. When they made obeisance to him, the ascetic said to the man and his wife, "Long life to you," but not to the child. When the parents of the child asked for the reason, the ascetic said that their son had only seven days to live and advised them to visit the Buddha and ask him whether there was any way of averting the child's fate. They did so, and the Buddha asked them to erect a pavilion outside the door of the house and get Buddhist monks to chant the paritta continuously for seven days with the child seated in their presence on a bench. On the seventh day, the Buddha himself came and hosts of *devas* [deities] gathered round him. At that time the yakkha (devil) Avaruddhaka also came to claim the child at the moment of his death for he had been granted the boon of eating the child. But on account of the presence of the devas he could not come near the child. All night long the Buddha himself recited the paritta and when the seventh day had passed the devil, unable to claim the child, went away. The critical moment was over and the Buddha declared that the boy would live for one hundred and twenty years and was renamed Āyuvaḍḍhana ["Prolonging Life"]. . . .

The collection of parittas known in Sinhala as the *Pirit-pota* is more widely known by the laity of Sri Lanka and Burma than any other Pali book. In Sri Lanka, . . . it forms an essential part of the meagre library of every Sinhalese household. Most of the Sinhalese people know some parts of these safety-runes which are in Pali, by heart, and every child is taught to recite some portion of them every morning and before retiring to bed in the evening. *Pirit* is heard every morning over the radio before the day's broadcasting programmes begin. The "Mahā Pirit" which includes the three sūtras, namely the *Mangala,* the *Ratana,* and the *Karaṇīya Metta Sutta,* is now available on Long Play records for use in every home. The parittas have been translated into Sinhala but they are recited in Pali. It is believed that the efficacy of the recital remains unaffected whether the reciter or the listener understands or not the meaning of what is chanted.

Pirit is chanted in temples or homes . . . [but] on special occasions for a full-fledged ceremony, a pavilion (pirit maṇdapaya) is erected for the purpose. Many temples have halls with a permanent pirit maṇdapaya. When a pirit ceremony is held this pavilion is gaily decorated. . . . Two chairs for the officiating monks (who sit while they chant) are placed near the table. . . . These chairs must face either the East or the North because the Buddha attained enlightenment facing the East and died with his head towards the North. Seats are also arranged for the other participating monks who sit around the table. A post called indrakhīla is planted securely and fastened on to the twin chairs. The threads drawn for decoration purposes are tied on to this post. Coconut oil lamps and pots filled with water are placed around and in the pavilion. The top of the pavilion is covered with white cloth. People sit outside the pavilion on mats and await the commencement of the ceremony which is announced by the beating of drums.

A lay-officer brings a new clay pot filled with water and places it in the pavilion. Then the *Pirit-pota* and a casket containing a relic of the Buddha (borne on the head of a lay-officer) are brought under a canopy of cloth held over them, accompanied by the beating of drums. The monks then come walking under a canopy of cloth also accompanied by the beating of the drums. When they approach the entrance to the hall, a layman washes their feet and another wipes them. Then they go walking on a carpet of white cloth and take their seats in the pavilion.

The relic represents the Buddha. It is believed to give the same efficacy to the proceedings as though the Buddha himself were actually present. The *Pirit-pota* represents the Dharma and the reciters, of course, the Sangha. The Triple Gem is therefore represented at this ceremony. This is an essential requirement. . . .

Before the chanting actually begins the reciters repeat the three-refuge formula [see 3.5.1], the Five Precepts and the paṭiccasamuppāda [see 3.3.1], and invoke the blessings of the gods. After this preparatory service the sacred thread (pirit nūla) is drawn round the interior of the pavilion, the end of which, after being fastened to the reading chairs and twisted round the neck of the pot of water, is placed on the table close to the relic and the reciters. Thus an unbroken and complete communication is maintained between each of the officiating priests, the relic, the *Pirit-pota* (i.e., the Triple Gem) and the water.

From the commencement of the ceremony until its conclusion the reading platform must not be vacated, neither must there be any break in the chanting. For this reason, when two officiating monks are to be relieved by others, one continues to chant while the other vacates and gives his seat to his successor and when he begins to chant the other monk vacates his seat and another takes his place. Two monks must be constantly officiating. When the ceremony continues for several days the chanting must continue night and day without intermission. . . . When the recitation of the sūtras constituting the *pirit* is concluded, it is recommenced, and in this way all the sūtras are recited over and over again.

On the morning of the seventh day [of a full-length ceremony], a grand procession is organised in order to send a messenger to a neighbouring temple or the *devāles* [shrines to the deities] within the temple precincts with a message to the gods. He takes with him four messages to the four guardian gods. The messenger is accompanied by armed and unarmed men and a few priests who proceed to the place where the gods are supposed to reside and invite them to attend the ceremony prior to its conclusion so that they may also partake of its benefits. . . . The gods and spirits are believed to answer the summons of the messenger and attend the ceremony. When the messenger and his company return the parittas are chanted more energetically than ever and a sermon is delivered to the gods, demons, and men, etc. The ceremony is brought to a close with the recital of . . . a benedictory sūtra and offerings of robes are made to the priest reciters.

Source: Reprinted by permission of the publisher from Lynn De Silva, *Buddhism: Beliefs and Practices in Sri Lanka,* 2nd ed. (Colombo: Ecumenical Institute, 1980), pp. 111–15 (slightly altered).

6.6 MEDITATIONAL ENDEAVORS: VISUALIZING THE VICTOR'S CAGE

In 3.5, we became acquainted with a number of basic Buddhist meditational practices. Although they are not followed by all monks and certainly not by all laypersons, most of them are still found in Sri Lanka and in Southeast Asia today, and some, in fact, as we shall see in 10.6, have been imported into the West. Practice in Theravāda lands, however, was not limited to such classic forms of meditation. The following selection is illustrative of a practice that has definite Tantric affinities; it involves the visualization of different beings and things and the association of them with various parts of the body. But it does this in a particularly Theravādin way: the Buddhas that are visualized on one's head are the twenty-eight Buddhas of the past and Gautama; the other beings, on various parts of the body, are Gautama's disciples, the arhats; finally, in addition, Pali texts commonly used as pirit are visualized all around, as though they formed a kind of protective barrier. Taking refuge in the Triple Gem represents, of course, a basic act in any devotional or meditational endeavor. Here we seem to have a more active form of refuge taking, in which the Buddha, Dharma, and Sangha are mentally constructed so as to form a protective Buddha's or Victor's Cage (Jinapañjara) around the meditator.

The verses setting forth this scenario are known throughout Southeast Asia but were perhaps composed in Thailand. In Sri Lanka, they form "a very important sutta recited in all pirit rituals,"[9] although they bear no resemblance to anything in the Pali canon. It is likely that they should be related to what has been called the tradition of "Tantric Theravāda." This comprises a wide variety of practices, many of them esoteric and yogic in nature, in which the path of liberation passes through the knowledge of the association of parts of the body with various Pali syllables, various texts, various Buddhas, and so on.[10]

Verses on the Victor's Cage

The buddhas who came to the seat of enlightenment,
who vanquished Māra and his elephant-mount,
who drank the ambrosia of the Four Noble Truths,
these great men, these leaders, these lordly sages,
these twenty-eight past buddhas beginning with Tanhaṃkara,
all are established above my head.
The Buddha is stationed in my head,
the Dharma in my eyes,
and the Sangha, source of all virtues,
is stationed in my chest.

[The Buddha's disciple] Anuruddha is in my heart, Sāriputta on my right,
Koṇḍañña is in back of me, and Moggallāna on my left.
Ānanda and Rāhula are posted at my right ear,
and Kassapa and Mahānāma, both, at my left ear.
Sobhita, best of sages, sits in splendor,
shining like the sun in back of the hair on my head.
That source of virtue, that great sage, that eloquent speaker,
the elder Kumārakassapa, is ever stationed in my mouth.
And the five elders Puṇṇa, Angulimāla, Upālī, Nanda, and Sīvalī,
are born as auspicious marks on my forehead.
The rest of the eighty great elders, victorious disciples of the Victor,
those eighty great elders, sons of the triumphant Victor,
glowing in moral conduct,
take their positions in various parts of my body.

In front of me, the Ratana sutta; to my right, the Metta sutta;
Behind me, the Dhajagga sutta, and to my left the Angulimāla paritta.
The Khandha and Mora parittas and the Āṭānāṭiya sutta
form a roof in the air over me,
while the other suttas are set up as a rampart around me,
seven walls maintained by the power and authority of the Buddha.

May all my inner and outer disturbances,
brought on by winds and bile and other such things,
be completely destroyed by the unending glory of the Victor,

---

[9]Lily De Silva, *Paritta* (Colombo: Department of Government Printing, 1981), p. 9.

[10]See, for instance, Lance Cousins, "Aspects of Esoteric Southern Buddhism," *Indian Insights* (London: Luzac Oriental, 1997), pp. 185–207; see also F. Bizot and F. Lagirarde, *La pureté par les mots,* Textes bouddhiques du Laos (Paris: Ecole Française d'Extrême-Orient, 1996).

as I go on, dwelling ever in the cage of the Completely Enlightened One.
And may all those eminent great men ever protect me
as I reside on earth, in the middle of the Victor's cage.
In this way I will be well guarded and well protected.
By the power of the Victor, disturbances are vanquished,
by the power of the Dharma, hosts of enemies are defeated,
by the power of the Sangha, obstacles are overcome;
Protected by the power of the True Dharma, I live in the Victor's cage.

Source: Translated from S. Sivaraksa, "Jinapañjaragāthā," *Journal of the Siam Society* 75 (1987): 299–300.[11]

6.7 WOMEN AND THE SANGHA: A TWENTIETH-CENTURY CASE

In 2.1.4, we examined the circumstances of the admission of women into the sangha by the Buddha. It should be pointed out, however, that in the Theravāda tradition, the ordination lineage for nuns (bhikkhunī) eventually died out (in part as a result of the additional regulations imposed upon them by the Vinaya). Strictly speaking, at least from the point of view of male orthodoxy, there are today no fully ordained Theravāda bhikkhunī in Sri Lanka, Thailand, or Myanmar. There are, however, many monastic movements of Theravāda women in these countries: women who devote themselves fully to the religious life, shaving their heads, wearing robes (of differing colors), and taking upon themselves the observance of various numbers of precepts (eight or ten). At the same time, various attempts are being made to try to revive the full Theravāda bhikkhunī ordination. This move has been supported by some, but it has been resisted by conservative forces within the sangha, who point out that according to the Vinaya, the presence of fully ordained nuns (not to mention willing monks) is required in order to ordain nuns, so that in their absence, such ordination is impossible. In effect, once the lineage has died out, it is dead. (There is one argument, however, that the Sri Lankan Theravāda bhikkhunī ordination was transmitted during the fifth century C.E. to China where it has survived and whence it could be reintroduced to Theravāda lands; see 8.7.1.)

The following selection tells the story of two pioneers in the bhikkhunī movement in Thailand and recalls some of the difficulties that they faced in the first half of the twentieth century.

Although . . . there has never been an official bhikkhuni sangha in Thailand, a few women have attempted to become bhikkhunis. In 1928, two young sisters, Sara and Chongdi Bhasit, with their father's encouragement, received the samaneri [female novice] ordination. At the time,

[11] Alternative English translation, Thanissaro Bhikkhu, "The Victors' Cage," unpublished manuscript (Valley Center, CA: Metta Monastery, n.d.).

Sara, the elder sister, was eighteen years old. Their father, Pra Panom Saranarin (alias Khlueng Bhasit), felt strongly that bhikkhunis needed to be represented in the Thai sangha. He hoped that bhikkhuni ordination would provide a meaningful way of religious life for women and also help improve their social status.

During an interview with Sara, who is now eighty-one years old, she did not want to disclose the name of the master who gave her ordination for fear that he might encounter difficulty in remaining in the sangha. At the time of their ordination, the Ven. Bhikkhu Ard of Wat Khaoyoi in Petburi province was suspected of having given ordination to these two women and was forced, as a consequence, to leave the sangha.

The two sisters remained samaneris and received bhikkhuni ordination in 1932. Apparently Sara and Chongdi received their vows only from monks. According to the ordination rules, proper bhikkhuni ordination requires that the preceptor giving ordination be a senior monk of at least ten years' standing, recognized and appointed as such by the sangha. A minimum of five monks must attend the ordination, and the applicant must first receive ordination from the bhikkhuni sangha before receiving it from the bhikkhu sangha. As there is no official Thai bhikkhuni sangha in existence, the Thai sangha did not consider Sara and Chongdi to have been properly ordained.

At the time in question, both sisters stayed at Wat Nariwong (literally, "female lineage") which had been built on land given them by their father in his own compound. Pra Panom Saranarin had offered the land to the sangha but had been refused, as they considered him someone who was going against Buddhist tradition. The temple was used as a center for Dharma discussion for local people interested in Buddhist teaching and practice.

During their residence at Wat Nariwong . . . the two bhikkhunis sometimes went for alms in the neighboring community. Although some people spoke harshly of them, others offered them food. They also traveled to different temples where they were given shelter with the mae jis [female lay practitioners], and they went on alms rounds, just like the monks.

During their travels, Sara and Chongdi stayed at Wat Pra Buddhapat in Saraburi province. It was local custom for laypeople to put only cooked rice in the bowl, placing other dishes on a tray held by the temple boy who followed the monks on alms rounds. The bhikkhunis had no temple boy to follow them, and for the first three days they received only cooked rice. When the local people realized this, they assured them that food would be brought for them to the temple. . . .

Pra Panom Saranarin was a controversial figure politically, who was involved in many publications . . . [that] reflected his progressive thinking. Most of his writing challenged the Thai government and raised issues about social injustice prevalent in the Thai society of his day. He was especially vocal about the decline of the sangha leadership. His printing press was closed down by the government many times. Pra Panom Saranarin's public criticism of both the government and the sangha placed him in a highly undesirable position. Subsequently, his daughters and the bhikkhuni sangha that he supported became targets of political wrath.

The sangha was opposed to both the samaneri and the bhikkhuni ordinations. The sangharaja [supreme patriarch] sent a personal letter to the mayor of Nonthaburi, the province where their home temple was situated, ordering the bhikkhunis to disrobe and declaring the ordination invalid. . . . Two monks, Pra Sasanasobhon of Wat Makut and Somdej Pra Buddhakosacaraya of Wat Sudat, stated that ordaining women was the act of a crazy person, and they reiterated the traditional view that women were the enemy of monks' purity.

There was a violent reaction in the public media as well. Newspapers generally ridiculed the ordination of women. *Thai Num* ("Young Thai Men") considered such ordination the enemy of Buddhism and an act of Devadatta's followers. *Lak Muang* ("City Post") considered the women's ordination a heretical act, deserving the death sentence. *Sri Krung* encouraged the government to punish these women. *Bangkok Karnmueng* ("Bangkok and Politics") suggested that if Pra Panom Saranarin was a good Buddhist, he should not allow his daughters to become heretics. Only one newspaper, *Ying Thai* ("Thai Women"), gave a positive report on the ordination of women.

Finally, police arrested the young bhikkhunis, and they were forced to appear in court at Nonthaburi. . . . [They] refused to give up their robes. They were charged with an act of disobedience to the Order of the Sangha. Sara was jailed for eight days, Chongdi for four. At their father's suggestion, they started wearing brown robes similar to those of Japanese monks when they were released, but as soon as police harassment stopped, they resumed wearing their yellow robes. . . .

Sara remained in robe as a bhikkhuni for two years before disrobing in the face of unrelenting pressure from society and from the Buddhist authorities. In total, she remained an ordained person for eight years—a mae ji for two years, a samaneri for four, and a bhikkhuni for two years. Interviewed in 1983, when she was seventy-three years old, . . . she still felt strongly about establishing a bhikkhuni sangha in Thailand, stating, "We should mend whatever is incomplete—a chair with a broken leg must be fixed. The Buddha established four groups of Buddhists: bhikkhus, bhikkhunis, laymen, and laywomen. As the bhikkhuni sangha is now missing, we have to reestablish this for the sake of completion."

Source: Reprinted by permission of the publisher from Chatsumarn Kabilsingh, *Thai Women in Buddhism* (Berkeley: Parallax Press, 1991), pp. 45–48 (slightly altered).

6.8 SANGHA AND SOCIETY

It should be clear by now that at no point in history have Buddhist monastics been completely disengaged from the social realities–the economics, politics, and social dynamics–of the world in which they live. Three examples of such interactions in modern times may be found in the following selections.

6.8.1 Monks and Money

According to the rules of the Vinaya, monks are not supposed to handle money; that is one of the things that differentiates them from the laity. That did not mean, of course, that some monasteries did not become rich. Historically, throughout the Theravāda world, the sangha was often the recipient of considerable donations, not only of food but also of wealth, of agricultural land, indeed of whole villages, which became attached in feudal times to particular monasteries. But that does not erase the dilemma for the individual monk, living day to day in a modern moneyed economy, a situation that is addressed in this selection.

It is interesting to note that thorough schooling in the rules of behaviour may bring about an awareness that there are certain precepts which are regularly broken. In rural areas there is a discrepancy between the accepted manner of behaviour and the official precepts, for example with regard to the handling of money. The 18th rule in the [Vinaya] category *nissaggiyā-pācittiyā* states clearly:

> Whatsoever Bhikkhu shall receive gold or silver, or get someone to receive it for him, or allow it to be kept in deposit for him—that is a Pācittiyā offence involving forfeiture.

According to this precept . . . monks may not possess nor handle money, and if they wish to rectify a breach of this rule they must forfeit the money handled. In principle, it would be possible for Thai monks to live without possessing or handling money. There are laymen who can hold the money which has been offered to the sangha, and the individual monks are provided with all basic material goods. The monk receives free clothing and food, free medicine in State hospitals and is assured of a roof above his head. When he performs a ceremony for lay people he often receives presents which include common household goods, such as toothpaste and soap so that he need not depend on buying them.

In practice, however, there are few monks who do not regularly break the rule. A monk handling money is a common sight; he may be seen paying for transport, for only the municipal bus services of Bangkok provide free travel for members of the sangha; in the rest of the country the bus companies charge a monk half price. The fare in taxis and boats is usually full price. When travelling a monk may be seen paying for his morning meal in a restaurant. In rural monasteries, many monks buy tobacco, tea, and Ovaltine.

It is not only the fact that many monks are used to spending money which makes it difficult to change the monkly behaviour more towards the letter of the rule, the laymen themselves often insist on giving money to individual members of the sangha. It is a generally accepted custom that all monks who assist at a ceremony in the house of a layman are remunerated for this service. All the invited monks come to the layman's house expecting to be rewarded financially, and their expectations are never in vain. Poor people will give less than rich ones, and it is not by accident that a chapter of monks often chants considerably longer in the house of a rich farmer than in the house of one who cannot afford to donate a great amount.

The people insist on making cash donations because they believe that there is a clear connection between the amount of money offered to the monks and the amount of beneficial *karma* received in return. . . . The giving of money to monks, though it contravenes an official rule, remains important to the people because they believe firmly in the possibility of an instantaneous effect of the beneficial *karma* that they gain through their donation. This immediate effect of merit is protective power, the keeping away of accidents, and good luck. [. . .]

[The following is a rather unusual situation but significant nonetheless]: . . . a well-to-do layman invited thirteen monks from three different monasteries to chant in his house. Many of the monks happened to be inexperienced, recently ordained monks, and the oldest, highest ranking monk present was more than 80 years old. This venerable bhikkhu chose to chant texts which almost none of the other members of the chapter knew, and the sound of the recitation became very meagre indeed.

The house-owner conferred softly with several other laymen present, and after the ceremony, when publicly announcing the amount of the donation, he stressed: "In this case we donate fifty *baht* [about $2.50] to each of the four members of the sangha who used their voices, and only half that amount to the remaining monks."

July 31, 1968. During a friendly talk, a monk complained that he had hoped to pay off his debts, but he had not won in the lottery this week. He had not spent any money on the lottery for some weeks now, but had the feeling that this time he might be lucky. Unfortunately it did not come true.

Question: Did you ever win a prize?

Answer: Yes, last year I got 200 *baht* for my 10 *baht* ticket.

Question: What would you do if you won a million *baht*?

Answer: I would give a generous sum to the monastery to build something, did you know that that is how the big *cetiya* [stūpa] had come to be built, as well as the school on the monastery grounds? Of course I would keep a good amount to set up a pleasant life.

Question: Do all monks buy in the lottery?

Answer: No, only a few can afford it. The Venerable X buys every week because he has a small pension from the government because his son was killed in the war.

Question: Does a monk have the same chance to win a prize as a layman?

Answer: Probably a monk has a better chance, after all he is apart by virtue of his discipline. But you cannot count on good luck, you never can reckon on the fact that merit will work instantaneously.

All the monks realize that gambling is officially frowned upon. Still, because it does not interfere with their private religious beliefs, they readily engage in such matters. The only concession to the written rules is usually that they engage a lay friend to purchase the lottery tickets.

Source: Reprinted by permission of the author from B. J. Terwiel, *Monks and Magic: An Analysis of Religious Ceremonies in Central Thailand* (London: Curzon Press, 1975), pp. 129–31, 110, 132–33 (slightly altered).

6.8.2 Leaving the Sangha

There is another aspect of the interaction of the sangha and society that needs to be considered here. Studies of Christian monasticism often lead Westerners into thinking of the careers of monks and nuns as lifetime commitments to the monastic life, and this assumption is sometimes applied to Buddhism. In modern-day Theravāda countries, however, this is not necessarily the case. Especially in Southeast Asia, the custom has grown for virtually all young men to spend at least some part of their youth in the yellow robes as members of the sangha. In Myanmar, this has resulted in the important tradition of the temporary ordination of boys as novices, a rite called shin-byu, which takes place around the time of puberty. The corresponding ceremony for girls, for whom the sangha is now closed, is an ear-piercing rite. In Thailand, it is customary for boys, before they marry, to become ordained and spend a token period (such as the three months of a rains retreat) in a monastery. In Cambodia, the tradition sometimes is for boys at puberty to spend some time as novices—in that way they repay their debt to their mother—and then, at age twenty or so, to do a second monastic stint as a monk. In that way, they repay their debt to their father. In all these cases, it is understood that these young men will not spend their entire lives as monks. Rather, their ordinations are rites of passage in their development as males on the road to becoming full members of society. At the same time, for their families and especially for their parents, the ordinations of these young men are important occasions for making merit, for of all merit-making occasions, the gift of a son to the sangha is the greatest.

Of course, many monks in Thailand and Myanmar do stay in the sangha until they die, but it is important to be able to think of monkhood in those countries not necessarily as a lifelong career but also—and this is true in the majority of cases—as a stage of life, an interim period that prepares laymen for success in society. There is no stigma attached to the act of disrobing, although it might be said that the longer a man is a monk, the better a layman he makes. King Mongkut, for example, spent almost thirty years as a monk before acceding to the throne at age forty-seven to become one of the great nineteenth-century monarchs of Siam (and to father no fewer than eighty-two children by the various wives of his harem, more than any other ruler of his dynasty). Leaving the order, then, is also an important rite of passage, the counterpart of the ceremonies of ordination which we looked at in 2.2.2.

Most newly ordained monks decide to leave the order after completion of their first Lenten season [rains retreat], after the *kathin* ceremony has marked the end of the period of the year when religious life is most intensive. The man who decides to leave the order must ask advice about an auspicious moment for doing so. A person with astrological knowledge tells him the most propitious day and usually insists that the ceremony should take place at the time of sunrise of that day. The insistence upon the moment of sunrise, the "birth" of a new day, could be an indication that leaving the sangha can be seen as a ritual rebirth; a man who "died" to the world when ordained is "born anew" when he leaves the order. Consistent with this view is the fact that ordination can take place on any day of the year. People do not try to select an auspicious day for becoming a monk; similarly, no special day can be set for death. In the same vein Rabibhadana writes:

> A man who was born at an unfortunate time, i.e., when the stars are not favorable, could select a propitious time for leaving the monkhood. He might then have his horoscope made, taking the time of his leaving the monkhood as the time of his birth. It is believed that by this means, the man would be able to escape the bad influence of the stars. . . .

Although it is recognized that the man who leaves the order breaks with what is noblest in a man's life, the ceremony is not a sad event and no stigma is attached to such a man. Every man who has passed at least one Lenten season in the order has the right to claim a position in adult lay society. It is advisable that a person who is going to leave the order should be happy and content about his decision; a man who is dejected and unsure of himself should remain in the security of the sangha until he feels more certain.

The day before leaving the order, a man must take leave of his fellow monks by prostrating himself in front of each of them and by asking forgiveness for any offence that he may have caused through his negligence. On the morning of the ceremony, the monk should dress in clean robes and renew his vows. . . . He must take some layman's clothes, candles, incense, flowers, his begging bowl in which he has poured some clean water and a bundle of twigs which still possess their foliage. All the twigs are taken from plants which have auspicious names or fortunate associations. . . .

With all these paraphernalia the monk must go towards the place where the ceremony will take place; usually this is the office of the abbot or the [hall of the temple]. The monk lights a candle and the incense and offers these together with the flowers while prostrating himself three times before the image of the Buddha. Meanwhile, the leader of the ceremony [usually the abbot] has taken the begging bowl with water and quickly murmurs some Pāli formulae whilst holding a lighted candle above the surface of the water, thus consecrating the contents of the vessel. . . .

The monk on whose instigation the ritual takes place is told that, if he wishes to change his mind about becoming a layman, he has a last opportunity to do so. When he has indicated that he is certain, he is asked to repeat three times the prescribed formula: "sikkhaṃ paccakkhāmi gihīti maṃ dhāretha" which can be translated as: "I leave the discipline, you should recognize me as a householder."

From the moment that the word *dhāretha* has sounded for the third time, the man is a monk no more, and he must therefore change into lay clothing. Upon returning to the scene of the ritual, the man who has just left the sangha must undergo several ritual acts which are intended to protect and guard him. The leader of the ceremony sprinkles him with consecrated water, using the bunch of leaves as a brush, whilst the other monks who had to be invited as witnesses chant some auspicious stanzas. The ex-monk is then instructed to go and bathe himself thoroughly, to rub himself with soap and rinse, and to return to the abbot afterwards. In the privacy of the room of the abbot, the layman is instructed to be a worthy member of the community, and he is prompted to request from the abbot to receive the Five Precepts of the layman.

Source: Reprinted by permission of the author from B. J. Terwiel, *Monks and Magic: An Analysis of Religious Ceremonies in Central Thailand* (London: Curzon Press, 1975), pp. 137–39.

6.8.3 Monks and Politics: The Views of Walpola Rahula

In 6.3 we saw that one of the traditional bifurcations in Theravāda countries has been that between forest-dwelling and town-dwelling monks. One modern-day expression of this divide may be seen in the so-called revival of Buddhism during the twentieth century in Sri Lanka. On one hand were those who thought that the primary duty of monks was to renounce society and devote themselves exclusively to a life of meditation; they were behind the foundation of a series of forest hermitages for "renouncers." On the other hand were the so-called "political monks," who felt that the primary duty of monastics was to involve themselves in the independence movement, social reform, elections, and bettering the lives of the people. Prominent in the latter group was the Venerable Walpola Ṛahula, a Sri Lankan monk well known in the West for his primer, *What the Buddha Taught.* In Sri Lanka, however, he was perhaps more famous for his *Bhikṣuvāge Urumaya,* written in Sinhalese in 1946 and translated into English as *The Heritage of the Bhikkhu.* In it, in a move that reflects his own interests in both Marxism and the Mahāyāna, he claims that throughout the history of Buddhism, monks have consistently been involved, along with laypersons, in improving not only the spiritual but also the material conditions of humanity. At the same time, Rahula is explicit in his critique of those who claim otherwise. These were first the British colonial rulers and, after independence in 1947, the English-educated lay elite, whose views that monks should have nothing to do with involvement in the world, according to Rahula, conveniently coincided with their own political agendas and desire for power.

[Politics involves] the development of such things as education, morality, health, sanitation, social and economic security, all of which are necessary and conducive to the good and well being of mankind both here and hereafter.

Now it is interesting to examine why some consider it unworthy of *bhikkhus* to engage in such noble and exalted service which is for the good and well being of humanity.

One reason for this attitude is the misunderstanding of politics and of Buddhism and the *bhikkhu*-life. Some people are of the opinion that *bhikkhus* need not participate in any activity intended for the progress and well being of the people and that they should live away from society, enjoying the requisites provided by the people, unmindful of what is happening to people, and intent only on their salvation—an utterly selfish and egoistic life! This is indeed a gross misconception and misunderstanding of Buddhism and the *bhikkhu*'s life. It loses sight entirely of the noble and lofty ideals and teachings of Buddhism.

The *bhikkhu* is not a selfish, cowardly individual thinking only of his happiness and salvation, unmindful of whatever happens to the rest of humanity. A true *bhikkhu* is an altruistic, heroic person who considers others' happiness more than his own. He, like the Bodhisattva Sumedha [see 1.4.1], will renounce his own *nirvāṇa* for the sake of others. Buddhism is built upon service to others. One who is concerned only with one's own happiness and salvation, unmindful of whatever happens to others, cannot be considered even to be an ordinary Buddhist, leave alone a Buddhist monk. [. . .]

Some people fear that political activities or social work will interfere with the piety of a *bhikkhu*. Yet, a *bhikkhu* who is bereft of virtue, whose mind and character are not developed through meditation, can never render any real service to the people. If anyone thinks that this is possible, it surely is a supreme deception. A *bhikkhu* engaged in social work must necessarily possess nobler and more exalted virtues and qualities than a *bhikkhu* living by himself and meditating in retirement in a forest. [. . .]

It is unthinkable that the present-day *bhikkhu* population of over 15,000 will, all of them, retire to the forest for meditation. Are they all to continue to live this meaningless and lazy life both in respect of themselves and of others, which is just another burden to the country and the nation? Or should they occupy themselves in a course of action that will be of use to themselves, to the country, to the nation, and to the religion?

This is not merely a religious question. This is a very grave question of religious, national, economic, and social import.

Another group of people who disapprove of *bhikkhus* participating in political activities is that wealthy, powerful, and aristocratic coterie which has inequitably usurped political as well as other powers and privileges in the country. They fear that once the *bhikkhus* become active in political issues their [own] unjust treatment of the poor might be publicly exposed, to the detriment of the power they enjoy. This fear, of course, is legitimate.

It is a well-known fact that in the recent past many high priests (*nāyaka theras*) and chief monks of temples belonging to several sects openly supported and campaigned in favor of certain candidates in the past general elections. . . . [However, they did so] neither with a conviction of the meaning of politics nor in accordance with any political principles, but merely at the request of wealthy and influential aristocratic leaders. It was simply surrender and subordination to the wealthy and the powerful. But today the situation is different. *Bhikkhus* who have acquired a good modern education have an insight into current problems, and through their devotion to their country, their nation, and their religion, have come forward freely and independently to tell the masses of their legitimate rights and privileges, without subordinating themselves to the will of the powerful and wealthy aristocrats. Those who have unjustly appropriated to themselves the power in the country are too well aware of the danger to which they are being exposed by the course of action taken by these *bhikkhus.* As a measure of self-preservation, therefore, as far as they are concerned, *bhikkhus* must be excluded from political activities.

Source: Reprinted by permission of the publisher from Walpola Rahula, *The Heritage of the Bhikkhu* (New York: Grove Press, 1974), pp. 125–28.

CHAPTER 7

Buddhists and the Practice of Buddhism: The Tibetan Cultural Area

Tibet is a country that historically has been both close to the great cultures of India and China, which surround it, and far distanced from them. What has linked it to its neighbors, at least since the seventh century C.E., has been its belief in Buddhism; what has distanced it has been its own distinct culture and the sheer facts of geography.

Buddhism was in its efflorescence in India when it was introduced, rather late, into Tibet, but there, after some hesitation, the teachings and practices of the Mahāyāna and Vajrayāna took root and continued to be worked out long after they had more or less vanished from the land of their birth. Nowhere else did Buddhist monasticism, and the educational system that went with it, attract such large numbers. Nowhere else did Buddhist ritual, art, and practice flourish quite so prolifically. Nowhere else were certain developments of Buddhist philosophy taken further and worked out more fully. Nowhere else did the Buddhist pantheon of Buddhas, bodhisattvas, and divinities mushroom more spectacularly.

The influence of Tibetan Buddhism, moreover, was not limited to Tibet. Historically, it spread in a variety of ways to the adjacent Himalayan regions of Ladakh, Nepal, Sikkim, and Bhutan, as well as northeastward to Mongolia, and through the Mongols and later the Manchus it extended its influence to China itself. In more recent times, especially since an unsuccessful uprising against the Chinese in 1959, many Tibetans, including the Dalai Lama and a large number of learned monks, have left their homeland and settled in India as well as in the West. This diaspora has had a tremendous influence on the course of Tibetan Buddhist studies, in that it has enabled scholars to become much better acquainted with what was once the poorly understood realm of a few hardy explorers.

7.1 MYTHIC HISTORY: SUBDUING THE DEMONS OF TIBET

In 6.1.1, we considered the story of the Buddha's visit to the island of Sri Lanka and of the Venerable Mahinda's conversion of Tissa, the Sri Lankan king. In Tibet, the legend of the establishment of Buddhism is associated with a number of figures. First, there is the early Tibetan king, Song-tsen-gam-po, who reigned in the seventh century C.E. and is thought to have been an incarnation of Avalokiteśvara (see 5.2.1), the patron bodhisattva of Tibet. Then, there are his two wives, the daughters of the king of Nepal and of the emperor of China, who are thought to have encouraged his propagation of Buddhism and are popularly believed to have been manifestations of different forms of the bodhisattva Tārā (see 5.2.2). Finally, in the eighth century, we come to two Indian Buddhist monks: the great Madhyamaka-Yogacāra scholar Śāntarakṣita and the Tantric exorcist, magician, and esotericist Padmasambhava, who is often credited with being the founder of the "old," or unreformed, sect of Tibetan Buddhism, the Nying-ma-pa, but in fact is revered by Tibetans of all schools.

One of the early problems faced by Buddhism in Tibet was dealing with indigenous forces, personified in the form of native "demons." In Sri Lanka, as we have seen, the mythic solution to this problem was to have the Buddha chase all the demons away. In Tibet, however, we find a slightly different scenario. The autochthonous demoness is first subdued, put down quite literally by the weight of monasteries built on top of her body. Subsequently, however, other demons arise, along with new opposition to Buddhism, and this necessitates new exorcistic measures. Indeed, Padmasambhava was invited to Tibet by Song-tsen-gam-po's successor, King Trhi-song-de-tsen, specifically to subdue indigenous demons who were blocking the building of the important early monastery of Sam-ye.

The following account is taken from a chronicle of Indian and Tibetan Buddhism written by the great fourteenth-century scholar and redactor of the Tibetan Buddhist canon, Bu-tön.

The king [Song-tsen-gam-po] then took in marriage Trhi-tsün, the daughter of the Nepalese king Aṃśuvarman. This princess brought with her images of [the Buddha] Akṣobhyavajra, [and of the bodhisattvas] Maitreya and Tārā, the latter being of sandalwood. After that the king married the Chinese princess Kong-jo, the daughter of the Chinese Emperor, who brought with her the statue of the Buddha which was afterwards placed in the [Jo-khang] temple [in Lhasa].

Thereupon [Queen] Trhi-tsün wished to build a monastery [to house the image], but had not the power of doing this. The king saw that the ground of Tibet was like the body of a demoness that had fallen on her back, and that it was necessary first to press this demoness down. Accordingly, on her right shoulder he caused to be built the monastery of Ka-tshel, on the left one, Trhan-duk, on the right leg, Tsang-dram, and on the left, Drom-pa-gyang—these being "the four monasteries of the four flanks." Then, he constructed on the [demoness's] right elbow, . . . left elbow, . . . right knee, . . . and left knee . . . [the monasteries known as] "the four subduers of the borders." Thereafter on the palm of her right hand . . . of her left hand, . . . on her right foot, . . . and her left foot, [four more monasteries] were built. . . . Then, in the middle of the lake [in Lhasa], the king made a foundation of stone covered with wood. Cement having been made out of the mould of the nāgas and earth having been brought with the help of a goat, the ground was levelled and the monastery of Lhasa [the Jo-khang] was built. From the working-tools heaped up in the northern projection of the temple there appeared by itself the form of Avalokiteśvara with eleven faces. . . .

[There follows an account of the fortunes of Buddhism under various kings. After several generations, Trhi-song-de-tsen came to the throne, while still very young. Certain ministers, who were opponents of Buddhism and supporters of the ancient indigenous religion, sought to take advantage of the situation]:

As the prince was still a child, the ministers violated the laws and customs, banished those who were acting according to the Doctrine, and made arrangements to send the statue of the Buddha back to China. But as three hundred men were incapable of moving it, they buried it in sand and made of the temple a slaughter-house. At that time, [two ministers died of accidents and] the other ministers said: "This is a punishment for our having buried the deity under sand." Accordingly, they hoisted the statue on a pair of mules and brought it to Kyi-rong in Mang-yül. . . .

Thereafter, Trhi-song-de-tsen, having attained the age of thirteen, ascended the throne. When the biography of his father and grandfather was related to him, the Doctrine was likewise mentioned in the narrative. The king got the sacred texts that had been concealed, expressed the wish to study them, and became full of faith. . . .

[Then the king] and other ministers, devoted to the Doctrine, . . . [sent to Nepal to invite the "ācārya bodhisattva," Śāntarakṣita, to come to Tibet.] With the Kashmirian Ananta as translator, he expounded in the palace for four months the teaching of the ten virtues, of the eighteen component elements of the individual, and of the twelve-membered causal chain. This brought the malignant deities of Tibet into a fury. The grassy plain [was devastated] by a flood, lightning struck [the hill of] Mar-po-ri, and diseases befalling men and cattle broke out. The Tibetan subjects declared that this was a consequence of the propagation of a false doctrine, and Śāntarakṣita was sent back to Nepal.

[After some time had passed, however, the decision was made to invite him to return.] When he had come back, the ācārya met the king . . . and said to him: "As the demons of Tibet are not subdued, they do not allow that one acts for the sake of the Doctrine. They are powerful and endowed with huge bodies. It is therefore necessary to subdue them. Now there exists a teacher called Padmasambhava who is endowed with great power and dexterity. You must invite him in order to pacify the devils."

The king [therefore sent a delegation to India to invite Padmasambhava, and] he gradually proceeded forward [to Tibet], subduing the malignant deities. . . . He met with the king and then . . . subdued all the Tibetan demons. Thereafter, he was invited to Sam-ye and he established his residence there.

The ācārya bodhisattva [Śāntarakṣita], in his turn, examined the ground [at Sam-ye], took the monastery of Odantapuri [in India] as a model, and made a plan [for the new monastery] containing the forms of

Mount Meru, the twelve continents, both the sun and the moon, all these surrounded by a circumference of iron. In the female-fire-hare-year the foundation was laid, and first of all the temple of Avalokiteśvara was built, and images, for which Tibetan men served as models, were sculptured. . . . In the female-earth-hare-year [775 C.E.] the work was accomplished. The ācārya bodhisattva and Padmasambhava performed the rites of consecration and a feast was celebrated during thirteen years.

Source: Reprinted from *History of Buddhism (Chos-hbyung) by Bu-ston,* trans. E. Obermiller (Heidelberg, 1931), 2:184–90 (slightly altered).

7.2 INTERACTIONS AND SYNCRETISM: BUDDHISM, SHAMANISM, AND BON IN NEPAL

The indigenous religious forces that long existed in Tibet and were opposed to the introduction of Buddhism in the seventh and eighth centuries are sometimes identified with the Bon religion. To do this, however, is to oversimplify greatly a complex question. Though it is undeniable that certain early indigenous practices have survived in Tibet, they should not be equated with the Bon religion that is practiced in Tibet and adjacent lands today. Nor should Bon be equated with "shamanism" or the undefined popular beliefs that are sometimes called Tibet's "nameless religion." Today the faith and practices of the Bon-po (followers of Bon) have been so influenced and defined by Tibetan Buddhism that some scholars prefer to think of Bon as a Buddhist sect or as a sort of mirror-image movement reacting to a dominant "orthodoxy." Others, however, would rather see it as a distinct religion in its own right, having affinities especially with some of the "unreformed" sects of Tibetan Buddhism (for example, the Nying-ma-pa and Ka-gyü-pa) and yet distinguishing itself from them.

Today the interaction among Bon, shamanism, folk religion, and Buddhism can best be seen, perhaps, in border regions where migrant Tibetan lamas have, fairly recently, settled and sought to propagate Buddhism in the face of more ancient traditions. The following example from the report of an anthropologist comes from a region of northern Nepal now settled by both Tibetans and the indigenous Gurung people, and it "provides insight into what may have occurred again and again in rural Tibet as Lamaism gradually triumphed over indigenous shamanic and later Bon practices."[1] The Tibetans coming into the area brought with them a famous and popular story of the miracle contest between a Buddhist saint, Milarepa (see 7.6), and a great Bon master, on the slopes of Tise mountain in southern Tibet (see 7.5.1). In the Buddhist telling of the story, Milarepa readily defeats the Bon master and proves himself superior. The Gurungs do not dispute this outcome of the contest, but in their telling of the story they identify themselves with the defeated Bon master, and "rescue" from the tale some positive points by adding to it a sequel.

[1]Stan Royal Mumford, *Himalayan Dialogue: Tibetan Lamas and Gurung Shamans in Nepal* (Madison: University of Wisconsin Press, 1989), p. 30.

In doing so, however, they transform the Bon master into the figure of an indigenous shaman and take the opportunity to praise their own oral traditions over the bookishness of the Buddhists. Clearly, the interactions of all these traditions can get very complicated.

My first project in collecting data on lama-shaman dialogues in [the district of] Gyasumdo was to elicit comment on the famed legend of the twelfth-century contest between the Tibetan lama Milarepa and the Bonpo Naro Bon Chung at the site of Mount Tise (Kailash) in Tibet. The legend had already been found to be prevalent among highland peoples in Nepal that have been influenced by Lamaism, and in Gyasumdo both Tibetan and Gurung communities knew the legend well. The Ghyabrẽ and Paju shamans unhesitatingly identify themselves with the Tibetan Bonpo . . . who "lost the contest" to Milarepa. They and the Tibetan lamas agree on the main kernel of the story, which I summarize here from taped interviews:

> Milarepa went with his disciples to Mount Tise. He met a Bonpo who challenged him to a contest of magical power to see which of them should control the mountain. After a few preliminary contests of flying over the lake in which they were both equal, they decided to see who could reach the top of Mount Tise first on the morning of the next day.
>
> Early in the morning the Bonpo, riding his drum, flew up the slope of the mountain. Milarepa's disciple awoke his master and pointed to the Bonpo nearing the top. At that moment a ray of sunlight broke over the top of the mountain and beamed down into the window of the hut. Milarepa instantly rode the sunbeam to the top of Mount Tise, arriving ahead of the Bonpo.
>
> Defeated, the Bonpo fell back, dropping his drum which rolled down the mountain slope and split in half. To this day, the drum of the Bonpo has only one side, while the drum of the lama still has two sides.

Apart from this core of the legend, which is agreed on, there is a sharp divergence between the interpretation of the lamas, who tell the story as quoted here, and that of the Ghyabrẽ and Paju shamans, who make additions. For Tibetans the story proves the superiority of the lama. In the versions of the Gurung shamans there are two changes. First, they elaborate on the "preliminary contests" prior to the climb of Mount Tise. The Bonpo had, after all, "proved equal" to the lama in the magical competition over the lake (Manasarowar), since both contestants had "jumped over it." Second, after the Bonpo was defeated on Mount Tise and dropped his drum, the version given by the Paju shaman adds the following:

> The Paju [Bonpo] was angry that he had lost the contest. In despair the Paju took all of his written texts and threw them into a fire, where they burned to ashes. Then he heard the voice of a god above: "Although you have destroyed your books you must do your rituals by remembering the knowledge that your books contained." The Paju ate the ashes of the burned texts and thus swallowed the knowledge. To this day, the lama has to read his texts, but the Paju chants his learning from memory.

The Paju knows that the lamas of Gyasumdo ridicule the Pajus for having no written texts. Hence when the legend is told in Gyasumdo, it comments on a present contest, as it were, an ongoing dialogue between rival practitioners. This becomes more obvious as the Paju shaman interprets his own version.

"How can the lamas perform exorcisms in the dark?" he asks. "Everyone knows that you must call your tutelary deity when it is dark, but the lamas can't even read their texts without light!" And what if the lama tries to chant in the dark? "Why, the guardian deity of the Paju might come and steal the lama's text and run away," chuckles the Paju, delighting in the image of the lama whose knowledge evaporates without his books.

The Paju's discourse is double voiced. He is willing to tell the story of his own "defeat" by lamas. But the Bonpo and the lama in his version were initially "equal" in magical capacity. Only when the Bonpo is tricked by the lama's ride on the sunbeam does the lama become superior, that is, in textual knowledge. On the other hand, the Paju retains another kind of superiority: "internal" memory from the swallowed ashes. This "internality" of the Paju's knowledge challenges the lama's definition of Buddhists as the "internal ones" (*nang-pa*) and shamanic ritual practice as external (*phyi*). "After all," adds the Paju, "when knowledge is written down it loses its power because anyone can read it," thus explaining why, in his view, the lamas have lost their ancient magical powers and the Paju shamans have not.

Source: Reprinted by permission of the publisher from Stan Royal Mumford, *Himalayan Dialogue: Tibetan Lamas and Gurung Shamans in Nepal* (Madison: University of Wisconsin Press, 1989), pp. 51–53.

7.3 DIVISIONAL ISSUES: SUDDEN VERSUS GRADUAL ENLIGHTENMENT

In 7.1, we saw how the Indian masters Padmasambhava and Śāntarakṣita, after dealing with the demons of Tibet, established the monastery of Sam-ye. Their success, however, should not efface the fact that Chinese Buddhist influence on Tibet was also strong at this time and that Chinese teachings, especially those of the Ch'an or Zen perspective, did not always harmonize well with the Indian ones. Some years later (about 792 C.E.), a great debate was held at the same monastery of Sam-ye, under the auspices of the Tibetan king. A Chinese monk, known in our source as the Hwa-shang, represented the Ch'an school and argued that Buddhist realization was a matter of "sudden enlightenment," which was not the result of a long practice of good works and progressive meditations but an instantaneous awakening to one's innately enlightened nature. The Indian master Kamalaśīla (see 4.4.1) represented the view of the "gradual path," which argued not only for the systematic practice of compassion but also that wisdom was to be approached progressively through study, logical investigation, and meditative contemplation.

According to legend, the stakes of the debate were high: whoever won would get to stay and propagate his view in Tibet; the other would have to leave. In fact, there is some debate about who won the debate. Most Tibetan sources (such as the one below) contend that the Indian "gradualist party" won, and they go on to suggest that some of the Chinese monks committed suicide in their humiliation and that Hwa-shang hired some thugs to murder Kamalaśīla. Chinese accounts of the debate, on the other hand, present the "subitist party" as the victors and suggest that the Tibetans, out of spite, persecuted some of their party. In any case, it is clear that both Indian and Chinese influences continued to be felt in Tibet after the debate. Ch'an inclinations did not suddenly disappear and can be found, for example, in the teachings of the Dzog-chen school, in which liberation is a result of the recognition of one's pure mind. And Indian influences continued as well and were reinforced by subsequent introductions of teachings from that country.

The debate at Sam-ye, moreover, can be seen as part of a much broader dispute between advocates of the "sudden" and the "gradual" paths. The same issue was debated, with equal divisiveness, by Buddhists in China, and a number of scholars have suggested that the sudden-gradual opposition can be taken as a paradigm for the understanding of many aspects of East Asian religions.

Thereafter the teacher Kamalaśīla arrived. The king seated himself in the middle, the Hwa-shang was given a place to his right and the teacher to his left side. The [gradualists] were placed so as to form the retinue of Kamalaśīla. The king, having handed to both wreaths of flowers, declared: "Ye two are to hold a controversy. To him who conquers, the vanquished must present his wreath and dare no longer abide here!"

Then the Hwa-shang spoke: "If one commits virtuous or sinful deeds, one comes to blissful or to evil births respectively. In such a way deliverance from saṃsāra is impossible, and there will always be impediments to the attainment of Buddhahood. Virtuous and sinful deeds are just like white and black clouds which alike obscure the sky. But he who has no thoughts and inclinations at all can be fully delivered from phenomenal life. The absence of any thought, search, or investigation brings about the non-perception of the reality of separate entities. In such a manner one can attain Buddhahood at once, like a bodhisattva who has attained the tenth stage."

To this Kamalaśīla himself answered as follows: "You say that one ought not to think about anything whatever. But this means the negation (or rejection) of the highest analytic wisdom. Now as the latter represents the foundation of the divine wisdom of a saint, the rejection of it necessarily leads to the negation of this sublime transcendental wisdom. If analytic wisdom is absent, what meditator can come to abide in a state where there is no constructive thought? If one has no thought concerning any of the elements of existence and does not direct the mind upon them, this does not mean that one can cease to remember all that one has experienced. If I think, 'I must not recall in my mind any element of existence,' such a thought will itself be an intense recollection and activity of the mind. If the mere absence of consciousness and recollection is regarded as sufficient, it follows that in a swoon or at the time of intoxication one comes to the state where there is no constructive thought. Now, in reality, without correct analysis there is no means of attaining the liberation from constructive thought. If we merely cease to reflect and have no discrimination, how can we come to the cognition of the non-substantiality of all the elements? And, without the cognition of non-substantiality, it is impossible to remove the obscurations. Therefore, the incorrect representation can be cast away only by means of the correct analytic wisdom. For this reason it is is not proper to say that one does not reflect, when in reality it is the reverse. Without recollection and correct activity of the mind, how can one come to remember the place of former residence and attain omniscience? And how will it be possible to extirpate the passions? But the yogin who reflects over an object by means of correct analytic wisdom, cognizes all the external and internal elements in the present, past, and future as non-substantial, has all thought construction pacified within him, and rejects all the evil doctrines. On this foundation he becomes skilful in expedients and in the manifestation of highest wisdom. And, having through this cleared all the obscurations, he can attain the state of a Buddha."

Thereafter the king said: "All the adherents of Kamalaśīla must likewise make their objections."

Accordingly Śrīghoṣa spoke as follows: "The Chinese are of the opinion that one has to enter the stage of a Buddha at once, but not by gradual practice. According to them, the six trancendental virtues [pāramitās] are to be taken as the mere negation of their opposites. Highest charity (dāna-pāramitā) is thus viewed only as the absence of greediness. The fact of abstaining from every kind of appropriation thus represents the highest transcendental charity. . . .

Then Jñānendra spoke: "The attainment of Buddhahood at once and the action by degrees must both be investigated. If the action by degrees is right, then in doing nothing you cannot be possessed of the factors of attainment. . . . But, if you attain Buddhahood at once, what are you doing at present? You must be Buddhas from the very beginning. . . . Now, when you ascend a mountain, you must do it step by step, but you are not capable of doing it all at once. In a similar manner, if it be difficult to attain the first stage (even by degrees), what is there to say of the attainment of omniscience? According to our point of view, it is necessary to become trained in the three kinds of analytic wisdom, then, on the basis of all the different subjects of scripture, to apprehend correctly the meaning of the latter, to receive training in the practice of the ten virtues, to attain steadfastness by the means of profound meditation, to enter the first stage, . . . and then, passing through gradual training on the ten stages, to attain Buddhahood by means of the ten virtues. If we admit your point of view, it follows that the accumulations of merit need not be brought to accomplishment, mental training is not required, and the knowledge of worldly matters is unneccessary. But, in such a case, how can the knowledge of everything cognizable be attained? If you do nothing and only sleep, you will not even take food and thus die of hunger! And, where and when are you to attain Buddhahood? If you walk without searching and investigating, you will fall; where and when can you thus cognize the Truth?"

Thus and more did he speak in detail, and the [subitists] were incapable of giving an answer. They gave the wreath of flowers to Kamalaśīla, and declared themselves vanquished. . . .

Thereafter the king gave the following order: "Henceforth, as concerns theory, one must adopt the system of Nāgārjuna. With regard to practice, one must become trained in the ten kinds of virtuous conduct and in the ten transcendental virtues. As to the subitist views, the propagation of these is not to be permitted!"

Source: Reprinted from *History of Buddhism (Chos-hbyung) by Bu-ston,* trans. E. Obermiller (Heidelberg, 1931), 2:193–96 (slightly altered).

7.4 REGULATION AND REFORM: THE EFFORTS OF ATĪŚA

The debate at Sam-ye reflected certain divergent tendencies within Buddhism in Tibet, but it did not mushroom into the growth of many sects. Those were to develop later over the course of history. It is commonly maintained that today there are four major sects of Tibetan Buddhism: the Nying-ma-pa, the Ka-gyü-pa, the Sa-kya-pa, and the Ge-luk-pa. However, the use of the word *sect* to describe these divisions is perhaps misleading. These are not sects in the rigid sense of the word; rather these are sects that should perhaps be thought of as several currents in one stream, which have split off but which continue to feed one another while pursuing the same basic course. What differentiates these currents from one another are their varying emphases on particular ways of interpreting common doctrines, on particular practices featured over others, and on particular lineages of gurus, both human and divine.[2]

The Nying-ma-pa, the "ancients," commonly trace their line back to Padmasambhava and base their doctrines and practices on a large number of "revealed" Tantric texts. These traditions, many of which have admixtures of Bon elements, are not always accepted by other schools.

The Ka-gyü-pa arose in Tibet around the eleventh century, beginning with the figure of Marpa (1012–96), who is said to have learned the six teachings of the Indian master Nāropa (956–1040). As a school, the Ka-gyü-pa is often thought to continue the line of the Indian siddhas (the perfected ones) and to lay particular emphasis on certain yogic practices (for example, tum-mo, the meditational development of an inner bodily heat), and on the quick path to enlightenment. Among Marpa's disciples figured Milarepa (see 7.6), one of the great saints of the Tibetan tradition.

---

[2]On this and the following paragraphs, see Giuseppe Tucci, *Tibetan Painted Scrolls* (Rome: Libreria dello Stato, 1949), 1:87–93.

The Sa-kya-pa are associated with the monastery and principality of Sakya as well as with the tradition of the Drok-mi (992–1072), who emphasized certain Tantras featuring the presence within ourselves of universal consciousness. The leader of the sect, being also the ruler of the Sakya territory, married in order to continue his line.

Finally the Ge-luk-pa, sometimes called the Yellow Hats, were the last of the Tibetan sects to emerge, and may be considered as a reform movement started by the great scholar Tsong-kha-pa (1357–1419). He emphasized learning, discipline, and celibacy (in contrast to the Nying-ma-pa and Ka-gyü-pa schools, in which monks might marry), and laid the foundations for the curriculum of great monastic universities, stressing dialectic, debate, and a whole hierarchy of degrees and examinations. In time, this sect also achieved political power with the ascendancy of the Dalai Lamas (see 7.8.1).

The Ge-luk-pa, however, were not the first reform movement in Tibetan Buddhist history. In fact they sometimes called themselves "the renewed Kadam-pa," thereby tracing their lineage back to the sect that was associated with the Indian master Atīśa (who arrived in Tibet in 1042) and with his disciple Drom-tön (1008–64). Atīśa (along with others) is sometimes credited with the second introduction of Buddhism into Tibet, after the devasting persecutions under King Lang-dar-ma (mid-ninth century). Without denying the Vajrayāna, Atīśa also emphasized the Perfection of Wisdom literature, Nāgārjuna's doctrines, and Asanga's descriptions of the bodhisattva path, as well as monastic discipline. The following excerpt from one of Atīśa's writings stresses the last.

Consider carefully these words of mine. Man's life in this *kali-yuga* [degenerate age] is generally short while the objects of knowledge are numerous. One is uncertain about how long one is going to live. Hasten to curb your desires with care. Do not say, "I am a bhikṣu," so long as you care for material wealth and livelihood. . . . You may be living in a monastery, but do not say, "I am a bhikṣu, I live in the monastery," . . . so long as you harbour worldly wishes or any thought of injuring others, . . . so long as you do not renounce the company of householders but continue to stay with them and waste your time by indulging in romantic and worldly gossips. Do not say, "I am a bhikṣu, a bodhisattva, . . ." if you cannot bear even a little injury by others or help others even a little. If you say anything like that, you will thereby be telling a great lie. . . .

Remember now what you promised before the gods and the gurus at the time of [your arousing the thought of enlightenment]. When you come across those who deserve to be forgiven, never say that it is difficult to forgive. Remember [that at the time of taking your bodhisattva vows, you promised] not to refuse even that which is difficult. . . .

The purpose of living in a monastery is to stop having intercourse with householders, to renounce partiality for relatives and to avoid the cause of distractions provoked by sexual and other desires. . . .

Even if you say, "I am acting according to Dharma," [in fact] Dharma and you will remain separate if you do not repeatedly correct your own mind by comparing it with the scriptures. . . . While meditating, do not count the number of years and months [devoted to it]; rather, try to find out how much or how little self-knowledge you have acquired in your mind and how much or how little control you have acquired over your habits. [. . .]

This kali-yuga is not the time for smiling; it is the time to have courage. It is not the time for holding high positions; it is time to hold a humble position. It is not the time to live in a crowd; it is time to take shelter in solitude. It is not the time to guide students; it is time to guide oneself. It is not the time to follow mere words; it is time to meditate on their true significance. It is not the time to be drifting; it is time to remain firm at one place.

Source: Reprinted by permission of the publisher from "Sayings of Atīśa B," trans. in Alaka Chattopadhyaya, *Atīśa and Tibet* (Calcutta: Indian Studies: Past and Present, 1967), pp. 540–42, 544 (slightly altered).[3]

7.5 RITUALS AND FESTIVALS

7.5.1 Pilgrimage to Mount Kailāsa

Among the many meritorious practices engaged in by Buddhists everywhere, the ritual of going on pilgrimage occupies an important and distinctive position. From Sri Lanka to Japan, Buddhist Asia is dotted with sacred sites that, like magnets with various degrees of strength, attract devotees and visitors.

In Tibet, one of the most powerful magnets for pilgrims (second perhaps only to the city of Lhasa) is Mount Kailāsa, the peak in the western Himalayas that the Tibetans call Gang Ti-se or Gang Rimpoche. Reputed to be located at the center of the world, and so to correspond to the Mount Meru of cosmological schemes, Gang Ti-se is a physically striking dome of almost twenty-two thousand feet that for centuries has attracted not only Buddhists and Bon-po from Tibet but Hindus from India as well.

For Tibetans it is also legendarily associated with the figure of Milarepa (see 7.6), and for that reason perhaps it is especially popular with members of the Ka-gyü-pa sect. But devotees of all denominations will journey hundreds of miles, often on foot, to reach the mountain. There, two features of Tibetan religious practice come to the fore: circumambulation and prostration.

The practice of circumambulation, going around a sacred object or site such as a stūpa or a temple (for Buddhists, this is always done in a clockwise direction), is a common act of veneration. On the Gang Ti-se pilgrimage, it is the mountain itself that is circumambulated, usually several times, on a circuit that covers over thirty miles. Prostration (placing one's body full length on the ground) is another common act of worship and discipline among Tibetans, and certain sacred sites are even equipped with special prostration boards on which this practice can be performed, often hundreds or even thousands of

[3]Original text: *Atīśa and Tibet,* pp. 555–60.

times. At Gang Ti-se, successive grand prostrations are used by some pilgrims as the means for advancing, body length by body length, all the way around the mountain, thereby measuring the entire circumambulation route with their own prostrate persons.

The following account of the Gang Ti-se pilgrimage by a Japanese sociologist, university professor, explorer, and mountaineer, Kazuhiko Tamamura, describes both the circumambulation route and the practice of prostration as he observed them in 1985.

What is known as the Gang Rimpoche [Mount Kailāsa] pilgrimage involves circumambulating the circumference of the sacred peak any number of times. . . . The pilgrims, coming from various directions, "appear" in Tarchen, the village near the base of the mountain [which serves as the takeoff point for the circumambulation path]. The word "appear" is entirely appropriate, for these people pay no attention to existing roads and simply take the shortest route. Some of them arrive, driving several dozen sheep on which they have loaded their baggage; some ride on horseback or in trucks or tractors; but the vast majority of them come on foot, their belongings on their back neatly packed in panniers made of willow branches. They carry staffs or tent poles in their hands in order to drive off ferocious dogs.

Except for those pilgrims travelling alone or in very small groups, most of the parties bring with them tents of white cotton cloth. As soon as they arrive in Tarchen, they set up these tents . . . and begin searching for fuel, yak dung, which they collect and carry in the folds of their aprons or shepherds' robes.

The fatigue of the long journey they have made to reach Tarchen is great [some have come on foot from Eastern Tibet as much as three thousand kilometers away], but the very next day after their arrival, they set out on the Gang Rimpoche pilgrimage circuit with eager anticipation. Their fervent desire to make the circuit of the holy mountain as soon as possible prompts them to take to the road again. . . .

The pilgrimage route around Gang Rimpoche is 52 kilometers long. If you were to extend your arms in front of you to make a circle corresponding to the route, Tarchen would be where your head is, and Gang Rimpoche itself would tower majestically from a spot just inside of the place where the tips of your fingers meet. The pilgrimage route thus leaves from Tarchen, at an altitude of 4,700 meters, follows the La Chu River upstream (corresponding to your left arm), crosses the Dorma Pass at 5,600 meters [located roughly where your right hand would be], and returns to Tarchen along a course that follows the Son Chu River (your right arm).

Tibetans make this circumambulation in one fourteen-hour day. If they were to spend the night on the road, they would require a good deal of baggage including their tents, so they choose to go all out and make the circuit in a day. It is also considered to be more meritorious to make the trip in a single day. . . . They make the circumambulation with the same joy and high spirits that we associate with going on a picnic, and return to Tarchen in the evening. Then, after resting in Tarchen for a day or two, they once again make the circuit. In this way, they go around the sacred mountain many times [13 and 26 times are popular numbers], and so end up staying in Tarchen for quite a long while. . . .

I myself had been thinking of taking up the challenge of the pilgrimage route and [after a few days interviewing pilgrims in Tarchen] I set out with plans to spend two nights and three days on the road. . . . In addition to my interpreter-guide, Dorje, I employed the services of two young men, Tashi (21) and Norbu (16) as porters. We set out from Tarchen on May 27th. . . . [At first] the way was virtually flat. There were no trees except for a shrub about fifty centimeters high called tama, and in general plants were of limited variety and few in number. . . .

A little while after leaving Tarchen, we encountered an old man coming from the opposite direction. Tibetan *Buddhists* make clockwise circumambulations, and so [since this man was going counterclockwise], I took him for a follower of the Bon religion [who do their circumambulations in a widdershins way]. It turned out, however, that he was a volunteer helping to rebuild the Chuk Gompa (monastery-temple), and was simply on his way back to Tarchen from work.

The peak of Gang Rimpoche had been visible from Tarchen, but it was now hidden by the foothills and we were not able to see it at all until we arrived at Changya Gang. At Changya Gang, there was a big pile of stones—some of them "maṇi stones" on which the mantra "OṂ MAṆI PADME HŪṂ" was written. Above the pitch-black hills that provided a backdrop for the stones, the white snow of Gang Rimpoche could be seen. The striking contrast was beautiful. Dorje faced the mountain and recited sūtras for about fifteen minutes.

From Changya Gang . . . it was forty minutes to Tarboche where a big festival called "Shaka Dawa" is held on the birthday of Śākyamuni. From there, it also took less than an hour to get to Chuk Gompa. . . . After leaving Tarchen that morning, we had met [besides the old man who was not a Bon-po] a number of village youths who were returning from having carried logs from Tarchen to Chuk Gompa [in order to rebuild the temple there]. In the past, there had been five gompa [monasteries] around Gang Rimpoche, but they had all been destroyed during the Cultural Revolution. . . . Tibet is now [1985] actively rebuilding its gompas. At the prefectural level, the decision was made to rebuild at the rate of two or three gompas a year; in the vicinity of Gang Rimpoche, Chuk Gompa in the West and Zurufuk Gompa in the East, were targeted for reconstruction this year. . . .

Chuk Gompa was located in the hills across the river. Since it had been completely demolished, I would probably have passed the spot without noticing it if Dorje had not pointed it out. . . . According to Ekai Kawaguchi [the Japanese Zen monk who visited this area in 1903], this gompa, which was under the control of the King of Bhutan, had the largest income of all the temples of its day, but now it was but a mound of debris. I stood on top of this rubble and gazed at Gang Rimpoche looming before me. The gompa was located so that the south slope of the Holy

Mountain could be seen at an angle. The vertical line of the face rising to the summit was truly like a ladder to heaven. Before it stood the crag known as the "Son of Gang Rimpoche," and the crag in the shape of a divine monkey in constant prayer. When I gazed below at the stacks of logs brought by the young people, they looked very small indeed.

From Chuk Gompa, the valley narrowed dramatically. . . . Many pilgrims had already overtaken us on the way. We now came across a party of three young people who had passed us some time before and were just finishing a meal by the river and preparing to set out again. The three were from the northern plateau of Chang Thang. After I finished interviewing them, . . . they set off at a brisk pace, spinning prayer wheels in their right hands and intoning "OṂ MAṆI PADME HŪṂ."

At Dirapūr Gompa [also destroyed during the Cultural Revolution], Gang Rimpoche appears as an enormous dome rising up from behind two hills on the left and right. The north face looms large and one has to strain to look upwards to take it in. . . . There is a narrow band of rock that runs along the center of the dome, rising upward towards the right. "Long ago, an evil deity lived on Gang Rimpoche. He took the mountain on his back and started to carry it to Sri Lanka." There was emotion in Dorje's voice as he offered this explanation. "Look, you can see the marks of the rope he used. But then Śākyamuni came here and persuaded the deity to change his mind. There is nothing that the Buddha cannot do. You remember the footprint of Śākyamuni which we saw on the way to Thamdon Dongang? There are footprints of Śākyamuni in four places around Gang Rimpoche. They tell us that no one can ever take the mountain away again."

The Buddha's footprint at Thamdon Dongang had been large, three or four times bigger than a normal human foot.

"Is it because Śākyamuni came here that Gang Rimpoche is a sacred mountain?"

"It is not holy just because Śākyamuni came here. Gang Rimpoche is at the center of the Himalayas. It is at the center of the world. . . ."

From Dirapūr, the way follows a branch of the La Chu called the Dorma La Chu. "La" means "pass" and the name means "the river that flows from the Dorma Pass." The left bank of the river was blocked by a large mound of sand so we were obliged to cross over to the right hand side. [We then spent the night, camping out at Charok Dongang.]

The next day, the weather was fair, without a cloud in the sky. Viewed from Charok Dongang, Gang Rimpoche was beautiful, the snow on the crest golden in the light of the early morning sun. I gazed at it transfixed for several minutes, even as I shivered in the cold.

From Charok Dongang to the Dorma Pass, the grade becomes steep and the altitude rises sharply. The path crosses a small river many times, and a thin film of ice had formed on the water. There was snow, but it was the consistency of slush. . . . We arrived at the top of the Dorma La at 10:40 after two hours of hard struggle. My altimeter measured 5,480 meters. There were many pilgrims at the pass. There was a huge boulder there that looked as though it had been dropped from heaven. The pilgrims circumambulated the boulder which was decorated with prayer flags and locks of human hair. Not just people but horses too were making the clockwise circuit of the boulder. But [as I was feeling unwell] I was not up to conducting any interviews and could only think of making the descent as quickly as possible.

The path going down from the Dorma La is very precipitous. The slope is so steep that it looked as though the pilgrims who were doing their circumambulation in grand prostrations [see below] were about to plunge head first down the mountain. Before us rose an imposing black peak punctuated by several sharp crags. . . .

At the bottom we arrived at a place called Shapje Daktok. It had taken us an hour and twenty minutes to reach it. . . .

Near the confluence of the Son Chu, we encountered a group of four young monks who were making the circumambulation doing grand prostrations. They said that they were from Ch'ing Hai Province [in northwest China]. [Later] we were overtaken by several parties of pilgrims. Before coming to Tarchen I had visited a farm family living near the border between Tibet and Nepal. The daughter of the family was in one of the groups that passed us. It was a group composed of four women. They went on singing songs as though they were on a hike. They told us they had all set out from Tarchen that morning. I suppose that without this sort of speed, it would not be possible for Tibetans to make the circumambulation in one day.

As we came out from the hills, the view opened dramatically. Before us was the peak of Namunani. The sight of it catching the evening sun encouraged me and [happy that I could finish my circuit of the mountain that night, a day early], I set out for the Tarchen resthouse and the sleep it promised. [. . .]

A Note on Grand Prostrations

The special feature of the Tibetan Buddhists' grand prostration is the repetition with which it is performed. In front of a temple, around a temple, facing holy ground, around holy ground, and, at times, on the way to temples and holy areas, the grand prostration is repeated constantly time and again. I could not help feeling a sense of awe at the rigorous and strenuous nature of the practice of Tibetan Buddhists which involved completing the 52 kilometer circuit around Gang Rimpoche by making grand prostrations. . . .

In Tibetan, this type of practice is called "kyang chak." "Kyang" means "to extend the body," and "chak" means "to worship." First, one holds one's two hands together on top of one's head, and one prays: "May the sins that I have committed up until now with this body be cleansed." Then one lowers the hands cupping them in front of one's face, and one says: "May the sins that I have committed up until now with this mouth be cleansed." Then one lowers one's hands further to chest level and says: "May the sins that I have committed up until now with this mind be cleansed." Then one falls to one's knees, forcefully extends the body forward, reaching the hands out as far as possible and bringing the palms together while flat on one's face. Then, getting up, one advances to the point to which one's hands extended, and one repeats the whole thing again. Each time, one can only move the distance one has measured out with one's body. Thus the ground that can be covered in a day is not very great. They say that it takes two weeks to cover the 52 kilometers around Gang Rimpoche by this method. . . . In the course of the circuit, any number of fords across rivers need to be made, but the pilgrims keep up their grand prostrations right across the stones in the stream.

Of the 145 pilgrims that I interviewed [during my stay in Tarchen], six had already gone around the mountain doing grand prostrations, [and twelve more were planning to do so,] including two nuns from Nepal. . . . If we assume that those who said they were going to do the prostrations did so, we can conclude that about 10 percent of the pilgrims around Gang Rimpoche make the circuit by prostrations.

Source: Translated and reprinted by permission of the author from Kazuhiko Tamamura, *Seizan Junrei* (Tokyo: Yama to Keikoku Sha, 1987), pp. 41–53, 147.

7.5.2 Magical Rites: Casting Spells

As we saw in 6.5.3, Buddhist ritual was not only directed toward venerating the Buddha, making merit, and achieving enlightenment. It could also be used for more down-to-earth purposes: for magical defense against evil spirits or wild animals or, conversely, for magical offense against beings whom one desired to subjugate. In India, the lines between mantras, magic, and meditation were sometimes difficult to draw. For example, the meditative practice of extending loving kindness (maitrī) toward all sentient beings was commonly applied in a very practical way: it was used in encounters with snakes or dangerous beasts who, suffused by the meditator's quiet love, decided that this human was no threat and went away. The amulets and spells described in the following Tibetan ritual manual, dating from around the tenth century C.E., are somewhat more active in nature and are directed toward a variety of ends, some of them more "worldly" than others.

To scare away snakes. On the lower step of the threshold, inscribe a triangle and another triangle upon that to form a six-pointed star: starting from the east, . . . write the six seeds [syllables] of the mantra [OṂ KURUKULLE HRĪḤ] at the six corners [of the star], with the seeds of the Law [SVĀ HĀ] in the midst thereof, and the syllable PHUḤ between them.

For a woman to subjugate her husband. On white birchbark, or on a cloth stained with menstrual blood, draw a seven-petaled lotus and write the seven syllables OṂ KU RU KU LLE SVĀ HĀ on the seven petals; and in the center of the lotus, between two HRĪḤS, write the name of the person to be subjugated; then roll it up into a little ball and fasten it upon the upper arm:

> and the husband becomes the woman's slave
> even a king becomes her servant
> but only a woman who is pure and virtuous
> may apply this mantra.

An amulet of protection. Draw a four-petaled lotus flower on a piece of birchbark: on the eastern petal draw an arrow, on the southern petal a bow, on the western petal a hand in the fearless gesture, and on the northern petal a lotus flower. Draw a moon in the center of the four petals and write thereon the name of the person to be protected, surrounded by the seven seeds OṂ KU RU KU LLE SVĀ HĀ. Draw a garland of lotus flowers all around the amulet and fasten it upon the upper arm; and whether you be a child or an old man or a youth, this magical amulet will protect you. . . .

Cowrie shell practices. If on a Tuesday you find a cowrie shell lying on its back, place it in the palm of your hand and recite the basic mantra eight hundred thousand times: then if you play at dice you will be victorious over your opponents.

Take a cowrie shell, bathe it, and make offerings before it for eight or twelve days, reciting the basic mantra one hundred and eight times; then wrap it up in silk and bind it on your upper arm: thereby you will become a great lord of wealth. . . .

To find treasure. Recite the mantra fifty times and place your feet upon the ground: wherever your feet begin to tremble, you know that there is buried treasure. If the upper part of your foot trembles, you are getting near; if the sole of your foot trembles, you are moving away from it. It is just as clear as if you were told where the treasure is, for he who holds this mantra sees beneath the earth as if it were day.

To walk on water. Take the milk of a black bitch and mix it with fresh butter; spread it gradually upon your boots and you will be able to walk upon the water.

To get rid of grey hair. After every meal, snuff up water through your nose while you recite the mantra and you will never have prematurely grey hair. . . .

Source: Reprinted by permission of Wadsworth, Inc. from Stephan Beyer, *The Buddhist Experience* (Encino, CA: Dickenson, 1974), pp. 138–39 (slightly altered).[4]

7.6 MEDITATIONAL ENDEAVORS: MILAREPA'S QUEST

Much can be learned about the practice of a religion and the quest for enlightenment from reading the life stories of some of its practitioners. One of the best known figures among the legends of Tibetan Buddhism was the eleventh-century saint Milarepa, whose lineage is basically the same as that of Maṇibhadrā (see 5.5.7). Milarepa's youth was spent mastering the practices of black magic so that he could wreak revenge on a cruel uncle who had

---

[4]Original text: *'Phags-ma sgrol-ma ku-ru-ku-lle'i rtog-pa* [*Ārya-tārā-kurukullā-kalpa*] [*The Rituals of the Goddess Kurukullā*], Peking Bka'-'gyur Rgyud CA 30b-45a (Tokyo: Suzuki Research Foundation, 1958), 3, no. 76.

oppressed him and his mother. In this he was successful, but then, undergoing a change of heart, he sought out a teacher who would impart to him certain initiations into the Dharma. The guru whom he found, Marpa, was a demanding, unconventional master, and their interactions as depicted in the following popular biography written by a fifteenth-century "mad" wandering yogin, Sang-gye-gyel-tshen, have become a classic expression of the Tibetan guru-disciple relationship. At the same time, their encounter well illustrates the importance, in meditational endeavors in Tibet, of receiving "empowerment" from one's teacher, a Tantric initiation without which contemplative practice will bear no fruit.

Now by this time I was beginning to get worried, and to suffer from my longing for the Law [Dharma]. Again and again I begged my master [Marpa] to teach it to me and to tell me how to practice it. Finally, he said: "I have many faithful disciples who come to me from central Tibet, but the nomads of Talung and Ling rob them on their way, steal their provisions, and prevent them from bringing me any offerings. Go cast down a hailstorm upon these people; that is the religious thing to do. Then I will give you my teachings."

So I sent a great hailstorm upon them, and I asked him again to teach me.

"Ridiculous," he said. "You send down a few lumps of hail, and you think that it earns you this Law that I struggled so hard to bring from India. You say you are a mighty magician; then if you really want the Law, go do some magic on the mountain men of Lhodra. They, too, have often robbed my disciples and have shown contempt for my authority. When I see that your magic has worked, I will give you my teachings and show you how to become a Buddha in this very life."

So I cast my magic spells and made feuds break out among the mountain men; I saw many of them die upon the sword, and was sick at heart.

"Well, you told the truth when you said you were a magician," my master said, and he started calling me his Great Magician.

I asked him to teach me how to become a Buddha.

"I went to India for these teachings at the risk of my life; I sacrificed my wealth, gave away my gold, and saved nothing. My teachings still breathe the breath of the goddesses who taught them, and you say you want them as a reward for your wickedness! Now that is a joke, and if it were only funny I could laugh at it. If I were anyone else I would have killed you by now. Go restore the harvest that you ruined and bring all the mountain men back to life. If you can do that I will give you the teachings, and if you cannot, then never return to my presence again."

His rebuke was as sharp as if he had struck me; and I cried bitterly in despair, as my master's wife tried to console me in my sorrow.

The next morning, my master himself came to me and said:

"We quarreled too much yesterday. Do not be so unhappy and do not be so impatient: I will give you the teachings eventually. You are a clever person, so just help me build a house for my son. When you finish it, not only will I give you the teachings, but I will provide you with food and clothing while you meditate upon them."

"But what will happen to me," I cried, "if I die in the meantime without the Law?"

"I guarantee that you will not die. Mine is not a Law which promises nothing: you are quite diligent, and if you can meditate upon my teachings it is up to you whether you become a Buddha or not. My tradition is different from all the rest; it is a lineage of great power."

I was quite happy at his good counsel, and I asked him to lay out the plan of the house for me.

Now this was not only a means to cleanse me of my sins; it was also a clever plot to build a tower overlooking a narrow pass, which my master and his relatives had all agreed not to fortify, so that no one would have a strategic advantage over the others. So my master took me to an eastern ridge of the mountain and said, "Build me a house like this."

So I started to build a circular house, as he had indicated; and I was only half finished when my master came and said, "I did not think enough about this. Tear this house down to its very foundation and take the earth and stones back where you found them."

I did as he ordered, and he took me to a western ridge of the mountain and said, "Now build me a house like this."

He seemed to be a bit drunk as he spoke to me, but I started to build the semi-circular house he had indicated, and I was only half finished when again he came and said: "Now this will not do at all. Take the earth and stones back where you found them."

Again I did as he ordered, and he took me to a northern peak and said: "My Great Magician, I drank a little too much beer last time. You really should not have listened to me. But now you can build me a really nice house right here."

"It is very difficult for me to keep building houses like this and then tearing them down again," I said, "and it is a waste of your money, too. Please think about it carefully this time."

"I am not drunk now, and I have thought about it quite carefully. A house for a mystic should be triangular, so build one for me: you will not have to tear this one down."

So I started to build a triangular house, and I had only finished a third of it when my master came and said: "Magician, whose house is this you are building? Who told you to do this?"

"You yourself told me to build such a house for your son," I replied.

"I do not remember telling you to do any such thing. You may well be right, but I was probably crazy at the time, or not in full possession of my faculties."

"I was afraid something like this might happen, and I begged you to think about it carefully, and you said that you had. You said that this time I would not have to tear it down, and you really seemed quite lucid about it."

And my master became furious and shouted at me: "Then who is your witness? Did you think to work magic upon us and cast us into a triangular house shaped like a pit of sacrifice? And if you sought not to enchant us, and you really want the Law—well, a house like this will anger all the local spirits. So take the earth and stones back where you found them. If you want the Law I can give it to you, and if you do not want it, then you can just go away."

I was miserable, but I wanted the Law: so I did as my master ordered, tore down the triangular house, and took the earth and stones back where I found them.

By this time there was quite a sore on my back, but my master would only have yelled at me had I shown it to him; nor did I show it to his wife, lest she think that I was bragging about how hard I was working. So I wept and did not show it to her, but I begged her help in asking for the Law.

So she went in to see my master and said to him: "Really, my lord, the child is miserable with all this useless building. Show a little compassion and give him the Law."

"Well, make me some nice food," he said, "and bring him to me."

So she brought me in with her when she took him his dinner, and he said to me: "Magician, you really should not tell such lies about things I never did. But if you want the Law I will give it to you."

And he taught me how to go for refuge, and he gave me the precepts and vows of a disciple. "This is the ordinary Law," he said. "If you want the special Law of my Tantric teachings, then you must act like this." And he told me briefly about the hardships suffered by his master in seeking the Law, and he added that it would be hard indeed for me to do such things. But I wept as the deepest faith awoke within me, and I vowed that I would do whatever my master said.

A few days went by, and my master invited me to go for a walk with him. We came to the narrow pass kept by his relatives, and he said: "Now you can build an ordinary square tower for me, nine storeys high, and with a turret as a tenth story. You will not have to tear this one down. When it is completed, I will give you the teachings, and I will give you the provisions you need while you are meditating upon them."

"May I ask your wife to be a witness to this?" I asked, and he agreed.

So my master laid out the ground plan while I went to ask his wife to come; and before them both I said: "I have built three houses now and torn them all down again. The first time, my master said he had not thought about it carefully; the second time, he said he was drunk; and the third time, he said he must have been crazy, for he could not remember telling me anything of the sort. And when I told him that he himself had given me the orders, he yelled at me and asked me who my witness was. So this time I am asking his wife to be my witness."

"Certainly I will be your witness," she said. "But my lord is such a tyrant that you cannot count on him for anything. He just keeps on building houses for no reason, and then for no reason tears them down again. And this place is not ours anyway, for we have all taken a vow not to build here. I have said as much to him, but he pays no attention to me."

"Just be a witness like you are supposed to!" he shouted. "I will do whatever I have said I will do. Stop concerning yourself with things that are none of your business, and leave me alone."

Now while I was laying the foundation for the square tower, three of my master's disciples rolled up a great boulder for sport, and I used it as the foundation stone just under the doorway. I had reached the second storey when my master came and looked at everything very carefully. Then he pointed to the rock that his three disciples had rolled up, and he said, "Magician, where did you get this rock?"

"Some of your disciples brought it here for sport."

"You cannot use their rock to build your tower! Take it out and put it back where it belongs."

"But you said I would not have to tear this building down."

"I did not say you could use my most advanced disciples as your servants! And you need not tear down the whole thing; just take out the foundation stone and put it back."

So I had to tear down the whole building to get to the stone, and I put it back where it came from. And my master said, "All right, now you can fetch it yourself, and put it in the foundation again."

So I took the rock, and with the strength of three men I dragged it back into place by myself, nor did I use my magic powers to help me. And I built the tower as before, and the rock became famous thereabouts as my Giant Stone.

Now as I was building the foundation, the relatives of my master were counseling together, and they felt that they should stop him from fortifying the pass where they had all vowed not to build. But some of them said: "Marpa has gone crazy. He has got himself a strong little disciple from the hills and has him building unorthodox houses on every ridge; then he has him tear them down again when they are only half finished and put the earth and stones back where he found them. He will tear this one down too. Just wait and see; there is still plenty of time to stop him."

But I was working on the tower without interruption and without tearing it down. I had reached the seventh storey—and another sore had appeared on my waist—when his relatives said: "This time he is not tearing it down. Tearing down the others was just a wicked plot to build this one. We must destroy it."

And so they prepared for war, but my master magically created an armed host which filled the tower inside and out. His relatives were terrified, and they could not discover where he had gotten such an army; and since they could not fight with him, they came to him secretly one by one and gave him presents, and submitted to him.

Now about this time Meton Tshonpo came to receive the initiation of Cakrasamvara, and my master's wife said to me, "This time we will somehow get you your initiation." For I had built a great tower without anyone giving me a piece of rock, or a basket of earth, or a jug of water, or a shovelful of clay, and I thought that this time at least I would be given an initiation. So I bowed down before my master, and took my place in the rows of his disciples.

"Magician," he said, "what fee have you brought for your initiation?"

"I have nearly finished the tower for your son. You promised you would give me the initiation and the teachings, and I am here hoping you will keep your word."

"Ridiculous," he said. "You build a turret a few feet high, and you think that it earns you this Law that I struggled so hard to bring from India. If you have a fee for your initiation, then bring it here, and if you do not, then you cannot stand in line for my profound Tantric initiation." And he hit me in the face and dragged me from the room by my hair.

I would have been happy to die right then, and I cried all through the night.

But my master's wife came to console me, and she said: "My lord is always saying that he brought the Law from India with the hope of benefiting all beings; he will teach it even to a dog that wanders in front of him, and finish by giving the animal all his merit. Do not worry. I do not know what he is doing, but think no evil of him."

The next morning, my master himself came to me and said: "Magician, leave off building the rest of the tower for a while and build me a courtyard with twelve pillars and a shrine room. When you finish that, I will give you the initiation and the teachings."

So I laid the foundation of the courtyard, as my master's wife brought me food to eat and a little beer to drink, and gave me what consolation she could.

And when the courtyard was almost finished, Tshurton Wange came to receive the initiation of Guhyasamāja; and my master's wife said to me, "This time we will somehow get you your initiation." So she gave me some butter, a roll of woolen cloth, and a small copper pot; and I set them out as offerings before my master and took my place in the rows of his disciples.

"Magician," he said, "what fee have you brought me, that you stand in line for my initiation?"

"This butter and cloth and copper pot," I said.

"Those are mine!" he shouted. "Those are things which my followers have given me! You cannot pay for your initiation with things that are mine already. If you have something of your own, then bring it here, and if you do not, then you cannot stand in line for my initiation." And he jumped up, yelling at me, and drove me out of the room with a volley of kicks.

I would have been happy to sink into the earth. I have killed many men with my magic spells, I thought, and this is my recompense for destroying the harvest with hailstorms. Or perhaps my master knows that I am unfit for the Law, or perhaps he just does not like me. But whatever the reason, what use is my sinful life without the Law? I might as well kill myself.

And my master's wife brought me some of the food from the ritual and sought to console me. But when she left, I had lost all taste for the food, and I cried all through the night.

The next morning my master came to see me again and said, "Just finish the courtyard and the turret, and I will give you the initiation and the teachings."

So I went back to work and had almost finished the courtyard when yet another sore broke out on my back. All three of my sores oozed pus and blood, and my whole back became an open wound. I showed it to my master's wife, reminded her of what my master had promised when I first started the tower, and begged her help in asking for the Law. She looked at my wounds, and began to cry, and said, "I will speak to my lord."

So she went in to my master and said: "The magician has worked so hard on your tower that all his limbs are cracked; he has three sores on his back which ooze pus and blood. Now I have heard of such sores on horses and donkeys, and seen them too, but I have never heard of a man with such sores, nor ever seen such a thing. We should be ashamed for other people to hear of it, and you are supposed to be such a great master! You should be ashamed of yourself. Have a little pity on him and give the child the Law, as you said you would when he finished the tower."

"I said I would give him the Law when he finished a tower ten storeys tall. Where are my ten storeys?"

"But he has built a courtyard larger than a ten-storey tower."

"I will give him the Law when he can finish the ten storeys without talking so much! But is his sore back really all that bad?". . . . And he turned aside and wept. . . .

[Had Milarepa been privy to this sign of his master's actual concern, he might perhaps have gone straight back to work, but instead he devises various other stratagems for getting the teachings, to the point of actually leaving Marpa for a while and seeking another teacher. All his schemes, however, come to naught, and he comes back. Eventually, after a series of more humiliations and refusals, the tower (symbolic of the ten stages of the bodhisattva path) does get built, and Marpa does agree, this time for real, to impart to him the teaching.]

"My anger is not like the anger of the world," said my master. "However it may appear, it is all for the sake of the Law, to banish pride, and to lead upon the path to enlightenment. You who are seated here may not understand, but you must not be shaken from devotion to your master. . . .

"And now I shall bless my faithful disciple, and give him the teachings so dear to the heart of an old man; I shall give him the provisions he needs while he meditates, and lead him to contemplation. So rejoice. . . ."

And my master said to his wife: "Set out the food and the excellent offerings upon the altar."

So she laid out the offerings to the masters and the high patron deities, food for the goddesses and protectors, and the excellent feast for my diamond brothers. And before the assembly my master appeared as all the high patron deities, and as their emblems; he appeared as a drop of brilliant light, and finally vanished. These many things Marpa showed . . . and I saw that my master was truly the Buddha himself: I felt immeasurable joy, and I thought that I too must obtain through contemplation power such as his. My master said: "My son, did you see? Did you believe?"

"I saw, and I could not help but believe," I replied. "And I thought that I too must do likewise through my contemplation."

"My son, that is good. And now you may go. I have shown you that all things are like an illusion, so do you experience likewise, adhering to the rocky wastes, the snowy ranges and the solitary forests. In these places make meditation your foremost aim."

Source: Reprinted by permission of Wadsworth, Inc. from Stephan Beyer, *The Buddhist Experience* (Encino, CA: Dickenson, 1974), pp. 175–84.[5]

---

[5]Original text: Sangs-rgyas rgyal-mtshan, *Mi-la ras-pa'i rnam-thar* [*The Life of Mi-la ras-pa*], ed. J. W. de Jong ('s-Gravenhage: Mouton, 1959), pp. 57–81, 102–3.

7.7 WOMEN AND THE SANGHA: THE ABBESS OF SAMDING AND ANI LOCHEN

Although female monastics (generically known as "ani") have long been an important part of the Tibetan sangha, the lineage of fully ordained nuns (Skt., bhikṣuṇī, Tib., gelongma) either never got transmitted to Tibet or died out there as it did in Theravāda countries. The basic ambiguity of women's position in Tibetan Buddhism is well reflected in the following two passages taken from the sacred biography of Yeshe Tsogyel, one of the chief Tantric consorts of Padmasambhava. At one point, Padmasambhava himself encourages Yeshe Tsogyel and extolls her meditational achievements:

> "Wonderful yoginī, practitioner of the secret teachings!
> The basis for realizing enlightenment is a human body.
> Male or female—there is no great difference.
> But if she develops the mind bent on enlightenment,
> the woman's body is better.
> From beginningless time,
> you have accumulated merit and wisdom,
> Now your good qualities are flawless—
> what an excellent woman you have become, a true Bodhisattma!"

A bit later on, however, Yeshe Tsogyel herself bemoans her fate:

> "I am a woman—I have little power to resist danger.
> Because of my inferior birth, everyone attacks me.
> If I go as a beggar, dogs attack me.
> If I have wealth and food, bandits attack me.
> If I do a great deal, the locals attack me.
> If I do nothing, gossips attack me.
> If anything goes wrong, they all attack me.
> Whatever I do , I have no chance for happiness.
> Because I am a woman, it is hard to follow the Dharma.
> It is hard even to stay alive!"[6]

With this ambiguity in mind, the following selection first reviews the variety of female religious practitioners in traditional Tibet and then presents briefly two prominent case histories.

In Tibet, prior to 1959, there existed a number of different types of women *chos-pa*, or religious practitioners. There were women *lha-khas* and *pa-mos* (i.e., "spirit-mediums"); there were female religious bards called *maṇi-pas;* and—representing what may be viewed as the two poles of Buddhist practice—there were the tantric adepts (like Yeshe Tsogyel)

[6] Tarthang Tulku, *Mother of Knowledge: The Enlightenment of Ye-shes mTsho-rgyal* (Berkeley: Dharma Publishing, 1985), pp. 102, 105, cited in Janice Willis, "Tibetan Ani-s: The Nun's Life in Tibet," *Feminine Ground: Essays on Women and Tibet* (Ithaca: Snow Lion, 1987), pp. 97, 96.

and the *anis,* or Buddhist nuns. . . . The type of women lauded in the sacred annals are the accomplished tantric practitioners: women like Ni-gu-ma, "wife" of the Indian *siddha,* Nāropa, who developed and taught her own system of the famed "six yogas." There is Dak-me-ma, Marpa's accomplished wife [see 7.6]; and Ma-chik-lab-dön-ma, Pha Dam-pa Sang-gye's chief consort and fashioner of the advanced meditative chöd rite. . . . All these women are *mudrās,* or "consorts" (to male tantric practitioners). Some are referred to simply as *yoginīs;* others are called human *ḍākinīs,* i.e., incarnations of the feminine principle of insight and wisdom itself. They are not your ordinary everyday Tibetan women practitioners.

On the other end of the spectrum there are the Tibetan Buddhist nuns, women who have quietly, and often with great diffciulties, continued to practice in accordance with the monastic rules laid down at Buddhism's very inception in India. . . . About this type of enrobed female practitioner the texts do not speak and very little information is presently available. No indigenous Tibetan literature, of whatever historical period, focuses upon them. [. . .]

While the earliest ordination of Tibetan monks (a solemn ceremony in which the Indian Ācārya, Śāntirakṣita, ordained the first seven indigenous Tibetans at Sam-ye monastery in the late eighth century) is an event well documented and much lauded in the major religious annals of the country, I have been unable to find a single reference to the earliest ordination of Tibetan nuns. There were, however, *ani* in Tibet; and though very few in number, there were even some *ani-khen-pos,* or Abbesses. . . . [Here are two examples]:

1. Samding was the State Nunnery of Tibet and its Abbess was regarded as the incarnation of the deity Dorje Phakmo (Skt. Vajravārāhī). Situated seventy miles southwest of Lhasa, on a slip of land some 14,512 feet high and overlooking the famed Yam-drok lake, the gompa was a most impressive sight. Waddell mused that Samding was "noteworthy as a monastery of monks as well as nuns, presided over by a female abbot." He continued his description as follows:

> This august woman is known throughout Tibet as Dorje-P'ag-mo, or "the diamond sow"; the abbesses of Samding being held to be successive appearances in mortal form of the Indian goddess, Vajravarahi. The present incarnation of this goddess is thirty-three years old (in 1899); and is described as being a clever and capable woman, with some claim to good looks, and of noble birth. She bears the name of Nag-dban Rin-ch'en Kun-bzan-mo dbAn-mo, signifying "The most precious power of speech, the female energy of all good." Under this lady the reputation which Samding has long enjoyed for the good morals of both monks and nuns has been well maintained. [. . .]

The early nineteenth century Tibetan work, *The Geography of Tibet,* mentions Samding . . . and terms the Abbess a *rig-ma* (i.e., a "wisdom-being"; also a synonym for *mudrā).* Both Taring and Waddell attribute the Abbess's high esteem to the fact that during the 1719 invasion of Tibet by the Dzungar Tartars she miraculously transformed herself and her followers into "a large herd of pigs" whose sight caused the Dzungars to flee in disgust. The convent was chiefly affiliated with the Nying-ma sect, but its Abbess is the only woman in Tibet venerated on a par with and "accorded privileges shared only by" the Pan-chen and Dalai Lamas.

2. In her wonderfully interesting autobiography, *Daughter of Tibet*, Rinchen Dolma Taring briefly mentions a saintly woman who commanded the respect of all the religious sects. This woman was called Ani Lochen. Sometimes a fuller title was given: "Shuksep Jetsun Lochen Rinpoche." Shuksep (*shugs gseb*, "Juniper Forest") named the location of Ani Lochen's nunnery, some thirty miles outside Lhasa. The titles "Jetsun" (rje-btsun) and "Rinpoche" are honorific ones, reserved for Tibet's most accomplished and treasured teachers.

Taring describes Ani Lochen as being the reincarnation of [the tantric consort] Ma-chik-lab-dön-ma, mentioned previously, and as also being affiliated primarily with the Nying-ma-pa sect. As a summary of Ani Lochen's life, Taring writes the following:

> She had been born in India in about 1820 . . . of a Nepalese mother and Tibetan father. From the age of six she preached, with a *thang-ka*, by singing of religion in a wonderfully melodious voice and whoever heard her found their hearts coming closer to religion. As a child she had a little goat to ride and when in her youth she went along the streets of Lhasa with her *thang-ka*, preaching from door to door, she caught the hearts of many Lhasa girls who became nuns and followed her. She was known as "Ani Lochen." . . . At the age of about forty Ani Lochen promised her mother that she would always stay in the mountains and meditate; later she found a place near Lhasa called Shuksep, where there was a cave in which Gyalwa Longchen Rabjampa had meditated. . . . Many nuns also came and there was a little nunnery nearby for about eighty women. People regularly visited Ani Lochen, for her cave was near Lhasa and she had many worshippers—lamas, monks, officials and women. Sometimes nuns would leave their nunnery to marry, but Ani Lochen always said, "Never mind—even if they have been nuns for only a week they will be different forever afterwards."

Source: Reprinted with permission of the author from Janice Willis, "Tibetan Ani-s: The Nun's Life in Tibet," *Feminine Ground: Essays on Women and Tibet* (Ithaca: Snow Lion, 1987), pp. 98–99, 104–06 (slightly altered).

7.8 SANGHA AND SOCIETY

It is sometimes said that in traditional Tibet 10 to 15 percent of the male population were monks. This made the sangha part of the very fabric of Tibetan society, in ways that were even more significant than those found in South and Southeast Asia. The following selections illustrate three involvements of Buddhism in Tibetan politics, economics, and society from the very highest to the most routine levels.

7.8.1 Dalai Lamas, Regents, China, and Tibet

Tibet has been unusual among the countries of the world to have adopted a system of government that features what has been called "rule by incarnation." Indeed, soon after the ascendancy of the Ge-luk-pa sect in the fifteenth century, there came the custom of investing political and spiritual authority in the line of Dalai Lamas. These men, as mentioned, are thought to be successive incarnations of Avalokiteśvara, the patron bodhisattva of Tibet. According to this system, when one Dalai Lama dies, a search is carried out for his reincarnation, who is then brought back to the capital, Lhasa, and installed in the Potala Palace. (Potala is the name for Avalokiteśvara's realm.) The story of the discovery in the 1930s of the present, or fourteenth, Dalai Lama is well known. Guided by the indications of his predecessor, the thirteenth Dalai Lama, before his death, as well as by certain oracular visions, the search party found him as a child in eastern Tibet and submitted him to a number of tests, which he successfully completed before being officially recognized. He was brought to Lhasa, where he was educated, ordained as a monk, and "enthroned" as the new ruler of Tibet in 1950, shortly before the Chinese takeover of his country. He now lives in exile in northern India, having fled there during an unsuccessful uprising against the Chinese in 1959.

Not all Dalai Lamas have been actual leaders, spiritual or secular, of their country. One of the drawbacks of the rule-by-incarnation system is that there tends to be a rather long period between the discovery of each new Dalai Lama and his attainment of sufficient maturity to rule. During this period of the Dalai Lama's minority, actual power is held by a regent, himself a monk and generally a part of a rather small circle of ecclesiastical dignitaries. Historically, especially during the nineteenth century, there was a tendency for some of these regents to seek to extend their power beyond the time of their regency, to dominate the Dalai Lama if he were not a forceful personality, or, as we shall see in the selection below, to make sure that his enthronement never took place. Indeed, during the period 1806–74, the ninth, tenth, eleventh, and twelfth Dalai Lamas all died young, some of them rather mysteriously.

But the Dalai Lamas and the regents were not the only players in this power game. The Panchen Lamas (whose seat was not at Lhasa but at the monastery of Tashilhunpo) were another important line of incarnations, of the Buddha Amitābha. Also influential were members of the Tibetan cabinet and leaders of the three great Ge-luk-pa monasteries near Lhasa—Sera, Drepung, and Ganden—veritable monastic universities housing thousands of monks. On the nonmonastic side of things were influential members of the Tibetan nobility, as well as the Chinese amban, the official representative of the Manchu emperor, who though ruling in distant Beijing claimed suzerainty over Tibet and was, at times of crisis, willing to enforce it.

The following account of events in Lhasa in the middle of the nineteenth century is taken from the travel memoirs of a Roman Catholic missionary, Evariste Huc, who happened (illegally) to be in Tibet at the time. Huc's report is not completely accurate and is sometimes sensationalistic. Nonetheless, it gives a firsthand flavor to events that shook the Tibetan capital in 1844, and it also makes clear two things that may still hold true about the Tibetan situation: that the interplay of forces there is very complex and that as much as Tibetans recognized and worried about the chaos and corruption of their own situation, they resented Chinese attempts to resolve their problems even more. The year 1959 was not the first time there was a popular uprising against Chinese interference, and not the first time such an uprising was quelled.

The violent deaths of the three Dalai Lamas who were the immediate predecessors of the one reigning today [1850] gave rise, in the year 1844, to an event that much preoccupied Tibet, Tartary, and even China. Because of its importance, something must be said about it here.

The incredible phenomenon of three Dalai Lamas dying in the prime of life plunged the population of Lhasa into a somber consternation. Gradually, whispered stories began to circulate, and the words "crime" and "assassination" were rumored abroad. It got to the point where one could even hear, in the streets of the city and in the monasteries, detailed accounts of the baleful events. People said that one Dalai Lama had been strangled, the other crushed to death by the collapse of the roof of his bedroom, and the third poisoned along with many of his relatives. The high lama of the great monastery of Ganden, who had been very devoted to the latter Dalai Lama, had suffered the same fate.

Public opinion named the regent as the perpetrator of these attacks. The four chief ministers were said to be fully aware of this, but they found themselves powerless to avenge the death of their sovereign; they were too weak to oppose the regent, who had the support of his numerous and influential friends.

The regent . . . was originally from a powerful principality in Kansu Province in Western China. Many of his relatives had been established in Lhasa for several generations, and they exercised a great deal of influence over the affairs of Tibet. The regent was still quite young when he was invested with his authority, which he was supposed to relinquish only to the Dalai Lama [when the latter came of age]. It is claimed that a few years after his accession to power, his ambitions and unbridled desire for domination became manifest. He used his great wealth and the influence of his relatives to surround himself with a coterie of courtiers who were entirely devoted to him. He strove especially to establish for himself partisans among the monks; and to that end he placed under his direct protection the famous monastery of Sera, situated a half-league from Lhasa and numbering over fifteen thousand resident monks. He lavished favors upon it, accorded it privileges and immense revenues, and placed many of its products in the various administrative ranks of his government.

The monks of Sera did not fail to respond with enthusiastic support for the regent. They regarded him as a saint of the highest order and gave accounts of his accomplishments that quite rivaled in magnitude and pomp the perfections of the Buddha. Having managed to muster the support of such a powerful faction, the regent no longer set any limits to his ambitions. Thus he caused the successive deaths of three young Dalai Lamas in order to keep for himself the power of the regency. At least, that is what we were told during our stay in Lhasa.

It was not easy to overthrow such a person whose power was so solidly propped up. The chief ministers could not come out openly against him without risking defeat. Nevertheless, they decided to work secretly toward the ruin of that execrable person.

The assembly of Hutukhtus elected a new Dalai Lama, or rather they found the child in whose body the spirit of the Living Buddha had been reincarnated. He was enthroned at the top of the Potala. The regent, along with all the other dignitaries, went and prostrated himself at his feet, worshiping him with great devotion while no doubt secretly promising himself to find an opportune moment to make him reincarnate a fourth time. The chief ministers, however, undertook secret measures to prevent a repeat of such a catastrophic event. They consulted with the Panchen Lama of Tashilhunpo and agreed that the way to stop the infamous projects of the regent was to oppose them with the irresistible power of the emperor of China. The Panchen Lama and the four chief ministers therefore drew up and signed a petition, which they sent secretly to Beijing.

There were three reasons why the Chinese government could not but accede to the Tibetans' request for protection in their grave circumstances. First of all, the Manchu dynasty had solemnly declared itself to be the protector of the Dalai Lama; second, the regent, being a native of the province of Kansu, was in some ways legally accountable to Chinese imperial justice; finally, politically speaking, this presented the court in Beijing with an excellent opportunity to establish its influence in Tibet and to realize its plans to usurp power there.

The request for intervention sent to Beijing by the Panchen Lama and the four chief ministers was received favorably. Immediately, it was decided that a new amban [representative] was to be sent to Lhasa, who would have the strength and prudence needed to overthrow the power of the regent. The emperor's choice for this difficult mission fell on Ch'i-shan, an official [of considerable administrative and judicial experience but with a mixed record of diplomatic success]. [. . .]

As soon as he arrived in Lhasa, Ch'i-shan consulted the Panchen Lama and the four chief ministers and had the regent put under arrest. Then he had all the people in the service of the accused submitted to interrogation. So as to assist them in declaring the truth, he had slivers of bamboo driven underneath their fingernails, and in this way, according to the Chinese, "truth was distinguished from falsehood and the true conduct of the regent was fully exposed." The latter, in fact, confessed to his crimes without even having to be questioned; he admitted guilt in having deprived the Dalai Lama of life three times and in having violently caused him to reincarnate, first by strangulation, secondly by suffocation, and thirdly by poisoning.

A formal record of the proceedings was drawn up in Chinese, Manchu, and Tibetan. The regent and his accomplices signed it. The Panchen Lama, the four chief ministers, and the Chinese amban all affixed their seal to it, and it was sent to Beijing by special courier. All this happened behind closed doors and in the greatest secrecy.

Three months later, the Tibetan capital was plunged into great uproar. An imperial edict, in three languages on yellow paper with winged dragons along the edges, had been posted on the great gate of the regent's palace. In it, after elevated reflections upon the duties of sovereigns and exhortations to potentates, monarchs, princes, magistrates, and people everywhere to walk in the ways of justice and virtue, . . . the emperor recalled the crimes of the regent and condemned him to perpetual exile on the shores of Sakhalin, on the other side of Manchuria. . . .

The citizens of Lhasa hurried to view these proclamations, which they were not accustomed to see posted on the walls of their city. The news of the condemnation of the regent spread quickly through the crowd. Numerous groups gathered and engaged in heated discussions, but in hushed tones. People were animated, and ripples of resentment ran through the crowd. The agitation that took over the Tibetan people was due less to the deserved fall of the regent than to the intervention of the Chinese authorities, intervention that made everyone feel offended and humiliated.

At the monastery of Sera, the opposition manifested itself with a different kind of energy. As soon as the news of the imperial edict was heard, there occurred a general and spontaneous insurrection. The fifteen thousand monks, who were all devoted to the cause of the regent, armed themselves with spears, rifles, sticks—anything they could find—and rushed to Lhasa, which was but a half-league away. The clouds of dust they stirred up in their riotous advance and the horrific clamor they raised made known their arrival to the residents of Lhasa. "The monks of Sera! Here come the monks of Sera!" That was the cry that broke out throughout the city and brought fright to every breast.

The monks descended like an avalanche on the residence of the Chinese envoy and smashed in the gates, yelling: "Death to Ch'i-shan! Death to the Chinese!" But the crowd found no one on whom they could vent their rage. The amban, forewarned in time of their coming, had run to hide in the home of one of the ministers, and the other members of his delegation had dispersed throughout the city.

The multitude of monks then split up into several groups. Some went to the palace of the regent, and others invaded the residence of the ministers, demanding that the Chinese envoy be handed over to them. There was, in that regard, a long and fierce struggle during which one of the four Tibetan ministers was torn to shreds and the others were injured more or less severely.

While these battles were taking place at the ministers' dwelling in an attempt to capture Ch'i-shan, the majority of the monks broke down the gates of the prison where their regent had been incarcerated, intending to carry him in triumph back to the monastery of Sera. But the regent expressed his vehement opposition to this plan and used his influence to calm down the monks. He told them that their reckless revolt had aggravated his situation instead of bettering it. "I am," he said to them, "the victim of a conspiracy. I will go to Beijing, explain things to the emperor, and return to you in triumph. But for now, we must obey the imperial decree. . . . So you should all return peacefully to your monastery."

These words did not alter the resolution of the monks, but, as night was falling, they returned to Sera, boisterously promising themselves to organize themselves better on the morrow.

The next day, the monks indeed roused themselves in their immense monastery, and prepared to invade the city of Lhasa once again. This time, however, to their great astonishment, they found in the plain, near their monastery, numerous tents and a multitude of well-armed Tibetan and Chinese troops. At the sight of them, the monks lost courage. The conch was sounded, and these makeshift soldiers threw down their arms, entered their cells, took up their books, and went peacefully to the sanctuary to recite their morning prayers.

Some days later, the regent, accompanied by a sizable escort, left on the road to Szechuan, going off docilely to the exile that had been assigned to him. . . .

Ch'i-shan, exulting in his triumph, wished to extend his power over the Tibetan accomplices of the regent. That plan, however, did not please the ministers, who declared that they alone reserved the right to pass judgment over people who were in no way Chinese dependents, and against whom the emperor had not been asked to offer protection. The amban did not push the point, but in order not to seem to cede to the Tibetan authorities, he replied officially that he would let them deal with these minor assassins, who were not worth the trouble of a representative of the great emperor.

Source: Translated from Régis-Evariste Huc, *Souvenirs d'un voyage dans la Tartarie et le Thibet pendant les années 1844, 1845, et 1846* (Paris, 1852; reprint ed., Beijing: Imprimerie des Lazaristes, 1924), 2:260–63, 266–69.

7.8.2 Life at Drepung Monastery

As part of the reform movement that established the Ge-luk-pa sect in the fifteenth century, Tsong-kha-pa founded the monastic university of Ganden in 1409. Before his death ten years later, two other great monasteries had been established, Drepung and Sera. These three monastic centers, all in the vicinity of Lhasa, soon became training centers for thousands of monks from all over Tibet and in no small way helped centralize Ge-luk-pa authority and make Lhasa the ecclesiastical and political capital of the country.

The largest of these monasteries was Drepung, which retained its prestige and influence for centuries, up until the abortive Tibetan uprising of 1959. At that time, its monastic estates and storehouses were confiscated by the Chinese and its administration was taken over by a work team of Communist party cadres, who appointed a Democratic Management Committee of monks from poor and deprived class backgrounds to run the place. By the mid-1960s, only about 7 percent of the original population of over ten thousand monks still lived there, and during the Cultural Revolution of 1966–76, although its buildings were not physically destroyed, it ceased functioning altogether as a monastery. Since then, Drepung has resumed some of its activities. The following selection describes its organization and functioning during its heyday in traditional Tibetan society.

The largest monastical institution in traditional Tibet was Drepung. Founded in 1416 by Jamyang Chöje and located about five miles west of Lhasa, it was a virtual town housing about ten thousand monks at the time of the Chinese invasion in 1950–51. It epitomized the institutionalization of mass monasticism in Tibet and was at that time the world's largest monastery.

Drepung was organized in a manner that resembled the segmentary structure of classic British universities like Oxford in that the overall entity, the monastery, was a combination of semiautonomous subunits known as *tratsang*. These are conventionally called "colleges" in the English literature, although there were no schools (with teaching faculties) in the Western sense. In 1959 Drepung consisted of four functioning colleges: Loseling, Goman, Deyang, and Ngagba. Each was a minimonastery with thousands of monks, an administrative structure headed by an abbot, and its own rules and traditions. Each was a corporate entity in the sense that it had an identity (a name), owned property and wealth, and had its own internal organization and leadership. The monks came and went over the decades, but the entity and its property endured. A monk's loyalties, in fact, were primarily rooted in his college.

The highest official of a college was the abbot. He held his office for a term of six years and could be renewed for another six-year term. He was appointed by the ruler (the Dalai Lama or in his minority, the regent) from a list containing six or seven ranked nominees submitted by the college in question. The ruler had the final authority over the appointment and could select someone not on the list, although this was rarely done. Nevertheless, power to choose the administrative leadership of colleges was one of the main ways that the Tibetan government maintained control over powerful and potentially unruly monasteries like Drepung. Under the abbot, various officials such as the *gegö* (disciplinary officer) and *nyerba* (economic manager) oversaw specific aspects of monastic life. Also, an "assembly" of the more senior monks periodically met to discuss collegewide issues.

Large monastic colleges were normally subdivided into smaller, named residential units know as *khamtsen*, or residence halls. . . . These units, similar to the colleges in terms of administrative structure, consisted of one or more buildings divided into apartments (*shag*) where the monks lived. Residence halls had a strong regional flavor since each khamtsen held rights to recruit monks from a specific geographic area or areas. Because great monasteries like Drepung recruited monks from all over the Tibetan cultural world as well as from non-Tibetan areas such as Mongolia, this system helped to facilitate the initial period of acculturation by situating a new monk in a residence together with others who spoke his dialect or language.

Drepung as a whole functioned as an alliance of colleges. There was no single abbot at the helm. Instead, monasterywide issues were decided by a council made up sometimes by the abbots of the different colleges and sometimes by the current and the former abbots. The monastery as a whole also owned property, and there were several important monasterywide monk stewards whose responsibility was to manage these. There were also monasterywide disciplinary officers.

At the level of the individual monk, Drepung's ten thousand members were divided into two broad categories—those who studied a formal curriculum of Buddhist theology and philosophy and those who did not. The former, known as *pechawa,* or bookish ones, were a small minority, amounting to only about 10 percent of the total monk population. These "scholar monks," as I shall refer to them, pursued a fixed curriculum that involved approximately fifteen classes or levels (*'dzin-grwa*), each of which took a year to complete. This curriculum emphasized learning Buddhist theology by means of extensive formal debating. Like much else in Drepung Monastery, the theological study program was conducted at the college rather than the monastic level. Three of Drepung's four colleges offered such a curriculum (Gomang, Loseling, and Deyang); the other, Ngagba, taught tantric rituals. The scholar monks in Goman, Loseling, and Deyang met three times a day to practice debating in their respective college's outdoor walled park called a *chöra* or dharma grove. The curriculum in each college used a slightly different set of texts, although in the end they all covered the same material. Monks pursuing this trajectory started in the lowest class and worked their way up until they were awarded one of several titles or degrees of *geshe* by their college's abbot. The title of geshe was sought by both monks and incarnate lamas of the Dalai Lama's Gelugpa sect, including the Dalai Lama himself. Monks came to Drepung from all over the Tibetan Buddhist world to see if they could master the difficult curriculum and obtain the degree of geshe. The intellectual greatness of the Gelugpa sect's monastic tradition was measured by the brilliance of these scholar monks.

The overwhelming majority of common monks—the *tramang* or *tragyü*—however, did not pursue this arduous course and were not involved in formal study. Many could not read much more than one or two prayer books, and some, in fact, were functionally illiterate, having memorized only a few basic prayers. These monks had some intermittent monastic work obligations in their early years but otherwise were free to do what they liked. However, because Drepung did not provide its monks with either meals via a communal kitchen or payments in kind and money sufficient to satisfy their needs, they had to spend a considerable amount of time in income-producing activities. Some monks, therefore, practiced trades like tailoring and medicine, some worked as servants for other monks, some engaged in trade, and still others left the monastery at peak agricultural times to work for farmers.

The reason for the monastery's financial shortfall was not a lack of resources. Drepung, for example, owned 151 agricultural estates and 540 pastoral areas, each of which had a population of hereditarily bound peasant families who worked the monastery's (or college's) land without wages as a corvée obligation. Drepung also was heavily involved in money- and grain-lending and had huge capital funds with thousands of loans outstanding at any give time. The monastery's inability to fund its monks, therefore, derived primarily from its decisions on how to utilize its income vis-à-vis its monks. On the one hand, Drepung allocated a substantial portion of monastic income to rituals and prayer chanting assemblies rather than to monks' salaries; on the other, it did not attempt to restrict the number of monks to the income it had available. Rather, it allowed all to join. Despite a traditional government-set ceiling of 7,700 monks, monasteries like Drepung made no attempt to determine how many monks they could realistically support and then admit only that many. How monks financed their monastic status was, by and large, their own problem.

The monks most affected by the insufficient funding were those who had made a commitment to study Buddhist theology full-time, that is, the scholar monks. They were sorely disadvantaged since they had no time to engage in trade or other income-producing activities because of their heavy academic burdens. Consequently, they typically were forced to lead extremely frugal lives unless they were able to find wealthy patrons to supplement their income or were themselves wealthy, as in the case of the incarnate lamas. Tales abound in Drepung of famous scholar monks so poor that they had to eat the staple food—*tsamba* (parched barley flour)—with water rather than tea, or worse, who had to eat the leftover dough from ritual offerings (*torma*).

Source: Reprinted by permission of the publisher from Melvyn C. Goldstein, "The Revival of Monastic Life in Drepung Monastery," in *Buddhism in Contemporary Tibet: Religious Revival and Cultural Identity*, ed. Melvyn C. Goldstein and Matthew T. Kapstein (Berkeley: University of California Press, 1998), pp. 20–22.

7.8.3 A Monk and a Beggar

In addition to monks training and living in monastic institutions such as Drepung, less affiliated individuals in Tibet led more peripatetic lives. Some of these were thought to be "crazy saints," enlightened wanderers who acted unconventionally. But it was often hard to distinguish such holymen and women from ordinary beggars. This ambiguity is nicely captured (and left unresolved) in the following snapshot of an encounter between an academically inclined monk and a seemingly ordinary beggar. The narrative is reconstructed from an account given by a member of a Tibetan aristocratic family remembering his life as a boy growing up on the huge estate of the Lhagyari family, in south-central Tibet in the 1940s. The Lhagyari claimed descent from the ancient Yarlung dynasty of Tibetan kings (see 7.1) and enjoyed a semiautonomous status in their relationship to the government in Lhasa. The setting for the story is the compound of the family's central estate house.

Hearing a flurry of activity below, Lobsang decided to see what was going on and stood up [and went] to the window. The courtyard below—ringed by large storage buildings and offices, workshops for craftsmen such as cobblers, and sheds for roasting barley and the like—was filled with people. It was the noise from the edge of the courtyard that held his attention. A large crowd . . . had gathered in the corner near a shed, and at the center a monk seemed to be arguing with one of the craftsmen.

As Lobsang watched, however, he realized that it was not one of his family servants but a man from the village whom he had seen only once or twice, a traveling beggar with glasses and a cane who always kept a young boy with him. Together, the two traveled through the countryside begging. They slept wherever the night found them and cooked whatever people gave them, and although the man always wore moderately respectable clothing, the child was covered only in rags. No one knew much about them. The man often beat the young child with a stick and constantly complained about him to anyone who was within earshot. One time when Lobsang and his father had chanced to meet them, the old man sat on a rock by the side of the road while the child approached their horses asking for alms. Lobsang's father had given them a piece of cheese from their supplies but told the old man to take better care of the child.

Now, as Lobsang listened to the loud argument, he realized that the child was the subject of dispute. The old man had been sitting outside waiting for alms during the arrival of the monks, and when he had become disgruntled, he had taken to beating the boy harshly with a stick. One of the women servants had objected, a crowd had formed around them, and finally a monk had taken the stick away from the man. Now everyone stood around the two, listening to them and talking to one another at the same time. Several women came out of the doors to the courtyard, wiping their hands on their wool aprons, and then stood in the crowd with their arms crossed in front of them, children holding on to their skirts.

The monk had stopped the beating out of compassionate feelings for the boy, but now he seemed to be enjoying the argument as a demonstration of his debating prowess. Most of the educated monks had been trained for years in logical analysis. They had learned techniques for debating, using stylized movements that involved stepping forward and slapping their hands before they made a point for the other side to answer. It seemed that the old man would be no match for a monk. But after initially yelling and telling the onloookers it was none of their business, the old man had begun to answer quite well, and the two were engaged. The onlookers drew back from the argument as they saw that the opponents were equally matched and that the old man was using reason.

The old man stated that the child was with him because of the boy's actions in a previous life and that severe beating was the only way to make him behave. Besides, the monk had surely been beaten often at the monastery when he misbehaved; in fact, all children were beaten like this, so there was nothing unusual in it. The monk responded that the man was no religious saint with special knowledge of previous lives and kept the child only for selfish reasons. The old man, who sat on the ground looking up only sporadically, asked the monk how he knew that a beggar was not a famous religious saint. This caused everyone in the crowd to wonder; it was apparent that they had all begun to suspect something of the kind themselves. If the old man was a religious ascetic, the beatings could be a way of helping the child to burn off bad karma. Clearly now, no one would interfere, and although the monk kept questioning, he had lost the force of his argument.

Source: Reprinted by permission of the publisher from Rebecca Redwood French, *The Golden Yoke: The Legal Cosmology of Buddhist Tibet* (Ithaca: Cornell University Press, 1995), pp. 222–23.

CHAPTER 8

Buddhists and the Practice of Buddhism: China

It is often pointed out that at about the same time that Buddhism spread from India to Sri Lanka and Southeast Asia, it also spread west and north to what is now Pakistan, Kashmir, and Afghanistan. From there it moved into Central Asia and, carried along the desert trade routes, entered China sometime around the first century C.E. Buddhism then spread throughout the rest of East Asia, through Korea to Japan, and southward to what is now northern Vietnam.

Such a quick overview does severe injustice to the complexities of the transmission, growth, and transformation of a religious tradition. It treats the peoples of certain regions (for example, Central Asia and Korea) as though they were mere conduits for the religions of others, and it views the spread of religious ideas and emotions as though they were a jet stream rather than a meandering river occasionally used to irrigate somebody's field. Properly speaking, separate chapters of readings should be given here at least for Central Asia, Korea, and Vietnam. Space, however, allows only for two—this one on China, and the next, Chapter 9, on Japan.

The Buddhism that was and is practiced in these regions is every bit as varied as that found in Tibet and in South and Southeast Asia and just as colored and enriched by its interactions with different indigenous and local traditions. Comparisons, however, may still be possible, and to facilitate them we shall use the same categories we employed in Chapters 6 and 7.

8.1 MYTHIC HISTORY: THE FIRST MONK, THE FIRST TEMPLE, AND THE EMPEROR MING

We shall start with a well-known legend about the introduction of Buddhism to China. In "histories" of Chinese Buddhism, the story is often told of the dream of the Emperor Ming (58–75 C.E.) of the Han dynasty. One night, he saw in his sleep a golden deity flying near his palace. The next day, his ministers informed him that this was a sage from faraway India, who had golden skin and could fly and who was called the Buddha. The emperor promptly sent some ambassadors to the western regions to find out more about this "Buddha" and his teachings, and they brought Buddhism back with them to Loyang, the capital of China at the time.

It is likely that this story was the fabrication of some second-century Buddhists in Loyang, wishing to make a claim for the primacy of their home community over other early Buddhist centers that had sprung up in China (in the south and the east). Depending on the source in which this tale is being recounted, however, various parts of it are featured over others. Some sources emphasize a text: the ambassadors are said to return and bring with them the *Sūtra in Forty-two Sections,* a compilation of verses attributed to the Buddha, widely thought to have been the first Buddhist sūtra translated into Chinese but most probably an apocryphal work compiled in China itself. Others stress a place: the White Horse Monastery (Pai-ma ssu) in Loyang, which eventually laid claim to having been the first Buddhist sanctuary established in China. There, the *Sūtra in Forty-two Sections* is said to have been kept. The following selection, taken from a compilation of biographies of eminent monks, focuses on a person: the Indian or Central Asian monk Kāśyapa Mātaṅga, thought to have been one of the first Buddhist monks in China. His story is hooked into the legend by making him the translator of the *Sūtra in Forty-two Sections* and by associating the place where he lived with the White Horse Monastery.

During the Yung P'ing era of the Han dynasty, the emperor dreamed one night that a golden man came to him flying through the air. He convened all his ministers in order to question them about the meaning of his dream. The knowledgeable Fu Yi respectfully offered this response: "Your minister has heard that in the western lands there is a god whose name is Buddha. Could he not have been the subject of your majesty's dream?"

The emperor thought so. Immediately, he sent Ts'ai Yin, the officer of the imperial guards, and Ts'ing Ching, an assistant at the academy, along with some others, to India to make inquiries about the Buddha's Doctrine. There, Ts'ai Yin and the others met Kāśyapa Mātaṅga and invited him to return with them to China.

Kāśyapa Mātaṅga, who had pledged to spread the Dharma widely, feared neither exhaustion nor suffering. Venturing across the Takla Makan Desert, he arrived at the city of Loyang. There he was welcomed by the Emperor Ming, who had a monastic dwelling built for him outside the western gate of the city.

He was the first Buddhist monk in China. But as the great Dharma was being transmitted there for the first time, there were as yet no converts to whom he could preach. For this reason, Kāśyapa Mātaṅga kept his deep understanding to himself. A few years later, he passed away in Loyang.

It is recorded that Kāśyapa Mātaṅga translated the *Sūtra in Forty-two Sections.* It was originally kept in the fourteenth bay of the stone room of the Imperial Library.

The place where Kāśyapa Mātaṅga lived, outside the western gate of the city of Loyang, is the [present-day] Pai-ma ssu [White Horse Monastery]. According to one account, once, when all the monasteries of the city were destroyed by a foreign king, only the Chao-t'i ssu monastery was left standing. At night, a white horse circumambulated the pagoda there, neighing mournfully. This was related to the king, and he immediately put a halt to the destruction of the monasteries. On account of this, he also had the name of the Chao-t'i ssu changed to Pai-ma ssu.

Source: Translated from Hui chiao, *Kao seng chuan* (Taishō shinshū daizōkyō, ed. J. Takakusu and K. Watanabe [Tokyo, 1924–29], no. 2059, 50:322c–323a].[1]

8.2 INTERACTIONS AND SYNCRETISM: BUDDHISM AND FILIAL PIETY IN CHINA

With the introduction of Buddhism into China, one of the questions that immediately arose was that of its relationship to indigenous Chinese religious and cultural traditions. Almost from the beginning, among the many accusations leveled against Buddhism by its detractors was that Buddhist monks were lacking in the basic Confucian ethic of filial piety. Not only did monks leave home and thereby abandon caring for their parents in their old age, but they did not marry or have children (thereby threatening the continuity of ancestral worship in their family). And by shaving their heads, they further insulted their parents by mutilating the bodies they had inherited from them.

Buddhism's response to these accusations was not long in coming and, in fact, had already been formulated somewhat in India in response to similar accusations from Hindu Brahmanical circles. First of all, Buddhists in China pointed to sūtras and other texts in their own tradition in which the Buddha seemed to advocate some sort of filial piety. For instance, there were the stories featuring the arhat Maudgalyāyana (Chinese: Mulien), who searched the whole cosmos for his deceased mother and then went to extraordinary measures to allay her suffering. This story of Mulien became very popular in East Asia, largely because of its advocacy of filial piety (see 2.5.4 and 9.5). Second, new texts, so-called "apocryphal sūtras" that were not translations from the Sanskrit but original compositions in Chinese, were created for the purpose of portraying the Buddha and Buddhism as solidly in the filial piety camp. Finally, Buddhist doctrine was adapted and used in various ways to argue for the actual superiority of the Buddhist ethic of filial piety over the Confucian one. For example, given the doctrine of an infinite number of previous births, Buddhists could argue that all beings might at some point have been one's parents in a past life. Consequently, the bodhisattva sentiment of compassion toward *all* beings was actually a kind of "great filial piety," which honored all one's parents in all one's lives and was not limited, as the Confucian ethic was, to one's parents in this life.

[1]Alternative French translation, Robert Shih, *Biographies des moines éminents (Kao Seng Tchouan) de Houei-kiao* (Louvain: Institut Orientaliste, 1968), pp. 1–2.

The following selection from a text entitled *Sūtra on a Filial Son* (Hsiao tzu ching), which may be a Chinese apocryphal work, does not go quite that far. Instead, it takes another popular tack and argues that a true act of filial piety consists not in physically supporting one's parents in this life but in converting them to Buddhism in order to save them from aeons of suffering in lower states of rebirth.

The Buddha addressed the assembly of monks: "A parent who is going to give birth to a child bears it for ten [lunar] months, during which her body grows heavy and she suffers from sickness. When it is about to be born, the mother is at risk, and the father is afraid. These feelings are difficult to describe. Once the baby is born, the mother puts it in the dry place and herself lies in the wet spot. She is so filled with sincerity that her blood changes to milk. She rubs the baby, wipes it, and bathes it. She dresses, feeds, and teaches it and admonishes it to be well-behaved toward teachers and friends and to have respect for its elders. When the child's expression is happy and peaceful, the parents are pleased; when the child is miserable, the parents feel anguish in their hearts. When the child goes out, they are concerned about it. When the child comes back in, they pay attention to it. Their hearts are very anxious that it might get into trouble. When the parents' loving concern is like this, how can the child repay it?"

The monks answered: "The child can only repay its parents' kindness by behaving with the utmost courtesy and serving them with a compassionate heart."

The Blessed One said: "If a child nurtures its parents by indulging their tastes for flavorful delicacies, by pleasing their ears with well-liked heavenly music, by dressing them splendidly in choice garments, by carrying them on their shoulders to the ends of the world, and repaying their kindness throughout their lives—can this be called filial piety?"

The monks replied: "There is no greater model of filial piety than this."

But the Blessed One said: "This is not really filial piety! If parents are stubborn and ignorant and do not revere the Triple Gem, if they are malicious and tyrannical, if they steal with impunity, if they have illicit sexual relations, if they use false language in defiance of the Way, if they are addicted to riotous behavior, if they are against righteousness and truth, if they are wicked and feisty, then their child should strive to admonish them in order to enlighten them. And if this does not work and they still remain unenlightened, the child should take further steps to convert them. . . . And if this still does not make them alter their ways, the child should wail and cry and stop taking food and drink. For the parents naturally love and feel tenderly toward their child, and although they do not understand, they would be anguished if it should die. In this way, they would be forced to capitulate and respect the Way.

"And if the parents then convert and honor the Buddha and the five precepts, they will become benevolent and not kill, they will become pure and deferential and not steal, they will become upright and chaste and not commit adultery, they will honor their word and not be deceiving, they will become filial and obedient and not be drunkards. In this way, within their group, parents will be kind and children filial, husbands will be upright and wives virtuous, families will be at peace and harmonious, and servants will be obedient. . . .

"In a world without filial piety, only this can bring about filial piety. Only this is able to make parents leave evil behind and do good, so that they come to honor the five precepts and stick to the threefold refuge. . . . If one is not successful in changing one's parents' ways by means of the Triple Gem, then even if one cultivates filial conduct, one would not truly be filial."

Source: Translated from *Hsiao tzu ching* (Taishō shinshū daizōkyō, ed. J. Takakusu and K. Watanabe [Tokyo, 1924–29], no. 687, 16:780b–c).[2]

8.3 DIVISIONAL ISSUES: DO ALL BEINGS HAVE THE BUDDHA-NATURE?

Not too long after the introduction of Buddhism into China, a story circulated about the Buddha and Ānanda meeting a poor woman on the street. Ānanda encouraged the Blessed One to speak to her and convert her, but the Buddha merely replied that she would be unreceptive to his teaching. Ānanda, however, urged the Buddha to approach her, certain that when she saw his glorious presence, she would rejoice and become receptive. So the Buddha went up to her, but she turned away and did not see him. He then used his magical powers to come at her from all sides at once, but she looked up in the air. He then flew up into the sky and came at her from above, but she looked down. Finally, he penetrated the earth and came up at her from below, but she covered her face with her hands. It was not that she was deliberately avoiding him, she simply never made contact with him. The Buddha then explained to Ānanda that his efforts were useless; some beings just could not be converted, could not be made receptive to the Dharma, because they simply were unable to see the Buddha.[3]

There are two possible ways of explaining the situation of this woman. One is to say that she is unreceptive because she has not yet planted the roots of merit that would enable her to be affected by the Buddha and the Dharma. This is tragic, but for her there is still hope that sometime in the future she may plant those roots and eventually be saved. The other view is that she acts as she does because her roots of merit have been completely cut off, destroyed. In that case, there is no hope that she will ever be enlightened.

[2]Alternative English translation, Alan Cole, *Mothers and Sons in Chinese Buddhism* (Stanford: Stanford University Press), pp. 68–73.

[3]The story can be found in the *Mahāprajñāpāramitā śāstra* (Taishō shinshū daizōkyō, ed. J. Takakusu and K. Watanabe [Tokyo, 1924–29], no. 1509, 25:125c–126a); French translation, Etienne Lamotte, *Le traité de la grande vertu de sagesse* (Louvain: Institut Orientaliste, 1949–80), 1:541.

The latter view formed the basis of the doctrine of the *icchantika,* a word whose etymology is uncertain but that signifies an individual who will never be able to mature in the teaching, who will never be able to develop the mind of enlightenment, who is permanently cut off from salvation. Obviously, such a doctrine had important repercussions for understanding the capacities and compassion of the Buddha, for the nature of the process of enlightenment, for the doctrine of the Tathāgatagarbha (see 4.3.5), and for a host of other issues.

This icchantika question, whether there were beings who were by nature excluded from potential Buddhahood, was much discussed in Chinese Buddhist circles in the early fifth century C.E. Part of the confusion on this issue stemmed from the very sūtras that Chinese Buddhists were reading at the time. The assertion of the incapacity of icchantikas to attain enlightenment was found in one version (Fa-hsien's translation) of the Mahāyāna *Mahāparinirvāṇa sūtra.* But in a second version of the same text (Dharmakṣema's translation), after the sūtra makes that assertion, it goes on to reverse itself and maintain just the opposite: that everyone, including the icchantikas, are destined for Buddhahood! Some later texts contended that this discrepancy was deliberate: that the first version of the sūtra had been written to rouse people of bad morals so that they would not rest assured that, whatever their behavior, they could still attain ultimate salvation; and that the second version had been written to make clear the true meaning of the teaching.

Be this as it may, at least one prominent monk is reputed to have found himself caught betwixt and between these two views. According to a well-known story, Tao-sheng, who died in 432 C.E., first read the first version of the sūtra and vehemently disagreed with its view. He was certain that the icchantika doctrine it contained was wrong and said so. For this he got into trouble with the upholders of orthodoxy and was expelled for what were deemed heretical views. When the second version of the sūtra arrived, however, he was vindicated. The following passage, taken from Tao-sheng's biography, tells the story of his stance.

When the *Nirvāṇa Sūtra* in six chapters [the first version, translated by Fa-hsien] reached the capital, Tao-sheng [disagreed with its view. He] inquired into the Buddha nature and deeply understood its [true] meaning. After that [despite the assertion of the sūtra], he was convinced that the *icchantika* could become Buddhas. At that time the *Large Nirvāṇa Sūtra* [the full second version, translated by Dharmakṣema] had not yet been brought to China; he stood, therefore, completely alone against the sangha which objected. The conservative party accused him of heretical views contradicting the Dharma. When the quarrel became more and more bitter it was brought before the full assembly and the expulsion of Tao-sheng was proposed. Tao-sheng, before the four divisions of the community, solemnly swore as follows: "In case my opinion does not correctly interpret the sūtra, I pray that in this incarnation my body may be covered with leprosy; but, if I am right, I beg that I may sit on the teacher's chair when I must pass from this life." With these words, he left the assembly in anger.

When the Northern edition [the second version] arrived, it said that the icchantika possess the Buddha nature; it corroborated completely his opinion. Tao-sheng, as soon as he got hold of it, studied it and it became a subject of his lectures. In the tenth month [of the year 432], in winter, he was sitting in the teacher's chair; he looked bright as if inspired and his voice went forth with unusual power. He had discussed his subject several times and had led his hearers into supramundane depths. All those present felt enlightened and comforted. Suddenly, when the lecture drew to its conclusion, the duster (in his hand) trembled and fell. He died leaning against the lectern in the orthodox posture with his face composed. His color being unchanged one could well believe that he was meditating. All Buddhists felt their loss deeply and mourning was general. The monks who had expelled him felt bitter remorse; they too believed (in the correctness of his opinion). That his spiritual mirror had been clear was now proved.

Source: Reprinted by permission of the publisher from Walter Liebenthal, "A Biography of Chu Tao-sheng," *Monumenta Nipponica* 11 (1955): 304–5 (slightly altered).

8.4 REGULATION AND REFORM: AN APOCRYPHAL MONASTIC CODE

For centuries, Buddhist monks in China, though belonging to various Mahāyāna schools, followed exclusively the approximately 250 disciplinary rules set forth in a Mainstream Buddhist monastic discipline (Vinaya). Eventually, however, the need was felt for a set of specifically Mahāyāna precepts, intended to establish a code of conduct more appropriate for bodhisattvas. The *Fanwang ching* (Sūtra of Brahma's Net) purports to be the translation of a Sanskrit original but was actually composed in China in the mid-fifth century C.E. It consists of ten major and forty-eight lesser precepts for bodhisattvas. Some of these were the usual moral interdictions against certain types of actions (e.g., killing, theft, lying, illicit sex, taking intoxicants); others went further and were more positive (e.g., vegetarianism, caring for the sick, helping the oppressed and downtrodden).

These so-called bodhisattva precepts tended to serve a dual role in the regulation of the Chinese sangha. On one hand, they were seen as the culmination of the monastic ordination ceremony; after agreeing to follow the ten precepts of a novice and then the 250 Mainstream Buddhist precepts of a monk, ordinands would now go on to take their fifty-eight bodhisattva vows. On the other hand, laypersons could also take the bodhisattva precepts (without taking the preliminary monastic vows) as an expression of their commitment to and support of Buddhism. Most of the precepts were written in such a way that they could be applied to both monastic and lay devotees, and thus they served to help break down the barriers among monks, nuns, and the laity and to give them all a sense of belonging to a common enterprise and community. This sense of the openness and inclusivity of the Mahāyāna sangha is reflected in the following passage from the fortieth lesser precept of the *Fanwang ching*, in which, in contrast to Mainstream Buddhist traditions (see 2.2.1), it is made clear that anyone can join the order (with the exception of those who have committed one of the seven great offenses). In the forty-first precept, however, certain specifications are added for performing preliminary purificatory penances for other misdeeds.

---

[40] When a Buddhist imparts the precepts to others, he should accord them no preferential treatment: everyone—kings, princes, ministers, officials, monks, nuns, laymen, laywomen, licentious men, licentious women, the lords of the eighteen Brahma worlds, the gods of the six realms of desire, people devoid of sexual organs, hermaphrodites, eunuchs, male and female slaves, all demons and divinities—may receive the precepts. . . . When such a person wishes to receive the precepts, the Dharma master should ask: "Have you committed any of the seven offenses of consequence?" for a bodhisattva who is a Dharma master must not impart the precepts to anyone who has done such acts in this lifetime. The seven offences of consequence are: shedding the blood of a buddha, patricide, matricide, killing one's teacher, killing one's preceptor, hindering the propagation of the Dharma, killing an arhat. Anyone who has committed such offenses, in this lifetime, may not receive the precepts, but all others may. . . .

[41] If someone has violated one of the ten major bodhisattva precepts [against killing, stealing, fornicating, lying, dealing in liquor, denouncing members of the sangha, self-aggrandizement, avarice, anger, or slandering the Triple Gem], they should express their penitence by reciting day and night, in front of the statues of buddhas and bodhisattvas, the ten major and forty-eight lesser precepts. Filled with regret, they should prostrate themselves repeatedly in front of the thousand buddhas of the Triple World, until they see a favorable sign. They should do this for one, two, three weeks, up to a whole year—it is important that a favorable sign be seen. If the Buddha comes and rubs the top of their head, if they see lights, or flowers, or any one of many other extraordinary signs, their sins are erased. If there is no favorable sign, the act of repentance is without fruit, and the person in question cannot, in this lifetime, receive the precepts.

Source: Translated from *Fan-wang ching* in J. J. M. DeGroot, *Le code du Mahāyāna en Chine* (Amsterdam: Johannes Müller, 1893), pp. 73–76.[4]

[4]Alternative English translation, Martine Batchelor, "The Bodhisattva Precepts," unpublished manuscript (Songwang Sa Monastery [Korea]: International Meditation Centre, 1983), pp. 28–30.

8.5 RITUALS AND FESTIVALS: ORDINATION AT PAO-HUA SHAN

The ordination of new monks in China, though it followed originally Indian patterns, evolved in time into a quite distinct process—some would call it an ordeal—during which ordinands not only took their vows but also were given a sort of "boot camp" training in monastic behavior and discipline.

Typically, at least in recent centuries, young Chinese entering the monastic life did so at small local "hereditary temples," where they had their heads shaved and were adopted by the local monk and given some rudimentary training. Ordination per se, however, generally occurred some years later in large public monasteries, along with novices from all over the country. One of the most famous of these large ordination monasteries was Pao-hua Shan in Kiangsu Province, where twice a year several hundred monks were ordained in ceremonies that lasted as long as fifty-three days.

Pao-hua Shan is sometimes thought of as the "West Point" of Chinese ordination monasteries. It prided itself on its strict discipline and the severity of its ordination masters. Ordinands generally spent the first two weeks there simply being schooled in "deportment," relearning how to walk, how to talk, how to eat, how to sleep, how to bow to the Buddha. Then there were several weeks devoted to the memorization and rememorization of liturgical texts. Finally came the monastic vows, which in China were threefold: one first took the novice's vows (the ten precepts; see 3.5.1). Then one took the bhikṣu's, or monk's vows (the 250 rules of the prātimokṣa code). Finally, one took the bodhisattva's vows (the fifty-eight precepts contained in the *Fan-wang ching;* see 8.4).

The following account is a personal reminiscence by a prominent Chinese monk, Chen-hua, who moved to Taiwan in 1948 but who was raised in the monastic system on the mainland during the 1930s and 1940s and who was ordained at Pao-hua Shan.

Having arrived outside the door of the guest department, the four of us did exactly as the rules prescribed. We put our bags down carefully against the pillars on either side of the covered walkway. Then we formed two rows, one on each side of the door. Lifting the foot nearest the door frame, we stepped into the room and then took two-and-a-half more steps. Still standing in two rows, we faced the front of the room and made three prostrations to the Buddha. Then we made a deep bow and stood with our hands joined before our chests, doing our best not to look past the end of our noses. With unrelaxed poise we awaited the advent of the guest prefect. Perhaps the guest prefect had important matters to take care of, or it could be that he was testing our level of endurance. At any rate, we stood there for a long long time, but no one came to greet us. My legs were trembling and my hands cold and aching. I was just considering pulling my hands into my sleeves to warm them when a short fat man in a light-brown, wide-sleeved robe suddenly walked by from behind. My eyes turned for an instant to get a look at his face and then immediately went back to looking at my nose, for the light in his eyes was like a sharp arrow that threatened to shoot in my direction. One glance at him sent a shudder of fright through my body.

The fat man stopped in front of us and rocked his body from side to side. Five words uttered in an incomparably harsh voice erupted from his mouth: "Prostrate yourselves to the Buddha!" We did as we were told. When our prostrations were completed, the brother ordinand standing next to me elbowed me and said, "Three prostrations to our master, the guest prefect!" The four of us got down on the floor again. As to whether or not he was really a guest prefect, only he himself knew. All the older monks at Pao-hua Mountain were qualified to bear themselves this way in front of new ordinands. Such rights were not limited to ordination instructors and guest prefects. The monk whom we assumed to be the guest prefect said, "One prostration." We answered with an "Amitābha," stood up and made another bow, joined our hands before our chests, and stood motionlessly. Without asking us a single question, the guest prefect ordered us to shoulder our bags and follow a young attendant to the guest hall. I thought I had seen the worst of Pao-hua Mountain's monastic code, which was known far and wide for its severity. As it turned out, the facts of the ordination sessions proved me totally wrong. [. . .]

[After several days spent in the guest hall], the day we had been waiting for, and the day we had been living in fear of as well, finally came. One morning after our morning meal of congee, the lay workman [in the guest hall] made the following announcement: "All new ordinands in this hall must shave their heads clean this morning. When finished, wait to be called for a bath. After your bath, each of you must pack your bag and prepare to go to the ordination hall." No one dared move slackly in response to this. Soon the room was thrown into busy confusion; we looked like a theater troupe preparing to move to the next town. When everything was in order, the workman led us to the steps before the main shrine hall. He joined his hands in salute and spoke a few soft words to the yellow-robed ordination instructors waiting there before leaving the scene. We stood there like sheep waiting for slaughter, putting up no resistance at all as the young ordination instructors with willow switches in their hands did with us exactly as they wished. They were probably influenced by the thought of Confucius who said, "Does Heaven say anything? Yet myriad things are all born from it." As they divided us into groups, they used their switches on the bare head of anyone who met their specifications and motioned him to the left or right without uttering a word. When everyone had been divided into groups on the basis of height, the group leaders wrote down the monastic name and style of each person and handed the lists to the instructors. Then came the roll call. When the ordination instructor called his name, one brother, who had probably been a serviceman, answered, "Here." He was given a few hard lashes on top of his head by the instructor, who warned him: "After this, when I call your monastic name, answer 'Amitābha,' not 'here'! Do you understand?" Our ordination brother's features took on a crestfallen appearance as he answered with a slow, unwilling "yes." So funny did this seem to the ordination instructors that they had to cover up their mouths with their hands and twist their necks from side to side in suppressed merriment.

The ordination instructors at Pao-hua Mountain were the most unreasonable, most unfeeling people I have ever come in contact with in my life. Their attitude toward ordinands was: "When in the right, give them three loads to carry; when in the wrong, make them carry three loads." That is to say, when they beat you and verbally abused you, whether you were in the right or not, your one and only permitted response was "Amitābha": sticking up for your rights was absolutely not permitted. One who failed to observe this ran the risk of being beaten to death.

I remember that on the first day of the ordination session, an instructor with a billy club in his hand spoke to us: "Since you've made your decision to come all this way and be ordained, you must rid yourselves of all the habits and failings you learned at your small temples. From now on you will walk, stand, sit, lie, and do everything else exactly as your ordination instructors tell you. If your instructor says that watermelons grow on papaya trees, you repeat after him: 'Watermelons grow on papaya trees.' If an instructor says eggplants grow on gourd vines, you repeat after him: 'Eggplants grow on gourd vines.' If anyone dares not to do as he is told, or tries to be clever, or says watermelons don't grow on papaya trees and eggplants don't grow on gourd vines, don't blame your instructor if he loses his compassion and beats you to death with a billy club. Should that happen, you'll be dragged under your bunk and left there until the end of the session, when all bodies will be taken to the body incinerator for cremation!"

Amitābha! A weak-nerved person would not need to go to such a place for ordination: merely hearing the above tirade would be enough to scare him into a horizontal position from which he would be a long time arising. I assure you, none of what I write here is sensationalism: such things actually happened during the last ordination session before this one.

Perhaps the hindrance from my past karma was too great or perhaps I was just unlucky: at any rate, it just so happened that a monk name Yen-hua was in my group. On the day groups were formed and roll was called (it was also the first day of the session), when the instructor began calling names from our group, he called the name "Yen-hua." Because he was a southerner and I could not clearly make out what he was saying, I caught only the word "hua" and thought he was calling me. I rapidly joined my hands before my chest and answered, "Amitābha." Hearing this, he lifted his head to have a good look at me and then switched me twice across the head. A painful, stinging sensation shot through my head.

"What is your name?" he barked.

"Amitābha. I am called Chen-hua."

"The name I called was Yen-hua. Why did you answer?"

"Amitābha! I . . . "

"You what?"

Seeing him raise the willow switch again, I stammered "I . . . I . . . I . . ." but dared not explain my mistake. Finally, I saved myself by repeating "Amitābha." [. . .]

In order to be fair, I must admit that while the ordination instructors bordered on the barbaric in their treatment of ordinands, they were certainly conscientious about instilling rules in us. They set an unfailingly good example in the four forms of solemn etiquette—walking, standing, sitting, and lying—and served as excellent teachers in this respect. As long as a person possessed a "root of goodness," he could gain much spiritual benefit during the session. Although the things studied were weighted in favor of form or *chieh-hsiang* [the external manifestation of the Vinaya commandments], the usefulness of this for maintaining the Buddhadharma could not be disparaged. Of course, if they had, in addition to the external manifestations of the commandments, imparted some understanding of the "theoretical doctrine of the Vinaya commandments" [*chieh-fa*] and of the "behavior that stems from the purifying effect of the commandments" [*chieh-hsing*], Pao-hua Mountain would truly have been deserving of its fame as the "Number One Mountain of the Vinaya School." What a pity that, like one who "knowing little, is satisfied" or "having drunk but shallowly, imbibes no more," they became bogged down with external forms. [. . .]

Pao-hua Mountain has long been notorious for its poor fare. Outsiders might have a hard time imagining how poor it was during the ordination session. People who stayed there used to say: "When you are supposed to be eating guest fare, you get bean curd leavings." The year I was ordained, which was also the year of victory in the War of Resistance, conditions had become so austere that not only outsiders find it impossible to imagine, but even people who were ordained there before us might not believe it. In the past, although the supposed guest fare was not really guest fare, at least they had bean curd leavings to eat. During our session, bean curd with meals was something no one even mentioned, much less was it guest fare: naturally there were no bean curd leavings to be seen. Someone might ask: "Don't tell me you had no vegetables at all with your rice!" There were, but they were no more than sour, malodorous pickled vegetables that had been kept I don't know how many years. Each one of us got a pinch of these with our rice gruel—just for embellishment. What is more, during the fifty-three-day ordination session, as I remember we had only four meals of boiled rice (on the first and fifteenth of each month): the rest of the time we ate rice gruel three times a day. [. . .]

Some things that happened in the ordination hall were . . . "not worth telling to outsiders," but in order to give readers an idea of the life of monks during ordination, I feel that a description is necessary. . . .

When the night patrolman's board sounded in the morning, there was not even time to rub one's eyes. We had to get out of our beds as quickly as lightning and fumble with our clothes in the murky lamplight. (In order to gain time, some monks went so far as to sleep fully clothed.) That done, we rushed to the bathroom, did our business, then rubbed some water on our faces on the way back to the hall. We put on our robes, made obeisance to Buddha, then sat on our bunks. The officer in charge poured a cup of water with a pinch of salt for each person. Anyone who had snacks could discreetly get them out and eat them. Those who did not got along with the salt water. When the drum had sounded three times, we filed out of the hall to the great shrine hall for morning devotions. This was at about half past three or four o'clock in the morning.

Morning devotions at Pao-hua Mountain were of a length rarely seen at other monasteries. [Just] the gatha [stanza] at the beginning of the *Suramgama Mantra* which reads "unmovable Tathāgata, who is subtle, profound, and upholds everything" had to be repeated for thirty to forty minutes. Perhaps because of the cold weather, some of the older ordinands had to ask leave to go to the restroom before the service was over. As the common saying has it: "You may interfere with heaven and interfere with earth, but you cannot interfere when nature calls." But during our session, this saying did not apply at all. If you felt a pressing need to go to the bathroom at a time which was not set aside for going to the bathroom and you asked an ordination instructor for permission, he would not only refuse your request but also "provide you with a meal of willow noodles" (hit you with a willow switch). Because of this, during devotions and ceremonial rehearsals, even if you needed to go so badly that you could not straighten up your waist, you had no choice but to bear it. If you truly could hold it no longer, you disregarded the consequences, blurted out your intentions, and lit out for the bathroom. Naturally you would have "willow noodles" to eat on your return.

Actually such hardships as morning devotions, dining hall fare, and chores still had a measure of flexibility. Only the "formal precept-takings at the three altars" were pure, unadulterated misery. What are they? In the first ceremony at the first altar we took *śrāmaṇera* [novitiate] precepts [*sha-mi chieh*]; in the second, *bhikṣu* [clerical] precepts [*pi-ch'iu chieh*]; and in the third, *bodhisattva* precepts [*p'u-sa chieh*]. The three stages were characterized by this saying: "*śrāmaṇera* are made to kneel, *bhikṣu* are beaten, and *bodhisattvas* have ordination scars burned on their heads." Judging from my personal experiences of "kneeling, beating, and burning," the most difficult to endure is kneeling rather than burning and beating. Why is this? Because burning and beating lasted only a short time. Also burning happened only once, and one was not beaten every day. Kneeling, however, was a common exercise. Readers who think I am contradicting myself might ask: "After saying that *śrāmaṇera* are made to kneel, how can you turn around and say that kneeling was a common exercise?" Actually, people only emphasized the fact that "*śrāmaṇera* are made to kneel" so they could come up with a clever, easily remembered saying. When we took our *bhikṣu* precepts and *bodhisattva* precepts, we kneeled just as we had before. . . . Just imagine! In the freezing winter cold of a north wind that pierced like a knife, we knelt on the coarse-grained stone slabs of the courtyard before the great shrine hall for at least two hours each time and waited for the end of the ceremony. As the three masters left for their quarters, the ordaining abbot congratulated us on taking the ten *śrāmaṇera* precepts (or *bhikṣu* precepts or *bodhisattva* precepts). We were frozen into corpselike stiffness, and it was all we could do to mechanically answer, "Amitābha."

Source: Reprinted by permission of the publisher from Chen-hua, "Random Talks about My Mendicant Life" (Tsan-hsüeh so-tan), trans. Denis Mair, in *Chinese Sociology and Anthropology* 13, no. 1 (1980): 36–37, 39–42, 45–46, 48–50.

8.6 MEDITATIONAL ENDEAVORS

8.6.1 The Platform Sūtra on Meditation and Wisdom

The story of Hui-neng, the sixth patriarch of Ch'an (Japanese Zen) Buddhism, is one of the best-known in the East Asian Buddhist world. According to this legend (which was fabricated by a later generation of monks pushing a partisan cause and set forth in a relatively late apocryphal text known as the *Platform Sūtra*), Hui-neng lived in the seventh century C.E. He was an illiterate kitchen monk living in the monastery of the fifth patriarch, Hung-jen, when the time came for the latter to pass on the mantle of his office. Accordingly, a contest was held in which monks were asked to write verses on the wall expressing their understanding. The head monk, generally considered to be a prime candidate for succession, wrote a verse comparing the body to the tree of enlightenment and the mind to a clear mirror and suggesting that, by continually polishing the mirror of the mind and not letting any dust collect on it, one can achieve realization. When Hui-neng heard about this, he had a verse of his own inscribed. There are several different versions of this, but one of them reads:

> *Bodhi* originally has no tree.
> The bright mirror also has no stand.
> Fundamentally there is not a single thing.
> Where could dust arise?[5]

For generations, scholars used this story to show a divergence between the so-called Northern School of Ch'an advocating gradual enlightenment (polishing the mirror) and the Southern School, which supported the view of "sudden enlightenment." In fact, modern scholarship has shown this to be a misleading conclusion and the situation to be far more complex. As one authority has put it, this story "should not be used to discuss either the historical or doctrinal development of early Ch'an Buddhism."[6] This does not mean, of course, that we should discount the *Platform Sūtra* that recounts this tale. Whatever its grounding in history and whatever its context, it became an important work for its presentation of the doctrine of inherent enlightenment and its equation of meditation (dhyāna) and wisdom (prajñā). The following is taken from a passage in which the author gives advice to meditators.

My good and learned friends, all people already possess enlightenment and wisdom; it is only because their minds are deluded that they cannot attain to realization themselves, but must seek out a spiritual guide to show them how to see their own nature.

My good and learned friends, to gain this realization is to gain true knowledge.

[5]See John R. McRae, *The Northern School and the Formation of Early Ch'an Buddhism* (Honolulu: University of Hawai'i Press, 1986), p. 237.

[6]John R. McRae, "Shen-hui and the Teaching of Sudden Enlightenment in Early Ch'an Buddhism," in *Sudden and Gradual: Approaches to Enlightenment in Chinese Thought*, ed. Peter N. Gregory (reprint ed., Delhi: Motilal Banarsidass, 1991), p. 229.

My good and learned friends, meditation and wisdom are the foundation of my teaching. But never make the mistake of saying that meditation and wisdom are different; they are one substance, not two; meditation is the substance of wisdom, and wisdom is the activity of meditation. Where there is wisdom, meditation is there, and where there is meditation, there is wisdom.

My good and learned friends, this means that meditation and wisdom are the same. Students of the Way, be careful: do not say that wisdom comes after meditation, or that meditation comes after wisdom, or that meditation and wisdom are different; to hold such a view implies that there is duality in the world.

If your words are good, but your heart is not, then your meditation and your wisdom will not be the same; but if your heart and words are both good, then inner and outer are of one piece, and your meditation and your wisdom are the same.

The practice of your own realization does not lie in argument. If you argue about what comes after what, you are deluded, you never settle the argument: you think that things really exist, and you never escape from birth and being and decay and death.

We are told to practice the meditation wherein we see all things as one, and this means simply to make your mind direct, whether walking or standing or sitting or lying down. The scriptures say: A direct mind is the object of the Way; a direct mind is the Pure Land.

Do not let your mind be crooked and your mouth speak of directness: if you say that all is one, yet do not see things deep and sharp, then you are no disciple of the Buddha; but to make your mind direct and to be attached to no event, is called the meditation wherein all is one.

Deluded people who like to label things say that this meditation, this direct mind, is to sit unmoving, to cast aside error and let no thoughts occur. If this were so, their teaching would simply turn us into inanimate objects, and set up a barricade upon the Way. But the Way should flow freely: why should we clog it like that? When the mind is not attached to events, then the Way flows freely; it is when the mind is attached that it gets all tangled up. . . .

My good and learned friends, how then are meditation and wisdom the same? They are like a lamp and its light: when there is a lamp, there is light, and there is no light without a lamp. The lamp is the substance of the light, and the light is the activity of the lamp. They have two names, but their substance is not two: my teaching of meditation and wisdom is like that.

My good and learned friends, in the Dharma there is no "sudden enlightenment" or "gradual enlightenment," but people may be intelligent or dull. The deluded understand gradually, and the realized practice suddenly. This realization is to know for yourself your original mind, to see for yourself your original nature, and then there is no difference. But without this realization you wander in the world for long eons.

My good and learned friends, my teaching from the very beginning has established no thought as its doctrine, no label as its substance, and no attachment as its foundation.

No label means to make no labels in the midst of labels; no thought means not to think in the midst of thought; no attachment is the original nature of man.

Thought after thought, and they do not stop; past thought and present thought and future thought, thought after thought continues on, and they never cease. But if you can detach just one of these thoughts from events [dharmas], you can separate the Body of Reality [Dharmakāya] from the Body of Form [rūpakāya], and in the midst of thought you will yet be without attachment. If a single thought is attached to an event, then all your thoughts will be attached, and this is called bondage; but if none of your thoughts is attached to anything, then this is freedom from bondage. Thus we take no attachment as our foundation.

My good and learned friends, no label means to be free of all labels; when you just stop sticking labels on it, the substance of your very nature is pure. Thus we take no label as our substance.

To be undefiled by the thought that things are real is called no thought. When your mind frees itself from thinking that things really exist, then your thoughts do not move toward events. But never cease being aware of things as they happen, or sit there trying to cast aside all your thoughts; to cut off thought completely is simply to die and then be reborn somewhere else. Students of the Way, take heed: if your mind is not aware of events, then you mislead yourself, and how much worse when you encourage others! Deluded, you do not see your own delusion, and you slander the teachings of the scriptures. Thus we take no thought as our doctrine.

Source: Reprinted by permission of Wadsworth, Inc. from Stephan Beyer, *The Buddhist Experience* (Encino, CA: Dickenson, 1974), pp. 162–63 (slightly altered).[7]

8.6.2 Constantly Sitting and Constantly Walking

Chih-i (538–597) is widely remembered as the founder of the T'ien-t'ai school of Chinese Buddhism. In his many writings, he not only systematized the sophisticated notion of the threefold truths that came to lie at the basis of T'ien-t'ai thought, but he also set forth multiple systems of meditation. In his *Treatise on the Great Calming and Discernment* (Mo-ho chih-kuan), he states that although there are numerous methods of practice, they may be summarized as comprising the samādhis of (1) constantly sitting, (2) constantly walking, (3) part sitting and part walking, and (4) neither sitting nor walking. These four kinds of practice, which involved a variety of meditational techniques, soon became one of the hallmarks of the T'ien-t'ai (and later, in Japan, of the Tendai) school. The following selection from an article by Daniel Stevenson describes the first two of these techniques.

---

[7]Original text and alternative English translation, Philip B. Yampolsky, *The Platform Sūtra of the Sixth Patriarch* (New York: Columbia University Press, 1967), pp. 5–7, 135–39.

Chih-i identifies the first of the four kinds of samādhi [the samādhi through constant sitting] with the practice known as *i-hsing san-mei,* rendered here as "one-practice samādhi.". . . As Chih-i describes it in the *Mo-ho chih-kuan,* one-practice samādhi is to be performed in a quiet room or a secluded and untrammeled spot. The essential requisite is that the immediate environs be free of any disturbance, human or otherwise. Only a single rope bed for meditation is to be placed in the hall; no other seats or daises should be added. The practice itself lasts for a fixed period of ninety days and may be performed alone or in a small group. Over the entire duration of this three-month period the meditator applies himself zealously to the practice of sitting motionless in the traditional "lotus" meditation posture. With the exception of brief stretches of walking meditation and attending to such necessities as eating and relieving himself, he vows never to sleep, lie down, stand, wander aimlessly about, or lean against any object for support. For this reason the practice is referred to as "constant sitting.". . .

Chih-i distinguishes two basic approaches to meditative practice in this one-practice samādhi: the radical approach of directly contemplating the reality of the Dharma-realm (or the Dharma-body of the Buddha) and the more expedient approach of concentrating the mind on the name, idealized image, and merits (the body of form) of a particular Buddha.

Providing that the meditator possesses the requisite meditative skill, the ideal approach is to "renounce all fallacious theories, cast aside all confused thinking, refrain from any random pondering, avoid seizing upon any characteristics, and simply absorb oneself completely in the direct experiencing of all objects as [identical to] the Dharmadhātu and in contemplating one's own [subjective] mind as [also] being uniform with the Dharmadhātu." [. . .]

If the meditator becomes exhausted, or illness and other forms of obstruction begin to overwhelm his powers of contemplation, or if he is a novice who has not yet developed the powers of meditative insight necessary to take up this first type of discernment effectively, then he turns to the second more tangible approach. Selecting a Buddha of his own choosing, he faces in the direction of that particular Buddha's realm and single-mindedly "invokes that Buddha's name, generates a deep sense of shame [over his own inability to practice as he should], repents, and entrusts his fate to him." [. . .]

By resorting to [invocation of the Buddha's] name, mindfulness is strengthened. [Once one] perceives the minor and major marks of the Buddha [through visualization], samādhi proper is complete. Once samādhi proper is complete, one perceives all the Buddhas. These Buddhas are perceived in the same manner as one sees one's own image reflected on the surface of water. This is known as the initial [experience of] samādhi. . . .

The radical approach of complete "non-abiding" and immediate identification with the Dharmadhātu and the expedient approach of fixing the mind on the Buddha's form and reciting his name were intended to function in close support of one another. If thoroughly pursued enough, either can convey the meditator to the same end, whereby, as Chih-i describes it, he "enters one-practice samādhi, perceives all the Buddhas face to face, and ascends to the stage of assurance of full bodhisattvahood."

Constantly walking samādhi is identified with the practice known as . . . *pratyutpanna* samādhi, [shorthand for] "the samādhi wherein one finds oneself standing face to face with all the Buddhas of the present age.". . . Like the one-practice samādhi, the *pratyutpanna* samādhi is to be performed in isolation. The meditator selects and adorns a hall for practice, prepares all the necessary accoutrements of offering, and lays out various delicacies, fruit, incense, and flowers. Having washed himself thoroughly, he changes into a new set of robes, which is to be worn at all times in the inner sanctuary where the practice is performed. Whenever he leaves this chamber to tend to necessities, he changes once again into an older set. The practice itself lasts for a fixed period of ninety days, over the duration of which the meditator must continuously circumambulate an altar to the Buddha Amitābha. He vows never to entertain worldly thoughts or desires, never to lie down or leave the hall, and, aside from the times when he eats his meals, never arbitrarily to sit down or stop to rest until the three months are completed. [. . .]

The meditative discernment itself centers around the visualization of the thirty-two major marks and eighty minor excellent qualities of the Buddha Amitābha. The practice is performed repeatedly, "in reverse order from the thousand-spoked wheels on the soles of his feet to the indiscernable *uṣṇīṣa* on the crown of his head, and then in the normal order from the crown of the head back to the thousand-spoked wheel." The visualization is carried out concurrently with the invocation of the Buddha's name and slow circumambulation of the hall so that, "step after step, recitation after recitation, recollection after recollection, [the practitioner's] mindfulness is wholly upon the Buddha Amitābha."

The devotional element in this practice, just as in the one-practice samādhi, undoubtedly plays a key role; however, as the practitioner becomes more skilled at constructing the mental image of the Buddha, the orientation of the visualization begins to shift radically. Eventually the eidetic image of Amitābha loses its devotional character altogether and instead becomes the basis for a simple dialectical investigation into the nature of mind and the noetic act itself. . . . Chih-i describes the technique as follows:

> Where does the Buddha that I am contemplating come from? [He does not come from somewhere else, and] I do not go off to reach him. Whatever [feature] I turn my attention to thereupon appears. This Buddha is simply mind perceiving mind. Mind is the [visualized] Buddha [that is the object, and likewise] mind is the [subjective] "I" [that sees the Buddha]. When it perceives the Buddha, mind is not itself aware of mind, nor does it itself perceive mind. When the mind gives rise to thoughts, then there is delusion. When it is free of thoughts, it is nirvāṇa.

Chih-i distinguishes three levels to [this] practice of "mindfulness of Buddha" (*nien-fo*). The first involves the mindfulness or contemplation of a Buddha through the visualization of the major marks and minor excellent qualities of his idealized physical form. The second is the contemplation of the more abstract qualities that mark a Buddha's spiritual omniscience, such as the forty qualities unique to a Buddha. The third and final stage involves the contemplation or mindfulness of Buddha as he is in his essence—the essential nature or true character of all phenomena. At this stage all vestiges of discrimination and dualistic thinking, together with any sense of Buddha being a real entity or an object of devotion, completely vanish, and reality stands directly revealed. . . . Chih-i explains:

> He does not cling to the [Buddha's] body of form, nor does he adhere to the [Buddha's essence] body of Dharma, but throughly realizes that all phenomena are eternally quiescent just like empty space.

Source: Reprinted by permission of the publisher from Daniel B. Stevenson, "The Four Kinds of Samādhi in Early T'ien-tai Buddhism," in *Traditions of Meditation in Chinese Buddhism*, ed. Peter N. Gregory, The Kuroda Institute Studies in East Asian Buddhism, no. 4 (Honolulu: University of Hawai'i Press, 1986), pp. 54–56, 58–60.

8.7 WOMEN AND THE SANGHA

8.7.1 The Arrival of the Sri Lankan Nuns

One of the Vinaya rules for the ordination of women states that they must be accepted into the community by both the order of nuns and the order of monks. Historically this has presented something of a dilemma: when and where there are no nuns already in the order, it would seem impossible to ordain new ones. Because the early Buddhist monastic missionaries to China from India were, as far as we know, all males, they faced this problem of the absence of nuns when female Chinese converts started wanting to be ordained. They got around it by invoking the example of the very first Buddhist nun, Mahāprajāpatī, who, after all, was ordained only by males (i.e., the Buddha) (see 2.1.4), and they also argued that the rules could be relaxed in "frontier lands" such as China. But there were some in both the bhikṣu and the bhikṣuṇī sangha who felt uncomfortable about this. The arrival of some nuns from Sri Lanka in the first half of the fifth century, therefore, caused a certain amount of excitement and was greeted as a chance to enhance the legitimacy of the nun's position. The following selection from a collection of biographies of Chinese nuns tells the story.

In the sixth year of the yüan-chia reign period [429 C.E.], a foreign boat captain named Nan-t'i brought some Buddhist nuns from Sri Lanka to the capital of the Sung dynasty. The Sri Lankan nuns stayed at Luminous Blessings Convent.

Not long after taking up residence there, they asked [the nun] Seng-kuo, "Before we came to this country, had foreign nuns ever been here?"

She replied, "No, there have not been any."

They asked again ["If that is the case,] how did the Chinese women who became nuns receive the monastic obligations from both the Assembly of Monks and the Assembly of Nuns [as they are required to do according to the rules?]"

Seng-kuo replied, "They received the obligations only from the Assembly of Monks."

"Those women who went through the ritual of entering the monastic life began the reception of the monastic obligations. This reception was an expedient to cause people to have great respect for the monastic life. Our eminent model for this expedient is the Buddha's own stepmother, Mahāprajāpatī, who was deemed to have accepted the full monastic obligation by taking on herself, and therefore for all women for all time, the eight special prohibitions incumbent on women wanting to lead the monastic life. [These she accepted from the Buddha only.] The five hundred women of the Buddha's clan who also left the household life at the same time as Mahāprajāpatī considered her as their instructor."

Although Seng-kuo agreed, she herself had a few doubts [about the validity of the rituals that had been observed in China regarding women leaving the household life]. Therefore she asked the central Asian missionary monk Gunavarman [who was an expert on the subject]. He agreed with her understanding of the situation.

She further inquired of him, "Is it possible to go through the ritual [of accepting the full monastic obligation] a second time?"

Gunavarman replied, "[The Buddhist threefold action of] morality, meditation, and wisdom progresses from the slight to the obvious. Therefore, receiving the monastic obligations a second time is of greater benefit than receiving them only once."

[Four years later] in the tenth year [433], Nan-t'i, the ship captain, brought eleven more nuns from Sri Lanka, including one named Tessara. The first group of nuns, who by this time had become fluent in Chinese, requested the Indian missionary monk Sanghavarman to preside over the ritual for bestowing the monastic rules on women at the ceremonial platform in Southern Grove Monastery. That day more than three hundred women accepted once again the full monastic obligation [this time from both the Assembly of Monks and the Assembly of Nuns].

Source: Reprinted by permission of the publisher from Kathryn Ann Tsai, *Lives of the Nuns* (Honolulu: University of Hawai'i Press, 1994), pp. 53–54.[8]

8.7.2 The Legend of Miao-shan

The story of the legendary Chinese princess Miao-shan, who defied her father's plans to marry her off and pursued a religious vocation, is significant for the intersection of several themes. First it shows the situation of a young

[8]Original text: Pao-ch'ang, *Pi-ch'iu-ni chuan* (Taishō shinshū daizōkyō, ed. J. Takakusu and K. Watanabe [Tokyo: 1924–29], no. 2063, vol. 50).

Chinese woman utterly dominated by her father and living in a context where filial piety is the norm. Second, it reflects a Buddhist solution to a classic dilemma: Miao-shan defies her father in order to become a nun, but because of this she is eventually able to save her father. Thus, despite her original apparent rejection of filial piety, in the end her sacrifice makes her a model of filial piety. Finally, Miao-shan is also thought of as a manifestation of the bodhisattva of compassion, the so-called Goddess of Mercy, Kuan-yin (Avalokiteśvara). Indeed, her legend may, in part, be responsible for the feminization of Avalokiteśvara as this deity's cult moved from India to China and he/she was transformed from a male bodhisattva into a female one.

Once in the past the Lü [Vinaya] Master [Tao-]hsüan dwelt in the Ling-kan ssu in the Chung-nan mountains, practising religion. In a vision, a *deva* [deity] attended him. The Master asked the *deva:* "I have heard that the Mahāsattva [great being, or bodhisattva] Kuan-yin has many links and manifestations on Sahā, this earth. In what place are they most abundant?"

The *deva* replied: "The Bodhisattva's appearances follow no fixed rule, but the pre-eminent site of his bodily manifestation is Hsiang-shan."

The Master enquired: "Where is this 'Hsiang-shan' now?"

The deva replied: "Over two hundred *li* to the south of Mount Sung there are three hills in a row. The middle one is Hsiang-shan—that is the Bodhisattva's place. To the north-east of the hill there was in the past a king whose name was King Miao-chuang-yen. His lady was named Pao-te. The king had no crown prince, only three daughters: the eldest Miao-yen, the second Miao-yin, the youngest Miao-shan. Of these three daughters two were already married. Only the third, in conduct and appearance far transcending the ordinary, always wore dirty clothes and took but one meal a day, never eating strongly flavoured food, and pursued this life of abstention and religious discipline without faltering in her resolve.

The king said to Miao-shan: "You are no longer a child now—you ought to take a husband."

Miao-shan said: "The river of desire has mighty waves, the sea of suffering has fathomless depths. I would never, for the sake of one lifetime of glory, plunge into aeons of misery. I earnestly desire to leave my home and pursue the way of religion."

The king angrily cast her out into the flower garden at the rear of the palace, cut off her food and drink, and made her mother strongly urge her to take a husband.

Miao-shan said: "Empty things come to an end—I desire what is infinite."

Furious at hearing this, the king summoned Hui-chen, a nun of the White Sparrow monastery, [and charged her] to take [Miao-shan] off to the monastery to grow vegetables, and to devise ways to induce her to return to the palace [by treating her harshly and giving her all the heaviest chores to do].

Miao-shan said [to the nun]: "Surely you have heard that those who obstruct someone's monastic vocation will suffer torments for countless aeons? Do you dare oppose the best interests of the Buddhist religion and willingly accept the retribution of hell?"

The nun answered: "I am under the king's orders. This is nothing to do with me."

Miao-shan would not consent. She remained firm in her desire to enter the order.

The nun reported it to the king, who in a great rage ordered troops to surround the monastery, behead the nuns and burn down their quarters.

[But] Miao-shan was taken off by a *nāga* spirit to the foot of Hsiang-shan, not a hair of her injured.

She built a hut and lived there, clothed in grass and eating from the trees, unrecognised by anyone.

Three years had passed by when the king, in return for his crimes of destroying a monastery and killing the religious, contracted jaundice and could find no rest.

Doctors could not cure him.

He advertised far and wide for someone to make him well.

At that point a strange monk appeared, saying: "I have a divine remedy which can cure Your Majesty's sickness."

The king asked: "What medicine do you have?"

The monk said: "If you use the arms and eyes of one free of anger to blend into a medicine and take it, then you will be cured."

The king said: "This medicine is hard to find."

The monks said: "No, it is not. There is a Hsiang-shan in the southwest of Your Majesty's dominion, and on the very peak of the hill is a holy one whose practice of religion has come to completion. This person has no anger. If you put your request to her she will certainly make the gift."

The king ordered an equerry to take incense into the hills and bow to the holy one, saying: "Our lord the king is sick. We venture to trouble you with a request for your arms and eyes in order to save the king's life. This will lead him to turn his mind to enlightenment."

Hearing this, the holy one gouged out her two eyes and severed both arms with a knife, handing them over to the equerry. At that moment, the whole earth shook. The equerry returned to the capital.

There they made the monk blend the medicine. The king took it and recovered from his sickness.

In solemn procession the king then went to Hsiang-shan, where he offered humble thanks and veneration.

He saw the holy one with no arms or eyes, physically defective. The king and his lady, looking from either side, were deeply moved to a painful thought: "The holy one looks very like our daughter."

The holy one said: "I am indeed Miao-shan. Your daughter has offered her arms and eyes to repay her father's love."

Hearing her words, the king embraced her with loud weeping. He said: "I was so evil that I have made my daughter suffer terrible pain."

The holy one said: "I suffer no pain. Having yielded up my mortal eyes I shall receive diamond eyes; having given up my human arms I shall receive golden-coloured arms. If my vow is true these results will certainly follow."

Heaven and earth then shook. And then the holy one was revealed as the All-merciful Bodhisattva Kuan-shih-yin of the Thousand Arms and Thousand Eyes, solemn and majestic in form, radiant with dazzling light, lofty and magnificent, like the moon amid the stars. The king and his lady, together with the entire population of the land, conceived goodness in their hearts and committed themselves to the Three Treasures.

Source: Reprinted by permission of the author from Glen Dudbridge, *The Legend of Miao-shan* (London: Ithaca Press, 1978), pp. 25–34.[9]

8.7.3 A Buddhist Attack on Sexism

Among the many targets for reform as China moved into the twentieth century was the status of women in society. Voices of change were raised from a variety of perspectives against such things as concubinage, foot binding, and traditional gender roles. T'an Ssu-t'ung (1865–98) was an intellectual, a reformer, and a martyr from Hunan Province who was eager to find solutions to what he perceived as China's decline and backwardness vis-à-vis the rest of the world. Starting off as an ethnocentrist, he then became a champion of westernization before finally turning to Buddhism as a vehicle for reform that could help him synthesize the Chinese and Western traditions. In his view, the oppression of women was in part related to male desires—what he here calls "lust"—and Buddhism, as a antidote to lust, could well be used to oppose sexism.

How can people be free from lust if they treat others as well as themselves as sex objects? Hence to regard men as superior to women is the most savage and unreasonable social custom. A man is allowed to have a large number of concubines to serve him, and can indulge himself in sex without restraint; but the penalty for a woman who has lapsed into lust is death. This in time leads to the practice of drowning female babies, and people tolerate doing what bees, ants, leopards, or tigers would not do. What can we say in defence of China when she is guilty of a crime for which even the loss of her nationhood cannot atone? Though the idea of "transforming women into men" is found in the Buddhist scriptures, it is confined to Hīnayāna teaching. Written in such Mahāyāna Buddhist sūtras as the *Garland Sūtra* and the *Vimalakīrti Sūtra* is the assertion that the female body should remain as it is, not needing to be changed into that of a male. There is nothing to suggest men are superior to women. If we understand that both men and women are the basic components of heaven and earth, that they both have countless virtues and have great things to do, that they are both equal and have the same roles to perform in society, and that originally they were not born into this world for the

[9]Original text: *Hsiao-shih chin-kang k'o-i hui-yao chu-chieh,* ed. Chüeh-lien, in *Dai Nihon zokuzōkyō,* ed. T. Nakano (Kyoto, 1905–12), 1:129a–b. For an updated translation of a portion of the text, see Glen Dudbridge, "Miao-shan on Stone: Two Early Inscriptions," *Harvard Journal of Asiatic Studies* 42 (1982): 589–614.

sake of lust, then we should also know that "beautiful women" are simply made up of powder and clothes. When the powder and clothes are taken away, they are but flesh and blood, no different from us and having no feminine beauty that we can be fond of. With this understanding, we can then guide people so that men and women can have social intercourse; we can liberate them so that they can get used to each other, until they feel spontaneous in each other's company and mutually forget their differences, as in the mutual intercourse of friends; at that stage, they will not be conscious of the sex difference, let alone lust.

Source: Reprinted by permission of the publisher from Chan Sin-wai, *Buddhism in Late Ch'ing Political Thought* (Hong Kong: Chinese University Press, 1985), pp. 109–10.[10]

8.8 SANGHA AND SOCIETY: THE COMMERCIALIZATION OF SERVICES

In all countries where Buddhism was established, the sangha became the recipient of donations. When these donations consisted of food and clothes, they were consumed and utilized. When they consisted of wealth and real estate, they were kept and reinvested in various ways. Thus some monasteries came to be owners of vast estates that were cultivated for them by others and whose income they enjoyed. At the same time, some gained local monopolies on certain commercial services, such as the milling of grain or the lending of money. And they became important employers of craftsmen, artists, construction workers, and others. In this way, Buddhist monasteries in China were economically significant and could become quite wealthy.

Not all monasteries, however, owned land. Those that did not sometimes had to depend on the rituals they performed for laypeople as a primary source of income. As the following selection makes clear, some of the money went to support the monks involved in the rites, but not all of it.

[S]ome of the large urban monasteries that did not have income from land . . . had no choice but to give priority to Buddhist services, which at some of them became "big business." For a firsthand and perhaps somewhat embittered description of this we shall hear from a monk who spent a year at the Fa-tsang Ssu in Shanghai. This temple was housed in a new building in the French concession, looking from the outside like any other house in the block. When he was living there in 1938, it had over a hundred monks in residence. Here is what he [said] about it.

> That was a place that really made money conducting Buddhist services. From morning to night, from the beginning of the year to the end, there

---

[10]Original text in *T'an Ssu-t'ung ch'üan-chi* [*The Complete Works of T'an Ssu-t'ung*], ed. Ts'ai Shang-ssu and Fang Hsing, 2 vols. (Beijing: Chung-hua shu-chü, 1981), 2:304.

were plenary masses. I was one of the ordinary monks. During the day I recited a penance—one penance took the whole day—and in the evening a *fang yen-k'ou* [ritual to help ancestors who have become hungry ghosts]. There was no time to rest. If you wanted to rest, you had to ask for leave, and this was very hard to get. If, for example, you said that you were sick, you would be told that since you could not recite penances, you should go to the buddha recitation hall and recite buddha's name. There it was possible to sleep—and still get your 25 cents a day [Chinese currency]. Laymen were willing to pay for this because the merit generated could be transferred to the deceased, just as in the case of a penance. Regardless of the type of work performed, the monastery charged one dollar per monk per day for daytime work, of which the monk got 25 cents; for an evening's work, the monastery charged $2, of which each celebrant at the lower table got 40 cents, while the three who presided got 80 cents. So in the course of twenty-four hours the ordinary monk could make 65 cents. But at that time 65 cents was a reasonable amount of money. We made a little more when we went out to perform services in people's homes—walking around the corpse on the first night, for example. They had to pay $1.50 per monk per night for this, out of which we got 50 cents apiece. Except when we were in people's homes, the monastery provided our food. We were not paid directly, but given bamboo slips each day. We kept these until the end of the half month, and then got a lump-sum in accordance with the slips we had accumulated.

If one was willing to stay there for many years and put up with the misery of the work, one could become an officer of the monastery and really make money. The abbot, the retired abbot, the manager, the guest prefect, the precentor, the proctor, and other high officers would each get a bamboo slip for each of the services performed in a given day, so that if ten groups of monks performed services, the abbot would get ten slips, whereas the monks participating would only get one apiece. The monastery used to cheat its patrons. They were laymen and did not understand. There should have been ten or twenty monks performing at each service, but because business was so good, there were not enough to go around and they would be divided into small groups—as few as three or four monks. Another way in which patrons were cheated was by pretending that the monks in the great shrine-hall were reciting a penance for only one family of worshippers. If the Wang family came they would be shown the monks reciting there and told that it was for the Wangs, and if the Chang family came they would be shown the same monks and told that it was for the Changs. When the monks left the shrine-hall to transfer merit in front of the tablet of the departed, they would do it first before the Wang tablet and then before the Chang tablet, each in its own hall for the occasion. The monastery used to make an enormous amount of money.

Ordinarily one could not leave the premises—except to perform Buddhist services at people's homes. It was like living in a prison. There was a meditation hall, but it was not a real one; it was just used for Buddhist services. There was no meditation. Life was harder physically at the Fatsang Ssu than it was at [the training center of] Chin Shan, but one made more money. It was like being in business.

The monk who told me this belonged to the rank and file. . . . His account reveals the same attitude toward the "higher-ups" that one finds among enlisted men in the army. Though most of what he said was confirmed, certain important details were contradicted by another informant who spent a year in the Fa-tsang Ssu at about the same time (1938–1939). Because he was well connected, he was given an apartment to live in and the rank of thurifer. He denied categorically that every high officer received one credit for each Buddhist service held, whether he attended or not. "That way officers would have made a *terrible* lot of money," he said. "How could the establishment have paid them?" What actually happened, he went on, was that one credit for each service was given to all the officers *collectively*. At the end of the month the total was divided up among them in equal shares as a solatium. Thus if there were ten officers and fifteen services a day, each officer received one and a half credits. "That other monk you were talking to remembered it wrong. He didn't know about it because he was never an officer himself."

According to this second informant the Fa-tsang Ssu was one of the three strictest monasteries in Shanghai. True, its work was almost entirely performing Buddhist services, but how else could it have survived? It had no land. The situation was different at the Liu-yün Ssu, where he had held office for many years. The Liu-yün Ssu received enough grain rent from farmland south of Shanghai to feed its residents four months of the year. Therefore it was able to operate a meditation hall where thirty to a hundred monks followed the same rules and schedule as at Chin Shan. They normally took no part in rites for the dead, which were manned by other residents in much the same way as at the Fa-tsang Ssu.

During his years as visitors' prefect this informant had often had the duty of dealing with the public, taking their orders for Buddhist services, keeping them company while these were under way, and collecting payment afterwards. He said that a typical conversation with a donor might run as follows:

Donor: "My father's sixtieth birthday is on the 18th and I would like to have a service performed."

Visitors' Prefect: "Would you like us to perform a one-day Longevity Penance or to recite the Longevity Sūtra for a day?"

Donor: "I'd like you to recite the Longevity Sūtra."

Prefect: "How many monks do you want to ask?"

Donor: "What is the minimum?"

Prefect: "With us here the minimum is seven."

Donor: What is the maximum?"

Prefect: "That's as you like—108, for example."

Donor: "This time I am afraid I cannot afford to ask too many."

Prefect: "Twenty-four, then, or twelve?"

Donor: "With twenty-four, how much would I have to give?"

Prefect: "The monks are now getting 40 cents apiece."

Donor: "Per day?"

Prefect: "That's what the monks get; our temple takes one dollar in all."

Donor: "All right, make it twelve monks. Then we will want to eat a vegetarian meal."

Prefect: "Do you want to have superior dishes or ordinary ones?"

Donor: "I want superior ones."

Prefect: "Preparing them on your behalf would be $12 per table."

Donor: "There would be thirty of us, which would be three tables. Let me see, the total would be about $50."

Prefect (perfunctorily): "Amitābha!"

Source: Reprinted with permission of the publisher from Holmes Welch, *The Practice of Chinese Buddhism 1900–1950* (Cambridge, MA: Harvard University Press, 1967), pp. 199–202.

CHAPTER 9

Buddhists and the Practice of Buddhism: Japan

To some extent, Japanese Buddhism may be thought of as a series of imports from China. Over the centuries, starting perhaps as early as 500 C.E., both lay devotees and monks traveled to the mainland, bringing back with them layer after layer of Buddhist teachings and practices along with other Chinese cultural traditions. At the same time, however, as the religion developed in Japan, it often did so along paths not followed on the mainland. The selections in this chapter will illustrate both continuities and discontinuities between these two major developments of East Asian Buddhism.

9.1. MYTHIC HISTORY: THE LEGEND OF PRINCE SHŌTOKU

The history of the introduction of Buddhism into Japan, like the history of its introduction into other countries, is narrated in legend. Though there is some evidence of foreign (Chinese and Korean) monks living in Japan early in the sixth century C.E., according to the *Chronicle of Japan* (*Nihongi*), it was in 552 that the king of the Korean kingdom of Paekche sent a Buddha image and a number of sūtras to the island, where they were received, honored, and used by members of the Soga clan in their bid for power and influence. For some years, the fate of Buddhism knew its ups and downs, until it became assured with the victory of the Sogas in the late sixth century. Thus it was that Prince Regent Shōtoku, who acceded to power about 592 with Soga support, came to be renowned as the father and establisher of Japanese Buddhism.

Shōtoku and his aunt, the empress Suiko, were interested in importing Chinese culture to Japan in an effort to consolidate the country, and they perceived Buddhism to be a part of that culture. Thus, in the famous seventeen-article "Constitution" of Japan, with which Prince Shōtoku is credited, we can read alongside the proposal to propagate a number of basically Confucian principles the injunction to revere sincerely the Triple Gem of the Buddha, Dharma, and Sangha.

In the popular tradition, Shōtoku's Buddhist affiliation was much emphasized. He came to be thought of as a bodhisattva who had been miraculously conceived, had been remarkably precocious, and had become a great scholar. (He is credited with commentaries on three important sūtras: the *Lion's Roar of Queen Śrīmālā* [see 4.3.5], the *Vimalakīrti nirdeśa* [see 4.4.4], and the *Lotus Sūtra* [see 4.1 and 5.2.1].) He is also said to have founded numerous early Buddhist monasteries, among them the Hōryūji (near Nara) and the Shitennōji (in present-day Osaka). The following passage from the first chapter of a collection of Buddhist tales compiled by the monk Chingen about 1040 C.E. gives some sense of the way his legend developed.

Prince Shōtoku was the second son of Emperor Toyohi [Yōmei]. The imperial consort, the mother of Prince Shōtoku, once dreamed that a gilded priest told her that he had vowed to save the people and would be conceived in her. The consort asked who he was and the priest replied that he was a bodhisattva residing in the West. The consort told the priest that her body was impure and asked him how and why he should remain in her. The priest responded that he would not mind the impurity, but just wished to contact a human being. Saying this, the priest leaped into her mouth. The consort woke and felt as if she had swallowed something. Afterwards, she knew that she was pregnant.

Eight months passed and the consort heard a voice talking in her abdomen. When the prince was born, red and yellow lights from the west suddenly illuminated the interior of the palace. The prince spoke well and understood matters concerning people.

About that time, the Buddhist writings first arrived in Japan as tribute from Kudara [Paekche in Korea]. The prince told the emperor that he wished to inspect them. The surprised emperor asked the prince his reason. The prince answered, "In my former existence, I lived in Nan-yüeh in China for several decades practicing the Buddhist Way."

At the age of six, the prince was a good-looking boy releasing a pleasant fragrance from his body. The fragrance impregnated the clothing of those who held the prince and was retained for several months.

One day, Nichira came to Japan from Kudara. He released radiance from his body. Nichira saw the prince dressed in old clothes following other children into a building. He pointed at the prince and said, "He is a Buddha." The surprised prince went away. Nichira took off his shoes and ran [after him]. . . . Kneeling on the ground, Nichira apologized and said to the prince respectfully, "I pay my respects to Kannon [the bodhisattva Avalokiteśvara], the king of [this] small eastern country who transmits the Law [Dharma]." As he spoke, Nichira released a great radiance from his body. The prince, too, emitted light from his forehead. The prince explained to those about him that Nichira had been his disciple when the prince had lived in China in his previous life. Since Nichira constantly worshipped Nitten [the sun god], his body released radiance.

Empress Suiko made Shōtoku the crown prince and left everything in his charge. One day when the prince was paying attention to political affairs, eight persons . . . came and all appealed simultaneously to him. The prince understood all the appeals and gave proper answers to each. So the government officials . . . called him the "Prince with Eight Ears. . . ."

There is a separate hall called the Dream Hall in the prince's palace compound. The prince bathed three times a month and entered the hall. When commenting on certain sūtras and not sure of the meaning, he used to go into the hall. A gilded person always appeared from the east and assisted the prince with appropriate meanings. . . .

For the first time in Japan, the prince drafted and instituted the Seventeen Articles of the Constitution which overjoyed the people.

Once when the empress requested the prince to present lectures on the *Shōmangyō* [*Lion's Roar of Queen Śrīmālā Sūtra*] for three days, the prince, dressed in priestly robes with a *shubi* staff in his hand, took the seat [as] a venerable master. After the prince finished his lectures, lotus blossoms a few feet in height fell from the sky.

The empress greatly marvelled when those flowers were presented on the following morning and she constructed a temple, the Tachibana Temple, where the blossoms had fallen. Again the empress had the prince give lectures on the *Hokekyō* [*Lotus Sūtra*] for seven days and granted him three hundred *chō* of rice fields in Harima Province, which were eventually donated to the Hōryūji Temple.

The prince's wife was from the Kashiwade clan. One day the prince said to his wife, "You have understood me and have done nothing against my will. I am now close to my end and I am going to have you buried with me in my grave. For many past decades until my old age, I have recited the *Hokekyō,* practiced the Buddhist way, become the crown prince of this small country, transmitted *The Lotus,* and propagated the deep meanings of the wonderful Law of the One Vehicle which provides salvation for all. . . ."

Hearing this, the princess wept, wetting her sleeves with tears. . . .

The prince bathed and dressed in new clothes. The princess, too, changed her clothes after bathing and lay down beside the prince. On the following morning, both the prince and princess did not wake up for a long time. The attendants opened the doors and found that the prince and his wife had already passed away. The prince was forty-nine years old.

Source: Reprinted by permission of the publisher from Yoshiko Kurata Dykstra, *Miraculous Tales of the* Lotus Sūtra *from Ancient Japan: The Dainihonkoku hokekyōkenki of Priest Chingen* (Hirakata City: Kansai University of Foreign Studies, 1983), pp. 24–27 (slightly altered).

9.2 INTERACTIONS AND SYNCRETISM: THE MONK MYŌE VISITS A SHINTŌ SHRINE

The relationship between Buddhism and Shintō, the indigenous faith of Japan, has varied over time, but for a considerable part of Japanese history a syncretic connection existed between the two faiths. One expression of this link lay in the theory of honji-suijaku, a doctrine of assimilation whereby certain Shintō divinities (kami) were said to be "manifestations" (suijaku) of the "original nature" (honji) of certain Buddhas and bodhisattvas. But the relationship between Shintō and Buddhism could be more complex than this, as the following story of the Buddhist priest Myōe (1173–1232) testifies. Myōe was a prominent monk of the Kegon (Chinese: Hua-yen) sect who developed the ambition to travel from Japan across China to India in search of the Dharma. He was also, however, a devotee of the god of the great Kasuga Shintō shrine in Nara, the ancient capital of Japan, where the Kegon sect had its headquarters. According to a famous legend, Myōe visited the Kasuga shrine to take his leave of the deity there, only to be told that he should not leave Japan, that there was nothing Buddhist in India that he could not find at home. Thus, we have a Shintō divinity (who is a manifestation of the Buddha) looking out for the interests of Japanese Buddhism by forbidding a Buddhist monk to go on a pilgrimage to the land of the Buddha, arguing that he is needed at home, where, in any case, the sacred sites of India and China could be found, some of them in the Kasuga shrine itself. (In this connection the well-known Deer Park of the Kasuga shrine at Nara is equated with the Deer Park at Sarnath in India, where the Buddha preached his first sermon.)

The tale was dramatized as a nō play by the famous Japanese playwright Zeami (1363–1443), from whose drama *The Dragon God of Kasuga* (Kasuga ryūjin) the following excerpts are taken.

Myōe: I am priest Myōe of Toga-no-o. Since it is our intention to travel to China and cross over to India, we now come to Nara to make a farewell visit to the Gracious Deity of Kasuga. [. . .] I would have a word with this [shrine] official.

Elder Official: Why, it's Priest Myōe of Toga-no-o, just now come on a pilgrimage! The gods will certainly be pleased to see you.

Myōe: My reason for this journey is really nothing special. I am planning to travel to China and then cross over to India, so I have come to the shrine for a farewell visit.

Elder Official: Such may be your determination, but what will the gods think of this? It is your wont to visit the shrine from the year's beginning through all the four seasons. And although you may miss an occasion, the gods can hardly wait for your arrival. They call you their Tarō [eldest son], and rely on [your companion] Priest Gedatsu as their Jirō [second son], for you are like a pair of eyes and a pair of hands to them. How could it please them for you to leave Japan to travel to China and cross over to India? Please abandon the idea.

Myōe: What you say is certainly true. But how could it be contrary to the wishes of the gods for us to cross China to India in order to venerate the sites associated with the Buddha's life?

Elder Official: This is unworthy of you. Were the Buddha living in the world today, then surely would it avail you to see and to hear him.

But nowadays the mountain of Kasuga is our Eagle Peak [Vulture's Peak in India, where the Buddha preached many sermons]. Moreover, when you come to visit the shrine, not only "along Nara Slope with palms joined" do people pay their respects, [but]:

Chorus: The plants and trees in Mikasa Grove [near the shrine]
The plants and trees in Mikasa Grove,
Bend down their branches
Although there is no wind.
And as morning breaks
On Kasuga's hills and plains,
Even the deer turn to you,
Paying respect with bended knee
And tilted antlers.
To seek elsewhere
For the real Pure Land
Even while witnessing such marvels
Is to have a longing for
"The endless autumn of Musashi plain."
It is better just to submit freely
To the gods on whom we depend,
And to venerate the divine will,
To venerate the divine will.

The Elder proceeds to stage center and is seated; Myōe sits beside him.

Myōe: Now then, please relate to me the facts about this shrine.

Elder Official: In this regard, I would remind you that the purpose of your trip to China and India is to visit the old ruins . . .

Chorus: . . . made famous by the Buddha's propagation of the Law. But if you would venerate Mt. T'ien T'ai [in China], you should journey to our own Mt. Hiei; and if you have a desire to visit Mt. Wu-t'ai, then pray at Yoshino or Tsukuba.

Elder Official: Of old it was on Holy Eagle Mount,

Chorus: But nowadays the Buddha is manifest at the shrine on this mountain as a Great Deity for the sake of all sentient beings,

Elder Official: So just as you would at the Mountain of the Eagle,

Chorus: Pay homage at the Mountain of Kasuga. The divine poem clearly states:

Know who I am!
Now that Śākyamuni Buddha
Has appeared,
Think of me as the clear moon
Shining over the land.

Thus, He has vowed that by means of the power of the gods through which the bodhisattvas work their myriad acts of compassion, He will shine His light on our illusions. Distressed that His Perfect Teaching was of no benefit to those of small capacity, he "removed his necklace and fine garments, put on a coarse, disheveled robe," and taught the Four Noble Truths. And the Deer Park where this transpired was this very site. On Kasuga Plain where the animals rouse themselves or recline—is this not the Deer Park?

Source: Reprinted by permission of the publisher from Robert Morrell, "Passage to India Denied: Zeami's Kasuga Ryūjin," *Monumenta Nipponica* 37 (1982): 190, 192–94.

9.3 DIVISIONAL ISSUES: THE RECITATION OF AMIDA'S NAME—ONCE OR MANY TIMES?

As Buddhism developed in East Asia, belief in the Pure Land of the Buddha Amitābha (Japanese: Amida) came to be one of its chief manifestations. In Japan, in particular, the notion of salvation by faith in the grace of the Buddha Amida experienced a great resurgence and development starting in the tenth and eleventh centuries. Amidism was one response to the widespread Japanese belief at that time that Buddhism had entered its final, most degenerate phase, the period of the "end of the Dharma" (mappō), when it was no longer possible for people to save themselves by their own efforts. By calling on the name of the Buddha Amida—by reciting the nembutsu, that is, the formula "NAMU AMIDA BUTSU"—devotees could expect to be saved by Amida, who, in one of his vows (see 5.4.1) had promised to welcome into his Pure Land (Jōdō) all those who called on him with faith.

The nembutsu quickly became the hallmark of Pure Land practice, and generally speaking, it was affirmed as being an expression of salvation by "other power" (tariki), that is, the power of the Buddha, as opposed to salvation by one's "own power" (jiriki), that is, by depending on one's own practice of meritorious good works or meditation. But this assertion was not without controversy. If one truly and completely depended on the "other power" of the Buddha, was it actually necessary to manifest one's own faith by reciting the nembutsu? Was such a belief—that by reciting the name of the Buddha Amida one could assure one's own salvation—not potentially a reassertion of "own power" notions in disguise? One solution to this question was to assert that the nembutsu was not an ordinary kind of efficacious action. It did not *bring about* one's salvation, rather, it was an expression of gratitude for the salvific power of Amida. This view was eventually fully worked out by Shinran (1173–1262), the founder of the True Pure Land sect (Jōdō Shinshū). More immediately, however, controversy raged around a very practical question: how often should one recite the nembutsu? Should one repeat it as many times as possible as a kind of mantra? Or should one recite it only occasionally—or just once—as a sincere assertion of one's faith in Amida, as a statement of conversion or rededication? Some popular preachers in late Heian times in Japan advocated the former view and emphasized the importance of numbers, setting examples by chanting as many as 120,000 nembutsus a day. Others pointed to Amida's Eighteenth Vow, which stated that if one called on him "ten times," a figure that was taken to mean with complete and perfect devotion, one would be welcomed in his Pure Land. Still others mixed Pure Land practice with the Avataṃsaka (Kegon) doctrine of the interpenetration of reality and asserted that each recitation of the nembutsu contained every recitation and every recitation contained each recitation.

The following solution to this question by Ryūkan (1148–1227), a disciple of Hōnen (1133–1212) and an influence on Shinran, advocates a somewhat different tack by recalling the importance of faith in the Buddha Amida at the moment of one's death. In this way, Ryūkan suggests that each nembutsu should be uttered as though it were one's only and last nembutsu, and, since one never knows when one may die, one should repeat this one nembutsu many times. Therefore, once-calling is inseparable from many-calling.

These days the practice of the nembutsu is being entangled in vigorous debate over the doctrines of once-calling and many-calling. This debate touches on matters of crucial importance and demands that we exercise great care. Both the advocacy of a position of once-calling that rejects many-calling and the advocacy of many-calling in denunciation of once-calling run counter to the essential meaning of the Primal [Eighteenth] Vow [of Amida] and fail to take into account the teaching of [the Chinese Pure Land patriarch] Shan-tao.

Many-calling is nothing but the accumulation of single callings, for human life is such that a person should consider each day that this may be his last, each minute that this may be the end. From the very moment of our birth, this realm of impermanence is merely a fleeting and temporary dwelling; our lives may be compared to a lantern flame before the wind, or likened to dew upon a blade of grass, and there is no escape anywhere for even a single person, whether wise or foolish, from the extinction of breath and the draining away of life. If our eyes may close forever even in this present instant, then we say "namu-amida-butsu," aspiring to be saved by Amida's Primal Vow and welcomed into the Pure Land of perfect bliss, based on our trust in the supreme virtues embodied in a single calling and our reliance on the great and vast benefit of that one calling. As life continues, this single calling becomes two or three callings; they accumulate, so that one moment becomes an hour, then two hours; a day or two; a month, a year, two years, ten or twenty years, eighty years. The immutable nature of our existence is expressed truly in the statement that we should wonder how it is that we are still alive today, and whether this very instant will be our last in this world. Therefore, Shan-tao prays, "May all people constantly desire that the excellent conditions and surroundings appear before them at the time of death," earnestly encouraging us to say the nembutsu from moment to moment, neither forgetting nor neglecting it for even a single instant, until the time we are actually born in the Pure Land.

If a person maintains that many-calling is necessary, even though there is no many-calling separate from once-calling, nor any once-calling apart from many-calling, then surely he is a greater enemy of the Pure Land teaching than those who simply ignore such passages of the *Larger Sūtra of Immeasurable Life* as the one that teaches: "When sentient beings hear the Name, say it even once in trust and joy, sincerely turn over merits toward the attainment of birth, and aspire to be born in that land, then they shall attain birth and dwell in the stage of non-retrogression." . . .

If, however, . . . you adhere single-mindedly to the position of birth through once-calling and declare that many-calling is erroneous, then do you intend to overlook the words of the Primal Vow, "Saying the Name even ten times," and ultimately take the teaching of saying the Name for one to seven days in the *Smaller Sūtra* to be pointless? Do you also regard as erroneous the teaching of Master Shan-tao? Based on these sūtra passages, he instructs us to practice without interruption for a long period of time: "With single-heartedness solely saying Amida's Name, whether walking, standing still, sitting, or lying down, regardless of the occasion, whether for long or short: this is called the act by which one's birth is truly settled, for it is in accordance with that Buddha's Vow." [. . .]

Those who adhere to once-calling as well as those who cling tenaciously to many-calling invariably meet with inauspicious deaths, for both deviate from the meaning of the Primal Vow. Consider this carefully. It cannot be said too often that you must avoid confusing the truth that many-calling is itself once-calling and that once-calling is many-calling. Namu-amida-butsu.

Source: Reprinted by permission of the publisher from Ryūkan, "The Clarification of Once-Calling and Many-Calling," trans. by Dennis Hirota et al., in Yoshifumi Ueda, ed., *Notes on Once-Calling and Many-Calling,* Shin Buddhism Translation Series (Kyoto: Hongwanji International Center, 1980), pp. 51–55.[1]

9.4 REGULATION AND REFORM: SAICHŌ'S DEATHBED ADMONITIONS

As Buddhism developed in East Asia, one of the matters that arose perennially was the size and composition of the sangha, something that could be regulated by the practice of ordination. In China, for example, ordination was a concern not only of the community of monks and nuns and lay believers but also of government authorities, because monastics were traditionally exempt from certain obligations to the state such as corvée labor and taxes. In fact, at various points in Chinese history the practice of selling ordination certificates to people seeking tax-free status was a lucrative one, and it resulted in government takeovers of the whole ordination procedure (in some cases, to crack down on a practice that had gotten out of hand; in others, so that corrupt government officials could cash in on it).

In Japan as well, ordination was an important issue. For some centuries after the introduction of Buddhism to Japan, all ordinations had to be in a

---

[1]Original text, Ryūkan, *Ichinen tanen fumbetsuji* (Taishō shinshū daizōkyō, ed. J. Takakusu and K. Watanabe [Tokyo, 1924–29], no. 2677, 83:919a–920a).

certain temple in the capital, Nara, thus, in effect, giving the central ecclesiastic authorities complete control over who became a monk. This ordination, moreover, consisted only in the administration of the bhikṣu precepts (the so-called Hīnayāna ordination) and not of the bodhisattva precepts (the so-called Mahāyāna ordination; see 8.4).

The Japanese monk Saichō, posthumously known as Dengyō Daishi (767–822), spent a good portion of his life fighting for the right to ordain monks outside of Nara and according to the bodhisattva precepts, a wish that was accorded to him only after his death. Saichō was renowned in Japan as the founder of the Tendai school. Breaking away from the early sects at Nara, he established his own monastic center on Mount Hiei, not far from Kyoto, which soon became the new capital. On Mount Hiei he could train monks in his own way. New disciples had to agree not to leave the mountain for an initial period of twelve years, during which they were expected to maintain strict discipline and to follow a regimen that included devotion to the *Lotus Sūtra* and to the Buddha Amitābha, as well as the performance of certain esoteric rituals. Eventually, four types of meditation that had been developed by the sixth-century Chinese T'ien-t'ai patriarch Chih-i were advocated (see 8.6.2).

In time, Mount Hiei became one of the most important formative centers of Japanese Buddhism, and many of the subsequent founders of Buddhist schools—Dōgen, Eisai, Hōnen, Shinran, Nichiren—spent part of their monastic careers there. Eventually, however, the monasteries of Mount Hiei also became powerful players in the political struggles of the capital, and with the vast armies of warrior-monks that they mustered, they affected military affairs as well. Finally, in the late sixteenth century, the shōgun Oda Nobunaga overran the mountain, slaughtered most of the monks, ransacked the monasteries and burned them to the ground. In doing so, he is reputed to have declared: "I did not destroy this monastery! This monastery destroyed this monastery."

Saichō could hardly have foreseen all this. His deathbed instructions to his disciples reveal a much simpler, stricter situation, with perhaps some initial signs of incipient problems. At the same time, they reiterate some of his own lifelong concerns.

I will not live much longer. After my death you must not mourn (for me).

Furthermore, my fellow monks on Hiei, the Buddha's precepts state that you may not drink liquor. Anyone who breaks (this rule) is not my fellow monk, nor is he a disciple of the Buddha. He should be expelled immediately and should not be allowed to step foot within the boundaries of the mountain. Nor is anyone who uses liquor as medicine to be allowed within the mountain temple's confines.

Women may not come near the temple and certainly may not enter its sacred precincts.

You should lecture extensively on the Mahāyāna *sūtras* everyday. You must carefully perform your religious practices in order that the Dharma may endure forever. You must diligently strive to benefit the nation and save sentient beings. My fellow monks, you must not tire in your practice of the four types of meditation. Esoteric initiation and the *goma* (Skt. *homa,* Esoteric fire ceremony) should be performed at the appropriate times. You should return your debt of gratitude to the nation by helping the Buddha's teachings to prosper.

[Saichō also left the following six admonitions for his disciples]:

1. Monks should sit according to the order in which they received the Mahāyāna precepts. On days when there is a general assembly (which includes monks who have received the Hīnayāna precepts), Tendai monks should conceal their bodhisattva practices and behave as Hīnayāna monks, sitting together with the Hīnayāna monks in the position of novices. An exception to this rule is allowed when one monk defers to another.
2. A monk's frame of mind should be as though he were first entering the Buddha's room, later wearing the Buddha's robes, and finally sitting in the Buddha's place.
3. For robes, the man of higher faculties uses dirty rags found at the side of the road. The man of medium faculties uses rough cloth, and the man of lower faculties uses robes (of cotton or flax) received from lay donors.
4. For food, the man of higher faculties begs, but without any thought about what he receives. The man of medium faculties begs while strictly adhering to the precepts. The man of lower faculties obtains his food from lay believers.
5. For his cell, the man of higher faculties uses a thatched hut made of bamboo brush. The man of medium faculties uses a three-room wooden house, and the man of lower faculties uses the whole monastery. You should obtain materials for building or for repairs by begging in the autumn, receiving one *masu* of rice in the provinces and one *mon* of coin in the towns.
6. For his bedding, the man of higher faculties uses bamboo brush and straw. The man of medium faculties uses one straw mat (mushiro) and one reed mat (komo). The man of lower faculties uses one bordered mat (tatami) and one straw mat.

We do not have the means to purchase large tracts of land, nor do we receive rich stipends of food. We do not dwell in the monasteries administered by the government-appointed monastic leaders. . . . In the morning you should beg for food. After offering a little (to the hungry ghosts), you should then present it to those practicing on the mountain. In the autumn, you should beg for a little cloth to cover your cold bodies. You should want nothing other than food and clothing.

Those who go out into the world in order to preach shall be exempted (from these rules).

Source: Reprinted by permission of the publisher from Paul Groner, *Saichō: The Establishment of the Japanese Tendai School* (Berkeley: Berkeley Buddhist Studies, 1984), pp. 158–61.

9.5 RITUALS AND FESTIVALS: RITES IN TENTH-CENTURY JAPAN

The *Sanbōe* (Illustrations of the Triple Gem) is a collection of Buddhist stories that was compiled in 984 C.E. by Minamoto Tamenori, a prominent Japanese official who presented the work to an imperial princess on the occasion of her becoming a nun. The third section of this book consists of short chapters describing and discussing various activities of the sangha, including a number of rituals and festivals that were in vogue in the temples around Kyoto at that time. Tamenori is not always very precise in describing the details of the rites, but he gives a good idea of the variety of practices that were to be found—some of them general and carried out in all temples, others specifically associated with particular places. In the passages that follow, we shall encounter the simple practice of building stone stūpas by the river bank; the urabon (obon) offering of food to the sangha in order to relieve the suffering of hungry ghosts, specifically of one's own ancestors; the continuous chanting of the Buddha's name by the monks on Mount Hiei; and the custom of liberating captive animals in order to make merit.

Stone Stūpas

The building of *stūpas* of stone is an act of devotion undertaken by many in the spring. Civil and military officials commission their assistants and lieutenants to see to the construction. Noble clans and royal households charge their retainers and courtiers with the task. They select a day and go to the river bank, and there they pile stones in the shape of a *stūpa.* Copies of the *Heart Sūtra* are gathered, and monks are invited to chant it and to worship at altars dedicated to the deity associated with the administration for that year, and prayers are offered for everyone in each sponsoring household. Many are inspired by the words of the presiding monk and are won over to the faith he expounds. Great joy is derived from the anticipation of the merit thus generated; much rice and wine are collected, and the faithful believe that this collection will help guard against famines and other misfortunes. But there are ignorant people who think of it merely as a pleasant excursion. They are responsible for setting the date of the annual observance, and they are the arbiters of taste regarding the adornments upon the altars, but in the evening they get drunk and collapse and tumble down in the streets. Nevertheless, they will reach the garden of merit, and they too shall plant their own good roots there. . . .

The Rite for the Dead

The Rite of the Dead was initiated in the age when the Buddha was in this world. In the *Urabon Sūtra* it is said: "When Maudgalyāyana [Chinese: Mulien, Japanese: Mokuren] attained the Six Supernatural Faculties and wanted to try to save his father and mother, to repay his obligation to them for having raised him, he discovered that his mother had been reborn in the Realm of Hungry Ghosts, where she suffered perpetual starvation. There was little left of her but skin hanging on bones. Grieving and weeping, Maudgalyāyana filled a bowl with rice and took it to her. She clutched the rice in her left hand, picked up a tiny bit of it with her right hand, and was about to eat it, but before she could put it in her mouth it turned to fire and then into cinders, so she could not eat it.

"Lamenting and grieving, Maudgalyāyana reported this to the Buddha, who said, 'Your mother's sins are very great. You cannot save her through your own efforts. On the fifteenth day of the seventh month, prepare a hundred delicacies and the Five Fruits and many other good things, put them on trays, and offer them to the Buddhas of the Ten Directions. On that day, all the Śrāvakas and Pratyekabuddhas and Bodhisattvas of the Ten Stages who have already sought and attained those states will temporarily appear in the guise of monks, and they will come and take the food. If you make this offering to these monks while they are holding confession, your own father and mother in this life and in seven other lives will escape the sufferings of the Evil Realms.'

"On that day, Maudgalyāyana's mother was saved from one *kalpa* [aeon] of suffering as a Hungry Ghost. Maudgalyāyana told the Buddha, 'My mother was saved through the power of the Three Jewels. What if all your disciples in future worlds were to do this, too?'

"The Buddha said, 'Let monks and nuns, kings and princes, prime ministers and counselors, chamberlains and officers and all the common people and all those who practice filial piety observe a day of rejoicing on this day when monks make their confession, and let them prepare delicacies, place them in trays, and offer them to the monks. Let them pray that their parents in this life may live for one hundred years without illness, that their fathers and mothers in seven other lives may be freed from the sufferings of Hungry Ghosts, and that they may be granted the pleasures of life in the Heavens. Those who cultivate filial piety must reflect upon it day after day, and obligations must be repaid year after year.' "

On this basis, this practice was observed in India and in China as well. It is observed by the government as well as the private citizenry of Japan.

The Continuous Nembutsu on Mount Hiei

The *Nembutsu* was introduced from China and practiced here first by Master Jikaku in the seventh year of the Jōgan era [865 C.E.]. . . . When the cool mid-autumn wind is blowing and the clear mid-month moon is shining, the meditation is begun at dawn, on the eleventh day of the eighth month, and it continues without interruption until the seventeenth. The two thousand monks of the monastery are divided into four watches. Their bodies constantly circle the Buddha, and all the sins of the body are negated. Their mouths constantly chant the *sūtra,* and all the transgressions of speech disappear. Their minds constantly contemplate the Buddha, and all confusion comes to an end.

In the *Amidakyō* it is said: "Any devout man or woman who is inspired with faith, remembers the name of Amida Buddha, and meditates upon it intensely for one day, two days, three days, or as many as seven days shall not falter even in the last moment before death, but shall immediately be reborn in Paradise." The seven-day length of this rite is based upon this passage.

Now this Buddha made a great vow for the sake of all sentient beings on this earth. The sentient beings of this earth have a great affinity with this Buddha. At the sound of one utterance of his name, sins from eighty billion *kalpas* of former life will be erased, and you will be reborn in that land where your outstretched arms can reach beyond the boundaries of a million billion lands. Those who want to reach the Pure Land must despise this world and pray for that one. Whether you are standing or sitting, despise your body for all its sufferings. Whether you are asleep or awake, pray for the joys of that other world. In the morning, when you see the lovely flowers of spring, you should yearn for the beauty of the Grove of Seven Rows, and in the evening, when you hear the autumn wind, you should imagine the sound of the rippling Waters of the Eight Good Qualities. At the end of each day let your heart follow the setting sun into the west. There is no doubt about the good effect of good intentions acted upon for one day or one instant. Trust in this, and even punishments for the Five Transgressions will be cancelled, and you will surely be reborn there.

The Liberation of Animals

Then [following an uprising in which many persons were killed], in an oracle, the deity said, "Many of the Hayato have been slain. To counteract this sin, a service for liberating animals should be held each year." On this basis, seashores and river banks in various provinces were chosen as the site for the performance of this auspicious ritual, the Liberation of Animals. Monks, laymen, and shrine officials of the province of Yamashiro buy a great many fish that fishermen and others who make their living from the sea are about to kill. Then the monks chant spells and prayers and return the fish to the water.

As the Buddha said, there are no sentient beings that do not cling to life. Their forms may vary, but the pains of the flesh are shared by all. In the *Bonmōkyō* it is said: "Cultivate compassion, and set living creatures free. All sentient beings of the Six Realms are our fathers and mothers from former lives. If you kill them and eat them, you are killing and eating your fathers and mothers. For this reason, always liberate living things. If you see someone about to kill a dumb beast, you should use some expedient means to save that animal."

And in *Rokudojikkyō* it is said: "Long ago, there was a man who went to market and saw someone selling a turtle. He asked how much it cost, and paid an exhorbitant price for it. He carried off his purchase and released it in a stream, and as he watched it swim away, he was filled with both joy and pity. Later, in the night, this turtle came knocking at his door. In amazement, the man went out to have a look, and the turtle said, 'I have been thinking about my debt to you for rescuing me and setting me free. But there is no way to repay you. All I can do is tell you what I know: a great flood is about to occur. Prepare your boats immediately.' The next morning the man went to the gate of the palace and asked that the king be informed of this. Since this man was known for his wisdom, the king took his advice and moved to high ground, whereupon the flood waters burst forth. Later, the king made the man prime minister. He led him by hand into the palace, and they sat next to one another and held discourse on the Way."

Source: Reprinted by permission of the publisher from Edward Kamens, *The Three Jewels: A Study and Translation of Minamoto Tamenori's Sanbōe* (Ann Arbor: Center for Japanese Studies, University of Michigan, 1988), pp. 279, 337–38, 342, 345–46 (slightly altered).

9.6 MEDITATIONAL ENDEAVORS: KŌANS AND HAKUIN'S FIRST SATORI

The practice of meditation is one of the hallmarks of Zen Buddhism (Chinese: Ch'an; Korean: Son), even though it is seriously undertaken only by a small minority of monks and nuns and by an even smaller percentage of laypersons. One of the features of a certain form of Zen meditation is the kōan (Chinese: kung-an), an apparently enigmatic account of the sayings or actions of some previous Zen master. In the context of training, kōans are typically assigned by Zen masters to their students in an effort to provide some concrete images that students can focus on as they wrestle with Buddhist concepts in the hopes of reaching some level of realization. That realization or awakening, called satori, is often communicated to and confirmed by one's teacher in the context of a personal interview.

For years, the study of kōans in the West, following the lead of scholars such as D. T. Suzuki, tended to focus on their mystical side, to see them as trying to shipwreck the use of logic and language and to push the Zen student to move beyond rationality. Today, it is more commonly realized that there are many types of kōans and that our study of them needs also to be grounded in their literary, social, historical, ritual and even folkloric contexts. To be sure, some kōans seem to revel in absurdity intended to put the meditator into a logical double bind. But it is probably better to think of most kōans as focal points for concentration rather than as conundrums to be solved. In this context, kōans are no more illogical than other classic objects of mindfulness such as one's breath, for example.

The first kōan that is sometimes given to meditators is called "Jōshū's 'Mu.'" "Mu" literally means "NO," and it is said to have been the answer that the Chinese Zen Master Jōshū (Chinese: Chao Chou) gave to a monk who asked him whether a dog had the Buddha-nature, a question not unrelated to doctrinal issues (see 8.3), even though Jōshū's answer goes far beyond doctrine. How does one "resolve" such a kōan? The following advice was given by the thirteenth-century Zen Master Hui-k'ai, who featured Jōshū's "Mu" [NO] as the first entry in his collection of kōans, the *Gateless Barrier* (*Wu-men kuan*):

> To practice meditation, you must pass through the barrier of the masters: subtle realizations require that you stop the wandering of your discursive thoughts. If you do not pass the barrier, if you do not stop your thoughts from wandering, then you are a ghost flitting among the weeds. . . . Do you want

to pass through this barrier? Then take your whole body, its three hundred and sixty joints and its eighty-four thousand pores, and concentrate upon this NO: day and night hold it in your hand. But do not make it an empty no, as in yes and no; it must be a red-hot iron ball you have swallowed, which you vomit and vomit, but cannot bring forth. Cast aside all your old misperceptions and mistakes: slowly, naturally, purely, the inner and outer become of a single piece; but (like a dumb man who has a dream) perhaps only you yourself will know it. Then suddenly you arise to startle the heavens and shake the earth; you take in your hand a magic sword; you meet the Buddha: kill him! you meet a master: kill him! In the midst of life and death you have reached the other shore, gaining great freedom; in the midst of the six destinies [of rebirth] you wander, playing in your contemplation. And how do you concentrate on the NO? With every bit of your strength. If you do not falter, you will light a lamp of the Law to benefit the world.

The dog: the Buddha-nature:
stern implacable command:
if you fall into yes and no
dead man.[2]

The following account is taken from the spiritual autobiography of the Japanese monk Hakuin (1685–1768). It relates his initial struggles with Jōshū's Mu as well as with other kōans and his first (of many) realizations of satori.

I related my understanding to the master one day during *dokusan* [a personal interview]. He said to me, "Commitment to the study of Zen has to be a true commitment. What about the dog and the Buddha-nature?"

"There's no way at all for hand or foot to touch it," I replied.

He suddenly reached out, grabbed my nose in his hand, and gave it a sharp push. "How's that for a firm touch!" he declared.

I was incapable of moving forward. I couldn't retreat. I couldn't spit out a single syllable.

After that, I was totally disheartened and frustrated. I sat red-eyed and miserable. My cheeks burned from the constant tears.

The master took pity on me. He gave me some [other] koans to work on: Sozan's Memorial Tower, the Ox Comes Through the Window, the Death of Nansen, Nansen's Flowering Shrub, Seishū's Hemp Robe, and Ummon's Dried Shit-stick.

"If you can get past one of these," he said, "you are worthy to be called a descendent of the Buddhas and patriarchs."

A great new upsurge of spirit rose inside me. With stiffened resolve, I chewed on those koans day and night, attacking them from the front, gnawing at them from all sides. But not the faintest glimmer of understanding came. Tearful and dejected, I sobbed out a vow: "Evil kings of

---

[2]English translation in Stephan Beyer, *The Buddhist Experience* (Encino, CA: Dickenson, 1974), pp. 262–63. Original text: Hui-k'ai, *Wu-men kuan* (Taishō shinshū daizōkyō, ed. J. Takakusu and K. Watanabe [Tokyo, 1924–29], no. 2005, 48:292c–293a).

the ten directions, demons of good and demons of evil, I call upon you all. If after seven days I fail to pass through one of these koans, come quick and snatch my life away."

Then I lit some incense, made my bows, and resumed my practice. I didn't stop for sleep. The master came and shouted abuse at me. I was doing "Zen-down-a-hole," he said. Then he told me, "You could go out and scour the whole world for a teacher who could raise up the fortunes of 'closed-door' Zen, but you'd never find one. You'd as soon see the morning star at noon."

I had my doubts about that. "After all," I reasoned, "there are great monasteries all over the place. Celebrated masters reside in them—they're numerous as sesame or flax. That old man in his wretched ramshackle old poorhouse of a temple—and that preposterous pride of his! I'd be better off leaving here for some other temple."

Still dejected, I took up my begging bowl early the next morning and went into the village below Iiyama castle. My mind was hard at work on my koans. It never left them. I stood before the gate of a house, my bowl in my hand, lost in a kind of trance.

A voice from within yelled, "Go on! Go somewhere else!" But I was so preoccupied I didn't even notice it. This must have angered the resident of the house, because she suddenly appeared, flourishing a broom upside down in her hand. She flew at me, flailing out wildly, whacking away at my head as if she was bent on dashing my brains out. My sedge hat lay in tatters. I was knocked down and ended heels up on the ground. I lost consciousness and lay there like a dead man.

All the neighbors, alarmed by the noise, appeared with apprehensive looks on their faces. "Oh, now look what that crazy old crone has done!" they cried, and vanished behind locked doors. There was total silence, not a stir or sign of life anywhere. Some people who happened to be passing by approached me in wonderment. They grabbed hold of me and propped me right side up.

"What's wrong!" "What happened?" they exclaimed.

As I regained consciousness, my eyes opened, and as they did, I found that the unsolvable and impenetrable koans I had been working on—all those poisoned cat's paws—were completely penetrated. Right to the root. They had suddenly ceased to exist. I clapped my hands and laughed great shouts of laughter, frightening the people who had gathered around me.

"He's lost his mind." "A crazy monk," they shouted, and shrank back from me. They turned heel and ran off without looking back.

I picked myself up from the ground, straightened my robes, and fixed the remnants of my hat back on my head. With a blissful smile on my face, slowly and exultantly I began to walk back toward [the temple]. . . . I smiled elatedly all the way back through the gates of Shōju's hermitage. The master was standing on the veranda. He took one look at me, and said, "I see that something good has happened to you. Try to tell me about it."

I advanced to where he was standing, and related at length what I had come to realize. He took his fan and stroked my back with it.

"I hope you live to be my age," he said. "Firmly resolve never to be satisfied with little, and devote your efforts now to after-satori practice. Those who content themselves with a small attainment never advance beyond the stage of the śrāvakas [disciples]. If you are ignorant of after-satori practice, you will end up without fail as one of those unfortunate lesser vehicle arhats, whose rewards are paltry indeed. . . . By 'after-satori' practice, I mean you must proceed on beyond your satori and devote yourself to further practice; and, when that bears fruit, continue still further. As you go on, you will arrive at a final, difficult barrier."

Source: Reprinted by permission of the publisher from Norman Waddell, trans., "Wild Ivy: The Spiritual Autobiography of Hakuin Ekaku," *The Eastern Buddhist* 15 (1982): 98–100.

9.7 WOMEN AND THE SANGHA: NICHIREN ON CHANTING AND MENSTRUATION

In Japan, just as in the rest of East Asia, the Confucian ethic of the "three subordinations" prevailed. According to this collective precept, a woman was as a child subordinate to her father, as a wife subordinate to her husband, and as a widow subordinate to her son. To this ethic was occasionally added the specifically Buddhist doctrine of the "five obstacles," which maintained that a woman was incapable of becoming a divinity in the heaven of Brahmā, Indra, or Māra or of becoming a cakravartin king or a Buddha. In addition, women were seen as more impure than men, in part because menstrual blood was deemed to be particularly polluting. Thus women were often forbidden from entering religious sites or participating in religious ceremonies during their monthly periods, or, in some cases, ever. (For instance, women were not allowed to set foot in the monastic precincts of sacred mountains such as Mount Hiei or Mount Koya.)

The thirteenth-century Buddhist leader Nichiren (1222–1282) lived at a time of great religious and social change in Japan. In his day, belief was widespread that Buddhism had reached the final and most decadent period of the Buddha's teaching, the period called mappō, "the end of the Dharma," when enlightenment, especially by one's own efforts, would be more or less impossible. In Nichiren's eyes, there were many signs of mappō in thirteenth-century Japan: the proliferation of "heresies" propounded by other Buddhist sects, the decline of law and order in the country, a series of natural disasters, the imminent threat of a Mongol invasion. But Japan could still be saved, could still be turned into a Buddha Land. All it would take would be for the people of the country as a whole to abandon their heretical beliefs, repent, and turn immediately to faith in the efficacy of the *Lotus Sūtra* (Japanese: *Myōhōrengekyō,* or, in abbreviated form, *Hokekyō*).

During the course of his career as a monk, Nichiren had come to believe that the *Lotus Sūtra* and only the *Lotus Sūtra* contained true teachings of the Buddha that were relevant to his day and age. So strong was his belief that he urged the Japanese government to suppress all Buddhist sects other than his own, and he did not hesitate to denounce them directly. At the same time, he did not refrain from criticizing Shintō divinities, such as Hachiman and the Sun Goddess Amaterasu, for having failed to protect the true Buddhism.

Nichiren's views got him into trouble with the government and with others. He was arrested, exiled twice, attacked by a mob, and almost executed, and his disciples were generally persecuted. In his later years, Nichiren seems to have toned down somewhat his urgent calls for immediate repentance. To the end of his life, however, Nichiren continued to encourage his disciples in their devotions and to urge them to recite the *Lotus Sūtra* or to repeat the *daimoku* (i.e., the title of the sūtra: *Namu Myōhō renge kyō* or "Praise to the Lotus of the Wonderful Dharma"). Among these followers were many women, mostly aristocrats, who took to corresponding with Nichiren about spiritual matters. The following selection is from his reply to the wife of Lord Daigaku Saburō, who had asked him certain questions about her chanting practice.

Letter on Menstruation

I have just read your letter in which you explain that, until recently, you had recited one chapter of the *Lotus Sūtra* every day, completing the recitation of the whole work in twenty-eight days, but that lately, for your daily devotions, you have recited only a single chapter, "The Bodhisatta Medicine King." You asked whether it was better, after all, for you to chant one chapter per day as you had been doing.

Now, when it comes to the *Lotus Sūtra* for one's daily devotions it is fine to read the entire work in eight scrolls and twenty-eight chapters, and it is fine to read just a single scroll, or a single chapter, or a single verse, or a single line, or even a single word. Alternatively, it is fine if one simply intones the seven characters, "Namu Myōhō Renge-kyō" (Hail to the Lotus Sūtra of the Marvelous Dharma!) only once a day, or only once in a lifetime. Also, even if one does not chant oneself, it is fine if just once in a lifetime one hears another person chant the *daimoku* and rejoices at that. Or one might hear someone else rejoicing and join in, and that hearing and rejoicing might be transmitted from one person to another to another. By the time it reaches the fiftieth person, the intention to express heartfelt joy will have grown progressively weaker and will have become uncertain, something as fuzzy as the thoughts of a one- or two-year-old child, or as undiscerning as a cow or horse. . . . Nevertheless, the merit of that person is a hundred thousand trillion times greater than the merit of those whose wisdom is as great as Śāriputra, Maudgalyāyana, Mañjuśrī, and Maitreya but who believes in sūtras other than the *Lotus Sūtra,* or who memorize all the various kinds of scripture. [. . .]

Also, in your letter you ask the following question. "Up until now as my regular religious practice I have venerated the seven chapters of the *daimoku* three times a day and made ten thousand repetitions of *Namu Ichijō Myōten* ("Hail to the Marvelous Single Vehicle Scripture!"). When I have my period, however, I do not read the sūtra or venerate *daimoku* and I suspend my intoning of the Ichijō Myōten, but I am wondering if this is permissible. During my period, should I forego these activities?

And how many days should I wait after my period ends before it is all right to resume my devotions?"

This is a matter that perplexes all women, and from ancient times many people have attempted to answer it. However, there is no place in all the Buddhist scripture where this point is expressly expounded upon, and as a result there is no one who has brought forward a definitive scriptural passage to serve as evidence. I, Nichiren, have read almost all of the Buddhist scriptures and while I have found passages that, for example, interdict the drinking of alcohol, the eating of meat, the consumption of the five piquant vegetables, or that prohibit sexual relations on specifically designated days or months, I have discovered nowhere in the scriptures a similar passage about the menstrual period.

When Śākyamuni Buddha was alive there were many young women who gave up the secular life to become nuns and not one of these was turned away because she was having her period. Reflecting on this, we can consider that menses is not an impurity that has come from outside, but a physiological phenomenon unique to women and necessary for the propagation of children. It is like a long illness. For example, feces and urine come out of our bodies but as long as we keep ourselves clean, they do us no particular harm. I feel that menstruation too, like feces, is not something that harms. That is why in India and China one hears of no particular alarm about menstruation.

Japan, however, is a land of the *kami.* That there were many things about the buddhas and bodhisattvas who manifested themselves as *kami* that do not conform with the sūtras and discourses is strange indeed, but it is owing to the customs of this land. If one does not heed those customs, one is subject to divine punishment. I, Nichiren, have researched the sūtras and discourses very thoroughly and I have found in them a teaching know as *zuihōbini,* the correct practice of discipline. In essence this teaching says that, provided it does not represent a serious breach of the Buddhist precepts, it is best not to run counter to the local customs of a country even if this involves some minor discrepancies with the precepts. However, wise men, unaware of this teaching of *zuihōbini,* strongly proclaim that the *kami* are demons and hence should not be revered. The end result is that they run the risk of harming the layman's faith. From what I have said above it would seem that the various *kami* of the Japanese nation dislike women's menstruation. Thus, it is best for people who are born in this country to avoid appearing before the *kami* at the time of their period.

The menstrual period, however, does not represent any obstacle to the daily practice of Buddhist devotions. Those who hold that it does do not genuinely believe in the *Lotus Sūtra* and are trying to do what they can to damage your faith. They do not tell you directly to abandon the *Lotus Sūtra,* rather they use your period as a pretext for distancing you from the *Lotus Sūtra.* Also, by intimidating you with the idea that practicing devotions to the *Lotus Sūtra* when you are menstruating represents a serious disrespect for the sacred sūtra, they are attempting to entice you into abandoning the *Lotus Sūtra* and committing a sin against the Dharma.

Keeping all these things clearly in mind, when you have your period, even if it lasts for a week, it is probably best during that time not to read the *Lotus Sūtra* but only to chant the *daimoku.*

Source: Translated by Sarah M. Strong from *St. Nichiren's Nyonin Gosho—Letters Addressed to Female Followers,* ed. Kyotsu Hori (Tokyo: Nichiren Shū Overseas Propagation Promotion Association, 1995), pp. 23–25, 37–41.

9.8 SANGHA AND SOCIETY

9.8.1 "Dear Abbot" Letters from Heian Japan

In addition to being members of a monastic community devoted to ritual, meditation, or study, Buddhist monks and nuns in East Asia (as indeed everywhere else) engaged in pastoral duties, counseling and advising the laity on a gamut of issues. This aspect of monasticism is often overlooked, but it was an important one and was one of the ways in which clerics had a significant effect on the daily lives of people.

The *Higashiyama Orai* is a remarkable eleventh-century text that has preserved a series of letters written to and by an anonymous Japanese priest, probably of the Shingon school, who lived not too far from the ancient capital of Kyoto. In this correspondence, which reads like the pages of a newspaper advice column, "parishioners" raise all sorts of issues with their cleric, seeking his advice on moral dilemmas or matters of ritual or doctrine. His answers are invariably learned, to the point, and filled with compassionate common sense.

Question: The child on whose behalf I am addressing you went one evening and played outside the house in an unlined red dress. Afterwards it was unwell, losing its appetite and sleeping badly. What is to be done?

Reply: Children under seven ought not to wear clothes of striking pattern or colour. A child under seven still counts as a baby and is exposed to many dangers. Ghosts and spirits are irresistibly attracted by bright colours, and if they do not get what they hope for, they revenge themselves by causing illness. In the monastic rules priests are forbidden to wander about outside the gates in the evening and to go near the water or under a bridge or near a butcher's shop or place of sacrifice. For by so doing they risk meeting ghosts. And if even priests are in danger, how much the more should ordinary people avoid roaming about outside the gates in the evening? Young children should wear green clothing till their seventh year. For this period of life corresponds to the Spring and green is the colour of Spring. That is why men speak of "green babes."

As regards the cure of your child, you should perform the appropriate ritual and scatter offerings (to the spirits). To scatter sugar as the Chinese soothsayers do nowadays is the worst possible thing. Use proper rice, even if it is only a handful. If incense is scattered, it must not be allowed to fall into the water. As to the ritual, it is difficult to describe in writing. You must come and see me. . . .

Question: In front of my modest house there is a small pond, where both frogs and snakes live side by side. The frogs feed on flies and the snakes feed on the frogs. I who know the story of the origin of the Three Branch Temple am deeply affected by the sight of these creatures that in retribution (for sins in previous lives) must live by preying upon one another. The frogs also cannot jump far and the snakes grip with a terrible force, so that the whole pond echoes continually with the noise of anguished croaking. The boys of the neighbourhood met at the edge of this pond. One of them wanted the other day to rescue the frogs. But others took the side of the snakes and said it would be cruel to deprive them of their nourishment. Another said that Heaven gave them the frogs to eat. I am perplexed. Is one showing compassion by rescuing the frogs or not? I shall be guided by your advice.

Reply: You may certainly help the frogs. The idea that Heaven made them for snakes to eat is nowhere found in the books of our religion nor in those of the laity. It is a question that must be decided by the magnitude of the suffering. If a frog is taken away from a snake, the snake does not necessarily die. But if a snake swallows a frog, the frog dies. . . . The pain of the snake in being deprived of its meal is slight. It can retire to its hole, lick the stones, chew the earth and get enough for its wants. But the frog suffers a most painful form of death, owing to its feeling of helplessness. When it is a question of small suffering or great, you must help the greater sufferer. This is to exercise the "bodhisattva's benefaction of allaying fear." Of all benefactions the saving of life is the greatest and cannot possibly be outweighed by the act of diverting food. [. . .]

Question: Recently when I was walking through the City I saw prayer-strips hung up along the streets of the various wards. To them were often attached locks of human hair. I asked the people in the street what this was for and they said: "Sick men give their hair as a substitute for their lives. It is an offering to the gods." Is this the real explanation? Pray inform me whether any text can be cited in support of the practice.

Reply: The offering of hair to purchase one's life is mentioned in the Holy Teaching. We are told that Prince Kalmāsapāda captured a thousand kings and was about to sacrifice them to the Mountain Spirit when he heard the four gāthās [stanzas] concerning Impermanence, Misery, Emptiness, and Non-existence of Self. He was thereupon converted and released the thousand kings. But in order to appease the Mountain Spirit he told each of the kings to offer to the Spirit a drop of blood and three locks of hair, as purchase for his life. The Spirit accepted these and did no harm. The story is summarized in *Jen Wang Ching* and told more amply in other sūtras. It is in accordance with this that people pluck out their hair and offer it to the Spirits in exchange for their lives. . . .

Question: One of our serving-girls gave birth this morning to a boy which has a full set of teeth like a grown-up child. Several of our neighbours tell us that such a monstrosity is of evil omen and say that a child born with teeth will grow into a demon. We are advised to expose it on the mountain-wilds. However, I am keeping it till I hear from you what should be done. . . .

Reply: I am glad to have your letter about the child born with teeth. The question is one that concerns the Art of Bodily Signs (hsiang-fa). From this science we learn that for a child to be born with teeth is a sign of great ability and by no means indicates misfortune. Here are one or two examples. In China the Empress Chen was born with teeth. Yet she was famous long afterwards for her talent and beauty and her presence at Court was sufficient to keep away all misfortunes and ills. During the Ch'i dynasty there was the priest T'an-yen who was born with teeth. Yet he became a Patriarch of the Avataṃsaka Sect and finally ascended to the Great Void at the gate of heaven. . . . Then there was the Śramaṇa Fa-li, whose teeth were full grown at birth. From the moment of his ordination he showed a profound understanding of the Great Teaching and his name travelled to the Four Oceans.

In our own country the Emperor Hanshō was born with teeth in the form of one single piece of bone and before his accession was known as the Prince with the Auspicious Tooth. During his reign absolute peace prevailed and the people were abundantly prosperous. . . . Keep the child, and when it grows up send it into the Buddhist Church.

Source: Reprinted by permission of the publisher from Arthur Waley, "An Eleventh Century Correspondence," in *Etudes d'orientalisme publiées par le Musée Guimet à la mémoire de Raymonde Linossier* (Paris: E. Leroux, 1932), 2:532–35, 545.[3]

9.8.2 Monks and Marriage in Korea

In India and Southeast Asia, for the most part, celibacy and homelessness remained marks of the lives of Buddhist monks and nuns. This was largely true in East Asia as well up until the modern period, even though in Japan in the early thirteenth century Shinran set an example for priests of his True Pure Land sect (Jōdo Shin shū) by getting married, thereby emphasizing the fact that salvation came only through the grace of Amida and not as a result of any actions or lifestyles of individuals. During the Meiji era in the nineteenth century, however, it became the universal practice for monks of all schools in Japan to marry, and temples, by and large, came to be inherited and passed on from father to son.

Following the Russo-Japanese War at the start of the twentieth century, Japan occupied and then officially annexed Korea. Korean Buddhism at that

[3]Original text in *Zoku gunsho ruiju,* ed. Hanawa Hokiichi (Tokyo, 1926), no. 359, 13b:1083b–84b, 1085a–86a.

time still formally advocated celibacy for monks, although there were several moves to "modernize" the sangha by allowing for a married clergy. Eventually these changes were approved by the Japanese government, and the result was a split in the Korean sangha between married and unmarried monks.

A key figure in this divisional dispute was a Korean monk and activist named Han Yongun (1894–1944). His advocacy of a married clergy for Korea was part of his tireless drive to make Korean Buddhism "relevant" in the modern age to both monastics and laypersons. It should be pointed out, however, that following the end of the Japanese occupation of Korea in 1945, a backlash occurred against having a married clergy, so that today most Korean monasteries have reverted to celibacy, even though the debate pushed by Han Yongun is still carried on.

Perhaps the most radical solution Han Yongun offered to this perceived split between the monks and the laity was for Korean Buddhism to allow monks to marry, a move that would controvert monastic standards of celibacy in place since virtually the inception of Buddhism in Korea. Apart from a small number of individual iconoclasts, Korean Buddhist monasticism had always been based on the institution of celibacy. Even during most of the Choson dynasty [1392–1910], when the tradition was weaker than any other time in its history, Buddhist monks still observed celibacy. It was not until the final years of the dynasty that adherence to the precepts became increasingly lax among the ecclesia. As contact with incoming Japanese missionary monks brought the news that that most materially advanced of Asian Buddhist nations permitted monks to take wives, some of the first widespread instances of marriage among Korean monks are noted. By the turn of the century, it had become common knowledge among Koreans that many monks were secretly marrying, regardless of the restrictions still in place. . . . Han Yongun felt that this increasingly common state of affairs should be acknowledged publicly and marriage officially allowed by the order. Monks who wished to marry would then no longer need to maintain the pretense of being celibate but could get on with their real vocation of studying, meditating, and teaching without inviting potential scandal or suffering pangs of guilt.

In March and September of 1910, Han Yongun sent separate petitions to the Japanese cabinet . . . and the monastery supervisory board, . . . asking that they lift restrictions on monks and nuns taking a spouse and allow both the freedom (but not the obligation) to marry. Yongun's arguments in favor of clergy marriages appeal to common sense, Buddhist doctrinal teachings, and the potential benefits of married monks to society, religion, and the government.

Social stratification within Buddhism between the celibate clergy and the married laity, Yongun explains, was inhibiting the religion's ability to adapt to the changing circumstances of modern life. In an argument remarkably similar to those proposed by reformists within the Catholic Church of our own age, celibacy, Yongun suggests, was no longer relevant in the present age of rapid social change. Because this precept remains in place, however, many monks who would remain in the order if allowed to marry were instead disrobing. Monks numbered only five to six thousand during Yongun's time, and their numbers would continue to remain small, he claimed, as long as this outdated restriction remained. And privately, many monks were ignoring the rule on celibacy and marrying anyway, causing unnecessary scruples. Because they are compelled to honor outmoded restrictions, the waning influence of Buddhist monks was weakening both society and religion, a process that would eventually lead to the demise of the religion. If monks were, however, allowed to marry and produce Buddhist offspring, Buddhism would be better able to compete with other religions and widen its own sphere of influence in society, thereby protecting its viability. . . .

In addition to these practical benefits accruing from allowing monks to marry, such basic doctrines of Korean Buddhism as "the unimpeded interpenetration of all phenomena" left no valid grounds for claiming that such a common human affair as marriage was unwholesome and thus deserving of being prohibited. The main reason monks were practicing celibacy, Yongun argued, was because of the Vinaya prohibition on sexual intercourse. But the cardinal Hwaom [Hua-yen] doctrine of interfusion offered an elegant solution to this restriction: since truth and falsity had no real essence, and merit and demerit had no fixed natures of their own, all such extremes were actually interfused. Thus celibacy and marriage were really no different and neither should be considered optimal for monastic practice. . . .

Neither the cabinet nor the monastery supervisory board responded to Yongun's petition. . . . Rebuffed by the government, he tried to lobby the ecclesiastical leaders of Korean Buddhism to accept such a move. In his "Essay on the Future of Buddhism and whether Monks and Nuns Should Be Allowed to Marry," . . . Han Yongun reiterated his arguments in systematic fashion. . . . [He] lists the four major arguments for maintaining the prohibition against marriage, and repudiates each.

1. Clergy marriage controverts ethical norms. Yongun replies that most people consider the greatest ethical sin to be a lack of filial piety. By not carrying on the lineage of the family, the celibate monk is offending the hundreds of thousands of generations of both ancestors and potential successors. Yongun here has simply revived an old argument, used often against Buddhism throughout its history in East Asia, that Buddhists were unfilial.
2. Clergy marriage injures the nation. Yongun replies that in civilized countries (meaning the West), where people are free to choose their own marriage partner, the population has expanded rapidly, allowing dramatic economic and social progress as well. When the liberal politicians of the Occident hear that Buddhist monks are prohibited from marrying, "they are suprised and feel sadness." While this may seem to us a rather naive position for Yongun to adopt, it is one that would appeal to the cultural and social inferiority Koreans were feeling during this period.

3. Clergy marriage impedes proselytization. Although Buddhists are trying to disseminate their religion throughout the world, Yongun explains, if they restrict marriage and do not allow potential converts to have a family, then who would have any interest in converting to Buddhism?
4. Clergy marriage inhibits moral development. Humans have strong desires for food and sex; indeed persons who have physical bodies but say they have no such desires are braggarts and liars. But if people forcibly try to repress their desires by clinging to the precepts, those desires will only become stronger, bringing immense grief to them and making any kind of happiness impossible. . . .

Han's petitions and lobbying to allow marriage initially gained little support within the order. In March, 1913, for example, at a meeting of the abbots of the thirty head monasteries, an agreement was reached prohibiting wives from living in the temples, as well as forbidding women from lodging overnight in the monasteries. But these restrictions were difficult to maintain, given the calls for secularization occurring among some of the reformers within the order and the support of the Japanese governor-general for a married clergy. Within a decade, monks maintaining celibacy were in the minority. Finally, in October, 1926, intense Japanese pressure compelled the head abbots to repeal the prohibition against marriage. From that point on monks were officially allowed to marry and eat meat. Within three years, some eighty percent of monasteries formally eliminated the restriction on having wives in residence, marking the end of an era for traditional Korean Buddhism and the beginnings of a new schism in the order between married priests (*taech'osung*) and celibate monks (*pikkusung*).

A married clergy created profound changes in Korean monastic life during the Japanese colonial period. Monks with families needed guaranteed sources of income, prompting monks to acccumulate private property and often take gainful employment. Such moves not only reduced the amount of property held in common by the monasteries, thus creating economic hardship for the bhikṣus who refused to take jobs, but also limited the amount of time spent in traditional monastic vocations, such as doctrinal study, meditation practice, and proselytization. Conveniently for the Japanese colonial administration as well, married monks were much more sedentary, tied as they were to their families and jobs, and thus much less able to travel freely about the country fomenting demonstrations, or possibly spying, as were the celibate monks.

Source: Reprinted by permission of the author from Robert E. Buswell, Jr., "Is Celibacy Anachronistic? Korean Debates over the Secularization of Buddhism during the Japanese Occupation Period," unpublished paper presented to the conference Toward an American Vinaya, Green Gulch Zen Center, Sausalito, California, June 3–8, 1990.

CHAPTER 10

Buddhists and the Practice of Buddhism: The West

It is common to think of Buddhism as an Asian religion. After all, its roots lie in India and, as we have seen in the last several chapters, its main branches have spread in other parts of Asia. But Buddhism is also a world religion, and its ability to adapt to a variety of different cultures is by no means limited to the Asian continent. Gradually over the last two centuries, and more and more rapidly over the last four decades, Buddhists and the practice of Buddhism have become part and parcel of the religious pluralism that now marks cultures in Western Europe and North America.

In this new context, at least three polarities—some of them new, some of them not—may be discerned. The first is a polarity between diversity and ecumenism. Buddhists and Buddhisms have come west from all parts of Asia, representing all schools of Buddhism. For perhaps the first time in history, adherents of Theravāda, Zen, Pure Land, Nichirenism, Vajrayāna, and other schools, representing multiple traditions from Sri Lanka, Thailand, Laos, Cambodia, China, Japan, Korea, Vietnam, and Tibet, coexist side by side in a single culture. On one hand, this has made some Buddhists in the West more acutely conscious of sectarian affiliations; on the other hand, it has served to break down some of those affiliations and promote "intra-Buddhist" dialogue or even the syncretistic combination of different traditions. This can take place at the individual level (a Westerner, for instance, might combine practices from Zen and Tibetan Buddhism), or at the institutional level (a single temple might mix different traditions).

Second, there is a polarity between Buddhists who are immigrants from different Asian countries and "non-Asian" persons who are converts to one form of Buddhism or another. For members of the first group, Buddhism tends to be caught up in a sense of cultural identity. For them, moreover, "rebirth and karma are often treated as existential facts, bodhisattvas as dynamic, personalized forces or cosmic entities. Liberation and awakening are essentially religious aspirations and rituals often retain an unambiguous sense of being efficacious."[1] For members of the second group, Buddhism is often

[1]Richard Hughes Seager, *Buddhism in America* (New York: Columbia University Press, 1999), p. 234.

caught up in forming a new identity, or it may be integrated with a basically secular outlook and seen as therapeutic or liberating but not as fundamentally "religious." Between these two poles is a third group, consisting of children of the first group, for whom Buddhism may serve as a way to hold onto or rediscover a cultural identity—to find and explore their roots—or it may be something to be jettisoned altogether.

Finally, there is also a polarity between what is known as "Engaged Buddhism" and what might be called the "Buddhism of Disengagement." The latter inclines towards meditation or other forms of practice, "retreats," and refuge from a turbulent world. The former emphasizes organizing in support of social justice, gender equity, environmental awareness, world peace, and other causes. Sometimes both tendencies are combined within single individuals or institutions. In some ways, this is but a new manifestation of an old polarity between "forest monks," who stress meditation and practice, and "town monks," who occupy themselves with the needs of their parishioners but applied now to both monastic and lay devotees. In other ways, however, it involves new departures.

10.1 MYTHIC HISTORIES: SMOKEY THE BEAR SŪTRA

Buddhism has not been established in the West long enough for it to develop myths about its first coming here. It has, however, spawned some creative speculation about that topic. Just as Buddhism, moving into China, resulted both in the translation of Sanskrit sūtras into Chinese and in the creation of new "apocryphal" texts aimed at responding to the new cultural situation, so too the interpretation of the Buddha's teachings has proceeded in the West.

The poet Gary Snyder's "Smokey the Bear Sūtra" has probably not achieved the status of a myth or even of an apocryphal text, but it is an example of syncretism in the making, and it shows us that that process does not always have to be deadly serious. It is a difficult poem to evaluate: part parody, it is, at the same time, obviously informed by Snyder's considerable knowledge of several forms of Buddhism, his environmental consciousness, and his abilities to see the East in the West and vice versa.

Once in the Jurassic, about 150 million years ago,
the Great Sun Buddha in this corner of the Infinite
Void gave a great Discourse to all the assembled elements
and energies: to the standing beings, the walking beings,
the flying beings, and the sitting beings—even grasses,
to the number of thirteen billion, each one born from a
seed, were assembled there: a Discourse concerning
Enlightenment on the planet Earth.

"In some future time, there will be a continent called
America. It will have great centers of power
such as Pyramid Lake, Walden Pond, Mt. Rainier, Big Sur,
Everglades, and so forth; and powerful nerves and channels

such as Columbia River, Mississippi River, and Grand Canyon.
The human race in that era will get into troubles all over
its head, and practically wreck everything in spite of
its own strong intelligent Buddha-nature.

"The twisting strata of the great mountains and the pulsings
of great volcanoes are my love burning deep in the earth.
My obstinate compassion is schist and basalt and
granite, to be mountains, to bring down the rain. In that
future American Era I shall enter a new form: to cure
the world of loveless knowledge that seeks with blind hunger;
and mindless rage eating food that will not fill it."

And he showed himself in his true form of

SMOKEY THE BEAR.

A handsome smokey-colored brown bear standing on his
hind legs, showing that he is aroused and watchful.

Bearing in his right paw the Shovel that digs to the
truth beneath appearances; cuts the roots of useless attachments, and flings damp sand on the fires of greed and war;

His left paw in the Mudra of Comradely Display—indicating
that all creatures have the full right to live to their limits
and that deer, rabbits, chipmunks, snakes, dandelions,
and lizards all grow in the realm of the Dharma;

Wearing the blue work overalls symbolic of slaves and
laborers, the countless men oppressed by a civilization
that claims to save but only destroys;

Wearing the broad-brimmed hat of the West, symbolic of
the forces that guard the Wilderness, which is the Natural
State of the Dharma and the True Path of man on earth;
all true paths lead through mountains—

With a halo of smoke and flame behind, the forest fires
of the kali-yuga, fires caused by the stupidity of those
who think things can be gained and lost whereas in truth all
is contained vast and free in the Blue Sky and Green Earth
of One Mind;

Round-bellied to show his kind nature and that the great
earth has food enough for everyone who loves her and trusts her;

Trampling underfoot wasteful freeways and needless
suburbs; smashing the worms of capitalism and totalitarianism;

Indicating the Task: his followers, becoming free of cars,
houses, canned food, universities, and shoes, master the
Three Mysteries of their own Body, Speech, and Mind; and
fearlessly chop down the rotten trees and prune out the
sick limbs of this country America and then burn the leftover trash.

Wrathful but Calm, Austere but Comic, Smokey the Bear will Illuminate those who would help him; but for those who would hinder or slander him,

HE WILL PUT THEM OUT.

Thus his great Mantra:
Namah samanta vajranam chanda maharoshana
Sphataya huṃ traka haṃ maṃ

"I DEDICATE MYSELF TO THE UNIVERSAL
DIAMOND BE THIS RAGING FURY DESTROYED"

And he will protect those who love woods and river, Gods and animals, hoboes and madmen, prisoners and sick people, musicians, playful women, and hopeful children;

And if anyone is threatened by advertising, air pollution, or the police, they should chant SMOKEY THE BEAR'S
WAR SPELL:
DROWN THEIR BUTTS
CRUSH THEIR BUTTS
DROWN THEIR BUTTS
CRUSH THEIR BUTTS

And SMOKEY THE BEAR will surely appear to put the enemy out with his vajra-shovel.
Now those who recite this Sūtra and then try to put it in practice will accumulate merit as countless as the sands of Arizona and Nevada,
Will help save the planet Earth from total oil slick,
Will enter the age of harmony of man and nature,
Will win the tender love and caresses of men, women, and beasts
Will always have ripe blackberries to eat and a sunny spot under a pine tree to sit at,

AND IN THE END WILL WIN HIGHEST PERFECT
ENLIGHTENMENT.

Thus have we heard.

Source: Reprinted by permission of the author from "Smokey the Bear Sūtra," in Gary Snyder, *The Fudo Trilogy* (Berkeley: Shaman Drum, 1973).

10.2 INTERACTIONS AND SYNCRETISM: THE EXPERIENCE OF A JEWISH BUDDHIST

As non-Buddhists have taken up Buddhist practice in the West, they have sometimes turned away from the religious traditions they were brought up in, but they have also sometimes found their original faiths deepened. It has long been remarked that a strikingly large number of "converts" to Buddhism in North America have come out of Jewish backgrounds. Indeed, estimates put the percentage of Jews or former Jews in Buddhist groups in the United States as over ten times higher than the percentage of Jews in the population at large, prompting some authors to popularize the term "Jubu" to denote this phenomenon. In particular, affinities have been felt between Tibetan and Jewish spiritual leaders, who have held a number of meetings exploring commonalities such as the experience of the diaspora. Sylvia Boorstein is an American meditation teacher and psychotherapist who describes herself as both a "faithful Jew" and a "passionate Buddhist." In the following selection, she describes how her experiences with meditation brought her back to the observances of her youth.

I was forty years old when I was introduced to Buddhist meditation, and I was surprised to find how much I loved monastic life. Some of my friends were surprised by my new schedule—going off at regular intervals for a week or two of "sitting."

"You *like* that?"

"How can you *stand* not talking?"

"No *reading* either? I'd go crazy! What do you *do* all day?"

I didn't try to explain a lot—I'm not sure, retrospectively, that I understood it myself, and anyway I was at the older edge of the wave of new meditators in the 1970s and my friends were generally too old to be "hip."

I think it was inevitable that Jews studying Buddhism and discovering the tranquillity, orderliness, and seriousness of meditation retreats would compare these new religious experiences with synagogue experiences. Jewish meditators routinely told me:

"No one sits quietly in *shul*!"

"We had a fifteen-second silent reflection, and then the music started. I couldn't even decide whom I was going to pray *for*, much less pray!"

"People are coming and going all the time."

"I don't believe in a God."

"The liturgy is sexist."

"There is nothing *spiritual* going on there."

I'd had some of those same thoughts myself.

A number of years had passed between my being an active member of a synagogue community and the beginning of my meditation practice. I wasn't looking for a new community. My family and friends and professional life were *full* of people whom I loved. I was looking for a practice. Indeed, the fact that retreats are *not* interactive was (and is) a great allure. I find the presence of other meditators a sustaining structure—my discipline in keeping the retreat schedule is silently supported by meditators around me practicing the same form in the same space. I was delighted to discover what a relief it is to be able to depend on everyone to leave me alone. Retreatants don't make eye contact. I feel I am being respected. I feel that everyone has said, "I know you can do this!"

Monasteries appeal to me. I've never been to Asia to practice meditation, and I've never spent many consecutive months intensively practicing in this country as many of my friends have. But I might have, had my life circumstances been different, because I love the quiet, the simplicity, and both the peacefulness of the contented, focused mind and the sometimes surprising (albeit temporal) bliss, rapture, and fireworks (yes indeed, *even* sitting, *especially* sitting still) of the radically clear mind. The monastic path, however, was never an option for me. I had a husband and four children when I discovered meditation—now I have grandchildren—and family life is *also* very appealing to me. I've tried to interpolate retreat practice into my family's schedule skillfully. It's been a bit like carrying a double major in college. When I think of all the retreats I've been part of over the last twenty years—a week here, two weeks there, ten days, and sometimes a whole month at a time—I think, "At *least* two years, maybe three, if I added it all up."

Some practice periods have been harder than others; they've all been different, but one experience has been consistent. At any retreat, anywhere, two or three days into the silence, I feel my mind (and my body) relax. "Aaaah," I think, "This is *it*. This is the proper way to live. In a graceful, cooperative, silent community. I wish I could stay here forever." Then, some time later—days, sometimes weeks—I begin to think about my family again and feel enthusiastic about resuming my relational life and my work life. Most often the transition back to regular life has been easy. The first few days are interesting—everyone seems busier and noisier than I remember—but I try to make the adjustment part of my practice. After all, an attachment to silence and slowness would be another attachment and would mean more suffering. I do love retreat practice, though, and I love teaching retreat discipline. And a year ago I joined a local synagogue.

Joining a synagogue after a twenty-year absence seems like it might mark some particular event—a particular insight, or even a particular birthday. That wasn't my experience. Belonging or not belonging for two decades had not been an issue. I didn't think about it. Synagogue membership seems yet another aspect of my current life, like prayers and Sabbath observance, that was absent for a while and has now become important. Each renewed practice has seemed timely. "Oh yes, I guess this *is* what I want to do." I never felt an obligation.

When I think about the forms of Jewish practice that have reentered my life I see—or at least I *think* I see—how they built on each other and how they were inspired by my monastic Buddhist meditation practice. Practicing mindfulness I felt peaceful and happy. Feeling peaceful and happy caused me to say blessings. Saying blessings reminded me of prayers, which I had found comforting as a child, and inspired me to pray again. My meditation experiences, especially those that presented themselves in terms of Scripture imagery, reminded me to read Scripture again. At some point I adjusted my reading schedule to the weekly Torah portion. I'm fairly sure my Sabbath observance is a direct consequence of my monastic practice. The possibility of a regularly scheduled day set aside for mindful recollection, meditation, and study—one that I could ritually celebrate with my family—is compelling.

Source: Reprinted by permission of HarperCollins Publishers from Sylvia Boorstein, *That's Funny, You Don't Look Buddhist* (New York: HarperSanFrancisco, 1997), pp. 140–43. Copyright © 1996 by Sylvia Boorstein and Sharon Lebell.

10.3 DIVISIONAL ISSUES: THE VENERATION OF RELICS

Among the persons who were instrumental in the late nineteenth century revival of Buddhism in Sri Lanka, the American theosophist Colonel Henry Steele Olcott played a unique role. Soon after he arrived on the island, along with Helena Petrovna Blavatsky, he established the Buddhist Theosophical Society, which helped organize Sri Lankan monks and laypersons in opposition to the forces of Christian missionaries. Olcott and the BTS founded schools, established Buddhist Sunday school programs, designed the Buddhist flag, convinced the colonial government to recognize Buddhist holidays, and spawned other organizations such as the Mahā Bodhi Society and the YMBA (Young Men's Buddhist Association). Olcott expressed his own views in a work called *A Buddhist Catechism,* which was published in both English and Sinhalese and widely distributed. In it he presents Buddhism not in traditional terms, but as "a rational, scientific religion that sets out an ethical path to liberation without the necessity of a god or a divine revelation."[2]

Olcott had considerable influence on a young Sri Lankan, Anagārika Dharmapāla, who as a layman was instrumental in reclaiming for Buddhism Bodhgaya (the Indian site where the Buddha attained enlightenment, which had passed into Hindu hands) and in spreading the Theravāda tradition to the West (Dharmapāla was an important presence at the World Parliament of Religions in Chicago in 1893). Dharmapāla and Olcott shared many views in common about the nature of Buddhism, but over time tensions developed between them and they parted ways. Interestingly, the occasion for their split came when Dharmapāla felt Olcott had failed to express proper respect for a relic of the Buddha.

Buddhists all over Asia have long venerated bodily relics of the Buddha (or of arhats or other great teachers; see 6.1.2 and 6.5.2). For Dharmapāla, they were important symbols to be held in high esteem; for Olcott, they were more like objects of curiosity, mere mementos of a deceased Master. In many ways, then, relics (as well as Buddhist images and other objects of devotion) came to epitomize the difference between two views of Buddhism as it moved into the twentieth century. In certain circles, belief in them and their efficacy became a definitional question about the bottom line of Buddhism, just like other issues debated by Western Buddhists, such as whether or not belief in

[2]George D. Bond, *The Buddhist Revival in Sri Lanka: Religious Tradition, Reinterpretation and Response* (Columbia: University of South Carolina Press, 1988), p. 50.

rebirth is a necessary part of the religion. Relics can thus be seen as a focal point for larger questions: Is Buddhism basically a "philosophy," or is it a "faith"? Is it a rational doctrine presenting a provable, experienceable world view, or is it a religion replete with rituals, beliefs, and "worship"?

The same issue of relics came up again in an interesting exchange between another American theosophist, Dr. Paul Carus of LaSalle, Illinois, and a Sri Lankan monk, the Venerable Alutgama Seelakkhandha. Carus himself was very influential in the spread of Buddhism in the West, not only through his own publication, *The Gospel of Buddhism,* but through his support of a young Japanese scholar, D. T. Suzuki, who became renowned for his popularization of Zen. When the Venerable Seelakkhandha wrote to Carus offering to send him some Pali books and some Buddha-relics, he was grateful but declined the latter, saying "I do not think that I would care for relics of human bodies, bones, teeth, or anything of that kind." Seelakkhandha promptly replied that these were not ordinary bones, these were relics "that are held most sacred. There is nothing more valuable to a Buddhist than a genuine relic." Although one could not obtain nirvāṇa (or any worldly benefit) by venerating relics, they did help purify the mind and give one courage to practice the Way. Carus, however, had his own views, which he expressed in the following selection from one of his letters to Seelakkhandha.

I wish to add a few words to my letter of yesterday with reference to the relics. I feel that if you were to send me one of those relics which you from *your* standpoint with good reasons consider so dear to you, you would be deprived of a treasure which would be less to me than it is to you. I would value these relics for historical reasons only. They would in my eyes be an evidence of the reverence in which you hold the memory of the Buddha and his saints, but otherwise they would only be to me objects of curiosity. According to my conception of Buddhism, the most sacred relics we have of the Buddha and his saints are the words which they left,—the Sūtras and all those ideas which can be verified in experience as valuable truths. Words, thoughts and ideas are not material things, they are spiritual. It is true that they are transferred by material means in books and manuscripts, and by the air vibrations of sounds, but it is not the paper of the book, or the fibres of the manuscript, or the sound-waves, that are sacred, but the ideas which are conveyed by them. Thus, all the treasures which I regard as holy are spiritual, and not material. The worship of relics, be they bones, hair, teeth, or any other substance of the body of a saint, is a mistake. They do not possess any other value than the remains of ordinary mortals. The soul of Buddha is not in his bones, but in his words, and I regard relic-worship as an incomplete stage of religious development in which devotees have not as yet attained to full philosophical clearness. Now, it certainly is of interest to me to have evidences of the religious zeal of Buddhists. The keeping sacred of relics is a *symptom of their devotion,* but that is all I see in the use of relics. And considering that these relics are more to you than to me, I feel that I should not deprive you of them. Therefore, do not send me relics except it be on the stipulated condition that you know what I think about them. Otherwise you might regret afterwards having sent them to a man in whose conception they possess no religious value.

Source: Reprinted from Paul Carus, "A Buddhist Priest's View of Relics," *The Open Court* 11 (1897): 123.

10.4 REGULATION AND REFORM: TOWARD AN ANDROGYNOUS RECONSTRUCTION OF BUDDHISM

One of the issues that Western Buddhists have been particularly sensitive to has been the sexism that has characterized many Buddhist monastic traditions. This is usually blamed for the failure of the Theravāda and Tibetan traditions to restore the lineage of fully ordained nuns as well as for the continued additional restrictions on women's status within the saṅgha. In the following selection, a scholar who is a feminist, a Buddhist, and a Westerner envisages the changes that will be required for things to be different.

Post-partriarchal monasticism does require some reconstruction from the present monastic practices. Some of these changes are nothing but restorations of what has been lost. Others would disrupt long-standing Buddhist practices that are male-dominant and disadvantageous to women. But none of them involves any major renovations to the basic structure and style of the monastic life.

The first, very obvious, reform is the restitution of full ordination for nuns in Theravādin and Tibetan Buddhism, in which it has been lost and has not been available for over a thousand years. Without this restoration, women are confined to perpetual novice status, in the Tibetan case, or to the status of "lay nuns," who receive no formal ordination ceremony at all, and wear white or other non-monastic colors, in Theravādin countries. Since the nuns' order, albeit with reservations and male hierarchy, was part of early Buddhism, it is hard to imagine opposition on Buddhist grounds. Even if no nuns' orders existed anywhere in the Buddhist world, it would be possible to reconstruct the order, if those in positions of authority cared enough about the quality of women's involvement in Buddhism. But the full ordination, including the ordination lineages and ceremonies, has survived in Chinese and Korean forms of Buddhism. In an age of international travel, receiving the ordination from these lineages presents no problems. [. . .]

The official [Tibetan] word about these ordinations is that they are under investigation to determine whether the ordination lineages are genuine and acceptable to the Tibetan Buddhist authorities. Given the urgency of the issue, such reactions and policies seem timid and unnecessary. Such recourse to legalism, which is not the religious concern usually dominant in Buddhism, and least of all, in Tibetan Buddhism, makes me suspicious that a smokescreen is being used to delay rectifying the denigration and objectification of women that occurs when there is any question about their abilities and rights to the monastic lifestyle. I doubt such caution would be employed if the issue concerned something of such vital importance to the male monastics. In fact, the monks' ordination has also been lost several times in various Buddhist countries throughout Buddhist history, but such lengthy investigations of the authenticity of the ordination lineage were not pursued when monks' ordination again became available. . . .

The situation in Theravādin countries is even more stark. Most of the monastic authorities are adamant in their opposition to recognizing nuns in Theravādin Buddhism, in large part because they are unwilling to recognize Mahāyāna ordination lineages as valid, even though those lineages derive historically from the same sources as their own ordination lineages. [. . .]

Even if the nuns' ordination were restored, that would not constitute an androgynous reconstruction of monasticism. [. . .] Formal subordination of nuns to monks is also part of the traditional monastic organization. The eight special rules [see 2.1.4] were a concession to the prevailing gender hierarchy of ancient India. They obviously have no relevance in post-patriarchal androgynous Buddhism, since their sole function is to subordinate all nuns to each and every monk. They involve a completely artificial gender hierarchy which has often inhibited nuns from functioning as religious authorities and teachers in Buddhism in general. Whatever hierarchy is necessary and appropriate in post-patriarchal Buddhism should be a hierarchy based on length of monastic standing and, even more, on accomplishments and abilities, which have little to do with gender. Men would then salute their female seniors in age and accomplishment, the practice that the Buddha objected to because not even heretical sects permitted women to be saluted by men. Since Buddhists have never worried about conventionality and being like everyone else in matters of doctrine, and, in fact, prided themselves on proclaiming truth, even if it goes "against the grain," it is painful to know that on this one issue, Buddhists have been so utterly conventional. It is time to go against the grain on this point too, since the humanity of half the Buddhist world is at stake.

The interactions of nuns and monks need to be reconsidered on one further important question. How much should the men's and women's orders be segregated for daily activities, study and practice? How much common life should the two orders engage in together? The *vinaya* rules limit quite severely the extent to which nuns and monks can interact on a regular basis for everyday activities. In the stories surrounding the formulation of these rules, most of the ordinances that separate the two orders resulted from gossip on the part of the laity that monks and nuns carried on sexual encounters under the pretext of meeting for joint religious ceremonies. . . . For reconstructing post-patriarchal Buddhism, such reasoning is hardly sufficient. Instead, it should be asked what kind of and how much interaction between the nuns and the monks would best facilitate the spiritual and intellectual development of both.

Regarding this question, arguments familiar from feminist debate will emerge. Sometimes, it is argued, quite persuasively, that women need the safety of their own assemblies, in which they will not be under subtle pressure to defer to men, and in which they would have to make decisions, learn to lead, and to manage their own affairs. If the nuns' order were truly autonomous, as it was not under the *vinaya* and the eight special rules, these benefits would happen of necessity.

Against this position is the argument that a completely segregated and separate group is more easily marginalized and ghettoized, as sometimes happens to the women's studies perspective in academic institutions. Unless the women's institutions have real power, they will then be financed on "soft money" and leftovers, which happened to the nuns throughout Buddhist history. It must also be asked whether "separate but equal" facilities can ever be a realistic possibility. . . . Why, to solve the problems of insufficient education and meditation training for nuns, should it be necessary to construct a whole parallel set of facilities and institutions when excellent ones already exist for men only? The current problems could probably be solved much more quickly and inexpensively if nuns simply trained with monks in the same classrooms and retreat centers, not as second-class inhabitants occupying the backs of those spaces, but as full-fledged equal members of the monastery.

Source: Reprinted by permission of the publisher from Rita M. Gross, *Buddhism after Patriarchy: A Feminist History, Analysis, and Reconstruction of Buddhism* (Albany: State University of New York Press, 1993), pp. 243–44, 246–47.

10.5 RITUALS AND FESTIVALS: THE BUDDHA'S BIRTHDAY IN LOS ANGELES

Three traditional popular festivals punctuate the Buddhist ritual year of Vietnamese émigré communities in the West: the Vu-Lan festival, which marks the end of the rains retreat and is usually celebrated in August; New Year's or Tet, which usually happens in February; and the Buddha's birthday on the full moon day in May. The following selection describes the celebrations at a Vietnamese temple in Los Angeles, which clearly serve multiple functions beyond just observing the birthday of the Buddha.

On this particular Sunday in May 1986, the 2,530th year since the birth of the Buddha, the Buddha's birthday is being celebrated in a big way. The Vietnamese Buddhist community seems to have the sense that . . . it has once more survived a difficult time against great odds, and that, though the future is uncertain and even perilous, there is much to be thankful for.

A large green parachute has been spread from roof to roof over the central couryard [of the temple]. Beneath this soft, translucent shelter, the

Vietnamese community and guests and friends are gathered. There is a large wooden platform in front. The Buddhist flag with its orange, white, red, yellow, and blue stripes is strung along the rooftops, and [is] in the hands of nearly everyone there. It is a bright, happy sort of flag—the same flag that [Ngo Dinh] Diem had forbidden the Buddhists of Hue to fly back in 1963. [. . .]

This year's celebration coincides with the United Nations International Year of Peace, and there is a representative from the U.N., as well as other dignitaries, representatives of the mayor's and governor's offices, and monks and nuns from other Buddhist traditions who now make their homes in Los Angeles and elsewhere in the United States. There are also a fair number of American Buddhists representing newer Buddhist groups.

There is no question that this is a Vietnamese celebration, but there is also no question that many others are included in it. This is due in no small part to the vision of the Most Venerable Thich Man Giac—the realization that in order for Buddhism to flourish in America, whether among Vietnamese or Americans or Vietnamese Americans, for that matter, it must adapt to its new home. "The customs of Americans are different from those of Asians," he says. "If we want Buddhism to develop and grow in the U.S., we must adapt to American customs."

Whatever the future may hold, today is a day to celebrate the continuing strength and resilience of the Vietnamese Buddhist traditions. The women have been cooking for days. Flowers and flags and balloons with the legend "Happy Birthday" are everywhere, particularly in the hands of toddlers bouncing around under the watchful eyes of slightly older brothers and sisters.

There are greetings and speeches from the platform, and there is chanting in praise of the Buddha in many of the languages of Buddhism—in Vietnamese, Korean, Japanese, Pali, and Sanskrit, and also in English. The president of the organizing committee of the celebration, Dr. Nguyen Thang Thai—a scholarly layman wearing a round black traditional hat that seems all brim—sums it all up when he says, "What happened in Vietnam—the misery and sorrow—has no end, but I want to make a solemn vow for peace and freedom in Vietnam." As is the custom on many Buddhist holidays, a number of pigeons are released, and then, as is the custom on this particular day, people file past a small figure of the Buddha and pour water over the image with a small ladle.

Berendo Street has been closed, or at least slowed down, by two motorcycle police, and the main concern is how to start and maneuver the float that is the centerpiece of the parade. The only way for the man driving to see out is through a few small holes bored in the flower-festooned wood panel that covers the front of the truck. The whole float is also covered with flowers. There is a large pink, white, red, yellow, and blue paper heart on one side framed by flowers, and on the other side is the Eight-spoked Wheel [of the Dharma]. Its spokes are made of flowers—red, orange, pale green, and pink, with blue in the center. On top of the float the Buddha stands, with the backdrop of India looking very blue and green and Himalayan cool in the Los Angeles heat. There are live trees on top of the float, too, with beautifully made orange and yellow paper flowers fixed in their leaves. Paper dragons with benevolent toothy smiles guard each side. Someone mentions that the monk in charge of getting the float ready hardly slept in a month. . . .

Finally, the Buddha's float begins to move slowly away from the curb toward the center of the street. There, four young girls wearing traditional Vietnamese clothes and with floral wreaths in their hair climb on top and take positions on the float.

First come two men holding a large banner that reads: "950 Million Buddhists All Over the World Happily Celebrate the Buddha's Birthday."

Then come four men, wearing traditional black robes, carrying an American flag, a Buddhist flag, the flag of the United Nations, and the yellow-and-red-striped flag of South Vietnam.

Then comes the Most Venerable Thich Man Giac, Supreme Abbot of Vietnamese Buddhists in America, wearing a bright yellow robe, a red transparent overrobe flecked with gold thread, and a high peaked hat. He is followed by four members of Long Hoa bearing a palanquin with a large incense burner. They are followed by more members of Long Hoa bearing flags from all over the world, and the green banners of Long Hoa, and by kids with lots of balloons.

Then a Vietnamese brass band, the players in dark trousers and white shirts.

Then the float with the Buddha and the four girls, moving slowly and carefully, guided by members of Long Hoa.

Then an oil painting of the Venerable Thich Quang-Duc—the first monk to immolate himself—his robes in flames, held aloft on a palanquin by four young men.

Then the banners, in various languages:

"There is No Religious Freedom in Vietnam."

"Long Live the Sacrificial Spirit of the Venerable Thich Quang-Duc."

"Long Live World Buddhism."

"Unity is Strength."

And, finally, "950 Million Buddhists All Over the World Unite with Other Religions to Serve World Peace."

Source: Reprinted with permission from Rick Fields, *Taking Refuge in L.A.: Life in a Vietnamese Buddhist Temple,* photographs by Don Farber (New York: Aperture Foundation, 1987), pp. 103–105.

10.6 MEDITATIONAL ENDEAVORS

10.6.1 Telephone Mindfulness

Thich Nhat Hanh is a Vietnamese Buddhist monk who presently lives at Plum Village, a monastic training center that he founded in southwestern France. His early activities in the 1960s in support of peace in his own country led to his being forced to remain in exile, where he has become a leader in the movement he dubbed "Engaged Buddhism." At the same time, he has been a prolific author on Buddhist traditions of contemplation and meditation and on adapting Buddhist teachings to Western circumstances. The following meditative contemplation, written in 1990, proposes using something as simple as answering the phone or making a call as an occasion for mindfulness and compassion. In the same work, Nhat Hanh also gives advice on how to watch television, how to drive a car, how to turn on and off a light, and other daily activities.

[Verse {gāthā}]:

Words can travel thousands of miles.
May my words create mutual understanding and love.
May they be as beautiful as gems,
as lovely as flowers.

When the telephone rings, the bell creates in us a kind of vibration, maybe some anxiety: "Who is calling? Is it good news or bad news?" There is a force which pulls us to the phone. We cannot resist. We are victims of our own telephone.

The next time you hear the phone ring, I recommend that you stay exactly where you are, and become aware of your breathing: "Breathing in, I calm my body. Breathing out, I smile." When the phone rings the second time, you can breathe again. I am sure that this time your smile will be more solid than before. When it rings the third time, you can continue practicing breathing, while moving slowly to the phone. You are your own master, walking like a Buddha to the phone, dwelling in mindfulness. When you pick up the phone, you know that you are smiling, not only for your own sake, but also for the sake of the other person. If you are irritated or angry, the other person will receive your negativity. But since you are smiling, how fortunate for him or her!

You can write down the telephone gatha and tape it onto your phone. I suggest that before you lift the receiver to make a call, you touch the phone, breathe in and out twice, and recite the four lines. Then pick up the phone and dial. When the bell rings, you know that your friend is breathing and smiling and will not pick up the phone until the third ring. So you continue to practice: "Breathing in, I calm my body. Breathing out, I smile." Both of you are close to your phones, breathing and smiling. This is very beautiful! You do not have to go into a meditation hall to do this wonderful practice. It is available in your house or office. Practicing telephone meditation can counteract stress and depression and bring the Buddha into your daily life.

Source: Reprinted by permission of the publisher from Thich Nhat Hanh, *Present Moment, Wonderful Moment: Mindfulness Verses for Daily Living* (Berkeley: Parallax Press, 1990), pp. 69–70.

10.6.2 A Guided Meditation

Buddhism in the West is not always about adaptation and change. It is also about transmission. Thanissaro Bhikkhu (Geoffrey DeGraff) is an American who was ordained in Thailand in 1976 and who, fifteen years later, returned to the United States, where he is now abbot of the Metta Forest Monastery near San Diego. His teacher in Thailand, Ajaan Fuang Jotiko, was a disciple of Ajaan Lee Dhammadaro, who belonged to the forest ascetic tradition revived, reformed, and given a new reputation for discipline by Ajaan Mun Bhuridatto in the early part of the twentieth century. One of the meditation techniques espoused by these teachers is their own version of the tradition of breathing mindfulness. In the following selection, Thanissaro Bhikkhu explains it for Westerners.

Sit comfortably erect, without leaning forward or back, left or right. Close your eyes and think thoughts of good will. Thoughts of good will go first to yourself, because if you can't think good will for yourself—if you can't feel a sincere desire for your own happiness—there's no way you can truly wish for the happiness of others. So just tell yourself, "May I find true happiness." Remind yourself that true happiness is something that comes from within, so this is not a selfish desire. In fact, if you find and develop the resources for happiness within you, you're able to radiate it out to other people. It's a happiness that doesn't depend on taking anything away from anyone else.

So now spread good will to other people. First, people who are close to your heart—your family, your parents, your very close friends: May they find true happiness, as well. Then spread those thoughts out in ever widening circles: people you know well, people you don't know so well, people you like, people you know and are neutral about, and even people you don't like. Don't let there be any limitations on your good will, for if there are, there will be limitations on your mind. Now spread thoughts of good will to people you don't even know—and not just people; all living beings of all kinds in all directions: east, west, north, south, above, and below, out to infinity. May they find true happiness, too.

Then bring your thoughts back to the present. If you want true happiness, you have to find it in the present, for the past is gone and the future is an uncertainty. So you have to dig down into the present. What do you have right here? You've got the body, sitting here and breathing. And you've got the mind, thinking and aware. So bring all these things together. Think about the breath and then be aware of the breath as it comes in and goes out. Keeping your thoughts directed to the breath: that's mindfulness. Being aware of the breath as it comes in and out: that's alertness. Keep those two aspects of the mind together. If you want, you can use a meditation word to strengthen your mindfulness. Try "Buddho," which means "awake." Think "bud-" with the in-breath, "dho" with the out.

Try to breathe as comfortably as possible. A very concrete way of learning how to provide for your own happiness in the immediate present—and at the same time, strengthening your alertness—is to let yourself breathe in a way that's comfortable. Experiment to see what kind of breathing feels best for the body right now. It might be long breathing, short breathing; in long, out short; or in short, out long. Heavy or light, fast or slow, shallow or deep. Once you find a rhythm that feels comfortable, stay with it for a while. Learn to savor the sensation of the breathing. Generally speaking, the smoother the texture of the breath, the better. Think of the breath, not simply as the air coming in and out of the lungs, but as the entire energy flow that courses through the body with each in-and-out breath. Be sensitive to the texture of the energy flow. You may find that the body changes after a while. One rhythm or texture may feel right for a while, and then something else will feel more comfortable. Learn how to listen and respond to what the body is telling you right now. What kind of breath energy does it need? How can you best provide for that need? If you feel tired, try to breathe in a way that energizes the body. If you feel tense, try to breathe in a way that's relaxing.

If your mind wanders off, gently bring it right back. If it wanders off ten times, a hundred times, bring it back ten times, a hundred times. Don't give in. This quality is called ardency. In other words, as soon as you realize that the mind has slipped away, you bring it right back. You don't spend time aimlessly sniffing at the flowers, looking at the sky, or listening to the birds. You've got work to do: work in learning how to breathe comfortably, how to let the mind settle down in a good space here in the present moment.

When the breath starts feeling comfortable, you can start exploring it in other areas of the body. If you simply stay with the comfortable breath in a narrow range, you'll tend to doze off. So consciously expand your awareness. A good place to focus first is right around the navel. Locate that part of the body in your awareness: where is it right now? Then notice: how does it feel there as you breathe in? How does it feel when you breathe out? Watch it for a couple of breaths, and notice if there's any sense of tension or tightness in that part of the body, either with the in-breath or with the out-breath. Is it tensing up as you breathe in? Are you holding onto the tension as you breathe out? Are you putting too much force on the out-breath? If you catch yourself doing any of these things, just relax. Think of that tension dissolving away in the sensation of the in-breath, the sensation of the out-breath. If you want, you can think of the breath energy coming into the body right there at the navel, working through any tension or tightness that you might feel there. . . .

Then move your awareness to the right—to the lower right-hand corner of your abdomen—and follow the same three steps there: (1) locate that general part of the body in your awareness; (2) notice how it feels as you breathe in, how it feels as you breathe out; and (3) if you sense any tension or tightness in the breath, just let it relax. . . . Now move your awareness to the left, to the lower left-hand corner of your abdomen, and follow the same three steps there.

Now move your awareness up to the solar plexus . . . and then to the right, to the right flank . . . to the left flank . . . to the middle of the chest. . . . After a while move up to the base of the throat... and then to the middle of the head. Be very careful with the breath energy in the head. Think of it very gently coming in, not only through the nose but also throught the eyes, the ears, down from the top of the head, in from the back of the neck, very gently working through and loosening up any tension you may feel, say, around your jaws, the back of your neck, around your eyes, or around your face. . . .

From there you can move your attention gradually down the back, out the legs, to the tips of the toes, the spaces between the toes. . . . Then repeat the process, beginning at the back of the neck and going down the shoulders, through the arms, past your wrists, and out through your fingers.

You can repeat this survey of the body as many times as you like until the mind feels ready to settle down.

Then let your attention return to any spot in the body where it feels most naturally settled and centered. Simply let your attention rest there, at one with the breath. At the same time let the range of your awareness spread out so that it fills the entire body, like the light of a candle in the middle of a room: the candle flame is in one spot, but its light fills the entire room. Or like a spider on a web: the spider's in one spot, but it knows the whole web. Be keen on maintaining that broadened sense of awareness. You'll find that it tends to shrink, like a balloon with a small hole in it, so keep broadening its range, thinking "whole body, whole body, breath in the whole body, from the top of the head down into the tips of the toes." Think of the breath energy coming in and out of the body through every pore. Make a point of staying with this centered, broadened awareness as long as you can. There's nothing else you have to think about right now, nowhere else to go, nothing else to do. Just stay with this centered, broadened awareness of the present. . . .

When the time comes to leave meditation, remind yourself that there's a skill to leaving. In other words, you don't just jump right out. My teacher, Ajaan Fuang, once said that when most people meditate, it's as if they're climbing a ladder up to the second story of a building: step-by-step-by-step, rung-by-rung, slowly up the ladder. But as soon as they get to the second story, they jump out the window. Don't let yourself be that way. Think of how much effort went into getting the mind centered. Don't throw it away.

The first step in leaving is to spread thoughts of good will once more to all the people around you. Then, before you open your eyes, remind yourself that even though you're going to have our eyes open, you want your attention to stay centered in the body, at the breath. Try to maintain that center as long as you can, as you get up, walk around, talk, listen, whatever. In other words, the skill of leaving meditation lies in learning how not to leave it, regardless of whatever else you may be doing. Act from that sense of being centered. If you can keep the mind centered in this way, you'll have a standard against which you can measure its movements, its reactions to the events around it and within it. Only when you have a solid center like this can you gain insight into the movements of the mind.

Source: Reprinted by permission of the author from Thanissaro Bhikkhu, *Noble Strategy* (Valley Center, CA: Metta Forest Monastery, 1999), pp. 37–41.

10.7 WOMEN AND THE SANGHA: LIVING AS A NUN IN THE WEST

One of the features of Buddhism in the West is a new ecumenism. Karma Lekshe Tsomo is a Western Budddhist nun who became a novice in the Tibetan tradition in France and later received full ordination as a nun in Korea and Taiwan. At the same time, she has also pursued an academic career. Her proposal for an "ideal Western Buddhist monastery" reflects not only her recognition of the realities of the context in which she finds herself but also the meeting of a variety of Buddhist traditions.

As the *Buddhadharma* goes to the West, it sometimes happens that Western people are inspired to lead celibate lives and receive ordination. The wish to become ordained may be a spontaneous impulse of the moment or it may be a reasoned decision based on practical considerations. In either case, there is usually a sincere commitment to the *Dharma* and a desire to devote more time to the practice. Almost all people received precepts with the best intentions, yet their lives following ordination take many different turns.

It is hard to visualize the effect that making such a serious commitment will have. Things are never exactly as we imagine. Ordination makes a deep impact upon the mind, often in ways that are inexpressible and imperceptible. Experiences differ, depending largely upon the extent to which we get caught up in judgments, labeling, and expectations. Nevertheless, we wake up the next day with a new perception of ourselves and our relationship to the world. We are faced with new feelings and practical realities that are complex in themselves, being further intensified by the responses of people around us. Even if nothing in particular changes, experiences register in new ways.

While the experience of living as a nun or monk within a loving supportive community will certainly differ from getting ordained and immediately being left completely on one's own, in either case the first teaching of the ordained life is often that we are born alone and die alone. There is no longer anything or anyone to lean on. Essentially the ordained life means relying on the inner experience of the teachings without external props. In a sense, Western people who have been raised to function independently may find it easier to adjust to such a life. The sense of aloneness which persists even in ordained community life is much harder for Asian people to cope with, since they are generally accustomed to a closely interdependent family life. After embarking upon "the homeless life," the monastic community often becomes a surrogate family for them.

The problems encountered by Western people in ordained life more often relate to discipline, emotional conflicts, and physical circumstances. A high percentage return to lay life. If ordained life is so conducive to practice and the people who enter it are so committed to the *Dharma,* what accounts for the high drop-out rate? Clearly, this is a question that requires in-depth research and should not be over-generalized. It is a very personal and individual matter, but a few thoughts on the subject may be in order.

Logic tells us that a decision to give up the celibate life may relate to problems in maintaining celibacy. It has become something of an "in" joke in ordained circles that no one gives up their vows due to an overwhelming desire to eat after noon. Some frankly admit to "falling in love." Others become ordained without having satisfactorily explored the limits of relationship and later find curiosity gets the better of them. Some find abstinence restrictive after ordination, though it was never a problem before.

Another problem relates to discipline and culturally conditioned value systems. A valid *Prāṭimokṣa* ordination is necessarily received in a particular *Vinaya* school, which at this point is transmitted through the medium of an Asian Buddhist tradition. The customs concomitant with the traditional lineage may complement individualistic Western lifestyles, but they may also conflict. The latter experience seems to be quite common.

While acknowledging and respecting the tremendous debt owed to Asian cultures, it is obvious that we Western Buddhists need time and space in which to find our own directions. We need to be strict, but not too rigid; to be open and flexible, but not sloppy. We need to learn from Asian Buddhist prototypes without being overwhelmed by Asian cultural components. We want to devise modes of practice which preserve the essence of the Buddha's teachings, yet are compatible with Western civilization. We should strive to preserve the most excellent values of East and West.

Accepting Buddhism does not mean forfeiting the positive aspects of our own religious and cultural heritages; however, becoming a nun or monk does imply adopting genuine Buddhist values authentically. One recommended method is to train closely with respected Asian exponents of monastic discipline during the first years of ordained life. Adjustments to Western cultural and social conditions can then be made on a solid foundation of understanding. Such training is an experience to be treasured. Similar to training in the martial arts, it requires humility and perseverance. While some people cite the hardships of traditional monastic training and the cultural adjustments it requires as reasons for giving up their vows, paradoxically, others cite the lack of such training as a reason. Certainly some experience of traditional training is important for nuns and monks, since they will be instrumental in the process of adapting traditional Buddhist institutions to the Western situation.

There is no doubt that Buddhism is a valuable spiritual path for large numbers of Western people, but is ordination a viable step when there are as yet very few monasteries in the West where they can stay and train? Is living on one's own a realistic alternative? What models should we look to in setting up monastic training centers and what problems can we expect to encounter in the process? Whose job is it to set up such centers and when are they going to get started?

There is a definite consensus on the need for centers where nuns and potential nuns can become accustomed to monastic life. Chaotic environments simply are not conducive to formal meditation practice and disciplined conduct. Living on one's own, isolated from a supportive sangha and vulnerable to the onslaught of worldly values, can be quite unsettling, especially in the beginning years. Ordained women need monasteries where they can study and attempt to live by the *Vinaya;* laywomen need protective surroundings where they can prepare for ordination and can gain experience in monastic values before making a lifelong commitment.

In addition to an intense awareness of the need for training centers, there is a recognition that monasteries for Westerners will differ in some important respects from Asian Buddhist models. Along with this recognition, there is growing concern that meaningful time-honored traditions not be discarded simply on the basis of superficial impressions. Even if they may appear exotic, extraneous, or constraining in the beginning, some traditions have symbolic or psychological significance that can be of great value in the practice. Wisdom and mature judgement are required to discern what will ultimately benefit and what will impede our spiritual growth. Nuns, monks, and others who have undergone many years of formal training have a special responsibility to understand traditions and interpret them for others. They can serve as cultural bridges, helping to bring about a graceful transition from ancient to modern practice.

There are some traditional practices that seem especially apt to arouse resistance—for instance, bowing. It is the custom of bowing to *bhikṣus,* the first of the eight important rules for *bhikṣuṇīs* [see 2.1.4], that is most difficult for Western women to countenance. This is understandable; Western people normally have difficulty bowing to anything, especially another human being, whether female or male. The Buddhist custom of bowing to statues of enlightened beings has been widely misinterpreted as "idol worship," causing great misunderstanding since it contravenes one of the ten commandments of the Judaeo-Christian faith. Actually the custom of bowing is meant to demonstrate respect for the enlightenment potential within all living beings, including oneself, and is not a display of worship or subservience at all. Bowing is also used as a practice for engendering humility. In some Buddhist countries the custom of bowing to senior nuns and monks is still widely practiced; in others, it is normally reserved for paying reverence to learned or realized masters. It derives from the ancient Indian custom of showing respect to elders; even in contemporary Sri Lanka and India, well-mannered children bow to their parents every morning.

By contrast, Western people do not always naturally engender respect along the lines of seniority. Most are accustomed to making independent decisions, and may resist authority and structures altogether unless they lead to tangible rewards and punishments. The large measure of social, economic, and academic freedom current in Western cultures stimulates individual creativity, even genius, but does little to promote personal discipline. Discipline is frequently labeled suppressive, constrictive, or authoritarian. For those seriously interested in developing self-discipline, therefore, periods of monastic training in traditional Asian monasteries will prove greatly instructive. There are also some monasteries in the West, such as the City of Ten Thousand Buddhas near Ukiah, California, where people may go to train. Eventually, new and creative operational structures will need to be developed which are suitable to the capabilities and temperaments of the members of new monastic communities. Those who display resistance to discipline altogether and an unwillingness to accommodate may simply be unsuited to monastic life.

It is likely that Western Buddhist monasteries will evolve their own models of organization. They may not be run strictly along the lines of Asian monastic institutions, but compatible features can be incorporated from traditional models. The structure of existing meditative communities should be studied and experienced to ascertain which features of each seem most desirable. These can then be implemented on an experimental basis to see which are most workable in the new monastic situation. Some features of traditional structures will be suitable, others can be adapted, some will be rejected, and surely the process of synthesizing will be informative. It would also be good to take a look at the organization of the Christian monastic institutions that have evolved for Western people over many generations.

To my mind, the ideal Western Buddhist monastery should be a sensitive blend of Asian and Western elements that is comfortable for all and still conducive to intensive practice. For example, I would like to see an international, non-sectarian monastery for women grow up somewhere in North America where nuns and prospective nuns could receive training and learn to live by the *Vinaya*. A meditation hall patterned on the Chinese, Japanese, or Korean model, *Vinaya* discipline on the Theravāda model, and a study program on the Tibetan model, with Western-style private rooms and a vegetarian diet would be a good combination to try. Years of communal living lead me to favor a careful admissions policy and small beginnings. I would like to experiment with a community composed exclusively of women who accept the administrative guidelines set forth in the *Vinaya* texts, and then gradually try to adapt them to Western living conditions. . . .

This is definitely a time for women to explore new ways of doing things. At the same time, many people feel the need for preserving the purity of meaningful traditions. Experiencing the beauty of each of the Buddhist traditions helps us to appreciate the beauty of Buddhist culture as a whole. There seems to be a danger, particularly in America, of adapting and rejecting things before they have been sufficiently digested. In recommending a respectful stance toward these ancient cultures, we are not speaking merely from an anthropological point of view; there is something of great historical significance at stake in the transmission of the *Dharma* to the West. As the first generation of Western Buddhists, we need to conscientiously embody the complete, authentic teachings of each tradition before we can begin to accurately translate them into our own cultural experience. We hope spiritual communities of women will play a special role in this process of religious and cultural transformation.

Source: Reprinted by permission of the publisher from Karma Lekshe Tsomo, "Living as a Nun in the West," *Sakyadhītā: Daughters of the Buddha,* ed. Karma Lekshe Tsomo (Ithaca: Snow Lion Publications, 1988), pp. 297–303.

10.8 SANGHA AND SOCIETY: ENGAGED BUDDHISTS IN CALIFORNIA

The term *Engaged Buddhism,* originally formulated by the Vietnamese monk Thich Nhat Hanh, has come to refer to a whole gamut of activities undertaken by Buddhists—both lay and monastic. In the West, these have ranged from involvement in peace movements, environmental activism, and working to end racial, ethnic, and gender-based discrimination to prison ministries, political activism, and other types of social action. The following selection describes the situation of some engaged Theravādin monks in Stockton, California, who have made their monastery into a neighborhood refuge for children.

The temple parking lot is teeming with kids. The younger ones are playing in a sandpile, while a group of older girls blasts the sounds of a Laotian pop group through a portable stereo. They range in age from two years to late adolescence. Most are Laotian-American, though some are of Thai, Hmong, or Cambodian descent. They come to the temple to worship and play, but mostly they come for a much-needed refuge from the violence of the streets.

"We established this temple with the kids in mind," explains Abbot Sombun. "There are all kinds of dangers in this neighborhood—guns, drugs, gangs. By keeping them off the streets, we're keeping them from harm.". . .

There are more Southeast Asian gangs *per capita* in Stockton than in any other city in the United States. They have names like Cambodian Mob Family, True Laos Crips, Eternal Wat Tribe, and Cambodians with Attitude. . . . Their exploits range in severity from substance abuse and "tagging" (graffiti vandalism) to drive-by shootings and gang warfare. But they are most renowned for their violent home invasions. Because many older Cambodians and Laotians grew to distrust public institutions during the wars in Southeast Asia, they now keep their cash savings at home rather than in banks. Southeast Asian gangs are well known for conducting paramilitary raids against such people and stripping them of their lifetime's savings. [. . .]

Wat Chansisamakidham was founded under the direction of Abbot Sombun in 1991. It is the regular gathering place for dozens of local youth. Some visit sporadically, but others are there every day. And a few—mostly older boys who come from large families with limited sleeping space—are there every night.

Many of the kids describe the temple as "a big family," and their analogy is apt in a number of ways. The building itself is a house, a decrepit Victorian mansion that the monks have striven diligently to refurbish over the years. Abbot Sombun is its master. He requires the kids to do their chores—to cook and clean for themselves and one another. The older kids look after the little ones, and those who can drive run errands for the rest.

The kids of this temple are unmistakably streetwise. They dress in hip-hop clothing and speak the language of gangsta rap. They all know gang members, and most say they've been pressured to join gangs on multiple occasions. A few, like twenty-year-old Lao Phimpa, are former gang members who attribute their reform to the intervention of the monks.

Surprisingly , the temple offers fairly little in terms of formal youth programs—beginning monastic training for boys and a summer school for children of both genders. Yet despite the relatively small number of specific activities for youth, it remains consistently popular with local kids. In fact, many of them claim the informality of the temple is the key to its success. They come not so much to participate in rigidly structured programs as to jump rope, shoot hoops, play hopscotch, and talk.

"I just come to kick it [hang out]," explains fifteen-year-old Khambi Vobouxasinh. "We feel safe here."

Among the nine monks who reside permanently at the temple is Ajahn Keerati Chatkaew. He is renowned among the kids for his relentless sense of humor and his ability to imitate their street jargon. He came to the United States reluctantly in 1994, just after receiving his ordination from Buddhist University in Bangkok.

"I didn't necessarily want to come here," he explains, "but my master told me I was destined to play some part in bringing the Buddha's teachings to the United States."

His master and others had insisted that America's need for the dharma was dire. They told the young monk that America was riddled with crime, that violent youth gangs roamed the streets, and that even children of Buddhist descent were forsaking their traditional ways and turning to lives of violence, crime, and substance abuse. [. . .]

Ajahn Keerati says his introduction to Stockton instantly changed his life. Not only did he suddenly realize the extent of America's inner-city gang problem, he also found his sense of purpose.

"The kids here need the monks," he explains. "Without this temple, they would have no place to play but the streets. They'd have no way to make positive friendships. And they might never learn the Buddha's teachings."

According to Ajahn Keerati, the mission of Wat Chansisamakidham is to give young locals a safe place to socialize and to teach them the traditional Buddhist virtues of non-violence and respect.

On the surface, this mission seems pretty simple. But in practice it has proven fairly complicated, because the monks of Wat Chansisamakidham maintain a delicate balance between the dictates of Theravāda tradition and the extenuating circumstances of inner-city America.

The harsh realities of life in downtown Stockton have forced them to reevaluate the traditional modes of relation between monks and young people. According to Ajahn Keerati, the authoritarianism that typifies Southeast Asian pedagogy has only limited applications in the United States.

"We've gotta be tough," he says, "but we can't be too tough, or they'll leave the temple and go to the gangs."

The key to attracting local kids to the temple, he says, is a non-traditional teaching style that emphasizes explanation over punishment.

"All the monks are really friendly here," says fourteen-year-old Patty Silasack. "In other temples, if you do something wrong, they hit you or yell at you. But here they take the time to explain to you *why* it was wrong."

The youth of Wat Chansisamakidham unanimously declare unqualified approval of their mentors' brand of engaged Buddhism. They claim the monks are exactly the type of active Buddhist role modes they require in order to stay more interested in the dharma than in the dangerous thrills of the streets.

But critics in the community claim that Abbot Sombun and his peers have violated age-old rules that require monks to disassociate themselves from secular distractions—especially the frivolity of child's play. The monks of Wat Chansisamakidham, they say, are not heroes but heretics.

It is hard to imagine, just by looking at him, that Abbot Sombun has been accused of reckless disregard for the rules of monastic non-attachment. . . . Yet his critics depict him as a shameless hedonist who has led his fellow monks—and their entire community—into spiritual ruin. They say that he has routinely violated the moral teachings of the Buddha and that his infractions have destroyed the integrity of the sangha. . . .

Opposition to the abbot's leadership is often heated, and the charges leveled against him and his fellow monks border on the fantastic. The wildest of them include drunkenness, gambling, gang affiliation, and watching pornography.

"That's ridiculous," says sixteen-year-old Johnny Kammanh in defense of the monks. "I've been here almost every day, and I never seen nothing like that."

"Besides," adds eleven-year-old Nancy Xayaseng, "those are exactly the things they've been teaching us to stay out of."

At present a group of approximately forty dissenters is taking legal action to remove the monks from the temple. However, the majority of the Chansisamakidham community continues to support the temple's leadership.

The conflict between the monk's opponents and their supporters is a contemporary version of the age-old struggle between religious conservatism and religious progressivism. The dissenting faction finds any variation from the traditions of Southeast Asia inexcusable. [Monks should be ritual practitioners and models of quiet reflection, not referees and guardians to a temple full of streetwise kids.] But the temple's supporters feel that modest adaptation to American ways is both inevitable and desirable.

The dissenters are incensed that the monks drive cars, but supporters claim the logistics of urban America make occasional driving a necessity. The dissenters lament the fact that the monks . . . do not strictly enforce the ancient rule requiring them to sit at a higher elevation than lay people. Supporters claim, however, that the occasional relaxation of this rule leads to an atmosphere of hospitality that can only be helpful in keeping Theravāda alive in America.

Source: Reprinted by permission of the author from Bob Easton-Waller, "Mean Street Monks," *Tricycle* 10, no. 2 (2000): 61, 63–65.

A Guide to the Transliteration and Pronunciation of Buddhist Terms

Buddhism is a pan-Asian religion and, as such, it has made use of the languages of a whole continent. The translations found in this anthology are taken, for the most part, from texts that exist in Sanskrit, Pali, Tibetan, Chinese, or Japanese. In addition, there are occasional references to words in Thai, Khmer, Burmese, Korean, and Sinhalese.

For purposes of discussion and in order to simplify matters, I have generally chosen to use Sanskrit forms for Buddhist terms that are difficult to translate. Thus, throughout this work, I speak of the Buddha's teaching as "Dharma" rather than as "Dhamma" (Pali), "Chö" (Tibetan), "Fa" (Chinese), or "Hō" (Japanese). Similarly, I employ such words as "karma," "nirvāṇa," "bodhisattva," and the like. Occasionally, however, when the context demands it, I have used non-Sanskrit (mostly Pali) terms. Also, in some instances (for example, "sangha"), I have retained a non-Sanskrit form because of its more common usage in English language textbooks. The language of all terms left untranslated is indicated in the glossary.

None of these languages is natively written in the Roman alphabet. All of them, however, can be transliterated into it. Of course, each system of transliteration carries with it its own set of pronunciation difficulties. The following comments are intended simply to help English readers overcome some of these, and not as complete phonetic guidelines.

Sanskrit and Pali Terms in these two languages have been transliterated with diacritical marks to aid in their pronunciation. A few basic rules are as follows:

1. A bar (called a macron) over a vowel makes it long. Thus:

   ā is sounded like the *a* in "barb,"

   ī like the *ea* in "eat,"

   ū like the *u* in "rhubarb."

Mnemonically, then, the long vowels can be remembered by the simple injunction to "Eat rhubarb!"

2. Short vowels are pronounced quite differently:

   a like the *u* in "but,"

   e like the *e* in "tray" (only more clipped),

   i like the *i* in "is,"

   o like the *o* in "so,"

   u like the *u* in "full."

   Mnemonically, then, one can think of the sentence: "But the tray is so full!"

3. **c** is always like the *ch* in "chest" (and never like the *c* in "country" or in "city"), while **ch** is sounded similarly but pronounced more emphatically and accompanied by a strong breath pulse, like the *ch+h* in "witch hunt."

4. **th** is always pronounced like the English letter *t* but also more emphatically, like the *t+h* in "hot house." It is never like the English *th* in "this" or "thing."

5. Similarly, **ph** is like that in "shepherd" and never like the English *ph* in "phone."

6. **ñ** is like the *ny* in "canyon."

7. Retroflex dots under letters (for example, **ṭ, ḍ, ṇ**) mean those letters should be pronounced with the tip of the tongue curled back up into the middle of the mouth. For Westerners unaccustomed to Indic sounds, it may be easier simply to sound them as an English *t, d,* or *n.*

   ṣ, however, should be pronounced like *sh* in "sheep,"

   ṛ like the *ri* in "rig,"

   ḷ like the second *l* in "little."

8. **ś** is difficult to differentiate from **ṣ** and may also be pronounced like the *sh* in "sheep," while plain **s** is pronounced as an *s* would be in English, as in "silly."

9. Finally, **ṃ** may be thought of as a completely nasal sound, somewhat like the *m* in "hum" when you are, in fact, humming, but more in the nose and the back of the mouth than on the lips.

10. All other letters can be pronounced as in English.

Chinese The transliteration used for Chinese terms here (except for a few modern place names such as Beijing) is the so-called Wade-Giles system. A few basic guidelines for its pronunciation (dismissing tonal distinctions) are as follows:

1. Pronounce **ch** (not followed by an apostrophe) like the *j* in "jar," but pronounce **ch'** (followed by an apostrophe) like the *ch* in

"chess." Thus "ching" is sounded like "jing" but "ch'ing" is sounded "ching."

2. Similarly, pronounce **k, p,** and **t** (not followed by an apostrophe) like the *g* in "good," the *b* in "baby," and the *d* in "darling." Pronounce **k', p',** and **t'** (followed by apostrophes) as though they were ordinary *k, p,* and *t* in English. Thus "Kuan Yin," "Pao-hua Shan," and "Tun-huang" are sounded "Guan Yin," "Bao-hua Shan," and "Dun-huang," but "K'uei-chi," "P'u-hsien," and "T'ien-t'ai" are sounded "Kuei-ji," "Pu-hsien," and "Tien-tai."
3. Pronounce **j** as though it were an *r*. Thus "jen" can be sounded as "ren."

Japanese The transliteration system used for Japanese terms here is the so-called Hepburn system. It causes few difficulties, but some guidelines should be kept in mind.

1. Vowels in Japanese are often kept said to be pronounced "in the Italian manner." This means that **o, e, i, a,** are sounded like the vowels in "do, "re," "mi," "fa," although the *e* in "re" should be short and clipped. The Japanese **u** is more problematic. Generally, it may be sounded like the *u* in "rhubarb," but often it is "whispered" and barely pronounced at all.
2. A macron over a vowel (for example, **ō** and **ū**) does not change that vowel's sound but makes it distinctly longer, as though it were pronounced twice in succession.
3. The Japanese **r** (the so-called "flapped" *r*) often sounds more like an English *d*. It is like the *d* sound found in the way some Americans pronounce the middle of the word "Betty."
4. Double consonants (**nn, pp, kk**) should be distinctly pronounced and not shortened and slurred together.
5. **g** is always hard and pronounced as the *g* in "goof" and never as the *g* in "gentle."
6. Finally, **y** should always be pronounced as the *y* in "quickly" and never as in "try."

Tibetan The transliteration system commonly used for transcribing Tibetan into the Roman alphabet makes it very difficult for persons unacquainted with the language even to come close to pronouncing it. For example, the name for the bodhisattva of compassion, pronounced Chen-re-zik, is more properly written sPyan-ras-gzigs. In order to spare the reader such stumbling blocks, I have chosen to render all Tibetan names and terms not as they are spelled but, with a few exceptions, according to a system used in Robinson and Johnson's *The Buddhist Religion* which makes them pronounceable for Westerners. This means that there are no rules to be listed here, except the reminders that umlauts over **ü** and **ö** should be pronounced as in German. Proper spellings for Tibetan terms are as follows:

Bu-tön (Bu-ston)
Chen-re-zik (Spyan-ras-gzigs)
chöd (gcod)
chörten (mchod-rten)
Dak-me-ma (BDag-med-ma)
Dorje Phakmo (Rdo-rje-phag-mo)
Drepung ('Bras-spung)
Drok-mi ('Brog-mi)
Dröl-ma (Sgrol-ma)
Drom-pa-gyang (Grom-pa-rgyang)
Drom-tön ('Brom-ston)
Dzog-chen (Rdzogs-chen)
Ganden (Dga'-ldan)
Gang Rimpoche (Gangs-rin-po-che)
Gang Tise (Gangs-ti-se)
gegö (dge-skos)
Ge-luk-pa (Dge-lugs-pa)
gompa (dgon-pa)
Gyantse (Rgyal-rtse)
Jetsun (Rje-btsun)
Ka-dam-pa (Bka'-gdams-pa)
Ka-gyü-pa (Bka'-brgyud-pa)
khamtsen (khang-mtshan)
kha-tak (kha-btags)
kyang-chak (rkyang-phyag)
Kyi-rong (Skyid-grong)
Lang-dar-ma (Glang-dar-ma)
Loseling (Blo-gsal-gling)
Ma-chik-lab-dön-ma (Ma-gcig-lab-sgron-ma)
Mar-po-ri (Dmar-po-ri)
Milarepa (Mi-la-ras-pa)
nyerba (gnyer-ba)
Nying-ma-pa (Rñing-ma-pa)
O-thang ('O-thang)
Pema Karpo (Pad-ma-dkar-po)
Pha Dampa-Sang-gye (Pha Dam-pa Sang-rgyas)
Sa-kya (Sa-skya)
Sa-kya-pa (Sa-skya-pa)
Sam-ye (Bsam-yas)
Samding (Bsam-sdings)
Sang-gye-gyel-tshen (Sangs-rgyas-rgyal-mtshan)
Sera (Se-ra)
Song-tsen-gam-po (Srong-btsan-sgam-po)
Tamdrin (Rta-mgrin)
Tashilhunpo (Bkra-shis-lhun-po)
torma (gtor-ma)
tragyii (grwa-dkyus)
tramang (grwa-dmangs)
tratsang (grwa-tshang)
Trhī-song-de-tsen (Khri-srong-lde-btsan)
Trhi-tsün (Khri-btsun)
Trhül-nang ('Phrul-snang)
tsamba (rtsam-pa)
Tsong-kha-pa (Tsong-kha-pa)
tülku (Sprul-sku)
tum-mo (Gtum-mo)
Yamdrok (Yar-'brog)
Yeshe Tsogyel (Ye-śes-mtsho-rgyal)

Glossary*

Abhidharma (Pali: *Abhidhamma*) Scholastic elaborations on the Teaching of the Buddha; one of the principal divisions of the Buddhist Canon.

Akṣobhya Savior Buddha of the Eastern Pure Land.

ālayavijñāna The storehouse or granary consciousness; the basic consciousness in Vijñānavāda philosophy.

Amitābha (Japanese: *Amida*) Savior Buddha of the Western Pure Land; the focus of faith for Buddhists of the Pure Land schools. Also named Amitayus.

anātman (Pali: *anattā*) The doctrine that there is no real, permanent, unchanging Self within individuals.

anitya (Pali: *anicca*) The doctrine of impermanence; along with anātman (no-Self) and duḥkha (suffering), one of the three characteristics of existence.

arhat A Buddhist saint; one who has attained enlightenment and is no longer subject to death and rebirth.

asura One of a class of supernatural beings whose fate is constantly to wage war against the devas (gods); sometimes translated as "titans."

Avalokiteśvara (Chinese: *Kuan-yin*; Japanese: *Kannon*; Tibetan: *Chen-re-zik*) Savior bodhisattva who embodies compassion; protector bodhisattva of Tibet.

Bhaiṣajyaguru (Japanese: *Yakushi*) Savior Buddha of Medicine or Healing Buddha.

bhikṣu (Pali: *bhikkhu*) Literally, a "beggar"; a fully ordained Buddhist monk.

bhikṣuṇī (Pali: *bhikkhunī*) Literally, a "beggar"; a fully ordained Buddhist nun.

bodhicitta The thought of enlightenment, or the mind set on enlightenment. The arousing of bodhicitta starts one on the bodhisattva path.

bodhisattva (Pali: *bodhisatta*) Anyone who has taken a vow to become a Buddha, who will attain that goal, and who, in the meantime, compassionately engages in assisting others; more specifically, the Buddha Gautama before his enlightenment.

Bodhi tree The tree of enlightenment; the particular tree in Bodhgaya, northern India, under which the Buddha attained enlightenment; any tree of that same species.

Brahmā The creator god in Hindu-Buddhist mythology.

caitya A monument or sanctuary that brings to mind the person of the Buddha or an event in his life; sometimes used as equivalent for *stūpa*.

cakravartin A "wheel-turning" monarch; a great king who rules the world according to Dharma.

*All terms are in Sanskrit unless otherwise specified.

Ch'an (Chinese; Japanese: *Zen*) School of Buddhism in China and Japan emphasizing meditation; the name "Ch'an" is considered to be the Chinese pronunciation of the Sanskrit word *dhyāna*.

daimoku (Japanese) In Nichiren Buddhism, the sacred title of the *Lotus Sūtra*.

Dalai Lama (Mongolian/Tibetan) Temporal and spiritual leader of Tibetan Buddhists; thought to be one of a line of successive incarnations of the bodhisattva Avalokiteśvara.

dāna The practice of giving, of making donations, especially to the sangha; one of the principal ways of making merit.

deva A god, a divinity, a status which, in Buddhism, is pleasurable and powerful but ultimately impermanent and still caught up in the cycle of saṃsāra. The deva realm is one of the realms of rebirth.

Devadatta A monk said to have been a cousin of the Buddha, and consistently portrayed as his rival and maligner.

Dharma (Pali: *Dhamma*) The Teaching of the Buddha, Truth, Law, Doctrine; a basic element of reality (in the latter sense, usually written *dharma*). The word has many meanings, but they mostly revolve around the notion of anything that is fundamentally true or real.

dhyāna (Pali: *jhāna*) Meditation; more specifically one of four or eight levels of trance attained in the course of meditative absorption.

duḥkha (Pali: *dukkha*) The first of the Four Noble Truths; suffering, unsatisfactoriness.

entering the stream The first step on the Path of enlightenment; a stream-enterer (srotāpanna) has only seven more rebirths to suffer before final liberation.

four-fold army The usual escort of a cakravartin king, consisting of elephants, chariots, cavalry, and infantry.

gandharva One of a class of minor divinities, often in attendance on other gods, sometimes portrayed as celestial musicians.

garuḍa A mythological, great, birdlike being; the traditional enemy of snakes (nāgas).

Gautama (Pali: *Gotama*) The clan name of the historical Buddha Śākyamuni; his personal name was Siddhārtha.

Great Man A person who is endowed with thirty-two auspicious bodily marks; can be either a Buddha or a cakravartin.

Hīnayāna Literally, the "Lesser Vehicle"; a derogatory term used by Mahāyānists to designate one of the principal divisions of Buddhism.

Indra The king of the gods in Hindu-Buddhist mythology; sometimes also called Śakra.

jātaka A story of a previous birth, a past life, often of the Buddha.

kali yuga The final, "degenerate" age of a world cycle.

kami (Japanese) Indigenous divinities of Japan.

karma Literally, "action," especially ritual, moral action; any deed that will bring about certain corresponding effects in this or a future lifetime; also, the law or principle governing these cause-and-effect relationships.

kaṭapūtana A type of preta.

kaṭhina (Thai: *kathin*) The cloth annually given by laypersons to Buddhist monks for them to dye and make into robes. The ceremonial giving of kaṭhina is held annually at the end of the rains retreat.

kiṃnara One of a class of minor divinities.

Kṣitigarbha (Chinese: *Ti-tsang;* Japanese: *Jizō*) Savior bodhisattva who protects beings on the six pathways of rebirth, especially those in hell; by extension a guardian of travelers and of children.

Mahāyāna Literally, the "Great Vehicle"; one of the principal divisions of Buddhism.

mahoraga A great serpent; one of a class of supernatural beings.

Mainstream Buddhism A nonderogatory term used instead of Hīnayāna (the Lesser Vehicle).

Maitreya (Pali: *Metteyya*) The next Buddha, due to come sometime in the future.

maṇḍala Literally, a "circle"; a structured arena for depicting and encountering a pantheon of Buddhas and bodhisattvas and various other levels of reality.

Mañjuśrī Savior bodhisattva who embodies wisdom, portrayed as carrying a sword and a book; in China, he is thought to dwell on Mount Wu-t'ai.

mantra A set of words or sounds endowed with spiritual or magical potency; sometimes translated as "spell."

mappō (Japanese) Literally, "the end of the Dharma"; the final period of the Buddha's Teaching when realization and enlightenment are very difficult.

Māra In Buddhist mythology, the highest god of the realm of desire, who is generally concerned with death and sensuality and is anxious to prevent beings from attaining enlightenment and thereby transcending his realm.

Mount Meru The mythic mountain thought to be at the center of the Buddhist cosmos and the dwelling place of the gods.

mudrā Literally, a "seal"; hand gesture with esoteric significance depicted iconographically or used in Vajrayāna ritual.

nāga A snake or snakelike supernatural being often associated with water.

nat (Burmese) An indigenous spirit or divinity.

nembutsu (Japanese) "Recollection of the Buddha"; the recitation of the mantra "NAMU AMIDA BUTSU" in praise of the Buddha Amida.

Nikāya A section of the Pali canon; a school or sect of Indian Buddhism.

nirvāṇa (Pali: *nibbāna*) The soteriological goal in Buddhism, characterized by the cessation of desire, ignorance, and hatred. Sometimes nirvāṇa is used to mean enlightenment; other times it is an equivalent for parinirvāṇa. (In the latter case, it is sometimes called "nirvāṇa without remainder.")

once-returner The second step on the Path of enlightenment; a once-returner (sakṛdāgāmin) has only one more rebirth to suffer before final liberation.

pāramitā One of six or ten perfections, the practice of which characterizes the life of a bodhisattva.

pārinirvāṇa The final nirvāṇa, occurring at the death of the Buddha or of any enlightened being, after which there is no more rebirth.

phī (Thai) An indigenous spirit or divinity.

pirit (Sinhalese; Pali: *paritta*) Any text chanted for its magical, protective power, generally by monks.

prajñā (Pali: *paññā*) Wisdom; understanding of the true nature of reality; one of the pāramitās.

prātimokṣa (Pali: *pātimokkha,* also *pāṭimokkha*) The list of rules governing monastic life which is formally recited and reaffirmed every fortnight by each assembled monastic community.

pratītya-samutpāda (Pali: *paticca-samuppāda*) "Interdependent origination"; the Buddhist doctrine of causality.

pratyekabuddha A person who, like the Buddha, attains enlightenment on his own, without the immediate help of a teacher, but who then, unlike the Buddha, does not share that enlightenment with others by preaching or founding a community.

pravāraṇā (Pali: *pavāraṇā*) A ceremony held each year at the end of the rains retreat in which members of the sangha ask each other's forgiveness for any offenses they have committed.

preta A ghost whose chief suffering is that of hunger and thirst; a spirit of the dead; the preta realm is one of the realms of rebirth.

Pure Land The paradisial realm of a Buddha in which devotees may be reborn after death; often specifically referring to the Western Pure Land of the Buddha Amitābha.

rains retreat The period of three months, in the monsoon season, during which monks and nuns are expected to reside in one place and devote themselves to their practice.

sādhana A Vajrayāna visualization-meditation, generally involving evocation and identification with a deity or Buddha.

Śākyamuni Literally, the "sage of the Śākya clan"; name given to the Buddha Gautama.

sal (Sanskrit: *śāla*) The kind of tree (*vatica robusta*) under which the Buddha attained pārinirvāṇa.

samādhi Meditative concentration; a trance state attained through yoga.

saṃsāra The process of death and rebirth, characterized by suffering, in which all beings are caught.

sangha The Buddhist community of monks and nuns (also taken to include laymen and laywomen); one of the three refuges of Buddhism. Also spelled *saṃgha* and *saṇgha.*

siddha An accomplished one; a Buddhist saint, especially of the Indo-Tibetan Tantric tradition.

śīla Morality; the upholding of Buddhist precepts; one of the pāramitās.

skandha (Pali: *khandha*) The five aggregates, or agglomerations, that constitute what is usually thought of as the individual Self. They are form, feelings, perceptions, karmic constituents, and consciousness.

smṛti (Pali: *sati*) Mindfulness, meditational recollection.

śramaṇa A striver, a quester; one who has abandoned the householder's life and set out on a religious quest, not necessarily a Buddhist one.

śrāvaka A disciple; one who hears the Dharma from a teacher; in Mahāyāna contexts, a follower of the Hīnayāna.

stream-winner (Sanskrit: *srotāpanna*) An enlightened person who has only seven more rebirths to suffer before final liberation.

stūpa A moundlike monument containing relics of the Buddha or some other object of veneration.

subitist English neologism for a follower of the path of sudden enlightenment.

śūnyatā Emptiness; the absence of any inherent self-existence; an important tenet in Mahāyāna Buddhism.

sūtra (Pali: *sutta*) Any doctrinal discourse attributed to the Buddha; one of the principal divisions of the Buddhist canon.

svabhāva Inherent self-existence; basic identity or nature of a thing.

Tārā (Tibetan: *Dröl-ma*) Female savior bodhisattva, often associated with Avalokiteśvara, and popular in Tibet.

Tathāgata An epithet of the Buddha often used by the Buddha in referring to himself; literally, the "Thus-Come One."

Tathāgatagarbha Literally, the "embryo or womb of the Tathāgata"; the principle of enlightenment that is within all beings.

Theravāda (Pali) Literally, the teaching of the elders; a sect of Nikāya Buddhism that became established in Sri Lanka and Southeast Asia.

thirty-three gods The thirty-three (trāyastriṃśa) divinities who inhabit the heaven of Indra, king of the gods.

trichiolomegachiliocosm English neologism for Trisāhasramahāsāhasralokadhātu, the largest imaginable unit in the expanse of space.

Tripiṭika (Pali: *Tipiṭaka*) Literally, the "three baskets"; the Buddhist canon, consisting of Vinaya, Sūtra, and Abhidharma texts.

Triple Gem The Three Jewels or Three Refuges that are the focal point of all Buddhists: the Buddha, the Dharma, and the Sangha.

tṛṣṇā (Pali: *taṇhā*) Literally, "thirst"; desire or craving which, along with ignorance, lies at the root of duḥkha.

upāya "Skillful means" in teaching the Dharma; good didactic strategy.

upoṣadha (Pali: *uposatha*) A weekly assembly of the sangha that all residents of a monastery are expected to attend and where laypersons may undertake to observe certain extra precepts.

Vairocana (Japanese: *Dainichi*) The centermost of a Vajrayāna set of five Buddhas arranged in a maṇḍala; the "cosmic" Buddha associated with the sun and figuring prominently in Japanese esoteric Buddhism.

Vajrayāna The "thunderbolt" or "diamond vehicle"; one of the principal divisions of Buddhism.

Vinaya The Discipline, or Code of Conduct, for monks and nuns; one of the principal divisions of the Buddhist canon.

wat (Thai) A Buddhist monastery-temple.

weikza (Burmese) A charismatic master having esoteric knowledge and thought to be endowed with supernatural powers.

yakṣa (Pali: *yakkha*) One of a class of supernatural beings, generally thought to be powerful and demonic but capable of being tamed and converted to the cause of Buddhism.

Yama God of the dead in the underworld.

Zen See *Ch'an.*

Subject Index

Text and Author Index